THEZAPATISTAREADER

THE
ZAPATISTA
READER

EDITED BY
TOM HAYDEN

THUNDER'S MOUTH PRESS / NATION BOOKS
NEW YORK

THE
ZAPATISTA
READER

Published by
Thunder's Mouth Press/Nation Books
161 William St., 16th Floor
New York, NY 10038

Nation Books is a co-publishing venture of the Nation Institute
and Avalon Publishing Group Incorporated.

The Zapatista Reader / edited by Tom Hayden.
p. cm.
Includes bibliographical references.

ISBN 1-56025-335-5 (pbk.)

1. Chiapas (Mexico)—History—Peasant Uprising, 1994- 2. Mexico—Politics and
government—1988- 3. Ejârcito Zapatista de Liberaciân Nacional (Mexico) 4. Marcos,
subcomandante. 5. Guerrillas—Mexico—Chiapas—History. I. Hayden, Tom.

F1256 .Z269 2001
972'.750836—dc21
2001043157

9 8 7 6 5 4 3

Printed in the United States of America
Distributed by Publishers Group West

CONTENTS

INTRODUCTION

TOM HAYDEN

AS this book of reflections on the Chiapas rebellion is published, the Zapatistas are silent. Less than a year ago, in March 2001, they captured the attention — and the hearts — of many across the world with their march to the Mexican capital demanding dignity for Indian people. It was an event similar in impact to the March on Washington in August 1963, a day permanently remembered as a moment from which there would be no return to the past. Even the newly elected Mexican president, Vicente Fox, like John F. Kennedy in that earlier time, endorsed constitutional reforms that promised self-determination for his country's ten million indigenous people.

But the reforms were blocked in the Mexican legislature, and the resulting compromise rejected by the Zapatistas. The core dispute revolved around whether Indian communities are "entities of public right," with control of their own historic territories and forms of representation, or communities subject to traditional municipal and state control. Worse, when the Zapatistas retreated back to their mountain enclaves, President Fox seemed to retreat from his early attempt to resolve the conflict as well. In June 2001, he even declared that there no longer was a conflict in Chiapas, and that "we shouldn't give any more space or situations of power to the Zapatista movement."

But neither Zapatista silence nor official dismissals are likely to be the end of the matter. The Zapatistas, relying on an Indian tradition, have observed long periods of silence before. Their obituary has been issued on earlier occasions as well. A conspicuous example was penned by Mexico's present foreign minister, Jorge Castañeda, as an independent observer three years ago. When 1,111 Zapatistas marched into Mexico City in September 1997, Castaneda wrote that they had reached a "dead end." While acknowledging that Subcomandante Marcos and the Zapatistas had "captured the imagination of the media and solidarity groups the world over," Castaneda argued that they were politically irrelevant to the new Mexico, and had been for two years.

Why do mainstream officials and observers so frequently pronounce the Zapatistas dead? Based on all the previous premature funerals, it seems likely that the rebellion will express itself again. But even in the unlikely case that it is over, "deactivated," to use President Fox's word, the Zapatista rebellion deserves serious public attention by anyone concerned with global injustice and resistance today. Following the terror attacks of September 11, 2001, it is understandable that many Americans distrust any form of rebellion, and support strengthening national security. September 11 also made the Mexican middle class more jittery about the Zapatistas. Anyone classified as associated with terrorism, however dimly, is likely to be marginalized if not arrested for questioning. No amount of law-and-order, however, can quell deepening unrest in a world demarcated so deeply by wealth and poverty. In addition, the Zapatista rebellion, which seeks to awaken and win over civil society, is entirely different than a religious fundamentalism which intends to take thousands of innocent lives. As Marcos tells the Spanish novelist Manuel Vázquez Montalbán in this book, "we wanted to go further and organize a politics which went beyond rancor. We go a lot deeper than fundamentalist movements . . ."

THE CHIAPAS REBELLION of January 1, 1994, was the first denunciation of a "new world order" from the viewpoint of that order's victims. That day marked the official beginning of the North American Free Trade Agreement (NAFTA) and more generally, the era of new global trade agreements dubbed the "New World Order" by President George Bush and implemented by President Bill Clinton. On that same day, thousands of masked Indians, declaring "NAFTA is Death!" began an armed uprising in the impoverished southern Mexico state of Chiapas. As they described their multicultural vision, the Indian rebels wanted "a world in which many worlds fit," not a monoworld with no space for them.

The globalization of trade and capital also caused a globalization of conscience and resistance. Demonstrations in support of the Zapatistas were staged in many countries, and the stream of international visitors to Chiapas grew by the day.

As a senator in the California legislature at the time, I was deeply stirred by the Chiapas uprising, and immediately dispatched a public letter to President Clinton warning against American intervention. Instead of modernizing

Yankee imperialism, I thought and wrote, it was a moment to address many festering issues. Would these trade agreements benefit anyone but global investors? Weren't California's and America's laws concerning labor and the environment undermined by these proposed new trade tribunals? Wasn't democracy itself at stake? Shouldn't our tax dollars be subsidizing human rights instead of environmental abuses?

My personal interest continued to grow. A Georgetown University law school study identified 95 California laws that could be challenged under NAFTA for interfering with international investors' rights. In the following years, I would visit Chiapas, lobby the Clinton Administration, question Mexican presidential candidates when they campaigned in California, protest the expulsion of California human rights activists, and hold screenings of documentaries on the Zapatistas.

In the middle of a hundred other duties, I couldn't get Chiapas out of my consciousness. I wasn't just thinking about NAFTA. The Chiapas revolt stirred crucial questions for progressives like myself who had participated in human rights and peace movements for decades. A new and pervasive cynicism proclaimed that revolutionary movements were out of fashion—obsolete like the 1960s era itself. Hate-dominated fundamentalisms started filling the void where political movements had failed. But Chiapas had stirred the revolutionary imagination far beyond Mexico. It pierced the seductive boredom of consumer society with haunting moral questions.

Chiapas raised from the hidden depths of our continental history an issue that our society seeks to forget: The Conquest of the Americas that left millions dead is the foundation on which our civilizations are built. To call the bloody events that began 500 years ago a genocide potentially undermines the legitimacy of all that many Americans, Mexicans, and Westerners hold dear. The integrity of our institutions seems to depend more on denying, rather than candidly confronting our original sins. Instead of calling it genocide, it is renamed a "tragic misunderstanding," a "dark chapter of the past," something regrettable but finished, not the responsibility of the present generation.

One facet of our schizophrenic American psyche is the capacity to annihilate people who stand in our way and then deny it. Interlaced with this terrifying frontier mentality is an opposite impulse, the democratic spirit of resistance to the oppression of monarchs and tyrants. Unable to reconcile these impulses, we prefer to forget the destruction from which democracy was built. Or we rationalize that, despite Indian wars and slavery, our "manifest destiny" has been to steadily dispense freedom and democracy to the world instead of expanding an empire. Even the history of slavery, I suspect, is consolingly if quietly interpreted by some as having resulted in a better life for African Americans in the long run than if they had remained in "backward" Africa.

But the claim that cultural destruction is an unfortunate prelude to a better, more democratic life is so transparently hollow that it cannot be asserted with public credibility. With a vanishing rationale, combined with an unwillingness to confront the past in the present, we become a country whose smugness grows in proportion to our denial. The toxic result is that we repeat the past again and again, through a process of transference, as we did during the slaughter of Vietnam. There always are new savages to tame, new resources to claim. And always there are flashbacks, ghosts to kill again.

In our arrogance we believe that we can be done with the past if the past is not done with us. Then, in January 1994, came another opportunity to confront the meaning of the Conquest and prove that the West had learned that crushing native peoples was wrong. Here was the chance for reparation, for healing, for a new beginning. Here were thousands of Mayans in rebellion against what they called "oblivion." Who was really masked, they were asking, those fighting for their identity in the jungle or those hiding their identity in the circles of power?

I have believed that even the Left—the broad movement derived from the Enlightenment and including liberals, free thinkers, socialists, communists, anticolonial nationalists—had a problem with this "Indian question." With honorable exceptions, the Left seemed to concur in the consensus that Indians were primitive, pre-modern, unfortunate people who were bypassed by history's inexorable machinery of progress. The Left was sorry for these Indians, but rarely in solidarity with them. Indian communities in the Americas remain the poorest of the poor. Some supported the token self-determination afforded by miserable, isolated reservation life. Others believed that the only hope lay in assimilation and education. The more ideological Left seemed to believe that Indians, like "backward" peasants everywhere, had to be transformed into a subgroup of an urban industrial proletariat. Few wanted to question the Conquest itself, the nightmare of the American soul.

The Zapatistas touched these deep feelings not only in myself but apparently in millions of others around the world. This book is meant to provide an opportunity to reflect on the meaning of both the Zapatistas and the global interest they have generated.

It is organized in three sections: The Story, a series of eyewitness accounts of the rebellion since 1994; The Word, a selection of lyrical literary and political writings and speeches mainly by Subcommandante Marcos; and The Commentaries, a range of exceptional essays on the Zapatistas by intellectuals and political leaders around the world.

PART OF THE fascination with Chiapas is that the rebellion occurred at the very moment when the traditional Left was in despair or disintegration. The Cold War was over. International capitalist commerce had prevailed over international revolution. But then who were these masked and multicolored Indians with makeshift weapons?

Seven years later, the experts have been confounded again and again. An unlikely new international movement has provided a ring of protection around the Chiapas rebels and Marcos. Mexico has passed through a crisis of authority, leading to the demise of its one-party state and the election of a new president in 2000 who spoke of Indian rights and a military pull-back from Chiapas. In March 2001, enormous throngs gathered at Mexico City's sacred plaza of revolution, the Zócalo, to welcome the reincarnated ghosts of Emeliano Zapata, the Zapatistas.

Inspired in large part by the Zapatista example, an international movement has arisen to physically confront and creatively challenge NAFTA and the World Trade Organization everywhere their power brokers choose to meet. The Seattle confrontation of 1999 is etched in American public consciousness as the most significant challenge to power-as-usual since the 1960s. The Seattle events helped trigger additional confrontations in Prague, Quebec City, Washington DC, and Genoa. The US government was forced to accept the rhetoric of protecting labor and environmental standards, although the executive branch—from Clinton to Bush—clearly favored a centralization of power over Congress and the states and municipalities. Two years after Seattle, the power brokers of the WTO were still demoralized and paralyzed internally, and forced to schedule their international meetings in the inaccessible reaches of Qatar.

But what sort of revolution do the Zapatistas promise? Since at least 1917, the concept of revolution has been synonymous with clandestine armed struggles—in Russia, China, Vietnam, Cuba, or with anticolonial movements led by a variety of parties and personalities seeking state power. The visions and political ideologies associated with those movements, which originally inspired millions and threatened ruling elites with their motivating clarity, have dissipated into dogma and bureaucracy. The Zapatistas, while rooted fundamentally in Mexican history, are also symbolic of the new forces of revolution which challenge modernity, monoculturalism, and the centralization of bureaucratic power without seeking to become new aggressors.

THE ZAPATISTA REVOLUTION originated in the culture of the Mexican— and Marxist—revolutionary left, the students and intellectuals who were hardened by massacres in Mexico during the 1960s and 1970s. But the significance of the Zapatistas is as much because of their break with the traditional Left as their continuity with other revolutionary movements. They harken back to the unfinished 1917 Mexican Revolution of Zapata which sought justice for landless Indians and campesinos. Like the 1916 Irish rebellion and war of independence, the Mexican Revolution lacked the vanguard party envisioned by Marx, Engels, and Lenin. It was laden with forces considered reactionary or superstitious by much of the Left, such as the Catholicism symbolized by the Virgin of Guadalupe and the indigenous peasant cultures suppressed 500 years ago by the Spanish Conquest.

Yet the Zapatista revolution cannot be understood without examining its roots in Catholic liberation theology and, more deeply, the continuing tradition of Indian resistance to the Conquest and subsequent usurpation of their lands and culture. Before there was a Marcos or an EZLN, there were catechists in Chiapas who had chosen the "preferential option for the poor," the slogan of liberation theology proclaimed at the 1968 Medellin, Colombia, conference. That meeting was attended by a conservative young priest named Samuel Ruíz who would become in time the best-known defender of the Indians since his Chiapas predecessor, Bartolomé de las Casas, five centuries before. The apostles of liberation theology learned to immerse themselves in, and give organizational energy to, the existing Mayan culture of resistance which continued to flicker in the mountains of Chiapas and throughout Central and Latin America. Instead of imposing their version of Christianity on the Indians, they realized that Christianity had to respect and adapt to the religious traditions of the indigenous. Jesus Christ was seen less as a Western figure sent to inspire the heathen and more like a cosmic symbol accessible through the Indians' own religious experiences. The interview with Bishop Ruíz contained in this volume is an important elaboration of this change in theological approach.

When the handful of future Zapatista cadres arrived in those same mountains in the early 1980s, they had to undergo a similar immersion before they could provide anything of value to the disenfranchised Indian communities. Just as the catechists could not export Jesus to Chiapas, neither could the Zapatistas export Marx or Mao.

Nothing might have happened, however, without the forces of globalization which required the Mexican government to scrap its constitutional protection of communal lands on which the Indian economy and culture depended. The prospective loss of those lands to the poorest of the poor was, as the Zapatista declaration put it, a genuine death sentence for a way of life. There was little for them to do but fight for dignity and land again.

Due mainly to Marcos, however, there is a diary, a poetry, an intellectual account, and an invaluable window into a movement that has an awareness of its novelty. "It has been remarked before that Marcos could use an editor," opines Tim Golden in an April 8, 2001 *New York Times* review of a *Our Word is Our Weapon* (Seven Stories Press, 2001), a recent collection of Marcos's writings. Titled "Revolution Rocks" in an apparent reference to Marcos's relationship with the rock band Rage Against the Machine, Golden's article is more lecture than review. Acknowledging Marcos's "gifts as a propagandist," the reviewer wonders if he has led the Indians astray with his radical chic posture.

Marcos should not be canonized, and some of the essays in this volume raise interesting questions about the strategy and direction of the Zapatista revolt. But the cynicism of the media does not seem to allow it to credit the achievements of the Zapatistas thus far in rescuing the "Indian question" from oblivion.

But as the Zapatista documents indicate, this is not a revolution aimed at a transference of political power to a new party, but a rebellion intended to prevent the triumph of amnesia. It is a sharp thorn jabbing into the cold heart of those who refuse to acknowledge the need for reparations to the indigenous. An issue that is 500 years old will not be settled in time for the evening news. And far from being an isolated phenomenon, the rebellion is part of a widespread pattern of confrontations and questioning of global institutions—institutions that only a few years ago projected an aura of inevitability. The wish of the ruling elites, most of all, is that a sense of weariness will settle into the consciousness of well-meaning people, that they will accept being entertained rather than engaged. Reading these pages, however, is likely to leave the reader anything but weary.

ZAPATISTAS:
A BRIEF HISTORICAL TIMELINE

TOM HANSEN

Adapted and expanded from Tom Hansen's timeline which originally appeared in *Our Word is Our Weapon: Selected Writings of Subcomandante Insurgent Marcos*, ed. Juana Ponce de Leon (Seven Stories, 2001)

Beginning of history
Mayan Indians settle area now known as Chiapas, Mexico.

1524–27
Spaniards conquer Mayan Indians, beginning five centuries of exploitation and repression.

Late 1500s
Mayan population reduced by 50% through disease and repression. Population doesn't begin to recover until the mid-seventeenth century.

1712
Tzeltal Indian rebellion brought on by Spanish tribute demands and crop failures. The Indians are brutally repressed.

1824
Chiapas leaves Guatemala to join a weak Mexican state, allowing relative autonomy for local elites, and beginning decades of Liberal/Conservative struggles for control over land and Indian labor. Both sides accrue huge landholdings, displacing indigenous owners, and many Indians are forced into virtual slavery.

1867–70

Indigenous communities rebel over taxation, control of markets, and religious freedom in Chamula. Violent repression again defeats the rebellion.

1876–1910

Dictatorship of Porfirio Díaz oversees accumulation of immense landholdings by local Mestizos. Chiapas economy is opened to international trade, with coffee, cacao, and mahogany the major exports.

1910–1920

Mexican revolution. In Chiapas the fight is over control of land and Indian labor. When General Álvaro Obregón becomes president in 1920, regional caciques declare loyalty in exchange for autonomy to govern Chiapas. Mexico's ensuing agrarian reform has limited impact in the state.

1929

The precursor to the PRI (Institutional Revolutionary Party) initiates 71 years of "the perfect dictatorship."

1934–1940

The populist presidency of Lázaro Cárdenas proclaims a common struggle with indigenous communities. Many indigenous Chiapanecos assume positions in PRI-controlled labor unions and peasant organizations. Although populism largely ended with Cárdenas's presidency, many indigenous political structures remain under PRI control for decades.

1940–70

Land reform under the ejido system (communally owned land) continues to lag in Chiapas, while large landowners consolidate their holdings. Cattle ranching becomes an important business as roads penetrate the state. Pressure for land from a booming indigenous population results in over 100,000 Indians moving to the Landandon jungle.

1960

Samuel Ruíz García is named Bishop of San Cristobal de las Casas. After the Medellin Council of Latin American Bishops in 1968, Ruíz begins to promote liberation theology and an Indigenous Catholicism.

1968

Student movement in Mexico City is brutally repressed, with hundreds murdered by government agents in the Tlatelolco Massacre. The repression convinces many activists to carry their struggles underground. Over the next decade, more than two dozen urban guerrilla groups develop throughout Mexico, with mainly student membership. The most active period of guerrilla activity is between 1971 and 1975. Most movements disintegrate under brutal repression and a dirty war, in which hundreds of activists "disappeared" and over 1,000 were killed.

1970s

Pressure for land precipitates organized local revolts against indigenous Caciques aligned with the PRI. Over the next two decades, 50,000 Indians are expelled from their communities for resisting local power structures, with many settling around large cities or in the Lacandón jungle.

1974

The Indigenous Congress is organized by the Diocese of San Cristobal at the invitation of the state governor. Over 1,200 delegates representing 300 communities demand land reform, education in native languages, health care, and labor rights. The Congress proves to be a historical juncture for indigenous grassroots organizing.

1979

Founding meeting of the National Coordinating Committee "Plan de Ayala." Two dozen peasant organizations declare themselves independent of the government.

1982

General Absalón Castellanos Domínguez becomes governor of Chiapas and oversees a dramatic increase in militarization to control land struggles. During his administration, 102 campesinos are assassinated, 327 disappear, 590 are imprisoned, 427 are kidnapped and tortured, 407 families are expelled from their homes, and security forces overrun 54 communities.

1983

Marcos and other activists from the National Liberation Forces (FLN) arrive in Chiapas. The Zapatista National Liberation Army (EZLN) is born on November 17 with three Indians and three Mestizos.

1985

Earthquake destroys large sections of Mexico City. Inadequate and corrupt response by government officials forces civil society to organize itself, marking an important break in PRI corporatist control.

1986

EZLN enters first indigenous community at invitation of local leaders.

1988

Fraudulent presidential elections on July 6 bring PRI candidate Carlos Salinas de Gortari to power. Opposition candidate Cuauhtemoc Cárdenas is ahead in polling when vote-counting computers suddenly crash. Three days later, Salinas is declared the winner.

1989

EZLN grows to over 1,300 armed members.

1992

President Salinas reforms Article 27 of the constitution, ending 75 years of land reform and allowing for privatization of ejidos. For many landless campesinos in Chiapas, this marks the end of hope of ever owning land.

1993

Zapatista communities approve a military offensive by the EZLN and form the Clandestine Indigenous Revolutionary Committee—General Command (CCRI-CG) to lead the struggle.

1994

NAFTA is implemented on January 1. On the same day, 3,000 members of the EZLN occupy six large towns and hundreds of ranches in an armed uprising. Within 24 hours the army responds, bombing indigenous communities and killing at least 145 Indians. Mexican civil society responds with massive demonstrations calling for an end to military repression, and a cease-fire is declared January 12.

Peace talks begin in February, but the government peace proposal is rejected by Zapatista communities.

In August the Zapatistas organize the National Democratic Convention. More than 6,000 people representing a broad range of civil society gather at

"Aguascalientes," a meeting place carved out of the jungle. Ernesto Zedillo is elected president in August, and Eduardo Robledo Rincón is elected governor amid widespread charges of fraud. Amado Avendano Figueroa, the PRD candidate, declares a "government in rebellion."

On December 19, the Zapatistas declare 38 autonomous indigenous municipalities, representing a serious challenge to local PRI power structures.

In December the Mexican peso tumbles, losing more than half of its value during the next two months. A US/IMF bailout of $50 billion does not mitigate dramatic increases in unemployment and loss of living standards during the following year. The majority of Mexicans suffer, while the elites enjoy the fruits of privatization and NAFTA.

1995

In January Chase Manhattan Bank issues a report calling for the Mexican government to "eliminate the Zapatistas." At this point, dozens of communities have publicly defined themselves as Zapatistas, representing well over 50,000 civilians.

On February 9, the army mounts a massive invasion in Zapatista areas of influence, especially in the Canadas, implementing a strategy of low intensity warfare (also known as civilian targeted warfare). Among other things, the army displaces almost 20,000 campesinos and turns "Aguascalientes" into an army base. The Zapatistas respond by constructing five new Aguascalientes (centers of indigenous resistance). During the next five years, over 60,000 troops occupy nearly every corner of the state, establishing army encampments just meters from most of the well-established Zapatista communities, and disrupting the lives, economy, and culture of indigenous communities.

In April peace talks resume, with both sides agreeing to focus discussions in six areas. In October talks begin in San Andrés Larrainzar on indigenous rights and culture.

In August the Zapatistas hold the first international consulta. Over 1,000,000 people vote, calling on the EZLN to transform itself into a new independent political force.

1996

In February the EZLN and the government sign the San Andrés Accords, outlining a program of land reform, indigenous autonomy, and cultural rights.

In March talks begin on democracy and justice, concluding with no agreement on August 12, as government representatives refuse to discuss Zapatista proposals and present nothing substantial of their own. Finally, on August 30, the EZLN suspends peace talks, demanding that government representatives actually be empowered to negotiate. In December Zedillo formally rejects the San Andrés accords.

In July/August, the Zapatistas organize the first Intercontinental Encuentro for Humanity and Against Neoliberalism. Several thousand people attend from Mexico and dozens of nations to discuss the role of civil society in confronting neoliberalism.

1997

The July 6 midterm elections mark significant gains for opposition parties—however, inside the "conflict zone" in Chiapas, abstention reaches 80 percent. Chiapas elections are notoriously fraudulent, and the high rate of abstention reflects a general mistrust of government in indigenous communities.

In September, 1, 111 members of the EZLN arrive in Mexico City for the founding of the Zapatista National Liberation Front (FZLN), the civil political arm of the indigenous movement.

On December 22, a paramilitary group affiliated with the PRI attacks a church in the community of Acteal, killing 45 indigenous campesinos, mostly women and children. Paramilitary activity has been growing throughout the state for several years as part of the strategy of civilian targeted warfare. Local PRI officials and army officers are implicated, but the intellectual authors are never brought to justice. Shortly thereafter, the Zedillo administration denies the existence of paramilitaries in Chiapas, and the army begins a campaign to disarm the EZLN, but not the paramilitary groups.

1998

In a twisted response to the Acteal Massacre, February marks the beginning of a campaign to expel foreign human rights observers from Chiapas, as the Zedillo administration tries to hide the truth from the world. Over 150 are expelled during the following two years.

Peace talks are still suspended, and the government continues to increase military presence throughout the state.

In April, the army begins to dismantle autonomous Zapatista communities. Over 1,000 troops and police invade four communities, destroying records and arresting community leaders. The actions culminate in the predawn invasion of San Juan de Libertad in June. At least eight civilians and one policeman are killed. The resulting outcry from civil society puts a temporary halt to the dismantling operations.

In June Bishop Samuel Ruíz García ends his efforts to mediate a peace, accusing the government of preferring the path of war and repression.

1999

In March the Zapatistas organize the Consulta on Indigenous Rights and Culture. Over 5,000 civilian Zapatistas conduct a weeklong program of popular education throughout the country. On March 21, over 3,000,000 Mexicans vote at thousands of polling places, agreeing that the San Andrés accords should be implemented.

In April state police occupy the autonomous community of San Andrés Sakamchem, site of the historic San Andrés accord, and install a PRI mayor. The following day, 3,000 unarmed Zapatistas nonviolently force the police to leave the town and reinstall their elected representatives.

In May the second National Encuentro of Civil Society draws 2,000 participants to discuss the March consulta.

In September the army occupies the remote village of Amador Hernández, the final link in plans to build a road that will encircle the Zapatistas in the Lacandón jungle. The community resists with nonviolent protests, but the military encampment remains.

2000

Presidential elections on July 2 and Chiapas state elections on August 20 dominate the political calendar. Vicente Fox of the National Action Party wins the presidency, ending 71 years of PRI rule.

Three days before the election, Tom Hansen of the Mexico Solidarity Network becomes the first expelled human rights observer to return legally to Mexico. This begins a process culminating in the legal return of many, but not all, expelled observers.

On August 21, Pablo Salazar, representing a PAN/PRD alliance, wins the governorship of Chiapas, ending decades of PRI domination.

Fox assumes the presidency on November 30 with promises to "resolve the problems in Chiapas in 15 minutes." Simultaneously, the Zapatistas end five months of silence, lambasting former President Zedillo and calling on the new administration to meet three demands before peace talks can resume: withdraw troops from seven of 250 military encampments in Chiapas, release all Zapatista political prisoners, and implement the San Andrés Accords. Fox responds by dismantling military checkpoints throughout the state. Over the next five months he gradually dismantles the seven army encampments—turning two into "social service centers"—and releases most of the political prisoners.

On December 5, Fox introduces constitutional reforms prepared by a Congressional peace commission (Cocopa) that would implement the San Andrés peace accords, giving indigenous communities autonomy, control over their natural resources, and respect for their traditional customs. Later, it becomes clear that Fox introduced the reforms with a series of secret commentaries encouraging Congress to modify the Cocopa proposal in significant ways.

2001

On February 24, two dozen Zapatista commanders, led by Subcomandante Marcos, begin an unprecedented two-week caravan from Chiapas to Mexico City to lobby for the Cocopa law. Hundreds of thousands of Mexican citizens greet the caravan, culminating in a 250,000-strong demonstration in Mexico City on March 11.

Despite a massive outpouring of support for the Zapatistas, both the Senate and House pass heavily modified versions of the Cocopa law in late April. The Zapatista Comandancia and the National Indigenous Congress immediately declare the law inconsistent with the San Andrés Accords and unacceptable, and begin national mobilizations in support of the original Cocopa law.

In June, 2001, President Vicente Fox and Central American presidents sign the Plan Puebla Panama agreement, outlining a neoliberal vision of economic development for southern Mexico and Central America. Tens of thousands of indigenous peoples will likely be resettled as transportation corridors and maquiladores link the Pacific and Atlantic, mainly for the benefit of transnational corporations. The Zapatista struggle continues, but with new challenges that look very much like the old challenges.

PART ONE

THE STORY

OPENING SHOTS

ANDREW KOPKIND

Originally appeared as an unsigned editorial in
The Nation, January 31, 1994.

THE armed insurgency against the Mexican government that began New Year's Day in the remote state of Chiapas draws heavily on symbols and styles of the past. The rebels call themselves Zapatistas, after the great Mexican revolutionary Emiliano Zapata, who led a peasant uprising 80 years ago; comparisons to the followers of Augusto Sandino and Farabundo Martí, in nearby Central American nations, inevitably leap to mind. Some of the guerrillas who have been interviewed speak admiringly of the Cuban revolution and say that communism is the one correct solution. The authorities respond with their own clichéd charges of international conspiracies and outside agitation. Worse, they bomb civilians, clear villages, and execute peasants death-squad style—tactics learned in dirty wars from Guatemala to Argentina, Angola to Vietnam.

And yet the revolt of the Chiapanecos is something stunningly new, the first shots of a rebellion consciously aimed at the new world order, the dire consequences of a history that did not die as predicted but intrudes in the most pernicious manner on the way of life of people always overlooked. It is a war against the globalization of the market, against the destruction of nature and the confiscation of resources, against the termination of indigenous peoples and their lands, against the growing maldistribution of wealth and the consequent decline in standards of living for all but the rich. It might be that the battle in Chiapas will end with the predictable bangs and whimpers heard whenever outnumbered, outgunned peasants without powerful international support are picked off and packed away. But the shots fired in Mexico in the first week of the new year have been heard around the world, and their echoes will not soon stop.

The Mayan tribes that inhabit the forests and secluded valleys of Chiapas have suffered without much relief since the Spanish Conquest 500 years ago; only the specifics of their misery have changed with the layers of history. Despite the rhetoric of the 1910 Mexican Revolution, the Indians were excluded from its benefits, however meager and stunted. For the most part they could not own land even when land reform laws were passed. They survived by subsistence farming, supplemented with a bit of cash from coffee, corn, and other agricultural commodities. And all the while they were brutally repressed by the "European" police, landlords, ranchers, and politicians of the dynastic PRI—the party that is revolutionary in name only and has ruled as a virtual dictatorship.

Things started going from bad to very bad for the peasants in the late 1980s when coffee prices slumped—not by an act of God or chance, but because President Bush orchestrated an end to the stable commodity markets to enforce his free-market ideology. Cappuccino drinkers in Seattle rejoiced; small coffee growers in Chiapas suffered.

About the same time, the Mexican government began speeding up its "modernization" program, which entailed across-the-board privatization of the economy and integration of the resulting structure into the US-led global system. In Chiapas, for instance, peasants could get ownership title or credit for their once-communal plots of land. Many took credit, but without a market for their surplus the land was soon foreclosed—and, with government and police help, wound up in the hands of big cattle ranchers. The Indians were pushed farther into the Chiapan rain forest, where they slashed and burned the land simply to survive for a few years—until that conveniently cleared land was grabbed by the ranchers. The Mayans inevitably have been forced to give up their life on the land (tiny Chiapas, with 3,000,000 inhabitants and thousands of refugees from the long war in Guatemala, has the highest indigenous population in the country) and join the city slum dwellers. Ultimately, the laws of population hydraulics push commensurate numbers of displaced and desperate people over the border to El Norte.

The passage of NAFTA provided the spark igniting the revolt, because its provisions so clearly imply the destruction of the Indian peasants' lives, culture, and history. Corn in the Mexican south cannot compete with the high-tech productivity in Bob Dole's Kansas or Tom Harkin's Iowa (both of whom voted for the treaty). The indigenous people are unequipped and ill-placed to become workers in export-oriented factories. The social services and land reforms brightly packaged by Mexican President Salinas as the

"Solidarity" plan are inadequate and do not protect the Mayans, who continue to be exploited by ranchers, oil companies, forest clearers, landlords, and police. In fact, the horrendous abuses documented by international human rights agencies have increased with the new economic pressures of the past several years. Local Catholic priests and bishops provide the only aid and comfort, but they are also under attack from the hierarchy.

The timing of the Zapatista invasion of several towns to coincide with NAFTA implementation shows how well the processes of history are understood: Mo' better in San Cristóbal de las Casas, it seems, than in Washington or L.A. It's not that the treaty itself causes all the grievances the guerrillas list, but the ideological underpinnings and political effects of the new globalism have suddenly become real and clear. A small army of Mayans can't reverse those effects, but the battle of Chiapas allows untold millions around the world to see that it's still possible to put up a fight.

ZAPATISTAS!
THE PHOENIX RISES

PACO IGNACIO TAIBO II

Originally appeared in
The Nation, March 28, 1994

I

THEY'VE come out of nowhere. From its perennially censorious perspective, the television repeatedly displays without understanding the faces of the Zapatista rebels, hooded by ski masks or covered with quintessentially Mexican paliacates (the red, yellow, and black bandannas worn by Mexican campesinos).

What the hell is this? Paloma wakes me up in midmorning and puts me in front of the TV. The Zapatista guerrilla army has taken half a dozen cities in Chiapas, including the state's traditional capital, San Cristóbal de las Casas.

The first words delivered by the rebels to the TV cameras are enunciated in shaky Spanish with a peculiar syntax: *Vinimo de aquí porque no*

aguantamos, ¿qué?, el ejército que persigue a nosotros. Vinimo a la guerra.
"We came here because we couldn't take it, see? The army is persecuting us. We came to the war."

Among the guerrillas are some officers, very few, whose speech gives away their urban origins; they could be members of a far left group, students who fled chronic unemployment to burrow into the jungle in what the language of the left called *trabajo de topo*, mole's work (teaching literacy classes, barefoot doctoring, organizing cooperatives), or schoolteachers who went through 20 years of ceaseless struggle in order to win the right to earn $200 a month and, in a handful of regions, to elect union representatives. But the vast majority are indigenous. Tzeltales, Choles, Mijes, Tojolabales. From the tribal babel of Chiapas, where the lingua franca of almost 60 percent of the population is not Spanish but one of the indigenous dialects.

Their weapons are indigenous, too. The images show an AK-47 here and there, an assault rifle stolen from the Mexican Army, but the majority are carrying shotguns and .22–caliber hunting rifles, even machetes and stakes, or wooden guns with a nail in the tip of the barrel. A lot of them are women and children. They're uniformed: green baseball caps, green pants, homemade black vests, *paliacates* around their necks or covering their faces.

The country enters the year 1994 with an insurrection and no one except the rebels understands anything.

II

They call themselves Zapatistas.

History repeats itself. In Mexico it always repeats itself. Neanderthal Marxists never get tired of reiterating that it repeats itself as farce, but that has nothing to do with it. It repeats itself as vengeance. In Mexico, the past voyages, rides, walks among us. Zapata is the key image: stubbornness, the dream cut short but not sold out.

III

In the first confrontation, 24 policemen died. In the fight for control of the town halls, the insurgents clashed with the state police, known as *judiciales*, and with the municipal police forces. The nation sees images of their dead bodies lying in the plazas. A lot of hate is stored up there. The judiciales are traditionally the landowners' white guards; they go into communities and ransack, make arrests, torture. Overheard on the second day of January in the Mexico City metro: *Los judiciales no son gente; no son personas.* "The judiciales aren't decent people; they aren't people."

IV

Are they crazy? How many of them are there? Where did the Zapatista army come from? Do they really think they can face in open combat a modern army that has air power, helicopters, heavy weapons, artillery?

In the first wave of attacks they've taken control of the entrances to the Lacandón jungle, the road from Chiapas to Guatemala and the second largest city in the state. The following day, they keep their promise and attack the military zone where the Thirty-first Army Division is headquartered. Then they disappear, falling back into the shadows. A reserve force of Zapatistas remains in Altamirano, Las Margaritas, and Ocosingo, the towns that serve as gateways to the jungle.

They have announced that they took up arms against a government founded on an electoral fraud, that they have decreed a new agrarian reform, that they will no longer endure any abuses by the police, the army, and the latifundios' caciques, that the North American Free Trade Agreement is the final kick in the stomach to the indigenous communities.

V

A couple days later, the coordinator of the coffee cooperatives of Chiapas will tell me that this rebellion was announced in advance. The air was full of forewarnings that the government didn't want to hear. No one would admit to being in the know.

An anthropologist friend who knows the region tells me that at the end of last summer the communities voted not to sow their crops. This, for groups that live from the precarious economy of corn, is death. There's no going back. He tells me that the rebel organization's work began 10 years ago. Looking back over the newspapers from the past few months I find bits of news here and there of clashes between the army, the police, and the indigenous communities.

At the end of March last year, the judiciales, in pursuit of an armed group that had killed two soldiers in an ambush, entered San Isidro Ocotal: Indigenous men—old men and one minor—were arrested. Some were tortured. In May, the same story. There were rumors of a guerrilla force. Everyone denied them. Soon afterward, the judiciales entered Patate Viejo, firing their guns. They assembled the residents of the small community in the basketball court, picked out eight at random, arrested them and took them to the penitentiary in Cerro Hueco. Mexico's Secretary of Gobernación (who is in charge of internal political affairs and police) acknowledged a few days after the fighting broke out that he knew of the existence of 15 guerrilla training centers.

VI

I haven't left the house in three days except to buy the newspaper. I talk on the phone, listen to the radio, watch television with the fascination of a blind man seeing an image for the first time.

An agrarianist friend explains to me that 15,000 indigenous people have died of hunger and easily curable diseases in Chiapas in the past few years. Without crop rotation, the fields are not very productive. The price of coffee has dropped, so the landowners have seized more land for cattle; they create conflicts between the communities and assassinate community leaders. Although the land cannot feed any more people, the population has been growing by 6 percent annually with the arrival of indigenous refugees from Guatemala and the internal migration of Indians whose land has been taken by the owners of the large haciendas. All this in a region where there is no electricity, 70 percent of the population is illiterate, most houses have no sewage systems or hookups for potable water, and the average monthly income of a family is less than $130.

VII

In *La Jornada*, I read a fascinating story. The night they took San Cristóbal, the Zapatistas burned the municipal archives, the financial records, the land titles. The director of the historical archive negotiated with them: "You aren't going to burn the historical archive. The papers there tell the history of the origin of this city. The history of the seventeenth-century campesino rebellions and the Tzeltal uprising are there." The Zapatista committee met. Not only did they not burn it, they posted someone to guard it.

VIII

In an amazing burst of lucidity, Toño García de León, one of our best anthropologists, foretold what was going to happen in a book published nine years ago, *Resistencia y Utopía*. García says, "The elements of the past are still here, as alive as phantoms and wandering souls. . . . The subsoil of Chiapas is full of murdered Indians, petrified forests, abandoned cities, and oceans of petroleum."

Chiapas lies at the asshole of the world, where Jesus Christ lost his serape and John Wayne lost his horse. After the nineteenth-century uprisings had ended, the governors had their pictures taken standing next to defeated midgets. The Mexican Revolution got here 20 years late, at a fraction of its original strength, leaving the large haciendas intact. The Lacandóns, a nearly extinct Indian tribe, buy electric lamps to put in rooms without electricity, towns without electricity, whole regions without electricity—in a state that has the country's largest hydroelectric dams. San Cristóbal, a gathering place for hippie tourists, has three Zen centers and hundreds of satellite dishes, and barefoot Indians walk through its streets unable to find work as bricklayers.

IX

A popular Mexican bandit of the 1920s, el Tigre de Santa Julia, died in a rather unseemly manner, trapped and pumped full of lead by the police while he was sitting on the toilet. When you're caught off guard, people say, "They got you like el Tigre de Santa Julia."

The Mexican state has been taken by surprise, like el Tigre de Santa Julia. Did they believe their own lies? Here are the results of the last few elections in Chiapas: According to official figures, the Institutional Revolutionary Party (PRI) won in 1976 with 97.7 percent of the vote, in 1982 with 90.2 percent, in 1988 with 89.9 percent.

Were they so stupid that they believed the official figures? They must have been the only ones.

People say Salinas had information on what was being planned and preferred to ignore it so as not to cast a shadow over the celebration of the implementation of NAFTA.

But elections are coming up. The chief opposition again is the Democratic Revolutionary Party (PRD), led by Cuauhtémoc Cárdenas. To confront it with a new electoral fraud while a civil war is brewing would throw gasoline on the flames.

X

In post-1968 Mexico, the forces of the new left opted to work for social organization among the masses. Thousands of students were mobilized by the union movement, the struggle in the slums, the slow work of assistance to campesino insurgent movements. A minority took up arms. There was never much sympathy between the two groups, who accused each other of being "ultras" and "reformists." The guerrillas, caught up in a crazed spiral of minor confrontations that led to new clashes until their final annihilation by the police, never took any interest in working with the people. They heated things up, and years of union or campesino work were often endangered by their sectarian adventures. In short, the majority of the Left was never attracted to the idea of armed struggle. But the Zapatista uprising generates a wave of sympathy.

"How could I not like them?" Ernesto, a university union organizer, tells me, "since I agree with their program for a new democracy, and since they're not some tiny group, they don't want to be anybody's vanguard, they don't impose their path, they're indigenous, they're an uprising of the masses and on top of that they've been screwed over even worse than I have."

XI

The army deployed 10,000 soldiers in the first days of the conflict, and the figure slowly rose to 17,000, one-third of the Mexican Army. Jeeps with machine guns, tanks, helicopters, German G-3 rifles, Saber planes.

XII

The dead will always be dead. The horror draws nearer. In the face of horror, political explanations are not moving. Reasons are harsh in wartime. I'm disturbed by the repeated sight of the bodies of campesinos, riddled with bullets, lying in ditches along the road. I see terrible images of a baby girl killed by a grenade fragment, her body lying in a cardboard box.

XIII

An enormous demonstration is held in Mexico City against the government's policy in Chiapas and for peace, with close to 150,000 attending. One of the chants: "First World, ha ha ha." Again we see the faces of the Old and New Left, but also of thousands of students joining the movement for the first time.

The Zapatistas are not alone. Their program and the faces and motives of the indigenous rebels are greeted with a massive outpouring of sympathy that is reflected in the press. Something new, something different, is happening.

XIV

The Department of Gobernación has decided to invent an enemy phantom. The real phantoms, the Chiapan rebels, aren't of much use in the great propaganda war that is being launched—they're too likable. One of the ski-masked comandantes, the one who led the occupation of San Cristóbal de las Casas and who said his name was Marcos, is chosen. He is useful because he appears to be from the city; he isn't indigenous and might even be foreign. A verbal portrait is disseminated across the country. His vital statistics: six feet tall, blond hair, green eyes, speaks three languages (where the hell did they come up with that one? and why not four languages, or five?).

The newspaper-reading sector of the country laughs at the absurdity. People call you on the phone to tell you that Marcos is their cousin, that he's the milkman. The phantom is welcomed in a wave of affection. The newsmagazine *Proceso* has just sanctified him by putting a close-up of him on the cover of its first issue on Chiapas. A Venezuelan biologist doing research on the endangered jaguars of the Lacandón jungle—and whose closest contact with a jaguar to date was the sight of some excrement—is arrested and beaten. The judiciales want him to confess to being the guerrilla commander in chief. Marcos himself laughs at his popularity in a joking letter to the media.

But does Commander Marcos really exist? Interviewed in the municipal palace of San Cristóbal at dawn on the first day of January, after the Zapatistas had made a clean sweep of the judiciales, the phantasmagoric Marcos avows that he is there to carry out the policies of a committee of indigenous campesinos; he is only a subcomandante, and he warns that the name "Marcos" is interchangeable—anyone can put on a ski mask and say "I am Marcos." He invites people to do so.

XV

"It's like Vietnam," says a soldier talking on the phone, overheard by an alert *La Jornada* reporter standing in line behind him. "They come out of the mist."

XVI

The jungle air is full of messages. At night, 150 short-wave radio stations saturate the ether over the ravines and footpaths with cryptic messages: "Six for Uruguay, do you copy?" "Truckloads of green cement passed in Paris." Zapatista bases identifying themselves as Two, Zero, and Thunder are the most important. The helicopters try to avoid the antennae that rise through the trees.

XVII

Bombs in the Distrito Federal of the capital. The war comes nearer to the monster city. The "bombers" aren't Zapatistas. A mini-sect of the extreme left, said to be fully infiltrated by the Department of Gobernación, is responsible. Even so, the feeling that the war is getting closer and could burst out of the TV screen and explode on the corner of your street sweeps the city for a week.

XVIII

The government tightens its grip. A general mobilization of the army has been ordered. Then, the armed resistance of the Zapatistas and the almost unanimous response of the intellectual community (with the lamentable exception of Octavio Paz, who weeps for a lost "modernity"), along with the demonstration in Mexico City, force the government to draw back. It changes its line, changes its personnel, dismisses the Secretary of Gobernación, the Attorney General, the governor of Chiapas. The soft line takes over. Manuel Camacho Solís, whom Salinas recently rejected as the PRI candidate for the presidency, is now Salinas's man once more and becomes a negotiator.

An amnesty is proclaimed.

In a desperate quest to end the conflict, economic support plans rapidly succeed one another, institutions are created to protect the indigenous people (from whom? from themselves?) and the official discourse adopts the critiques of the left and incorporates them, chameleonlike. The jaguar is a Mexican species. The Venezuelan biologist should have known that.

A cease-fire is declared—a tense cease-fire.

///

XIX

On TV there are images of soldiers vaccinating children and distributing food. The women standing in line for food in Ocosingo's plaza don't get any the second day if they don't bring their husbands. The soldiers distributing food are there to identify Zapatistas.

XX

Rumors again. Phone calls from journalist friends, low-voiced conversations during a Cárdenas rally on the esplanade of the Insurgentes metro station. Provocations are expected. There will be armed clashes. Does the army want to avenge the affront? The country grows uneasy once more. In Quintana Roo, only four kilometers from the Disneyland with real sharks known as Cancún, the judiciales arrest campesino leaders supposedly because they were armed. A secretary photographs a judiciale taking AK-47 bullets out of his sock and putting them inside a roll of toilet paper in the offices of the campesino union: This will be the proof. The judiciales unleash an enormous operation in the state of Guerrero. During the meeting of a powerful organization of agrarian unions on the Isthmus of Tehauntepec in the state of Oaxaca, many voices are heard protesting against the pacifism of the leaders: "If we'd rebelled, people wouldn't have died from the epidemic, there would be a hospital by now and the fraud would have fallen flat on its ass." The states of Tabasco and Michoacán are worried. The Cárdenas-led opposition won the elections there, and a spectacular fraud was carried out. During the past two years, campesino community leaders who were members of the PRD have been assassinated.

XXI

The Zapatistas aren't in any hurry. They're waging a masterful media war, keeping up the pressure while dissidents across the country go on the alert and mobilize. The pressure must be kept up in order to establish non-fraudulent conditions for the next elections.

A space for the social movements opens. Some of the townships that were occupied in the coastal region of Chiapas throw out mayors accused of fraud; indigenous communities in Oaxaca, Michoacán and Puebla mobilize; 10,000 teachers in Chiapas march to demand a 100 percent increase in salary. During this impasse, Zapatismo acquires social legitimacy through T-shirts, posters, continuous declarations of allegiance.

The electoral campaign of the left and center left, a broad front led by Cárdenas, is growing and has adopted the Zapatistas' program as its own. A ring is forming around the PRI that will make it difficult for the party to stage more fraudulent elections in August.

Are we nearing the end of the oldest dictatorship in the world? From 1920 to 1994 they have governed this country in the name of modernity and a betrayed revolution. Has their moment passed?

XXII

For now we're walking on shadows, disturbed and filled with hope. We are waking up with the distinct feeling that we slept among phantoms.

THE MEDIA SPECTACLE
COMES TO MEXICO

OCTAVIO PAZ

Originally appeared in
New Perspectives Quarterly, Spring 1994.

MEXICO CITY — The media spectacle so well perfected by our neighbors to the North has finally come to Mexico. During the months of crisis in Chiapas, television has involuntarily revealed to us a curious spectacle which combines religious liturgy with civic ceremony. The enchantment of certain images — in the original and powerful sense of the word enchantment: magical spell — is intensified because it reminds us of the romanticism of those scenes in novels and films in which masked conspirators appear gathered together in a catacomb around an altar (in this case, the domes of a cathedral). To all this one must add the illusion of seeing an historical deed "live." Which is, in fact, true: we have seen it, but staged and with makeup.

It is true that politics borders on the one side with theater and on the other with religion. Symbols are a central element in these rites. Like the theatrical scene or the mass, the political act is a representation. That is why the principal initiation to politics is not through the treatises of our political theorists but through Shakespeare's theater. Therefore, what sets apart our era from the preceding ones is the double preeminence of news and the image over reality. Through the image, time loses continuity and consistency to the benefit of the instantaneous sensation; through news, the true reality is always something else; it is over there. I see it but I don't touch it; nor do I think it; unutterable, it disappears in a wink.

For more than 30 years we have lived in what a French writer has called "a society of spectacles." In the world of spectacles, things occur as they do in the real world and at the same time, they occur in another way, in the magical space and time of representation. They are here and they are there.

It is not arbitrary for me to use a language reminiscent of that of the clergy; the ancients had visions, we have television.

But the civilization of the spectacle is cruel. The spectators have no memory—because of that they also lack remorse and true conscience. They live tied to what is new, and it doesn't matter what it is so long as it is new. They quickly forget and scarcely blink at the scenes of death and destruction of the Persian Gulf War or at the curves, contortions, and tremulos of Madonna and of Michael Jackson. Commandants and bishops are condemned to suffer the same fate: they also await the Great Yawn, anonymous and universal, which is the Apocalypse and Final judgement of the society of spectacle.

We are condemned to this new version of hell; those who appear on the screen and those of us who watch. Is there an escape? I don't know. One must seek it.

In order to attempt it, we must turn off the television, close the newspaper or the magazine, and go out for a walk. But walk where? Outside or within? It doesn't matter if it is through the streets of our city, populated with phantoms like ourselves, or through the imaginary plazas of dreams explored with eyes closed, unconscious in the cold light of dawn.

The point is to walk inward or outward among known specters or among strangers with whom we converse every day, losing ourselves in the city or in our thoughts, touching the hand of a neighbor, questioning the child entombed within; to stop being images, to become again what we are; men and women, blood and time.

CHIAPAS: THE WORDS AND THE GESTURES

It is not pointless with regard to the negotiations of San Cristóbal to dedicate a brief commentary to another aspect of the Chiapas conflict. I refer to its influence on the attitudes of many of our intellectuals and above all, on public opinion in Mexico City.

I begin with an obvious observation; the conflict has been the cause of little spilt blood but much flowing of ink. The seas of ink which darken our newspapers at first produced an intellectual tickle: Now they provoke an invincible yawn. But tedium cannot and should not justify our silence in view of certain heedless opinions.

For example, one of the more unscrupulous Latin American intellectuals was inspired to say that the Chiapas Movement "was the first post-communist revolution of the twenty-first century." Now a half dozen parrots are imperturbably repeating this absurdity.

It is hardly necessary to point out that the Chiapas matter is not a revolution either by its proportions—it involves four districts—or by its doctrine or ideology. The rebels are not proposing to change the world, the distinctive sign of all true revolutions—even less, our country. Their program does not advocate change in the social or economic system. Nor is the movement "postmodern," as others have stated. Their demands, many of them justified, are directed toward mending traditional abuses and injustices against the indigenous communities and asking for the establishment of an authentic democracy. This last point is an aspiration as old as the Revolution of 1910. With this "historical" criteria, Madero would be Mexico's "first postmodern revolutionary."

Nevertheless, the Chiapas rebels are indeed decidedly ultramodern in the most precise sense: through their style. It is a question of an aesthetic definition more than a political one. Beginning with their first public appearance on the first day of January, they revealed a noteworthy control over an art that the modern media has evolved to a dangerous perfection: public relations. Later, during the discussions and negotiations in the Cathedral of San Cristóbal, each one of their presentations has had the solemnity of a ritual and the seduction of a spectacle. Beginning with their attire—the black and blue knit masks, the colored neck scarves and their master of the use of symbols like the national flag and religious images—they offer the spectacle of hooded characters that television simultaneously brings close and and then draws away on the screen; close up and yet remote, a hallucinatory museum of wax figures.

The spokesperson for the rebels, Marcos, stands out as well through an art forgotten by our politicians and ideologues: rhetoric. The language of the leaders of the PRI is a language of bureaucrats: phrases constructed of cardboard and plastic; that of Subcommandante Marcos, although uneven and full of ups and downs like a roller coaster, is imaginative and lively. His pastiches of evangelical language and more frequently, of indigenous eloquence with its recurring formulas, its metaphors and mytonomy, are almost always fortunate. Sometimes he is artless and coarse; other times brilliant and eloquent; others, satirical and realistic; again, brutal and sentimental. A stylized prose; cadenced and uneven. His strength is not reason but emotion and unction: the pulpit and the rally.

Although the political texts of the rebels are principally destined for the masses, they seem well thought out and written to seduce or irritate an elite—that middle class that flocks to literary cafes, reads cultural supplements, goes to exhibitions and lectures, loves rock and Mozart, takes part in avant-garde spectacles and attends marches. Thanks to his rhetoric and undeniable theatrical talent, Subcommandant Marcos has won the opinion battle. In this, not in a supposed "postmodernity," rests the secret of his popularity among intellectuals and among the vast sectors of the middle class in Mexico City.

THEUNMASKING

ALMA GUILLERMOPRIETO

Originally appeared in
The New Yorker, March 13, 1995.

March 3

ON the evening of February 9, at a press conference in Mexico City that had been announced less than two hours before, an aide to the attorney general played a strange game of peekaboo with photographers and a crowd of sweating, jostling reporters. In his right hand the aide held an oversized black-and-white slide of a ski mask and a pair of large, dark eyes, and in his left a black-and-white photograph of a Milquetoasty-looking young man with a beard and large, dark eyes. After we were allowed to study the two for a few seconds, the aide slipped the slide over the photograph. Voilà! Subcomandante Marcos, the dashing leader of an Indian peasant revolt in southeastern Mexico, the hero of a thousand fervent letters addressed to the Mexican nation, the postmodern revolutionary who has contributed mightily to what in this turbulent year, with its hemorrhaging economy and political murder scandals, looks like the steady crumbling of a 66-year-old regime—this masked idol is a Clark Kent. His name, the attorney general announced, is Rafael Sebastián Guillén, and he is a philosophy graduate and former university professor. The aide continued imposing the slide of Marcos on the photograph of Guillén and flipping them apart again—now we saw him, now we didn't—until the storm of camera flashes subsided, and then we left.

The revelation of Marcos's identity was part of a two-pronged strategy by President Ernesto Zedillo Ponce de León to break the stalemate that has existed in the state of Chiapas since the Ejercito Zapatista de Liberation National, or EZLN—a ragtag army of Mayan peasants led by Subcomandante Marcos—rose up in revolt there, on January 1, 1994. Even as we watched the slide show, Army troops were preparing to move into the mountainous and overwhelmingly rural southeastern part of Chiapas—almost on the border with Guatemala—where the Zapatistas had maintained their unofficially recognized *territorio liberado* for 13 months. Villages were being retaken without a fight, and their inhabitants, including the Zapatista fighters among them, were fleeing into the ravines and the jungle-covered mountains. President Zedillo said that the Army was going into the area only to provide backing for the federal agents who would attempt to serve Marcos with an arrest warrant, but this was a transparent excuse, for thousands of troops swarmed in, and have continued to take positions farther and farther inside the territory.

Before the offensive began, the stalemate between the Zapatistas and the government had lasted so long that it seemed permanent. All actual fighting ended barely twelve days after the New Year's Day rebellion got under way last year, in the lovely town of San Cristóbal de las Casas. The peasant army had vowed in its declaration of war that it would march to Mexico City and overthrow the government of President Carlos Salinas de Gortari, but, instead, it suffered significant losses and scored no military victories. It did, however, capture Mexicans' imagination: televised interviews of Mayan peasants in makeshift uniforms, who said that they were fighting not only for a change in their own desperate circumstances but to rid the nation of a corrupt and slothfiil regime, brought thousands of demonstrators out into the streets all over Mexico during the first days.of January, demanding an end to what threatened to turn into an Army slaughter of the armed Zapatistas and their families.

Faced with the politically volatile option of turning the Army against its own people, Salinas, on January 12, called for a ceasefire. Thereafter, and through the transfer of power in December from Salinas to Ernesto Zedillo, following the Presidential elections last August, talks and attempts at talks promoted by both sides led to no fruitful agreement, but they at least kept the ceasefire from breaking down. Even in December, when the Zapatistas pushed beyond their control zone to protest the stalemate and what they saw as massive fraud in the elections for governor of Chiapas, the rebels and the government troops managed to come within a few hundred feet of each other without a shot being fired.

The Army's offensive certainly appears to have taken Marcos completely by surprise. Much of the anxious speculation about what will happen next in Chiapas centers on his personality and his aims—on what he believes in and to what lengths he is willing to take the war. Will he negotiate to keep his peasant troops from suffering further? Does he really want nothing less than the overthrow of the government? And is he in fact the man in the photograph?

As FAR AS I could tell on the night of the attorney general's press conference, as I tried to make the 10-year-old ID shot of a bland Rafael Guillén jibe with my recollection of the masked man I had talked with last April, the ski-masked slide we were being shown could have been slipped just as persuasively over a photograph of Richard Nixon. The Marcos whom I and other journalists interviewed in the Zapatista control zone was a mesmerizing personality—self-possessed, considerate, ironic, and theatrical. He liked to make journalists spend hours, or days, waiting for him, and then he would appear in the dead of night and talk endlessly, puffing on a pipe, tugging at the uncomfortable ski mask, and asking as many questions as he answered—uncannily well informed about the intellectual and media world beyond Chiapas. When I said that it was delusionary to think that the Zapatistas could really take Mexico City, he answered, "Weren't we there already by January second? We were everywhere, on the lips of everyone—in the subway, on the radio. And our flag was in the Zócalo"—the central plaza.

While the resemblance between Guillén's eyes and Marcos's—the only part of his physiognomy we are all acquainted with—is not conclusive (Marcos's are a hazel-brown, for one, and the photograph is black-and-white), the account of the EZLN's history and Marcos's role in it which the Attorney General's office has been leaking to the press does coincide with much that has been said privately about Marcos in Chiapas for some time.

According to what can be pieced together from these convergent accounts, the EZLN has its roots in the Latin American guerrilla movements that sprang up in Mexico beginning in the tumultuous 1960s. In the early 1970s, one of those guerrilla groups, the Fuerzas de Liberación Nacional, or FLN, had a training camp in Chiapas, near Ocosingo, a town that sits on the edge of what later became the Zapatista control zone. In 1974, the Army raided that camp, arrested several of the guerrillas, and "disappeared" three others, including a woman whose first name was Elisa. People here have speculated that one of the guerrillas who survived—the brother of one of the disappeared men—took refuge in the north of Mexico for a few years and then returned to Chiapas, using the code name Germán. He was either accompanied by, or eventually joined by a dozen others, among them a second-year woman medical student, who had been captured in a raid on another FLN camp. After spending a few months in jail, she had been granted a presidential amnesty. In Chiapas, she took the code name Elisa—presumably in honor of the disappeared guerrilla from the Ocosingo camp. Sometime around 1984, a year after the EZLN's official founding, a young; bright philosophy graduate who was known first as Zacarías and then, much more recently, as Marcos, linked up with these comrades in Chiapas. The government claims that Subcomandante Marcos—that is, Rafael Guillén—is the son of a prosperous furniture retailer from Tampico, and was a leftist activist student and a teacher at a Mexico City university before he left for Chiapas. It also claims that, although Comandante Germán is still at large, Comandante Elisa was captured two days before the February 10 offensive.

At the university, a fairly radical enclave called the Universidad Autónoma Metropolitana, which was founded in 1973, people certainly remember Guillén. In the early 1980s, a friend of mine who taught there recalls, the faculty saw social activism as part of its mandate. "We wanted to put the emphasis as much on practice as on theory, and we understood that it was our duty to give back to the community what we received from it," he says. "We were all radicals, particularly those of us in the Design Science and Arts Division. But no one was more radical than a group of young, brilliant, serious, and hardworking teachers in the Department of Theory and Analysis. Guillén and Silvia"—Silvia Hernández, an EZLN founding member—"were in the middle of that group. I thought we were perhaps too sectarian, but they beat us. They kept strictly to themselves, like a little family. But they came up with very original, very creative projects: They were big on Althusser"—Louis Althusser, the French philosopher—"on his theories of ideology and communication, and on something they called *grá-fica monumental*. Before they left the school, they did a wonderful mural for the auditorium—it's still there today."

MY FRIEND COULD not say for certain, at twelve years' remove, whether the man he remembered as Rafael Guillén would prove to be Marcos. Most reporters who have interviewed Marcos have no opinion on his like-ness to Guillén's mug shot, but none of us could fail to notice how much Marcos talks like one of Guillén's brothers—Alfonso Guillén, a university professor in Baja California Sur, who was shown on television on February 9 being hounded by reporters as he tried to explain, with much of Marcos's striking calmness and courtesy, why he had not seen his brother Rafael in several years. There were other clues as well: before the Army incursion, the "capital" of the Zapatistas' *territorio liberado* was an impressively large per-formance space built out of nothing in a clearing in the jungle and presided over by an amphitheater whose benches covered the entire face of a steep triangular hill and whose rostrum was fronted with socialist-realist paint-ings—surrealist, in their jungle surroundings—that recalled the mural at the university.

Marcos's preoccupation with symbolic language is certainly worthy of a student of Althusser. He has created his own dazzling image as a masked *mito genial*—his term, meaning an inspired act of mythmaking. He has staged a very real, threatening war on the Mexican state based on almost no firepower and a brilliant use of Mexicans' most resonant images: the Rev-olution, the peasants' unending struggle for dignity and recognition, the betrayed Emiliano Zapata. And he has used his writing: What we know about Marcos is mostly what he has written about himself. "How do you manage to write so much?" he asked me enviously when he showed up at last on the night we talked, in a hamlet in the Zapatista control zone in April. I pointed out that writing was what I did for a living, whereas he had a revolution to run and nevertheless managed to produce reams of copy. (Rather more than my output, in fact. The collected letters and commu-niqués he published in the Mexican press in the first eight months of last year alone have just been turned into a good-sized book.) It had not dawned on me then that the most visible and critical part of the Zapatistas' revolu-tion was the letters that the Mexican press publishes regularly—particularly the long, sometimes poetic, sometimes irreverent, personified postscripts that are the subcomandante's contribution to epistolary art. Now swagger-ing, now full of righteous fury, now impudent and hip, the Marcos of the postscripts is at all times both elusive and intimate, and this seductive knack has allowed him to become a faceless stand-in for all the oppressed, an anonymous vessel for all fantasies from the sexual to the bellicose, a star.

Marcos's letters exhibit an intense, self-involved romanticism, and so did Rafael Guillén's senior thesis at the university, which was ostensibly about Althusser and really about himself. Guillén wrote, "One thing is certain: the philosopher is 'different'; he belongs to a strange lineage of 'sensibilities that keep themselves at a prudent distance from the trite'; he can reflect with a brilliant phrase that will eventually pass into posterity on the death of an ant squashed as it tries to cross a busy street at 8 P.M. . . . His hair is disorderly and his beard unkempt, his gaze is continually ecstatic, as in an orgasm not yet achieved; cigarettes and coffee are part of his persona." Marcos, too, likes to come up with little fables about ants and rather personal things about sex. ("The anchor's long chain . . . groans when it is detached from its moist bed like our sex from the feminine belly," he wrote last August.)

WHEN MARCOS ARRIVED in Chiapas to join his friends—lugging too many books through the jungle, by his own account—he found fertile ground for a rebellion. The southeastern part of the state, where the revolt first took hold, and where the Zapatistas eventually set up their control zone, is one of the most backward in all Mexico, but it is also an area whose inhabitants were already familiar with and eager for ideological debate. The region is known as Las Cañadas, or the Canyons. It has no paved roads, no phones, little electricity, hardly any working schools, and a soaring population-growth rate. It was settled by campesino migrants from other parts of the state and from the rest of Mexico, most of them Mayan Indians who speak Tojolabal, Tzeltal, and Tzotzil, and little Spanish, and came to what used to be the nearly uninhabited Lacandón jungle in search of land where they could grow their corn and raise their families in peace. For years, the Bishop of San Cristóbal, Samuel Ruíz, had preached Indian rights and egalitarianism in the hamlets of Las Cañadas, and also for years radical activists had done organizing work in the communities—sometimes in agreement with Bishop Ruíz's network of priests and deacons, sometimes at odds with them.

The radicals' work was increasingly successful as the land ran out and, once cleared of its jungle covering, turned stingy. Government repression helped, and so did private attacks. Chiapas is an actively racist state; its cattle ranchers enlisted moonlighting policemen, soldiers, and ranch hands to terrorize—and, fairly often, to murder—the Indian peasants who, with Bishop Ruíz's encouragement, were daring to organize themselves. People from Chiapas who know Las Cañadas well say that Marcos, Germán, and Elisa usurped the Church's existing network of priests and deacons to promote "self-defense brigades," and gained credibility among the population by offering health services. (Whether the demure dark-haired former medical student who was presented to the press as Elisa, and is married to a freelance television producer—also under arrest—is really the EZLN comandante is uncertain. She has disavowed her initial confession, saying that government agents blindfolded her and threatened the life of her two-year-old son to make her sign it, but, as far as I know, she has not specifically denied that she is Elisa.)

According to several accounts, the guerrillas' work added to the divisions in the by-now radicalized communities. Some of Bishop Ruíz's most deeply committed followers abandoned him to join the EZLN. So did many of the campesinos initially organized by the radicals, whose leaders had by the late 1980s embarked on a series of close alliances with the government. On the other hand, many campesinos who had opted for the guerrillas' self-defense courses were offended by their theories of dialectical materialism and by their denial of the existence of God. (In the process of becoming "Indianized," Marcos told me, "there was a certain amount of clashing while we made the adjustment between our orthodox way of seeing the world in terms of bourgeois and proletarians to the community's worldview," and I assume that he was referring to the clash over religion.)

Sometime around 1993, the guerrillas themselves appear to have suffered, if not a split, at least a serious difference of opinion. People say they have heard stories that Marcos, on the basis of his organizing work, was convinced that Las Cañadas was ripe for an insurrection that would set off a revolutionary spark throughout Mexico. Apparently, neither Germán nor Elisa felt this to be the case, and they left the zone.

IT SEEMS UNLIKELY that the government found out what we now know about the EZLN from Elisa and the other guerrillas captured the day of the attorney general's press conference. For all the mystery surrounding the Zapatistas, the rebels had plenty of connections to both the Salinas and the Zedillo administrations, and it makes more sense to guess that information gathered from these sources had been known and kept for use at the moment when the government might decide that further attempts to reach a negotiated settlement with the Zapatistas would be fruitless. One former radical who has joined the establishment is Adolfo Orive, a founder of Politica Popular, the radical movement that first organized the Indian peasants in Las Cañadas; he is now Zedillo's chief adviser on rural affairs. Another is a ruling-party *diputado*, or member of the House of Representatives, who for years was part of the EZLN's high command, and is now known to the Zapatistas as a traitor. And then there is Raúl Salinas de Gortari, the "troublesome brother" of the former President, as the newsweekly *Proceso* called him in a prescient cover story last year. Raúl Salinas is a very wealthy man, an engineer with a postgraduate degree from a French university, a sometime litterateur. He has also, of course, just been indicted on charges of conspiring to murder his former brother-in-law José Francisco Ruíz Massieu, the secretary-general of the ruling party, who was assassinated last September. And he is a former Maoist who, together with Orive and, apparently, Comandante Germán, was active in Politica Popular, nearly two decades ago.

The warrant for the arrest of Rafael Guillén announced on February 9 has allowed the Zedillo administration to leak much of its hoarded information and rumor, but the government has not succeeded in what appears to have been its primary goal. The plan to disillusion Marcos's admirers with the revelation that the daring guerrilla is a sappy-looking academic full of old-line Marxist dogma worked for about 72 hours. A young acquaintance of mine who used to swoon at Marcos's name took one look at Guillén's photograph and said "Guácala!"—"Yuck!" That was on a Thursday. The following Sunday, the Mexico City papers received the first communiqué from Marcos since he, his troops, and his campesino followers retreated from their villages into the hills. It had three of his trademark addendums, in which the postscript itself becomes a character in a drama, and a signoff:

P. S. that rabidly applauds this new "success" of the government police: I heard they've found another "Marcos," and that he's from Tampico. That doesn't sound bad, the port is nice. I remember when I used to work as a bouncer in a brothel in Ciudad Madero [near Tampico], in the days when [a corrupt oilworkers'-union leader] used to do the same thing to the regional economy that Salinas did with the stock market; inject money into it to hide poverty. . . .

P.S. that despite the circumstances does not abandon its narcissism: So . . . Is this new Subcomandante Marcos good-looking? Because lately they've been assigning me really ugly ones and my feminine correspondence gets ruined.

P.S. *that counts time and ammunition:* I have 300 bullets, so try to bring 299 soldiers and police to get me. (Legend has it that I don't miss a shot, would you like to find out if it's true?) Why 299, if there's 300 bullets? Well, because the last one is for yours truly. It turns out that one gets fond of things like this, and a bullet seems to be the only consolation for this solitary heart.

Vale again. *Salud,* and can it be that there will be a little spot for me in her heart?

[signed] The Sup [Subcomandante], rearranging his ski mask with macabre flirtatiousness.

In five short paragraphs, the Sup reestablished his credentials as an outlaw hero, brought sex into the issue, and, yanking back the mask his pursuers had torn off, donned it once more. Two demonstrations were called by solidarity committees in Mexico City to protest the military attack on the Zapatistas and the arrest warrants on the EZLN leadership; according to press reports, tens of thousands of people showed up.

THERE WAS A very real sense in which, during the past 13 months, Marcos fought the Zapatista war singlehanded. It was, after all, a public-relations war, and the Indian fighters—most of whom spoke little Spanish, and for whom the government had provided, at most, a few years of elementary schooling—were not equipped for the sophisticated exchanges with the government and the Mexican public which such a war required. It was Marcos who wrote the letters, and also the communiqués signed by something called the Clandestine Indigenous Revolutionary Committee—General Command, which is supposedly the highest authority within the EZLN. (It is more likely the body, consisting of village authorities, that makes the real decisions affecting daily life in the Zapatista zone, while Marcos himself seems to have decisive influence, if not absolute power, in questions having to do with war and relations with the central government.) It was Marcos who granted the vast majority of the interviews—or, at least, the ones that got quoted. It was he who drew up the list of accredited "war correspondents," and signed our laminated mint-green credentials. It was he who stage-managed the moving EZLN events at which glamorous visitors from Mexico City and abroad watched Indian peasants parade in homemade uniforms, carrying hunting rifles and other guns and—in the absence of real weapons—carved wood imitations of guns. And it was his adroit manipulation of this array of symbolic weapons that mobilized public opinion in favor of the EZLN and kept the war the Zapatistas had invited at bay.

Marcos, however, cannot fight a real war by himself, and, on the basis of the Army's stunning advance over the last three weeks, it seems that any attempt by the EZLN troops to take on the Mexican Army can end only in tragedy. The total number of dead that reporters have reliably been able to come up with for the offensive is fewer than 10, and this is because, rather than fight, the Zapatistas and their families fled by the thousand into the jungly, ravine-crossed mountains that stand between their homes, in the former control zone, and what remains of the Lacandón jungle.

Just about a year ago, the government, desperate to appease the rebels of Las Cañadas, offered a settlement involving a cornucopia of social-works projects—health clinics and roads and electrification programs—and the insurgent peasants proudly turned down the offer, declaring that they wanted democracy as well. Less than a month ago, they were a defiant force, the improbable vanguard of a leftist movement that had finally managed to pose a real challenge to Zedillo's decrepit ruling party. Now the Zapatistas are terrified, sick with fear and hunger and in awe of the display of tanks and cannon the Army has ostentatiously deployed throughout the former control zone. Marcos continues to produce communiqués, but they are days late in arriving, evidently because an excellent communications network that included faxes and a satellite phone is no longer in place. As he did throughout the 13 months of ceasefire, he continues to warn that, although the Zapatistas want peace, and have therefore refrained from war, they can be pushed only so far.

But it is hard to see how much farther the rebels can be pushed without calling it defeat. Those of us who watched the repeated Zapatista military parades last year, and saw the carved wood weapons, assumed that the 400 or so troops who used to march were representative of thousands of others, and that the wooden weapons could, on the day of reckoning, be turned in for something to fight with. Perhaps we were wrong. "The EZLN is not willing to hold a dialogue in humiliating conditions," a recent communiqué stated. In other words, the EZLN has been humiliated. An amnesty law sent to Congress by Zedillo will most likely be approved. It is a surrender treaty disguised as a dialogue offer, and there is a good chance that the Zapatistas will sign it;. significant numbers of their supporters are already starting to return to the villages.

THE NEW PROMINENCE of the military establishment is only one of the worrying aspects of the Chiapas conflict. In the space of two weeks, the evening news led off with three different military ceremonies attended by

Zedillo. Although the Zapatistas' support network in the United States pumped up the Internet with reports of widespread killing by the Army, reporters could find no trace of these events, and it appears instead that the military has behaved with remarkable restraint by Latin-American standards. By these standards, restraint means that many peasants who did not flee have been arbitrarily detained in their villages, and are being threatened, beaten, asphyxiated, or deprived of food, so that they will denounce the Zapatistas among them. Essentially, the remilitarization of the Chiapas conflict means that the Mexican Army has been turned into an occupying force.

Then, there is the economic disaster that it has been Zedillo's lot to preside over. The best that can be expected is that the Mexican economy will remain in recession for at least a year, and it is not clear how money can be found to buy stability in Chiapas, where the economy has collapsed. Who will pay the taxes to pay for the public works demanded not only by the Zapatistas but now by virtually all of Chiapas's impoverished peasant population? And where is the land that can satisfy the campesinos' hunger, now that so much of the Lacandón jungle has been deforested and settled?

There was a phrase one heard everywhere last year, stated sometimes fearfully, sometimes with joy: *"Los indios perdieron el miedo"* — "The Indians are no longer afraid." Made fearless by the armed Zapatistas, *los indios* invaded some 2,000 cattle ranches and coffee farms. The owners are threatening to take up arms in defense of their land. *Los indios* also did fierce, bloody battle with each other over issues of religion and politics, which always had their roots in land disputes. Even if the Zapatistas are brought to their knees, these conflicts remain unresolved.

THERE IS A dreamlike quality about the speed with which the world that the Zapatistas created in their stronghold is being dismantled. Their pride, their monument, the capital of their *territorio liberado* — a ceremonial space baptized Aguascalientes, in honor of the site of the constitutional convention that was called by the revolutionaries of 1914, and in which Emiliano Zapata played a preponderant role — is gone. The Zapatistas built Aguascalientes last July in preparation for a National Democratic Convention called by Marcos, which was attended by thousands of Mexican delegates and hundreds of reporters from all over the world. Mexicans are lavish hosts, and the impoverished Indians of Las Cañadas were no exception. They cleared the jungle to build guesthouses, a kitchen, parking lots, even a library with makeshift bookshelves, so that their literate guests could feel at home. And they built the amphitheater, with a primitive rostrum to rival the one in the national Congress, in Mexico City, and gave it as a backdrop two enormous Mexican flags, just like the ones in Congress. In front of the rostrum, there was a parade space for the marching troops. For the audience, an entire hillside was covered with benches made out of split logs. It was a gigantic effort, worthy of the importance that the campesinos of Chiapas felt they had attained, and it took Army troops less than a week to dismantle the entire compound, log by log.

When I arrived at the site last week, government soldiers were planting the last of several hundred saplings in the holes where Y-posts had once held the benches of the amphitheater on the hill. I asked the colonel in charge of the operation why the government had felt that it was necessary to return Aguascalientes to the jungle. "I think that in Mexico the era calls for more wooded spaces," he said, explaining the issue ecologically. "The problem is that anyone can think of cutting down a tree, but no one thinks of planting one back."

I asked him why the troops seemed so relaxed, as if they had no fear of an enemy attack. "You're the one who says there are Zapatistas," he answered. "I've been stationed in the region eight months and I haven't seen one yet."

It took an hour to travel about 10 miles down a gutted road from the nearest town to another village in the region. The campesinos there had taken to the hills when they heard of the Army's approach, abandoning their yard animals and their supplies of corn, but days later, figuring that if they didn't reclaim their homes the Army would take them over, they had returned. Since then, they had not dared to leave the village to work their fields. Yet the radical fury of their discourse, their innocence of the world, their stubborn hope that the Zapatistas might yet manage to terrify the government into giving them a place in the world, was startling. "We don't know what the government looks like, where it sits, or what its palace is like," a woman said, in broken Spanish. She was choking with rage. "We are ignorant, but what I want to know is this: Do the bourgeois, the rich people's children, sleep on the floor, the way ours do? Do helicopters come and terrify them?"

"Let the government take its helicopters, tanks, and cars out of here," a man said, "because everyone knows that the Zapatistas aren't just a handful, so if it doesn't they will take revenge. Is it a crime to want what they want? We want justice, liberty, and democracy." And he added, with no apparent sense that one wish was infinitely smaller than the other, "We want the government to take us into account."

I told him that Aguascalientes was no more, and other villagers came close to hear the news.

"They didn't have to carry the logs to build it," the man said quietly. "Was it so much in their way that they had to destroy it?"

THE MARCOS MYSTERY:
A CHAT WITH THE SUBCOMMANDER OF SPIN

JOEL SIMON

Originally appeared in
Columbia Journalism Review, September 1994.

IN the July issue of *Vanity Fair*, Subcommander Marcos, the masked leader of Mexico's Zapatista Army of National Liberation, describes himself as a "brilliant myth." Despite the volume of ink that has been spilled about him, that's exactly what he remains. No journalist has figured out who Marcos is, really, and until someone does, he will continue to invent and reinvent the image of himself that he disseminates to visiting journalists. The mystery of Marcos helps continue to make him a good story, despite a lot of exposure; his secret identity allows him to be both elusive and accessible at the same time.

By the time I set out to interview Marcos this past March, three to five carloads of journalists were arriving every day at the Zapatista checkpoint heading into the Lacandón jungle. In San Cristóbal de las Casas, I had teamed up with Susan Ferriss of the *San Francisco Examiner* and photographer Ricardo Sandoval. At the Zapatista checkpoint, Bill Weinberg of *High Times* magazine and WBAI radio in New York joined our group. After two days of waiting, a Zapatista militiaman came to tell us that we would be permitted through the checkpoint.

The decision about who gets through is made by Marcos himself and those denied access are never explicitly told they will not be let in. Mexican journalists grumble that the foreign press gets preferential treatment. I'm not sure how Marcos decides whom to let in and whom to exclude, but he certainly has a remarkable knowledge of the US press. He asked Ferriss of the Hearst-owned *Examiner* what had ever become of Patty Hearst, and when he met Weinberg he blurted out the correct frequency for WBAI—99.5.

Inside the Zapatista camps, Marcos likes to make everyone wait for an interview, and in fact he seems to show up only after a journalist throws a tantrum or starts packing up to get ready to leave. In our case that was after almost a week. Through a courier, we sent a letter to Marcos letting him know that we had a flight the next morning and couldn't wait any longer. Late that night, he pushed open the door of the shack where we were sleeping, climbed into an empty bed, and lay there smoking a pipe until we noticed him. When he inhaled, the glowing tobacco illuminated a prominent nose, which was barely contained by his ski mask; a pair of tired-looking, greenish eyes; and a weatherbeaten, gray military cap adorned with three plastic stars. He spoke mostly in Spanish, occasionally lapsing into fluent, accented English.

It took me a while to make the transition from sleep and unfortunately our colleague Bill Weinberg was unable to do it. He woke up briefly when Marcos came in, and then went back to sleep convinced that the wise-cracking guy joking about his sex life couldn't possibly be a guerrilla commander, even if he did have a bandolier of red shotgun cartridges strung across his chest. But Marcos has a conscience; he gave Weinberg an exclusive interview the next morning.

Part of the explanation for the theatrics—long waits, dramatic midnight appearances—may be a legitimate security concern. The nocturnal visits can also be explained by Marcos's reported insomnia. But his antics also seem calculated to make for good copy. He tells different stories about his past during each interview.

For example, Marcos told us that during the *Vanity Fair* interview the week before he had invented stories about his early years. "I told them that I became a revolutionary because my parents had a bad divorce," he joked. "I told them a whole bunch of lies that I don't remember right now." (In fact he told them just the opposite—that he had a normal childhood and home life in northern Mexico.)

Marcos has said that he learned military strategy by reading CIA manuals, but he is less forthcoming about how he mastered the fine art of media relations. What is clear is that he began cultivating favorable press the moment the Zapatista uprising began. After the Zapatistas marched into San Cristóbal, virtually unopposed, on January 1, Marcos called out to Mexican journalists by name and invited them to take his picture (how he recognized them after supposedly spending a decade in the jungle remains a mystery). Within the first two months, he had granted extensive interviews to a number of publications, including the Mexican dailies *La Jornada* and *El Financiero*, and *The New York Times*. "We did not go to war on January 1 to kill or have them kill us," Marcos was quoted in the *Times* as saying. "We went to make ourselves heard."

In July, Marcos sent a facetious communique in which he both mocked journalists and revealed his knowledge of their trade: "Everything You Wanted to Know About El Sup [Marcos's nickname] but Were Afraid to Ask." It supplies reporters with a format and multiple choices for their pieces on the subcommander. "At last we arrived at (a valley/a forest/a clearing/a bar/a Metro station/a pressroom)," the communique says at one point. "There we found (El Sup/a transgressor of the law/a ski mask with a pronounced nose/a professional of violence). His eyes are (black/coffee/green/blue/red/honey-colored/oatmeal-colored/yogurt-colored/granola-colored). He lit his pipe while he sat on a (rocking chair/swivel chair/throne . . .)."

But while Marcos pretends to be tired of the ceaseless interviews, he also seems to accept that entertaining journalists is part of his job. Every positive story written about Marcos or the Zapatistas raises the political cost of a Mexican army assault on the ragtag rebels. Good press—in Mexico and in the US—is the Zapatistas' strongest defense.

Marcos's decidedly informal approach to interviews has occasionally gotten him in trouble. When he joked with a *San Francisco Chronicle* reporter that he had been fired from a restaurant in San Francisco for being gay, the Mexican press ran headlines claiming that Marcos had "admitted" that he was homosexual. (While the *Chronicle* article suggested that Marcos was joking, its pull quote did not.)

Marcos's response was interesting. The story could not be literally true, he asserted, because he was not a real person, but a myth. "Marcos is gay in San Francisco," noted a communique the subcommander penned in response to the controversy. "[He is] black in South Africa, an Asian in Europe, a Chicano in San Ysidro, an anarchist in Spain, a Palestinian in Israel . . . a pacifist in Bosnia, a housewife alone on a Saturday night in any neighborhood in any city in Mexico . . . a single woman on the Metro at 10:00 P.M.

"Marcos is all the exploited, marginalized, and oppressed minorities, resisting and saying, 'Enough,' " the communique concluded.

CHIAPASCHRONICLE

EDUARDO GALEANO

Originally appeared in *La Jornada,* August 7, 1996.
Translated by Mark Fried.

RAIN

"It's raining yesterday," a local tells me on the road leading out of San Cristóbal de las Casas. Yesterday was little Saint Christopher's Day, which is always rainy, but this year was dry, and that's why today's rain is yesterday's.

On the way to the village of Oventic, under a downpour, the phrase buzzes around my head. In Chiapas it's raining yesterday, and not only because little Saint Christopher forgot to drench us.

HOME

The forgotten of the earth have opened their home to us. They have to be the most generous, these people who are the poorest among the poorest of the poor. We who are gathered here in the Zapatista communities of the Lacandón jungle and the highlands of Chiapas have come from more than 40 countries.

"Come and offer your voice," invited the owners of the house.

With machetes, they have constructed pyramids out of tree trunks to shelter us from the incessant rain. Huddled together in the mud, amid skinny dogs and barefoot children, we share ideas, doubts, plans, ravings. For an entire week 5,000 of us, women and men who refuse to believe that the law of the market is the law of human nature, get soaked together: from Mexico's Superbarrio to Argentina's Mothers of the Plaza de Mayo, by way of Brazil's landless peasants, and feminists, homosexuals, unionists, and ecologists from all over.

Our hosts wear masks. "Behind these ski masks," they say, "we are you."

MIST

The mist is the jungle's ski mask. That way she hides her persecuted children. From the mist they emerge, to the mist they return: people who dress in majestic clothing, who walk on air, who speak quietly or remain silent. These princes condemned to servitude were the first and are the last. Their land has been taken, their words denied, their memory outlawed. But they have known how to take refuge in the mist, in mystery, and from here they have emerged, masked, to unmask the power that humiliates them.

The Maya, sons and daughters of the days, are made of time. "In the earth of time," says Marcos, "we scribble what we call history."

Marcos, the spokesperson, came from elsewhere. He spoke to them; they did not understand. Then he entered the mist, he learned to listen and was able to speak. Now he speaks from them: His is the voice of voices.

AIRPLANES

Every so often an airplane or a helicopter flies over the five remote communities where this crowded international gathering is occurring. It's the military telling the Indians, "They'll be leaving, but we'll remain."

Already this happened in Guadalupe Tepeyac. Once a community, now it's a base. That's where the first gathering in solidarity with the Zapatistas took place. Thousands of people came. When they left, the army invaded. In February of last year the army grabbed land, homes, and possessions, expelled the Indians, and took everything they had built during half a century of laboring to open up the jungle. Since then, however, the Zapatista movement has grown. The stronger its voice resounds in the world, the less impunity the powerful can enjoy.

"Alone, we can't save ourselves," say the Zapatistas. And they add, "No one can."

EXORCISM

When a community misbehaved and its men refused to be slaves on the haciendas, the troops would take them away, never to be seen again. Sick and tired of dying by the bullet or by hunger, the Indians took up arms. They had more sticks than guns, but they took up arms.

As in Guatemala, the neighboring land where other Maya live, it wasn't the guerrillas who provoked repression. Rather it was repression that made the guerrilla war inevitable. Of the community delegates who attended the First Indigenous Congress of Chiapas in 1974, few survived. In El Quiché, in Guatemala, between 1976 and 1978 the government murdered 168 leaders of cooperatives that had flourished in the region. Four years later, using the guerrillas as an alibi, the Guatemalan army reduced 440 Maya communities to ashes.

On one side of the border, as on the other, the victims are Indians, and so are the soldiers. These Indians used against other Indians are under the command of mestizo officers who, with every crime, perform a ferocious act of exorcism against half their blood.

WORLD

When the year 1994 still smelled of a newborn babe, the Zapatistas poured water on the party the Mexican government was throwing to celebrate money's newfound freedom. Using the mouths of their rifles, the voices never listened to spoke and made themselves heard.

But the Zapatistas would prefer their guns to fall silent. This is not a movement enamored of death; it doesn't take pleasure in shooting bullets or slogans, and it doesn't wish to take power. It comes from the farthest reaches of time and from the greatest depths of the earth: It has much to denounce, but also much to celebrate. After all, five centuries of horror have not been able to exterminate these communities or their 1,000-year-old ways of working and living in human solidarity and in communion with nature.

The Zapatistas would prefer to advance their cause peacefully, by helping to unearth the hidden strengths of human dignity. Against the horror, they use humor. It takes a lot of laughing to make a new world, says Marcos, because otherwise the new world will come out so square it won't turn.

RAIN

Chiapas hopes to become a focal point of resistance against infamy and stupidity, and it's doing just that. So are those of us who have been immersed in discussion over the past few days. Here in this community called La Realidad, where everything is lacking but desire, rain falls relentlessly. The roar of the downpour drowns out the voices making leaden pronouncements or endless speeches, but we get the gist of it despite the thundering, because the urge for justice and the luminous diversity of the world are well worth the effort. Meanwhile, as that fellow from San Cristóbal, whose last name could be Cortázar, might say, the rain that rains and rains and rains is raining tomorrow.

GUERRILLAS IN THE MIST

ANDRES OPPENHEIMER

Originally appeared in *New Republic*,
June 17, 1996.

MORE than two years after their uprising began, Mexico's Zapatista rebels and their charismatic leader, Subcommander Marcos, have lost momentum. Militarily, they remain surrounded by the Mexican army in a remote corner of the southern state of Chiapas. Politically, marathon peace talks with the government have disappeared from the front page and may soon break off altogether. Yet, for all their woes, the Zapatistas have one thing going for them: they continue to fascinate socially conscious activists and radical chic celebrities in Europe and the US.

In recent weeks, Oliver Stone and actor Edward James Olmos have made separate pilgrimages to Chiapas for widely publicized meetings with Subcommander Marcos. The Hollywood tourists had barely left when a new convoy headed by former French First Lady Danielle Mitterrand arrived for her own encounter with the ski-masked guerrilla leader. French guerrilla-turned-government-adviser Regis Debray was next to pose with Marcos—the latest in a long list of writers working on books or documentaries about the rebel hero. Sensing a publicity coup, Benetton, the Italian clothing firm, offered Marcos a juicy modeling contract (he turned it down).

The US media are not immune to the hype. "What Robin Hood was to the people of Sherwood Forest, Subcommander Marcos has become to the people of Mexico—a fighter for the rights of peasants who are trapped in poverty by the large landowners," declared the voice-over for a *60 Minutes* profile of Marcos a few months after the January 1, 1994, rebellion. Reflecting an image of the rebel leader held by many (including me) at the time, normally hard-nosed correspondent Ed Bradley prompted: "What you are asking for is basic individual rights? . . . What we call in the United States life, liberty, and the pursuit of happiness?" Marcos nodded, "Yes."

Well, Marcos wanted that—and much more. His force, described in most US and European newspapers simply as an "Indian army," was actually born as the rural wing of the National Liberation Forces (NLF), a white-dominated Marxist guerrilla group founded in 1969 and based in Mexico City. The Zapatistas altered their rhetoric after the rebellion, when Marcos discovered the public relations value of casting his uprising as a struggle for Indian rights—but the organization was created by, and in large measure remains under the control of, not indigenous peasants, but white intellectuals. The main difference between the Zapatistas and previous Latin American guerrillas is that Marcos succeeded where Che Guevara and so many others had failed: The middle-class rebel leaders won the allegiance of scores of Indian communities.

According to its own documents, the NLF had by 1980 adopted a Maoist strategy of "prolonged popular war," which would combine urban and rural guerrilla actions throughout the country with massive protests by the civilian population to wear down the government and ultimately topple it. Taking charge of the plan's rural strategy, a group of young Marxist philosophy and sociology professors at the Autonomous Metropolitan University of Mexico (UAM)—including Rafael Sebastián Guillén, who the government would later identify as Subcommander Marcos—moved to Chiapas.

By the early 1990s, they had built a sizable force made up of Mexico City intellectuals, Mayan peasant leaders, and officials of local Archdiocese lay groups. The NLF's military wing in Chiapas was led by three subcommanders—Subcommander Marcos, in charge of the Osocingo area; Subcommander Daniel, who headed the Altamirano region; and Subcommander Pedro, who led troops in the Las Margaritas area—all light-skinned intellectuals from Mexico City. In 1993, shortly before the rebellion, NLF leaders issued a Declaration of Principles stating that their goal was "to establish the dictatorship of the proletariat, understood as a government of the workers that will stave off counterrevolution and begin the construction of socialism in Mexico."

To be sure, Subcommander Marcos deserves praise for drawing world attention to the dismal conditions of the Chiapas Indians and the rampant government corruption in that state (and most of Mexico, for that matter). In addition to the now widely cited poverty statistics—in many of Chiapas's Indian villages, nearly 70 percent of the homes lack electricity and half the population lacks potable drinking water—free trade and the removal of a decades-old law that granted peasants lifelong property rights over their lands had wreaked havoc on Mayan communities, which were already suffering from a steep decline in world coffee prices. Neither the government nor its conservative opposition seemed particularly concerned.

Adding to these indignities was the mounting evidence of grotesque government waste. Arriving in San Cristóbal de las Casas, the city where the Zapatista rebellion started, the first thing I noticed was a monumental edifice—by far the tallest building in town—with hundreds of helmeted construction workers laboring at full steam. A huge sign in front of the building proclaimed: "Theater of the City: For the well-being of the people of Chiapas."

It was an $11 million state-of-the-art theater and opera house, not far from where the fighting was taking place. With 1,000 seats and a sunken pit for a 100-member symphony orchestra, the theater was to serve a city and several surrounding Indian towns that together had fewer than 100,000 residents, most of whom couldn't even afford the pair of shoes required to enter it. As if to drive home the contrast between rich and poor in Chiapas, the new theater was going up right next to a crumbling government building where hundreds of homeless Indians from the nearby town of San Juan Chamulas had taken refuge.

The city was also remodeling its old colonial theater at a cost of more than $1 million. San Cristóbal would soon have two state-of-the-art theaters. It would be able to present itself as a cultural center with more theater seats per capita than Paris or New York and, perhaps not coincidentally, as the only such center with a guerrilla uprising in its midst.

I suspect that Subcommander Marcos is sincerely appalled at the government's indifference to the Mayans' plight. But, before the 1994 uprising, Indian rights had never been central to his organization's rhetoric. Like other Marxist groups, the NLF interpreted its country's problems in class rather than racial or cultural terms. Even after the uprising, the Zapatistas' first official communiques made only marginal references to Indian rights. The Mexican Awakener, the group's first known official publication, virtually ignored the particular concerns of Indians as an ethnic group. The Zapatista revolution, it said, was a struggle by "the poor, the exploited, and the miserable of Mexico" against "the oppressive government and the big national and foreign exploiters of the people."

Only after the first week of fighting, when the Zapatista rebels had made headlines worldwide, would Subcommander Marcos begin to deemphasize class struggle and focus on the Indian aspects of the rebellion. Mexico's intelligence services would soon draw their own conclusion. Somebody—perhaps Zapatista friends in the Roman Catholic Church or rebel sympathizers in the United States or Europe—had seen the international reaction to the uprising and had given Marcos a precious piece of advice: Forget the socialist mumbo-jumbo and play the Indian card. That was what was drawing attention in New York, Paris, Madrid, and Mexico City, and what helped turn the Chiapas rebels into media stars.

When I interviewed him in the Chiapas jungle, Marcos freely admitted that he had adjusted his political message after the rebellion. "The change resulted from a decision by the [Zapatista] Committee to respond to government charges that we were foreigners and 'professionals of violence,' " he said, citing the term used by the Salinas government to describe the rebels in the first days of fighting. "The Committee said, 'We must emphasize our Mexican and Indian roots and show that this is not a movement financed by foreign governments, Castro, or anything of the sort. We have to show people that this is a Mexican and Indian movement.' "

When I mentioned to a Mexican source with close ties to the Zapatista leadership that the NLF's 1993 Declaration of Principles calling for a "dictatorship of the proletariat" was hardly that of a group committed to representative democracy, he played down the document's significance without denying its authenticity. It was a morale-boosting internal statement aimed at the Zapatistas' Mayan troops and written in a Marxist rhetoric that Indian political activists had become used to hearing for the past three decades, he said. You could not change that language overnight, throwing your troops into ideological confusion at a time when you were preparing to launch your all-out offensive.

Maybe so. Indeed, Subcommander Marcos may have convinced himself by the time of the uprising that communism's days were over. But his political history should at least raise questions about the sincerity of his moderate, post-insurrection rhetoric. While the Zapatista uprising cannot be explained away as the work of a small group of Mexico City radicals, it wasn't exactly a spontaneous Indian rebellion, either. It was a long-planned offensive by a white-dominated Marxist guerrilla group that found considerable support among Mayan communities in a place wrecked by government corruption.

For all his personal charm, Subcommander Marcos has yet to unequivocally state that he no longer believes in class struggle and that he has come to terms with what the National Liberation Forces used to call "bourgeois democracy." Until that happens, he runs the risk of being seen by many Mexicans, even those legitimately outraged by the country's glaring disparities of wealth, as a charismatic but marginal figure—a fashionable curiosity for Hollywood celebrities in search of excitement.

WOMEN'S BATTLE FOR RESPECT
INCH BY INCH

ELENA PONIATOWSKA

Originally appeared in
The Los Angeles Times, September 8, 1997.

WOMEN dominate Mexico's pantheon, from Cortes's mistress, Malinche, who enabled the Spanish to conquer Mexico in 1521, to the Virgin of Guadalupe, the Little Mother, or Tohantzin, of all of Mexico's downtrodden. Yet in the late twentieth century, Mexican women still struggle for respect. Even the guerrilla women in Chiapas are victims of their men's macho attitudes.

Surprising as it may sound, the first uprising of the EZLN (Zapatista National Liberation Army) was not on the first day of January 1994, but in March 1993. At that time, the Zapatistas were discussing what were to become the laws of the revolution. "Major Susana" was given the responsibility to canvass women in dozens of communities about the revolutionary laws they wanted.

When the revolutionary committee met to vote on laws, they considered, one by one, the justice commissions, agrarian laws, war taxes, the rights and obligations of the embattled villages and those of women. Susana presented the proposals that she had gathered from the minds of thousands of indigenous women. Susana began to read and, as she advanced in her discourse, the committee assembly became more and more agitated. Whispers and comments could be heard in the Chol, Tzeltal, Tzotzil, Tojolabal, Mame, Zoque and Castilian languages.

Susana didn't hesitate; she continued her declarations against everything and everyone:

> We do not wish to be obliged to marry someone we don't love. We want
> to have the children we want and can care for. We want the right to a position
> in the community. We want the right to say what we think and have it be
> respected. We want the right to study and even to be truck drivers.

And thus it went until she finished. At the end there was a heavy silence. The "laws of women" that were just heard signified for the indigenous communities a true revolution.

While the women in the assembly were receiving the translations in their various dialects, the men simply looked at one another, nervous, distressed. A feminine applause broke the silence, followed by songs and commentaries.

After the "women's laws" were approved unanimously, a Tzetzal man was heard saying, "The good thing is that my wife doesn't understand Spanish, because if she did. . . ." A female Tzotzil insurgent with the rank of major in the infantry started in at him: "You're screwed, because we're going to translate it into all of our dialects." The impertinent man could only lower his gaze.

This is the truth: The first uprising of the EZLN was in March 1993, and was headed by women Zapatistas. No one disagreed with them, and as expected, they won.

Women make up 52 percent of Mexico's population; only 19 percent of them finish elementary school. Since 1970, these statistics, provided by the National Institute of Geography and Information, hardly have changed at all. Although women have few opportunities to study, they take great advantage of them, and their dropout is almost always due to overwhelming factors as marriage, pregnancy, or lack of money.

On Mother's Day, which is a national holiday in Mexico, "little mothers" (as they are called) are treated with gifts of washing machines, vacuum cleaners, or at least one of those magic mops with a built-in wringer. The gifts serve to reinforce the image of women as having no place, no value but in the home, obligated to and controlled by men. Yet the perception of women's place in society is changing, slowly, as (perhaps) in the Zapatista declaration, and dramatically, as in the case of Claudia Rodríguez.

Claudia and her husband, Jorge Cruz, have a wonderful marriage. He does half of the household work and takes care of their five children. He has a free night out when he needs one, as does she. One night, Claudia decided to have a night out with her friend Victoria. Claudia danced all night in a bar with a man who later followed her home. On a walkway over the Metro, the man, who was very drunk, tried to rape Claudia. She took a gun from her purse and shot and killed him.

Everything was against Claudia—tradition, religion, society—yet Mexican feminist associations and lawyers got her out of jail after only a year and 11 days, truly a miracle in Mexico's male-dominated society.

This experience has changed many women's perspectives.

As the respected feminist television newscaster and writ[e]
ria Llamas says: "Claudia's case drew attention to the sexist
macho Mexican justice deals with women, especially poo[r]
have not had access to an education. There is hope that it w ....-
dent in a country where women are considered guilty when they have been
abused, raped, or victimized."

US TRAINS THOUSANDS
OF MEXICAN SOLDIERS

PASCAL BELTRÁN DEL RÍO

Originally appeared in
Proceso, May 3, 1998.

WASHINGTON, DC—Mexico has become the principal provider of military
personnel for training programs offered by the US Armed Forces.

As a result of closer ties between the Pentagon and the [Mexican] Secretary of National Defense, formalized in a series of agreements announced
in March 1996, and despite the scandals regarding links with drug traffickers that have shaken the Mexican Army since last year, the majority of
the students at US military training centers are from the Mexican military.

The war on drugs, which has replaced the battle against communism on
the priority list of US military, is the focal point of this new cooperation,
according to statements by both countries' governments. "As you know,
there are historic sensibilities between the United States and Mexico, and
the two armies have had very little contact," explains Lieutenant Colonel
Bill Darley of the Pentagon Press Corps.

"If this relationship exists now, it is because there is a situation of crisis
and its purpose is to alleviate a mutual problem," he adds, in reference to
drug trafficking.

According to Darley, the instruction that Mexican soldiers receive in the
US is focused on the war against drugs.

Some weeks ago controversy erupted when *The Washington Post*
reported that the anti-drug tactics that the Pentagon teaches are "similar to

the counterinsurgency methods that they used in the preparation of Latin American officers during the Cold War."

The official Mexican news agency Notimax tried to deny this by reproducing statements by Secretary of State Madeline Albright in an address to Congress: "We are not involved in any counterinsurgency training and the Mexican government has not requested said training," she said.

Another controversy arose when both *The New York Times* and *The Washington Post* reported in late December of last year that the Mexican military not only receives anti-drug training from its US counterparts but also from the Central Intelligence Agency (CIA), whose agents participate in the Anti-Drug Intelligence Center of the Army, also known as CIAN. (This information was neither confirmed nor denied by the Mexican and US governments.)

According to official information from the US government, the anti-drug training that the Pentagon has provided to the Mexican military since 1996 has reached $41.1 million. Mexico received another $3 million in aid during this period as part of the training and international military education program (IMET), financed by the United States State Department. The data regarding the number of Mexican military personnel that have received military training in the US during the last two years, however, is not completely clear. Some statistics have been published by the US press; others have been compiled by the Latin America Working Group, and still others were provided to *Proceso* by the Pentagon.

Section 10–04 of the Defense Department's budget finances the Pentagon's anti-drug training of Mexican soldiers. The report about this budget section from fiscal year 1997 (October 1996 to September 1997) indicates that during that time period training was provided to 829 Mexican soldiers.

Apart from this information, it is officially known that the IMET program provided training to 221 persons in 1996 and to 192 in 1997; and, according to estimates, will provide training to 190 in 1998. In all, 603 Mexican soldiers will have received instruction from the IMET between 1996 and 1998.

A large part of the training offered by this program is provided at the School of the Americas, located at Fort Benning, Georgia. This base has been strongly criticized for having had, among its 60,000 graduates, some who later distinguished themselves as torturers, murderers, and dictators in Latin America. In the past, it was revealed that an instructor at the school used a manual that taught torture.

Revelations like this, and the collapse of the Socialist Bloc, plunged the School of the Americas into crisis during the latter part of the last decade. Last September, the House of Representatives nearly approved a proposal that would have reduced the budget of the institution so much that it would have had to close. The initiative was defeated by just seven votes.

Nevertheless, the School of the Americas (SOA) is trying to remodel its academic program. Among the anti-drug training courses, there are now human rights courses, among other subjects.

The number of students is growing, according to a recent report by *The Boston Globe*. Among those that have contributed most to this growth are Mexican military personnel. According to the *Globe* report, in 1994, 15 Mexicans attended the School of the Americas; last year 333 attended.

School of the Americas Watch (SOAW), an NGO which is campaigning for the closure of the school, revealed that "at least 13 of the high-ranking military personnel involved in the conflict [in Chiapas] are graduates" of the School of the Americas, including General Juan Lopez Ortiz, who, according to certain versions, oversaw the offensive against the Zapatista rebels in Ocosingo in January 1994, after which several people were found executed.

SOAW has also identified as former students of the school three of the officers mentioned in the military intelligence documents obtained by *Proceso* last year, which detail ties between drug traffickers and high-ranking Army officers: Col. Augusto Moises García Ochoa, Head of the Anti-Drug Intelligence Center, who, according to SOAW data, took a course on Jungle Operations in 1997; Lieutenant Colonel Gerardo Rene Herrera Huizar, who testified against Colonel Pablo Castellanos, was at the School of the Americas in 1980 to take a course on Patrol Operations; and General Fernán Pérez Casanova, who received visits from Irma Lizzete Ibarra Navejat, the former beauty queen who was murdered last year in Guadalajara, studied counterinsurgency in 1962.

According to data from the Latin American Working Group and information appearing in the US press, between 1996 and 1997 almost 500 Mexican officers came to the School of the Americas.

By the end of this year, it is estimated that a total of 3,000 will have participated in training courses in the United States (the Pentagon handles an average of 1,000 per year) since the tightening of relations between the two military authorities began.

THE MEXICAN GREEN BERETS

According to *The New York Times*, of those 3,000 Mexican soldiers, "328 young officers will have completed special 12- and 13-week programs," which have the goal of creating a corps of anti-drug specialists. Those officers, the paper said in an article published last December, are then sent to train units of special air forces (known as GAFE) which are stationed in the headquarters of the 12 regions and 40 zones that make up the military geography of Mexico.

The 328 officers to which the *Times* refers are being trained at Fort Bragg, North Carolina, headquarters of the Special Forces of the US Army. A special anti-narcotics school operates at that same military installation. Eric Olson, an analyst with the NGO Washington Office on Latin America, which monitors the military cooperation between Mexico and the US, claims that within the current anti-narcotic training program there is a cloak or cover of disinformation which prevents discovering, among other things, the names of the Mexican officers that participate in the courses.

Olson says it is important to know these names because "one of the GAFE units, created with US training, was apparently responsible for the events in Zapopan last year." Olson is referring to the kidnapping of 18 young people on December 14, 1997 in the town of San Juan de Ocotlan. During these events, a young man, Salvador López Jiménez, lost his life. In early January, a military judge from Region 5 issued a formal verdict of imprisonment against a chief, 11 officers and 15 soldiers belonging to the GAFE (Special Forces Air Transport Group) that operated in the area.

Joy Olson of the Latin American Working Group confirms: "Up until now we have not been able to find out the names of Mexican military personnel trained in the United States."

Lieutenant Colonel Darley says that it is up to the Mexican government, not the United States, to decide whether to make public the names of the soldiers who have received training. But he remarks: "If I were in their position, I wouldn't do it, because it would make those soldiers targets of the criminal organizations they are trying to fight against."

Asked directly, Darley revealed that the Mexican military personnel receive training at 17 installations of the US Armed Forces: Bolling Air Force Base, located outside Washington, D.C.; Randolph Air Force Base and Lackland Air Force Base in Texas; Fort Wachuca, Arizona; Fort Benning, Georgia; Fort Bragg, North Carolina; Fort Rucker and Fort McCullen, Alabama; Fort Eutis and Norfolk Navy Base, Virginia; Camp Pendleton, California; Pensacola Naval Base, Florida; Indian Town Gap, Pennsylvania; Rodman Naval Station, Panama, and other installations in the cities of Indianapolis, San Antonio, and San Diego.

MEXICO'S SECRET WAR

LUIS HERNÁNDEZ NAVARRO

Originally appeared in *NACLA Report on the Americas*,
May/June 1999.

IN considering the current status of the conflict in southeastern Mexico, four fundamental realities must be kept in mind. First, despite the contrary claims of the Mexican government, there is a war in the state of Chiapas. This stage of the conflict began on January 1, 1994, when the Zapatista National Liberation Army (EZLN) declared war on the Mexican army and federal government—a declaration that has not been retracted despite the group's agreement just 12 days after the uprising to abide by a cease-fire. In Chiapas, two armed parties confront each other, although only one of them—the federal government—has actively employed arms since the cease-fire.

The insurgents have been formally recognized under law as the EZLN. On March 11, 1995, Congress promulgated the "Law for Dialogue, Conciliation, and Dignified Peace in Chiapas" and created the Commission of Concordance and Pacification (COCOPA), an organism meant to facilitate negotiations between the government and the insurgency. This legal framework designed to resolve the conflict explicitly stated that its objective was to seek peace. Peace, as defined by the *American Heritage Dictionary*, is "the absence of war," while war is "a state of open, armed, often prolonged conflict carried on between nations, states, or parties." So the legal framework for defining the peace process acknowledges the war in Chiapas. The two parties began formal peace negotiations in 1994, resulting in the February 16, 1996 signing of four documents on indigenous rights and culture in the town of San Andrés, Chiapas.

The war in Chiapas has produced only 12 days of open combat. On January 12, 1994, both sides agreed on a truce. But this truce has been broken on two occasions by the federal government: in February 1995, when it unsuccessfully tried to capture the Zapatista leadership, and in early 1998, when it launched political and military offensives against the autonomous municipalities of Ricardo Flores Magon, Tierra y Libertad, and San Juan la Libertad. The Zapatistas have never used arms against civilians, and since the January 12 truce have not even employed them against the Army. On the contrary, they have respected the truce and confronted hostile military movements in their communities with peaceful civic resistance.

But the existence of a truce—defined as "a temporary suspension of hostilities"—is not the same as peace. The situation in Chiapas over the past five years has been far from peaceful. To confront the growing indigenous rebellion, the government, despite its denial that a state of war exists, has applied a war strategy. Some 60,000 troops have been positioned in key points in 66 of Chiapas's 111 municipalities. At least nine paramilitary groups operate in 27 municipalities and have been responsible for hundreds of civilian assassinations. More than 150 foreign human rights observers have been expelled from the country. The federal government has repeatedly and publicly attacked the official organizations established for mediating and facilitating the peace talks, to the point of forcing the most important mediating body—the National Mediating Commission (CONAI), headed by Don Samuel Ruíz, the Bishop of San Cristóbal—to dissolve itself, citing a lack of cooperation on the part of the government.

Any real strategy for peace, of course, would have to begin with social reforms. The Zapatista uprising has a military dimension, but Zapatismo is not strictly a military phenomenon. On the contrary, the military manifestation represents the last resort of people confronting a volatile mix of agrarian, ethnic, and social problems. By 1994, these problems had been aggravated by a crisis in the regional system of political and economic control, and further inflamed by profound changes on the national level, especially the official cancellation of land reform programs and the privatization of communal lands brought about by the presidential reform of Article 27 of the Constitution.

When the government denies that there is a war in Chiapas, it is seeking a way out of the conflict that avoids the negotiation of substantive reforms. It creates a smokescreen to cover up the fact that its real strategy and on-the-ground plan is the military defeat of the EZLN. The extreme tension that characterizes life in Chiapas now threatens to provoke a new phase of confrontations. To pretend the conflict in Chiapas can be reduced to a bunch of secondary problems amplified in the context of intercommunity violence only serves to accelerate a dangerous dynamic of political polarization, social breakdown, and violent provocations by diverse actors and security forces in the area.

Second, the government's position once again notwithstanding, the conflict in Chiapas is national in scope. From the government's perspective, the strength of the EZLN has been unduly exaggerated—its impact, says the government, is basically local, not national. Government officials have worked hard, in Mexico and abroad, to sell the idea that Zapatismo is neither a national force nor truly representative of the interests of even a fraction of the nation's 10 million indigenous people. They insist that the EZLN's range of influence is limited to a handful of scattered townships in Chiapas. According to this logic, too much has already been conceded to an organization that has scant military capacity and not nearly the stature of the armed movements that once challenged state power in El Salvador and Guatemala.

Despite the propaganda, the general public does not appear to share the government's perspective. According to a recent survey of the Mexico City–based Rosenblueth Foundation, only 17 percent of the Mexican population believe that the conflict in Chiapas is strictly local, while 73 percent think it has national repercussions. At the same time, 44 percent think that the EZLN legitimately represents indigenous peoples, while 40 percent say it does not.

Aside from the military force of the EZLN, Zapatismo is a political force with national and international impact and influence. The rebels have managed to generate an enormous current of support and sympathy for their cause, or at least in favor of a peaceful and lasting solution to the conflict. The same survey shows that 73 percent of Mexicans think that the indigenous populations had legitimate reasons to rebel against the government in 1994, and 68 percent believe that the government still has not improved conditions for indigenous peoples. Fifty-seven percent state that the government has not made its best effort to achieve peace. The conflict in Chiapas has received extensive coverage in the mass media, obliging President Ernesto Zedillo to make a record number of trips to the state to publicly promote his failing policies.

The war in Chiapas and the transition to democracy in Mexico have intertwined in such a way that there is no real possibility of resolving one without the other. The administration sought to use the partial success of the midterm elections of 1997 as proof that the nation as a whole opted for reforms through elections and that the Zapatistas were passe. But this line of argument did not succeed in isolating the Zapatistas. Given the power relations in play and the urgency to end the armed uprising by resolving issues pending on the national agenda—including the rights of Indian peoples—the price to pay for peace is nothing short of the transformation of the conservative regime which rules Mexico.

The supposedly nonexistent war in Chiapas has also conditioned much of Mexico's foreign policy. In negotiations for a free-trade agreement with the European Union, in discussions among human rights experts at the UN, and even in the recent visit of Pope John Paul II to Mexico, the Mexican government just cannot seem to escape the issue of Chiapas. To its great discomfort, when the eyes of the world turn to Mexico, they see Chiapas.

The governmental coordinator of the nonexistent dialogue, Emilio Rabasa, travels all over the world attending to what he calls "just a regional political conflict." And he has to, because no other liberation movement in recent times has achieved the network of solidarity that the Zapatistas have today. The Chiapas problem has become an international issue, drawing over 50,000 people into the streets of Rome for a solidarity march and causing President Zedillo to sweat under the collar in a recent encounter with human rights groups in France. In his recent visit to Mexico, even France's conservative president, Jacques Chirac, diplomatically reminded the Mexican government that it should comply with the agreements signed with the EZLN in San Andrés.

The Mexican government cannot achieve an internal consensus to move into open warfare. Nor does it have the option of forcing the rebels into conventional politics without first conceding reforms. The current impasse is in part the result of the nature of the conflict. It is far from simply a local problem.

The third fundamental reality is the newness of the EZLN, and hence its attraction. The Zapatista movement broke onto the international stage just when the dreams of peoples' liberation have been sundered by the decreed "end of history." It emerged just when the idea of revolution, so costly to social-change projects, had fallen into disuse and was seen as an eccentricity. Whether it set out to or not, among the most important consequences of the Zapatista movement in our times is that it has stimulated dreams of social change, and resisted the idea that all emancipatory projects must be sacrificed to global integration. It accomplished this through the symbolic force of the image of armed revolution that still holds sway for many parts of the population, as well as through the moral force that indigenous struggles have acquired, especially in Europe. Finally, the nature of the Zapatista project itself was surprisingly distant from the traditional image of the guerrilla as an armed party struggling to take state power. In the long run, after the cult of the rifles wore off, what remained as the fundamental proposal of the Zapatista Mexican indigenous rebels was something else: a new political project.

The EZLN is not a Marxist-Leninist vanguard whose objective is to take over state power through violent means to install socialism. It was not in 1994, and is even less so now. To characterize it as such is to purposely conjure up visions of Cold War demons in a misguided attempt to delegitimize Zapatismo. But false stereotypes prohibit any real understanding of the movement, its proposals, and its undeniable political success.

In their first public document, the "Declaration of the Lacandón Jungle," the rebels declared war on the government but did not exhort the people to destroy the bourgeois state. Instead, they proposed that the legislative and judicial powers restore the legality and stability of the nation by impeaching President Carlos Salinas. The proposal struck a responsive chord given that the opposition had declared the Salinas government illegitimate ever since he came to office through the fraudulent presidential elections of 1988. These accusations of illegitimacy were fueled by Salinas' decision to decree the privatizing reforms to Article 27 of the Constitution and by the assassination of over 500 members of the opposition Party of the Democratic Revolution (PRD) during his term.

From the start, the rebellion attempted to respect the framework of the law, citing Article 39 of the Constitution to argue the legitimacy of their uprising. Article 39 establishes that national sovereignty resides essentially and originally in the people, and that they have the right, at all times, to alter or modify their form of government. The EZLN did not seek to subvert the Mexican state, but to replace the existing political regime and transform its economic policies. Five years after the uprising, in its latest communiqué, it reiterates its demands for "recognition of the rights of Indian peoples and democracy, liberty and justice for all Mexican men and women." These demands, the Zapatistas claim, constitute the necessary foundations for peace.

Zapatismo has won legitimacy on the same terrain in which the regime has lost it. Its demands go to the heart of the nation's problems: the absence of democracy, the shrinking protective state, loss of sovereignty, the disappearance of social safety nets, the cancellation of land reform, the lack of recognition of the rights of Indian peoples. It has won legitimacy by explaining itself in its own terms, by naming the intolerable, by constructing a new language, by stimulating the will to aspire to higher and different kinds of goals, by appealing to the collective imagination, and by tuning its discourse to harmonize with the sentiments of a large portion of civil society.

Many aspects of the new Zapatismo form part of a new terrain within traditional leftist discourse — the search for values accepted by the community in rebellion and supported by daily practices, the role of dialogue in establishing shared critieria, the demand for dignity, the struggle for the right to be different, the confluence of the social and the political, the combination of the ethnic and the democratic struggle, the importance of popular sovereignty, and the refusal to seek to conquer power and the determination to transform it.

The Zapatistas moreover have rearticulated and relaunched the new Indian struggle from a perspective of "difference" that has profound implications for the birth of a new model of the nation. The French sociologist Alan Touraine has defined and defended this perspective. "Identity and otherness are inseparable," he writes, "and, in a universe dominated by the impersonal forces of the financial markets, they should be defended together if the goal is to avoid the situation where the only effective resistance to its domination come from sectarian fundamentalisms. Democratic multiculturalism is the main objective of social change movements today, much as industrial democracy was years ago. It cannot be reduced to tolerance or accepting limited particularisms, nor can it be confused with a cultural relativism charged with violence." At stake, says Mexican journalist Luis Villoro, is nothing less than "the reform of the national project. We have to reinvent the nation we want."

Chiapas is not the former Yugoslavia, nor do Indian demands in Mexico share the antidemocratic ethnicism of other movements. The politics of identity proposed by the Zapatistas does not seek control over national territory or secession from the nation. It seeks to change the country.

The dominant reality is that the Mexican government has no plan for peace. The latest interruption in the peace process is in large part due to the fact that the government views the means to resolve the conflict in Chiapas as a scheme of negotiations and not as a peace process. Its primary goal is not to achieve peace but to recover the political and military initiative. Any real peace policy must seek to resolve the root causes of the rebellion and assure the continuity of negotiations as part of a state policy that transcends the immediate interests of the government and the parties. A scheme of negotiations consists, on the other hand, of merely applying diverse measures to "contain" the enemy while trying to defeat it, meanwhile manipulating the conflict in the interests of national political objectives.

The government's scheme of negotiations aims to minimize the actors, to "Chiapanize" the conflict, and to offer the Zapatistas a plan of civil reinsertion that bypasses any real negotiation of their demands. In the latest phase, it has sought to retake the initiative by presenting a proposal for constitutional reforms on indigenous rights and culture that diverges significantly from the commitments agreed to in San Andrés. It has also set out to eliminate mediating bodies. It has chipped away at the legal framework and institutional context that have made peace talks possible.

In this way, the laudable advances that took place during the negotiation process such as maintaining the military truce, incorporating the army directly into the dialogue, involving political parties as facilitators, and encouraging the participation of civil society, have all been abandoned. Likewise, the economic aid funneled into the region has served to buffer social discontent and help some political clients, but not to develop the state, create effective institutions, or to resolve the causes of the conflict.

The government's decision to monopolize the negotiations and dismantle mediating bodies not unconditionally allied to its interests provoked, first, the destruction of CONAI and later the erosion of COCOPA. These actions made it virtually impossible to solve the conflict in the short run, and increased the possibility of having to resort to international mediation.

But this governmental strategy has failed. During 1998, in the midst of the worst offensives against the EZLN in the conflict zone, the communities resisted the military offensive, the autonomous townships continued to function, the conflict remained a major national issue, and the Zapatistas significantly increased their influence abroad.

Peace processes in other countries have taught us that paralysis in negotiations is frequently linked to insufficient commitment on the part of one of the major actors. To break an impasse requires recognition of the adversary, dialogue, compliance with all previous agreements, and finally, unified negotiating mandates. In the case of Chiapas, the insurgency should be recognized as a legitimate actor, the government should reaffirm the path of dialogue as a solution to the conflict, it should comply with all agreed-on commitments, and its negotiators should sustain a unified position which they are capable of implementing.

Only two of the four necessary conditions for breaking the Chiapas impasse have been met. The EZLN has been recognized as a legitimate actor since the first negotiations in the Cathedral of San Cristóbal de las Casas. Since then, both parties have insisted on dialogue as the only means of resolving the conflict, although the federal government has broken its commitment on several occasions. It failed to comply with the agreements on indigenous

rights and culture and practically boycotted the second round of negotiations on democracy and justice. Neither the mediating bodies nor the facilitators—the backbone of any negotiation—had sufficient strength to oblige
the government to comply with its commitments. This has aggravated the
disorder that periodically reigns within the ranks of the federal government,
especially now that a contested process of presidential succession has
begun. Over and over, the declarations of different government officials
contradict one another on official strategy.

The government's noncompliance with the accords on indigenous rights
and culture is the main reason, although not the only one, for the impasse in
negotiations with the EZLN. From the EZLN's point of view, only if the government complies with the terms it agreed to can the paralysis be unblocked.
Only in this way can the government's insistence on its willingness to
engage in dialogue be credible. Today the indigenous reforms depend on
it, and tomorrow the lives of the rebels may be at stake. If in the future the
Zapatistas negotiate their insertion into the civil arena and the government
does not respect their lives or their liberty, there will be no chance of rene-
gotiating—as is now still possible—the San Andrés accords.

But without confidence and credibility on the part of the government,
there can be no negotiation. And without compliance with accords already
signed, there can be no confidence or credibility.

COMIC RELIEF, NEA-STYLE*

JoAnn Wypijewski

Originally appeared in *The Nation*,
April 19, 1999.

THE world is a bleak canvas, all black and white, with only some grays "so
that the black and the white [don't] bump into each other so hard." The
gods are quarrelsome and bored. They begin looking for true colors, find

*A review of *The Story of Colors*, by Subcomandante Marcos. Illustrated by Domitila Dominguez.
Translated by Anne Bar Din. Cinco Puntos. 40 pp. $15.95.

them by various ingenious and accidental means, paint the world anew and, in the end, make sure that the people never "forget how many colors there are and how many ways of thinking."

Representative Ralph Regula says this children's story—presented in Spanish and in English, illustrated with boldly hued, fantastical images of birds and beasts, of gods bearing little resemblance to those in pre-Columbian art, of people smoking or lying in each other's arms, of the Zapatistas' inspired pamphleteer with trademark ski mask and pipe—"isn't appropriate for American children." In commenting on the National Endowment for the Arts' recent decision to break its $7,500 promise to Cinco Puntos Press for production of the book, Regula said NEA chief William Ivey did "exactly the right thing in stopping the grant."

He's right. The decision got the book on the cover of the *New York Times*; within 24 hours the Lannan Foundation came forward with $15,000, and booksellers ordered 3,000 copies. This—on top of the 500 bought directly by people who kept phones trilling for a day and a half at Bobby and Susie Byrd's home-publishing office in El Paso—guaranteed a sellout of the first printing of 5,000. The Byrds protested Ivey's decision (virtually unprecedented in that it came after the award had been granted and all that was left was to cut the check), but without it they wouldn't now be planning a second print run. For small publishers, getting their books noticed and getting people to buy them has always been more important than government beneficence. And for Colectivo Callejero, the artists' collective in Guadalajara that first published *La Historia de los Colores* two years ago and was granted all royalties from the US edition by Subcomandante Marcos, more American sales could help finance a reprinting of the Mexican edition (only 2,000 originally run)—or at least bolster the collective's regular work of producing subversively beautiful art for the people.

So, more money for Cinco Puntos, more money for the Colectivo and, for us (and those delicate "American children"), more opportunity to read this magical book. As Marcos has declared many times in the Zapatistas' communiques, "everything for everyone, nothing for ourselves."

There is another, less material reason to find gratification in the NEA's refusal to honor its monetary pledge—and here I shall put to one side the flashpoint question of whether any artist should desire a state seal of approval. Since they burst into public consciousness on January 1, 1994, the Zapatistas have often been discussed as if they were an art installation: the guerrilleros in the mountains, unseen but everywhere represented, most famously in the communiqués but also in the masked dolls backpackers return with from Chiapas; in the snacks and condoms and assorted goods bearing their image that suddenly appeared on the streets of Mexico City from producers excited to exploit so seemingly romantic a rebellion; in the hearts of the world's radicals longing for a reminder that just because, as Marcos wrote, the enemy is "shoving the struggle for democracy, liberty, and justice into the corner reserved for utopias and impossibilities," it needn't be so.

They've been called "postmodern" so regularly—even, bizarrely, on the flap of *The Story of Colors*, which also applies the word to Dominguez's pictures, rich though they are with the influence of her Mazatecan culture— and still no one knows what it means. Maybe the word stuck because Marcos is so fond of attaching postscripts to his letters and pronouncements, or because he regularly mixes jokes and storytelling with polemic, or because noncombatants in that New Year's uprising marched with wooden guns to signal sympathy with those bearing real ones, shooting hot lead.

It certainly isn't there because the Zapatistas bleed like real revolutionaries, or propagandize like real revolutionaries (the best of whom always suited "form and content" to the times), or aim to dislodge every brick in the wall of power—political, economic, cultural, ideological—like real revolutionaries. And it isn't because, with only 2,000 troops under arms, the Zapatistas have so discomfited the Mexican government and its US sponsors that a 1995 memo from Chase Manhattan Bank urged their "elimination," and today one-third of the Mexican Army is deployed in the mountains, villages, and forest remnants of Chiapas. No, the only postmodern turn on this story is a parlor game of supposition: If, instead of being an intellectual and a revolutionary and a storyteller, Marcos were an intellectual-turned-revolutionary-turned-storyteller playing for arts grants behind a guerrilla's mask; and if the US government, straightening its own mask as patron of the arts, were to find his "work" a "provocative" commodity worthy of its subventions; if, in other words, the joke was on us! Marcos, and now the NEA, have spared us that agony.

The Story of Colors joins all the other stories, easily mistaken for charming digressions, in Marcos's political writing. Some may see it as a traditional creation myth, but it's not. The gods, in their bickering and fatigued bumbling, in their longing for a beauty of their own making and for comfort in a draught of pozol, are not too different from the people, who more than once are imagined making love ("a nice way to become tired and then go to sleep") and drawing deep on tobacco. "These gods," after all, are "not like the first ones, the seven gods who gave birth to the world." These gods don't even know "who made the birds. Or why."

Cinco Puntos, which specializes in bilingual children's books and literature of the border (its lively list can be found at www.cincopuntos.com), says *The Story of Colors* is a bit of "holiness" from an indigenous culture "that cannot be measured in dollars or defined by politics." Bobby Byrd says it "is essentially about diversity and tolerance." But I don't think it's those things either.

In *Shadows of Tender Fury*, a wonderful compendium of the letters and communiques of Subcomandante Marcos published a couple of years ago by Monthly Review Press, the figure of Old Antonio, who narrates the tale of the colors in this book and who, in real life, invited the Zapatistas into the first community they organized back in 1985, frequently appears as the Zaps' guide to the history and traditions—even the geography—of Chiapas. He is their link to the past and the future, the one who confirms for them that, indeed, there are no words in the native languages of Chiapas with which to translate the term "to give up."

Here, Antonio offers an allegory not of "diversity"—a timid, lackluster thing—but of dissatisfaction and its creative possibilities. The world that seems fixed and oppressive can be changed; the "gods" can be anyone, but what they make they must safeguard against forgetfulness in case the spirit of revolt should dim or be tamped down. And so the gods, who color the world with a thrilling abandon, use the last of their pigment to paint the feathers of the macaw, a bird revered in the highlands, "because they didn't want to forget the colors or lose them."

It's no minor matter that the Zapatistas call themselves after Zapata, or that, while insisting upon the absolute integrity of indigenous culture, they speak to the whole of the country, invoking a radical nationalism that is inconceivable, because it is historically impossible, in the United States. In a sense, Marcos has been telling the story of colors in different ways since he first explained the Zapatista struggle to a curious world. In a February 14, 1994, letter (reprinted in *Shadows*) to a coalition of workers, campesinos, students, and intellectuals called the National Coordination of Civic Action for National Liberation, Marcos wrote:

> The oldest of the old of our peoples spoke words to us, words that came from very far away, about when our lives were not, about when our voice was silenced. And the truth journeyed in the words of the oldest of the old of our peoples. And we learned through the words of the oldest of the old that the long night of pain of our people came from the hands and words of the powerful, that our misery was wealth for a few, that on the bones and dust of our ancestors and our children, the powerful built themselves a house, and that in that

house our feet could not enter, and that the light that lit it fed itself on the darkness of our houses, and that its abundant table filled itself on the emptiness of our stomachs, and that their luxuries were born of our misery. . . .

But the truth that traveled on the paths of the word of the oldest of the old of our peoples was not just of pain and death. In the word of the oldest of the old also came hope for our history. And in their word appeared the image of one like us: Emiliano Zapata. And in it we saw the place toward which our feet should walk in order to be true, and our history of struggle returned to our blood, and our hands were filled with the cries of our people, and dignity returned once again to our mouths, and in our eyes we saw a new world.

Not a folktale new world; folktales aren't dangerous.

KING OF THE JUNGLE

MICHAEL McCAUGHAN

Originally appeared in *Irish Times*,
August 5, 1999.

WHEN Subcommander Marcos went to the Chiapas jungle and joined a group of armed rebels in August 1983, he carried a dozen books in his backpack. Among them were novels by Gabriel García Márquez, Mario Vargas Llosa, and Julio Cortázar, much to the amusement of his fellow rebels who insisted he also carry his share of bullets, food, and equipment.

One by one the books were left behind, as the 27-year-old city kid learned the first rule of life as a guerrilla: "One kilo weighs two after an hour. After two hours, it weighs four and you just want to dump the whole f—king lot."

Marcos's skill in bringing books to life around the campfire led to a change of heart among his companions. "Every time I left a book behind, someone would offer to carry it for me. 'A story is going to come out of that,' they would say." Marcos was soon in demand as a rent-a-scribe, writing letters for his lovesick compañeros. "Tell me what to say to this woman so she'll fall in love with me," they pleaded.

Ten years later Subcomandante Marcos appeared to the rest of the world when he led an armed uprising by Zapatista rebels on January 1 1994, seizing the tourist town of San Cristóbal de las Casas and shaking Mexico's one-party political system to its roots. The government moved swiftly to capture the masked rebel, drawing up a rough approximation of a man of "25 years, clean-shaven with big hazel-colored eyes, a prominent nose, speaks two languages." Mexican women sat up and began to pay attention.

Police and Army troops arrested and imprisoned "Marcos" in two different towns on the same day, identified him as a Venezuelan birdwatcher, an alcoholic bricklayer, and a 66-year-old priest who had spent the previous two years in hospital recovering from a car crash.

A week later Marcos was pronounced dead, only to be resurrected and captured as "foreign agitator," Marcos Rojas, a Mexican who fought with the Sandinistas in the Nicaraguan revolution. The myth grew.

The Zapatistas took their name and inspiration from independence hero, Emiliano Zapata, a Zapotec Indian who fought for land and freedom during Mexico's first revolution in 1910. The neo-Zapatistas' short-lived military attack was followed by a more sustained literary strike, as Marcos retreated to his jungle headquartes and sent a stream of communiques to the national media, who doubled circulation when they printed the rebel message in full. Marcos anticipated his own death during the doomed uprising but found he had been granted a stay of execution and now felt he was "living on borrowed time." A torrent of writings followed—scraps of songs and poems, references to soap operas, the Beatles, Shakespeare, and Neruda, an uncontrollable stream of consciousness born of the miracle of being alive.

Marcos's writings blended allegoric folktales with sharp political satire, drawing on the indigenous wisdom learned during the years spent among the Indian communities. One recurring character was "Old Antonio," a wise elder who passed on advice and wisdom to the impatient guerrilla leader.

The Marcos letters acted as a crucial bridge between "profound" Mexico—of indigenous custom and communal identity—and "imaginary" Mexico, of credit cards, factories, and Hollywood films.

"Facing the mountains we speak to our dead so that their words will guide us along the path that we must walk. The drums sound and in the voices of the land we hear our pain and our history." (Second Declaration of the Lacandón Jungle, June 1994.) When the first round of rebel government talks ended in March 1994, Marcos staggered out of San Cristóbal's Cathedral under the weight of 2,000 letters sent to him from every corner of Mexico, from laid-off oil workers to smitten señoritas, and even an eight-year-old girl wondering how she could become Marcos's "subcommander-ess."

Along with the fan mail came the dolls, socks, T-shirts, posters, and even "condoms for an uprising" which sold out as fast as they appeared.

OCTAVIO PAZ, MEXICO'S Nobel laureate and a highly conservative states-man, recognized Marcos's "imaginative and lively prose" which had "eas-ily won the war of opinions." The French intellectual, Regis Debray, trekked into the jungle and vouched for Marcos, ranking him the greatest living writer in Latin America. Carlos Fuentes exchanged letters with him, while the king of magical realism, García Márquez, acknowledged that events in Mexico made him want to "throw his books into the sea." It was hardly news when this year's Nobel literature prize-winner, José Saramago, announced he would dedicate his remaining years to the Zapatista cause.

The Zapatista headquarters looked like Studio 54 at times, with Oliver Stone prowling the undergrowth on horseback, Danielle Mitterrand chat-ting to locals about the Kurds, or the Benetton PR chief hunched over a campfire, waiting to find out if the rebels would agree to an ad campaign. (They didn't.) When Bianca Jagger turned up she was refused entry as she arrived with Robert Torricelli, a US Congressman who lent his name to an embargo-tightening law against Cuba.

The master of ceremonies was the pipe-smoking Marcos, while the indigenous authority, the Clandestine Revolutionary Committee (CCRI), stayed in the background, happy to have a fluent, eloquent Spanish-speaker taking care of PR.

After yet another round of who-is-Marcos questions by journalists, the rebel revealed his identity: "Marcos is gay in San Francisco, black in South Africa, Palestinian in Israel, Jewish in Germany, a woman alone in the Metro at 10:00 P.M., a landless peasant, all the minorities searching for a word, their word, which would make a majority out us, the eternally frag-mented ones."

In February 1995 the Mexican Army advanced against rebel positions, with Marcos narrowly avoiding capture when Army helicopters almost landed on the roof of his jungle hut. The next communiqué was a diary extract, in which he described how he threw up after drinking his urine in the jungle and how Eva, a five-year-old local, was going to kill him for leaving her copy of The Jungle Books behind in the panicky exit. This was a far cry from Che Guevara's epic Bolivian diary.

On a visit to rebel villages, this journalist heard talk of a children's book, written by Marcos, about the history of colors, which circulated by hand from village to village. In the book, Marcos lights up his trademark pipe, sits down beside village elder Antonio, and a story unfolds, about how mythical gods grew tired of the universe, because it was tinted only in gray. The gods held a meeting and agreed to look for more colors. The first color, red, was discovered after one god tripped up and split his head open with a stone.

"Another god was looking for colors when he heard a child laughing," wrote Marcos. "He snuck up on the child, snatched his laugh and left him in tears. That's why they say that children can be laughing one minute and all of a sudden they are crying. The god stole the child's laugh and they called this seventh color yellow." When the gods went to sleep they pinned the seven colors to the tail of the macaw bird so that they would remember where they had left them.

The story was published by a worker's collective in nearby Oaxaca state, who then passed it on to a bilingual US publisher, Cinco Puntos, based in El Paso, Texas. *The Story of Colors* was translated into English and published last March, with the pledge of a grant by the US National Endowment for the Arts (NEA).

Cinco Puntos press is a shoestring operation, publishing bilingual books, many of them with border themes. The Colors book cost $15,000 to print, with the NEA grant paying half of the cost. Marcos appeared in a photo on the inside flap, while Indigo Girls singer Amy Ray wrote the back cover blurb.

When NEA chairman William J. Ivey saw the book, he cancelled the grant, saying he feared some of the royalties might end up in the hands of armed rebels in Mexico. Bobby Byrd, co-director of Cinco Puntos press, dismissed the claim as ridiculous, as he had already agreed that no part of the money would go to Marcos, who does not believe in copyright and had formally waived his rights in prior talks.

The publishers feel that the NEA got cold feet after reading the text, which includes references to lovemaking and smoking, which are frowned upon in conservative US circles. Ivey denied that the content of the book had anything to do with the decision to cancel funding. The controversy did no harm to book sales, as the first print run sold out within three days. The book is now in its third edition, with 17,000 copies sold.

The Story of Colors concludes with the iridescent macaw strutting about the world, "just in case men and women forget how many colors there are and how many ways of thinking, and that the world will be happy if all the colors and ways of thinking have their place."

IN CHIAPAS

TOM HAYDEN

It is more than probable that with more time Emiliano Zapata will emerge as the great and pure man of Mexico and will take a parallel position to the Virgin of Guadalupe as the human patron of the freedom of Mexico.

—JOHN STEINBECK, 1948

We are the continent of desire. We are always at a rolling boil. Isn't that preferable to the rigid cold solitude of the poorly named First World, a dictatorship of technocrats and accountants that wishes to convert us into a great factory of Puritan zombies?

—EDUARDO GARCÍA AGUILAR, 1998

THE Zapatista community of Amador Hernández, in the Lacandón jungle of Chiapas, is as far from global markets, media centers, and metropoles as physically possible. Yet the January 1994 Zapatista rebellion, beginning in tiny hamlets such as this—mere dots in a dot.com world—has managed to survive and challenge the faraway power centers of government and finance in a pivotal test of whether the globalization of capital is prompting the globalization of conscience.

I traveled to Amador Hernández, a village of 500 indigenous Tzoltzil-speaking Mayans, and several other highlands communities under Zapatistia control, in February 2000. I was flown by a beer-drinking pilot through the rainforest mist, in a a journey out of Western time and space. As the small plane bumped down in a jungle meadow, I felt alternately haunted and fascinated. Haunted because I was about to witness a current-day confrontation between the indigenous of the Americas and the colonizers, militarizers, and modernizers, which had left lakes of blood in its wake for 500 years. Fascinated by the indigenous will to survive—to wage "war against oblivion"—incarnated in the Zapatista front.

North Americans like John Steinbeck have been enchanted by Mexican revolutionaries before. Like those previous gringo romanticos, I had been drawn to the cause of indigenous for many years. I was raised, like most North Americans, with a dimmed and sanitized view of their genocidal fate. When discussed at all by my parents or teachers, I was led to believe that it was all a tragic misunderstanding between Europeans and the local Indians, that the fatalities were caused by accidental Western germs infecting vulnerable people, and, in any case, it was an inevitable stage of progressive development. It was not until the 1960s jarred my own sense of identity, and an Indian band seized Alcatraz Island, that I sat down on a Berkeley floor to read *Bury My Heart at Wounded Knee* and experienced a life-altering realization that America and the West had been destroying native people for 500 years. I then saw Vietnam for what it was, not a "mistake" or a Cold War confrontation, but a continuation of the Conquest of the indigenous. The US bombing campaigns had names like "Rolling Thunder," our helicopters were called Apaches. The jargon was the same, with only the labels changed: "the only good gook is a dead gook." The defoliation of crops had begun long before William Westmoreland, with Kit Carson. The Harvard-based doctrine of "forced urbanization" and the Pentagon strategy of "fighting their birth rate" were aimed at destroying ancient cultures attached spiritually to land and ancestors.

Flying over the Chiapas highlands 30 years later, I was reminded of the jungles of Vietnam, the rainforests of Brazil, the mountains of El Salvador, all the fault lines of the war between the forces of market modernity and the world of the wretched of the earth. So much starvation, so many genocides, so much overpowering technology, so many Che Guevaras dead in the long struggle to challenge the West. And as a result, so much resignation, weariness, cynicism had taken root, from the barrios of the poor to lecture halls of the left. Worst of all, the West was oblivious to the oblivion the Zapatistas were fighting. One mindset floated in the bubble of modernity while the other tried to shake off a 500-year nightmare.

But then on January 1, 1994—on the very first day of the North American Free Trade Agreement—came an armed uprising by the stones the builders forgot, in a town named for Christopher Columbus himself. Out of oblivion came thousands of masked Mayans, invoking the cultural identity of the indigenous and the land reforms of Zapata. And amidst their leadership was a masked mestizo, a spokesperson named only Marcos. Having been disillusioned all my life by cults of personality, I nonetheless became intrigued like millions of others by this subcomandante. He came from my generation, that of 1968. He was an intellectual. He chose the path of armed struggle when others were giving it up, in a time that was considered postrevolutionary despite its unending poverty and humiliation. With a handful of compañeros, he endured the utter isolation of the mountains, eating insects, repeating to themselves "we're okay, we're okay" in the darkness of the Montes Azules biosphere, the last wilderness of the Lacandón jungle.

By his mask and generic name, by becoming iconic, Marcos seemed to deflect any cult surrounding his own inaccessible personality. The most crucial aspect of his transformation seemed to come from contact with the local Indians. As he listened to their stories and followed their ways, the indigenous ghosts within his ladino identity gradually seemed to come alive. As he would later say, instead of the classic model of the guerrilla penetrating the community, the Indian communities penetrated the guerilla until it became an Indian army in Indian time and space. To seek such a transformation, recognizing and reclaiming our collective indigenous roots—my own were Irish—was a personal Holy Grail. Just as Marcos had come to terms with the indigenous within the Mexican, by coming to know Mexico, North Americans could, in the phrase of Octavio Paz, "learn to understand an unacknowledged part of themselves."

In short, I felt slightly like another in the long line of crazy gringos seeking rebirth in Mexico.

But as a North American, I too opposed NAFTA for its assertion of commercial values over any others. As a state senator, and a former California official appointee to a binational border commission, I believed in policies that would improve opportunities for Mexican campesinos on their historic lands, not rupture their traditions for a future of emigration or maquilladoras. As a human rights activist, it seemed to me that international observers were all that stood between the indians and what they called oblivion (*el olvido*).

In that sense, we of the North were being invited, challenged, to do our part in resisting a Conquest 500 years old. The past was not over. We could not lament the atrocities of "manifest destiny" as if it was finished, beyond anything we could reverse. The past was present, and we had a choice to break with it.

I realized I was in Chiapas as a meditation, to explore how resistance was possible to the New World Order first vocalized by George Bush and implemented by Bill Clinton. After 18 years in legislative politics, I had concluded that the corporate market mentality was fast eclipsing the democratic process, human rights, and environmental concerns in a flood of campaign dollars and claims about the "inevitability" of globalization. For example, NAFTA and the World Trade Organization (WTO) threatened to negate over 90 California laws which, in NAFTA-speak, interfered with investor rights. Looking southward, American multinationals like Monsanto and Novartis were marketing cheap, genetically modified corn and seed to Mexico, disrupting the traditional Indian culture—where corn is sacred—and forcing countless campesinos to migrate from their jungle canyons to the cement ones of southern California. Already Los Angeles was home to 5,000 Mayans from one region of El Salvador, near neighbors of the Chiapanecos, destroyed in the US-sponsored intervention of the 1980s. They huddled together in wretched apartment houses, relived their war traumas on their own, without supportive services, attended syncretic Mayan–Christian evangelical services, earned cash as day laborers, scavengers, or garment workers, were frequently stopped, searched, and sometimes deported, and raised a generation of lost children. Potentially tens of thousands would be forced to join them on the emigrant trail as their traditional lands were modernized out of existence.

Could the Zapatistas stop anything as inexorable as this? Their uprising, with the slogan "NAFTA is Death!" certainly surprised, and temporarily challenged, the NAFTA elite with its claim to invincibility. And in November 1999, just two months before my Chiapas visit, I had been in the streets of Seattle at the birth of another rebellion against NAFTA. Led by young rebels in an improbable alliance with labor unions, the "battle of Seattle" actually stopped an international meeting of the WTO from completing its business. The conflict was joined: direct participatory democracy versus the globalists with their secret tribunals who were usurping the traditional powers of elected governments. A key inspiration for the Seattle uprising was the example of the Zapatistas, whose slogans and imagery filled the air. To avoid police and tear gassing, hundreds of protestors wore ski-masks like the Zapatistas, asserting that they were unmasking the invisible global trade bureaucracy. I had not seen any demonstrations on this scale since the 1960s. The poisonous pepper spray felt familiar, even bracing, after so many years of political hot air. But was it real, or were Chiapas and Seattle like the Oglala ghost dances of the 1890s, the last cry (*grito*) of history's rearguard before our fate was sealed?

I RESOLVED TO make travel arrangements diplomatically, by first visiting the large Mexican consulate in Los Angeles and explaining my general purposes. Mexicans generally were sensitive to Yanqui interference in their internal affairs, and the Mexican government had not hestitated to expel scores of international observers, including Californians. On the other hand, relations between California and Mexico were warming after eight years of Governor Pete Wilson's immigrant-bashing, and I hoped they would grant me visa privileges to travel to Zapatista zones. The delicate problem was that the Mexican government denied that there was a war, or a military crisis, in Chiapas. The conflict was an embarrassment to the sovereignty of the federal state and a serious concern to foreign investors. If I explicitly asked to meet the Zapatistas, Mexican officials would have to acknowledge the existence of an insurrection on their national soil. If I expressed any sympathy for the rebels, I would be legitimizing their insurrection against the state that was providing a visa. So I chose an indirect, more discreet request for travel papers. Browsing through glossy brochures in the consulate which depicted Chiapas as a charming place of archeological interest, I described to the officials my genuine desire to visit the ancient ruins at Palenque. After assuring me that tourists are safer in Chiapas than any part of Mexico "because of the Army presence," the Mexican official noted that I could visit Palenque by taking roads which happened to pass through Zapatista communities. The message was that I could visit the rebel areas, but not officially so. It was obvious that the Zapatistas were not the only masked ones in this conflict. The state wore a diplomatic mask of sorts too. Having completed our nondiscussion of the nonwar, the consul general graciously provided a "distinguished visitor" visa—which would prove useful at army checkpoints in the jungle.

AND NOW I was staring at Mayan children running barefoot in multicolored clothing as our small plane bounced along a grassy strip in Amador Hernández. Behind them was a multicolored wall-mural of Emiliano Zapata, the revolutionary ambushed by the Mexican government—which then coopted his image, and whose political descendants, the Partido Revolucionario Institutional (PRI) were now confronted by his ghost in the jungle. Around me was a small cluster of wooden cabins—perhaps 25 in number—in a several-acre clearing in the rainforest. A few children ran loose with their dogs. Women in Mayan dress stood in doorways. Trails ran into the forest darkness. Masked men approached on horseback and dismounted. Historically a faceless people, their masks now made them recognizable to the world while they remained invisible to surveillance cameras.

Amador Hernández was one of 33 autonomous "communities in resistance" that had risen in arms on January 1, 1994, and which now existed as liberated zones outside the structure of the Mexican state. On the edge of the Montes Azules biosphere, Amador became a center of rapid criss-crossing road construction as the Mexican Army sought to encircle and isolate the Zapatistas. Besides their military use, the roads were opening access to the remaining hardwoods and potentially significant oil reserves that lay below the jungle floor. Not minutes away was an Army base from which attacks could be launched on the hamlet where we stood.

We dropped our backpacks in an open-air village center and, after a drink of water, I sat on a large log interviewing two masked men about their masked history. Amador Hernández, made up of indigenous Tojolabal-speaking Mayans, had been driven from nearby lands a generation ago, and never benefited from 20 years of official Mexican development promises. For survival, they planted subsistance crops. Occasionally government representatives would try to force them out of the jungle, which contains vast untapped oil reserves.

"We started organizing resistance to the displacement on our own," one rebel recounted to me, "and then one day in 1982 or '83, I can't remember when, about a dozen compañeros came walking through the jungle and starting talking with us.

"They asked us if we were ready to stop drinking and start organizing, because the government was fucking us up with alcohol. We saw how the brothers were fighting in El Salvador and Nicaragua, so we said yes, why not?"

Those 1982 visitors to this jungle clearing were the original Zapatistas, one of them to become known as "Marcos." It was their earliest appearance as organizers among the indigenous. I tried to imagine the moment. The idea of one-to-one, patient, grass roots organizing of a movement—any movement, much less a movement toward armed insurrection—is improbable, to say the least, in this age of globalized entertainment media and technofixes. How had the Zapatistas come so far? What made them believe a rebellion could be launched from these jungle meadows? What made these Indians put down alcohol and reach for their weapons?

The Zapatistas emerged in the 1960s from disillusionment with a Mexican state that permitted the 1968 slaughter of student activists in Mexico City and likewise smothered all dissent. They chose to move to the poorest, most forgotten areas of southern Mexico, not unlike those Americans who organized in Mississippi in 1960. In those days, any Mayan walking in the towns of Chiapas had to step off the sidewalks to let a white Mexican pass. The social order was controlled by armed ranchers employing vigilante justice. Organized paramilitary-style in groups with names like "white guards" or "peace and justice," the vigilantes often enough were Indians themselves who, through self-hate and material benefits, had become cowboys.

A tradition of Indian autonomy and resistance was still alive in Chiapas as well. They had learned to survive under many forms of oppression, but in the early 1990s their world became more threatened than ever. In preparing for NAFTA, the Mexican government cancelled Article 27 of its constitution, the cornerstone of Zapata's revolution of 1910–1919. Under the historic Article 27, Indian communal landholdings were protected from sale or privatization. But under NAFTA this guarantee was redefined as an obsolete barrier to investment. With the removal of Article 27, Indian farmers would be threatened with loss of their remaining lands and flooded by cheap imports from the US. Thus, the Zapatistas labeled NAFTA "a death sentence," and Indian communities all over the Chiapas Highlands made preparations for war.

But it was not simply the rapidly worsening conditions that made the rebellion possible. The Zapatistas had also prepared. They metamorphized into an indigenous army. Left behind was the vocabulary of Marxism with its primary emphasis on class; the Zapatistas constituted themselves as descendents of the original Zapata and the land reform tradition. In place of a political party, they were instigating a movement. Instead of expecting proletarian revolution, they chose to challenge and galvanize all sectors of what they called "civil society." In place of the seizure of power, they followed the Indian (and anarchist) path of disavowing power: "for everyone, everything," they declared, "for ourselves, nothing." In place of a new "Internationale" (of the Marxist or Tricontinental variety), they spoke of awaking the world's conscience. In place of a revolutionary war to overthrow the state, they used their guns to show their determination and demand attention, then turned to words and websites to make their case. These were armed intellectuals in a supposedly postrevolutionary time, intent on making history in defiance of the best-selling thesis proclaiming the "end of history." The Zapatistas were committed to the end of modern history as we know it, and to a revindication of the history of the indigenous whose plight is the enduring contradiction at the center of modernity's claims of "progress."

As their several "Declarations from the Lacandón Jungle" make clear, the Zapatista vision has evolved and transformed from a traditional class-based Marxism to a deep identification with the Mayan, not only in the jungles of Chiapas but the Mayan in all Mexicans and the indigenous spirit around the world. I had previously visited ancient Mayan sacred centers in the Yucatan, Guatemala, and Belize, always coming away shaken by the original, unexplained death of these ancient societies and their second death through the process of modern forgetting. Wandering amid those magnificent temples, courtyards, and ballfields—and realizing that the jungles are filled with many more as yet undiscovered—made one abandon any notion that these were primitive or backward civilizations. These were people who actually discovered and studied the cycles of time and the seasons, things we take for granted like the watches on our wrist. They lived amid myriad explosions of color, flowers, skies full of plumed birds, and survived in the dangerous world of the jaguar as well. While I offered support to indigenous struggles all over the Americas, I too assumed that the 500-year war was in its final stages, that the Conquest had succeeded, that extinctions would continue their grisly toll until the end. We who cared for endangered cultures and species were only able to work within the parameters of the Conquest itself, the Conquest we now called the modern world, salvaging what we could of tribal cultures and fragmented ecosystems.

When Marcos and the Zapatistas showed, if only for a moment, that there was an alternative, that the Conquest itself could be challenged one more time, it electrified those like myself who believed, with Carolyn Forche, that "everywhere and always, go after that which is lost." The battle of the EZLN suggested more than another resistance against repressive landowners and paramilitaries. It suggested the deeper possibility of a reversal of forced assimilation on all levels from psychic to political. It suggested that we could reclaim the indigenous roots that lie mangled beneath the architecture of our modern selves.

The declarations of Marcos and the Zapatistas are translated in several places, including the historical reader *Rebellion in Chiapas* (1999) by Harvard historian John Womack. One that reflects the Indian tone and worldview is the "Fourth Declaration" of January 1996, which reads in part:

> Our blood and our word lit a small fire in the mountain, and we walked it along the path that goes to the house of might and money (their march to Mexico City). Brothers and sisters of other races and languages, of another color, but of the same heart, protected our light and drank in it their own fires. . . .
>
> The arrogant want to put out a rebellion that their ignorance locates in the dawn of 1994. But the rebellion that today has a dark face and a true language was not born today. It spoke in other languages and in other lands. [The declaration goes on to list 70 indigenous dialects.]

Many worlds walk in the world. Many worlds are made. Many worlds make us. . . . In the world of the mighty one only the great and their servants fit. In the world we want we all fit. The world we want is one where many worlds fit. . . .

The flower of the word does not die, although our steps walk in silence. In silence the word is sown. So that it may flower shouting, it goes quiet. The word becomes a soldier in order not to die in oblivion. To live the word dies, sown forever in the womb of the world. Only those who surrender their history will return to oblivion.

These were armed guerrillas like no others. Not simply fighting for their cultural identity or negotiating for a niche in the modern state, they seemed to be fighting by using their identity as a weapon itself, challenging the government and Mexican society to think, see, feel, and respond to indigenous identity. They wanted to heal the modern world not by overthrowing or smashing it, but by a cultural re-Conquest of Mexico and the modern world. In this re-Conquest, they seemed to say, the indigenous in everyone, the indigenous in every culture and nation, would overthrow its guards of forgetting and re-emerge as a source of wisdom.

I WAS READING the declaration of "the word in the womb of the world," perched on my log, when the nearby trail into the jungle triggered a memory of seeing the path of Che Guevara in the Bolivian jungle. I had seen that actual path in a documentary based on Che's Bolivian diary filmed by the late Robert Kramer. I had first met Kramer in Newark, New Jersey in 1965 where I was working as a community organizer. He made a radical *noir* film about our community organizing project suggesting that our work was a treadmill without end. Later, when our reformism had disintegrated into urban violence, Kramer made the film *Ice* which prefigured the Weather Underground. He became an American exile in France, and from there went to Bolivia where he documented Che's diaries from his jungle camp to the place of his capture and assassination. The Guevara film, shot with a handheld camera, traverses the jungle trails as Che walked them. The emptiness of the jungle trail visually suggested the isolation of Che's group from the indigenous peasants and Bolivia's civil society. I had seen a representation of that same path once before, at the memorial where Che's remains are buried in Pinar del Río, Cuba. The green, dimly lit trail adjacent to Che's small coffin represents an invitation to future guerrillas and, I realized, was identical to the trail that entered the Lacandón jungle where I sat on the log.

I was thinking about these Zapatistas on the trail of Che—and how they, unlike Che, had taken great pains to become immersed in the indigenous world—when one of my masked guides motioned that it was time to go. We were to follow the trail into the jungle and to the Army base where, every day for the past six months, the people of Amador Hernández had staged nonviolent demonstrations against the presence of the Mexican Army.

We hiked for about a kilometer, over a streambed, through a series of pacific meadows, until coming to a small encampment. There were perhaps 150 villagers, men, women and children in the bright garb of the Tzoltzil people. All but the smallest children were masked. Just then a large US-made military helicopter appeared over the hill behind us. It circled around our march and descending into the trees just ahead where, I realized, the Mexican Army was waiting for us.

As we marched into the canopied shade of the jungle, I heard the beginning of familiar chants ahead. "El pueblo, unido, jamá será vencido/The people, united, will never be defeated." The voices intermingled with strains of music that also seemed familiar, but from where? I climbed a hill where the Zapatistas were massed, raising their fists at a presence I couldn't see in the shadows of trees and vines. There were large rolls of barbed wire along the trail, and camouflaged combat soldiers on the other side. What was that music? It was now louder than the Zapatista chanting and coming from enormous loudspeakers being held aloft by the Mexican soldiers.

It was *La Traviata*! A European opera in the Mayan jungle. A concert behind the concertina wire. The music was meant to drown out the chanting and, on a deeper level, remind the Mexican soldiers of the civilized (and European) values they were defending against these uncultured Indian peasants. After a few minutes, *La Traviata* was replaced by a blaring martial anthem that I couldn't place. In a few minutes, the Zapatistas moved further along the concertina wire, forcing the Mexican troops to gather up their musical equipment, giving the Zapatistas a few minutes to chant again and speak to the Mexican soldiers guarding the fence. "We are your brothers and sisters. You don't want to fight us. You don't want to kill our women and children. You must stop fighting for Zedillo, stop destroying our forest," one after another would say.

The Mexican soldiers at the line were few in number, perhaps 20, with as many as 400 enclosed in a dimly visible encampment behind us. The most prominent, wearing both civilian and military garb, were videotaping the masked faces of each individual protester in the crowd.

The ostensible purpose of the base was road-building to connect remote jungle communities like Amador Hernández to the outside world. In times past, the villagers would have wanted the road because, for example, it required eight hours walking to carry someone to the nearest hospital. But only *after* the Zapatista uprising did the Army come to the jungle, and not for community development. The demonstrators were protesting the project because of its real purpose: to allow the Mexican military to encircle the Zapatista-controlled territory. With helicopters and armored vehicles the army could reach Amador Hernández in 10 minutes. Standing in its way would be this same throng of nonviolent protestors, nothing more. The troops, perhaps supercharged by *La Traviata*, would storm and unmask these peon troublemakers and, in the process, also unmask the repressive nature of the state. For that official unmasking to occur, I realized, it would require an alert public opinion across Mexico and internationally.

After two hours of chanting amid *La Traviata*, the community of Amador Hernández marched back to their encampment and village. It had been a good day, the sun was shining, and my presence had brought a journalist from *La Jornada* and a photographer from the Associated Press. With or without visitors, the community had been demonstrating at the concertina wire every day for the past six months. In the rainy season, they said with smiles, they had to crawl most of the way because boots were sucked off by the mud.

It was a lovely dusk as I sat waiting for the small plane to return us from the jungle to the city. Dogs rolled in the grass nearby as children poked at my camera. The villagers' ears heard the drone of the plane long before I did. As I piled my things aboard and said goodbye, the village returned to routine, which called for raising children, growing corn, and now included making preparations for raising their voices over *La Traviata*. As the plane lifted me up into the rainforest clouds, Amador Hernández became a disappearing green patch in the Lancondon below. I looked at my tourist map. The village didn't exist.

In April, two months later, I received word that the Mexican army was expanding its base behind the barbed wire, and now occupied the pedestrian bridge to control the campesinos' passage between the two sides of the river. According to *La Jornada*, however, "the indigenous abandoned that *hamaca* [bridge], and they went and put one up in another place, far from the soldiers." Finally, in 2001, newly elected Mexican President Vicente Fox ordered the Army's withdrawal from the Amador Hernández base to spur peace talks with the Zapatistas.

THE UNITED STATES is invisibly present in Chiapas. The remoteness of the struggle on the ground, combined with the American helicopters in the air, contributes to an invisible US counterinsurgency role designed to evade American and Mexican public notice. There is little or no American media in Chiapas, and none can reach the highlands without government approval. The modern journalistic credo "if it bleeds, it leads" apparently does not apply when the blood being spilled is Mayan.

The military presence represents a new post-Vietnam strategy to keep American antiwar instincts dormant by constructing Chiapas as a complex, distant, age-old conflict among Mexicans, of no security concern to the United States. But according to Harvard's John Womack in a 1999 study, "for the last few years, the US government, in particular the Defense Department, has wanted 'low intensity' warfare in Mexico." The US Ambassador to Mexico was quoted in 1996 saying that our government was willing to provide intelligence and training for the fight against rebel movements (AP, Sept. 9, 1996). Huey helicopters, surveillance planes, and electronic night vision systems have been sold or donated by the US to Mexico (*El Financiero*, Aug 3–9, 1998). Thousands of Mexican soldiers have been trained at US military bases, and hundreds of officers at the School of the Americas in Fort Benning, Georgia and at Fort Bragg, North Carolina (*Proceso*, May 3, 1998). Though rationalized by the military's "war on drugs," there is no way to "limit the uses to which they put our counternarcotics training because that can be used just as easily for counterinsurgency", according to a specialist as the US Army War College. (*El Financiero International*, August 3–9, 1998).

In addition, under President Clinton the United States increasingly has financial investments to protect from rude insurgencies. The $20 billion Mexican bailout of 1995 benefited Chase Manhattan, J. P. Morgan, Merrill Lynch, Saloman Brothers, and Goldman Sachs, which included Treasury Secretary Robert Rubin as a partner. Chase Manhattan, it may be remembered, was the source of a notorious 1994 memo which stated that "the government will need to eliminate the Zapatistas to demonstrate their effective control of the national territory and of security policy" (IPS, Feb. 13, 1994). On this level, the conflict is between the credibility of the modern state in protecting investors, versus protecting indigenous people on lands containing rich natural and biological resources.

The political dimension of low-intensity warfare consists of hushing up the conflict in every way. Even though there are between 40,000 and 50,000 Mexican troops in Chiapas, it is never described as a "war" in officialspeak. Potentially critical US constituencies are lulled or neutralized.

One American group that could make a major difference, the new generation of Latino politicians, has been quiet on the whole, in the tradition of previous immigrants entering the mainstream. With notable exceptions, the new Latino leaders apparently prefer not to publicly criticize the Mexican government, fearing that their comments might fuel American xenophobia. Further, their need to seek acceptance and respectability in the United States would hardly be advanced if they supported masked revolutionaries who conjure up the gringo fear of Zapata living or dead. When President Zedillo, sinking in controversies, visited Sacramento in 2000, he was hosted by the Latino legislative caucus and Governor Gray Davis in a setting that precluded any public references to the conflict in Chiapas. As Zedillo spoke of economic partnerships with California, posed for photo opportunities, and shook hands all around, even the press remained respectfully silent. Outside, a few protestors with puppets and EZLN masks tried to generate attention, looking like a forlorn contingent of losers. I passed a bilingual letter to Zedillo through an aide, asking that Californians be allowed to travel in Chiapas without harassment, and never heard back.

The other possibility of mass discontent lies with organized labor, which is angered at job loss from NAFTA and turning toward plans to organize Mexican immigrants to the States. But the AFL-CIO thus far has ignored the connection between repression in Chiapas and the instability that drives thousands of Mexicans north to the border. This neutrality may in the future be replaced by solidarity as the ranks of labor swell with Latino workers. But for now, the opposition to US Mexico policy is left to circles of conscious intellectuals, clerics, artists, and students, who have seen through the sophisticated public relations of American-sponsored counterinsurgency. Despite all the limits, the Zapatista message has broken through to this conscience constituency around the world largely over the Internet.

The point is that the Chiapas Indians and their Zapatista allies have two encirclements to elude. One has been that of the Mexican Army. The other, in some ways more formidable, is *perception management* by the United States, designed to make the indigenous return to the oblivion where they have been placed for five centuries. If this seems stretched, consider that the top campaign consultant to Francisco Labastida, the PRI's losing presidential candidate in 2000 was James Carville, President Clinton's de facto minister of propaganda. The PRI's pollster was Stanley Greenberg, also the president's longtime confidant. On every level, therefore, from the banks to the military to presidential politics, the Clinton Administration was involved in orchestrating the fate of Chiapas. Of the three major candidates for the presidency in 2000, two proposed a military pullout from Chiapas.

Only the PRI candidate managed by Clinton's consultants supported the policies of military pressure and encirclement.

THE 500-YEAR-OLD Cathedral of San Bartolomé de las Casas looms heavily over the charming city of San Cristóbal. A large, shabby stone colonial structure with a dark, candlelit interior, the cathedral remains open to worshippers. On its steps, from dawn to dusk, come Indian vendors selling handmade clothing and crafts, including miniature Zapatista dolls, to European and North American tourists. Graffiti on the cathedral walls proclaim support for the armed struggle of the Zapatistas.

Bartolomé, as the locals call him even now, was a Dominican bishop sent to Chiapas in the 1540s, and one of the most fascinating figures in the history of the Conquest, representing the road not taken. He first sailed to the Americas with Columbus in 1502, returning many times. At some point he became morally repelled by the torture and exploitation of the indigenous, as recorded in vivid detail in his diaries, where he described the Indians as "the most guileless, the most devoid of wickedness and duplicity [with] no desire to possess worldly goods" (de las Casas, *The Devastation of the Indies: A Brief Account*, Johns Hopkins University Press, Baltimore, 1992, pp. 28–29).

In numerous religious and intellectual forums, most famously in a debate with Gines de Sepulveda in 1550 in Valladolid, de las Casas argued passionately that the indigenous people were human beings with souls (although, for whatever reason, he did not always extend the same recognition to African slaves). For his troubles, he faced scorn, harassment, and death threats as the designated "Protector of the Indians" until his death in 1566 at the age of 92.

Just as his cathedral still stands, the sixteenth-century bishop is very much alive today among the Indians of Chiapas. His name was invoked familiarly, for example, in testimony at the 1974 Congreso Indígena de Chiapas, the convention that initiated the most recent cycle of the 500-year Indian revolt. A statement from the minutes of that 1974 meeting tells the story from the native viewpoint:

> Columbus came with his compañeros to know the people here and to bother them. With them came Brother Bartolomé de las Casas [who] saw that it was very bad what his other compañeros were doing . . . Right here in San Cristóbal Brother Bartolomé de las Casas was defending the Indian. I

believe we all know the church that's to one side of the Church of Santo Domingo, up from the union hall. . . . Well, comrades, now Brother Bartolomé de las Casas is no longer alive. It's only in his name that we're holding this congreso. So where is the liberty Brother Bartolomé left? We've been suffering injustice for 500 years, and we're still in the same situation (Womack, p. 150).

This long history nurtured the deep religious root of the insurgency in Chiapas, which blended later with the Zapatista root into the present uprising. And nurturing the spiritual root was a modern Brother Bartolomé in the person of Bishop Samuel Ruíz García—known, sometimes disparagingly as "the Indians' Prophet." Hardly a born revolutionary, Samuel Ruíz received a conventional Catholic education at the College Pío Latinoamerico in Rome before coming to Chiapas in 1960. But traveling by foot or mule through the impoverished Indian highlands changed him, as it changed the Zapatistas a decade later and de las Casas five centuries before.

In 1968 Ruíz participated in the historic conference in Medellin, Columbia, when the Latin America bishops embraced liberation theology with its "special preference for the poor." The Medellin manifesto recalled that Jesus was sent to "liberate the poor from slavery, hunger, misery, oppression, and ignorance" and mandated development of "grassroots organizations for the redress and consolidation of their rights and the search for true justice." With that in mind, Ruíz began to inspire, train, and empower a mass movement of the indigenous across Chiapas, organized by thousands of disciplined catechists. By the time of the Zapatista uprising, Ruíz had became a principal sponsor and mediator of sporadic peace talks, the only leader the Indians would trust. Like the murdered Archibishop Oscar Romero in El Salvador, Ruíz was subject to severe pressures from the Catholic hierarchy, periodic death threats, and constant scapegoating by conservative landowners who blamed him for stirring up their Indian servants and laborers. At the time of my visit, the Bishop, age 75, was entering the Church's mandatory period of retirement, much to the relief of those in power.

ATTEMPTING TO UNDERMINE a robed Samuel Ruíz was more difficult than raising doubts about masked Zapatistas. The most sophisticated sowing of doubts appeared in *The New York Review of Books*, a respected publication that has moved significantly to the right since the 1960s. The *Review* published a lengthy article in December 1999 by Mexican intellectual Enrique Krauze. The original piece appeared in the Spanish-language publication *Letras Libres**, with a cover drawing of a benign and lofty Bishop Ruíz standing over the bodies of Mayan peasants presumably sacrificed as a result of his liberation theology. In his magisterial 1997 history of Mexico, Krauze concludes that Chiapas will be remembered only as a "limited and isolated phenomenon" (*Mexico, Biography of Power: A History of Modern Mexico, 1818–1996*, HarperCollins, p. 794). Racism, he wrote, is "not a special feature of Mexican consciousness" (787) except in special cases like traditional Chiapas. Thus the acknowledged poverty and oppression in Chiapas, in Krauze's view, deserve attention but are not national in scope, an argument much like the American one in the 1960s that Mississippi's racial problems were isolated to the old Confederacy.

Krauze acknowledges that "Don Samuel" is a "true incarnation of Isaiah or Amos" whose struggle for justice has been "impressive and moving." But his *New York Review* piece also depicts the Bishop as a religious truebeliever whose attitudes toward violence and compromise are "ambiguous," and who polarizes communities in ways that can lead to tragedies like the Acteal massacre of December 22, 1997, the paramilitary killing of 45 Indians at a highlands village which caused international embarrassment for the Mexican government. The bishop's teachings serve, according to Krauze, to "intensify the exclusiveness" of the Indians, and "feed the temptation toward martyrdom as a means of triumph over injustice."

Nowhere, however, does the Krauze article mention that all 45 victims of the Acteal massacre were praying at the time of their deaths. Or that 43 were shot in the back, while two were bludgeoned in the head. Twenty were women—including four who were pregnant—and 18 were children. The shootings went on for nine hours and though Mexican troops were only a few minutes away, they did not enter the site until the bloodletting was finished. The Acteal massacre was carried out through a counterinsurgency technique as old as the Conquest itself—the arming of paramilitary units composed of Indians willing to kill other Indians for advantage.

I had met Bishop Ruíz in Mexico City, a stocky, jovial, plaid-shirted down-to-earth man who attended a private dinner with a group from Northern Ireland, including Gerry Adams, displaying an exhibition of the "disappeared" from the 1972 Bloody Sunday massacre. The Bishop suggested that I visit Acteal and see conditions for myself. So, after returning to San Cristóbal from the trip to Amador Hernández in the eastern highlands, I found myself caravaning north of San Cristóbal—in heavy rain through military checkpoints up

---

*See page 395 of this book.

winding roads—until we reached a clearing at the foot of the village. We parked next to an immense structure like a tree trunk carved from wood, which, I realized as I peered through the fog, depicted the agonized faces of Acteal's dead.

I was accompanied, guided actually, by Ophelia Medina, the respected Mexican actress who has changed her life to support the Zapatista communities with food, medicine, and solidarity. We met first inside a tent in Mexico City in 1995 where she was fasting in protest of the military occupation of Chiapas. Tall, dramatic, looking eerily like the artist Frieda Kahlo she played in a Mexican film, Medina poured out her reasons for joining the rebellion. "The most important value of this rebellion is to make us Mexicans aware that inside of us there is an an Indian that we have not allowed to talk because we think it's a stupid person. The color of our skin defines our being. But the skin is only a border. When we cross it we enter an inner world, one of community, a different way of thinking, a hope for the future." No wonder Medina is reviled or dismissed by many Mexicans, I thought. Here she was, their symbol of First World, European beauty and taste, now marching in the mud of Chiapas wearing indigenous pants, taking lessons in the native language, changing herself from the inside out. Not unlike Jane Fonda transforming from Barbarella to friend of the Indians at Alcatraz, the Black Panthers, and the Vietnamese peasants.

I followed Medina down 50 yards of steps that had turned into a small waterfall, and walked uncertainly into the village. It reminded me of entering the heavy, unchanging emptiness of Wounded Knee where the Sioux were slaughtered in 1890 (and where, incidentally, the Sioux staged protests in solidarity with the Acteal victims). Before me was an unoccupied, open-walled community center used for religious services and assemblies. A small child stood in a doorway, nose running, sobbing, and I remembered someone saying that newborn babies in Acteal are becoming smaller due to the lack of medicine and malnutrition. It seemed to be raining tears. There were low ravines on both sides of the path where I stood, the places where villagers were hunted down and shot on that day in December. Except for the little girl, the inhabitants of the shanties around me were shuttered inside. Unlike Amador Hernández, Acteal was loaded with grief.

We passed a red brick building, the only one of its kind, and entered a one-room structure nearby—Acteal's "city hall." Inside sat a circle of survivors of the massacre to tell us their story. The room had a dirt floor in which numerous Pepsi bottle caps were pressed. The light came through an open door. I noticed a photo of Archbishop Romero, a calendar, maps of the mountains, and a large poster of a black and yellow bee pollinating a flower.

The community was known as Acteal of the Bees (*las abejas*) to distinguish it from an adjacent Acteal controlled by the Zapatistas. The difference between the neighboring hamlets is that *las abejas*, while supporting the goals of the Zapatistas, is a devout religious group that prays constantly and practices strict nonviolence—a fact that couldn't have escaped the paramilitaries responsible for the massacre. Two years later, the community still had not recovered its pre-massacre population. Nearby communities—Pohlo and Juan Diego de X'oyep were two we visited—are filled with refugees from the time of the massacre, still unable to move back to lands taken by landlords and paramilitaries.

These were the people who, in the account of Enrique Krauze, were manipulated by Bishop Ruíz and liberation theology into their own martyrdom. They sat in a small circle, wearing combinations of tattered jackets with traditional Indian garb. They looked down or away. They were prepared to speak, however, and brought notebooks to record the occasion.

Amid this melancholy, I asked them about their religious beliefs and, in particular, why they remained so nonviolent. They answered readily, in both Tzoltzil and Spanish, while still looking away. A dark-skinned man wrapped in a heavy blue blanket said "the bees" began organizing seven years ago. "We knew the government didn't recognize us, and since the authorities won't protect us, we put ourselves in the hands of God. We call ourselves "the bees" because bees are unified—they diversify their labor but they all work together. We knew the government was giving weapons to the paramilitaries. Christmas was near, so many of us were praying all the time, hoping our Lord would help them see the light. For two days we fasted, but we could not finish because they came to kill us. We were completely surprised. Some stayed in prayer, and others tried to run into our canyons. They hunted us all day long while we prayed."

Their account was confirmed by eyewitnesses. During the massacre, one *abeja* ran up the very road from which we had descended, begging an Army commander to intervene. Nothing was done. During the same hours, an Army spokesman told a reporter there was no news, *sin novedad*. (John Ross, *The War Against Oblivion*, Common Courage Press, 2000, pp. 241–242.)

How could a Krauze cast blame on these people, or Bishop Ruíz, for provoking their own massacre by their devout nonviolence? If they had been armed Zapatistas, the massacre would have been unlikely. Only a profound discomfort with liberation theology, and with Indian autonomy, could cause Krauze to blame the victims for stirring such genocidal passions. The scene they described brought to mind Picasso's *Guernica* painting, the photographs of My Lai, and, of course, images of frozen bodies at Wounded Kneee. I put down my notebook, feeling as much like an intruder as a witness. There was a stoicism about these people, based in the centuries, that would sustain them. But would there be a global conscience large enough to add Acteal to its long list of unanswered wrongs?

It finally stopped raining, so *las abejas* led us a few yards over to the brick building I had noticed before. Inside was a chilly rectangular chamber decorated with flowers and small family photographs of Indian faces. Below our feet, I realized, under a cement landing, the bodies of the 45 dead had been laid to rest. The killings had been barbarous. I remembered reading an autopsy report on "Corpse #16," for example, a "female cadaver, approximately 32 years old, who died of perforation to her abdominal viscera by a cutting instrument—the abdominal cavity was opened up and the product of approximately 28 weeks extracted." (Ross, p. 240.) Corpse #16 and her baby were beneath my feet. We all knelt down. Medina spread newly gathered flowers in a ceremonial arrangement on the floor. Not everyone's photo was on the wall, they said, because some of the victims had never had a photograph taken in their lives. They asked if I would tell people on "the outside" what had happened here. I felt like the question came from 500 years before. I could not speak, so I nodded yes.

An unresolved issue is how far up the Mexican ladder of power the official complicity in Acteal extended. Human rights observers had documented the links between paramilitaries, the army, and Chiapas landowners and government officials. John Ross calls the vigilantes the "Frankenstein love children" of the Mexican army and landowners. But what of the US role? How could one know in an age of "plausible deniability," covert operations, or low-intensity warfare? Instead of holding liberation theology responsible for this tragedy, why didn't publications like the *New York Review* explore whether American advisors and officials foster a mentality of bloodletting by the extremists on "our side?" Thousands of Mexican army officers, after all, were trained in counterinsurgency techniques at the School of the Americas, known to critics as the "School of Assassins." Our military advisors and strategists blinked at death squads in El Salvador, our CIA hired thugs in Guatemala. President Clinton had even apologized to the new Guatemalan government for our part in that dirty war. How long would it take to establish the murky truth in Chiapas?

President Clinton wrote me about these concerns on March 25, 1994, just after the Zapatista uprising. The relevant part reads as follows:

"I assure you that my administration is working hard to protect human rights in Mexico and other countries. In meetings with President Salinas and Foreign Minister Camacho, Ambassador Jones stressed the importance of Army restraint and respect for human rights in dealing with the recent skirmishes. As I continue to monitor the situation in Mexico, I will keep your ideas in mind.

Sincerely,
Bill Clinton

I am sure there is some truth in this reassuring letter. But not the whole truth. Chiapas has become more than the "skirmish" Clinton originally imagined. Even if the White House counsels restraint, even if a massacre like Acteal was the handiwork of isolated thugs, it is clear by now that the US government is implicated through NAFTA in a simmering crisis in Chiapas which can explode into more Acteals at any moment. The US Administration persists in sinking us deeper into a brave new world of globalization that requires counterinsurgency if it is to prosper. America remains the policeman of the world, this time wearing masks of our own, masks far more effective than those of the Zapatistas: the masks which are the uniforms of the armies we train and the mercenaries we foster.

While I was in Chiapas, President Zedillo was in Davos, Switzerland, speaking at a WTO conference on the aftermath of Seattle. His speech was a classic example of the new corporate globalizer's mantra. The low wages of workers in developing countries—and how long developing countries have been developing!—represent a "step toward better opportunities" as well as an escape from "extreme rural poverty or a marginal occupation." The environmental price is acceptable, he added, since more trade equals more growth without which the funding to clean the damaged environment would be unavailable. We wreck the environment, in other words, to generate the capital necessary to restore it. (See *Los Angeles Times*, March 7, 2000 for the full text.)

Zedillo zealously branded all opponents of the WTO "globalphobics," a turn of phrase surely applauded among the besieged insiders of the WTO. The dismissive label served two purposes: first, to brand the critics as antimodern and therefore irrelevant, and second, to politically blame North American (white) protectionists and environmentalist zealots for holding back Mexico's development.

To which Subcommandante Marcos responded over jungle Internet that the Zapatistas welcomed all "Zedillo-phobics, all global-phobics, even all phobic-phobics" to join the struggle against neo-liberalism. It was not a question of globalization versus protectionists phobias, he understood, it was a question of global corporatism versus global conscience.

Memories of Chiapas can make one lonely in America. The process of forgetting is seductive when the alternative is grief. I left the gravesites of Chiapas and returned home to California. I wrote a letter summarizing my trip to the Mexican consul-general, and received no answer. I wrote James Carville urging him to lobby the PRI for a Chiapas pullout, but there was no answer. To my surprise, the most conservative presidential candidate, Vicente Fox, did respond to questions I submitted through a Mexican reporter in Sacramento, Xochitl Arellano. On May 8, 2000, Fox said straightforwardly, "we could remove the two great obstacles that exist to reach an agreement. One has to do with the military presence, which we are willing to take out from their original positions, and number two, use the agreements of San Andreas Larrainzar as a point of departure for this negotiation. I think we are ready also if an interview with Commandante Marcos happens."

I was not surprised, therefore, when the newly elected Fox took the bold initiative to invite the Zapatistas to present their case in Mexico City and begin negotiations after prisoner releases and troop withdrawals to passive positions. In March, 2001, hundreds of thousands of Mexicans welcomed Marcos and the other commandantes to Mexico City in a scene reminiscent of the August 1963 March on Washington. While a historic moment of opportunity, however, it was neither a love-feast nor an end to the conflict. President Fox's own party unanimously opposed letting the Zapatistas into the halls of power which the Panistas had seized after 80 years of PRI domination. Marcos sparred with Fox, suggesting that the Presidente was trying to co-opt the Zapatistas. Others feared a new Chinameca, named after the place where Zapata was ambushed and assassinated. After an extraordinary week of celebration, oratory, and negotiations, the EZLN commandantes left the city for Las Cañadas of Chiapas once again, this time with discreet security from the Mexican Army.

No one can say what the future holds, but then no one expected the rebellion to come this far.

Marcos and the EZLN, while raising hopes for a settlement of the 500-year-old question of Indian autonomy, continue to remain infectious irritants in the body of the globalizers. The Zapatistas hope that world opinion will not only protect their struggle but challenge the New World Order. They do not want to become merely the reform wing of that New World Order, not even modern day Bartolomés railing against the Conquest. They seem deeply satisfied for now to insist on the relevence of dreamers—armed dreamers to be sure—against the visionless nightmares of modernity.

For precisely this reason, both the media and many influential observers write them off as a romantic fringe. Jorge Castañeda, the respected Mexican author chosen by Fox to be Secretary of Foreign Affairs, is one of those. On several occasions Castañeda has predicted the demise of the Zapatistas, blaming Marcos for missed opportunities to enter the political process (as Castañeda, a man of the left, has done by joining the Fox regime). By not joining the "political game," Castañeda has written, Marcos is bungling his chance and in danger of fading to the margins (see Yve Le Bot interview with Marcos, citing Castañeda, in Womack, p. 321). In his biography of Che Guevara, *Compañero*, Castañeda made the same argument, that the fate of revolutionary leaders is to become at best cultural icons, not political or military winners.

This argument, however, understates the achievements of revolutionaries like Marcos who have shaken Mexico, shaken NAFTA and the WTO, and once again raised the question of the indigenous out of the dustbins of history. From a narrower revolutionary perspective, Marcos and his comrades have succeeded where others, even el Che, have failed, in truly modifying and adapting themselves to the Indian world. In his perceptive book on the Maya, *The Heart of the Sky* (1992), Peter Canby interviewed a Guatemalan Indian about the guerrillas in his country so close to Chiapas. "The guerrillas used efficacious methods. They spoke to the Maya in their own languages. But their approach had one fundamental flaw. Their interest in the Maya derived from a theoretical conclusion that the Indians had a revolutionary potential that the guerrillas could use. They therefore wanted to proletarianize the Indians until they were not longer Indians. To them, it was all about a conflict of classes. . . . Because of this, many Indians felt that if the guerrillas had won, it would only have been a change of masters.") (Canby, New York, Cadansha International, p. 339.)

In the 1960s, we learned that the role of an organizer is to organize himself or herself out of a job, to awaken the powerless to dream of their possibilities of leadership and self-determination. We were to be a *catalytic* vanguard but not an organizational vanguard seeking power, for power, as we chanted, was "to the people." We were a mystery to the establishment always hungry to identify leaders for purposes of co-optation or elimination, and a mystery as well to those liberals and leftists who believed in institutionalized agencies of change. I learned much later that these debates were at the center of many efforts to change the world long before the 1960s, including the Mexican revolution.

Marcos and the commandantes appear to be the latest incarnation of the same dream. And even if Casteneda is proven right in his political realism, we all should wonder if that is a good thing. Should utopianism be cauterized from the souls of those who oppose injustice? Or is Marcos right, that dreams are a function of the human character worthy of defending? Zapatismo takes the risk of becoming "just another organization," he has said, "or on the contrary, contributing something truly new." (Womack, 326.)

Having experienced pragmatism for 40 years since the utopian blessed communities and youthful visions of the 1960s, I can testify that the world needs "something truly new." Not that social reforms should be rejected or scorned, but those reforms lose their vitality, their meaning, if they lack all connection to dreaming. They become means of cooptation which finally sap all our righteousness. We in the West have lost the dreaming capacity that evolved as a spiritual and survival resource among our native predecessors over many thousands of years. Now, dialectically, the dreamless tides of globalization are giving rise to a new global resistance on behalf of dreamers.

In the beginning is not the party, not the program, not the constituency, and certainly not the weapons. In the beginning is the dream, which parties, programs, constituencies, and weapons must serve. Without the dream, the means become the ends and the world of power is reproduced. That is the message from Chiapas that the globalizers can neither understand nor suppress.

MEXICO'S DIRTY WAR

BILL WEINBERG

Originally appeared in *In These Times*,
February 21, 2000.

WHEN the security forces in Mexico's militarized southern state of Chiapas persecute foreign sympathizers of the local rebel Indians, it makes headlines. On January 3, Greg Ruggiero, an editor working on a collection of writings by verbose guerrilla leader Subcomandante Marcos for New York's

Seven Stories Press, was detained at the mountain village of San Andrés Larrainzar, held for six hours, and interrogated. He had his 90-day tourist visa revoked and was ordered to leave the country within a week. His story made *The New York Times*.

Kerry Appel, a Denver-based organic coffee importer working with indigenous cooperatives, was also picked up at a roadblock—and banned from Mexico for three years for alleged visa violations. His story also was picked up by the international press. These were just two of 47 foreigners detained by authorities in Chiapas over New Year's, the anniversary of the Zapatista uprising that shook the state in 1994.

But every day the Maya Indians of Chiapas face a far more dire human rights situation—and the world media have paid little note. Ruggiero, back in New York, describes the Chiapas he witnessed as pervaded by "roadblock after roadblock of heavily armed military troops searching vehicles and videotaping, photographing, and harassing travelers of all nationalities."

With the Chiapas peace process at a long impasse and the government resorting to "dirty war" tactics to reconsolidate control over the state, the Indians face not only harassment, but terror. Mercedes Osuna, director of Enlace Civil, a human rights monitoring group based in the Chiapas highland town of San Cristóbal de las Casas, says arbitrary detentions are common. She counts more than 100 political prisoners in Chiapas and says 20,000 Chiapas Indians are "displaced by the terror implemented by paramilitary groups, living in conditions of extreme misery, without sufficient food, shelter, clothes, or medicine. There is at least one dying each week."

The Zapatista National Liberation Army (EZLN) chose January 1, 1994 to launch its uprising because it was the day that NAFTA took effect. They called NAFTA a "death sentence" against Mexico's Indians. Under constitutional changes pushed through in preparation for the treaty by then-President Carlos Salinas, the communal peasant lands known as *ejidos* could be legally privatized or used as loan collateral. This robbed the residents of the "inalienable" village lands that Emiliano Zapata fought for in the Revolution of 1910–1919. But the measures were approved by Congress and all 32 state legislatures, then all under the control of the corrupt, entrenched Institutional Revolutionary Party (PRI). Subcomandante Marcos has said that this constitutional reform "was the door that was closed on the indigenous to survive in a legal and peaceful manner."

The New Year's uprising was followed by 12 days of war in the Chiapas Highlands. After huge peace protests in Mexico City, the government and rebels agreed to talk. But the dialogue was stalled by President Ernesto

Zedillo's refusal to accept the San Andrés Accords, a peace proposal the Zapatistas hashed out with congressional negotiators in a painstaking process. The accords (named for San Andrés Larrainzar, where they were negotiated) call for changes to the Mexican constitution to recognize the autonomy of indigenous peoples—provisions already found in the Colombian and Nicaraguan constitutions. Acceptance of the accords was the EZLN's one precondition for laying down its arms and transforming itself into a civil organization. But the Zedillo government called the accords a dangerous call for "separatism," and vetoed them.

The EZLN remains holed up in the Lacandón Selva, the lowland rainforest region of Chiapas, while the highland communities are bitterly divided between rebel and PRI loyalists. But despite the state of siege, the EZLN has not been goaded into using its weapons. Therefore, the 60,000 federal army troops in Chiapas are still bound by certain restraints. The EZLN has been able to help build and coordinate a national movement from its besieged territory, holding high-profile gatherings in La Realidad, the jungle settlement that serves as the rebels' unofficial capital.

Chiapas has been costly for the PRI. Analysts across the Mexican spectrum acknowledge that the Chiapas rebellion was critical in the nation's tentative democratic opening. Since 1994, the PRI has struggled to maintain control as Zapatista-inspired rebel movements have emerged in Oaxaca and Guerrero. In the 1997 elections, the party lost control of the lower house of Congress for the first time. Then last November, the PRI held its first-ever presidential primary to select a candidate for the 2000 elections.

But just like in the bad old days before such extravagances as primaries, the regime's favorite candidate, Francisco Labastida, won the nomination. Labastida is a former federal Interior Secretary who had been appointed with the implicit mission of pacifying Chiapas. Cuauhtémoc Cárdenas of the left-opposition Party of the Democratic Revolution (PRD), whose victory was stolen by fraud in 1988, will challenge Labastida. The right-opposition National Action Party (PAN) is fronting former Guanajuato Governor Vicente Fox, who advocates freewheeling cowboy capitalism. Pacifying Chiapas remains a top issue. A Labastida victory would point to continued Army–paramilitary collaboration in Chiapas.

Immediately after the PRI primary, Mary Robinson, the UN High Commissioner for Human Rights, toured Mexico in response to the deteriorating situation in Chiapas and elsewhere. Robinson criticized the regime for covering up crimes by security forces in Chiapas, Oaxaca, and Guerrero, saying "government reports do not always match reality."

In Chiapas, Robinson met with both state legislators and Tzotzil Maya women who had survived the December 22, 1997 massacre at the highland hamlet of Acteal, which briefly brought the ongoing crisis to the world's attention. The killers, organized in a paramilitary group called Red Mask, gunned down 21 women, 15 children, and 9 men, targeted because they were Zapatista sympathizers. After the massacre, leaked government documents revealed that the network of paramilitary groups had been established under the direction of officers from the Rancho Nuevo army base outside San Cristóbal at the behest of military intelligence. Some of the officers involved were graduates of the US Army's School of the Americas. (Last year, Mexico received $500 million in US military aid, plus helicopters and other equipment—all in the guise of narcotics enforcement.) Last September, Jacinto Arias, former PRI mayor of Chenalho, was sentenced to 35 years in prison for his role in the massacre. More than 100 suspects have been arrested in the case—including 12 police officers and a soldier. But in January, Arias and 23 co-conspirators had their sentences unexpectedly overturned, hardening local perceptions that no justice is possible within the system.

Since Acteal, the paramilitaries have avoided indiscretions such as killing 45 people in a single day, so as to avert undue media attention. But the grisly terror campaign grinds on. At Sabanilla, in the north of the state, Osuna reports that in recent weeks 52 Chol Maya families have been expelled by the Orwellian-named paramilitary group Peace and Justice, and are waiting in the mountains for some guarantee of safety before they will return home. In Sabanilla and nearby villages, Peace and Justice is engaged in a violent struggle against campesinos loyal to the Zapatistas and the PRD for control of the municipal governments.

On January 5, 29 Tzotzil Maya were arrested by state police while working in their coffee fields near the highland hamlet of Polho. Two of the detained are still being held at the harsh Cerro Hueco state prison in Tuxtla Gutiérrez, the state capital, accused of murder and revenge attacks on village chieftains, or *caciques*. Through La Voz de Cerro Hueco, a political prisoner's organization, the men have proclaimed their innocence, and are backed up by Polho's pro-Zapatista indigenous authorities. The men, Manuel Gutiérrez and Antonio Arias, were expelled by caciques from their native hamlet of Tzanembolom in 1997 under threat of death. The crimes they are accused of took place there a year later, when they were already in exile in Polho. "They were persecuted for opposing the paramilitaries," Osuna says.

The government also has exploited the stalemate to encircle the Zapatistas with military roads. Since August, there has been a standoff at the jungle settlement of Amador Hernández, with Zapatista-loyalist Tzeltal Maya campesinos blocking an army roadbuilding crew from advancing into the tropical forest. Many Lacandón Selva settlements have been occupied by the federal troops, but the rebel authorities of these settlements, the "autonomous municipalities" loyal to the EZLN, continue to function clandestinely in the shadow of the Army. They have issued press statements accusing the occupying Army forces of harassing Indian women, illegal logging, and plundering the area's wildlife for sport and profit.

The critical issue of subsoil rights underlies this struggle over land and autonomy. *La Jornada*, Mexico City's aggressively investigative national daily, recently found that for the first time since the 1994 uprising, the Mexican government has resumed oil exploration in the Lacandón Selva, signaling a return to long-delayed plans to push into Chiapas from the petroleum heartland of Tabasco state to the north on the Gulf Coast. Pemex, the state oil monopoly, is both a top supplier to the United States and the top moneymaker for the Mexican regime.

Making matters worse for Chiapas, Bishop Samuel Ruíz García, for generations the relentless advocate and beloved "grandfather" of the Maya, submitted his resignation to the Vatican on November 3, upon reaching the customary retirement age of 75. A Nobel Peace Prize nominee, Ruíz was seen by many as the one man standing between Chiapas and total war. Ruíz brokered the EZLN–government peace dialogue, only to step down as a negotiator to protest the deadlock two years ago. But the Fray Bartolomé Human Rights Center that his diocese led remained at the forefront of documenting abuses in the Maya lands of Chiapas. Ruíz, who says the church must learn to recognize "God working among the Indians," has been the target of numerous death threats in recent years. In 1997, his motorcade was sprayed with gunfire on a tour of the state's northern zone.

Many presumed that Ruíz would be succeeded by his loyal Bishop Coadjutor Raúl Vera. But on December 30, the Vatican abruptly announced Vera was being transferred to Saltillo, far away at the other end of the country. This decision sparked local protests and suspicion in the press that the "dark hand" of the government was behind the move. Mexico's new Papal Nuncio Justo Mullor insisted the decision was "purely ecclesiastical."

The veto of Vera's ascendance to the diocese was said to have been arranged by Mullor's long-reigning predecessor, Girolamo Prigione, whose personal mission had been to purge the Mexican church of liberation theology influences. He succeeded in rotating the progressive Bishop Sergio Méndez Arceo out of the Diocese of Cuernavaca in Morelos state, and had asked Ruíz to resign in late 1993—just before the Zapatista uprising suddenly made him indispensable. Now, the official moves against his legacy at the diocese signal "a very dangerous moment," Osuna says.

The year in Chiapas ended—as the anniversary of the 1994 uprising approached—on the traditional note of paranoia. Army and state police troops flooded into the Lacandón Selva, with the Chiapas government warning (on no evidence) that the EZLN was planning "new acts of violence." At Amador Hernández, where the army still maintained a heavily fortified post, the Tzeltal jungle settlers resorted to political theater to lampoon the hyped threat of Zapatista violence. Calling themselves the Zapatista Air Force, the Indians pelted the troops with dozens of paper airplanes. On each one was a message to the young conscripts: "Soldiers, we know that poverty has made you sell your lives and souls. I also am poor, as are millions. But you are worse off, for defending our exploiter—Zedillo and his group of moneybags."

POSTSCRIPT

MARCH 2001

THE PEOPLE OF THE
COLOR OF THE EARTH
Zapatista Communiqué of March 11, 2001.

Translated by Irlandesa

EDITOR'S note: This is a remarkable document, comparable to Rev. Martin Luther King's "I Have a Dream" speech of August, 1963, delivered at the Lincoln Memorial in the US capitol before a throng of hundreds of thousands.

It may be the most important expression of the indigenous dream in the last century.

The occasion itself—250,000 in the Zócalo, the heart of Mexico profundo—magnified the power of the declaration translated here many times over.

The invisible name themselves, restoring their identities from the oblivion they resist. In naming themselves, they become a mirror in which all who are not indigenous can see themselves as well. The real Mexico is thus revealed.

Further, in naming themselves they name who they are not and will not be: not the ones who aspire to take power, not the ones who reduce everything to market transactions, and emphatically not a passing fad.

Finally, in naming themselves they express the integration of the human community and the natural world. They are the People of Corn, the People of the Color of the Earth.

Contained within the vision is a political summary as well. It transcends the conventional boundaries of politics and violence by stating a new paradigm: "We are here to say we are here. . . . [The powerful] do not want to say it because to say it is to admit it and to admit is to see that everything has changed, and no longer because something is changing, but because everything is changing and is changed in the process." The Zapatistas will always be rebels, but as a mirror and not a vanguard party, not the road, not the guide, because struggle itself is a complex and many-colored as the natural world from which all living forms arise. The Zapatistas are suggesting nothing less than restoring the ecology of humanity ("a world where many worlds can fit"), starting with the "first people" who face extinction.

If the inclusion of the People of the Color of the Earth is agreed, if they no longer face oblivion, the communiqué suggests that revolution can come "without war as a house and a road."

That is why the style and form of the communiqué is as important, is synonymous with its substance. It challenges the audience, from the powerful to all of civic society, to remake themselves by assimilating into indigenous consciousness, by accepting the Other within, just as the original EZLN guerrillas did in the mountains.

Mexico City:

We have arrived.

We are here.

We are the National Indigenous Congress and Zapatistas who are, together, greeting you.

If the grandstand where we are is where it is, it is not by accident. It is because, from the very beginning, the government has been at our backs. [The speaking platform was erected in front of the presidential palace] Sometimes with helicopters, sometimes with paramilitaries, sometimes with planes, sometimes with tanks, sometimes with soldiers, sometimes with the police, sometimes with offers for the buying and selling of consciences, sometimes with offers for surrender, sometimes with lies, sometimes with strident statements, sometimes with forgetting, sometimes with expectant silences. Sometimes, like today, with impotent silences.

That is why the government never sees us, that is why it does not listen to us.

If they quickened their pace a bit, they might catch up with us.

They could see us then, and listen to us.

They could understand the long and firm perspective of the one who is persecuted and who, nonetheless, is not worried, because he knows that it is the steps that follow which require attention and determination.

Brother, Sister:

Indigenous, worker, campesino, teacher, student, neighbor, housewife, driver, fisherman, taxi driver, stevedore, office worker, street vendor, unemployed, media worker, professional worker, religious person, homosexual, lesbian, transsexual, artist, intellectual, militant, activist, sailor, soldier, sportsman, legislator, bureaucrat, man, woman, child, young person, old one. Brother, sister of the National Indigenous Congress, now rainbow of the best of the Indian peoples of Mexico: We should not have been here. (After hearing this, I'm sure that the one at my back is applauding like crazy for the first time. So I'm going to repeat it) We should not have been here.

The ones who should have been here are the Zapatista indigenous communities, their seven years of struggle and resistance, their ear and their looking. The Zapatista people. The men, children, women and old ones, support bases of the Zapatista Army of National Liberation, who are the feet that walk us, the voice that speaks to us, the looking which makes us visible, the ear which makes us heard.

The ones who should have been here are the insurgent women and men, their persistent shadow, their silent strength, their memory risen. The insurgent women and men. The women and men who make up the regular troops of the EZLN and who are guardian and heart of our peoples.

It is they who deserve to see you and to listen to you and to speak with you. We should not have been here.

Nonetheless, we are. And we are next to them, the men and women who are the Indian peoples of all Mexico. The Indian peoples, the first inhabitants, the first talkers, the first listeners. Those who, being first, are the last to appear and to perish . . .

Indigenous brother, sister.

Tenek.

We come from very far away.

Tlahuica.

We walk time.

Tlapaneco.

We walk the land.

Tojolabal.

We are the bow and the arrow.

Totonaco.

Wind walked.

Triqui.

We are the blood and the heart.

Tzeltal.

The warrior and the guardian.

Tzotzil.

The embrace of the compañero.

Wixaritari.

They assume us to be defeated.

Yaqui.

Mute.
Zapoteco.
Silenced.
Zoque.
We have much time in our hands.
Maya.
We came here to give ourselves a name.
Kumiai.
We came here to say "we are."
Mayo.
We came here to be gazed upon.
Mazahua.
To see ourselves being looked upon.
Mazateco.
Our name is spoken here for our journey.
Mixe.

THIS IS WHAT we are:
    The one who flourishes within the hills.
    The one who sings.
    The one who guards and nurtures the ancient word.
    The one who speaks.
    The one who is of maize.
    The one who resides in the mountain.
    The one who walks the land.
    The one who shares the idea.
    The true we.
    The true man.
    The ancestor.
    The Señor of the net.
    The one who respects history.
    The one who is people of humble custom.
    The one who speaks with flowers.
    The one who is rain.
    The one who has knowledge to govern.
    The hunter of arrows.
    The one who is sand.
    The one who is river.
    The one who is desert.

The one who is the sea.
The different one.
The one who is person.
The swift walker.
The one who is good.
The one who is mountain.
The one who is painted in color.
The one who speaks the right word.
The one who has three hearts.
The one who is father and older brother.
The one who walks the night.
The one who works.
The one who is man.
The one who walks from the clouds.
The one who hears the word.
The one who shares the blood and the idea.
The son of the sun.
The one who goes from one side to the other.
The one who walks in the fog.
The one who is mysterious.
The one who speaks the word.
The one who governs in the mountain.
The one who is brother, sister.
Amuzgo.
Our name says all of this.
Cora.
And it says more.
Cuicateco.
But it is hardly heard.
Chinanteco.
Another name covers our name.
Chocholteco.
We came here to be ourselves.
Chol.
We are the mirror for seeing ourselves and for being ourselves.
Chontal.
We, those who are the color of the earth.
Guariji'o.
Here, we no longer feel shame for the color of our skin.

Huasteco.
Language.
Huave.
Clothing.
Kikapu'.
Dance.
Kukapa'.
Song.
Mame.
Size.
Matlatzinca.
History.
Mixteco.
Here, there is no longer embarrassment.
Nahuatl.
Here we feel the pride of our being the color we are, the color of the earth.
Ñahñu.
Here the dignity which is seeing ourselves being seen being the color of the earth which we are.
O'Odham.
Here is the voice which births us and inspires us.
Pame.
Here, the silence is no longer.
Popoluca.
Here, the shout.
Purepecha.
Here, the place that was concealed.
Rara'muri.
Here the dark light, the time and the feeling.
Indigenous and non-indigenous Brother, Sister:
We are a mirror.
We are here in order to see each other and to show each other, so you may look upon us, so you may look at yourself, so that the other looks in our looking.
We are here and we are a mirror.
Not reality, but merely its reflection.
Not light, but merely a glimmer.
Not a path, but merely a few steps.
Not a guide, but merely one of the many routes which lead to tomorrow.

///

BROTHER, SISTER MEXICO City:

When we say "we are," we are also saying "we are not" and "we shall not be."

That is why it is good for those who have money and the ones who peddle it to take note of the word, to listen to it carefully, and to look with care at what they do not want to see.

We are not those who aspire to make themselves powerful and then impose their way and their word. We will not be.

We are not those who put a price on our own dignity—or anyone else's—and convert the struggle into a market, where politics is the business of sellers who are fighting, not about programs, but for clients. We will not be.

We are not those who expect pardon and handouts from one who feigns to help, when he is, in reality, buying, and who does not pardon, but humiliates the one who, by merely existing, is a defiance and challenge and claim and demand. We will not be.

We are not those who wait, naively, for justice to come from above, when it only comes from below. Liberty can only be achieved by everyone. Democracy is at every level and is fought for all the time. We will not be.

We are not the passing fashion which will be made into songs and filed in the calendar of defeats which this country flaunts with such nostalgia. We will not be.

We are not the cunning calculation which falsifies the word and conceals a new fakery within it. We are not the simulated peace longing for eternal war. We are not those who say "three," and then "two" or "four" or "all" or "nothing." We will not be.

WE ARE, AND we shall be, one more in the march:

Of Indigenous Dignity.

Of the Color of the Earth. That which unveils and reveals the many Mexicos which are hidden and suffer under Mexico.

We are not their spokespeople. We are one voice among all those voices. An echo which dignity repeats among all the voices.

We join with them, we are made one with them. We will continue to be echo. We are, and we shall be, a voice. We are a reflection and a shout. We shall always be.

We can be with or without face, armed with fire or without, but we are Zapatistas: We are and we shall always be.

///

NINETY YEARS AGO the powerful asked those from below by whose authority Zapata was called: "With whose permission, Señores?"

And those from below responded—and we respond: "With ours."

And with our permission, for exactly 90 years, we have been shouting, and they call us "rebels." And today we are repeating: we are rebels.

Rebels we shall be. But we want to be so with everyone we are. Without war as house and path.

Because so speaks the color of the earth: The struggle has many paths, and it has but one destiny: to be one with all the colors which clothe the earth.

BROTHER, SISTER:

Up there they say that this is the end of a tremor. That everything will pass except their being above us.

Up there they say that you are here to watch in morbid fascination—to hear without listening to anything. They say we are few, that we are weak. That we are nothing more than a photograph, an anecdote, a spectacle, a perishable product whose expiration date is close at hand.

Up there they say that you will leave us alone. That we shall return alone and empty to the land from which we came.

Up there they say that forgetting is defeat, and they want to wait for you to forget and to fail and to be defeated.

There is something they know, but they do not want to say it: There will be no more forgetting, and defeat shall not be the crown for the color of the earth. They do not want to say so, because saying it is recognizing it, and recognizing it is seeing that everything has changed, and nothing will change now without everyone changed, changing.

This movement, the one of the color of the earth, is yours, and because it is yours, it is ours.

Now there is no longer the "you" and the "we," because now we are all the color of the earth—and it is what they fear. It is the hour for the fox and the one he serves to listen to us. It is the hour for the fox and the one who commands him to see us.

Our word says one single thing. Our looking looks at one single thing: the constitutional recognition of indigenous rights and culture. A dignified place for the color of the earth.

It is the hour in which this country ceases to be a disgrace, clothed only in the color of money.

It is the hour of the Indian peoples, of the color of the earth, of all the colors we are below, and all of the colors we are in spite of the color of money. We are rebels because the land rebels if someone is selling and buying it as if the land did not exist, as if the color of the earth did not exist.

MEXICO CITY:

We are here. We are here as the rebellious color of the earth which shouts:

Democracy!
Liberty!
Justice!

MEXICO:

We did not come to tell you what to do, or to guide you along any path. We came in order to humbly, respectfully, ask you to help us. For you to not allow another day to dawn without this flag having an honorable place for we who are the color of the earth.

From the Zócalo in Mexico City
   Clandestine Revolutionary Indigenous Committee—
   General Command of the Zapatista Army of National Liberation
Mexico, March 2001

THE UNKNOWN ICON

NAOMI KLEIN

Originally appeared in *The Guardian* (London),
March 3, 2001.

I'VE never been to Chiapas. I've never made the pilgrimage to the Lacandón jungle. I've never sat in the mud and the mist in La Realidad. I've never begged, pleaded, or posed to get an audience with Subcomandante Marcos, the masked man, the faceless face of Mexico's Zapatista National Liberation Army. I know people who have. Lots of them. In 1994, the summer after the Zapatista rebellion, caravans to Chiapas were all the rage in North American activist circles: Friends got together and raised money for second-hand vans, filled them with supplies, then drove south to San Cristóbal de las Casas and left the vans behind. I didn't pay much attention at the time. Back then, Zapatista-mania looked suspiciously like just another cause for guilty lefties with a Latin American fetish: another Marxist rebel army, another macho leader, another chance to go south and buy color-ful textiles. Hadn't we heard this story before? Hadn't it ended badly? Last week, there was another caravan in Chiapas. But this was different. First, it didn't end in San Cristóbal de las Casas; it started there, and is now criss-crossing the Mexican countryside before the planned grand entrance into Mexico City on March 11. The caravan, nicknamed the "Zapatour" by the Mexican press, is being led by the council of 24 Zapatista commanders, in full uniform and masks (though no weapons), including Subcoman-dante Marcos himself. Because it is unheard of for the Zapatista command to travel outside Chiapas (and there are vigilantes threatening deadly duels with Marcos all along the way), the Zapatour needs tight security. The Red Cross turned down the job, so protection is being provided by several hun-dred anarchists from Italy who call themselves Ya Basta! (meaning "Enough is enough!"), after the defiant phrase used in the Zapatistas' dec-laration of war. Hundreds of students, small farmers, and activists have joined the roadshow, and thousands greet them along the way. Unlike those early visitors to Chiapas, these travelers say they are there not because they are "in solidarity" with the Zapatistas, but because they are Zapatistas. Some even claim to be Subcomandante Marcos himself—they say we are all Marcos.

Perhaps only a man who never takes off his mask, who hides his real name, could lead this caravan of renegades, rebels, loners, and anarchists on this two-week trek. These are people who have learned to steer clear of charismatic leaders with one-size-fits-all ideologies. These aren't party loy-alists; these are members of groups that pride themselves on their autonomy and lack of hierarchy. Marcos—with his black wool mask, two eyes and pipe—seems to be an anti-leader tailor-made for this suspicious, critical lot. Not only does he refuse to show his face, undercutting (and simultaneously augmenting) his own celebrity, but Marcos's story is of a man who came to his leadership, not through swaggering certainty, but by coming to terms with political uncertainty, by learning to follow.

Though there is no confirmation of Marcos's real identity, the most repeated legend that surrounds him goes like this: an urban Marxist intellectual and activist, Marcos was wanted by the state and was no longer safe in the cities. He fled to the mountains of Chiapas in southeast Mexico filled with revolutionary rhetoric and certainty, there to convert the poor indigenous masses to the cause of armed proletarian revolution against the bourgeoisie. He said the workers of the world must unite, and the Mayans just stared at him. They said they weren't workers and, besides, land wasn't property but the heart of their community. Having failed as a Marxist missionary, Marcos immersed himself in Mayan culture. The more he learned, the less he knew. Out of this process, a new kind of army emerged, the EZLN, the Zapatista National Liberation Army, which was not controlled by an elite of guerrilla commanders but by the communities themselves, through clandestine councils and open assemblies. "Our army," says Marcos, "became scandalously Indian." That meant that he wasn't a commander barking orders, but a subcomandante, a conduit for the will of the councils. His first words said in the new persona were: "Through me speaks the will of the Zapatista National Liberation Army."

Further subjugating himself, Marcos says that he is not a leader to those who seek him out, but that his black mask is a mirror, reflecting each of their own struggles; that a Zapatista is anyone anywhere fighting injustice, that "We are you." He once said, "Marcos is gay in San Francisco, black in South Africa, an Asian in Europe, a Chicano in San Ysidro, an anarchist in Spain, a Palestinian in Israel, a Mayan Indian in the streets of San Cristóbal, a Jew in Germany, a Gypsy in Poland, a Mohawk in Quebec, a pacifist in Bosnia, a single woman on the Metro at 10:00 P.M., a peasant without land, a gang member in the slums, an unemployed worker, an unhappy student and, of course, a Zapatista in the mountains."

"This non-self," writes Juana Ponce de León who has collected and edited Marcos's writings in *Our Word Is Our Weapon*, "makes it possible for Marcos to become the spokesperson for indigenous communities. He is transparent, and he is iconographic." Yet the paradox of Marcos and the Zapatistas is that, despite the masks, the non-selves, the mystery, their struggle is about the opposite of anonymity—it is about the right to be seen. When the Zapatistas took up arms and said *Ya Basta!* in 1994, it was a revolt against their invisibility. Like so many others left behind by globalization, the Mayans of Chiapas had fallen off the economic map: "Below in the cities," the EZLN command stated, "we did not exist. Our lives were worth less than those of machines or animals. We were like stones, like weeds in the road. We were silenced. We were faceless." By arming and masking themselves, the Zapatistas explain, they weren't joining some *Star Trek*–like

Borg universe of people without identities fighting in common cause: they were forcing the world to stop ignoring their plight, to see their long neglected faces. The Zapatistas are "the voice that arms itself to be heard. The face that hides itself to be seen."

Meanwhile, Marcos himself—the supposed non-self, the conduit, the mirror—writes in a tone so personal and poetic, so completely and unmistakably his own, that he is constantly undercutting and subverting the anonymity that comes from his mask and pseudonym. It is often said that the Zapatistas' best weapon is the Internet, but their true secret weapon is their language. In *Our Word Is Our Weapon*, we read manifestos and war cries that are also poems, legends, and riffs. A character emerges behind the mask, a personality. Marcos is a revolutionary who writes long meditative letters to Uruguayan poet Eduardo Galeano about the meaning of silence; who describes colonialism as a series of "bad jokes badly told," who quotes Lewis Carroll, Shakespeare, and Borges. Who writes that resistance takes place "any time any man or woman rebels to the point of tearing off the clothes resignation has woven for them and cynicism has dyed grey." And who then sends whimsical mock telegrams to all of "civil society": THE GRAYS HOPE TO WIN. STOP. RAINBOW NEEDED URGENTLY.

Marcos seems keenly aware of himself as an irresistible romantic hero. He's an Isabel Allende character in reverse—not the poor peasant who becomes a Marxist rebel, but a Marxist intellectual who becomes a poor peasant. He plays with this character, flirts with it, saying that he can't reveal his real identity for fear of disappointing his female fans. Perhaps wary that this game was getting a little out of hand, Marcos chose the eve of Valentine's Day this year to break the bad news: he is married, and deeply in love, and her name is La Mar ("the Sea"—what else would it be?).

This is a movement keenly aware of the power of words and symbols. Rumor has it that when the 24-strong Zapatista command arrives in Mexico City, they hope to ride downtown on horseback, like indigenous conquistadors. There will be a massive rally, and concerts, and they will ask to address the Congress. There, they will demand that legislators pass an Indigenous Bill of Rights, a law that came out of the Zapatistas' failed peace negotiations with president Ernesto Zedillo, who was defeated in recent elections. Vicente Fox, his successor who famously bragged during the campaign that he could solve the Zapatista problem "in 15 minutes," has asked for a meeting with Marcos, but has so far been refused—not until the bill is passed, says Marcos, not until more Army troops are withdrawn from Zapatista territory, not until all Zapatista political prisoners are freed.

Marcos has been betrayed before, and accuses Fox of staging a "simulation of peace" before the peace negotiations have even restarted. What is clear in all this jostling for position is that something radical has changed in the balance of power in Mexico. The Zapatistas are calling the shots now— which is significant, because they have lost the habit of firing shots. What started as a small, armed insurrection has in the past seven years turned into what now looks more like a peaceful mass movement. It has helped topple the corrupt 71-year reign of the Institutional Revolutionary Party, and has placed indigenous rights at the center of the Mexican political agenda.

Which is why Marcos gets angry when he is looked on as just another guy with a gun: "What other guerrilla force has convened a national democratic movement, civic and peaceful, so that armed struggle becomes useless?" he asks. "What other guerrilla force asks its bases of support about what it should do before doing it? What other guerrilla force has struggled to achieve a democratic space and not take power? What other guerrilla force has relied more on words than on bullets?"

The Zapatistas chose January 1, 1994, the day the North American Free Trade Agreement (NAFTA) came into force, to "declare war" on the Mexican army, launching an insurrection and briefly taking control of the city of San Cristóbal de las Casas and five Chiapas towns. They sent out a communiqué explaining that NAFTA, which banned subsidies to indigenous farm cooperatives, would be a "summary execution" for 4,000,000 indigenous Mexicans in Chiapas, the country's poorest province.

Nearly 100 years had passed since the Mexican revolution promised to return indigenous land through agrarian reform; after all these broken promises, NAFTA was simply the last straw. "We are the product of 500 years of struggle . . . but today we say *Ya Basta!* Enough is enough." The rebels called themselves Zapatistas, taking their name from Emiliano Zapata, the slain hero of the 1910 revolution who, along with a ragtag peasant army, fought for lands held by large landowners to be returned to indigenous and peasant farmers.

In the seven years since, the Zapatistas have come to represent two forces at once: first, rebels struggling against grinding poverty and humiliation in the mountains of Chiapas and, on top of this, theorists of a new movement, another way to think about power, resistance, and globalization. This theory—Zapatismo—not only turns classic guerrilla tactics inside out, but flips much of left-wing politics on its head.

I may never have made the pilgrimage to Chiapas, but I have watched the Zapatistas' ideas spread through activist circles, passed along second- and thirdhand: a phrase, a way to run a meeting, a metaphor that twists your brain around. Unlike classic revolutionaries, who preach through bullhorns and from pulpits, Marcos has spread the Zapatista word through riddles: Revolutionaries who don't want power. People who must hide their faces to be seen. A world with many worlds in it.

A movement of one "no" and many "yesses."

These phrases seem simple at first, but don't be fooled. They have a way of burrowing into the consciousness, cropping up in strange places, being repeated until they take on this quality of truth—but not absolute truth: a truth, as the Zapatistas might say, with many truths in it. In Canada, where I'm from, indigenous uprising is always symbolized by a blockade: a phys- ical barrier to stop the golf course from being built on a native burial site, to block the construction of a hydroelectric dam, or to keep an old-growth forest from being logged. The Zapatista uprising was a new way to protect land and culture: Rather than locking out the world, the Zapatistas flung open the doors and invited the world inside. Chiapas was transformed— despite its poverty, despite being under constant military siege—into a global gathering place for activists, intellectuals, and indigenous groups.

From the first communiqué, the Zapatistas invited the international community "to watch over and regulate our battles." The summer after the uprising, they hosted a National Democratic Convention in the jungle; 6,000 people attended, most from Mexico. In 1996, they hosted the first Encuentro (or meeting) for Humanity and against Neo-Liberalism. Some 3,000 activists traveled to Chiapas to meet with others from around the world.

Marcos himself is a one-man Web: he is a compulsive communicator, constantly reaching out, drawing connections between different issues and struggles. His communiqués are filled with lists of groups that he imagines are Zapatista allies—small shopkeepers, retired people and the disabled, workers and campesinos. He writes to political prisoners Mumia Abu Jamal and Leonard Peltier. He is pen-pal with some of Latin America's best- known novelists. He writes letters addressed "to the people of world."

When the uprising began, the government attempted to play down the incident as a "local" problem, an ethnic dispute easily contained. The strategic victory of the Zapatistas was to change the terms: to insist that what was going on in Chiapas could not be written off as a narrow "ethnic" strug- gle, that it was universal. They did this by clearly naming their enemy not only as the Mexican state but as the set of economic policies known as "neoliberalism." Marcos insisted that the poverty and desperation in

Chiapas was simply a more advanced version of something happening all around the world. He pointed to the huge numbers of people who were being left behind by prosperity, whose land and work made that prosperity possible. "The new distribution of the world excludes minorities," Marcos has said. "The indigenous, youth, women, homosexuals, lesbians, people of color, immigrants, workers, peasants; the majority who make up the world basements are presented, for power, as disposable. The distribution of the world excludes the majorities."

The Zapatistas staged an open insurrection, one that anyone could join, as long as they thought of themselves as outsiders. By conservative estimates, there are now 45,000 Zapatista-related websites, based in 26 countries. Marcos's communiqués are available in at least 14 languages. And then there is the Zapatista cottage industry: black T-shirts with red five-pointed stars, white T-shirts with EZLN printed in black. There are baseball hats, black EZLN ski masks, Mayan-made dolls and trucks. There are posters, including one of Comandante Ramona, the much-loved EZLN matriarch, as the Mona Lisa.

It looked like fun, but it was also influential. Many who attended the first *encuentros* went on to play key roles in the protests against the World Trade Organization in Seattle and the World Bank and IMF in Washington DC, arriving with a new taste for direct action, for collective decision-making and decentralized organising. When the insurrection began, the Mexican military was convinced it would be able to squash the Zapatistas' jungle uprising like a bug. It sent in heavy artillery, conducted air raids, mobilized thousands of soldiers. Only, instead of standing on a squashed bug, the government found itself surrounded by a swarm of international activists, buzzing around Chiapas. In a study commissioned by the US military from the Rand Corporation, the EZLN is studied as "a new mode of conflict— netwar—in which the protagonists depend on using network forms of organization, doctrine, strategy, and technology." This is dangerous, according to Rand, because what starts as "a war of the flea" can quickly turn into "a war of the swarm."

The ring around the rebels has not protected the Zapatistas entirely. In December 1997, there was the brutal Acteal massacre in which 45 Zapatista supporters were killed, most of them women and children. And the situation in Chiapas is still desperate, with thousands displaced from their homes. But it is also true that the situation would probably have been much worse, potentially with far greater intervention from the US military, had it not been for this international swarm. The Rand Corporation study states that the global activist attention arrived "during a period when the United States may have been tacitly interested in seeing a forceful crackdown on the rebels."

So it's worth asking: What are the ideas that proved so powerful that thousands have taken it upon themselves to disseminate them around the world? A few years ago, the idea of the rebels traveling to Mexico City to address the congress would have been impossible to imagine. The prospect of masked guerrillas (even masked guerrillas who have left their arms at home) entering a hall of political power signals one thing: revolution. But Zapatistas aren't interested in overthrowing the state or naming their leader, Marcos, as president. If anything, they want less state power over their lives. And, besides, Marcos says that as soon as peace has been negotiated he will take off his mask and disappear.

What does it mean to be a revolutionary who is not trying to stage a revolution? This is one of the key Zapatista paradoxes. In one of his many communiqués, Marcos writes that "it is not necessary to conquer the world. It is sufficient to make it new." He adds: "Us. Today." What sets the Zapatistas apart from your average Marxist guerrilla insurgents is that their goal is not to win control, but to seize and build autonomous spaces where "democracy, liberty, and justice" can thrive.

Although the Zapatistas have articulated certain key goals of their resistance (control over land, direct political representation, and the right to protect their language and culture), they insist they are not interested in "the Revolution," but rather in "a revolution that makes revolution possible."

Marcos believes that what he has learned in Chiapas about non-hierarchical decisionmaking, decentralized organizing, and deep community democracy holds answers for the non-indigenous world as well—if only it is willing to listen. This is a kind of organizing that doesn't compartmentalize the community into workers, warriors, farmers and students, but instead seeks to organize communities as a whole, across sectors and across generations, creating "social movements." For the Zapatistas, these autonomous zones aren't about isolationism or dropping out, 1960s-style. Quite the opposite: Marcos is convinced that these free spaces, born of reclaimed land, communal agriculture, resistance to privatization, will eventually create counter-powers to the state simply by existing as alternatives.

This is the essence of Zapatismo, and explains much of its ap global call to revolution that tells you not to wait for the revolution, stand where you stand, to fight with your own weapon. It could be camera, words, ideas, "hope"—all of these, Marcos has written, "are also weapons." It's a revolution in miniature that says, "Yes, you can try this at home." This organizing model has spread throughout Latin America and the world. You can see it in the anarchist squats of Italy (called "social centers") and in the Landless Peasants' Movement of Brazil, which seizes tracts of unused farmland and uses them for sustainable agriculture, markets, and schools under the slogan *Ocupar, Resistir, Producir* (Occupy, Resist, Produce). These same ideas were forcefully expressed by the students of the National Autonomous University of Mexico during last year's long and militant occupation of their campus. Zapata once said the land belongs to those who work it; their banners blared: WE SAY THAT THE UNIVERSITY BELONGS TO THOSE WHO STUDY IN IT.

Zapatismo, according to Marcos, is not a doctrine but "an intuition." And he is consciously trying to appeal to something that exists outside the intellect, something uncynical in us, that he found in himself in the mountains of Chiapas: wonder, a suspension of disbelief, myth and magic. So, instead of issuing manifestos, he tries to riff his way into this place, with long meditations, flights of fancy, dreaming out loud. This is, in a way, a kind of intellectual guerrilla warfare: Marcos won't meet his opponents head-on, but instead surrounds them from all directions.

A month ago, I got an email from Greg Ruggiero, the publisher of Marcos's collected writings. He wrote that when Marcos enters Mexico City next week, it will be "the equivalent of Martin Luther King Jr.'s March on Washington." I stared at the sentence for a long time. I have seen the clip of King's "I Have a Dream" speech maybe 10,000 times, though usually through ads selling mutual funds, cable news or computers and the like. Having grown up after history ended, it never occurred to me that I might see a capital-H history moment to match it.

Next thing I knew, I was on the phone talking to airlines, canceling engagements, making crazy excuses, mumbling about Zapatistas and Martin Luther King. Who cares that I dropped my introduction to Spanish course? Or that I've never been to Mexico City, let alone Chiapas? Marcos says I am a Zapatista and I am suddenly thinking, "Yes, yes, I am. I have to be in Mexico City on March 11. It's like Martin Luther King Jr.'s March on Washington." Only now, as March 11 approaches, it occurs to me that it's not like that at all. History is being made in Mexico City this week, but it's a smaller, lower-case, humbler kind of history than you see in those news clips. A history that says, "I can't make your history for you. But I can tell you that history is yours to make."

It also occurs to me that Marcos isn't Martin Luther King; he is King's very modern progeny, born of a bittersweet marriage of vision and necessity. This masked man who calls himself Marcos is the descendant of King, Che Guevara, Malcolm X, Emiliano Zapata, and all the other heroes who preached from pulpits only to be shot down one by one, leaving bodies of followers wandering around blind and disoriented because they lost their heads.

In their place, the world now has a new kind of hero, one who listens more than he speaks, who preaches in riddles not in certainties, a leader who doesn't show his face, who says his mask is really a mirror. And in the Zapatistas, we have not one dream of a revolution, but a dreaming revolution. "This is our dream," writes Marcos, "the Zapatista paradox—one that takes away sleep. The only dream that is dreamed awake, sleepless. The history that is born and nurtured from below."

FROM THE SUBSOIL
TO THE MASK THAT REVEALS
The Visible Indian

CARLOS MONSIVAÍS

Appeared in *Proceso*,
March 3, 2001.

Translated by Mark Fried.

PROLOGUE ON COMPARISONS

In one of his great classic poems, "Yerbas del Tarahumara," Don Alfonso Reyes described the Indians' arrival in Chihuahua: "Into the towns trickles the herd / Of human animals with rags on their backs." And the close-up is devastating:

Naked and sun-baked
Tough in their shiny blotchy skin,
Blackened from the wind and sun, they animate
The streets of Chihuahua,

Slow and suspicious,
With all the springs of fear coiled tight,
Like meek panthers.

There, in the first decades of the twentieth century, are the Indians "with the mute patience of ants."

FEBRUARY 24, 2001: SAN CRISTÓBAL DE LAS CASAS

Just before 10:00 P.M. the plaza of San Cristóbal fills up with 15,000 or 20,000 people from the Indian groups of Chiapas: Tzoltales, Tzotziles, Tojolobales, Choles. Waiting for them caused a five-hour delay in the send-off rally for the Zapatista march, the Caravan of Peace or ZapaTour, if we can use the language of political tourism. Nearly all of them are quite young, they've given up traditional clothing, they show no trace of "the ancient herd of human animals" and, evidently, they've traded in their "springs of fear" for astonishment and restrained joy. Their bandanas and ski masks show they are members of the EZLN's community base of support, and their secondhand clothing indicates a nearly furtive entrance into modernity, into the Eden of late consumption, where museum-piece sweaters, jackets, and Levis, so very out of fashion, find resurrection.

From the rooftops, the genuine upper crust of San Cristóbal arrogancy—the ones who shouted at Bishop Samuel Ruíz, "You're a devil!"—step out of their private world of angry racism to verify the extent of the tourist boom. Across from the cathedral the Indians, and not only they, shout "Marcos! Marcos! Marcos!" and whoever has no faith in the strongman approach to leadership had better withhold his vote. These Zapatistas, most of them men, have changed (or at least that's how I perceive them from the heights of my generalizations) in the seven years since they let their springs of aggressiveness fly like panthers set free. Their body language has changed, as has the rhythm of their advance (no kidding around until later on, back in the communities), and most unexpected is their gaze. These young people look and accept being looked at. They convey a sense of newness: no longer do they consider themselves perennially excluded from the vision of others. They know they are perceived, and the end of their invisibility makes them happy and reinforces their adherence to the EZLN.

Now they sing the national anthem, another sign of belonging, and immediately afterward, the Zapatista anthem (to the tune of "Carabina 30–30"):

We men, children, and women
will always go the distance,
for our country cries out and needs us,
needs every step of the Zapatistas.

The rhyme is a big stretch, but the spirit isn't. On the contrary, it's relaxed and their conviction is moving. Here in what is practically the official birth-place of the EZLN (and what follows is a reading of glances since the ban-danas hide their faces and the lighting is bad), those in attendance feel they are included in the speech. It's not what they would have said, but they feel as if they themselves were saying it. The leader voices the thinking of his followers, something not at all unusual, backed by seven years of support under very adverse conditions. (Don't forget that the participants in oblig-atory tourism at PRI rallies, what we call "carreo," neither heard nor per-ceived any substantive sound besides the name of the candidate or the official in question.) In San Cristóbal what's inspiring is the intuitive, relaxed, powerful sense of being inside the discourse. "That's about me, even if those aren't my words or my concepts, they are my demands," could be a synthesis of the response.

Marcos's speech in San Cristóbal was typical and a classic: the message wrapped in rhetoric, yearning to communicate through the breath of poetry. The tale of their origins is told through reiteration, tracing fatefully a genesis intuited from the apocalypse of peoples "on the road to cultural extinction." Marcos repeats the demand for inclusion:

"We Mexican Indians are Indians and we are Mexicans. We want to be Indians and we want to be Mexicans. But the lord with a lot of tongue and not much ear, the one who governs, offers us lies instead of a flag. Ours is the march of Indian dignity. The march of those of us who are the color of the earth and the march of all who are all the colors of the earth."

In line with his deeds, Marcos insists on adding the Indians to the nation. They were never considered, so they aren't excluded; they've never been invited, so they haven't been snubbed. And the high point of the speech, couched in self-praise like a letter of introduction to broader Mexico, is the proclamation of original belonging. The Zapatistas are memory, chal-lenging oblivion and extermination:

"Compañeros and compañeras of the EZLN: For seven years we have resisted all sorts of attack. They've attacked us with bombs and bullets, with torture and jailings, with lies and calumny, with scorn and neglect. But we have survived. We are the rebels of dignity. We are the forgotten heart of our country. We are the very first memory. We are the brown blood in the mountains that illuminates our history. We are those who struggle and live and die. We are those who say, 'For everyone, everything; nothing for ourselves.' We are the Zapatistas, the smallest of these lands. We salute the communities who lead us and care for us."

Those who seek to enlarge the narrow official version of Mexico speak in the name of the first inhabitants. He repeats: "The march begins on Flag Day. Patriotism is reborn in those called 'unpatriotic' by the governor of Querétaro, Ignacio Loyola."

REFLECTIONS FROM THE LONG WAIT IN THE PLAZA OF SAN CRISTÓBAL

In his classic work, *Invisible Man,* novelist Ralph Ellison takes up the condition of blacks in the United States, who are all the same in the eyes of racists. The situation of Indians in Latin America is even more dramatic, incorporated as they are into nations through religion and the rudiments of language, promptly unincorporated through exploitation and cultural and political isolation. Observing the blend of patience and impatience of those present, I begin to perceive the reasons for the durability of the EZLN: Its sticking power isn't due to the spirit of armed resistance (with its fatal implications), nor even to the charisma of its leadership, but rather to the way in which they have brought the Indians of the zones some social visibility. The oft-repeated phrase in Zapatista speeches: "The world is watching us," is in the end a sign of existence: "Someone sees us! We acquire bodily presence. And, if they watch us, it is because we decided to exist by resisting."

In a society as racist as Mexico's, to acquire visibility today means to become the object of commentaries that mix modern prejudice with feelings of guilt. But we have to acknowledge the magnitude of the changes. In 1913, Querido Moheno, one of Victoriano Huerta's congressmen, didn't mince words when referring to the threat from Emiliano Zapata's troops surrounding the capital: "It's the surfacing of the subsoil." And nearly 90 years later this trip from the subsoil to the surface, amid a deluge of cameras and tape recorders belonging to the most important publications and TV networks, is the truest and most significant march. The beginning of the historic leap is the social visibility acquired right now by 25 people, but it's going to affect another 10 million who to date have been background scenery, nomadic shapes, shadows in markets, objects of gibes that mock their way of speaking "Castilla," the bouncy gait, the innocence previous to knowledge, the "Love ya more than my eyes / More than my eyes I love ya / But I love my eyes more / 'Cause my eyes saw ya." Ever since Cuauhté-moc on his knees and Benito Juárez on the rise, Indians have had no polit-ical archetypes to identify with when faced with such alarmed, offended, amused disdain. Régalo Madaleno, Tizoc, India María are humorous or melodramatic figures, but more than anything they are characters created as entertainment by the cultural industry, and in this case the underlying message is about selecting or rejecting role models. Before, in that very near yet remote before, only one Indian was conceivable, the one frozen on the long march of civilization, the one singled out by (bad) luck to inhabit the monolithic globe where past and future mixed as they spun around a degraded and lethal present.

Everything said for and against Marcos and his savvy media skills is meaningless if divorced from the fact that the focus of interest and the heart of the Zapatista movement is not individual, but community-based. That indigenous groups from all over give their staffs of authority to the EZLN leadership, that demonstrators identify themselves to strangers as Indians, that the march evokes a variety of passionate and enthusiastic responses — all of this grows from the recuperation or incorporation of Indianness into the notion of nation. This genuine broadening of vision of what constitutes Mexico is not demagoguery, although there's no shortage of speeches and slogans rooted in the lexicon of exaltation, nor has it come too late because the Indians are still here; it is simply an idea whose time has come. Why did it take so long? Because racism has been a historic component of national life and because the PRI barred the gate against ideas. True, the Zapatista march couldn't have taken place without the July 2 fall of the PRI, of the all-powerful president and his sexennial cast of capricious and hysterical seers. True, July 2 can also be explained by the pent-up need of ever larger groups to take up unpredictable causes, be they indigenous rights or the rights of minorities or majorities (women).

RALLIES IN THE LIGHT OF HISTORY
ARMED ROUNDTABLE DURING THE LONG PAUSES ON THE ZAPATISTA MARCH

"The news media are the front-line para-Zapatista army. Seven years of making them news, and let's see who can manage to dislodge them from what's now their natural niche of being attention-worthy."

"They were already news on January 7, 1994. Remember them: masked, defiant, carrying ancient rifles and a challenge to the IMF and the Free

Trade Agreement. The images and the aggressive message reinforced one another."

"The focal point is Marcos. The others can't muster anything close to his eloquence or his spontaneous humor. In one sense, it's a one-man movement."

"Not at all. Marcos and the community are indivisible. Those thousands upon thousands of Indians in struggle may need a leader, but the leader did not invent the reasons they embraced the cause. Imagine Marcos in another movement."

"What a pointless argument! Marcos even awakens interest among the most skeptical, the ones who have no desire to be fooled by utopias. But what underpins the Zapatistas' support is not an exceptional communicator, but a moral rejection of neoliberalism."

"That may well be why the ski masks worked so well. After the fall of the Berlin Wall, a new stage-set was needed, one without the Caudillo's beard or Papa Joe Stalin's whiskers. Though the last thing we need now are Caudillos or Papas."

"What's most incredible about this moment, the adjective on everyone's lips, is 'historic.' Why? Because nothing like this ever happened before? Is that enough to make it historic?"

"It's historic for reasons that barely require listing. Making their way to Mexico City are the catalysts of a change in the collective notion of indigenousness. A rebel group is traveling unarmed, and what's most impressive is that never have so many people, each on his or her own, believed they embody civil society. If you notice, civil society in practice is turning out to be an arena for those who have nothing, an invented realm that gathers strength and the power of persuasion when on the rise, and then becomes lethargic, but never disappears. The proponents of the widest range of causes consider themselves to belong to civil society, neighbors who don't want a gas station near their homes, defenders of historical patrimony, environmentalists, defenders of animals who oppose the cruelty of bullfighting. . . . 'Madame Civil Society' who has been made fun of so much turns out to be a synonym for 'the people' divided into sectors. Many times, Marcos and the EZLN have trusted civil society in vain; on other occasions, such as now, civil society has responded."

"Look closely at one portion of the crowd. Note what's left of the Left: self-proclaimed activists from '68, Cardenistas from '88, those radicalized by the second Aguascalientes Convention, escapees from strategic voting.

It's curious. The past of all those components of the left gets reawakened with the simple announcement that protest and dissidence continues."

"But remember this crucial point: On July 2, 2000 a dissident won the presidency of the country."

"A dissident promoted by the most orthodox gringo-style marketing techniques in the world."

"Yes, and most of his big backers were people who can only read with their appetite, as the poet would say, but Fox heads up a legitimate regime and that makes the cultural and ideological battle even sharper. Take a peek at today's debate. Those who praise the EZLN and those who write it off agree on one point: the motives for the uprising are irreproachable, the prostration of Indians is morally and intellectually intolerable."

"Look, there's talk of peace and they say it's a virtual peace because there's no fighting and that makes room for nuances: Yes, there is such a thing as a low-intensity war; people die every day in the communities—and look at Acteal. The paramilitary forces and the militarization of the region are unfortunately real. But that aside, the peace they speak of is not the opposite of a theater of war, but of the oppressive disorder made up of social violence, the frustration of the immense majority, the blocking of fair responses to issues like employment, health, education, and housing, the concentration of resources in the hands of a morally and numerically insignificant minority. While we insist on peace, and on ChiaPeace, what we don't want is a return to the first of January of 1994. Rather, the end of urban devastation and post-Rulfian village tragedies."

"That rhetoric is very entertaining and it works for advertising a concert, but by exalting Indian rights aren't you abetting anachronisms? A country that expects its Indians and its most unredeemable poor to catch up, and I mean now, is going nowhere fast. No use denying it, development is an impatient process and—as anthropologists point out in every one of their doctoral theses—Indian time is quite something else. If we're talking about a 'caravan of hope,' we'd better be clear about the speed. Under globalization, there's only one time, and there's nothing to be done about it."

"I suggest this symposium slow down for a moment. Are we talking about Indian rights without the EZLN? At least acknowledge their contribution. In 1994 more than a few insisted that their violent beginning was pointless. Democratic development would take care of things. Yet violence existed and it was one-sided. Since January 6, 1994 the EZLN hasn't fired a shot, but the deaths of those first few days are what is driving the demand for peace."

"Is it possible to forget the sectarianism of some of the EZLN's proposals, the ones based on National Liberation Front militarism?"

"No, we can't forget, but memory also ought to take into account the PRI, the political bosses, the big landowners, the semi-slave system on the plantations, the 600-grams-a-kilo merchants, the alcohol monopolies, the mayors who jailed or disappeared dissidents, what all of them have been. Without comparing or justifying, the fact is that the proposals of Marcos and the EZLN have changed radically. Frankly, those of their adversaries and enemies have not."

THE RALLY: THE RESPONSIBILITY OF THOSE LISTENING

In Oaxaca, the spirit is more festive than in San Cristóbal, or more festive according to my traditional understanding of community jubilation. The frenzy, repeated a thousand times, comes from wanting to see, to hear, to witness Marcos, who is probably turning into a media-made myth. And is this because of the ski mask? What is covered is revealed? In this epoch of the empire of the close-up, don't we need to see all facial features? When Marcos signs the peace agreement, won't he need plastic surgery to permanently add the ski mask to his expression? Is the absence of a face the message? Such worries are pointless. The historic aspect of this march still uses ski masks and could care less if PAN leader Diego Fernández de Cevallos refuses to speak with people in masks. Those who will, in their own way, number in the millions.

As the 20 or 30 articles I read this morning pointed out, the marketing duel, the poll fight at the OK Corral, is between Vicente Fox and Marcos. Who's going up, who's going down, whose numbers are flat? Who will top the charisma meter? Fox evicted the PRI from the presidential residence at Los Pinos; Marcos leads a movement that through a combination of intransigence and the Internet has demonstrated the advantages of resisting. Fox, who was a businessman, envisions a nation of 110 million businessmen; Marcos, who is a mestizo, longs for a nation that respects itself by respecting its minorities.

"We want autonomy so that the majority always rules, not just every so often. So that he who leads does so by obeying. So that being the government becomes a responsibility to and a labor for the collective, rather than a way to get rich at the expense of the governed. So that it is no longer a crime to be an Indian, to live as an Indian, to think as an Indian, to dress as an Indian, to speak as an Indian, to love as an Indian, to be the color of an Indian."

Just as Fox's discourse presumes everything is already resolved—even the celebration of the solutions' centennial—that of Marcos tends to alternate between political clarity and enigmas. What does it mean "to think as an Indian"? What is it in this day and age "to be an Indian"? Nevertheless, these questions indicate progress. Ten years back, who would have posed them to a national and international public?

WHERE, DESPITE ITS MILLENNIAL PRESTIGE, RAIN DOES NOT DISRUPT A RALLY

No matter how you look at it, the march is a success. If only one group comes out to meet the Zapatistas in Tehuacán, Puebla, Orizaba, Pachuca, Actopan, it's one that could in no way be undervalued. On February 28 in Ixmiquilpan, in Ñahñu territory, a ghost town from the mining boom, they held the most climatic rally I can recall, in the strictest sense of the word. After two hours of civic/mystic litany ("¡*Zapata vive, vive, la lucha sigue, sigue!*"), the caravan arrives and Marcosista jubilation lets loose. A lady shouts: "Get off the bus, we want to see you!" The bus moves on and the woman, happily disappointed, consoles herself with, "He didn't want to get off, the son of a gun. What a peach!"

Ñahñu dances and music begin along with the rain, rising to meet the intensity of the gathering storm. With a savvy I can respect, the subcommander asks the thousands about to get soaked to take shelter from the downpour, but they answer with a categoric "*Nooo!*" Two commanders, David and Zebedeo, speak, and are mercifully brief. The storm grows and the crowd, anxious to hear Marcos, holds their ground. (Here I make use of the transcription by Jesús Ramírez Cuevas in *La Jornada*).

Marcos speaks:

"If I've got it right, Ixmiquilpan means place of sterile clouds. Seems like that's no longer the case—something changed today."

Inside the plaza, the rain becomes a backdrop of its own, a natural downpour of fertility and destruction. It would seem to counsel surrender, prudent eviction. Someone wants to save Marcos from the humid conditions, but he refuses: "No, if they get wet, so will I." Applause.

The speech starts off like a lecture, obligatory since the march is also a way to connect with indispensable learnings. Marcos distinguishes between "their democracy and that of those on the bottom," between their freedom and ours, between their justice and ours:

" . . . their justice is a prostitute, and what's worse, a cheap one. How many bankers are in jail? How many businessmen? How many big landowners? How many landlords? . . . No sir, the jails are filled with poor people, Indians, laborers, employees: That is their justice. The justice of those on top has a price and being unable to pay it is a crime."

The storm lets loose. The lightning is, if you manage to see it, highly decorative. People persevere, with attention and pleasure, building themselves a Noah's Ark or a refuge or a cosmic umbrella. (Metaphors fail, not so the power of the rain.) Marcos persists with his lesson:

"We've brought a present to the Mezquital Valley. We brought this rain. No, that's not true. We looked in our packs, and we looked in our rucksacks, and we found nothing worthy of you. We brought you questions: Is the EZLN the vanguard of the Mexican Indian movement?"

"Yessss," shouts the crowd.

I'm floored. The terrible history of "vanguardism" flashes through my mind, the arrogance of showing the people (civil society) the way. Seconds later, Marcos dispels my foreboding.

"No way. The vanguard of the national Indian movement is made up of the Indian peoples of all Mexico."

This line of questioning is risky, but for once it came out right.

"The second question: Are you happy here with the EZLN?"

"Yesss!"

"Are we wet? No, not that one. Are we happy to have met?"

Who could doubt the response.

"Should the EZLN surrender?"

"Nooo."

"Will the EZLN sell out?"

"Nooo."

Marcos, wet, happy, humidly charismatic, caps it off: "We in the EZLN know we are not alone. Yes, we know we are not alone."

As much as I'd like to wait a few years before using it, the adjective "historical" keeps circling me. What I've seen—the crowd in the rain—is a show, but what lies beneath it, each person's decision, is the greatest show of all.

MARCOS MARCHES
ON MEXICO CITY

IGNACIO RAMONET

Originally appeared in *Le Monde Diplomatique*,
April 2001.

Translated by Ed Emery.

ON March 11 Marcos made a triumphal entry into the Mexican capital, escorted by 23 other EZLN commanders and by sympathizers from around the world (Nobel prize–winning author José Saramago, screenwriter Oliver Stone, trade unionist José Bové, actor Robert Redford, novelist Manuel Vázquez Montalbán, Euro MP Sami Naïr and Danielle Mitterrand were all part of the lineup). In a grand, symbolic gesture he had followed the route taken by Emiliano Zapata in 1914 at the time of the Mexican revolution. There, in the huge Plaza Zócalo in the heart of the capital, with a crowd of more than 100,000 supporters, Marcos addressed the people of Mexico in the name of 10 million Indians: "Here we are. We are the forgotten heart of this country, and we represent the dignity of rebellion."

A few days before the march started, we met Marcos, flanked by Comandante Tacho and Mayor Moisés, in the little village of La Realidad (with its 450 inhabitants). The village is 1,000 kilometers south of Mexico City, 1,500 meters up the side of a rainy mountain surrounded by dense jungle, close to his secret headquarters.

Wearing his usual black mask and a faded cap of indefinable color, he had his old submachine-gun on his back and a satellite phone close at hand. He explained why the Zapatistas were marching on Mexico City: "This is not Marcos's march nor the EZLN's. It is the march of the poor, the march of all the Indian peoples. It's intended to show that the days of fear are over. Our aim is to get the Mexican Congress to recognize the identity of indigenous people as 'collective subjects' by right. Mexico's constitution doesn't recognize Indians. We want the government to accept that Mexico has a variety of peoples; that our indigenous peoples have their own political, social, and economic forms of organization; and that they have a strong connection to the land, to their communities, their roots, and their history.

"We are not asking for an autonomy that will exclude others. We are not calling for independence. We don't want to proclaim the birth of the Maya nation, or fragment the country into lots of small indigenous countries. We are just asking for the recognition of the rights of an important part of Mexican society which has its own forms of organization that it wants to be legally recognized.

"Our aim is peace. A peace based on a dialogue which is not a sham. A dialogue that will lay the groundwork for rebuilding Chiapas and make it possible for the EZLN to enter ordinary political life. Peace can only be had by recognizing the autonomy of the indigenous peoples. This recognition is an important precondition for the EZLN to end its clandestine existence, give up armed struggle, participate openly in regular politics and also fight the dangers of globalization."

After a nine-month silence Marcos's December 2 communiqué announcing the march was a bombshell. It arrived on the eve of the inauguration of Mexico's new president, Vicente Fox, and politicians across the board were caught off guard. It was a bold move at a delicate moment.

On July 2 last year the Institutional Revolutionary Party (PRI), in power for over 70 years, lost the presidential election to Fox of the right-wing National Action Party (PAN). And unlike the strong whiff of electoral fraud surrounding the election of his predecessors Carlos Salinas (1988–94) and Ernesto Zedillo (1994–2000), Fox's election has been unanimously accepted as the voters' true choice. For the first time in a long while, with Fox's inauguration on December 1, 2000, Mexico has a president whose legitimacy seems irrefutable.

Marcos has admitted as much in a letter to the incoming president: "Unlike your predecessor, Zedillo, who achieved power by criminal means, supported by the corrupt monstrosity of the state–party system, you arrive at the presidency thanks to the people's rejection of the PRI. You must realize that you won the election, but you were not the one who routed the PRI. It was the citizens of Mexico who did it. And not only those who voted against the ruling party, but also those generations, past and present, who have fought back against the authoritarianism, crime and impunity that PRI governments have built up over the past 71 years."

During the election campaign Fox promised to settle the Zapatista problem, peacefully and politically, "in 15 minutes." Marcos's march caught him in his honeymoon period. He has been forced to deal with the indigenous issue here and now. Carlos Monsiváis, who just had his own long interview with Marcos, told us "The march was a stroke of genius. The government will have to work to a timetable set by Marcos. That gives him the initiative. And Fox has to accept it—partly because he's being pushed by national and international pressure, and partly because, by coming to talk to the new government in Mexico City, Marcos is giving it a legitimacy that he never gave the Salinas and Zedillo regimes—which the Zapatistas and many other Mexicans saw as frauds and cheats."

Anthropologist André Aubry, who is head of the diocesan archives in San Cristóbal de Las Casas and an associate of the former bishop Samuel Ruíz, points out that "Marcos isn't asking for the earth. By organizing this march he is simply challenging President Fox to say what kind of Mexican nation he means to build. Marcos is just asking for the Indians to be part of that nation."

Fox can handle this. Once the surprise was over, he responded favorably to the Zapatista march. First he calmed the hotheads in his own camp—like the governor of Queretaro State, who branded the Zapatista commanders "traitors" and threatened them with death. Then he publicly accepted the march as representing "a hope for Mexico." After all, could he be outdone by President Andrés Pastrana in Colombia, who on February 8 went to the region controlled by his country's main guerrilla forces and had face-to-face talks with their legendary rebel leader, Manuel Marulanda?

On January 26 Fox declared, to reassure worried investors, that "Nobody need fear the EZLN march on Mexico City. We must not be afraid to include all Mexicans in a project that aims to give everyone access to development. The march will be peaceful and we should reach a peace agreement in Chiapas."

Then Fox virtually began promoting the march. "My government is in favor of the march," he declared. "We have to believe the EZLN and give it the chance to prove that it really wants peace. What is at stake is our nascent democracy, and we must show that it is flexible enough to absorb different forms of thinking, even the most radical." And Fox had no qualms about taking up Zapatista arguments about the terrible fate of the Indians. "Five hundred years of suffering is enough! Enough of ignoring indigenous people, and failing to integrate the poor and the marginalized! Mexico's Indians have been subjected to racist humiliation, to public and private policy designed to exclude them, keep them out of education and development, and prevent them from expressing their rights as free citizens."

But Fox's enthusiasm for the march did not impress Marcos. He told us: "The president is trying to appropriate the Zapatista march, virtually presenting it as a Foxist march. His strategy is to pressure the EZLN by telling the world that peace has already been achieved, and if it's not signed, it's the Zapatistas' fault. This is a kind of blackmail. He wants the EZLN to surrender unconditionally. But he knows perfectly well that, before entering into full negotiations, we were asking for three small signs of goodwill on his part: the release of all Zapatista prisoners, a withdrawal of the army from seven military positions, and ratification of the San Andrés accords on the rights of indigenous people, signed by the government in 1996 but never implemented."

When the march set off on February 24 the authorities released only 60 out of 100 Zapatista prisoners and the armed forces withdrew from only four of the seven positions demanded by Marcos. Nor have the San Andrés accords been ratified. As Dr. Aubry explains, "If Fox can't fulfil the three conditions set by the Zapatistas, it means he doesn't really have the power: He isn't in charge and he has the Army on top of him. After all, since 1920 it's been traditional in Mexico to settle political problems by military means. That's what his predecessors, Salinas and Zedillo, tried to do with the Zapatistas. They failed. If Fox wants to succeed, and if he truly wants peace as he is forever claiming, he has to show that he really is president and that he does run the army; and as a sign of goodwill he must accept the Zapatistas' three conditions. For their part, they have shown their desire for peace by coming out of hiding and traveling to Mexico City unarmed. Marcos has given the president until March 11 to accept those conditions. Fox should make an effort to agree to them because the future of the Indians depends on it. And ·Mexico owes the Indians a lot."

For the past 500 years the indigenous peoples have been hunted, exploited, humiliated, and partially exterminated, and their lives have been appalling. The brutal experiences of the Chiapas Indians at the hands of the conquistadors were described by the Dominican priest Bartolomé de las Casas, bishop of San Cristóbal, in his book A Brief Account of the Destruction of the Indies (1522). His powerful account makes it easy to understand the nightmare of the Indians' suffering during the conquest.

After Mexico's independence in 1810, and even after the 1911 revolution (fought under the banner of Tierra y Libertad), the Indians' conditions did not improve. Their exploitation and marginalization continued, and so did their gradual extermination by the big cacao and coffee plantation owners with their gangs of hired killers and paramilitaries. The constitution still does not recognize the existence of the indigenous people (10 percent of the population). On the grounds that most of them are half-caste, Mexico officially promotes the image of people of mixed race but shows a contemptuous disregard for its real Indians.

Marcos explains: "Of all the people of Mexico, the Indians are the most forgotten. They are seen as second-class citizens, an embarrassment to the country. But we aren't rubbish. We are people with a history and a wisdom that goes back thousands of years. We may be downtrodden and forgotten but we're not yet dead! And our aspiration is to become citizens like everyone else. We want to be part of Mexico, without losing our identity, without being forced to give up our culture, without ceasing to be Indians. Mexico owes us a debt—a debt two centuries old, that can only settle by recognizing our rights."

The Indians have been victims of a kind of silent genocide. Forgotten by everyone, almost invisible, they have been condemned to sit and watch as their languages and their age-old values were slowly destroyed. It was to stop this inexorable decline that Marcos and his Zapatistas began their uprising.

With their roots in the green mountains of Chiapas and the rainforests of southern Mexico near the frontier with Guatemala, the Zapatistas have been fighting for the past seven years to publicize the plight of the indigenous communities. "To be an Indian in Mexico is not just to have a particular physical appearance," explains writer and essayist Carlos Montemayor, author of a key book on the Zapatista uprising. "It is also to speak an Indian language, to live on ancestral land, to practice traditional customs, and to hold the age-old values of the community within which you live. In Chiapas a third of the population is indigenous, more than a million people. With the exception of the Zoques (related to the Popolocas and the Mixes), most groups belong to Mexico's Maya family (Tzotzils, Tzeltals, Cholans, Tojolabals, Lacandóns, Mames, Mochos, Kakchikeles, 12 linguistic groups in all). But recent major migrations have greatly changed the social, ideological, and political composition of the sub-regions of the Lacandón jungle, the EZLN's main social base. You can reckon that at least 200,000 indigenous peoples of one race or another support the EZLN in Chiapas."

Chiapas is a rich state. It has Mexico's biggest oil and natural gas reserves, as well as supplying the country with 40 percent of its hydroelectricity. (It enabled Mexico to supply the United States with electricity during the recent power cuts in California.) Herman Bellinghausen, a leading expert on the Zapatista uprising, points out that despite the state's huge wealth, "a third of the children in Chiapas still have no schooling, and barely one student in a hundred makes it to university. Among the indigenous peoples illiteracy runs at more than 50 percent and mortality rates are 40 percent higher than in Mexico City."

It was to protest against the Indians' fate and focus world attention on these communities, among the most forsaken in the world, that Marcos and the EZLN launched their uprising on January 1, 1994. After battles that left them with dozens dead, the Zapatistas carried out a one-day occupation of four towns in Chiapas, including San Cristóbal de las Casas (population 50,000).

"The remarkable thing about this movement," says Bellinghausen, "is that Marcos understands that there is a new possibility for the traditional kind of guerrilla movements that existed in Latin America during the second half of the twentieth century. He also knows that the end of the Cold War, the fall of the Berlin Wall and demise of the Soviet Union, and now the globalization offensive, have all radically changed world politics and transformed the structures of power. He realizes that countries' policies are run by more than just political forces: You have to reckon with the financial markets and the free-market thinking expressed in the North American Free Trade Agreement (NAFTA)."

That is why the Zapatistas chose January 1, 1994—the day NAFTA came into force between Mexico, the US, and Canada—to make their explosive entry onto the Mexican political scene. Marcos was defending the cause of the Indians, but he was also using that day to issue a first symbolic challenge to the globalization process. It was several years before tangible new initiatives against globalization began to appear: international mobilisation against the Multilateral Agreement on Investments (MAI) in 1998, demonstrations at the World Trade Organization (WTO) summit in Seattle in 1999, and the Davos protests last year.

Marcos was the first to construct a theory linking globalization to the marginalization of the poor peoples of the South. He explained it to us in his schoolmasterish way: "After the fall of the Berlin wall, a new superpower appeared, stimulated by neoliberal policies. Although the big winner of the Cold War—which we could call the Third World War—was the US, a new power began to emerge over and above it, a financial superpower which began issuing global directives. This produced what we refer to broadly as globalization. For globalization, the ideal would be a world transformed into one big business, with an executive board made up of the IMF, the World Bank, the OECD, the WTO, and the president of the US. In that situation, governments of other countries would function just as representatives of the executive board—local managers, if you like.

"And what you in France at *Le Monde Diplomatique* describe as pensée unique supplies the ideological glue needed to convince the world that globalization is irreversible and that any other project would be utopian, unrealistic. At the world level, the big battle now taking place—which we could call the Fourth World War—has its own lineup of forces. On one side are the supporters of the global economy, and on the other is everyone who, in one way or another, is resisting it. Anything that obstructs the onward march of globalization is now under threat of destruction."

When we ask Marcos to explain how this relates to the dramatic situation of indigenous peoples, he replies: "In its desire for hegemony, globalization addresses the question of culture. It wants a cultural homogenization of the world. To an extent economic globalization means the American way of life. The law of the market rules everywhere. It doesn't just govern the workings of governments, but also the media, education, even the family. Individuals only have a place in this society if they can produce and buy. So market criteria eliminate a whole section of humanity that offers no prospect of profits. Which is the situation of all the indigenous peoples of Latin America. Globalization requires their elimination—through open warfare if necessary, and otherwise through a silent war. This war argues that the Indians have no role in advancing globalization, can't be integrated into it, and may even pose a serious problem through their potential for rebellion."

In the course of organizing the fight in the indigenous communities of Chiapas, Marcos has analyzed his tactics and reframed them to match the present world political context and the globalization process. He is a practical idealist, a media-conscious strategist who uses the internet as a weapon to reach the world through communiqués, articles, stories, poems. He has set up solidarity links with hundreds of activist organizations and minority rights campaigns. He is far more original and effective in media terms than the Mexican government. On January 12, 1994, just 11 days after the start of the uprising, Marcos abandoned the use of weapons. Not a shot would be fired by the Zapatistas; instead they would opt for nonviolent struggle to win the hearts and minds of a world public opinion increasingly concerned about Indian rights.

Marcos's language is a mixture of poetry and politics, message and metaphor, as we heard in the speech he made when the march set off from San Cristóbal de las Casas on February 24. "Mexican Indians, we are Indians and we are Mexicans. And we want to be both. But that man with the loud voice and the deaf ears, the one who governs us, is offering us no flag, only lies. Ours is a march for the dignity of the indigenous people: the march of those who are the color of the earth. The march of those who are all the colors of the very heart of the earth. Seven years ago the dignity of the indigenous people demanded a place on the Mexican national flag. And we, who are the color of the earth, demanded it then with fire. And with fire and lies came the reply from the dzul, the powerful one, who own the money whose smell infects the color of the earth. It was then that we saw other voices and heard other colors.

"Today we are marching for the Mexican flag to become ours, and in exchange we are offering the cloth of suffering and poverty. We are marching for good government, and they offer us discord. We are marching for justice, and they offer us charity. We are marching for freedom, and they offer us slavery through debt. We are marching for an end to death, and they offer us a peace made up of deafening lies.

"Just as our ancestors resisted the wars of conquest, we have resisted the wars of forgetting. Our resistance isn't over, but it's no longer alone. Millions of beating hearts, in Mexico and all the five continents, are with us. We are all marching side by side. With them, we shall march to that capital that was built on our backs, that despises us. We shall go with them and with the Mexican flag."

Marcos is a charismatic leader and promotes a new style of political action ("lead by obeying") which is free of arrogance and conceit. Having opted for the word instead of the gun, he has also made his mark as a writer of talent, full of wit and humor and always ready to cite his favorite authors, known for their optimism of the will and pessimism of the intellect (such as Gramsci, Cervantes, Lewis Carroll, Brecht, Julio Cortázar, Borges).

Marcos is marching on Mexico City but he is not after power: "The problem isn't one of taking power," he told us with a smile. "We know that the space once occupied by power is now empty. We know that the struggle for power is a struggle for a lie. What is needed in these times of globalization is to build a new relationship between government and citizens. If a peace deal is signed, the EZLN will cease making politics in the ways we've done so far. We'll do politics differently, without masks, without weapons, but still for the same ideas. We have come to understand that we're a kind of mirror, and in our own way we reflect other resistance movements around the world. That's why we feel solidarity with other struggles: Homosexuals and lesbians who suffer all kinds of persecution and discrimination. Migrants facing all the racist laws that are being set up against them. The authorities want people to deny their identities, the color of their skins, their origins, the country of their birth. . . . They want them to feel like criminals for having been born the way they were, with that color, in that place, as though they should be punished for it."

When will he remove his mask? Régis Debray asked him the question in 1996. Marcos replied: "On the day when an indigenous person has the same rights as a white person in any part of the republic, when the one-party-state no longer exists, when elections no longer automatically mean fraud." Unbelievable as it once seemed, that second condition has now been fulfilled. And if the march succeeds and we are to believe Vicente Fox, the first may shortly come about too.

I asked Marcos the same question, as evening drew in and the rain started and the shadows crept up on La Realidad (no electricity there). "You can rest assured," he replied, "that we want to get rid of our masks and our weapons as quickly as possible. We want to conduct politics in the broad light of day. But we won't take off our masks just in exchange for promises. The rights of the Indians must be recognized. If the government refuses, not only will we take up arms again, but so will other movements, far more radical, intolerant, desperate, and violent than ours. Because here, as elsewhere, the ethnic question can easily create fundamentalist movements ready for all kinds of murderous madness.

"On the other hand, if things go as we hope and Indian rights are finally recognized, Marcos will cease to be subcomandante, leader, myth. . . . People will realize that the Zapatistas' main weapon was not the gun, but words. And when the dust raised by our uprising settles, people will discover a simple truth: In this whole struggle and thinking process, Marcos was just one more fighter. That's why I say, 'If you want to know who Marcos is, see who's hidden behind the mask, then take a mirror and look at yourself. The face you see there will be face of Marcos, because we are all Marcos.' "

Night fell on La Realidad. Galaxies of glowworms shone in the darkness. Taking a break from the march, Marcos and his two Zapatista friends went off into the forest, disappearing into the vegetation and the shadows. To a great extent the future of the Indian peoples of Mexico depends on a successful outcome to this march. But will it bring results? José Saramago, the Nobel prize-winning writer, was optimistic: "The Zapatistas covered their faces to make themselves visible, and now, in effect, we have finally seen them. They are marching on the capital of Mexico. And when they make their entry on March 11, Mexico City will become the capital of the world."

INDIAN IS BEAUTIFUL

HOMERO ARIDJIS

Translated by Russell Cobb.

THE act staged by Marcos in the Zócalo on Sunday, March 11 was full of political symbolism: the Cathedral to the right, city hall on the left, the Mexican flag in the middle of the plaza, the Zapatista high command with their backs turned to the balcony of the National Palace (the most important political space in the country). This is where the President of the Republic gives the traditional "shout of independence." Marcos's lyrical shout evoked indigenous poetry in its rhetoric. The Zapatistas' arrival in the Zócalo was by way of the Avenue 20 de Noviembre, which commemorates the Mexican Revolution. In fact, the event in the Zócalo was a symbolic political overthrow. Of course, if someone (Marcos) gains political space, someone else (Fox) loses it.

In the crowds one could see everything from government bureaucrats to high society ladies masquerading as leftists, to angry youths ready to join in the armed struggle, as well as a great many others who believe that the moment in which there should be justice for the indigenous people had finally arrived. Also in attendance were many foreign intellectuals whose revolutionary expectations were on the rise — not in their own countries, of course: "This is only a prologue to what is getting ready to happen" (José Saramago), "And now what? The response has to be a mass movement." (Manuel Vázquez Montalbán). The Left, which had been extinguished after the collapse of communism in Eastern Europe, could take a new turn. There is no other movement on the horizon against globalization and materialism than this political romanticism.

Seven years ago I wrote that in 1994 the Ejército Zapatista de Liberación Nacional not only called attention to the plight of the indigenous peoples, but to the plight of all the indigenous in Mexico, a Mexico torn apart between its indigenous past and its attempts to insert itself into the economic future of North America. Disconnected Yanomanis, Paraguayan Aches, Peruvian Yaguas, Nicaraguan Miskitos, Panamanian Guaymis,

Mexican Tarahumaras and Huicholes, Mayas from Mexico and Guatemala, Colombian Guambians, Chilean Mapuches, among others, are groups affected by urban and rural overpopulation, settlements of colonizers, industrial development and toxic dumps, the construction of highways, hydroelectric dams, and tourist complexes, military raids and aggression from miners, ranchers, loggers, and drug traffickers who violate their rights and move into their habitat. It is imperative that Latin American governments take indigenous peoples into account in their development plans (for example: the Puebla-Panama plan) and in their definitions of free-trade zones. If not, Latin America will become full of Chiapases.

Some time ago, people began asking me questions: Has Marcos's revolutionary rhetoric stirred up social discontent in Mexico? Could members of the far Left or far Right detonate a social bomb? Is Subcomandante Marcos, deliberately, or President Fox, subconsciously, arousing the rebellious Mexico? Will Mexico become a country of constant demands and threats of indigenous uprisings and invasions of land and nature reserves? Will we see the end of the Montes Azules biosphere reserve, now that the Aric has invaded 250 acres of the Lacandón village of Naha and begun cutting down trees with no hindrance whatsoever? How will Marcos spend his political capital? Will he return to Chiapas? Will he found a Zapatista political party, merging with the PRD with an eye toward the 2006 presidential elections? Could Fox have foreseen that he would celebrate his 100 days in office with the Zapatistas in the Zócalo? Will Fox's government have the political and economic capacity to satisfy the Zapatistas' demands and the expectations of all the indigenous peoples? Will Marcos meet the expectations of the Mexican and international Left? Will the president be able to present to Mexicans a national plan of social justice and prosperity for the entire population—regardless of ethnic background? Mexico is waiting for answers.

Meanwhile, the Zapatista movement is changing the image of indigenous people in Mexico and Latin America. These are our compatriots whom we are used to seeing begging on city streets, in village markets, and on the roadsides. They are not the only ones in the indigenous world to have suffered abject poverty: María Sabina, the priestess of magic mushrooms and the most important visionary poet of Latin America in the twentieth century went hungry in her childhood, and it was not the rhetorical hunger that our intellectual courtesans speak of, but real hunger lived out on a daily basis.

"Indian is beautiful," the world now says, thanks to the Zapatista movement—paraphrasing the African American slogan. After suffering discrimination, abuse, and poverty during the conquest and the colonial period, the Independence years, Maximilian's empire, and the reign of Porfirio Díaz, and the Mexican Revolution, and under the 71-year rule of the PRI, it is time that our ethnic groups become part of the Mexican body economic and politic.

"Indian is beautiful," they exclaimed in the Zócalo on Sunday, March 11; even the children of the PRI political and economic bourgeoisie, always eager for exciting social happenings. Watch out: When the rebel is accepted by the bourgeoisie, he becomes inoffensive (Rilke).

Vindicating the image of indigenous people is important, as after the end of the Cold War and the collapse of communism, Latin America has been of little political and cultural interest to the Western capitalist powers, beginning with the United States, a country used to seeing us as a market for its goods and a supplier of natural resources, and as an immigration and drug problem. The United States shows more interest in remote cultures— Asia, Africa, or the Balkans—than in ours, as if the USA were not of this continent. You only need watch movies or television programs made in the USA to know that the so-called "Latinos" are not part of their ethnic quotas. In the media summaries of the twentieth century and the second millennium, the indigenous world did not exist.

The historical disdain for Latin American on the part of Western countries continues, and in the eyes of some we are not even newsworthy. This disdain has been fed by the defeatism, corruption, and mediocrity of our government officials. The Zapatista movement of indigenous affirmation will have a domino effect, moving beyond national borders and eventually extending to other parts of Latin America.

This affirmation has taken centuries in the making, considering that Fray Bartolomé de las Casas, the first defender of Indian rights, denounced abuses against the native population in his *Brief History of the Destruction of the Indies* and defended them with the *New Laws* (1543) and while he was Bishop of Chiapas (1545). And Chiapas, a state with 3.9 million inhabitants of whom 1.3 million are indigenous, has only been part of Mexico since 1824; before then it belonged to Guatemala.

From now on, and deservedly, our country and the world can say "Indian is beautiful."

TWOLASCASIANPOEMS

HOMERO ARIDJIS

Translated by Betty Ferber.

Because scant bread is the indigent's life
And whosoever takes it is a bloodthirsty man.
He kills his fellow who would deprive him of his sustenance
And spills blood if he holds back the laborer's wages.

SAD TYRANTS, CAPTAINS OF DEATH

One vernal day that outlasts its year,
Fray Bartolomé de las Casas, ex-Bishop of Chiapas,
The waxen candle of the dying in his hand,
Urges his friends to keep up the fight for the Indian;
Because then as now, in these lands without rest or reason,
Sad tyrants, captains of death,
Governors who misgovern the people,
With guns and speeches
Rob the poor of their bread and wages.

CONQUISTADORS ALL

Conquistadors every one: Hernan Cortés, Pedro de Alvarado,
Nuño de Guzmán, Francisco Pizarro—whose memory Fray
Bartolomé de las Casas wished to see
Vanish off the face of the earth forever—
As though they had never left the number of the living,
Rage on under other names
Across these misadventurous lands.

THE ZAPATISTA ARMY
OF NATIONAL LIBERATION
Part of the Latin American Revolutionary Tradition
—But also very Different

SAUL LANDAU

SCHOLARS and even politically savvy people often refer to the Zapatista Army of National Liberation (EZLN) as a modern guerrilla movement, a term that connotes a history of revolutionary insurrection in the twentieth century and in particular Latin America. In fact, the EZLN has scant resemblance to Mao tse Tung's' Chinese guerrillas or to Fidel Castro's forces in the Sierra Maestre. The masked Mayan Indian army that staged a dramatic insurrection in Chiapas in January, 1994, announced a new kind of politics with a dramatic piece of live—and bloody—theater.

Led by Subcomandante Marcos, a non-Indian former university professor, a premodern indigenous people expressed both their immediate grievances and demands and offered their stinging critique of corporate globalization. Moreover, they used postmodern technology (the Internet) to do so. But underneath the humble words of the "sup" lay strong remnants of the Marxist-Leninist ideology, and especially the version elaborated by Fidel Castro.

Castro had established his Cuban model as exemplary for all Latin American revolutionaries when he defied the dictum: You can make revolution with the army, without the army, but never against the army. In 1959, Fidel Castro's small guerrilla force smashed dictator Fulgencio Batista's 50,000-man, US-supplied army and the regime that depended on it. Twenty years later, using a similar model, the Sandinistas dislodged Somoza and his National Guard in Nicaragua.

From the 1960s through the later 1970s, revolutionaries throughout Latin America launched guerrilla insurrections but failed to win power as US-backed counterinsurgency programs and the use of systematic torture unraveled the fragile connections between the clandestine bases in the cities and the rural warriors.

In Venezuela, the Dominican Republic, Brazil, Peru, Uruguay, Colombia, and Argentina, bands of Castro-Guevara inspired revolutionary combatants failed to topple the governments, which by the mid-1970s had turned into military dictatorships in much of South and Central America.

In October 1967, Che Guevara, the patron saint of twentieth-century guerrillas, died a captive of US-trained Rangers in Bolivia. He and his Cuban-trained band failed to apply successfully what Castro had insisted would spark a revolution that would spread through South America.

The successful Cuban model of guerrilla warfare that Castro promulgated with his apostle Guevara involved a combined mountain-city struggle. Each guerrilla *foco*, a mobile band whose members' revolutionary will provides the courage and stamina to suffer the deprivations of guerrilla life, requires an infrastructure. The intelligence, supplies, weapons, and fresh recruits come from an urban underground network. This clandestine fifth column also carries out educational and armed actions to force the regime to withdraw some of its troops from the rural guerrilla front and also to try to repress the fifth columnists, thus making more enemies among the already skeptical populace.

The guerrilla defeats the army, according to this model, by choosing the field of battle and the time of engagement, and by ambushing the less mobile and much less enthusiastic regular armed forces. In the 1980s, Subcomandante Marcos and his urban intellectuals became guerrilla warriors in this tradition as they established their foco in the remote Montes Azules in Chiapas's Lacandón jungle.

In November 1995, I mentioned to Marcos that Fidel Castro had said that guerrilla life requires more sacrifice than any other commitment. People who brave gunfire and torture in cities often find themselves unable to withstand the rigors of guerrilla life.

"It was a very tough time," Marcos recalled of the early days in 1983–84. "I don't know how to measure deprivation because seeing the indigenous conditions I would say that if anyone lives worse than guerrillas it is the indigenous people here."

Marcos talked of how difficult it was "especially for someone from the city. The only thing that allowed you to survive was the hope that something would come from everything we were doing. It was an irrational expectation, totally loony, because there was nothing, absolutely nothing, that would validate what we were doing—not world news, nor anything."

Marcos looked behind him at the Blue Mountains some 20 forbidding miles away, waving his hand at them. "We are talking about a group of four, five, six people in the mid-1980s, and we kept repeating to ourselves all day, all night, 'We are good. This is what we have to do.' But there was nothing outside of us to confirm that what we were doing made sense."

"Moreover, the mountain was rejecting us. The mountain made us hungry, sick. It pushed rain and cold on us. The aggression of animals, insects, all this was saying: 'Go, get out of here, you have no business here.' "

Comandante Elisa (Gloria Benavides), who had arrived with a group intending to establish a foco before Marcos and his comrades, agreed. "I got used to going around with a hunger pain in my stomach, or I'd have diarrhea." She laughed. Eventually, she continued, "we established close relations with the indigenous people. They began to trust us." But they did not join the nascent guerrilla foco. Indeed, they continued to get their radical education from the teachings of Bishop Samuel Ruíz of San Cristóbal de las Casas, who had trained catechysts to preach the word in religious and social terms.

Marcos puffed on his crooked stem pipe, exhaled, and continued. "The entire world was telling us the same thing. The socialist camp was collapsing, the armed struggle was being completely abandoned, and we were like some nuts clinging to a dream: Dreaming, yes, that was the truth."

"We were dreaming that what we were doing was going to be good for something, and we didn't have ambitious dreams. Don't think that we were fantasizing about taking power and then becoming great presidents or emulating Castro or Lenin or whatever. We were thinking that at least we were going to help the indigenous people transform their lives in a radical and irreversible way so that the past would not return."

By the mid-1980s, Elisa said "we still weren't having much success in convincing the local people of our truth." The city radical went to the mountains to teach the local peasants about fulfilling their destiny as guerrilla warriors who would liberate Mexico. But the indigenous people learned only some of their lessons. And in turn, the Mayan militants taught the urban intellectual revolutionaries, as Marcos and Elisa both tell it, to convert their latent guerrilla foco into the vanguard of a people's army.

From their utopian aim of winning state power, they turned to becoming organizers of an indigenous army designed primarily to protect the vulnerable communities against the incursions of voracious cattle barons and sugar and coffee plantation owners. The constant erosion of indigenous land over decades, the periodic need for the villagers to move deeper into the jungle because of aggressive behavior by the economic elite of Chiapas—linked always to PRI political power in the state—made the creation of a defense force necessary. And, given the difficulties of communication and coordination between Mayans in the region, many of whom don't speak Spanish, but do speak seven different dialects, and of their lack of education and military training, the arrival of the revolutionaries presented the villagers with an opportunity for cooptation.

In turn, the Mayans willingly learned some of the Marxist discourse of those brave and selfless souls who had become their military commanders. Marcos and his comrades taught a worldview that made sense to indigenous people who had previously been exposed to a radical theology. The three-decade-long work of Bishop Samuel Ruíz of San Cristóbal de las Casas laid the intellectual groundwork for the revolutionary discourse of Marcos and his comrades.

Marcos, the Indians discovered, had the unique ability to lead their military training, formulate strategic plans—like the January 1 assault on eight Chiapas municipalities—and at the same time, to articulate arguments and ideology that helped bring together militants from the seven different Mayan regional language groups.

At a ceremony, the village leaders anointed Marcos as their military commander. They made him one of them—handing him the sacred corn, the redeeming rifle—and they smeared blood on his face to consecrate the rite. Marcos and his comrades now held the responsibility of leading an indigenous army, first against the White Guards—the mercenary thugs of the voracious cattle barons and sugar and coffee plantation owners who enjoyed close ties to the ruling PRI machine. These armed thugs would pick off militant villagers, rape their women, or have the Chiapas authorities arrest particularly "uppity" types. Moreover, the constant eviction of villagers from their indigenous land forced the Mayan people to move villages ever deeper into the uninviting jungle. The aggressive behavior of the economic elite of Chiapas—linked always to PRI political power in the state—made the creation of a defense force a necessity.

Although concrete circumstances dictated the changes in Marcos and his comrades' goals, those goals nevertheless remained in their minds, as part of a larger revolutionary movement. Like all serious Latin American leftists, they had visited Havana and Managua, revolutionary Meccas in the glorious and heady days of the late 1970s and early 1980s when both the Cuban and Nicaraguan revolutions appeared destined to succeed.

Then they witnessed the decline of the Soviet Bloc, the erosive years of the Contra War and the shocking 1990 electoral loss in Nicaragua. With Washington promising permanent war if the vote went wrong, the Nicaraguan majority chose peace and voted the Sandinistas out of office. In 1991, with the Soviet Union gone and no hope for outside backing, the

Salvadoran revolutionary FMLN negotiated a political agreement with the right wing government and Guatemalan guerrillas opened peace talks shortly afterward. In Peru, the future of the Shining Path looked downright dim. The Tupac Amaru still existed, but without much popular support.

Without a Soviet Union to write an insurance policy on revolutionary Third World governments, the very notion of armed struggle as the first step on the path toward building a socialist Third World state appeared impossible. Marcos and his comrades had made a pragmatic transition, but it corresponded closely to world reality.

In 1992, Jorge Castañeda in *Utopia Unarmed* wrote the obituary on the Fidel Castro-Che Guevara model of armed insurrection as the exclusive revolutionary route to state power. Indeed, Castaneda said, armed struggle as a tactic and strategy belonged to the past. In the post-Soviet world, where corporate globalization held sway, the idea of overthrowing governments by force and violence and setting up a socialist state in the Third World seemed inconceivable. Small states became captives of multilateral lending organizations and transnational trading patterns.

On January 1, 1994, shortly after Castaneda's book appeared, thousands of armed and masked Mayan Indians took eight municipalities in the State of Chiapas by arms. Radical pundits had a good laugh at Castaneda's expense. But in fact Castaneda was correct. Armed struggle as a means to achieve state power in Latin America had become passé.

The Mayan insurrection had a different purpose: to call the world's attention to the plight of indigenous people and to the corruption and fraud behind the façade of prosperity and democracy in Mexico. The Zapatistas also claimed to have timed their uprising to coincide with the day that NAFTA (The North American Free Trade Agreement) went into effect.

The uprising, in which Zapatistas and Mexican army units held several bloody firefights, ended 12 days after it started when President Carlos Salinas called a cease fire. The Zapatistas retreated to their villages in the Lacandón jungle. They had made their point: their shots were heard round the world. As Mexican leaders crowed about how far they had advanced, as Henry Kissinger gloated over Mexico's democracy and Carlos Salinas's near-miraculous effort to clean up corruption, thousands of very angry Indians with lists of just demands that only the coldest-hearted could deny had offered a different version of Mexico. The Zapatista assault burst President Salinas's public relations bubble about Mexican democracy, modernity, and prosperity, but it did not alter Castaneda's conclusion: In 1994, armed struggle was no longer the road to state power. On the walls of San Cristóbal de las Casas, the old colonial city of Chiapas, Zapatista warriors pasted their declaration of war. The words did not refer to a guerrilla-style confrontation with Mexico's armed forces, much less to facing the vastly superior force and armaments army-to-army. Rather, the declaration referred to a list of basic demands and grievances, a declaration of rights, along with a plea for an end to the decades of PRI corruption and the installation of real democracy—a kind of Port Huron statement of the Lacandón jungle. Some revolutionaries understood the uprising as the beginning of a new round of armed struggle, but the term "armed theater" would have better fit the January 1 events. Thanks to the Mayan rebellion, televised and seen on the Internet, the indigenous people of Mexico—and by extension, the world—became actors on the world stage—or at least the media stage.

The Zapatistas also had made plans to take strategic installations in Tuxtla Guttiérez, Chiapas's capital city about 50 mountainous miles from San Cristóbal. Indeed, some of them thought that if Chiapas fell . . . well, on to Mexico City. But armies traditionally make optimal plans and feel lucky to achieve minimal objectives. Once the EZLN came into contact with Mexican Air Force jets and laser-guided Army artillery, they realized that their mismatched weapons and low supply of ammunition could not stand up to a force that would actually fight. Some dreamers thought that Mexican soldiers would not fire against Indians, or would have not stomach for war. The street fighting in Ocosingo and other towns proved that Mexican soldiers would fight and that President Salinas would call on his Air Force to use rockets against suspected rebel positions. So Marcos and the members of the decision making Clandestine Revolutionary Indigenous Committee opted quickly for the minimal objective: Their shot in Chiapas was heard round the world. Their live theater scenario had worked.

By February, 1994, people from all over Mexico and the rest of the world had descended on the Chiapan highlands and walked in solidarity rings around the Church where the government and Zapatista officials discussed peace under the auspices of Bishop Samuel Ruíz.

Underneath what appeared to be a new kind of politics, representing premodern indigenous people by using postmodern technology to inform the world of the horrors that globalization or neoliberalism was wreaking on their lives, lay remnants of the old, armed struggle agenda, pieces of an ideology that still rang true to Marcos and some of his comrades. But their language, instead of sounding the same old harangue against imperialism, attacked neoliberalism and the free trade and market ideologies of the transnational corporations.

Subcomandante Marcos, who emerged on January 1 as the spokesman for the EZLN, also still belonged to the older Castro-Guevara tradition. But a wholly new kind of radical politics effectively covered the remnants of the older and more sectarian ideology linked to the armed struggle agenda.

Marcos's mentor, Che Guevara, had failed to confront the indigenous issue in Bolivia. Like Castro, Che showed little interest in indigenous questions; rather, class struggle and imperialism were his ideological guideposts. But neither Castro nor Che seriously questioned their ideology or method despite consistent failures. The foco model had failed to take into account African religious customs in the Congo, where Che and Cuba's best guerrilla warriors confronted behavior that confounded their epistemology.

Cuban-backed uprisings in Argentina and Venezuela had fizzled similarly, and in October 1967, when Che and his foco met their tragic fate in Bolivia, the armed struggle imperative seemed finally bankrupt. Castro blamed Che's failure on the failure of the Bolivian Communist Party to provide the guerrillas with supplies, intelligence, weapons, fresh recruits and communications—elements necessary for the Cuban model to prevail. But Castro's foco theory depends upon an urban support network that did not materialize in Bolivia, and it is difficult to conceive of Che being successful without dealing with indigenous issues—above and beyond imperialism and class struggle.

The Zapatistas, led by Marcos, their poet-warrior, changed Mexican history. Without their uprising, the PRI might well have remained entrenched in power. Marcos not only challenged the establishment, provoked the complacent, and lit a spark to the passive, he forced the entire thinking world to begin to deal with the issues that surround indigenous people in the age of corporate globalization. And the Zapatistas, now home in Chiapas after successfully presenting their analysis to the Mexican Congress, with President Vicente Fox as their unlikely advocate, have not finished their historical tasks.

They have won some rights; others remain to be achieved. But as long as the neoliberal order dictates the way people live, where they work, and all terms of economic and environmental life, we can look to the mountains and jungles of Chiapas for creative ideas about how to resist—short of seizing state power through guerrilla war.

THE TWILIGHT OF THE
REVOLUTIONARIES?

JORGE MANCILLAS

"WE apologize for the inconveniences, but this is a revolution," said Sub-comandante Marcos on the morning of January 1, 1994, to a confused and alarmed group of tourists visiting San Cristóbal de Las Casas. After late night New Year's eve celebrations, the tourists had been woken by gunshots and the sounds of the Zapatistas' rubber boots as they marched swiftly through the cobblestone streets of this charming colonial city nestled in the highlands of Chiapas. The sight of uniformed armed rebels was initially frightening. Yet their courteous manner and their orderly actions after they took over city hall assuaged their concerns.

But the roads were blocked. Could they leave if they wished? the tourists asked. What about their safety if the Mexican army attacked the city? A Frenchman asked if he could take photographs. None of the fighters could understand their questions, so Marcos was sent for, the only one who spoke English and whose assignment was to lead the assault on the police head-quarters. "We have reservations to visit the ruins of Palenque," cried a Swiss couple, demanding to know if they were free to leave. "Please forgive us," Marcos responded courteously, "this is a revolution." Asking for a notebook, he scrawled out a few safe conduct passes, telling the tourists to show them to those guarding the roadblocks.

Marcos's use of the word revolution was not accidental. No one then mistook their uprising—timed to coincide with the day the North American Free Trade Agreement took effect—for anything other than the emergence of an armed revolutionary movement intent on overthrowing the Mexican Government. In their "Declaration of the Lacandón Jungle"—distributed widely by the insurgents—they cited the "people's . . . unalienable right to alter or modify their form of government" provided by the Mexican constitution, declared war on the Mexican Army and called for "the overthrow of the dictator," President Carlos Salinas de Gortari.

As part of their Manifesto, they issued a set of laws covering areas such as urban and agrarian reform, labor, industry and commerce, social security, and justice to take effect in rural and urban "zones controlled by the EZLN." When asking the "people of Mexico" to support their plans they committed themselves to fighting "until we achieve the fulfillment of these basic demands of our people by forming a free and democratic government for our country." They instructed the leaders of their revolutionary armed forces to "change the authorities of the places which fall under the power of the revolution, according to the will of the people and as indicated by the law of revolutionary government," commanding them to "advance toward the capital of the nation, defeating the Mexican Federal Army. . . ."

Seven years later, on March 11, 2001, when 23 commanders of the EZLN and a now-familiar Subcomandante Marcos marched on Mexico City they had undergone a significant transformation. The proclaimed goal of their march on Mexico City was to rally "civil society" and lobby for the passage by Congress of legislation protecting the rights of indigenous people and granting their communities autonomy. Ironically, the legislation was introduced and supported by President Vicente Fox, of the conservative PAN (National Action Party). From armed revolutionaries calling on the people to overthrow the government, to photogenic media-savvy rebels championing the cause of indigenous people, the transformation of the Zapatistas from revolutionaries to narrow-cause rebels is symptomatic of a worldwide retreat of a demoralized, defeated (or at times coopted) Left.

THROUGHOUT THE TWENTIETH century, the Left, just as it was all over the world, was a force to be reckoned with in Mexican politics. Mexico experienced the first social revolution of the century in 1910, when armed peasants and middle- and upper-class dissenters challenged the rule of the dictator, Porfirio Díaz. The regime which emerged from the 10-year struggle created a party which, while it twice changed its name (From National Revolutionary Party, to Party of the Mexican Revolution to Revolutionary Institutional Party, or PRI), always clung to the label of "revolutionary." It survived international revolutionary upsurges and internal challenges from a substantial Communist Party in the 1930s, mass urban mobilizations in the 1960s, and significant military challenges from rural and urban guerrillas in the 1970s, by adopting a populist rhetoric and embracing revolutionary regimes abroad, including aiding the revolutionary regimes of Cuba and Nicaragua. Every significant political challenge to the Mexican Government, every major independent peasant or union movement—not to mention several armed guerrilla movements—was led by leftists inspired by a socialist vision for Mexico.

By the end of 1993, however, on the eve of the EZLN uprising, the Mexican Left was in retreat. In 25 years it had gone from being a force of militant political protest, of radical union and peasant organizing, to a political opposition with most of its energy concentrated in the electoral arena.

The watershed was the wave of massive demonstrations for democracy that shook the PRI regime in the summer of 1968, when Mexico was preparing to host the Olympics. The student movement rallied behind it independent labor and peasant organizations and was supported by almost all Mexicans, except the political and economic elite. It was finally suppressed by a massacre of hundreds of civilians attending a rally in Tlalteloco square the night of October 2. A massive wave of arrests, kidnappings, and torture followed. Student, trade union, and political leaders disappeared, and the authorities clamped down on public protest and political activity. The events of 1968 were branded into the consciousness of a whole generation whose commitment to challenge PRI power was reaffirmed.

The violent suppression of another peaceful demonstration, this time on June 10, 1971, confirmed to many that there were few options for opening the political process via peaceful means. Rural and urban guerrilla groups flowered throughout Mexico, among them the FLN (National Liberation Front) the forerunner of the EZLN, which Marcos joined late in that decade.

It was an unequal war, fought by young inexperienced idealists in their twenties, some still teenagers, armed with guns snatched away from street policemen, or bought in California or Texas (with money obtained through assaults on small businesses) and smuggled into Mexico. A few guerrilla groups survived long enough to develop tight professional organizations and become experienced enough to stage kidnappings of right-wing industrialists or to assault banks. There were a few skirmishes with army units, primarily in the southern state of Guerrero—where two rural guerrilla groups developed a significant political base—and in Chihuahua, as well as a few kidnappings of figures tied to the regime. But by and large, for nearly a decade, Mexico lived through its own version of a dirty war, with a systematic hunting and annihilation (onsite or after kidnapping and torturing) of hundreds of young people driven by a vision of a free, just society.

I WAS RESCUED from an early death by a young professor, Alfonso Peralta, who persuaded a handful of us in Baja California to leave one such group and instead embrace the path of patiently building a national political organization.

We had helped organize and build "Colonia Tierra y Libertad," an autonomous community of 10,000 squatters who in 1973 took over a steep hillside on the outskirts of Tijuana after their homes in the Tijuana riverbed had been destroyed to give way to a commercial, industrial, and tourist development. Their efforts were met with the brutal demolition of their humble homes and the torture and disappearance of some of their leaders. Those of us who escaped were easily recruited by an emerging national urban guerrilla organization. Five of us were persuaded by Alfonso to leave and join his underground political party. Several of those who were not persuaded did not live long after that.

But fighting for democracy, organizing independent labor unions or democratic currents in government-controlled ones was not much safer. It meant dodging bullets in the dark after meetings of dissident members of the oil workers union; enduring threats and persecution while organizing auto workers, teachers, or university employees; being subjected to continual surveillance or being jailed for belonging to "illegal" organizations; and on occasion, having to go underground.

None of us, of course, had violated a single law. In 1977, Alfonso Peralta was shot in front of his students as he left his classroom in México City. To this day, I am still haunted by the image of his horrified students watching the growing pool of blood as his body lay limp, his brilliant intellect forever silenced.

I narrowly escaped a couple of kidnapping attempts in 1978. Others who did not were brutally tortured or assassinated. My own vulnerability was brought home when I was jailed in a tiny dark cell with a group of common criminals, after I was arrested for proselytizing for my own group. Hours later, I was pushed into a torture chamber, with large stains of blood—some dry, some still fresh—on the hard, cold concrete walls and floor. I was lucky, thanks to the efforts of my union, to be freed quickly and before the national police learned of my capture.

BY THE END of that year, it was clear to me, as it was for many in my generation of political activists, that I did not have long to live, and that my death was going to be meaningless. Many gave up and tried to reconstruct our lives. Some steered their political organizations into entities more acceptable to the regime. They were rewarded with legal status, generous governmental stipends, and entered the electoral arena. Ironically, our efforts had forced a political reform and an opening of the electoral and political system, but the PRI wasted no effort in turning this to their advantage by coopting the political organizations it found most threatening into the safer arena of electoral and parliamentary politics.

A few of us left the country. Some, like me, left quietly and focused our efforts into supporting revolutionary movements in Central America. Others, like Hector Marroquín, became symbols of political persecution in Mexico, as they launched campaigns for political asylum. Unbeknownst to all of us, Marcos and a few survivors of the FLN left for the most remote rural areas of Mexico, clinging to a dream that seemed to be fading.

By 1993, all that remained of the communists, socialists, Trotskyists, Maoists, and several guerrilla movements had either closed ranks behind former PRI-ista Cuauhtémoc Cárdenas, merged into his party, the PRD, and embraced electoral politics—or barely survived unnoticed as one of a handful of tiny grouplets swamped by the tidal wave of Cárdenas's new party. And after Cárdenas's failure to claim his narrow electoral triumph in 1988, when Salinas had, by any objective account, manipulated the electoral results to snatch the presidency away from him, the PRD's fortunes declined.

Then, unexpectedly, where everyone least expected it, the Zapatistas emerged, challenging not only the Salinas government, but the new international order.

I WAS WOKEN early January 1, 1994, by a phone call from an old friend from Mexico City, who relayed the news to me. For months, we had heard persistent rumors of the presence of a guerrilla group in Chiapas, but were somewhat incredulous. But that morning, the personal reports from several friends were unequivocal. A guerrilla army had taken over four cities. The next day, as I watched the clouds turn scarlet red as the sun set over the Pacific Ocean, it suddenly hit me. I did not know who these guerrillas were—for all I knew they could turn out to be one of those awful brutal aberrations like the *Sendero Luminoso* (Shining Path) or the Khmer Rouge—but I was extremely familiar with the Mexican government and its methods. Given the size of the rebel army and their success in keeping their existence secret, there were going to be consequences for the civilian population. I called some friends, Tom Hayden and Jodie Evans first among them, and in a couple of days, with the support of Jerry Brown, we put together a human rights delegation.

We arrived in San Cristóbal in the midst of the shooting war, bombs still being dropped from Mexican Air Force planes over villages, strafing by helicopters over unidentified targets. Together with the journalists who had arrived from all over the world, we were constrained by the cordoning off of one quarter of the region by the Mexican Army. We interviewed refugees as they streamed by the hundreds into San Cristóbal. We repeatedly challenged the military roadblocks—hundreds of human rights activists, arms locked, wearing makeshift white vests—to no avail. At night, imprisoned in our hotel rooms by the military curfew, we watched the bright flashes on the other side of the mountains and heard the explosions like distant thunder.

Finally, after a demonstration of 100,000 in Mexico City and increasing international pressure, President Salinas ordered a cease fire. After quick cleanup operations (hundreds of bodies were flown by helicopter into the Tuxtla stadium, where they were cremated), the roads were opened up.

Everywhere we drove, the sea of white flags over the roofs of every hut in the countryside was clear evidence that something monstrous had descended over the region. In spite of the extensive clean up, the signs were hard to miss: the puddles of dried blood clumsily hidden under layers of lime everywhere in the Ocosingo market where a battle had raged for hours. The eerie quiet in abandoned villages like San Antonio de Los Baños, with most of their huts ransacked. The bullet-ridden mini bus by Rancho Nuevo, drenched in blood mixed with abandoned—and unmistakably civilian—personal effects. The civilians in the mass graves we discovered by the IMSS clinic in Ocosingo. And most of all, the expressions of fear, caution, and mistrust in the faces of civilians.

During those days, amid the chaos and confusion of the Fray Bartolomé de Las Casas human rights center in San Cristóbal, I kept running into old friends. They had arrived at the same conclusions as I, and reacted the same way. At night, after harrowing days collecting evidence of the brutality of the actions of the Mexican army against civilians, we exchanged personal stories and tried to piece the pieces together and figure out who the Zapatistas were.

Given the past preeminence of the Mexican Left, it was natural that many assumed that the Zapatistas had their origins in one of its currents. Even as late as the summer of 1995, when the Zapatistas had reshaped their image to present themselves as an autonomous representative organization of the communities of the highlands of Chiapas, and had been dissected publicly for a year and a half, some were still probing their origins.

IT WAS A humid August morning and the sun had not risen yet over "La Realidad," the small hamlet nestled on the southern side of a long ravine at the southeastern edge of the highlands, where Marcos, Tacho, and other comandantes had retreated after the governments military offensive of February 1995. Several hundred attendees of the First Intercontinental Meeting for Humanity and against Neoliberalism slept in hammocks and sleeping bags under the rustic makeshift facilities built in the jungle. As I went for a walk at first light, I ran into Comandante Tacho, and together with a friend from the Mexican electrical workers union, began a conversation with him. A couple of Italian journalists joined us a few minutes later. At one point, one of them turned on his tape recorder and began probing.

"But what are your origins?" he asked intently, after mentioning how most groups do not arise spontaneously, but are founded by committed cadre formed by an ideological current. "Where did the Zapatista movement come from?"

Tacho paused for a moment, gazing into the distance. "We came from the depths of oblivion," he replied in a soft yet intense voice. "From an abyss so deep, our voices could not be heard. So dark, we could not be seen. We emerged from the deepest depths of oblivion."

Clearly, the communities which they call their "base of support," and all but a few of their combatants, do come from isolated hamlets and villages of the highlands of Chiapas. They are in every possible way a phenomenon that reflects those indigenous communities. But what triggered the formation of the EZLN was the arrival in the summer of 1983 in Chiapas of roughly 12 members of the FLN, one of the few surviving armed Marxist revolutionary movements in Mexico.

After a few months, only four remained, and during their efforts to win converts to their movement, they were transformed by the communities who embraced them and their message of revolution. When they entered the public arena with their masterfully organized military actions on New Year's Day 1994, they were still committed to a deep transformation of Mexican society. Yet, what started as a harbinger of a renewed challenge to the "new world order" of global capitalism, found itself cornered and able only to survive by adopting an image—which gradually became content—that could insure its physical and political survival.

Clearly, the Zapatistas ignited a spirit of defiance throughout the country—from a popular takeover of city hall at the small municipality of San Mateo Atenco, only a short drive from Mexico City, in the first weeks after the Zapatista uprising, to countless individual actions. On January 16, 1994, having spent a harrowing week heading a human rights delegation in Chiapas during the second week of the uprising—in the midst of the shooting war for the first four days, then documenting the deaths of civilians at the hands of the Mexican Army—I waited to meet Francisco Mendoza, a friend and a journalist who helped us communicate our activities and findings to the Mexican press.

We were to meet with the Secretary of Gobernación to submit our preliminary report and demand they investigate multiple violations of human rights. Mendoza was delayed when his taxi driver spotted a fancy limousine double parked in front of a government office. The driver swiftly drove by the back door of the limo and prevented the passenger, dressed in an expensive suit, from leaving the car. He yelled and waved at a traffic policeman standing a short distance away, demanding that he make the limousine move and park legally. Looking furiously at the stunned fat cat, he said firmly "No more, this no longer takes place here, get out of here! If the Indians are willing to die for a better country," he said in a softer voice, turning toward Mendoza, who watched from the back seat, "this is the least I can do. *Go!*" he yelled again to the limousine driver, and did not budge until the limousine drove away.

But in spite of a wave of isolated incidents, including the detonation of a bomb at a Mexico City shopping center, and a demonstration by 100,000 in support of the Zapatistas in Mexico City 12 days into the rebellion, the rest of the country did not rise up against the government. The support and sympathy the rebels garnered stayed the hand of President Salinas and eventually led to negotiations. But they found themselves politically and militarily encircled in Chiapas. This, even though throughout 1994 the nation was rocked by the eruption of a shooting war between warring factions within the PRI—starting with the assassination of Presidential candidate Luis Donaldo Colosio on March 23 and the party's Secretary General José Francisco Ruíz Massieu on September 28—the resignation of Interior Minister Carpizo, massive capital flight ($17 billion in six months) and a financial meltdown in December. The political system seemed to be coming apart at the hinges, yet the Mexican Left could do no better than focus on Cárdenas's Presidential candidacy and was at a loss after their defeat at the polling booth. In fact, while supportive of the Zapatistas, for electoral reasons, they distanced themselves from the rebels' "methods."

To be sure, the Zapatistas led several attempts at creating a national movement, each time with more and more limited goals. In the second "Declaration of the Lacandón Jungle" issued in June 1994, they convened a National Democratic Convention in Zapatista territory (held that August) and called for the formation of a Constituent Assembly to reform the Mexican Constitution. They proposed a redefinition of the question of power, liberty, and justice and a change in the culture within political parties. In January 1995, in the third "Declaration of the Lacandón Jungle" they called for the creation of a National Liberation Movement to fight for a laundry list of national issues. In 1996, in the second anniversary of their uprising, they issued their fourth "Declaration of the Lacandón Jungle" announcing their decision to pursue politics of a new type, nonpartisan, independent, and peaceful, and which did not pursue the seizure of power. On July 1998, in the fifth "Declaration of the Lacandón Jungle" the EZLN proposed a Law of Rights and Culture of Indigenous People. On March 1999, Zapatista supporters throughout Mexico organized an informal national referendum in which 95 percent of participants asked for respect for the rights of indigenous people. From then on, the defense of those rights became the central focus of the EZLN.

LAST MARCH, IN Mexico City, Marcos, during multiple speeches and interviews, clearly defined the Zapatistas' current goals and identity. They are rebels, not revolutionaries, he pointed out in several interviews. They do not seek power or the responsibility of implementing policies to solve the nation's problems; their role is simply to identify problems and demand their solution, as he told María Elena Salinas of Univisión. They are a movement of the Indigenous people of Chiapas. Their immediate goal is the passage of the Law of Rights and Culture of Indigenous People.

Their criticism was aimed at President Fox and his party, the PAN. Yet, Fox's government was, for better or for worse, legitimately elected by Mexicans, and Fox's team succeeded in doing what the Zapatistas and the left failed by military or political means: removing the PRI from power after seven decades of continuous rule. And the Zapatistas' criticism was devoid of specifics, they offered no alternative policies and stressed that they did not intend to become a national political party or join one.

Marcos criticized the Cuban and Central American revolutionaries, and chose Martin Luther King, Gandhi, and Mandela as figures who better exemplified what they wanted to achieve. In his relations with Mexican and international political groups and currents over a period of seven years, they attempted alliances with political groups, but, while accepting anyone's support, they ended by narrowing their close relations to figures like Danielle Mitterand, writers like Eduardo Galeano and José Saramago, and groups of "rebels" from various countries who challenge the ethics of neoliberalism.

Marcos and the small group of FLN cadre who moved to Chiapas in 1983 survived while other leftist movements were annihilated, withered away into oblivion, assimilated into the political institutions or were coopted, because they adapted to their surroundings. Since 1994, the Zapatistas managed to survive militarily and politically in an adverse environment, because they narrowed their image and goals to become the expression of a segment of the population whose attraction to the general public became irresistible.

Their success in surviving and impacting the national and international conscience—no small feat—was based on a constant transformation and adaptation to changing political circumstances. But this transformation carried with it the loss of a longterm alternative proposal for Mexican society, a vision of what deep changes are necessary in its economic relations and political system to achieve the goals of justice, liberty, and real democracy for everyone in the nation. The Zapatistas need a consistent strategy to achieve those goals and make them sustainable, because any sustained progress for the indigenous people in Chiapas requires a transformation of economic and power relations throughout the nation. Mexico has had progressive legislation for 83 years, but its implementation and enforcement has been another matter.

And that will be the fate of any legislation on the rights of indigenous people, unless there is a change in the institutions? And what of their economic, medical, and educational needs, even while they manage to preserve their culture and gain some degree of autonomy? During an exchange with sympathetic reporters in Mexico City, Marcos recently told a moving story of a little girl who died in his arms because they did not have a *mejoral* to lower her fever. A reporter asked him—reminding him of that the central point of his efforts is the preservation of indigenous traditions and culture—"well, why did they not use one of their traditional herbs?" He tried to raise a legitimate point: how do you resolve the contradiction between the defense of their culture and traditions, and the realization that the technology which humanity has collectively developed as cultures meet, exchange knowledge, and create a universal culture, has much to offer and will better address traditional problems? Well, needless to say, the reporter almost got lynched.

Yet, the nation's political reality has left the Zapatistas with few choices. And while they received considerable international support, it never crossed a critical threshold. Marcos himself often pondered out loud why their solidarity movement in the United States never approached the magnitude of CISPES (the Salvadorean support movement) or the movement in solidarity with the Sandinistas in Nicaragua. After all, none of the leaders of those revolutionary movements received the favorable coverage the Zapatistas got, including a piece during CBS's *60 Minutes* and the publishing of pieces by Marcos in the op-ed pages of the *LA Times*. Part of the explanation lies in the EZLN's decision to anoint individuals with little or no political or organizational presence as "official representatives." But support among US Latinos and Chicanos was limited to a few grassroots organizations, and prominent individuals and elected officials were almost universally silent. Latino elected officials had labored so hard to gain respectability in the corridors of power that they were not willing to compromise their image by associating themselves with the rebels. In addition, most of them had supported NAFTA and were (and are) anxious to build relationships with Mexican Government officials.

The predicament of the Zapatistas is indicative of an international reality. Revolutionaries—governments, parties, currents, intellectuals, individuals—are rapidly withering away and seen more and more as unwanted relics of a failed social evolutionary experiment. And "rebels" are stepping into that vacuum. While for a century and a half the Left was primarily a current of various political organizations that fought for one or another version of socialism, it is now becoming primarily a collection of protest groups and individuals: opponents of neoliberalism and economic globalization (which Marxists always favored but on the basis of different economic relations), groups and individuals whose goal is the humanization of capitalism, rather than its overthrow, with an amorphous and undefined "civil society" at the lead. Gone is the concept of classes and class struggle. Groups are increasingly critical of political parties and the view that is necessary to seize the institutions of political power to effectively and sustainably make economic and political change.

There is an implied acceptance of the immutability of the current economic system and a rejection, as failed because of an implied inherent bureaucratic nature, of alternative economic systems based on planned economies. And therein lies one of the fallacies which has become widely accepted: That the struggle of the twentieth century was between proponents of free markets and promoters of planned economies run by central bureaucracies. The central issue was not the nature of the markets, but who would own the means of production, regardless of how goods would then be exchanged—whether democracy should extend also to the economic realm or remain an illusion of the political process, always distorted by political realities and imperatives that inevitably stem from the concentration of wealth in a few hands.

Yet, the predominant discourse in what appears as the left these days is increasingly dominated by concepts like civil society, citizens, plurality, the defense of social or ethnic identity, with social classes or economically derived identities not entering the picture. Increasingly, actions which in any way affect the functioning of the engines of economic production or build organized political power are becoming rare, socially unacceptable, or outmoded, and being substituted by events, actions which more and more have the nature of spectacles which generate images fit for prime time news—turtle suits, painted faces, brown uniforms, and ski-masks; breaking windows at McDonald's or Starbucks. Symbolism substitutes for substance.

The Zapatistas did not have many options. In the new political framework that their insurrection helped create in Mexico, they did not find a way to present an alternative proposal and a way to organize around them. This is not their fault or shortcoming as much as a reflection of a vacuum of leadership in the rest of the nation and the political realities it created, which the Zapatistas alone were in no position to change. The electoral Left channeled much of the sentiment of defiance they created in 1994, only to lead those who followed into disillusionment and skepticism. Yet, believing that they would be the beneficiaries, the PRD and the electoral Left continued to help convince Mexicans, who were presented with no viable alternative means, that legitimate elections and an experiment in democracy was the way forward. And the Right was better prepared than the Mexican left to capitalize on those advances as well as on the Zapatistas' blows to the legitimacy of the PRI government. Unable at first—and unwilling later—to extend and channel their political influence into a national organized structure that can capture spaces in the political institutions, the Zapatistas can be said to have helped pave the way for the Right's takeover: Surely an unintended outcome, but part of the reality that must be faced and contended with.

In the end, perhaps Rosario Ibarra de Piedra said it best when casually assessing the contribution of the Zapatistas. She was almost 70 as we walked on the mud at La Realidad. With her wrinkled face and gray hair barely protected from the sun by a straw hat, and her eyes shining with inextinguishable energy, we sat down under the shade of a tree and watched the hundreds of visitors milling around the hamlet: young rebels from various countries attending the Zapatista-sponsored meeting against neoliberalism. We reminisced about the last 20 years. We had met in 1976, when, her son having been kidnapped by the Mexican Government, she had began her crusade on behalf of those "disappeared, tortured, persecuted, or exiled" for political reasons. She had founded Mexico's human rights movement and become, in the words of The New York Times, a pillar of the Mexican Left. A candidate for President in 1982 and a Congresswoman in 1994, she was at the epicenter of events and witnessed from a privileged vantage and with exceptional clarity the transformation of Mexico's political landscape.

"Hope," she said, "the Zapatistas represent hope, and we must preserve hope at all costs." I agreed and—always the biologist—I replied that hope is like a seed. No matter how gray and hopeless things may look at times, the least we must do is preserve our hopes and the vision of better things to come until once more we find fertile ground.

Who knows the best way forward for humanity? Many believe they do and fight doggedly to bring their own vision to reality. Determinedly, with sacrifice, or brutally. But we cannot let go of the belief that there is a better way to live than by parasitic relationships in which so few concentrate so much, so many suffer endlessly, in which our environment gets plundered and our collective future squandered.

There has to be a better way. The Zapatistas reminded us of the strength of the human spirit, of the value of determination, altruism, willingness to sacrifice, honesty.

The Uruguayan writer Eduardo Galeano put it well. Following a parade of notables speaking endlessly in support of the Zapatistas at La Realidad, Galeano rose to speak and the assembly of hundreds quietened down. He simply said, "I am here and support the Zapatistas, because in a world full of lies, I believe and trust them."

And believe we must.

The future of the Zapatistas in the new reality of Mexican politics is uncertain. But their contribution has been enormous. They have injected new hope and renewed faith in the possibilities of social change, while reminding us all that it requires the willingness to make personal sacrifices. They have brought renewed attention and legitimacy to the rights and contributions—not just the plight—of indigenous people. Their denunciations of the consequences of economic globalization for the forgotten millions have helped take some of the steam from the triumphant marketing of neoliberal economic policies.

Unfortunately, while the Zapatistas have provided an example of resilience, and how to resist and fight the system, they have not shown how to transform it. That remains the unresolved question, as revolutionaries are replaced by rebels, and capitalism, transformed, triumphant, reinvigorated, continues to expand and entrench itself. And the human suffering and economic and social dysfunction it creates goes eloquently denounced but ineffectively challenged.

THE INVISIBLE**SIGHT**

Salvador Carrasco

> Sightless, unless
> The eyes reappear
> —T. S. Eliot, *The Hollow Men*

IN Mexico we are force-fed many of the mythical episodes from our history. Throughout childhood, we are told certain stories over and over until they lose all meaning. We are told, for example, that the Spaniards put a torch to the soles of the feet of the last Aztec emperor, Cuauhtémoc, so that he'd reveal where Moctezuma's treasure was hidden. His stoicism and refusal to speak became legendary. We hear about it at home and in school and see pictures of it in books and on giant murals until at last it becomes like a song we've heard a thousand times without ever stopping to consider its meaning.

Film gives us a wonderful opportunity to add new dimensions to such stagnant historical models. A good historical film can make people feel as if they're experiencing those events for the first time, perhaps even understanding them in a new way.

It was my hope in making *The Other Conquest* to do just that: To shed new light on old events, which have come to seem so familiar that we are deceived into mistaking familiarity for clarity.

In many ways, *The Other Conquest* is a film that should not have been. Many a face I'd rather forget in the government-sponsored film institute in Mexico tried to stop it from being made—and once made, from being recognized. The very fact that over a million people went to see it anyway, making it the largest-grossing dramatic film in Mexican history, was a cultural breakthrough. Perhaps they felt uneasy about it because it threatened to change the way people viewed Mexican films and Mexican history. In the United States, it has helped to encourage the acceptance of so-called Latino films. But perhaps its worst sin was to question the very roots of Mexican culture, which grew out of the clash between the Aztecs and Spanish into the tangle that it is today. And as with those stagnant myths that we are meant to accept without thinking, the official history of the Conquest was not meant to be questioned because of the embarrassing things that it might say about the situation of Mexican Indians today. The truth is: The Conquest is not over. And it's not perfectly clear who is doing the conquering.

The story of *The Other Conquest* follows the attempts of a Franciscan priest, Friar Diego of La Coruña, to convert a young Aztec scribe to Christianity in the aftermath of the Spanish Conquest. Topiltzin, the fictitious son of Emperor Moctezuma, survived the 1520 massacre at the Great Temple only to find his people dead, their culture shattered.

The opening scene, in which Topiltzin crawls out from under a corpse to find his own mother brutally murdered by the Spanish, sets the tone for the whole film; for as a result of the Conquest, the surviving Aztecs found themselves in a state of cultural orphanage, having lost their families, homes, language, temples, and gods—a situation that hasn't changed much in the intervening five centuries.

When Topiltzin is captured, he is brought by Friar Diego to face the Conqueror of Mexico, Hernando Cortés. There he discovers that his sister, Tecuichpo (the historical Doña Isabel), has become Cortés's mistress and interpreter. At her insistence, the Conqueror spares Topiltzin's life and orders Tecuichpo to help Friar Diego convert him to Spanish Christian ways—but only after being punished for his crimes. He is renamed Tomás and then placed before a life-sized statue of the Virgin, where he is brutally whipped and the soles of his feet burned with a torch. His brother attempts to rescue him, only to be beheaded by a soldier. When the ordeal is over, Topiltzin is kept under house arrest at the Franciscan Monastery of Our Lady of Light to undergo the battle for his soul.

There, subjected to an escalating series of catastrophes and tortures—physical, mental, and spiritual—Topiltzin experiences hell on earth, as he fights to retain his own identity and religion against the onslaughts of Christian mythology, which is doubly confusing because of its similarity to his native Aztec beliefs. Both religions are given to phantasmagoric representations, which gradually blend in his mind to form one distorted—a new, other—reality. Topiltzin's war cry becomes: "You can conquer my body, but my spirit . . . never!" As his mind descends into hallucination, the Christian and Aztec images merge until the Virgin Mary and Tonantzin, the Aztec Mother Goddess, become indistinguishable.

Fearing for his sanity, Friar Diego locks him in his cell, but Topiltzin manages to escape on a personal crusade to conquer Her in whose name inconceivable things have been done. If he absorbs the Virgin's powers, if he fuses with her, redemption will follow. For Topiltzin, to conquer is not to destroy, but to appropriate the main symbol of his oppressors in order to regain what he had lost. So who is in fact conquering whom? After all, historically speaking, the patron saint of Mexico (and of all the Americas, as of Pope John Paul II) is the dark-skinned, indigenous Virgin of Guadalupe.

Is Topiltzin's conversion (or madness) real? Is he simply trying to retain his own beliefs under the guise of the new creed? Those questions torment Friar Diego, and despite the Franciscan's attempts to keep Tomás (Topiltzin) from consummating his obsession with the Virgin, he finally allows Providence to decide whether Tomás's mission is legitimate or not. For better or worse, Providence, God, fate, historical necessity, or life's mutability—whatever one calls that mysterious force that holds the strings of our existence—chooses *mestizaje*, the fusion of indigenous and European bloods. And thus, from unhealed wounds, a new nation is born, leaving Indians bleeding on the fringes, trapped in a state of cultural orphanage. Indians have been transformed from creators of pyramids to the base of the social pyramid.

THE OTHER CONQUEST attempts to explore the remarkable process of the Spanish Conquest on several levels, along with its relevance to modern Mexico, which seems all the more poignant today, as the Zapatistas have peacefully marched into the capital.

In other parts of the world, encounters between European and native peoples have traditionally been resolved through genocide. The indigenous peoples of Mexico, however, managed to survive their violent incorporation into the life of New Spain. The process of conquest, conversion, and colonization was not complete, and in some cases, it was reversed. The mestizo fusion of races that resulted certainly was not the consummation of an idealized process of harmonious interaction. And yet, it is not useful to adopt a facile Manichean point of view that sees history as a Hollywood story with good guys and bad guys.

On one hand, there exists an imperialist version that bestows a positive sign, an unconditional justification, upon everything Spanish, as if the historical mission of Spain had been fulfilled with the Conquest of America. We might call this vision of history the White Legend. On the other hand we have the Black Legend, which overlooks historical complexities, portraying the Spaniards as a gang of faceless barbarians and the Indians as pure victims.

It doesn't take much knowledge of Mexican or Latin American history to see the obvious parallels between Topiltzin's story and the contemporary plight of Indians. And that may be the main reason why three different administrations of the Mexican Institute of Cinema (IMCINE) refused to finance or support *The Other Conquest*, despite the appalling shortage of films about the fall of the Aztec empire.

Then as now, our main intention was to make a modest contribution by heightening interest in a topic so vast that it deserves to be treated with a multiplicity of voices, stories, and points of view. I simply wanted people to talk about the Conquest. Historically, Mexico has always been a land of repressed voices. Now, between the Zapatistas and the Popocatepetl volcano, it seems that Mexico can't wait to erupt. It is fitting that in one of his press releases, Subcommander Marcos wrote: "We are worried, as is everyone, about Popocatepetl and the anxious sky hovering above so many people. . . . "

As is often the case in Mexico, we might never know the real reasons for the official opposition to our film. Throughout the seven years it took to make *The Other Conquest*, we heard a litany of excuses: that the subject matter was "too delicate" (precisely the reason to make it); that people just wanted to be entertained and did not want to confront those issues (as if a film needed to be thoughtless to be entertaining); that they should not help to finance a director who had studied film at NYU rather than in Mexico (despite the fact that I was born and raised in Mexico, and that the subject of the movie could not be more Mexican); that a film with an Indian protagonist, partly spoken in Nahuatl, and with such "artistic pretenses" wasn't commercial, and therefore nobody (and they meant *nobody*) would bother to see it.

When *The Other Conquest* was released in April 1999 by Twentieth Century Fox, it broke box-office records in Mexico, consolidating itself as the number one movie, even against big Hollywood productions such as Mel Gibson's *Payback*. TOPILTZIN BEATS MEL, read a newspaper headline after opening weekend.

Though many Mexican industry people have chosen to ignore it, the fact remains that *The Other Conquest* has opened the doors for the stream of acclaimed Mexican films that has followed. A noteworthy exception is Matthias Ehrenberg, the producer of the highly successful comedy *Sexo, pudor y lágrimas*, who has repeatedly voiced this opinion.

The point here is not to blow my own horn, but rather to highlight that, by having flocked to theaters and video stores despite every institutional effort to suppress it, the Mexican people have expressed precisely what the film itself meant to express: the indefatigability of the culture. Whether they're aware of it or not, IMCINE sought to prevent the film from being made—and once made, distributed—partly because it was a mirror of the culture. And people went to see it for the very same reason. And that despite some rather Orwellian efforts to all-but-ban the film (which presumably would have made it too tempting to resist, as was the case with *Herod's Law*, a recent Mexican film boycotted by its own producer, IMCINE).

A month before our premiere in Mexico City, *The Other Conquest* played at a film festival in Guadalajara. The audience screening was packed. It was so quiet during the film that we could hear people breathing. At the end of the film, there was thunderous applause. When Damián Delgado, the actor who plays Topiltzin, was asked to step to the front of the auditorium, the audience gave him a standing ovation that lasted over three minutes.

Notwithstanding, the morning newspaper reported that the screening had been an utter disappointment, and that the film had left the audience cold. (It turns out that the writer hadn't even attended the screening.) During the rest of that week, all those connected with the festival did their best to pretend that *The Other Conquest* didn't exist. Media and industry people blatantly ignored our presence there. I am not an Indian. Like many Mexicans, I'm of Spanish descent. But for the first time, I had a taste of what Indians in Mexico are exposed to, day in day out—the ontological paradox of being there without being there.

I had a public confrontation with one of the heads of IMCINE because they had published a book called *Mexican Cinema*, which was being sent to film festivals worldwide. *The Other Conquest* wasn't even mentioned in the book. Making a film in Mexico outside of the establishment can be a draining experience. People often ask me why *The Other Conquest* wasn't the official Mexican entry for the Oscars. We learned that the small jury in charge of choosing what to send to the Academy was comprised of competing directors, producers, and actors. When I complained, the only thing that the head of the IMCINE could think of to say in his defense was, "They won't vote for themselves." This is not so much an issue of corruption but of culture.

When *The Other Conquest* was selected for the American Film Institute International Film Festival in Los Angeles, our friend Neil Cohen picked up on the fact that it was the first Spanish-language film ever entered in the AFI competition. That led to a cover story in the *Calendar* section of the

Los Angeles Times. When we arrived at the Chinese Theater in Hollywood for the screening, there was a huge line. I thought it was for the new *Star Wars* installment, but the people were there, in fact, to see Topiltzin's story. It was a diverse crowd, both Latino and non-Latino, wealthy and working class, young and old. A group of youngsters had even come from San Diego wearing the official uniform of the Mexican soccer team. Ambassador Jesús Reyes Heroles had flown in from Washington, DC. Mexican pop stars were there, limos and all, expecting to see God-knows-what kind of film.

The second screening at AFI was just as packed, even though it took place on a Monday at 4:30 P.M. Hundreds of people had to be turned away, and they complained bitterly that they had a right to see "their film." Mexican Consul José Ángel Pescador later told us that he had received many similar calls at the Consulate in subsequent weeks. Witnessing that, I knew that the film was no longer mine. It had a life of its own.

THE OFFICIAL PREMIERE in Mexico on April 1, 1999 was attended by Mexico's President, Ernesto Zedillo, along with the Ministers of Culture and Education, among others, and the General Director of IMCINE. By a fateful coincidence, it took place on the eve of the National Indigenous Referendum. When Topiltzin's feet were burned by the Spaniards, the president sank down in his seat, while the First Lady let out an involuntary shriek of horror. When the film was over, Zedillo shook my hand and said, "Congratulations. Very powerful. I'm glad I saw it; it gives one a lot to think about." He started to walk away, then turned and added: "Did González Torres really let you do all this?"

A Jesuit and Dean of the Ibero-American University in Mexico, Enrique González Torres was one of our main co-producers. He once received death threats for being "the man behind Marcos." It wasn't a matter of his letting me do those things: González Torres's faith in the movie was and still is a great source of inspiration for me. He was absolutely respectful of the content of the film, and the reason that he supported us (through a non-profit organization called FAPRODE) was, in his own words, because "this film sends out a clear message about the Indians' humanity and their often neglected role in the history and constitution of modern Mexico."

Twentieth Century Fox placed a huge billboard on the Periférico, one of Mexico City's main arteries, where an average of 650,000 people would see it every day. The key art was the face of Topiltzin in profile, bathed in a ray of light—based on a striking photograph taken by my wife, Andrea. One day I drove the most commercial and densely populated stretch of the

Periférico, about 20 miles long. Among the hundreds of billboards, there were only two indigenous faces: one was Topiltzin; the other one appeared in an ad from the National Crime Prevention Organization, warning women not to go out alone at night because they could be raped (presumably by Topiltzin's evil twin).

Guadalupe Loaeza published a wonderful essay about *The Other Conquest* in the *Revista Cultural El Angel* in April 1999. She wrote, "Doesn't the type of Mexican that we use in our ad campaigns about crime look just like Topiltzin? Why do we have to show these dark-skinned Mexicans as if they were violent, the violators, the perpetual aggressors? Why the hell are we still so racist, so much like the Spaniards who came to conquer us so many years ago?"

That emblematic image of Topiltzin has played a crucial role in the life of the film. We were consciously trying to create an icon, a powerful symbol, so that when people mentioned the title of the film, something tangible would come to mind. On how many other occasions have indigenous people seen themselves represented with a positive connotation—as Topiltzin was—on a movie poster, a billboard, in bus shelters, on flyers, and even on placemats at the popular VIPS restaurants? For Indians who are all but invisible in Mexico, it was a real breakthrough. And for all who tried to make *The Other Conquest* just as invisible, it was an infuriating defeat.

ONE DAY, DAMIÁN (Topiltzin) and I arrived for a television interview at Televisa, which held a virtual monopoly on entertainment in Mexico at the time. Without so much as glancing at Damián, the guard at the entrance told me, "You can go in, but your chauffeur has to wait for you outside." When I explained that I was actually accompanying him, that he was the star of the movie *The Other Conquest,* the guard chuckled as if I'd told a joke. Then he must have seen something in my eyes that suggested that I wasn't joking. He let us in. The surreal part of that exchange was that the guard was an Indian, too. He could have been Damián's brother.

I was ashamed that Damián had to endure such humiliation to promote our movie. As we walked down the corridor toward our interview, he said, "Don't worry, there's hardly a day that doesn't happen to me. I'm immune now." To become immune or to become Marcos, that is the question facing Mexicans now more than ever.

When we finally arrived on the set, the girl who was going to interview us asked me if the star was delayed. "No," I said, pointing at the allegedly invisible man standing next to me. "This is Damián."

"Of course," she said, obviously flustered. "I'm so scatty sometimes. . . ." *No*, I thought, *You're a racist. We're all racists. We just don't know it.*

Which proves that in Mexico, not even showing an Indian's face 40 feet across to millions of people, or playing in 100 movie theaters, or being one of the top video rentals at Blockbuster, or appearing ubiquitously on all media . . . can make him any less invisible.

THE OTHER CONQUEST opened in 75 theaters in Los Angeles in April 2000. In many ways, Los Angeles is the city where the whole world has collided, so an LA release is extremely challenging and indicative of a film's worldwide potential. Despite all the resistance we encountered, yet again, to theatrical distribution, the results exceeded everyone's expectations. The film quickly became the top foreign-language film in the US, grossing $1 million, even though it was playing in only one city. It performed as well in Latino as in non-Latino areas, in commercial as in art-house theaters. Damián and I went to the Laemmle's Theater in Santa Monica to gauge people's reactions. We were used to seeing people come out of the theater in a bit of a trance. But nothing had prepared us for a man in his seventies who, emerging from the show, spotted Damián. He seemed frozen in the doorway. People had to walk around him. Leaning on his cane, he stared at Damián for about a minute and then began trembling uncontrollably. Then he embraced Damián and burst out crying like a baby. Sobbing, the man thanked him for telling his story, because this was the story of his people, too. He was Jewish. Moments like that justify everything.

IN MEXICO THE star of the film was the film itself. In the US the star was Damián. That speaks volumes about our cultural differences. At festivals in the US, people approached Damián to get his autograph, to touch him or chat with him. They wanted to have their picture taken with him. They invited him to colleges, introduced him to the gay scene, offered to buy him an exotic meal, asked him to join parades. He was mobbed at the Cinco de Mayo parade on Broadway in downtown Los Angeles. Those sorts of responses seem unmistakably American to a Mexican.

There's a scene in *The Other Conquest* in which Topiltzin has a confrontation with his older brother, Alanpoyatzin, who is trying to convince him to give in to the Spaniards and go to work with him at the new, hybrid market. The dialog is in Nahuatl with subtitles.

⫻

BROTHER: "I want you to join us. Tell them you've changed. You can still be with our gods secretly."

TOPILTZIN: "So this is what you've come for? Go back to them!"

BROTHER: "We must adapt to survive."

TOPILTZIN: "I don't adapt. I know who I am!"

While audiences in the US usually applaud at that point in the film, the only place I saw it happen in Mexico was at a screening in Milpa Alta, where there are still over a million people who speak Nahuatl. That audience also laughed with great pride whenever the Indians deliberately mistranslated what the Spaniards said. Language is a powerful way of getting back at the enemy, as many señoras in Mexico have experienced when their maids talk back to them in Nahuatl.

In general people in Mexico, while respectful of Damián, treated him with the same formality with which they'd approach an Aztec codex in a museum. It's all about context: In a glass case you may be beautiful, but court my daughter, and you're a dead man. Serve me and I'm gracious to you; raise your voice and I'll put you behind bars.

After experiencing so much visibility and notoriety, Damián was expected to land a substantial acting job in Mexico, if not in the United States. What he got instead was a casting call for a Televisa soap opera. He was dismissed before even having a chance to read because he was "too short."

Damián's acting professor at the UNAM, Héctor Mendoza, one of Mexico's most revered theater directors, had warned Damián that he was too "short, thin, and dark" (*chaparro, flaco y moreno*) to make it as an actor, that he'd better quit while he could. Thank the Virgin of Guadalupe he didn't listen to him. The talented actors who played Indian roles in our film would all eventually complain that, nine out of ten times, the parts they were offered were those of maids, wetbacks, pimps, drug dealers, prostitutes, gang members, or Indian "props"—as in *The Mask of Zorro*—to provide atmosphere. Not that there's anything intrinsically wrong with these roles (laden as they are with negative connotations), but it gets to be frustrating if those are the only choices. It seems that in film and television, both in the US and Mexico, the dark cloud of five centuries of oppression lingers on. I don't think the solution is so much to fulfill ethnic quotas, but to create more interesting roles for minorities.

I'm often asked how I went about the research to write the screenplay of *The Other Conquest*. . . . I read a lot, and I grew up in Mexico. Take the case of a longtime family friend, Laura. She is an insanely jealous middle-class woman with a masters degree in psychology, of all things. When her husband began to receive anonymous love letters, Laura spent her day sitting on a stool, half-hidden behind a kitchen curtain, waiting for the culprit to show herself. Her husband, Víctor, thought the whole thing was amusing, even flattering. He had a clear conscience. But Laura, nevertheless, worked herself up to the verge of a full-blown depression. Then the truth came out: The letters were from the maid at the house across the street. Like all maids in Mexico, she was Indian. When Laura found out, the whole thing became a big joke. In fact, Laura loved to tell the story at parties: "Can you imagine that poor little Indian (*esa pobre indita*), as if Víctor would ever go for that?" For all practical purposes, her rival wasn't a woman, perhaps not even a human being, and was therefore no threat.

If you think that unusual, consider the case of a four-year-old boy who, playing a war game with his older brother and a friend, had the housemaid kneel at his feet, sentenced her to death, and proceeded to execute her with a .22 caliber rifle. The bullet entered her cheekbone and lodged in her brain, killing her instantly. She was the enemy. She was also 12 and an Indian ("Playing at War Three Little Boys Execute a Servant," Excélsior; December 18, 1951). The boy, Carlos Salinas, went on to become President of Mexico. Needless to say, the whole incident was swept under the rug, as if a stray dog had been accidentally run over by a car. The story had no effect whatsoever on his political career. The boy's mother declared it was the maid's fault, though she conceded that "she was a very hard worker and very clean." And we ask what the fuss is all about in Chiapas. . . .

When the Spaniards arrived in Mexico in the first half of the sixteenth century, several of their apologists (particularly Juan Ginés de Sepúlveda) supplied them with the proper excuses for taking the land away from the Indians and for treating them in ways that ought to defy our imagination. In his tremendously popular *Democrates II* (*Concerning the Just Cause of the War Against the Indians*), Ginés wrote that in accordance with Aristotelian principles, "Indians are inferior to the Spaniards just as children are to adults, women to men, and, indeed, one might even say, as apes are to men." If *The Other Conquest*, the Zapatistas, and being Mexican are about anything at all, it is about that very issue.

THERE IS NO doubt that artistic works such as *The Other Conquest* touch a profound nerve; and for that reason, many more should be made. A movie creates a self-contained world that can bring complex situations to life in a very accessible way; more so than the hollow retelling of them that we get as part of the official discourse. Movies—and the self-contained realities they create—imprint themselves indelibly on the mind. And it's not even necessary to understand all the nuances. We are captivated by unforgettable moments—images and events that won't ever leave us. People sit in the dark and pay unconditional attention for two hours. You can't skim a movie. You have to watch every frame. Not only are people immersed in that world, but they do so collectively, creating a new intimacy, a new community of sharing and belonging—in effect, a new culture unique to that film.

Ideally, every filmmaker should feel a tremendous sense of moral responsibility before, during, and after undertaking an effort to, in effect, play God and create a new world.

Instead, time and time again, Indians are portrayed as bloodthirsty barbarians, which helps explain why a high-school student once told me that what shocked her most about *The Other Conquest* was to realize that the Aztecs did not live in caves. Sometimes the well-intended attempts to depict them as pure, flawless, mystical creatures does them an even greater disservice, showing them as noble but passive savages, devoid of any signs of cultural resistance, unquestioningly accepting whatever is imposed on them by their oppressors.

The Mission, for instance, has many virtues but regrettably falls into that trap. Its colonialist viewpoint is so completely assimilated in its makers' minds that the words the Indians speak in the film are not even given subtitles, presumably because what they have to say could not be of interest.

In *The Other Conquest* we tried to portray more complex characters, ones who were taking an active role in shaping their own destiny within the context of their indigenous culture. The characters in the film show us that, even under the worst circumstances, people will struggle to achieve their own conquests.

So what is the other conquest? In one sense, it is the conquest carried out by the indigenous people, who appropriated European religious forms and made them their own. Catholicism in Mexico today bears little resemblance to that brought over by the Spaniards in 1519. In that sense, the Aztecs (unlike, for example, the Plains Indians, who along with their culture were wiped out) were as much Conquerors as the Spanish. That reverse conquest is embodied in Topiltzin's melding of the Aztec Mother Goddess with the Catholic Virgin Mary and in his Christlike self-sacrifice, which makes him transcend his enemies and become a symbolic figure.

Topiltzin is by no means a flawless hero. In fact, like many rebels, he finds it easier to sacrifice himself to an abstraction (the redemption of his people, paradoxically a Christian notion) than to sacrifice himself for another person, as his half-sister or his older brother do in order to save Topiltzin's own life. When they're captured by the Spaniards, his brother reassures Topiltzin: "I'll make sure that you live, not die for us. You shall become the voice of eternal fire."

It never ceases to surprise me the way many of us refuse to acknowledge events such as those in the Conquest and those of Chiapas. People treat them as if they were taking place in some obscure, remote land. Like the massacre at Acteal, despite the fact that videotape of the slaughtered men, women, and children was aired on national television. We deny that it happened, but deep inside we know it happened in our country, in our backyard, in our bedrooms, and inside our heads. And the denial, as much as the events themselves, is tearing us apart as a nation, even as it forces us to confront who we really are.

The more we delve into our own culture, the more we discover universal values. We all have a bit of Topiltzin in us. We look within and around us and cannot figure out what it means to be Mexican. Then we look in the mirror and realize that we're the product of a tragic, bloody birth. If you think the Spanish exterminated the Aztecs, look around you. They're still here. Look at Damián. He's not a myth, he's a modern, educated man, and yet so Aztec that a time machine or a film could have plucked him out from under a corpse during the massacre at the Great Temple in 1520 and set down here among us. Damián's reality is the very reason that we feel compelled to make him invisible. The profound implications of his existence are otherwise too painful to contemplate.

But, thank Marcos, the events in Chiapas have made the Damiáns of our world come out of the woodwork—and the woods. We try, consciously or unconsciously, but we can no longer make them disappear, and attempting to do so only makes them that much more visible. Mexico is entering a new political era. One of the main challenges, the true measure of success, will be whether Indians, who have moved invisibly among us these 500 years, at last become not only a part of our country's renovated psyche and conscience, but also a key force in its everyday decision making process. And then, only then, will there be no need to wear those ski masks whose underlying purpose is to emphasize the eyes we dared not meet, perhaps not because they were invisible after all, but because we were too afraid they'd stare us down. Now we have the unique opportunity to look into those eyes again, regain our sight as a nation, and at long last, restore a fundamental part of our identity.

MARCOS SPEAKS

An interview with Subcomandante Marcos

GABRIEL GARCÍA MARQUÉZ AND CAMBIO

Originally appeared in *Revista Cambio*,
March 24, 2001.
Translated by Russell Cobb.

SUBCOMANDANTE Marcos arrived in the Lacandón jungle of Chiapas in southeast Mexico in 1984 and lived there for 17 years with the indigenous Tzotzils and Tzeltals until March 11. Then Marcos led a march across half the country culminating in a gigantic demonstration in the Plaza de la Constitución—better known as the Zócalo—in Mexico City.

In this place of enormous historic connotations, the head of the Zapatista Army of National Liberation, unarmed, made the official decision to turn the Zapatistas into an honest political movement. Since that day, Mexicans have been waiting with bated breath since they know that, to a large extent, the fate of their country depends on the gestures of this mysterious masked man and the handful of leaders that together make up the *comandancia*.

Their mission is to achieve congressional approval for a law granting indigenous rights and sit down face to face at the bargaining table with the government of Vicente Fox.

Marcos and his people moved into the National School of Anthropology and History (ENAH) in the south of the city where classrooms function as makeshift dorms and student meeting rooms have become the center of worldwide public opinion. All of this is due to the school's present occupants and the whirlwind of breaking news items.

The Subcomandante has yet to convince Congress to allow him to present his concerns about the indigenous rights law in front of a congressional plenary. The split between the political parties is so deep that it has impeded any sort of consensus on the topic. Meanwhile, Marcos and President Fox are trying unsuccessfully to come to an agreement about what the best first step will be to initiate peace talks between the rebels and the government.

Last week ended in incredible suspense. The Zapatistas announced their intention to return to Chiapas, since they believed the political mainstream was closing off the path to dialogue. To tie them up in Mexico City, Fox responded with an order to vacate military bases in the conflict zone, and proclaimed that he would liberate Zapatista guerrillas still in prison. The fear that the Zapatistas generated when they arrived in Mexico City was only surpassed by a feeling of general uneasiness that they might go back home with empty hands.

By way of a long chain of messages handed down through friends in common, Subcomandante Marcos decided to speak with the journalists of Cambio. The date was set for one evening last week at 9:30. Police agents guarded the main entryway to the School of Anthropology, while a group of students keeps guard 24 hours a day over the classroom where the Zapatistas stay. After going through two security details, we arrived at a meeting room decorated with only a table and three chairs. Five minutes later Marcos entered and spoke with us.

Cambio: Seven years after the Zapatistas announced that they would one day triumphantly arrive in Mexico City, you come to the capital and find the Zócalo completely full. What did you feel when you climbed up on the platform and saw the whole spectacle?

Marcos: Following the Zapatista tradition of anticlimax, the worst place to see a demonstration in the Zócalo is onstage. The sun was very strong, there was a lot of smog, we had headaches, and we started to get very worried counting all the people that were fainting in front of us. I was telling my partner Tacho that we should hurry up because by the time we got to speak, no one would be left in the plaza. You couldn't see the entire extension of it. The distance between the crowd and us due to security problems was also an issue and we didn't find out what happened in the Zócalo until the next day when we read the accounts and saw the photos. In this sense, and taking into account what others have said about it, we do think this moment was the culmination of an era. We think our words, our discourse, on that day were in the most appropriate and precise and that we surprised a lot of people who thought we would try to take the palace or call for a general insurrection. We also surprised people who thought that we would limit ourselves to the purely rhetorical or lyrical. I believe that we achieved a certain balance and that, one way or another, the EZLN was speaking in the Zócalo on March eleventh—not about the year 2001, but about something that has yet to be completed: the notion that the definitive defeat of racism is an issue for state policy, an issue for education, and an issue for all of Mexican society. We are very close to resolving this, but we still have a way to go. Like we military men say, the war may be won, but there are a few battles still to be fought. Finally, I think, what March eleventh meant was that it was time to give up our arms, since military strength was not what was giving us a connection to society, and that our best bet was a pacific demonstration that would yield results. Only the Mexican State doesn't understand this—the government in particular doesn't understand.

Cambio: You used the expression "as we military men say." For us Colombians who are used to the discourse of the guerrillas, yours doesn't sound very military. How much of you and your movement are military, and how would you describe the war in which you have fought?

Marcos: We all work from within an army: the Zapatista Army of National Liberation. The structure is military. Subcomandante Marcos is the military leader of an army. However, this army is unlike any other because what we are proposing is to cease being an army. The military man is an absurdity because he must always rely on weapons to be able to convince others that his ideas are the ones that should be followed, and in this sense our movement has no future if it is military. If the EZLN perpetuates itself as a military organization, it is bound to fail. As a position toward the world, as an ideological option, it would fail. And the worst that could happen—apart from failure—would be that it comes to power and installs itself as a revolutionary army. For us, that would be failure. What would be a victory for a political-military organization of the 1960s or 1970s, like those that came on the scene as national liberation movements, for us would be failure. We have seen that the victories these movements achieved turned out to be masks for their own defeat because what was left unresolved was the place for the people, for civil society. Basically, these are disputes between two hegemonies. There is an oppressive power from on high that decides for society and a group of elitists that decides how to guide the country down the right path. This group throws the other out of power, assumes control, and then decides for society what's best for it. For us this is a battle between hegemonies, and there is always one good side and one bad side: The side that's winning is the good side while the side that's losing is the bad side. But for the rest of society, there are no fundamental changes. There arrives a moment in which the EZLN sees itself as surpassed by what *Zapatismo* represents. The "E" (for *ejército* or army) of the acronym becomes insignificant, such that for us to mobilize without being armed is, in a certain sense, a relief. In fact, the accouterments weigh less than before and we feel that the military paraphernalia is less of a burden when the time comes to engage in dialogue. One cannot reconstruct the world or society, nor reconstruct national sovereignty—which has been destroyed—through a dispute in which hegemonic powers try to impose themselves on society. The world, and specifically Mexican society, is composed of different groups and the various relationships that need to be constructed between these groups should be based on respect and tolerance—terms that never appear in any of the official political or military discourses of the 1970s and 1980s. Reality has arrived to cash in its check, as always occurs, and for the movements of armies of national liberation, the cost of the bill has been high.

Cambio: You seem to differ with the traditional Left also in the sectors of society that you represent. Is this so?

Marcos: I'll point out two shortcomings of the revolutionary Left in Latin America. One concerns the indigenous peoples—which we represent—and the other concerns so-called minority groups. Even if we took off our ski masks we would not be as marginalized as gays, lesbians, and transsexuals. These sectors of society have not only been ignored by the traditional Left in Latin America during previous decades—an ignorance which still persists today—but the theoretical model of Marxist–Leninism has been to leave them out or consider them as part of the problem to be eliminated. The homosexual, for example, is suspected as a traitor, as a malignant force for the movement and for the socialist state. And the Indian is a backward element that impedes the forces of production . . . blah, blah, blah. So the only thing left to do is to eliminate these sectors, which means, for some, to quarantine them or to put them in reeducation centers, while for others this means assimilating them into the productive process and transforming them into a qualified labor force. Proletarians, to put it in their terms.

Cambio: Guerrillas usually talk in terms of majorities. It's surprising that in your discourse you talk in terms of minorities, when you could talk about the poor or the exploited. Why do you do this?

Marcos: Every vanguard assumes it is a representative of the majority. In our case, we think that this is not only a falsity but also, even in the best of cases, it doesn't go beyond good intentions and, in the worst of cases, it is a clear example of cooptation. When social forces come in to play, one realizes that the vanguard is not so vanguard and the people who it supposedly represents don't recognize themselves within it. When the EZLN renounces being in the vanguard, it is recognizing its real horizons. To think that we can do this — that we can speak for those beyond ourselves — is political masturbation. And in many cases, it's not even that, since one doesn't experience the pleasure of onanism — just the one that can be obtained in pamphlets that make everyone seem alike. We are trying to be honest with ourselves and one could say that it is an issue of human solidarity. No. We could even be cynical and say that being honest has been productive only in that we just represent some indigenous communities in a zone in the southeast of Mexico. But our message has been able to grab the attention of a lot more people. We have arrived at that point. That's it. In all the speeches that we churned out along the march, we kept saying to the people and to ourselves that we couldn't put an end to all of our struggles. We imagined that the hidden Mexico was ready to be brought to the surface, that there were so many injustices, so many wounds, and so many demands. . . . In our minds we had the image of a plough, digging up dirt when we started the march. We had to be honest and tell people that we weren't going to be in the vanguard of any of this. We were coming to present our demands and hopefully start a chain reaction in which the people could present others. But that's a different story.

Cambio: Did you come up with the speeches town by town until you arrived in Mexico City, or did you design them from the start to be said in this way, so that the last had the greatest impact?

Marcos: Well, there's an official and an unofficial version. The official version is that we realized in the moment what we had to do, but the real version is that our discourse was made up as we went along during these seven years. There's a moment in which the EZLN's version of Zapatismo is surpassed by many things. We are not responding to what we were before 1994, nor to what we were in the first days of 1994 when we were fighting, but to a series of ethical commitments that we have been acquiring over the past seven years. What happened is that we wanted to carry this plough but we ended up uprooting only the plants that were at our feet as we walked. In each plaza we said, "we did not come to direct you, we did not come to tell you what to do, but to ask for your help." Even so, during the march we received a million complaints that had their origins in problems that came before the Mexican Revolution and that people had been waiting this long to be addressed. If we could sum up the Zapatista message of today, it would be, "No one will do it for us." We must reorganize and rethink our political duties so that this will be possible. When we say no to leaders, we are also saying no to ourselves.

Cambio: You and the Zapatistas are at the height of your prestige, the PRI has fallen from power, there is a project in Congress to create a statute for the indigenous people, and the negotiations that you have suggested can now begin. How do you see this panorama?

Marcos: The struggle is like that between a time clock that checks the schedule of workers—which is President Fox's timepiece, and an hourglass of sand—which is our timepiece. The struggle then becomes how Fox can accustom himself to our way of keeping time, and us to his way. It's not going to be all or nothing. We both have to understand that we have to come up with another way of keeping time, and this new timepiece will set the pace for dialogue and, finally, for peace. We are in their space now, the seat of political power, where politicians are in the middle of what becomes developed. We are with an organization that is incapable when it comes time to effect political action—at least, this kind of political action. We are clumsy, babbling, and well-intentioned. On the other side are people that operate well with these codes. The dispute is between whether political decisions are going to be made by politicians or by us. I think, once again, that it is not going to be either or. When we declared war, we had to defy the government and now that we are making peace we not only have to defy the government but the entire Mexican State. There is not a table from which we can speak with the government—we have to build one. The challenge now is to convince the government to build this table and that it should sit down at it and that it will win because if it doesn't, then it is going to lose.

Cambio: Who should sit at this table?

Marcos: On one side, the government, and, on the other, us.

Cambio: Is Fox accepting this table when he says that he wants to speak with you and that you two can speak in the palace or any place you want?

Marcos: What he is really saying is that he wants to bask in the media spotlight because this has not yet become a real process of dialogue and negotiation but is still a popularity contest. Fox wants to have his picture taken to guarantee his presence in the media. The process of peace is not constructed as a media event but with dialogue. This process is built not by photo ops, but by giving out the right signs, sitting down, and dedicating oneself to it. We are available to talk with Fox if he is going to be responsible in the dialogue and negotiation until it is taken to its conclusion. But we would ask him, "So, who is going to govern the country while you are meeting with us, because this is going to be an arduous process?" Well, what could I tell Colombians about this? They know that the process of negotiation and dialogue during an armed conflict is difficult, and it is not possible for the chief executive to dedicate all his time to it. Let him name a commission and with this commission we will build the table. We do not have any illusions about getting our picture taken with Vicente Fox.

Cambio: In this long, drawn out process, are you going to continue dressed like this, a guerrilla in a university classroom? What's a day with you like?

Marcos: I get up, give interviews, and then go back to bed [laughter]. We speak with some of the groups I have mentioned. We talk with a ton of worlds — or subworlds, depending on how persecuted they are and how much they are marginalized — that the Zapatista discourse has touched. What we are doing is comparable to having two tables and one of those little swivel chairs that we had when I was young. We are at a moment when we can sit at one table with Congress and at another table the various communities of Mexico City. But it disturbs us that Congress is giving us the type of treatment that it gives any group that asks to be heard: it tells them to wait because it is tending to other matters. If it's going to be like that, then there's going to be a lot of damage because it's not just the indigenous laws that are in play here. People won't stand it if the government only pays attention to them on election day. It will

also be a sign for other more radical groups, which have been growing recently, that political negotiation is ineffective.

Cambio: In passing you mentioned that there were swivel chairs
when you were young. How old are you?

Marcos: I am 518 years old [laughter].

Cambio: Does the dialogue that you are proposing look for new mechanisms for popular participation in decision-making or are you
behind the way the government makes decisions for the country?

Marcos: Dialogue only means that we agree that the dispute between the
government and us takes place on another terrain. What is on the
table does not include the economic model, but rather how we are
going to debate it. This is something that Vicente Fox has to understand. We are not going to become "Foxistas" at the roundtable. What
the roundtable has to construct is a way for these masks to come off
with dignity, so that no one has to put military paraphernalia back on.
The challenge is not only that we have to build the table but that have
to create an interlocutor. We have to have this person constructed as
a man of the state and not as a marketing product or a design by
imagemakers. It's not easy—war was easier. But with war there is
much that is irredeemable and in politics you can always redeem.

Cambio: Your uniform is strange: an old handkerchief tied to your
neck and a beat-up cap. But at the same time you carry around a
flashlight here that you don't need, a communications device that
looks really sophisticated, and you also have a watch on each wrist.
Are they symbols? What does all this mean?

Marcos: The flashlight is because they have stuffed us in here where
there's no light and the radio is for my imagemakers who tell me
what to respond to reporters' questions. No, seriously. This is a
walkie-talkie that can safely communicate with our people in the
jungle so that they inform us if there's any problem. We have
received various death threats. The handkerchief was new and red
when we took San Cristóbal seven years ago. The cap is the same
one I wore when I arrived in the Lacandón forest eighteen years
ago. With one watch I arrived in the jungle and the other is from
when the cease-fire began. When the two times coincide on the
watches, it means that Zapatismo is finished as an army and that a
new stage follows—another watch and another time.

Cambio: How do you see the guerrilla war in Colombia and the
armed conflict in general in our country?

Marcos: From this vantage point, I see very little—what they let through the filters of the mass media: the process of dialogue and negotiation that is going on right now, the difficulties that have emerged from this process. From what I've been able to see, it's a traditional process of dialogue—there's nothing new there. Both sides are sitting down at the table and at the same time both sides are engaging their military forces in order to reinforce their position at the bargaining table. Or, it could be the opposite, because we don't know what each side has in mind. It could be that the bargaining table is producing an advantageous situation for a military conflict. We don't pay much attention to the accusations of ties to drug trafficking because it wouldn't be the first time that a government accused someone of that, only to have it turn out to be false. We'll give the rebels the benefit of the doubt. We don't classify them as good or bad, but we do take a certain distance, as we do with other armed groups in Mexico, since we don't consider it ethical that the ends always justify the means when the end is the triumph of the revolution. Everything, including dragging civilians into it, for example. It is not ethical that the seizure of power includes the actions of all revolutionary groups. We don't believe that the end justifies the means. We believe that, finally, the ends are the means. We construct our objective at the same time that we come up with the means to fight for them. In this sense, the value we give to the word, to honesty and sincerity is huge, although sometimes we are guilty of being a little naive. For example, on the first of January 1994, before we attacked the army, we told them that we were going to attack them. They didn't believe us. Sometimes this gives us results, and sometimes it doesn't. But we are satisfied with the fact that as an organization we are constructing an identity.

Cambio: Do you think it's possible to negotiate for peace while in the midst of a war, as is happening in Colombia?

Marcos: It's very easy and very irresponsible to speculate from here about what is happening over there. The process of dialogue and negotiation cannot be successful if all the parties do not renounce winning. If one of the parties uses the process of dialogue as a means to see who can defeat the adversary, then sooner or later, the process will fail. In this case the terrain of military confrontation is moving to the negotiation table. For dialogue to succeed, both sides need to believe that they can win something. There has to be an exit that signifies victory for both sides, or, in the worst case scenario, a defeat for both sides—just that the confrontation doesn't continue as is. Of course it's difficult, especially in movements that have been around for a long time, as in the case of the guerilla war in Colombia. Each side has been damaged so much and there are still so many debts yet to be repaid . . . but I don't think it's ever too late to try.

Cambio: Do you still have time to read in the middle of all this mess?

Marcos: Yes, because if not . . . what would we do? In the armies that came before us, soldiers took the time to clean their weapons and rally themselves. In this case our weapons are our words, so we have to depend on our arsenal all the time.

Cambio: Everything you say—in terms of form and content—demonstrates a literary background on your part. Where does this come from and how did you achieve it?

Marcos: It has to do with my childhood. In my family, words had a very special value. The way we went out into the world was through language. We didn't learn to read in school but by reading newspapers. My mother and father made us read books that rapidly permitted us to approach new things. Some way or another, we acquired a consciousness of language not as a way of communicating with each other but as a way of building something. As if it were more of a pleasure than a duty or assignment. When the age of catacombs arrives, the word is not highly valued for the intellectual bourgeoisie. It is relegated to a secondary level. It's when we are in the indigenous communities that language is like a catapult. You realize that words fail you when you try to express certain things and this obliges you to work on your language skills, to go over and over words to arm and disarm them.

Cambio: Couldn't it be the other way around? Couldn't it be this control over language that permits this new era?

Marcos: It's like a blender. You don't know what is thrown in first and what you end up with is a cocktail.

Cambio: Can we talk about your family?

Marcos: It was a middle-class family. My father, the head of the family, was a rural teacher in the days of (Lázaro) Cárdenas when, according to him, they cut off teachers' ears for being communists. My mother, also a rural teacher, finally moved and we became a middle-class family, I mean, a family without any real difficulties. All of this was in the provinces, where the cultural horizon is the society pages of the local newspaper. The world outside—or the great city, Mexico City—was the great attraction because of its bookstores. Finally, there were book fairs out in the provinces and there we could get some books. García Márquez, Fuentes, Monsiváis, Vargas Llosa—independently of how he thinks—just to mention a few, all came through my parents. My parents made us read them. *One Hundred Years of Solitude* was meant to explain what the province was in those days and *The Death of Artemio Cruz* was to explain what had happened to the Revolution. *Days to Save* was to explain what was happening to the middle class. To some extent, although naked, our portrait was *The City and the Dogs*. All those things were there. We were coming out into the word in the same way we were coming to know literature. And this shaped us, I believe. We didn't get to know the world through a newswire but through a novel, an essay, or a poem. And this made us very different. This was the looking glass that our parents gave us, as others might use the mass media as a looking glass or just an opaque glass so that no one can see what is going on.

Cambio: Where was *Don Quixote* in the middle of all these readings?

Marcos: They gave me a beautiful book when I was twelve—a hardcover. It was *Don Quixote de la Mancha*. I had already read it, but in juvenile editions. It was an expensive book, a very special present that I was waiting for. Shakespeare arrived after that. But if I could say the order in which the books arrived, it would first be the "boom" literature of Latin America, then Cervantes, then García Lorca, then there was a time of all poetry. Thus, you [pointing to García Márquez] are partly responsible for all this.

Cambio: Did the existentialists and Sartre come into all this?

Marcos: No. We arrived at them later. Explicitly existentialist, and before that, revolutionary literature we arrived at already very "molded"—as the orthodox would say. So that by the time we got to Marx and Engels we were very contaminated by the sarcasm and humor of literature.

Cambio: There were no readings of political theory?

Marcos: In the first stage, no. From our ABCs we went on to literature and then on to theoretical and political texts about the time we got to high school.

Cambio: Did your schoolmates think you were, or could be, a communist?

Marcos: No, I don't think so. The most they ever said to me was that I was a radish—red on the outside and white on the inside.

Cambio: What are you reading now?

Marcos: I have *Don Quixote* by the bedside and I regularly carry around *Romancero Gitano* by García Lorca. *Don Quixote* is the best book out there on political theory, followed by *Hamlet* and *Macbeth*. There is no better way to understand the tragedy and the comedy of the Mexican political system than *Hamlet, Macbeth,* and *Don Quixote*. They're much better than any column of political analysis.

Cambio: Do you write by hand or on a computer?

Marcos: On a computer. On the march I had to write by hand because I had no time to work, though. I write a rough draft, then another and another. You think I'm joking but it's like the seventh draft by the time I'm done.

Cambio: What book are you working on?

Marcos: What I was trying to write was absurd: It was an attempt to explain ourselves to ourselves, which is almost impossible. We have to realize that we are a paradox, because a revolutionary army doesn't propose to seize power because an army doesn't fight if that's its job. All the paradoxes we have encountered: that we have grown and become strong in a sector completely alienated from cultural channels.

Cambio: If everyone knows who you are, why the ski mask?

Marcos: A bit of leftover coquetry. They don't know who I am, and they don't care. What's in play here is what Subcomandante Marcos is, and not what he was.

THE STORY OF THE BOOT
AND THE CHESSBOARD

JOHN ROSS

MEXICO CITY (March 26)—Subcomandante Marcos, the charismatic spokesperson for the Mayan Indian rebel Zapatista Army of National Liberation (EZLN) often spins yarns that have a prophetic ring. The tale he told recently to visiting European luminaries (Nobel laureate Jorge Saramago was in the audience) was in this literary vein. An Indian lost in the big city happened upon a chess tournament, the Subcomandante related. He was fascinated by the game but did not understand it well and kept asking the players why they made the moves they made. "Shush!" the chess masters advised the visitor, they were trying to concentrate on their moves. The Indian continued to observe the match and when he at last thought he had figured it out, he removed his muddy boot and plunked it down square on pawns. "Check?" he asked the distraught players innocently.

The 24 leaders of the EZLN's general command currently encamped in Mexico City, have been embroiled in a similar high-stakes chess game ever since they arrived in the capitol after a 15-day, 3,000-kilometer odyssey that took them from the jungles and highlands of Chiapas through the Indian heartland of southern and central Mexico—a "March for Indian Dignity" which culminated in a triumphal rally in Mexico City's central plaza, the Zócalo, on March 11.

The EZLN's mission in this urban jungle: to convince the majority of members of the Mexican congress that an Indian Rights agreement the comandantes signed six years ago with the government should have constitutional standing.

At every stop along their dusty, colorful trail up to the capital, the Zapatistas advised cheering throngs of their intention to address the 628 deputies and senators who compose the federal legislature, from the highest tribune in the land—the podium of Congress. But many members of Congress had other plans.

The chess match over taking that podium, a potent patriotic and political symbol, was joined hours after the EZLN filled the Zócalo with 160,000 jubilant supporters. COCOPA, the multiparty legislative commission that oversaw the 1996 agreement on Indian Rights and Culture between the rebels and the government that is the source of the proposed new law, came knocking on the gates of the National Anthropology school where the EZLN had set up base camp, to deliver an invitation from congressional leaders to a meeting with 20 members of commissions assigned to introduce the Indian Rights bill in both houses of Congress. This was not quite the appearance before Congress that the EZLN had in mind.

Labeling the invite, which was unsigned and typed on blank white paper, "humiliating," the comandantes turned it down flat. "We didn't come all this way to knock on doors to beg for an audience. Indian rights are a national clamor. We will not be treated like second-class bureaucrats assigned to some subcommittee," Subcomandante Marcos remonstrated, making it abundantly clear that the rebels wanted to speak from the podium of Congress.

Indeed, the treatment of Indian farmers by their government when they journey from remote provinces to plead their cases with federal authorities is at the root of the Zapatistas' rebellion. Sensing that they were being ignored, that they were literally *sin rostros* ("without faces") to the government bureaucrats who studiously avoided them, the Indians picked up the gun and put on the ski-mask in 1994 to be noticed.

Having rebuffed Congress's first offer, the rebels hunkered down at the anthropology school and awaited a second overture. To while away the hours, they met with Indians and students and members of prominent rock and roll bands. They huddled with international intellectuals and accepted an invitation to address the European Parliament if their own Congress refused them an audience. Marcos invited in the neighbors and told fables about his famous pet beetle, Durito. One day, the comandantes toured the Indian suburbs of the megalopolis—with over a million Indians in residence, the greater Mexico City area holds the most important concentration of indigenous people on the continent.

The Zapatistas also made the rounds of Mexico City universities. A megarally at the National Autonomous University (UNAM), an institution torn asunder by a recent student strike and the alma mater of Subcomandante Marcos if he is who the government says he is, drew upwards of 40,000 under sun-scorched spring skies.

At the more working class National Polytechnic Institute in the industrial north of the city, Subcomandante Marcos fanned the flames of class warfare: "the rich think this country is their hacienda and we are the peons who do the work. . . . They take our land and in one night they build an airport and we never fly in their airplanes. . . . When we say we are hungry, they say just hang on (*aguantar*) . . . When we are sick or complain about the low pay, they say just hang on. Basta Ya! (Enough!)—we are not going to *aguantar*, anymore . . ."

If the Zapatista agitation was allowed to continue, Claudio González, a powerful businessman, warned freshman president Vicente Fox "we are going to lose foreign investment."

For a week, the comandantes waited for a fresh overture from the nation's Congress and when none was forthcoming, Marcos took the microphone at the daily press conference down at the anthropology school to announce that the EZLN, which had previously vowed to stay on until Indian Rights were incorporated into the Constitution, was going home to Chiapas. A virtually all-white Congress had closed its doors to the March for Indian Dignity. Hard-liners in Fox's own National Action (PAN) Party and confederates in the once-ruling (71 years) Institutional Revolutionary Party (PRI) which Fox displaced in presidential elections last July, had joined forces to keep 10 million Indians from talking.

At the top of the list was National Action's senate leader Diego Fernàndez de Cevallos, a bewhiskered, megalomaniacal blueblood who was PAN's presidential candidate in 1994 and hails from the party's rightist wing. Fernández repeatedly insisted he would not permit Indians "who wear socks on their heads" into Congress.

Others on this racist roster included the PRI's Manuel Bartlett, a onetime Interior Secretary who engineered the theft of the 1988 presidential election from Left leader Cuauhtémoc Cárdenas, and Eduardo Andrade, a loudmouthed PRI legislator who recently burst into a television studio in a drunken rage and challenged Fernandez de Cevallos to a few rounds of fisticuffs.

Acting as if they had the moral authority to defend Congress from the Indian hordes, this motley alliance argued that only members of the legislature could speak from its tribunes. Historians pointed out that dozens of nonmembers have addressed both houses for years, including one rehabilitated sex murderer.

The EZLN's decision to return to Chiapas hit the chess table with all the force of the Indian's muddy boot in Marcos's parable. The message of

Congress's failure to respond to the Indians was painfully clear. Mexico, a nation steeped in 500 years of racism, had refused once again to listen to its first peoples. History had come knocking on the door of Congress and the politicians and their parties had sent it home.

The Zapatistas' threatened leavetaking doused President Fox like a pail of cold water. Since his inauguration last December, Fox had invested virtually his entire political credibility in achieving peace in Chiapas—and now the rebels were going home, dashing any hope of an early settlement.

The President offered a flurry of enticements to head the comandantes off at the city limits. Two of the three "signals" the Zapatistas had demanded to resume dialogue with the government were immediately posted. A handful of remaining EZLN-affiliated prisoners were immediately set free, and three military bases close by EZLN strongholds were dismantled and converted by edict into "Indigenous Community Development Centers." The comandantes responded to this gambit by reminding Fox that the military bases had been illegally sited on Indian lands in the first place.

Parlaying his personal popularity, Vicente Fox also offered to meet with Subcomandante Marcos "face to face and eye to eye" (apparently none of the other comandantes were to be included in this tête-à-tête), a sales pitch he repeated during a March 21 swing through California.

But the EZLN was adamant. The comandantes had not come to Mexico City to give Fox a photo op but rather to address the legislature. Moreover, the third signal they had asked for, the passage of the Indian Rights Bill, was still hanging before a Congress that would not listen to them. They were packing. A farewell rally was scheduled for March 22 on the sidewalk outside the gargantuan building that is home to the Chamber of Deputies, the lower house of Congress, at the exact hour that the lawmakers would finally take up debate on allowing the ski-masked rebels to address them. The pieces were in place for the showdown.

"This is a decisive day in our history," Luis Hernández Navarro, a veteran Zapatista advisor and an editor at the Left daily *La Jornada*, counseled listeners during a morning radio interview March 22. Even as the rebel supporters gathered by the thousands outside Congress, word spread that, across town, the Mexican Senate had opted by a razor-thin five-vote majority not to allow the Indians into their august chambers. Angry epithets filled the hot afternoon. "*Portazo! Portazo!*" (Break down the doors!) the seething crowd began to chant.

Then, with 20,000 Zapatista sympathizers prepared to storm the premises and the comandantes mournfully tendering their goodbyes from a flatbed truck parked on a street ironically named for the rebels' namesake, Emiliano Zapata, the deputies began to vote.

The results stunned the crowd and the nation.

Contrary to all expectations, the Chamber of Deputies voted that afternoon 220 to 210 to allow the EZLN to address the nation from the tribune of Congress. The decisive margin was cast by the PRI, longtime foe of the Zapatista Army of National Liberation, which voted the insurgents' cause up March 22 just to *"chingar el PAN"* (fuck PAN).

Outside on Emiliano Zapata Street, tens of thousands jumped for joy. "The door to dialogue may just have opened," Subcomandante Marcos told a late night press conference, adding that the comandantes had postponed their imminent departure. (The EZLN in tandem with the National Indigenous Congress (CNI), a representative assembly of the nation's 57 distinct Indian peoples, are scheduled to make their case before Congress Wednesday, March 28.)

"The door to dialogue is indeed open," a relieved Vicente Fox told the nation the morning after. The battle over the EZLN's access to Congress pitted Fox against his own party which voted unanimously to deny the Indians admittance, and the bruised feelings could cripple the president's legislative agenda for the foreseeable future.

Although the EZLN has won the chance to defend the Indian Rights Bill before Congress, the measure's passage is not assured. Many of the senators and deputies who voted to allow the comandantes to speak have expressed vehement opposition to the bill. Indeed, the five-vote net margin of victory March 22 is hardly large enough to enact constitutional changes that require a two-thirds majority in both houses.

Moreover, a recent poll conducted by *Milenio*, a national daily, anticipates that six out of every 10 members of Congress will vote against the Indian Rights Bill if it is not amended. EZLN is on record as opposing modifications. The chess match is not settled yet. Indeed, chess aficionados prone to calculate opponents' future moves might want to consider what Subcomandante Marcos's Indian will do with his other boot.

WORDS OF COMANDANTA ESTHER
AT THE CONGRESS OF THE UNION

Translated by Irlandesa.

HONORABLE Congress of the Union:

Legislators, men and women, from the Political Coordinating Committee of the Chamber of Deputies:

Legislators, men and women, from the Joint Committees of Constitutional Issues and of Indigenous Affairs of the Chamber of Deputies:

Legislators, men and women, from the Committees of Constitutional Issues, of Indigenous Affairs, and of Legislative Studies of the Senate:

Legislators, men and women, of the Commission of Concordance and Peace:

Deputies:

Senators:

Brothers and sisters from the National Indigenous Congress:

Brothers and sisters of all the Indian peoples of Mexico:

Brothers and sisters from other countries:

People of Mexico:

Through my voice speaks the voice of the Zapatista Army of National Liberation.

The word that our voice is bringing is an outcry.

But our word is one of respect for this tribune and for all of those who are listening to it.

You will not receive either insults or rudeness from us.

We shall not do the same thing which took place on the first of December of 2000, in disrespect of these legislative halls.

The word we bring is true.

We did not come to humiliate anyone.

We did not come to defeat anyone.

We did not come to replace anyone.

We did not come to legislate.

We came so that you could listen to us and we could listen to you.

We came to engage in dialogue.

We realize that our presence in this tribune led to bitter discussions and confrontations.

There were those who counted on our using this opportunity to insult or to settle overdue accounts, who said that it was all part of a strategy to gain public popularity.

Those who thought like that are not present.

But there were those who counted on and trusted our word. It was they who opened this door of dialogue for us, and they are the ones who are present.

We are Zapatistas. We shall not betray the trust and faith that many in this Parliament and among the people of Mexico put in our word.

Those who chose to lend an attentive ear to our respectful word won. Those who chose to close the doors to dialogue because they feared a confrontation lost. Because the Zapatistas are bringing the word of truth and respect.

Some might have thought that this tribune would be occupied by Sup-Marcos, and that it would be he who would be giving this main message of the Zapatistas.

You can now see that it is not so.

Subcomandante Insurgente Marcos is that, a Subcomandante. We are the comandantes, those who command jointly, the ones who govern our peoples, obeying. We gave the Sup and those who share hopes and dreams with him the mission of bringing us to this tribune. They, our guerreros and guerreras, accomplished that mission, thanks to the support of the popular mobilization in Mexico and in the world.

Now it is our hour.

The respect we are offering the Congress of the Union is one of content, but also of form.

The military chief of a rebel army is not in this tribune. The ones who represent the civil part of the EZLN are here. The political and organizational leadership of a legitimate, honest, and consistent movement are here, which is, in addition, a movement which is legal, due to the Law for Dialogue, Conciliation, and a Dignified Peace in Chiapas.

We are thus demonstrating that we are not interested in provoking resentments or suspicions in anyone.

And so it is I, an indigenous woman. No one will have any reason to feel attacked, humiliated, or degraded by my occupying this tribune and speaking today. Those who are not here now already knew that they would refuse to listen to what an indigenous woman was coming to say to them, and they would refuse to speak because it would be I who was listening to them.

My name is Esther, but that is not important now. I am a Zapatista, but that is not important at this moment either.

This tribune is a symbol. That is why it caused so much controversy. That is why we wanted to speak in it, and that is why some did not want us to be here. And it is also a symbol that it is I, a poor, indigenous and Zapatista woman, who would be having the first word, and that the main message of our word as Zapatistas would be mine.

A few days ago, in these legislative halls, there was a very heated discussion, and, in a very close vote, the majority position won.

Those who thought differently, and worked accordingly, were not sent to jail, nor were they pursued, let alone killed.

Here, in this Congress, there are marked differences, some of them even contradictory, and there is respect for those differences. But, even with these differences, the Congress does not come apart, is not balkanized, does not fragment into many little congresses. Its regulations are constructed precisely for those differences. And, without losing what makes each individual different, unity is maintained, and, with it, the possibility of advancing by mutual agreement.

That is the country we Zapatistas want.

A country where difference is recognized and respected.

Where being and thinking differently is no reason for going to jail, for being persecuted, or for dying.

Here, in this Legislative Palace, there are seven empty places corresponding to the seven indigenous who could not be present. They were not able to be here with us because the difference which makes us indigenous is not recognized nor respected.

Of the seven who are absent, one died in the first days of January 1994, two others are imprisoned for having opposed the felling of trees, another two are in jail for defending fishing as a means of livelihood and opposing pirate fishermen, and the remaining two have arrest warrants against them for the same cause. As indigenous, the seven fought for their rights and, as indigenous, they were met with the responses of death, jail, and persecution.

In this Congress, there are various political forces, and each one of them joins together and works with complete autonomy. Their methods of reaching agreements and the rules of their internal coexistence can be looked upon with approval or disapproval, but they are respected, and no one is persecuted for being from one or the other parliamentary wing, for being from the Right, from the Center or from the Left. At the point at which it becomes necessary, everyone reaches agreement, and they unite in order to achieve something they believe to be good for the country. If they are not all in agreement, then the majority reaches agreement, and the minority accepts and works according to the majority agreement.

The legislators are from a political party, from a certain ideological orientation, but they are, at the same time, legislators of all Mexican men and women, regardless of the political party someone belongs to or what their ideas are.

That is how we Zapatistas want Mexico to be.

Where indigenous will be indigenous and Mexicans.

Where respect for difference is balanced with respect for what makes us equals.

Where difference is not a reason for death, jail, persecution, mockery, humiliation, racism.

Where, formed by differences, ours is a sovereign and independent nation, and not a colony where lootings, unfairness and shame abound.

Where, in the defining moments of our history, all of us rise above our differences to realize what we have in common: being Mexican.

This is one of those historic moments.

In this Congress the federal Executive does not govern, nor do the Zapatistas. Nor does any political party govern it. The Congress of the Union is made up of differences, but everyone has in common the fact of their being legislators and concern for national well-being.

That difference and that equality are presenting them with the opportunity to see very far ahead and to make out, at the present moment, the hour to come.

Our hour, the hour of the Mexican indigenous, has come.

We are asking that our differences and our being Mexicans be recognized.

Fortunately for the Indian peoples and for the country, a group of legislators like you drew up a proposal for constitutional reforms which safeguards the recognition of the indigenous, while maintaining and reinforcing national sovereignty.

That is the COCOPA legislative proposal, named because it was members of the Commission of Concordance and Peace of the Congress of the Union, Deputies, and Senators, who drew it up.

WE ARE NOT unaware of the fact that this COCOPA proposal has received some criticism.

For the last four years there has been a debate which no other legislative proposal has received throughout the history of the federal legislature in

Mexico. In this debate, all the criticisms were scrupulously refuted, both in theory and in practice.

This proposal was accused of balkanizing the country, ignoring that the country is already divided. One Mexico produces wealth, another appropriates that wealth, and another has to stretch out its hand for charity.

We, the indigenous, live in this fragmented country, condemned to shame for being the color we are, for the language we speak, for the clothes which cover us, for the music and the dance which speak our sadness and joy, for our history.

This proposal is accused of creating Indian reservations, ignoring that we indigenous are already living apart, separated from the rest of the Mexicans, and, in danger of extinction.

This proposal is accused of promoting a backward legal system, ignoring that the current one only promotes confrontation, punishes the poor, and gives impunity to the rich. It condemns our color and turns our language into crime.

This proposal is accused of creating exceptions in political life, ignoring that in the current one the one who governs does not govern, rather he turns his public position into a source of his own wealth, and he knows himself to be beyond punishment and untouchable as long as his term in office does not end.

My indigenous brothers and sisters who will be following me at this tribune will be speaking of this in more detail. I would like to speak a little about the criticism of the COCOPA law for legalizing discrimination and marginalization of the indigenous woman.

Deputies, Ladies and Gentlemen.

Senators.

I would like to explain to you the situation of the indigenous women who are living in our communities, considering that respect for women is supposedly guaranteed in the Constitution.

The situation is very hard. For many years we have suffered pain, forgetting, contempt, marginalization, and oppression.

We suffer from forgetting because no one remembers us. They send us to live in the corners of the mountains, so that no one will come any more to visit us or to see how we are living. Meanwhile, we do not have drinkable water, electricity, schools, dignified housing, roads, clinics — let alone hospitals — while many of our sisters, women, children and old ones die from curable illnesses, malnutrition, and childbirth, because there are no clinics or hospitals where they can be treated.

•

Only in the city, where the rich live, do they indeed have hospitals with good care, and the rich have all the services. For us, even in the city, we do not receive any benefits, because we do not have any money. There is no way to come back: If there were we would not have come to the city. We return to the road, dead already.

It is the women who feel the pain of childbirth. They see their children die in their arms from malnutrition, for lack of care. They see their children without shoes, without clothing, because they do not have enough money to buy them. Because it is the women who care for the homes, they see that they do not have enough for food. They also carry water for two or three hours, walking with pitchers, carrying their children, and they do everything that is to be done in the kitchen.

FROM THE TIME we are very young, we begin doing simple things. When we are bigger, we go out to work in the fields, to plant, to weed, and carry our children.

Meanwhile the men go out to work in the coffee plantations and cane fields, to earn a little money in order to scrape by with their families. Sometimes they do not come back, because they die from illnesses. They have no time to return to their homes, or, if they do return, they return sick, without money, sometimes already dead.

And so the woman is left with more pain, because she is left alone caring for her children. We also suffer from contempt and marginalization from the moment we are born, because they do not take good care of us, since, as girls, they do not think we are worth anything. We do not know how to think or work, how to live our lives. That is why many of us women are illiterate, because we did not have the opportunity to go to school.

Then, when we are a bit older, our fathers make us marry by force. It does not matter if we do not want to, they do not ask for our consent. They abuse our decisions. As women, they beat us; we are mistreated by our own husbands or relatives. We cannot say anything, because they tell us we do not have a right to defend ourselves.

The mestizos and the wealthy mock us indigenous women because of our way of dressing, of speaking, our language, our way of praying and of curing, and for our color, which is the color of the earth we work. We are always in the land, because we live there. Nor do they allow us to participate in any other work. They say we are filthy, because, since we are indigenous, we do not bathe.

We, the indigenouus women, do not have the same opportunities as the men, who have the right to decide everything.

Only they have the right to the land, and women do not have rights since we do not work the land. Since we are not human beings, we suffer inequality.

The bad governments taught us this entire situation.

We indigenous women do not have good food. We do not have dignified housing. We do not have health services or education. We have no work programs, and so we scrape by in poverty. This poverty is because of abandonment by the government, which has never taken notice of us as indigenous, and they have not taken us into account. They treat us just like any other thing. They say they send us help like Progresa, but they do so for the purpose of destroying us and dividing us.

And that is simply the way life, and death, is for us, the indigenous women.

And they tell us that the COCOPA law is going to make them marginalize us. It is the current law which allows them to marginalize us and to humiliate us. That is why we decided to organize in order to fight as Zapatista women—in order to change the situation, because we are already tired of so much suffering, without having our rights.

I am not telling you all of this so that you will pity us or save us from those abuses. We have fought to change them, and we will continue to do so.

But we need for our fight to be recognized in the laws, because up until now we have not been recognized. We have been seen only as women, and even then not fully. In addition to being women, we are indigenous, and we are not recognized.

We know which are good and which are bad uses and customs. The bad ones are hitting and beating a woman, buying and selling her, marrying her by force against her will, not allowing her to participate in the assembly, not allowing her to leave the house.

That is why we want the indigenous rights and culture law to be approved. It is very important for us, the indigenous women of all of Mexico. It is going to allow us to be recognized and respected as the women and indigenous people that we are.

That means that we want our manner of dressing recognized, along with our way of speaking, of governing, of organizing, of praying, of curing, our method of working in collectives, of respecting the land and of understanding life—which is nature, of which we are a part.

Our rights as women are also included in this law, so that no one will any longer be able to prevent our participation in life, our dignity and safety in any kind of work—the same as men.

That is why we want to tell all the Deputies and Senators to carry out their duties, to be true representatives of the people.

You said you were going to serve the people, that you are going to make laws for the people. Carry out your word, what you committed yourselves to with the people.

It is the moment for approving the COCOPA legislative proposal. Those who voted for you, and those who did not but who are also people, continue thirsting for peace, for justice.

Do not allow anyone to any longer put our dignity to shame.

We are asking you as women, as poor, as indigenous, and as Zapatistas.

Legislators, ladies and gentlemen:

You have been sensitive to an outcry which is not only the Zapatistas', nor just of the Indian peoples, but of all the people of Mexico—not only of those who are poor like us, but also of people of comfortable means.

Your sensitivity as legislators allowed a light to illuminate the dark night in which we indigenous are born, grow up, live, and die.

That light is dialogue.

We are certain that you do not confuse justice with charity, and that you recognize, despite our differences the equality which, as human beings and as Mexicans, we share with you and with all the people of Mexico.

We applaud your listening to us, and that is why we want to take advantage of your attentive ear in order to tell you something important:

The announcement of the military vacating Guadalupe Tepeyac, La Garrucha and Rio Euseba, and the measures which are being taken in order to carry this out, have not gone unnoticed by the EZLN.

Señor Vicente Fox is responding now to one of the questions which our people made to him through us:

He is the supreme commander of the federal Army, and the army follows his orders, whether for good or bad.

In this case, his orders have been a sign of peace, and that is why we, the comandantes and comandantas of the EZLN, are also giving orders of peace to our forces:

First, we are ordering Subcomandante Insurgente Marcos, as military chief of the regular and irregular forces of the EZLN, to carry out whatever is necessary in order to see that no military advance by our troops is made into the positions which have been vacated by the federal Army, and for him to order our forces to maintain their current positions in the mountains.

We will not respond to a sign of peace with a sign of war. Zapatistas arms will not replace government arms. The civilians living in those places vacated by the federal Army have our word that our military forces will not be employed to resolve conflicts or disputes.

We are inviting national and international civil observers to set up peace camps and observation posts in those places, and to certify that there is no armed presence by the Zapatistas.

Second, we are giving instructions to architect Fernando Yañez Muñoz to, in the shortest possible time, put himself in contact with the Commission of Concordance and Peace and with Government Peace Commissioner Senator Luis H. Álvarez, and to propose that together they travel to the southeast state of Chiapas and certify personally that the seven positions are free of all military presence and thus, one of the three signs demanded by the EZLN for the resumption of dialogue has been fulfilled.

Third, we are also instructing architect Fernando Yañez Muñoz to become official liaison for the EZLN with the government peace commissioner, and to work in coordination in order to achieve the fulfillment, as quickly as possible, of the two remaining signs, so that dialogue may be formally resumed: the release of all Zapatista prisoners, and the Constitutional recognition of indigenous rights and culture according to the COCOPA legislative proposal.

The federal executive now has, from this moment on, a secure, trustworthy, and discreet means for making progress in the conditions which will allow direct dialogue between the peace commissioner and the EZLN. We hope he makes good use of him.

Fourth, we are respectfully requesting the Congress of the Union, given that it is here where the door to dialogue and peace have been opened, to facilitate a place within its walls so that there can be—if the government peace commissioner accepts it—this first meeting between the federal government and the EZLN liaison.

In the case of a refusal by the Congress of the Union, which we would understand, architect Yañez is instructed to see that the meeting is held in a neutral and appropriate place, and that the public is informed as to what is agreed upon there.

Legislators, ladies and gentlemen:

In this way we are making clear our will for dialogue, for the building of accords, and for achieving peace.

If the path to peace in Chiapas can be seen with optimism now, it is thanks to the mobilization of many people in Mexico and in the world. We would most especially like to thank them.

It has also been made possible by a group of legislators, men and women, who are now in front of me, who have opened their ears and their hearts to a word which is legitimate and just. To a word which has on its side reason, history, truth, and justice—which, nonetheless, does not yet have the law on its side.

When indigenous rights and culture are constitutionally recognized in accord with the COCOPA legislative proposal, the law will begin joining its hour with the hour of the Indian peoples.

The legislators who today opened their door and hearts to us, will then have the satisfaction of having fulfilled their duties. And that is not measured in money, but in dignity.

Then, on that day, millions of Mexican men and women, and those from other countries, will know that all the suffering they have endured during these days, and in those to come, has not been in vain.

And if we are indigenous today, afterward we will be all those others who are dead, persecuted, and imprisoned because of their difference.

Legislators, ladies and gentlemen:

I am an indigenous and Zapatista woman.

Through my voice spoke not just the hundreds of thousands of Zapatistas of the Mexican southeast. Millions of indigenous from throughout the country and the majority of the Mexican people also spoke. My voice did not lack respect for anyone, nor did it come to ask for charity. My voice came to ask for justice, liberty, and democracy for the Indian peoples. My voice demanded, and demands, the Constitutional recognition of our rights and our culture.

And I am going to end my word with a cry which all of you, those who are here and those who are not, are going to be in agreement with:

With the Indian Peoples!
Viva Mexico!
Viva Mexico!
Viva Mexico!
Democracy!
Liberty!
Justice!
Thank you very much.

From the San Lázaro Legislative Palace, Congress of the Union.
Clandestine Revolutionary Indigenous Committee—
General Command of the Zapatista Army of National Liberation.
Mexico, March 2001.

PART TWO

THE WORD

THE WRITINGS OF INSURGENT
SUBCOMANDANTE MARCOS AND THE EZLN

Editorial Notes by Tom Hayden

TESTIMONIES OF THE FIRST DAY

Originally appeared in
La Jornada, January 19, 1994.

BY all accounts the uprising was a complete surprise. The operation itself, carried out by 600 Indians in the predawn hours, occurred without death or injury. The Zapatistas seized the city hall, destroyed land deeds in the registrar's office, and proclaimed their existence from the balcony over the central square. At the same time, they occupied five other municipalities across Chiapas.

It was a surprise for deeper reasons. Although evidence of the new guerrilla formation had existed for over a year—in May 1993, the Mexican Army had actually skirmished with the EZLN—there were powerful forces of denial at work. The oblivion in which the Indians existed served to blind the authorities to preparations for rebellion. The obsession with NAFTA and the business climate discouraged public discussion of any threats to stability. The state and its armed forces felt invincible.

It is clear from these spontaneous "testimonies of the first day" that the Zapatistas were prepared not only with military weapons (ranging from AK-47s to fake wooden rifles) but with what they called the weapon of the word. In addition to militant slogans—*Basta Ya!*—they brought an unexpected philosophical perspective to the public square. Never has war been declared with such intellectual style.

Take the matter of the masks. In other conflicts in the world masks are worn for military and security reasons. But when Marcos is asked about the EZLN masks, he replies with an unexpected mixture of humor and philosophy. Handsome ones like himself have to be protected, he says, only to take the statement back a moment later. The masks signify many things. One is to be anonymous, to avoid a cult of personality ("no protagonism"). Thus, from the very first day, the cult of Marcos will surround a person who is unknown. "Our leadership is collective and we have to submit to them," he notes. And finally, the mask is about having a "collective heart." Everyone, no matter how degraded, how literate, whatever their physical physique, can feel "that it is enough to have dignity and put on a mask."

In these interviews, even as San Cristóbal is occupied by masked guerrillas risking their lives, Marcos notes that "the path we have chosen is just one, not the only one . . . nor do we think that it is the best of all paths." But it was the only path available to the indigenous of Chiapas, he adds, and invites "all of the people to do the same, not to rise up in arms, but to struggle for a truly free and democratic government." This was the initial call for an awakening of "civic society" that received increasing emphasis in Zapatista strategy. Marcos went on to explain that the EZLN had no desire to "monopolize the vanguard" or "stingily claim the qualifications of revolutionary," but a desire to demonstrate dignity and patriotism and "you should do the same, within your ideology, within your means."

It was clear from the beginning that the Zapatistas were not calling for an overthrow of the Mexican state, but the replacement of the Salinas de Gortari administration, which was widely believed to have stolen the previous presidential election and sold the nation's patrimony to NAFTA. As prophecy, the Zapatista strategy was not far wrong. It called for a "transitional government" to replace Salinas and hold "clean, real elections." In the meantime, the Zapatistas would initiate land reforms protecting indigenous rights in the zones they controlled. As history turned out, by 2001 the Mexican people threw out the ruling Partido Revolucionario Institutional (PRI) and two Mexican presidents had offered to negotiate constitutional autonomy for Mexico's indigenous.

There is an emphasis here on the plight of the indigenous, who are described as the majority of the combatants. Someone needed to "give a lesson in dignity," says Marcos, in a succinct description of the uprising, "and this fell to the most ancient inhabitants of this country that is now called Mexico." The indigenous are the catalyst to a larger awakening.

Humor runs through the commentary, which is quite extraordinary given the stress of the life-and-death situation in which the Zapatistas placed themselves that day. In San Cristóbal, no one would die, but in Ococinco and elsewhere scores of combatants died in 12 subsequent days of war.

Marcos laughs about infiltrating San Cristóbal while people were sleeping off the New Year's festivities. "We fell on you, but like a slap," not a marauding army of bloodthirsty guerrillas. To a Swiss couple with tickets for Palenque, he said sympathetically, "forgive us, but this is a revolution" (Ross, p. 20).

"If the way of the arms only served to make us heard, then that was good," said the EZLN's Commandante Tacho years later. "Our word is our weapon," Marcos would add. What kind of guerrillas were these? A friend of mine in El Salvador, a former commandante who fought in the mountains and in the cities, said with a quizzical shrug, "as I was trained, the purpose of an army is to fight wars." The implication was that the EZLN was a guerrilla theater group, not a guerrilla army.

But that analysis discounted their years of military training, the formation of an army of several thousand trained combatants, their limited but successful battles against the Mexican Army, and their successful evasion of counteroffensives designed to capture their leadership. The Zapatistas *were* an army—and much more. And Marcos clearly was an intellectual—but much more. In a time of widespread apathy and hopelessness, that touched a very deep chord.

(The following are excerpted transcriptions that were published in *La Jornada*. They were recorded in San Cristóbal de las Casas just after the EZLN liberated the city on January 1, 1994, and the transcription was published in *La Jornada* on January 19. They begin with Subcommander Marcos answering questions after reading the declaration of war from the balcony of the Municipal Presidential Palace.)

Q: Have there been any losses?

Marcos: No. Neither ours nor the enemy's. Only in Ocosingo. There were two dead and two wounded and four prisoners on their side.

Q: The military zone is here, less than 12 kilometers away. They have not responded?

M: You have to take into account that it is a difficult situation, because this is the command of the thirty-first Military Zone. And they attack the back and three fronts. It is not as though you say, okay, now I will come and finish with San Cristóbal.

Q: Why are some of you masked and others not, although you are all from the same movement?

M: Those of us who are more handsome always have to protect ourselves. . . . What is happening is that, in this case, the officers are those who are masked, for two reasons. The primary one is that we have to watch out for protagonism—in other words, that people do not promote themselves too much. It is about being anonymous, not because we fear for ourselves, but rather so that they cannot corrupt us. . . . We know that our leadership is collective and that we have to submit to them. Even though you happen to be listening to me now because I am here, in other places others, masked in the same way, are talking. This masked person today is called Marcos here and tomorrow will be called Pedro in Margaritas or José in Ocosingo or Alfredo in Altamirano or whatever he is called.

Finally, the one who speaks is a more collective heart, not a caudillo. That is what I want you to understand, not a caudillo in the old style, in that image. The only image that you will have is that those who make this happen are masked. And the time will come when the people will realize that it is enough to have dignity and put on a mask and say: Well then, I can do this too, and I do not need to be of a particular physique. That is the truth, and for that reason, you should not believe what I said when I said I was very handsome. I am doing propaganda for myself.

Q: And women are in this movement voluntarily?

M: Did someone obligate you to come? They are Tzotziles, Tzeltales, Tojolabales—Indians.

Q: What is the average age?

M: A scandalous twenty-two years old. It has gone up. When we started it was sixteen years. Then, four years ago, it was twenty, and now the average age is between twenty-two and twenty-three years old. There are people much younger than that, but the average of the troops is that. Those who have masks are officials or people that . . .

Q: Command?

M: No, that will not check out. You are going to check out all that you see with what you read. You will check Tupamaros, Montoneros, the Sandinista Front (Frente Sandinista), twenty-sixth of July Movement (Movimiento 26 de Julio), URNG. Nothing will check out. "They are a mess." "They are going to win." This is an organization that has been preparing itself for over 10 years without a single assault, robbery, or kidnapping. "Where did they get money for what they did?" "Who protected them for so long?" They are going to say that we were part of the government. Today had to come so that we could demonstrate that we are not.

Q: How many people make up the Zapatista Army? Can you tell us?

M: I will tell you that there are thousands, and that they are all moved to take these actions.

Q: Will there be more?

M: Of course. After this, here, when we leave here, when we advance, we are certain that more will join us. Three or four hours ago we received information that an element of the Federal Army deserted and joined our ranks. They have offered to show us the location of the barracks. No, they will not show us tactics. We know more than they.

Q: Who was the source?

M: A deserter from the Army who joined our ranks.

Q: Is it safe for the press to enter into the zones?

M: In our zones, with us, you will not have problems, but I am sure that the Army will not let information pass through. Or that your editorial boards or your bosses will not let you publish it.

Q: Can you provide the resources of the city hall for our work—like the phone lines and fax?

M: Go in and look for them if you like. Oh, you're asking. . . . I was already up there looking for a telephone because I had to talk to Human Rights, to the National Commission. No, man, they have stolen everything. There are computers and all of that, there is communication. The only thing I can guarantee is where we move, and if you present your newspaper credentials, they will let you pass.

Q: Are you only here, in the state of Chiapas?

M: No.

M: . . . We hope that the people understand that the causes that have moved us to do this are just, and that the path that we have chosen is just one, not the only one. Nor do we think that it is the best of all paths. We only think that this is one that needs to be taken and we invite people to do the same, not to rise up in arms, but to struggle for a truly free and democratic government in Mexico that can fulfill the aspirations of each and every person. We do not want a dictatorship of another kind, nor anything out of this world, like international Communism. We want justice where there is now not even minimum subsistence—such as in the whole state of Chiapas. And one can say: Well, soon I am going to rise up in arms. No, but do demonstrate your agreement, each person where you work, students, teachers, and all of that, make count what they have denied us until now, which is the right to have an opinion, to feel, to dissent. That is what we want. We resorted to this because, well, because they did not leave us any other way, really.

Q: Do you think the conditions are right to do what you are doing?

M: Yes, we think that the time is ripe at an international level. We think that at the international level there is a sensibility for the Mexican people to rise up against a dictatorship of such long standing, in this case of a party, as it was in Europe. And at the national level, there is much discontent, but what was needed was for someone to give a lesson in dignity, and this fell to the most ancient inhabitants of this country that is now called Mexico, but when they were here it did not have a name, that name. It fell to the lowest citizens of this country to raise their heads, with dignity. And this should be a lesson for all. We cannot let ourselves be treated this way, and we have to try to construct a better world, a world truly for everyone, and not only for a few, as the current regime does. This is what we want. We do not want to monopolize the vanguard or say that we are the light, the only alternative, or stingily claim the qualification of revolutionary for one or another current. We say, look at what happened. That is what we had to do.

We have dignity, patriotism and we are demonstrating it. You should do the same, within your ideology, within your means, within your beliefs, and make your human condition count.

Q: It is speculated that you are a member of some political party.

M: Well, they have asked this question often, if we are a member of the PRD or of the PAN or some faction within the PRI that is against [then-Presidential-candidate Luis Donaldo] Colosio.

But the truth, we tell you sincerely, is that the political parties do not come to Indigenous people in Chiapas. They do not come and the people are tired of butting their heads against the wall. For that reason, we grew here, precisely because the political parties do not have consensus.

Q: Don't you think that people are afraid of you?

M: I think that they did not have bigger problems than us . . . Well, more than fear. That yes, but that we would rape and mutilate and all of that, no. But aside from that, I hope that the fear has gone. You should understand than any mess that we could have made here we would have done at dawn, when you were sleeping; that is, you should recognize that. You realized what was going on when the morning was quite advanced, when we were already here. You drank a toast to the new year and went to sleep, and we fell on you, but like a slap. I think that the force is not against everyone, quite the opposite.

Q: Why did you pick those four towns, did you have that already planned?

M: We have everything planned.

Q: In the state [of Chiapas]?

M: Comita'n, Tuxtla, Palenque, Arteaga, Tapachula . . .

Q: Not just four towns?

M: Well wait, and we'll be right behind you. Everything is planned down to the hut of Tres Marías and the Cuernavaca-Mexico highway. And from there we have planned how to enter. Some say that we should stay and eat some quesadillas in Tres Marías . . . The plan is to go on to all of the towns. We will go on to all of the towns. The thing is that we are the majority. That is the truth. But we will try to follow the bosses of San Cristóbal and not cause any problems to the civil population and try to convince the Army to come over from the side of injustice.

The immediate objective is that our agricultural laws begin to operate in the liberated zones, that the campesinos organize themselves, taking land, respecting small rural property and working in collectives, ignoring all of the debts with the government. Banrural (Banco de Crédito Rural), all of the taken assets, all of that, we don't know anything about in the rural zone because where we move those laws will start to operate, that is, the old Constitution before they reformed it. That is the immediate plan that we have, that is, to organize the rural life of this country according to the will of the majority of our compañeros. That is, that there be land, because there is land, and that it be distributed, because they just said that they were not going to give any more out.

So before it was running around in Agrarian Reform, which they would probably give you. Well now, even if you run around, they won't give it to you. That is what Hank González and Salinas de Gortari said when they said: Land reform is over.

Q: Listen, what about the stores?

M: I said a little while ago up there that businesses will be permitted to open. We will not do anything to private commerce, only to the government. But everything, the mini-buses, the gas stations, we are not prohibiting them from opening. We guarantee them that we will not attack any store because the law about that says . . .

Q: Could tomorrow be a normal day?

M: Yes, let's see if you can live with that. In any case you will have to live always with that threat over your head, until the problem of social justice for these people is resolved, they will come back any moment. You were always scared of the black legend that we would kill you, rape you and mutilate you, and you saw that we didn't.

///

[In the tape a man can be heard who, with difficulty, reads a document.]

I am going to communicate some of the decisions that our Clandestine Revolutionary Indigenous Committee, leadership of our revolution, has decreed today:

First: that the stores and businesses that belong to the oppressor government be opened so that the people of San Cristóbal can take from them what they need. Only the stores and businesses that belong to the federal and state government, nothing against local commerce.

Second decree: directed at the command of the 31st Military Zone with headquarters in Rancho Nuevo, of the federal government, to invite the body of officers, classes and troops to abandon the ranks of the evil government and pass, with all of their instruments and all of their experience, to the side of the struggle of the people. In case the garrison of the 31st Military Zone does not accept the abandonment of the cause of the evil government and embrace the cause of the people, then I am ordered to ask for the unconditional surrender of those barracks at the date and time that it be communicated appropriately. I make public, therefore, the offer for the 31st Military Zone and the battalions and units of the Federal Army to abandon the federal government and join our cause in one single army, respecting their ranks and their chain of command. [applause]

It has already been agreed and tomorrow a commission is ready to certify that we did not harm anyone: It will be allowed to leave on the side of Tuxtla. After this time [six in the morning] when the delegation is formed and can see that nothing happened to them, you will be able to leave the city on the side I already mentioned, and you will be able to come here for a safe conduct so that they will let you pass. We are speaking with the National Human Rights Commission so that there can be a representative of theirs on the other side to guarantee the passage of tourists without being harmed by the federal troops. This is a negotiation that we are doing. What we can guarantee is that when this delegation is formed, we will let them out. What happens beyond our lines? Go at your own risk. That's clear. Here they are fewer, but some people have approached us to ask how they can help us. I have told them clearly that what we hope is that they will understand the justice of our demands.

You may not agree with the path that we have chosen, but you have to understand that the conditions that brought us to this are very cruel and very desperate. If you can understand that, it is a great help to us. If you realize that we have done everything possible to respect your lives, your goods, because the problem is not with you, and if you can also take it into account, because right now the press and the propaganda are saying very much that we are raping, stealing, robbing gasoline stations, looting businesses and many things that you have seen with your own eyes, we have not done here in San Cristóbal. If anyone would like to go further [applause] . . . Also, here a person is telling me to make public the guarantees that we give to all civilians regardless of their political affiliation, nationality, race, or creed, that they will not be touched by our forces.

Whenever we can, what I want to say to people that want to go further, if you can give some food or money, it would be welcome. You know that we do not steal. Whoever wants to help us in something more material, they can give us that, food and money. If you cannot or do not want to, it is enough [to] understand why we did this. Then, we will be satisfied.

We will continue towards the regular troops of the Zapatista National Liberation Army and the orders that our leadership gives us to go where they direct us. Now they are sending us to Rancho Nuevo. Well, it will be there. If it is on the other side, then to the other side we'll go. But it should be clear that we are inviting the federal troops to come over to our side. That is all, if you have any question, that is all I can say. Don't worry about your goods or your persons. They will be respected, as will your liberty. In case of problems, we are not going to take hostages or take anyone by force with us to protect us. In the case that we have to leave, or that we have to fight, that is the guarantee, that we will not take civilians or hostages . . . [vigorous applause].

We will fight until the fall of the capital of the Republic. My compañeros have said it very clearly in their declaration of war, that their fundamental demands imply the creation of a transitional government that calls for elections, clean, real elections, and for that they are calling for the House of Deputies and the House of Senators to disregard and unseat the illegitimate president, Carlos Salinas de Gortari, and from among them a coalition government of various parties and people of known prestige; a transitional government that would call for clean elections so that the will of the people could win. That is what the compañeros explain. I was ready to talk with anyone but the only thing they have sent is airplanes. That should be clear: We have not denied the dialogue to anyone. There has been no attempt, other than that of the National Human Rights Commission, which did approach us to ask for the free passage of foreigners. All of us are Mexicans. The movement is national, and among our troops that fight here are people who have visited various states of the Republic but mainly the troops that are here are Chia-panecos and mainly Indigenous. We are not requiring the reaching of an accord as a condition for leaving San Cristóbal. We may leave even though there is no accord, according to orders that may tell us to leave and attack another place. We would have to march to other places. In this case Tuxtla, since if the order is that we have to go there, we have nothing to do here. What I want you to understand is our situation here. We have not prohibited any commerce, not the gas stations, not the bus stations, not the mini-buses, not that, nor have we prohibited the radio stations. The only thing we have pro-hibited is leaving the city because we cannot guarantee that the federal troops will respect you. As for the rest, we have not done anything but get things a bit dirty. That we have done, but we will try to fix that as well, very soon. So we advise with this, then, to the small and medium businesses, that they will not be touched, only the business that is of the federal and state government.

[Marcos is speaking again.]

M: Let me finish.
Q: Wait a minute.
M: Of course, finish.
Q: Compañeros of Chiapas, Indians, permit me a minute, if you were brought tortillas, water, pozolito, would you accept it?
M: Yes, of course. That is what we are eating. That is the situation. What has to continue is our advance to Mexico City. We started this very day. Today the North American Free Trade Agreement begins, which is nothing more than a death sentence to the Indige-nous ethnicities of Mexico, who are perfectly dispensable in the modernization program of Salinas de Gortari. Then the com-pañeros decided to rise up on that same day to respond to the decree of death that the Free Trade Agreement gives them, with the decree of life that is given by rising up in arms to demand lib-erty and democracy, which will take them to the solution to their problems. This is the reason that we have risen up today. Any other questions, because they are going to cut me off?
Q: We don't want free trade. What is happening?
M: What I know is nothing more than you know. There were displays of adherence and sympathy in four or five states of the Republic, among them Veracruz, Oaxaca, Puebla and another state in the North that I can't remember. Our organization will also speak on

a national level. A column was lost as they entered and then they went in there, they left to look, but we are not going to enter any civilian house. We did not do it when you were sleeping [applause], and won't now that you are awake. I think we did well, because you did not awaken until very late. [applause]

FIRST DECLARATION FROM THE
LACANDÓN JUNGLE
EZLN's Declaration of War
"Today we say 'enough is enough!' (Ya Basta!)"

THIS is the declaration of war read by the EZLN commandantes from the balcony of the Palacio Municipal on the morning of January 1, 1994, the first day of NAFTA.

The declaration is terse and intense, fitting the purpose of going to war. It locates itself within the long struggle of Mexican history, making no reference to other revolutionary traditions. It claims the authority of the Mexican Constitution, Article 39 of which declares an "inalienable right to alter" the form of government when it becomes repressive. Its focus is on the particular Mexican problem of having a "dictatorship" of a single party (the PRI) in charge of both the state and the Army. The declaration therefore calls on "other branches of the nation's government" to depose Carlos de Gortari Salinas and "restore the legality and the stability of the nation." It declares belligerent status for the EZLN and calls for international monitoring of the Geneva conventions on warfare. And finally, it summarizes its platform in a series of historic code words of Mexican revolutionaries: work, land, housing, food, health care, education, independence, liberty, democracy, justice, and peace.

The Zapatistas thus break quickly from calls for socialism or vanguard notions of replacing the state with a "dictatorship of the proletariat" or any other new apparatus. They are careful to tailor their demands to restructure the state consistently with the Constitution. The declaration is a mixture of armed struggle and reformism.

The declaration also proposes to advance on Mexico City while "conquering the Mexican federal Army," a concept that seems hopelessly out of touch with reality.

What did the Zapatistas mean? Marcos later described a plan to seize the hydroelectric facilities near the Chiapas capital, which provide 45 percent of Mexican power, but did not explain how the plan was thwarted or dropped. In any case, the gap between the declaration's military rhetoric and the reality of EZLN uprisings in only five towns reinforced the official Mexican line that the rebellion was merely a local one marginal to the country's overall security.

The scholar John Womack makes the important point that the declaration includes no mention of Indians. Did the Zapatista emphasis on the indigenous only grow as they realized the limits on their national liberation project? It is unclear. The declaration itself begins with the words, "we are a product of 500 years of struggle," an unmistakable though indirect reference to the Conquest of the indigenous. Marcos's interviews on January 1 made explicit reference to the Indian character of the uprising and the army's composition. Later, Marcos claimed that the declaration's drafting committee, including indigenous members, chose intentionally to focus on the national issue. If that is so, the emphasis on the Indian roots of the struggle, on the Indian as the repressed soul and constituency of Mexico, became explicit and primary only later.

TO THE PEOPLE OF MEXICO:
MEXICAN BROTHERS AND SISTERS:

We are a product of 500 years of struggle: first against slavery, then during the War of Independence against Spain led by insurgents, then to avoid being absorbed by North American imperialism, then to promulgate our constitution and expel the French empire from our soil. Later the dictatorship of Porfirio Díaz denied us the just application of the Reform laws and the people rebelled; leaders like Villa and Zapata emerged: poor men just like us. We have been denied the most elemental preparation so they can use us as cannon fodder and pillage the wealth of our country. They don't care that we have nothing, absolutely nothing, not even a roof over our heads—no land, no work, no health care, no food, no education. Nor are we able to freely and democratically elect our political representatives, nor is there independence from foreigners, nor is there peace or justice for ourselves and our children.

But today, we say ENOUGH IS ENOUGH.

We are the inheritors of the true builders of our nation. We are the dispossessed. We are millions and we call upon our brothers and sisters to join this struggle, so that we will not die of hunger due to the insatiable ambition of a 70-year dictatorship led by a clique of traitors that represent the most conservative and sellout groups. They are the same ones that opposed Hidalgo and Morelos, the same ones that betrayed Vicente Guerrero, the same ones that sold half our country to the foreign invader, the same ones that imported a European prince to rule our country, the same ones that formed the "scientific" Porfirsta dictatorship, the same ones that opposed the Petroleum Expropriation, the same ones that massacred the railroad workers in 1958 and the students in 1968, the same ones that today take everything from us, absolutely everything.

To prevent the continuation of the above and as our last hope, after having tried to utilize all legal means based on our Constitution, we apply Article 39 of our Constitution which says:

> National Sovereignty essentially and originally resides in the people. All political power emanates from the people and its purpose is to help the people. The people have, at all times, the inalienable right to alter or modify their form of government.

Therefore, according to our constitution, we declare the following to the Mexican federal Army, the pillar of the Mexican dictatorship that we suffer from, monopolized by a one-party system and led by Carlos Salinas de Gortari, the maximum and illegitimate federal executive that today holds power.

According to this declaration of war, we ask that other powers of the nation advocate to restore the legitimacy and the stability of the nation by overthrowing the dictator.

We also ask that international organizations and the International Red Cross watch over and regulate our battles, so that our efforts are carried out while still protecting our civilian population. We declare now and always that we are subject to the Geneva Accord, with the EZLN as the fighting arm of our liberation struggle. We have the Mexican people on our side, and we have the beloved tri-colored flag. We use black and red in our uniforms as a symbol of our working people on strike. Our flag carries the letters EZLN, for Zapatista National Liberation Army, and we always carry our flag into combat.

Before we begin, we refuse any effort to disgrace our just cause by accusing us of being drug traffickers, drug guerrillas, thieves, or other names that might by used by our enemies. Our struggle follows the Constitution, which is held high by its call for justice and equality.

Therefore, according to this declaration of war, we give our military forces, the EZLN, the following orders:

First: Advance to the capital of the country, overcoming the Mexican federal Army, protecting during your advance the civilian population, and permitting the people in liberated area the right to freely and democratically elect their own administrative authorities.

Second: Respect the lives of prisoners and turn over all wounded to the International Red Cross.

Third: Initiate summary judgments against all soldiers of the Mexican federal Army and the political police that have received training or have been paid by foreigners, accused of being traitors to our country, and against all those who have repressed the civil population and robbed or stolen from or attempted crimes against the good of the people.

Fourth: Form new troops with all those Mexicans who show their interest in joining our struggle, including enemy soldiers who turn themselves in without having fought against us, and who promise to take orders from the General Command of the Zapatista National Liberation Army.

Fifth: We ask for the unconditional surrender of the enemy's headquarters before we begin any combat to avoid any loss of lives.

Sixth: Suspend the robbery of our natural resources in the areas controlled by the EZLN.

TO THE PEOPLE OF MEXICO:

We, the men and women of the EZLN, full and free, are conscious that the war that we have declared is a last resort, but also a just one. The dictators have been applying an undeclared genocidal war against our people for many years. Therefore we ask for your participation in and support of this plan that struggles for work, land, housing, food, health care, education, independence, freedom, democracy, justice, and peace. We declare that we will not stop fighting until the basic demands of our people have been met by forming a government of our country that is free and democratic.

JOIN THE INSURGENT FORCES OF THE
ZAPATISTA NATIONAL LIBERATION ARMY.

General Command of the EZLN
1993

SECOND DECLARATION
FROM THE LACANDÓN JUNGLE
"Today we say: We will not surrender!"

THIS declaration was issued six months after the January 1994 uprising.

The 12-day shooting war ended in Chiapas on January 12. Guerrillas did not rise in other parts of Mexico. But "civil society" awakened, with thousands of protestors in Mexico City and elsewhere. Their opposition to Salinas's military offensive was effective. The Zapatistas took careful note of civil society's other demand: to give peace a chance, to negotiate, to build a nonviolent alternative to another round of violence. The shadow of violence then darkened the land as the PRI's presidential candidate, Luis Donaldo Colosio, was assassinated by a "lone gunman" at point blank range. Meanwhile, peace negotiations between the Indians of the EZLN and the Salinas government began in San Cristóbal in February, but soon collapsed.

The Second Declaration credited civil society for preventing an all-out military offensive by the Salinas regime. It accepted a cease-fire to permit civil society to organize further, to create a nonviolent alternative. It expressed a vision of civil society as the birthplace of a new political culture which eventually might give rise to "political parties of a new type," but in the meantime served as "the waiting room of the new Mexico." Finally, it called for a coming together of Mexicans of all backgrounds in a "democratic, national convention"—which occurred in August, when thousands trekked to the jungle for a weeklong dialogue.

Womack notes that the Second Declaration lacks any reference to Indians, but he misses the clear emergence of an Indian consciousness, mythic symbols, and language. The dead of the mountains have spoken to the people of corn, asking that they "organize the dignity that resists and does not sell itself." Here for the first time is the Zapatista slogan, "For everyone, everything, for ourselves, nothing." On one level, this represents an affirmation that the EZLN does not seek power, is not a new caste of caudillos. But it appears here not as a slogan (like *Basta Ya!*) but in an Indian cadence: "The drums sounded, and in the voice of the land our pain spoke, and our history spoke our pain and our history spoke. 'For everyone, everything,' our dead say. So long as this is not so, there will be nothing for us."

It is difficult to believe that this was a mere strategic and tactical shift in rhetoric and priorities. That this is not an EZLN retreat to only an "Indian agenda" is clear from the call to the larger civil society. But the declaration marks the beginning of an explicitly Indian emphasis. Perhaps the struggle itself had uncovered and expressed its true nature, the voice of the Mexico profundo described by Guillermo Bonfil as the indigenous tradition lying hidden under the modern Mexican character and state. (See Guillermo Bonfil, Mexico Profundo: Una Civilizacion Negada [The Deep Mexico: A Civilization Denied], Mexico City: Grijalbo, 1989. Also see Enrique Rajchenberg and Catherine Heau-Lambert, "History and Symbolism in the Zapatista Movement," in *Reinventing Revolution in Mexico,* ed. John Holloway and Eloina Pelaez, London, Pluto Press, 1998, p. 24.)

Those who bear swords aren't the only ones who lose blood or who shine with the fleeting light of military glory. They aren't the only ones who should have a voice in designating the leaders of the government of a people who want democracy; this right to choose belongs to every citizen who has fought in the press or in the courts. It belongs to every citizen who identifies with the ideals of the Revolution and who has fought against the despotism that has ignored our laws. Tyranny isn't eliminated just by fighting on the battlefield; dictatorships and empires are also overthrown by launching cries of freedom and terrible threats against those who are executing the people. . . . Historical events have shown us that the destruction of tyranny and the overthrow of all evil governments are the work of ideas together with the sword. It is therefore an absurdity, an aberration, an outrageous despotism to deny the people the right to elect their government. The people's sovereignty is formed by all those people in society who are conscious of their rights and who, whether civilian or armed, love freedom and justice and work for the good of the country.

—PAULINO MARTINEZ, Zapatista delegate to the Revolutionary Sovereignty Convention, Aguascalientes, Mexico, on behalf of Emiliano Zapata.
OCTOBER 27, 1914

///

To the people of Mexico:

To the peoples and governments of the world:

Brothers and Sisters:

The Zapatista National Liberation Army, on a war footing against the government since January 1, 1994, addresses itself to you in order to make known its opinion.

Mexican Brothers and Sisters:

In December, 1993, we said, "Enough!" On January 1, 1994, we called on the legislative and judicial powers to assume their constitutional responsibility and to restrain the genocidal policies that the federal executive imposes on our people. We base our constitutional right in the application of Article 39 of the Constitution of the United Mexican States:

> National sovereignty essentially and originally resides in the people. All political power emanates from the people and its purpose is to help the people. The people have, at all times, the inalienable right to alter or modify their form of government.

The government responded to this call with a policy of extermination and lies. The powers in Mexico ignored our just demand and permitted a massacre. However, this massacre only lasted 12 days. Another force, a force superior to any political or military power, imposed its will on the parties involved in the conflict. Civil society assumed the duty of preserving our country. It showed its disapproval of the massacre and it forced a dialogue with the government. We understand that the ascendancy of the political party that has been in power for so long cannot be allowed to continue. We understand that this party, a party that has kept the fruits of every Mexican's labor for itself, cannot be allowed to continue. We understand that the corruption of the presidential elections that sustains this party impedes our freedom and should not be allowed to continue. We understand that the culture of fraud is the method with which this party imposes and impedes democracy. We understand that justice only exists for the corrupt and powerful. We understand that we must construct a society in which those who lead do so with the will of the people. There is no other path.

This is understood by every honest Mexican in civil society. Only those who have based their success on the theft of the public trust, those who protect criminals and murderers by prostituting justice, those who resort to political murder and electoral fraud in order to impose their will, are opposed to our demands.

These antiquated politicians plan to roll back history and erase the cry from the national consciousness that was taken up by the country after January 1, 1994. Enough!

We will not permit this. Today we do not call on those weak powers in Mexico that refuse to assume their constitutional duties and which permit themselves to be controlled by the federal executive. If the legislature and the judges have no dignity, then others who do understand that they must serve the people, and not the individual, will step forward. Our call transcends the question of presidential terms or the upcoming election. Our sovereignty resides in civil society. Only the people can alter or modify our form of government. It is to them that we address this Second Declaration from the Lacandón Jungle.

First: We have respected the international conventions of warfare while we have carried out our military actions. These conventions have allowed us to be recognized as a belligerent force by national and foreign forces. We will continue to respect these conventions.

Second: We order all of our regular and irregular forces, both inside national territory and outside the country, to continue to obey the unilateral cease-fire. We will continue to respect the cease-fire in order to permit civil society to organize toward the goal of achieving a transition to democracy in our country.

Third: We condemn the threats against civilian society brought about by the militarization of the country, both in terms of personal and modern repressive equipment, during this time leading up to the federal elections. Without a doubt, the Salinas government is trying to impose its will by fraud. We will not permit this.

Fourth: We propose to all independent political parties that are suffering from intimidation and repression of political rights—the same intimidation and repression that our people have suffered for the last 65 years—that they declare themselves in favor of a government transition toward democracy.

Fifth: We reject the manipulation and the attempts to separate our just demands from the demands of the Mexican people. We are Mexicans, and we will not put aside our demands nor our arms until we have democracy, freedom, and justice for all.

Sixth: We reiterate our disposition toward finding a political solution to the transition to democracy in Mexico. We call upon civil society to retake the protagonist's role that it first took up in order to stop the military phase of the war. We call upon civil society to organize itself in order to direct the peaceful efforts toward democracy, freedom, and justice. Democratic change is the only alternative to war.

Seventh: We call on all honest sectors of civil society to attend a National Dialogue for Democracy, Freedom and Justice.

FOR THIS REASON WE SAY:

Brothers and Sisters:

After the start of the war in January, 1994, the organized cry of the Mexican people stopped the fighting and called for a dialogue between the contending forces. The federal government responded to the just demands of the EZLN with a series of offers that didn't touch on the essential problem: the lack of justice, freedom, and democracy in Mexican territory.

The offers with which the federal government responded to the demands of the EZLN were limited by the system of the political party in power. This system has made possible sectors in the Mexican countryside that have superseded the power of the Constitution, and whose roots have maintained the party in power. This system has made possible the existence and belligerence of the caciques, the omnipotent power of the ranchers and businessmen, and the spread of drug trafficking. Just the fact that the government offered us the so-called proposals for a dignified peace in Chiapas provoked tremendous agitation and an open defiance by these sectors. The single-party political system is trying to maneuver within this reduced horizon. It can't alienate these sectors without attacking itself, yet it can't leave things as they are without having to face the anger of the campesinos and indigenous peoples. In other words, to go through with the proposals would necessarily mean the death of the state party system. By suicide or execution, the death of the current Mexican political system is a necessary precondition for the transition to democracy in our country. There will be no real solutions in Chiapas until the situation in Mexico as a whole is resolved.

The EZLN understands that the problem of poverty in Mexico isn't due just to a lack of resources. Our fundamental understanding and position is that whatever efforts are made will only postpone the problem if these efforts aren't made within the context of new local, regional, and national political relationships—relationships marked by democracy, freedom, and justice. The problem of power is not a question of who rules, but of who exercises power. If it is exercised by a majority of the people, the political parties will be obligated to put their proposals forward to the people instead of merely relating to each other.

Looking at the problem of power within the context of democracy, freedom, and justice will create a new political culture within the parties. A new type of political leader will be born and, without a doubt, new types of political parties will be born as well.

We aren't proposing a new world, but something preceding a new world: an antechamber looking into the new Mexico. In this sense, this revolution will not end in a new class, faction of a class, or group in power. It will end in a free and democratic space for political struggle. This free and democratic space will be born on the rotting cadaver of the state party system and the tradition of fixed presidential succession. A new political relationship will be born, a relationship based not in the confrontation of political organizations with each other, but in the confrontation of their political proposals with different social classes. Political leadership will depend on the support of these social classes, and not on the mere exercise of power. In this new political relationship, different political proposals (socialism, capitalism, social democracy, liberalism, Christian democracy, etc.) will have to convince a majority of the nation that their proposal is the best for the country. The groups in power will be watched by the people in such a way that they will be obligated to give a regular accounting of themselves, and the people will be able to decide whether those groups remain in power or not. The plebiscite is a regulated form of confrontation among the nation, political parties, and power, and it merits a place in the highest law of the country.

Current Mexican law is too constricting for these new political relationships between the governed and the governors. A national democratic convention is needed from which a provisional or transitional government can emerge, be it by the resignation of the federal executive or by an election.

This national democratic convention and transitional government should lead to the creation of a new constitution, and, in the context of this new constitution, new elections should be held. The pain that this process will bring to the country will be less than the damage that would be caused by a civil war. The prophecy of the southeast is valid for the entire country. We can learn from what has already occurred so that there is less pain during the birth of the new Mexico.

The EZLN has its idea of what system and proposal are best for the country. The political maturity of the EZLN as a representative of a sector of the nation is shown by the fact that it doesn't want to impose its proposal on the country. The EZLN demands what is shown by its own example: the political maturity of Mexico and the right for all to decide, freely and democratically, the course that Mexico must take. Not only will a better and more just Mexico emerge from this historic synthesis, but a new Mexico as well. This is why we are gambling our lives: so that the Mexicans of the future can inherit a country in which it isn't shameful to live.

The EZLN, in a democratic exercise without precedent in an armed organization, consulted its component bases about whether or not to sign the peace accords presented by the federal government. The indigenous bases of the EZLN, seeing that the central demands of democracy, freedom, and justice have yet to be resolved, decided against signing the government's proposal.

Under siege and under pressure from different sectors that threatened us with extermination if the peace accords weren't signed, we Zapatistas reaffirmed our commitment to achieve a peace with justice and dignity. In our struggle, the dignified struggle of our ancestors has found a home. The cry of dignity of the insurgent Vincente Guererro, "Live for the country or die for freedom," once again sounds from our throats. We cannot accept an undignified peace.

Our path sprang out of the impossibility of struggling peacefully for our elemental rights as human beings. The most valuable of these rights is the right to decide, freely and democratically, what form the government will take. Now the possibility of a peaceful change to democracy and freedom confronts a new test: the electoral process that will take place this August. There are those who are betting on the outcome of the elections and the post-election period. There are those who are predicting apathy and disillusionment. They hope to profit from the blood of those who fall in the struggles, both violent and peaceful, in the cities and in the countryside. They found their political project in the conflict they hope will come after the elections. They hope that the political demobilization will once again open the door to war. They say that they will save the country.

Others hope that the armed conflict will restart before the elections so that they can take advantage of the chaotic situation to keep themselves in power. Just as they did before, when they usurped popular will with electoral fraud, these people hope to take advantage of a pre-electoral civil war in order to prolong the agony of a dictatorship that has already lasted decades. There are others, sterile naysayers, who reason that war is inevitable and who are waiting to watch their enemy's cadaver float by . . . or their friend's cadaver. The sectarians suppose, erroneously, that just the firing of a gun will bring about the dawn that our people have waited for since night fell upon Mexican soil with the death of Villa and Zapata.

Every one of these people who steals hope supposes that behind our weapons are ambition and an agenda that will guide us to the future. They are wrong. Behind our weapons is another weapon: reason. Hope gives life to both of our weapons. We won't let them steal our hope.

The hope that came with the trigger came about at the beginning of the year. It is precisely now that the hope that comes with political mobilization takes up the protagonist's role that belongs to it by right and reason. The flag is now in the hands of those who have names and faces, good and honest people who have the same goal that we yearn for. Our greetings to these men and women—and our hope that you can carry the flag to where it should be. We will be standing there waiting for you with dignity. If the flag should fall, we will be there to pick it up again.

Now is the time for hope to organize itself and to walk forward in the valleys and in the cities, as it did in the mountains of the southeast. Fight with your weapons; don't worry about ours. We know how to resist to the end. We know how to wait. . . . And we know what to do if the doors through which dignity walks close once again.

This is why we address our brothers and sisters in different nongovernmental organizations, in campesino and indigenous organizations, workers in the cities and in the countryside, teachers and students, housewives and squatters, artists and intellectuals, members of independent political parties, Mexicans.

We call all of you to a national dialogue with the theme of democracy, freedom, and justice. For this reason, we put forward the following invitation to a national democratic convention:

WE, THE ZAPATISTA National Liberation Army, fighting to achieve the democracy, freedom, and justice that our country deserves, and considering that:

One: The supreme government has usurped the legality that we inherited from the hero of the Mexican Revolution.

Two: The Constitution that exists doesn't reflect the popular will of the Mexican people.

Three: The resignation of the federal executive usurper isn't enough and that a new law is necessary for the new country that will be born from the struggles of all honest Mexicans.

Four: Every form of struggle is necessary in order to achieve the transition to democracy in Mexico.

Considering these things, we call for a sovereign and revolutionary national democratic convention from which will come a transitional government and a new national law, a new Constitution that will guarantee the legal fulfillment of the people's will.

This sovereign revolutionary convention will be national in that all states of the federation will be represented. It will be plural in the sense that all patriotic sectors will be represented. It will be democratic in the way in which it will make decisions by national consultations.

The convention will be presided over, freely and voluntarily, by civilians, prestigious public figures, regardless of their political affiliation, race, religion, sex, or age.

The convention will be launched by local, state, and regional committees in every ejido, settlement, school, and factory. These committees of the convention will be in charge of collecting the people's proposals for the new Constitution and the demands to be completed by the new government that comes out of the convention.

The convention should demand free and democratic elections and should fight for the people's will to be respected.

The Zapatista National Liberation Army will recognize the national democratic convention as the authentic representative of the interests of the Mexican people in their transition to democracy.

The Zapatista National Liberation Army is now to be found throughout national territory and is in a position to offer itself to the Mexican people as an army to guarantee that the people's will is carried out.

For the first meeting of the National Democratic Convention, the EZLN offers as a meeting place a Zapatista settlement with all of the resources to be found there.

The date and place of the first session of the National Democratic Convention will be announced when it is appropriate to do so.

MEXICAN BROTHERS AND Sisters:

Our struggle continues. The Zapatista flag still waves in the mountains of the Mexican southeast and today we say: We will not surrender!

Facing the mountains we speak to our dead so that their words will guide us along the path that we must walk.

The drums sound, and in the voices from the land we hear our pain and our history.

"Everything for everyone," say our dead. "As long as this is not true, there will be nothing for us.

"Find in your hearts the voices of those for whom we fight. Invite them to walk the dignified path of those who have no faces. Call them to resist. Let no one receive anything from those who rule. Ask them to reject the handouts from the powerful. Let all the good people in this land organize with dignity. Let them resist and not sell out.

"Don't surrender! Resist! Resist with dignity in the lands of the true men and women! Let the mountains shelter the pain of the people of this land. Don't surrender! Resist! Don't sell out! Resist!"

Our dead spoke these words from their hearts. We have seen that the words of our dead are good, that there is truth in what they say and dignity in their counsel. For this reason we call on our brother and sister Mexicans to resist with us. We call on the indigenous campesinos to resist with us. We call on the workers, squatters, housewives, students, teachers, intellectuals, writers—on all those with dignity—to resist with us. The government doesn't want democracy in our land. We will accept nothing that comes from the rotting heart of the government, not a single coin nor a single dose of medication, not a single stone nor a single grain of food. We will not accept the handouts that the government offers in exchange for our dignity.

We will not take anything from the supreme government. Although they increase our pain and sorrow, although death may accompany us, although we may see others selling themselves to the hand that oppresses them, although everything may hurt and sorrow may cry out from the rocks, we will not accept anything. We will resist. We will not take anything from the government. We will resist until those who are in power exercise their power while obeying the people's will.

BROTHERS AND SISTERS:

Don't sell out. Resist with us. Don't surrender. Resist with us. Repeat along with us, "We will not surrender! We will resist!" Let these words be heard not only in the mountains of the Mexican southeast, but in the north and on the peninsulas. Let it be heard on both coasts. Let it be heard in the center of the country. Let it cry out in the valleys and in the mountains. Let it sound in the cities and in the countryside. Unite your voices, brothers and sisters. Cry out with us: "We will not surrender! We will resist!"

Let dignity break the siege and lift off of us the filthy hands with which the government is trying to strangle us. We are all under siege. They will not let democracy, freedom, and justice enter Mexican territory. Brothers and sisters, we are all under siege. We will not surrender! We will resist! We have dignity! We will not sell out!

What good are the riches of the powerful if they aren't able to buy the most valuable thing in these lands? If the dignity of the Mexican people has no price, then what good is the power of the powerful?

Dignity will not surrender!
Dignity will resist!
Democracy!
Freedom!
Justice!

From the mountains of the Mexican Southeast,
Clandestine Revolutionary Indigenous Committee—
General Command of the Zapatista National Liberation Army
Mexico, June, 1994.

THIRD DECLARATION FROM
THE LACANDÓN JUNGLE
The EZLN Calls for the Formation of a National Liberation Movement

Translated by Cecilia Rodriguez and Cindy Arnold.

A year after the EZLN uprising, Mexico continued to reverberate with shocks. On September 28, 1994, the secretary-general of the PRI was assassinated, an event that appeared connected to internal tensions in the ruling party. The following year PRI candidate Ernesto Ponce de Leon Zedillo was elected president, another US-trained-technocrat at the helm of the Mexican state. In December, the peso collapsed, beginning a 1930s-style depression across Mexico. Zedillo, who blamed the Zapatistas, threatened a tightening military encirclement of Chiapas.

But the Zapatistas went on the offensive in unpredicted ways. In the Chiapas state, pro-Zapatista journalist Amado Avendano, was defeated in a fraudulent election. Immediately, the pro-Zapatista "civil society" turned to civil disobedience, disrupting transportation and communications across the state. While 25,000 marched in San Cristóbal, the EZLN seized control of several communities and declared them autonomous zones. Avendano became the pro-Zapatista "governor in resistance," creating a virtual situation of parallel power (he was almost killed in a mysterious traffic "accident"). Then in December, the EZLN launched a surprise response to the Army siege by suddenly appearing in 38 more municipalities. Marcos wrote Zedillo saying "it is my duty to inform you that you have an Indian rebellion in the Nation's southeast."

In this context the EZLN once again called for civil society to step up its resistance lest the bloodshed resume. This time they linked the indigenous question with the national question explicitly. The tone of the declaration overall is similar to the declaration of war one year earlier, with its intense demands that the "bad government" (*mal gobierno*) be replaced at once by a transitional one able to guarantee "clean elections, credibility, equity, and nonpartisan and nongovernmental civic participation."

The earth and its dead are mentioned only briefly. This is a warning note, not without reason. Just a month after the declaration was issued, Zedillo ordered the Mexican Army to hunt down and capture Marcos and the EZLN high command in the Lacandón. The Army failed, not because civil society prevented them, but because the EZLN eluded them.

However, the Zedillo military offensive energized civil society to respond with protests. One hundred thousand marched in Mexico City. Hunger strikes broke out. The army offensive ended in February.

One year after the Zapatista uprising, today we say:

> The motherland lives! And she is ours! We have been disgraced, it is true; our luck has been bad many times, but the cause of Mexico, which is the cause of the people's rights and justice, has not succumbed. It has not died and it will not die because there still exist committed Mexicans, in whose hearts burn the sacred fire of patriotism. Wherever in the Republic weapons are clenched and the national banner flies, there—as well as here— will thrive the right of protest against force.

Understand the gullible man who has accepted the sad mission of being the instrument for enslaving a free people: His vacillating throne does not rest on the free will of the nation, but rather on the blood and corpses of thousands of Mexicans who have been sacrificed because they defended their freedom and their rights.

Mexicans: Those who have the disgrace to live under the dominion of the usurpers, do not resign yourselves to putting up with the yoke of oppression that weighs on you. Do not delude yourselves with the perfidious insinuations of the followers of the consummated deeds, because they are and have been always the followers of despotism. The existence of arbitrary power is a permanent violation of people's rights and Justice, which neither the passage of time nor arms can ever justify, and whose destruction is necessary to honor Mexico and humanity.

I declare myself: in action and deeds, just as resolute as in the first day.

—BENITO JUAREZ, JANUARY 1865, CHIHUAHUA

To the people of Mexico:

To the peoples and governments of the world:

Brothers and sisters:

The first day of January of 1994 we released the "First Declaration of the Lacandón Jungle." On June 10, 1994 we released the "Second Declaration of the Lacandón Jungle." Both were inspired by the fervor of the struggle for democracy, liberty, and justice for all Mexicans.

In the first one we called upon the Mexican people to take up arms against the bad government, as the principal obstacle to democracy in our country. In the second one we called Mexicans to a civic and peaceful effort. This was the national democratic convention, which was to achieve the profound changes that the nation demanded.

While the supreme government demonstrated its falseness and haughtiness, we, by one gesture after another, dedicated ourselves to showing the Mexican people the justness of our demands and the dignity that motivated our struggle. Our weapons were put aside so that the legal struggle could demonstrate its possibilities . . . and its limitations. In the "Second Declaration of the Lacandón Jungle" the EZLN attempted to avoid the reinitiation of hostilities and to look for a political, dignified, and just solution to resolve the demands contained in the 11 points of our program for struggle:

housing, land, work, food, health, education, justice, independence, liberty, democracy, and peace.

The pre-electoral process in August 1994 brought hope to many that the transition to democracy was possible by means of the electoral process. Knowing that elections are not, in the current conditions, the road to democratic change, the EZLN accepted being put to one side in order to give legal political opposition forces the opportunity to struggle. The EZLN pledged its word and its effort to seeking a peaceful transition to democracy. In the national democratic convention the EZLN sought to become a civic and peaceful force—one which, without opposing the electoral process, would also not be consumed by it, and that would seek new forms of struggle that would include more democratic sectors in Mexico as well as linking itself with democratic movements in other parts of the world. August 21 ended the illusions of an immediate change through peaceful means. An electoral process that is corrupt, immoral, unfair, and illegitimate culminated in a new mockery of the goodwill of the citizens.

The party-state system reaffirmed its antidemocratic vocation and imposed, in all parts and at all levels, its arrogance. In the face of an unprecedented level of voter participation, the Mexican political system opted for intervention—and cut off people's hopes for the electoral process.

Reports from the National Democratic Convention, the Civic Alliance, and the Commission for Truth brought to light what the mass media had hidden, with shameful complicity: a gigantic fraud. The multitude of irregularities, the corruption, the cheating, the intimidation, the robbery, and the lying made the elections the dirtiest ones in Mexico's history. The high absentee rates in the local elections in Veracruz, Tlaxcala, and Tabasco showed that skepticism reigned within civil society in Mexico. Not satisfied with this, the party-state system repeated the fraud of August, imposing governors, mayors, and local congresses. As at the end of the nineteenth century, when the traitors held "elections" to justify the French intervention, today we are told that the nation approves of the continuation of an authoritarian imposition. The electoral process of August 1994 is a state crime. They should be judged as criminals and held responsible for this mockery.

On the other side, gradualism and hesitation appear in the words of the opposition members who accept this great fraud as a series of small "irregularities." A great dilemma in the struggle for democracy in Mexico reappears: The civic struggle bets upon a transition "without pain," a final blow which will light the road to democracy, and only prolongs the agony.

The case of Chiapas is only one of the consequences of this political system. Ignoring the longings of the people of Chiapas, the government repeated its dosage of imposition and domination.

Confronted by a broad movement of repudiation, the party-state system opts to repeat to society the lie of its triumph and to exacerbate the confrontations. The present polarization in southeastern Mexico is the responsibility of the government and demonstrates its incapacity to resolve, at their roots, the political and social problems of Mexico. Through corruption and repression the government tries to resolve a problem that can only be solved when the legitimate triumph of the will of the people of Chiapas is recognized. The EZLN has maintained itself, until now, at the margins of the popular mobilizations, even though it has been subjected to a great campaign of defamation and indiscriminate repression.

Waiting for signs of the government's willingness to accept a political, just, and dignified solution to the conflict, the EZLN watched, powerlessly, as the best sons and daughters of the dignity of Chiapas were assassinated, jailed, and threatened. The EZLN watched as their indigenous brothers and sisters in Guerrero, Oaxaca, Tabasco, Chihuahua, and Veracruz were repressed and received mockery as an answer to their demands for a solution to their living conditions.

During all of this period the EZLN resisted not only the military blockade and the threats and the intimidations by federal forces—they also resisted a campaign of slander and lies. During the first days of 1994, the government accused us of receiving foreign military support and financing. They tried to force us to give up our flags in exchange for money and government posts. They tried to delegitimize our struggle by reducing the national problem to a local indigenous context.

Meanwhile the supreme government prepared a military solution for the indigenous rebellion in Chiapas and in the nation despair and impatience arose. While claiming a desire for dialogue (that barely hid their desire to liquidate the Zapatista movement through asphyxiation), the bad government let time and death run rampant through the indigenous communities in the country.

Meanwhile the Revolutionary Institutional Party, the political arm of organized crime and drug traffickers, went into its most acute phase of decomposition, resorting to assassination as a method of solving its internal conflicts. Incapable of a civilized dialogue within its own party, the PRI bloodied the national soil. The shame of seeing the national colors usurped by the emblem of the PRI continues for all Mexicans.

The government and the country again forgot the original inhabitants of these lands. Cynicism and laziness returned to take possession of the nation. Along with their rights to the minimal conditions of life with dignity, the indigenous peoples were denied the right to govern according to their own reason and will. The deaths of our members became useless. Seeing that they did not leave us with any other alternative, the EZLN risked breaking the military blockade that surrounded it, and marched with the help of other indigenous brothers who were fed up with the despair and misery and tired of peaceful means. Seeking at all costs to avoid bloodying Mexican soil with the brothers' blood, the EZLN saw itself obliged to call the nation's attention anew to the grave conditions of Mexican indigenous life. We called attention especially to those who supposedly had received government help, and yet continued living in the misery that they inherited, year after year, for more than five centuries. With the offensive in December 1994, the EZLN sought to show—to Mexico and to the world—its proud indigenous essence and the impossibility of resolving the local situation without profound changes in political, economic, and social relations throughout the country.

The indigenous question will not have a solution if there is not a *radical* transformation of the national pact. The only means of incorporating, with justice and dignity, the indigenous of the nation, is to recognize the characteristics of their own social, political, and cultural organization. Autonomy is not separation; it is integration of the most humble and forgotten minorities of contemporary Mexico. This is how the EZLN understood the issue since its founding, and this is how the indigenous communities who make up the leadership of our organization have defined it.

Today we repeat: *Our struggle is national.*

We have been criticized for asking for too much. The Zapatistas, it is said, should be satisfied with the handouts that the bad government offers us. Those who are willing to die for a just and legitimate cause have the right to ask for everything. We Zapatistas are willing to give up the only thing we have, life, to demand democracy, liberty, and justice for all Mexicans.

Today we reaffirm: *For everyone, everything; nothing for us!*

At the end of 1994 the economic farce with which Salinas had deceived the nation and the international economy exploded. The nation of money called the grand gentlemen of power and arrogance to dinner, and they did not hesitate in betraying the soil and sky in which they prospered with Mexican blood. The economic crisis awoke Mexicans from the sweet and stupefying dream of entry into the first world. The nightmare of unemployment, scarcity, and misery will now be even more wearing for the majority of Mexicans.

1994, the year that has just ended, has shown the real face of the brutal system that dominates us. The economic, political, social, and repressive program of neoliberalism has demonstrated its inefficiency, its deceptions, and the cruel injustice that is its essence. Neoliberalism as a doctrine and as a reality should be flung into the trash heap of national history.

BROTHERS AND SISTERS:

Today, in the middle of this crisis, decisive action by all honest Mexicans is necessary in order to achieve a real and profound change in the destinies of the nation.

Today, after having called the people of Mexico first to arms and later to a civic and peaceful struggle, we now call them to struggle *by all means, at all levels, and in all parts of the country* for democracy, liberty, and justice, by means of this:

THIRD DECLARATION FROM THE LACANDÓN JUNGLE

We call to all social and political forces of the country, to all honest Mexicans, to all of those who struggle for the democratization of the national reality, to form a *national liberation movement*, including the national democratic convention and *all* forces, without distinction by religious creed, race, or political ideology, who are against the system of the state party. This national liberation movement will struggle from a common accord, by all means, at all levels, for the installation of a transitional government, a new constitutional body, a new Constitution, and the destruction of the party-state system. We call upon the national democratic convention and citizen Cuahtémoc Cárdenas Solorzano to head up this national liberation movement, as a broad opposition front.

We call upon the workers of the republic, the workers in the countryside and the cities, the neighborhood residents, the teachers and the students of Mexico, the women of Mexico, the young people of the whole country, the honest artists and intellectuals, the responsible religious members, the community-based militants of the different political organizations, to take up the means and forms of struggle that they consider possible and necessary, to struggle for the end of the party-state system, incorporating themselves into the national democratic convention if they do not belong to a party, and to the National Liberation Movement if they are active in any of the political opposition forces.

For now, in keeping with the spirit of this III Declaration of the Lacandón Jungle, we declare:

First: that from the federal government's custody be taken the Mexican flag, the justice system of the nation, the Mexican hymn, and the national emblem. These will now be under the care of the resistance forces until legality, legitimacy, and sovereignty are restored to all of the national territory.

Second: The original Constitution of the United Mexican States is declared valid, as written on February 5th, 1917, with the incorporation of the Revolutionary Laws of 1993 and inclusion of the Statutes of Autonomy for the indigenous regions, and will be held as valid until a new constitutional body is installed and a new Constitution is written.

Third: We call for the people of Mexico to struggle for recognition for the transitional governments to democracy. These shall be social and political organizations, defined by distinct communities for themselves, which maintain the federal pact agreed upon in the 1917 Constitution, and which are included without regard for religious creed, social class, political ideology, race, or sex, in the national liberation movement.

The EZLN will support the civilian population in the task of restoring legality, order, legitimacy, and national sovereignty, and in the struggle for the formation and installation of a national transitional government for democracy with the following characteristics:

1. The liquidation of the system of party-state and separation of the government from the PRI
2. The reform of electoral law in a way that guarantees clean elections, legitimacy, equity, nonpartisan and nongovernmental citizen participation, recognition of all national, regional, and local political forces, and that convenes new general elections in the federation
3. The convening of a body for the creation of a new Constitution
4. The recognition of the right of the indigenous groups to inclusive autonomy and citizenship
5. The reorientation of the national economic program, putting aside lies and deceptions, and favoring the most dispossessed sectors in the country, the workers and the peasants who are the principal producers of the wealth that others appropriate.

///

BROTHERS AND SISTERS:

Peace will come hand in hand with democracy, liberty, and justice for all Mexicans. Our path cannot find the peace and justice which our dead demand if it is at the cost of our Mexican dignity. The earth does not rest: It walks in our hearts. The mockery to our dead demands that we struggle to wash away their shame. We will resist. The oppression and the arrogance will be overthrown.

As with Benito Juarez in the face of French intervention, the Motherland marches today at the side of the patriotic forces, against the anti-democratic forces and authorities. Today we say:

The Motherland lives! And she is ours!
Democracy!
Liberty!
Justice!
From the mountains of Southeastern Mexico
Clandestine Indigenous Revolutionary Committee
—General Command of the Zapatista National Liberation Army
Mexico, January 1995

FOURTH DECLARATION
FROM THE LACANDÓN JUNGLE

TWO years had passed since the uprising. Having survived the Army's offensive, having preserved its expanded autonomous zone, having begun to negotiate with the Zedillo government on Indian autonomy at San Andres, the EZLN once again called for a national liberation movement and this time took steps to create it. Forty thousand pro-Zapatista activists fanned out across Mexico for an independent national referendum on their platform. By late August, 1.2 million people had expressed their preferences. Ninety percent approved a "broad opposition front," though only 57 percent for the EZLN's restructuring into an independent political force. Back in Chiapas, the EZLN continued building more encampments for its "encounters" with civil society.

This declaration is by far the most lyrical and most Indian, beginning with its statement that "the flower of the word will not die." It names scores of Indian communities. It speaks of struggling against oblivion. The description of solidarity from civil society sounds five centuries in the making. Its statement that "the world we want is one where many worlds fit" would touch people across the world. The declaration, while programmatically calling for a national liberation front, marks the passage of Zapatismo into the lyrical world of Mexico profundo. In a war for indigenous identity against oblivion, the identity itself comes to the foreground. To make a revolution, the identity *profundo* must be reclaimed, and "only those who surrender their history will return to oblivion."

TODAY WE SAY: WE ARE HERE. WE ARE REBEL DIGNITY, THE FORGOTTEN OF THE HOMELAND

All those communities, all those who work the land, all whom we invite to stand on our side so that together we may give life a single struggle, so that we may walk with your help.

We must continue to struggle until the land is our own, property of the people, of our grandfathers, and out of the shadow of those who loom over us, who command us. Together we must raise with the strength of our hearts and our hands held high, that beautiful banner of the dignity and freedom of we who work the land. We must continue to struggle until we defeat those who have crowned themselves, those who have helped to take the land from others, those who make much money with the labor of people like us, those who mock us in their estates. That is our obligation of honor, if we want to be called men of honesty and good inhabitants of our communities.

Now more than ever we need to be united, with all our hearts and all our efforts in that great task of marvelous and true unity, with those who began the struggle, who preserve purity in their heart, guard their principles, and do not lose faith in a good life.

We beg that those who receive this manifesto pass it on to all the men and women of those communities.

—REFORM, LIBERTY, Justice and Law Chief General of the
Southern Liberation Army Emiliano Zapata
[original Zapatista manifesto written in Nahuatl]

I

To the People of Mexico:

To the peoples and governments of the world:

Brothers and sisters:

The flower of the word will not die. The masked face which today has a name may die, but the word which came from the depth of history and the earth can no longer be cut by the arrogance of the powerful. We were born of the night. We live in the night. We will die in her. But there will be light tomorrow for others, for all those who today weep at the night, for those who have been denied the day, for those for whom death is a gift, for those who are denied life. The light will be for all of them. For everyone, everything. For us pain and anguish, for us the joy of rebellion, for us a future denied, for us the dignity of insurrection. For us, nothing.

Our fight has been to make ourselves heard, and the evil government screams arrogance and closes its ears with its cannon.

Our fight is caused by hunger, and the gifts of the evil government are lead and paper for the stomachs of our children.

Our fight is for a roof over our heads which has dignity, and the evil government destroys our homes and our history.

Our fight is for knowledge, and the evil government distributes ignorance and disdain.

Our fight is for the land, and the evil government gives us cemeteries.

Our fight is for a job which is just and dignified, and the evil government buys and sells our bodies and our shames.

Our fight is for life, and the evil government offers death as our future.

Our fight is for respect for our right to sovereignty and self-government, and the evil government imposes laws of the few on the many.

Our fight is for liberty of thought, and the evil government builds jails and graves.

Our fight is for justice, and the evil government consists of criminals and assassins.

Our fight is for history, and the evil government proposes to erase history.

Our fight is for the homeland, and the evil government dreams with the flag and the language of foreigners.

Our fight is for peace, and the evil government brings war and destruction.

Housing, land, employment, food, education, independence, democracy, liberty, justice, and peace. These were our banners at the dawn of 1994. These were our demands during that long night of 500 years. These, today, are our necessities.

Our blood and our word have lit a small fire in the mountain. We walk a path against the house of money and the powerful. Brothers and sisters of other races and languages, of other colors — but with the same heart — now protect our light and drink of the same fire.

The powerful came to extinguish us with violent wind, but our light grew in other lights. The rich still dream about extinguishing the first light. But their attempts are useless; there are now too many lights, and they have all become the first.

The arrogant wish to extinguish a rebellion which they mistakenly believe began in the dawn of 1994. But the rebellion which now has a dark face and an indigenous language was not born today. It spoke before with other languages and in other lands. This rebellion against injustice spoke in many mountains and many histories. It has already spoken in Nahuatl, Paipai, Kiliwa, Cucapa, Cochimi, Kumiai, Yuma, Seri, Chontal, Chinanteco, Pame, Chichimeca, Otomi, Mazahua, Matlatzinca, Ocuilteco, Zapoteco, Solteco, Chatino, Papabuco, Mixteco, Cucateco, Triqui, Amuzzgo, Mazateco, Chocho, Ixcaateco, Huave, Tlapaneco, Totonaca, Tepehua, Populuca, Mixe, Zoque, Huasteco, Lacandón, Mayo, Chol, Tzeltal, Tzotzil, Tojolabal, Mame, Teco, Ixil, Aguacateco, Motocintleco, Chicomucelteco.

They want to take the land so that our feet have nothing to stand on. They want to take our history so that we and our word will be forgotten and die. They do not want Indians. They want us dead.

The powerful want our silence. When we were silent, we died; without the word we did not exist. We fight against this loss of memory, against death, and for life. We fight the fear of death because we have ceased to exist in memory.

When the homeland speaks its Indian heart, it will have dignity and memory.

BROTHERS AND SISTERS:

On January 1, 1995, after breaking the military blockade with which the evil government pretended to submerge us in surrender and isolation, we called upon the people to construct a broad opposition front which would unite those democratic voices which exist against the state-party system: the national liberation movement. Although the beginning of this effort at unity encountered many problems, it lives still in the thoughts of those men and women who reject conformity when they see their homeland under the rule of the powerful and of foreign money. This broad opposition front, after following a route filled with difficulty and misunderstandings, is about to concretize its first proposals and agreements for coordinated action. The long process of this organizing effort will bear fruit this new year. We Zapatistas salute the birth of this movement for national liberation and we hope that among those who form it there will always be a zeal for unity and a respect for differences.

Once the dialogue with the government began, the commitment of the EZLN to a political solution to the war begun in 1994 was betrayed. Pretending to want dialogue, the evil government opted for a cowardly military solution, and with stupid and clumsy arguments unleashed military and police persecution with the objective of assassinating the leadership of the EZLN. The EZLN met this attack with serene resistance, tolerating the blows of thousands of soldiers assisted by the sophisticated death machinery and technical assistance of foreigners who wanted to end the cry for dignity coming from the mountains of the Mexican southeast. An order to retreat allowed the Zapatista forces to conserve their military power, their moral authority, and their political force and historic reason—our principal weapon against a fraudulent government. The great mobilizations of national and international civil society stopped the treacherous offensive and forced the government into dialogue and negotiation. Thousands of innocent civilians were taken prisoner by the evil government and still remain in jail—kept as hostages by the terrorists who govern us. The federal forces had no military victory other than the destruction of a library, an auditorium for cultural events, a dance floor, and the pillage of the few belongings of the indigenous people of the Lacandón jungle. This murderous attempt was covered up with the governmental lie of "recuperating national sovereignty."

Ignoring Article 39 of the Constitution which it swore to uphold on December 1, 1994, the government reduced the Mexican Army to the role of an army of occupation. It gave the Army the task of salvaging the organized crime which has become government, and deployed the Army to attack its own Mexican brothers.

Meanwhile, the true loss of national sovereignty was concretized in secret pacts and public deals with the owners of money and foreign governments. Today, as thousands of federal soldiers harass and provoke a people armed with wooden guns and the word of dignity, the high officials finish selling off the wealth of the great Mexican nation and destroy the little that was left.

Once it took up that dialogue for peace again, forced by the pressure of international and national civil society, the government delegation demonstrated its true motivation for the peace negotiations. The neo-conquerors of the indigenous people distinguished themselves by their attitude, their arrogance, their racism, and their constant humiliation which caused failure after failure in the dialogue at San Andres. Betting upon the exhaustion and frustration of the Zapatistas, the government delegation placed all its energies into breaking the dialogue, confident that it would then have the political cover it needed for the use of armed force, securing by force what it could not secure by reason.

Once the EZLN understood that the government would not concentrate seriously on the national conflict, it undertook a peace initiative in an attempt to revive the failed dialogue and negotiations. It called civil society to a national and international dialogue in its search for a new peace; it called for a plebiscite for peace and democracy in order to hear national and international opinion about its demands and future.

With the enthusiastic participation of the members of the national democratic convention, with thousands of volunteer citizens with democratic hopes, with the mobilization of international solidarity groups and groups of young people, and with the invaluable help of the brothers and sisters of the National Civic Alliance during the months of August and September 1995, a civic and unprecedented experiment was carried out. Never before in the history of the world or the nation had a peaceful civil society negotiated with a clandestine and armed group. More than a 1.3 million voices were heard in this encounter with democratic wills. As a result of this plebiscite, the legitimacy of the Zapatista demands were ratified, and a new push was given to the broad opposition front which had become stagnated and clearly expressed the will to see the Zapatistas participating in the civic political life of the country. The massive participation of international civil society called attention to the necessity of constructing those spaces where the different aspirations for democratic change could find expression. The EZLN considers the results of this national and international dialogue very serious and will now begin the political and organizational work necessary to comply with those messages.

Three new initiatives were launched by the Zapatistas as responses to the success of the plebiscite for peace and democracy.

The first initiative is a call for an intercontinental dialogue in opposition to neoliberalism. The other two initiatives are more national in character:

the formation of civic committees to discuss major national problems and form the seeds of a nonpartisan political force, and the construction of new Aguascalientes as places for encounters between civil society and Zapatismo.

Three months after these three initiatives were launched, the call for the intercontinental dialogue for humanity and against neoliberalism is almost complete, more than 200 civic committees have been organized throughout the Mexican republic, and today, 5 new Aguascalientes will be inaugurated: in the community of La Garrucha, in Oventic, in Morelia, in La Realidad, and the first and last one in the hearts of all the honest men and women who live in the world. In the midst of threats and poverty, the indigenous Zapatista communities and civil society have managed to raise these centers of civic and peaceful resistance as a gathering place for Mexican culture and cultures of the world.

The new national dialogue had its first test under the rationale for Discussion Table Number One in San Andres. When the government professed ignorance regarding the original inhabitants of these lands, the advisors and guests of the EZLN began such a new and rich dialogue that it overwhelmed the limitations of the discussion table in San Andres. It had to be relocated to its rightful place: the nation. The indigenous Mexicans, the ones always forced to listen, to obey, to accept, to resign themselves, recounted the wisdom which is in their walk. The image of the ignorant Indian, which the powerful had disseminated for national consumption, was shattered, and the indigenous pride and dignity returned to history in order to take the place it deserves: that of complete and capable citizens.

Independently of San Andres negotiations, the dialogue begun by the different ethnic groups and their representatives will continue now within the indigenous national forum, and it will have rhythm and achievements which the indigenous people themselves will agree upon and decide.

On the national political scene, the criminality of Salinismo was rediscovered, and it destablized the state-party system. The apologists for Salinas, who reformed and altered the Constitution, now have amnesia and are among the most enthusiastic persecutors of the man under whom they acquired their wealth. The National Action Party, the most faithful ally of Salinas de Gortari, began to show real possibilities of replacing the Institutional Revolutionary Party (PRI) at the summit of political power and demonstrated its own repressive, intolerant, and reactionary nature. Those who see hope in the rise of neo-PANism forget that replacing one dictator with another is not democracy. They applaud the new inquisition, which through a democratic façade pretends to moralistically sanction the last remains of a country which was once a world wonder and today provides material for police action and scandals. A constant presence from the government has been repression and impunity. Massacres of indigenous people in Guerrero, Oaxaca, and the Huasteca ratify government policy toward indigenous peoples. The authoritarianism in the UNAM toward the movement of those students wishing to democratize the College of Sciences and Humanities is a manifestation of the corruption which seeps into academia from politics. The detention of the leaders of El Barzon is another manifestation of treachery as a method of dialogue. The bestial repression of the regent Espinoza spills into street fascism in Mexico City. The reforms to the Social Security law increase the democratization of misery. The support for the privatization of the banks secures unity between the state-party system and money. These political crimes have no solution because they are committed by those who are supposed to prosecute criminals; the economic crisis makes corruption even more prevalent in government spheres. Today government and crime are synonymous.

While the legal opposition dedicated itself to finding the center in a dying nation, large sectors of the population became even more skeptical toward political parties, and searched fruitlessly for a new kind of political organization.

Like a star, the dignified and heroic resistance of the indigenous Zapatista communities illuminated 1995 and wrote a brighter chapter in Mexican history. In Tepoztlan, in the workers of SUTAUR-100, in El Barzon—to mention just a few places and movements—popular resistance found dignified representation.

In summary, 1995 was a time of two different and contradictory national projects.

On the one hand, the national project of the powerful entails the total destruction of the Mexican nation, the negation of its history, the sale of its sovereignty, treachery and crime as supreme values, hypocrisy and deceit as a method of government, destabilization and insecurity as a national program, repression and intolerance as a plan for economic development. This project finds its criminal face in the PRI and its pretense of democracy in PAN.

On the other hand, there is the project of a transition to democracy— not transition within a corrupt system that simulates change in order for everything to remain the same, but transition to democracy as a way of rebuilding the nation. This project calls for the defense of national sovereignty, justice and hope as aspirations, truth and obedient government as a guide for leadership, the stability and security created by democracy and liberty, and dialogue, tolerance, and inclusion as a new way of making politics. This project must still be created, not as a homogeneous political force or built around a charismatic individual, but as a broad opposition movement capable of gathering the sentiments of the nation.

We are in the midst of a great war that has shaken Mexico at the end of the twentieth century. The war between those who intend to perpetuate the social, cultural, and political regime that betrays the nation and those who struggle for a democratic, just, and free change. The Zapatista war is only a part of that great war—part of a struggle between a history that aspires for a future and an amnesia with foreign roots.

A plural, tolerant, inclusive, democratic, just, free, and new society is only possible today, in a new nation. The powerful will not be the ones to construct it. The powerful are only the salesmen of the remains of a destroyed country, one devastated by the subversives and destabilizers who govern it.

The new opposition lacks something decisive. We are opposed to a national project which implies its destruction, but we lack a proposal for a new nation, a proposal for reconstruction.

The EZLN's effort for a transition to democracy has been in the vanguard of the new opposition. In spite of the persecution and the threats, beyond the lies and deceits, the EZLN has remained honest and accountable as it forged ahead in its struggle for democracy, liberty, and justice for all Mexicans.

Today, the struggle for democracy, liberty, and justice in Mexico is a struggle for national liberation.

II

Today, with the heart of Emiliano Zapata and having heard the voice of all our brothers and sisters, we call upon the people of Mexico to participate in a new stage of the struggle for national liberation and the construction of a new nation, through this Fourth Declaration of the Lacandón Jungle in which we call upon all honest men and women to participate in the new national political force which is born today: the Zapatista Front for National Liberation—a civic and peaceful organization, independent and democratic, Mexican and national, which will struggle for democracy, liberty, and justice in Mexico. The Zapatista Front for National Liberation is born today and we invite the participation of the workers of the Republic, the workers in the field and in the city, the indigenous people, the squatters, the teachers and students, Mexican women, the youth in all the nation, honest artists and intellectuals, religious people who are accountable—all Mexican people who do not want power but want democracy, liberty, and justice for ourselves and for our children.

We invite national civic society, those without a party, from every social movement—all Mexicans—to construct this new political force:

- A new political force that will be national, and based on the EZLN.
- A new political force that forms part of a broad opposition movement, the National Liberation Movement, as a space for citizen political action together with other political forces of the independent opposition—where popular wills may encounter and coordinate united actions with one another.
- A political force whose members do not aspire to elective positions or government offices. A political force which does not aspire to take power. A force which is not a political party.
- A political force that can organize the ideas and proposals of citizens while remaining obedient to its members. A political force that can help solve the collective problems without the intervention of political parties and of the government. We do not need permission in order to be free. The role of the government should be chosen by society and it is society's right to make that choice.
- A political force that struggles against the concentration of wealth in the hands of a few and against the centralization of power. A political force whose members do not have any pay or privilege beyond the satisfaction of having fulfilled their commitment.
- A political force with local, state, and regional organization that grows from civic committees of dialogue.
- A political force which is called a *front* because it incorporates organizational efforts that are nonpartisan, and has many levels of participation and many forms of struggle.
- A political force called *Zapatista* because it is born with the hope and the indigenous heart which, together with the EZLN, descended from the Mexican mountains.
- A political force with a program of struggle with 13 points: those contained in the First Declaration of the Lacandón Jungle and added to throughout the past two years of insurgency. A political

force which struggles against the state-party system—and for a new constituency and a new constitution. A political force which does not struggle to take political power but instead strives for a democracy whose leaders govern by obeying.

We call upon all those men and women of Mexico, both the indigenous and those who are not indigenous; we call upon all the peoples who form this nation—upon those who agree to struggle for housing, land, work, bread, health, education, information, culture, independence, democracy, justice, liberty, and peace; upon those who understand that the state-party system is the main obstacle to a transition to democracy in Mexico; upon those who know that democracy does not mean substituting new dictatorship for those in absolute power but government of the people, for the people, and by the people; upon those who agree with the need to create a new Magna Carta which incorporates the principal demands of the Mexican people and the guarantees that Article 39 be complied with through plebiscites and referendums; upon those who do not aspire to public privileges or elected posts; upon those who have heart, will, and wisdom on the left side of their chest; upon those who want to stop being spectators and are willing to go without pay or privilege other than participation in national reconstruction; upon those who want to construct something new and good, to become a part of the Zapatista Front for National Liberation.

Those citizens who aren't members of a party, those social and political organizations, those civic committees of dialogue, movements, and groups—all those who do not aspire to take power and who subscribe to this Fourth Declaration of the Lacandón Jungle commit themselves to participate in a dialogue to formulate its organic structure, its plan of action, and its declaration of principles for this Zapatista Front for National Liberation.

Today, January 1, 1996, the Zapatista Army of National Liberation signs this Fourth Declaration of the Lacandón Jungle. We invite all the people of Mexico to subscribe to it.

III

Brothers and Sisters:

Many words walk in the world. Many worlds are made. Many worlds are made for us. There are words and worlds which are lies and injustices. There are words and worlds which are truths and truthful. We make true words. We have been made from true words.

In the world of the powerful there is no space for anyone but themselves and their servants. In the world we want, everyone fits.

In the world we want, many worlds fit. The nation which we are building is one where all communities and languages fit, where all steps may walk, where all may laugh, where all may live the dawn.

We speak of unity even when we are silent. Softly and gently we speak the words which find the unity that will embrace us in history and that will discard the abandonment which confronts and destroys one another.

Our word, our song, and our cry, is so that most dead will no longer die. We live fighting so that we may live singing.

Long live the word. Long live *Enough is Enough!* Long live the night which becomes a soldier in order not to die in oblivion. In order to live the word dies, its seed germinating forever in the womb of the earth. By being born and living we die, but we will always live. Only those who give up their history are consigned to oblivion.

We are here. We do not surrender. Zapata is alive, and in spite of everything, the struggle continues.

From the mountains of the Mexican Southeast.
Subcomandante Insurgente Marcos
Indigenous Clandestine Revolutionary Committee General
Command of the Zapatista Army of National Liberation Mexico,
January, 1996

OF TREES, CRIMINALS,
AND ODONTOLOGY:
LETTER TO CARLOS MONSIVAÍS

September–November 1995

Translated by Cecilia Rodriguez.

IF one accepts the seeming chaos of this reflection on *The Rituals of Chaos*, by one of Marcos's intellectual heroes, Carlos Monsivaís, it may stand as a lasting contribution to the Left.

Chaos itself is an actor in the argument, which shifts from abstract mathematical theory to Durito's account of his visit to Mexico City during the Zapatistas' national referendum, finally revolving around a critique of Machiavellianism.

What is the thread running through this multilevel mixture? The most important point is the description and rejection of the sixteenth century philosophy of Niccolo Machiavelli. In *The Prince*, Machiavelli's counsel to the incumbent ruler was to maintain an equilibrium of an almost mathematical nature. For Machiavelli, modern governance was not about achieving justice but about placating and balancing what we today call "special interests." The purpose of politics was to maintain power, nothing more. Machiavelli drew a fundamental line between morality and statecraft, asserting that amorality was the essential ingredient of successful rule. "The fact is that a man who wants to act virtuously in every way necessarily comes to grief among so many who are not virtuous." Machiavelli's theories matched the emergent philosophy of the universe as a great machine. Thomas Hobbes's notion of *Leviathan* rested on the premise that "life is but a motion of limbs." Isaac Newton furnished a further note on power by stating that "every body continues in its state of rest . . . unless it is compelled to change that state by forces impressed on it."

Marcos is an intellectual insurgente against all this. In the fable of Durito, the beetle is crushed under a tiny piano, but emerges to show that the small upholds the large "in history and nature." Durito's complaint is that Marcos won't add a seventh question to the six on the Zapatista's national referendum on public attitudes toward the rebellion. The seventh question Durito proposes is an invocation of Don Quixote's classic idealism: "Are you in agreement that gallant knighthood should be added to the National Professional Register?" Clearly Marcos wants to rescue Don Quixote from the birdbath of ridicule and rehabilitate the "gallant night" as an idealist, a task akin to rescuing the Indians from oblivion. In an interview with Gabriel García Márquez, in fact, Marcos said that "*Don Quixote* is the best book out there on political theory, followed by *Hamlet* and *Macbeth*." Durito is apparently Marcos's Sancho Panza.

There is a further point by Durito, that the EZLN's plebiscite has only six questions, when the uneven number seven would give it "the charm of asymmetry." Leaving the analogy to Don Quixote and Sancho Panza, Marcos returns to the significance of mathematical logic which, he says, differs from algebra because the point represents a conjunction, an "and," a relationship, a hinge between mirrors. "In the mirror, chaos is a reflection of the logical order and the logical order a reflection of chaos."

The modern Machiavellians, he is saying, have elevated a mathematical equilibrium-based politics, one organized by power technicians, to a level of dogma disguised as "efficiency." He is surely referring to the Harvard-trained elite of technocrats operating the Mexican state in the service of the econometric logic of NAFTA, a world of premises completely alien to that of the indigenous.

What is interesting is that Marcos includes the Left in his critique of the either-or politics of inverted images. "Where the Right dominates, now the Left will do . . . where the bourgeoisie, now the proletariat."

Against this Machiavellian ethos, Marcos and the EZLN offer an alternative politics of the spirit—not a touchy-feely spirit, but a spirit that can endure, resist, and overcome the technicians of the state. This is a humble view for a guerrilla. A new political morality won't emerge from an army willing to kill, Marcos writes; that new morality will have to emerge from the indigenous tradition itself, in combination with the continuing ideals of the Mexican Revolution. In this context, it is worth noting the echo of the original Emiliano Zapata, whose political leadership personified a distinct quality of the Mexican Revolution. Unlike reform liberalism or revolutionary Marxism, Zapata's vision of power and leadership was instinctively toward decentralization, self-governance, rooted in land and communal tradition more than hierarchical structures. This may have been its fatal vulnerability; after Zapata's assassination his figure was coopted into a bureaucratized party and state—aptly named the "Partido Revolucionario Institucional"—against which the Zapatista rebellion was aimed. Seen this way, Marcos is resurrecting Zapata's original vision after a near-century of failure by political parties and nation states of all kinds to address the enduring question of how to preserve the indigenous culture and the land on which it rests.

Marcos does not even revive the offer of the Left to create a better world. Instead, like Albert Camus in the French Resistance, he simply says "it is necessary to try to be better." Political morality must be separated from taking power. Or perhaps, he opines, there can be a way to create political relationships—between people and power, for example—that will eventually give rise to a new politics and even "create new politicians." The new politics will not be hammered out through force against force, but through the creation of a new type of force altogether—perhaps through the development of leadership having to "rule by obeying" the consensus of the community. The point, in mathematics and politics, is never a final one, but "a sign of unity, something which is added."

If this is difficult to comprehend, Marcos deepens the argument by questioning whether basic meanings and relationships can be expressed at all in the mechanical language of politics. The best ideas are never expressed because when they are materialized as words they become discrete, standing alone, not in relation to others. And what does this have to do with dentistry? The failure of the Indians to follow orders gives Marcos a pain in the molars. The molars create pain so that dentists and torturers will be employed, not to mention toothpaste vendors.

"Dentistry" is the name of this bureaucracy designed in response to suffering, "and is as heavy as the bill."

To: Carlos Monsivais,
Mexico, D. F.
From: Subcomandante Insurgente Marcos
Mountains of the Mexican Southeast
Chiapas, Mexico

Master[teacher],
I* send you a greeting and claim receipt of the book *The Rituals of Chaos*. I read it while running from one of those impasses that the Supreme Government calls the Dialogues of San Andres.

Vale. Health and try finding out if Alice manages to find the Red Queen and resolve the enigma to which the last P.S. invites.

From the mountains of the Mexican Southeast,
Subcomandante Insurgente Marcos
Mexico, Fall 1995

P.S. He recalls, a little late, the principal reason behind this chaotic epistle and titles it:

EHT RORRIM DNA OTIRUD
(OF POLITICS, DENTISTRY, AND MORALITY)

In that instant I saw the Apocalypse face to face. And I understood that the holy terror about the Final Judgement lies in a demonic intuition: One will not live to see it. And I looked into the eyeball of the Beast with seven heads and ten horns, and among its horns ten crowns, and on each head a blasphemous name. And the people applauded it and took pictures and videos, and recorded its exclusive declarations, while, with a clarity which

---

*Translator's note: Throughout his text Marcos plays with the formal and informal pronoun, implying doubt as to his right to be informal with Monsivais.

would become a painful burden, I had the belated realization: The
most horrible nightmare is that one which definitely excludes us."
—CARLOS MONSIVAÍS, *The Rituals of Chaos*

A point is the hinge which binds two mirrors, which face to face, spread out
to the sides like wings for flying over a chaotic era. That's the *point*, a hinge.

"Look on page 250" Durito says, as he unpacks his bags. And I look hur-
riedly and murmur,

"Page . . . 250 . . . mmh . . . yes, here it is," I say with satisfaction.

Or the one which excludes us momentarily, I think, while Durito insists
on hauling his tiny piano on top of what is already his tiny desk, to show me
how it is that the small holds up the large, in history and in nature. The
argument falls together with the piano and Durito who rolls under, after
that rickety operation, with the piano and the desk on top of his shell. I finish reading that part of the book and search for the pipe, the tobacco, and
Durito (in that order). Durito has no intention of coming out from under
the catastrophe which is on top of him, and a tiny column of smoke
announces two things: The first is the location of my tobacco, and the second that Durito is alive.

I light the pipe and the memories, which are one. Something about the
text takes me back many years. That was a sweet and simple time. All we
had to worry about was food. The books were few but they were good, and
rereading one meant finding new books inside it. And this is relevant
because Durito has brought me this book as a gift, and has pointed out a
text on page 250 to tell me that something is still pending, because there
are more important things than pointing out for example, that books are
made of pages, and pages, added to branches and roots, make trees and
shrubbery. The trees, as everyone knows, are for guarding the night, which
by day is idle. Among branches and leaves, the night destributes its round-
ness the same way in which a woman shares her curves inside moist and
breathless embraces. In spite of this sensual mission, the trees take time for
other things. For example, they tend to house many different kinds of animals, mammals, oviparous animals, arthropods, and other rhyming syllables
which serve only to show that children grow up. Sometimes, the trees also
house masked men. These are, no doubt, delinquents and outlaws. The
covered face and the fact that they live in treees no doubt means that they
are persecuted characters. These type of people live in the night, even by
day, in the trees. That is the reason for their passion and drive to love the
trees. It is also true that in the trees rest beetles like . . .

Durito interrupts me from the depths of the modern sculpture made by the piano and desk on top of his head.

"Do you have a lighter?"

"That sculpture should be called something like *Chaos on a Smoking Beetle*," I say as I throw the lighter to him.

"Don't offend me with your ridicule. All you show is your ignorance. It's clear you've never read Umberto Eco, who writes about the open work of art. This lovely sculpture is the best demonstration of modern and revolutionary art, and it shows how the artist so commits himself to his work that he becomes a part of it."

"And what's it called?"

"That's the tricky part. It should have a name if it's to be respectable. That is why it is an "open" work of art. As you know my dear "Guatson," the "open" work of art is not finished but becomes so within the process of circulation and consumption in the artistic market. Elementary. In this way the spectator stops being one and becomes a "co-artist" of the work of art. Zedillo, for example could call his work something like *My Government Program* and put it at Los Pinos*; Salinas de Gortari could call his *My Economic and Political Legacy* and house it at Almoloya, and the neoliberals could call theirs *Our Proposal for a New World Order*. And you . . . what would you call this work of art?" Durito asks me.

I stare with a critical eye and answer "Mmmh . . . something like *Beetle Buried Under a Piano and a Desk*."

"Bah! That's just descriptive," Durito complains.

As we talk the rituals of the night go on slowly: the sound of an airplane, the smoke of the pipe, the loneliness, the discreet scandal of the crickets, the luminous and drawn-out blinking of the fireflies, the heaviness of the heart, and above, the stardust of the Milky Way. Maybe it'll rain. The past months have had inconsistent rain; even the seasons seem disoriented and cannot find themselves within so much coming and going. Durito asks me for the name of the author of the book.

"Monsiváis," I answer.

"Oh, Carlos!" Durito says with a familiarity which surprises me. I ask if he knows Monsiváis's work.

"Of course! History is a subject we share . . . but you should keep writing. I have other things to do," Durito answers.

---

*Translator's note: Los Pinos is the Mexican white house. Almoloya is a Mexican federal prison.

///

I DELAY BECAUSE at the beginning of this letter I was unable to resolve the dilemma of whether to use the informal or formal pronoun in order to address you[sir]. Durito is a firm supporter of the axiom, there is no problem large enough that it cannot be avoided. And so with that philosophic corpus, I've decided, once again, to leave the solution to this dilemma pending and continue with the soft pendulum which takes us from *you* to *sir*.

So then I decide. I bite the pipe in determination. I take on a look of a Southeastern-governor-willing-to-defend-the-popular-will-at-all-costs-who-sees-how-things-are-and-provokes-them and undertake the rude task of writing to you[sir].

I must look like a real phenomenon; too bad I have no witnesses (Durito is already snoring underneath the ruins of his work of art), too bad I sent all the mirrors in that writing called something like *Mirrors: The Mexico Found Among the Nights of Day And the Crystal of the Moon*. What? That wasn't the title? Oh well, no matter. The thing is I now need a mirror to check myself for that delirious glow of genius getting ready to abort his own best idea. What? A self-imposed goal? Why? In order to abort? But no! You[sir] must agree with me that the best ideas are those which are never expressed. The moment they go inside the jail of language, they are materialized, they become letters, words, phrases, paragraphs, pages . . . even books if you're careless and give them free reign. And once there, ideas become tangible — they can be weighed, measured, compared. Then they are really boring, in addition to the fact that they become independent and do not obey orders of any kind. I understand that to you[sir] it matters little that orders go unobeyed, but for a military leader like myself it is a true pain in the molars. The molars, as all scientists with postgraduate degrees know, are pieces of bone which exist in order to give jobs to dentists, and in order to make the toothpaste industry flower, and in order that the profession of shameful torture exist: dentistry. The word "dentistry" is an idea made language and once so, becomes measurable and classifiable; it has nine letters, syllables, and is as heavy as the bill which must be paid after you leave the waiting room . . .

"Definitely," Durito says.

"WHAT?" IS ALL I can muster in response to Durito's interruption.

"There's no doubt that this plebiscite excludes beetles," Durito continues, who to all appearances was not asleep but reviewing papers even beneath the chaos on top of him.

"This plebiscite left out all beetles and is a form of racism and apartheid. I shall take my protests to all pertinent international organizations."

It's useless to try to explain things to Durito. He insists that the Seventh Question was missing, and its wording was something like, "Are you in agreement that gallant knighthood should be added to the National Professional Register?"

I explain to him that I sent various postscripts making discreet insinuations to the CND [National Democratic Convention] and the Civic Alliance, but no one noticed.

"It's insulting that that question is missing. It's a matter of aesthetics. Whose silly idea is it to have a plebiscite with six questions? Even numbers are anti-aesthetic. Uneven numbers, however, have the charm of asymmetry. It's strange to me that someone as asymmetrical as you, my big-nosed shieldbearer, should not have fixed a detail like that."

I pretend to be offended and keep silent. An atrocious noise is heard from the north. The lightning bolts tear the dark curtain which dilutes the distance between mountains and sky.

Durito tries to console me by telling me a story (which I can't understand too well from under the modern sculpture) about how he once had a practice which specialized in the big toe of the left foot. I appreciate the subtle insinuation which Durito offers in order to help me concentrate on the subject of this article, which is something like "Ethics and Political Parties" or "Politics and Morality" or "The new Left, New Morality, and New Politics, or "We are all Prigione"* or. . . . Just now a thunderbolt jolted me so that I even forgot about the Apocalypse, and Durito says that it serves me well for picking on members of the high clergy, and I tell him I'm not picking on him, I'm just looking for a g-o-o-o-o-d title for this article, so that it impresses some ambassador who will copy it.

"What about this one . . . The Lovely Lie and the Lost Cause."

Durito says I've lost my mind, and he'd rather go to sleep, and that I should wake him once civil society arrives to save him from the ruins. Then I realize that I now have all the necessary elements for the article: title, characters (political parties, the ambassador, the papal nuncio, the political spectrum and civil society), a polemics (that one about the relationship between morality and politics) in which to stick my nose—and for which I have plenty of nose. Now I only need a subject to justify the paragraphs, the stamps, the request to Juan Villoro of the weekly *Jornada*, in order to

*Translator's note: A reactionary moralistic Vatican representative in Mexico City.

have an audience for such a "beautiful" story, and the excuse to renew that amiable epistolary exchange which we began shortly before the Convention a year ago. Do you remember?

My other me comes near and says that if I'm going to get into polemics, I should be serious about it, because you can't play with the nuncios and the Machiavellians. "And if you don't believe me just ask Castillo Peraza, who demonstrated the efficiency of his political ethics in Yucatan," my other me says as he leaves to watch the beans cook.

All polemics are nightmares, not just for the polemicists, but for the readers as well. That's why it occurs to me that it's not worth it, especially when I remember that prophesy of a certain Salinista intellectual (who now has amnesia) in December of 1993, who foresaw great victories for Salinas in 1994, since he had all "the marbles" in his pocket.

It occurs to me that I cannot remain a spectator and that I should take sides. So I take sides—in this case, the side of those who do not have a party, and who, together with Durito create a "wave," and no small one either; being that Durito has so many feet and hands that it appears to be a "wave" of Mexican fans during the last games of the World Cup.

But Durito is dreaming with Brigitte Bardot; he's let out a sigh which is more like a stray lament, so I can't count on him and I should concentrate on the discussion. And the most important part of the discussion is the relationship between morality and politics, even more so, between morality and political parties, and between politics and power.

However, there is reasoning beyond this, and the problem of the relationship between morality and politics is overcome or displaced by the relationship between politics and "success," and politics and "efficiency." Machiavelli revives the argument that, in politics, the "superior" morality is the "efficient" one, and efficiency is measured in quotas of power, or, in the exact amount of access to power. And from here comes the Machiavellian juggle which defines democratic change as the political opposition made government. The National Action Party is the example, they say, of this political "success," this political morality.

But then they correct and rearrange themselves: The accumulation of power, they say, serves to contain the antagonism that pluralistic societies guard inside themselves. Power is exerted in order to defend society from itself!

Let's leave this new reference for measuring political efficiency pending, and return to the original. Not to polemicize with those who measure "success" and political "efficiency" in the number of governor's offices, mayor's offices, and congressional seats they hold, but to reclaim the evidence of "success" which has so many followers in the actual government of Carlos Salinas De Gortari.

Is "success" in politics defined as efficiency? Are politics more successful based on the efficiency of their products? In such a case, Carlos Salinas de Gortari deserves a monument, and not a police investigation due to his alleged complicity in the murders of J. F. Ruiz Massieu and Luis D. Colosio. His politics were "efficient" because they kept the entire country living in virtual reality, which was eventually torn up by real reality. The knowledge of this reality was acquired through the mass media. A great "success," no doubt. The "efficient" politics and economics of Carlos Salinas de Gortari deserves applause from National Action and from those orphaned intellectuals—and not just from them but from the powerful businessmen and high clergy members who now complain about having been deceived. Together they used to praise one another about having "all the marbles." The consequences of the Salinista "success" are suffered today by all Mexicans, not just the poorest ones.

After all, isn't "political efficiency" as perennial in Mexico as an administration? Sometimes it is less. The government of Ernesto Zedillo is an excellent example of "successes" as durable as the pages of a calendar without pictures.

The other problem, the one about the quotas of power, points out that the efficiency of a democratic change lies in the alternation of power. The alternation of power is not synonymous with democratic change, or with "efficiency," but with indulgences and divorces in the form of projects. The politics followed by National Action in Baja California, Jalisco, and Chihuahua are far from being another "way" of making politics, and are sufficiently authoritarian in order to adjust the length of the skirts (Guadalajara) and the uncovering of the human body (Monterrey).

The alternation of power is a separate problem, and perhaps a rebound to the polemics of the master Tomas Segovia with Matias Vegoso: "Well, the ideal of bipartisan government is tied to this position, not just because bipartisanism is its only manifestation, but because until today it is the only concrete manifestation of a 'nonideological' government, in other words, of a 'technical' government." The first thing I have to say (and surely not the most important) is that this position gives clear proof of the continuation of ideologies and not of their end. The conviction that a "technical" government is better than an "ideological" one is in itself an ideology, a conditioning and distorting belief toward reality, exactly the same way in which the conviction of a "positive" truth is better than the "metaphysical" truth, which in itself is a metaphysical conviction.

(Sure, I interrupt, and now there is talk of "tripartisanship" but the problem remains.) Tomas Segovia continues: "In the same way, I advise you as a friend to remember that to defend neoliberalism you must remember that it is only an ideology, and nothing more." Don't you understand that this is a most astute, and insidious ideology? There is nothing more ideological than to say: "Everyone else is ideological; I am the only one who is lucid."

Here I could deduce in my favor those arguments of the master Tomas Segovia with Matias Vegoso, but in addition to the fact that I do not have his authorization, this discussion would take me to my other problem: the morality of immorality (or should I say amorality?). *Mutatis Mutandis*: the ideology of no ideology. And from here we can jump to the problem of knowledge and the intellectuals who produce and distribute this truth.

The process followed by some intellectuals is typical: From criticism of the powerful they go on to criticize from the summit of the powerful.

With Salinas they showed that knowledge exists to serve the powerful. Then they collaborated to give theoretical substance to him. Their logic, no matter how you look at it, arrived at the same result: The powerful cannot be wrong when they analyze reality, and if they are wrong, it is reality's problem not the powerful's.

It is a painful but inevitable truth; the powerful have not only managed to gather around them a group of "brilliant" intellectuals; they have also produced a team of analysts capable of theorizing today on the future hardening of the powerful (regardless of whether the images in the mirror of the powerful belong to the PRI or PAN).

Machiavelli is today the head of a group of intellectuals who seek to give theoretical-ideological substance to the repression to come (in this line you can find Porfirio Diaz's grandson and his *Rebellion of the Pipeline.* * This is the fundamental contribution of its elite; the evolution from the justification of a stupid system to theorization about the imbecility yet to come. These are the new kinds organic intellectuals in power. They are capable of seeing beyond power. They represent the image of what organic intellectuals of neoliberalism aspire to be. They will leave their books. . . .

I STOP HERE in order to restock the pipe and rest my back. Now, a grey weight adds a new layer to the heavy theater curtain of the night. There are noises which come from the "open" work of Durito, evidence that he is not

---

*Translator's note: Here the book's title is changed from *Ravine* to what the Subcomandante believes to be the government's official view on their history.

asleep and is still working. A small column of smoke rises between the drawers of the desk and the keyboard of the piano. Somewhere, beneath that scribble which pretends to be a sculpture, Durito is reading or writing.

In the fire, the dance of the colors ends and little by little turns black. In the mountains the sounds and the colors change constantly. And what to say about the inevitable changing of the day into afternoon, of afternoon into the night, of night into the day. . . .

I'VE GOT TO get back to the article. Machiavelli is revisited and converted not into a guide, but into an elegant garment which disguises cynicism as intellectuality. Now there is an ethic of "efficient politics" which justifies whatever means necessary to obtain "results" (or quotas of power). This political ethic should put distance between it and "private ethics" whose "efficiency" is zero, because it adheres to a loyalty to principles.

Once again efficiency and its results in addition to the theme of political morality is confined by "private ethics" to the ideology of the "salvation of the soul." In front of the moralists, Machiavelli and his contemporary equals propose their "science," their "technology": efficiency. One must hold to these.

This "nonideological" doctrine has followers and adherents, in addition to the Salinista intellectuals and neo-PANists. The ambassador displays, in all its details, the doctrine of cynicism and efficiency before the applause of the intellectuals who have no memory: If I assault it, it speaks; if it speaks, it assaults.

The ambassador does not represent just himself. He represents a political position, a form of making politics characterized by the undefined eleven months of the present Salinas administration without Salinas. The ambassador is a part of the corps of presidential "counselors" who recommend that Zedillo assault in order to speak. The high cost of these assaults, they say, can be minimized because of the composition of the mass media.

I DON'T REMEMBER the name of the movie (maybe the master Barbachano remembers) but I do remember that a main actor was Peter Fonda. I remember the plot clearly. It was about a group of brilliant Harvard students who raped a woman. She accused them in a public hearing and they responded that she was only a prostitute. Their lawyer defended them by using their grades and good families. They're found innocent. The woman commits suicide. As adults, the "juniors" look for stronger emotions and they dedicate themselves to hunting down vacationing couples on weekends. And "hunting" is no figurative term; after the standard rape, the "juniors" free the couple to run into the countryside, and they hunt them down with shotguns.

I don't remember the ending, but it's one of those where justice is done, where Hollywood resolves on the screen what in reality often goes unpunished.

Today, the modern "juniors" have found that they have a country to play with. One of them is at Los Pinos and the other in Bucareli. They're tired of playing Nintendo so now they play at hunting down "the bad guys" in a game of real war. They give their prey time to escape, and move their game pieces to surround them and make the game more interesting. But it appears that the country is in no mood for games and mobilizes and protests. The "juniors" find themselves in a quandary because the game grows longer and they can't catch the "bad guys." Then the ambassador appears to save (?) them: "It was all planned" he says to us. "The dead are not dead, the war is not the war, the displaced are not displaced. We always wanted to talk and we only sent thousands of soldiers to tell the 'bad guys' that we wanted to talk."

Meanwhile, reality approaches . . . and the mass media tries to impose itself on reality. Forgetfullness begins to take over the government's stories; they forget the fall of the stock market, the devaluation of the peso, the "negotiations" of San Andres as a window dressing to hide the true indigenous politics of neoliberalism, instability, jealousy and distrust, ungovernability and uncertainty. They forget their principal objective, according to Machiavelli: They've had no results; they've not been "efficient."

They forget that they defend a lost cause, and the ambassador knows this but he forgets it when he's giving exclusive interviews. The last declarations of the government are clear; they forget reality, they forget that with each passing moment there are fewer of them who believe in the lovely lies and who support lost causes.

Meanwhile, the modern Machiavellians complain about our morality. Their view is that in politics there is no good and bad, and therefore the affair cannot be settled by classifying factions. And here they claim that it is not easy to resolve the relationship between ethics and politics by classifying factions as bad or good. In other words "If the Machiavelli of the nostalgic Salinista intellectual is bad, then we, who do not agree with him, are good." It remains tempting to take this polemic further, but I think that when you [sir] pointed out that "If efficiency in the manner of neoliberalism has taken us to the present tragic situation, the cult for doctrinaire purity, which has not had such costly results, has also not taken us far" (*Proceso* 966). You pointed out a new problem that is worth examining.

From the Left the alternative to Machiavelli is not more attractive. But "doctrinaire purity" is not the problem. It's a mirror which offers itself as an alternative and simplifies political relationships (and human ones as well, but that is another subject) into an inversion. This is the fundamental ethic of "revolutionary science," that scientific knowledge produces an inverse morality to capitalism. So altruism is the response to egotism, collectivity to privatization, social context to individualism.

But this knowledge remains inside a mirror; like a fundamental morality, it does not contribute anything new. The image is not a new one, but an inverted one. The alternative moral and political proposal is in a mirror: Where the Right dominates, now the Left will do so; where the white dominates, now the black; where the one above, now the one below; where the bourgeoisie, now the proletariat, and so on. Each one is the same, but inverted. And this ethic is what is recorded (or was) in all the spectrum of the Left.

The modern Machiavellians say, and say well, that we offer nothing better than they do: cynicism and efficiency. They claim that we criticize them from a new "morality" as criminal as theirs (well, they don't say that theirs is a criminal morality, but that ours is) and that we want to reduce politics to a struggle between black and white, forgetting that there are many grays. This may be true, but we do not just say that the morality of the resurrected Machiavelli is cynical and criminal, we also point out that it is *inefficient.* . . .

DURITO INTERRUPTS AGAIN to say I must be prudent when I talk about morality. "Your immorality is public knowledge," Durito says, trying to overlook his failure to bring the videos, those with a lot of X's, that I asked him to bring from the capital.

"We're not talking about that kind of morality. And stop lecturing me like a Panista mayor," I say in my own defense.

"I'd never do that. But it's my responsibility to deter you from your perverted cinematic preferences. Instead of those I brought you something more constructive. They're the pictures of my trip to the DF."

This said, Durito threw an envelope at me. In it are pictures of different sizes and subjects. In one of them Durito is standing in Chapultepec.

"You don't look too happy in this picture at the zoo," I said.

Durito answers (from under the desk), that the picture was taken after he was detained by a guard from the zoo. Seems the man mistook Durito for a dwarf rhinoceros and was determined to take him back to a cage. Durito argued using different lessons about botany, zoology, mammology, anthropology, and even gallant knighthood, but he wound up penned with the rhinos. He escaped somehow, when the guard took a break.

He was so happy to be free he decided to take a picture when he looked exactly like a white rhinoceros. He was that pale. He was that scared, he says.

And then there were other pictures with Durito in different poses and urban backgrounds.

There was one with Durito among many feet. He wanted me to notice that none of the feet wore boots, and that made Durito applaud. I told him not to be so enthusiastic, that Espinosa [the Mexico City mayor] had not yet shown his claws.

There was a picture with a lot of people in it. Durito took that one so that I wouldn't feel so lonely.

There was another one of Durito and another beetle. In the background you could see the buildings of University City. I asked him who the other beetle was.

"It's not a he, it's a she," he answered with a long sigh.

No more pictures. Durito was silent and all you could hear were sighs which emanated from the sculpture. I turned back to the indignation of Machiavelli at my criticism of efficiency.

IN VIEW OF this morality and this criticism does this mean that we offer an alternative? Is this the blasphemy which knocks down the adopted Machiavellians? A new morality? A better morality? A more successful morality? More efficient? Is that what we offer? No. The Zapatistas believe it is necessary to construct a new political relationship, whose source will not only be neoZapatismo. We believe that that relationship should act upon itself. This relationship will be so new that it will not only be a new politics, but create new politicians—a new form of defining the arena of politics and those who practice it.

I won't argue why a new political morality won't come solely from neoZapatismo; its enough to say that our existence is also old. We have undertaken the argument of weapons (no matter how much J. Castañeda, in the hopes of salvaging his book from failure, denies them and claims that only in name are we an army), and together with them, we use the argument of force. Whether the weapons are old or new or have gone largely unused does not change the situation. The fact is that we were and are willing to use them. We are willing to die for our ideals, yes. But we are also willing to kill. That is why an army, whether "lame" or revolutionary, heroic or not, cannot produce a new political morality—or rather, a political morality superior to that which oppresses us a good part of the day and much of the night. The night still keeps some surprises, and I'm sure that many hairs will be torn out trying to figure out what . . .

"THINGS ARE NOT that simple," Durito says. "Maybe I did not bring you the videos you wanted and that's why you want to lay on my noble shoulders a blame much heavier than this piano and desk. But I did bring some things for the Zapatistas: bracelets, headbands, earrings, hairclasps. I worked ten nights straight to get these things. . . . "

SPEAKING OF NIGHTS, the one today shows the sharp horns of a bull-moon which, new, returns from the west. Her clouds are gone, and without a cape to help her, the night fights the bull alone and in silence. Her enthusiasm is not dampened by the storm stirring in the east, and among her treasures are as many comets as rhinestones on the suit of the best bullfighter.

And there I was, trying to decide whether I would rise to her defense, when I was held back by the wide smile painted inside the horns of the moon. Ten times I sought to avoid her, and 10 times the stars demanded that I continue the passes of the bullfight.

Then I tossed the article aside and moved toward the center of the nightly stadium, asking Durito to play a pasodoble. He said I should go back to my writing because I'd taken too much time to finish it, and he would not help me. I left the round pending and returned to the article and the problem of political morality. The thousand heads thrust forward by the light barely peeked and shook the wall of the night gently. . . .

WHAT WAS I saying? Oh yes! Our criticism of Machiavelli does not mean that we are better, superior, or best. But we do say that it is necessary to try to be better. The problem is not which political morality is better or more efficient, but what is necessary for a new political morality.

In any case, it's not the diluted cynicism of those intellectuals, anxious to find a theoretical explanation for chaos, which will produce a new or more efficient political morality. In terms of the political parties, Machiavelli produces a complicated scale of rewards; once legalized as alternatives to power, all of their pettiness (secrets, negotiations, opportunisms, pragmatisms, and betrayals) do not weigh enough to shift the balance in their favor.

However, the nature of that "pettiness" soon makes a historic payment. And the higher the position reached with those "small and great political wits," the larger the payment that history demands. Once again, Carlos Salinas de Gortari is an example made historic lesson (which, it seems, no one in the political class wants to learn).

Is it a better world that we offer? No: We do not offer a new world. Machiavelli does, and he says it is not possible to be better, to conform with the grays that populate Mexican politics and the necessity to keep them from being antagonistic, thus diluting them into grayer grays. We disagree, and not just because of the mediocrity of that sad view of "not one or the other," but because it is a lie, it has no future, and sooner or later reality comes—with that pigheadedness that reality assumes, and with the tendency to decompose medium tones and sharpen even the most neutral gray . . .

"SEVEN QUESTIONS. THAT was the correct thing to do," Durito says, refusing to let go of his disagreement with the National Plebiscite. I try to distract him and ask him about Pegasus. Durito's voice breaks as he answers.

"What happened to Pegasus is part of that daily tragedy which lives and dies in the DF. Pegasus was an amiable and intelligent beast, but too patient for the traffic of Mexico City. I had just disguised him as a compact car, since he refused to be a Metro car and was afraid of sliding in the rain. Things were going well, but as it turns out Pegasus was a she and she fell in love with a bus from Route 100. The last time I saw her she was collecting money in a can for the resistance fund. But I don't regret it, I'm sure she will learn good things. I told her to write but she didn't know where to send the letter."

A tremor shook the sky. I stare at the place where Durito is. A silence and a cloud of smoke surrounds the sculpture. I try to encourage Durito and ask him to tell me more about his trip to the capital.

"What else can I tell you? I saw what is to be seen in a large or small city: injustice and anger, arrogance and rebellion, great wealth in the hands of a few and a poverty which each day claims more people. It was worth seeing. For many, fear is no more; for others it disguises itself as prudence. Some say it could be worse; others will never have it so bad. There is no unanimity, except about the repudiation of everything that is government."

Durito lights the pipe and continues.

"One early morning I was about to go to sleep in one of the few remaining trees of the Alameda. And the city was another, different from the one that lives during the day. From high in the tree I saw a patrol car going by slowly. It stopped in front of a woman and one of the officers stepped out of the car. His demonic look gave him away. My intuition was correct: I knew instantly what was going to happen. The woman did not move, and waited for the officer as though she knew him. Silently, she gave him a roll of bills and he put it away as he looked to the sides. He said goodbye by trying to pinch the woman's cheeks but she brushed his hand aside brusquely. He returned to the vehicle, and the patrol car left instantly."

Durito is quiet for a long time. I suppose he has finished and returned to his paperwork, and I should return to mine: Instead of discussing which political morality is better or more "efficient" we should discuss the necessity of fighting for the creation of a space in which a new political morality may be born. The problem starts with this:

Should political morality always be defined in relationship with power? Maybe, but that is not the same as saying "in relationship to the taking of power." Perhaps, for example, the new political morality will be constructed in a new space that will not require the taking or retention of power, but the counterweight and opposition that contains and obliges the power to "rule by obeying."

"Rule by obedience" may not be within the concepts of "political science" and may be devalued by the morality of "efficiency" which defines the political activity which we suffer. But in the end, confronted by the judgement of history, the "efficiency" and "success" of the morality of cynicism is naked unto itself. Once it looks at itself in the mirror of its accomplishments, the fear it inspires in its enemies (who will always be the majority) turns against it.

On the other side, the side of the "pure" ones, the saint learns he is a demon, and the inverse image of cynicism discovers that it has made intolerance into direction and religion, in the measuring cup of a political project. The puritanism of National Action, for example, is a part of the sample that remains unexhausted in the Mexican right wing.

Well, the dawn is coming, and with it, time to say goodbye. Maybe I didn't understand the polemic of the resurrected Machiavelli to which I was invited, and I see now that I presented (and did not resolve) more polemical lines than the original ones. That's not bad; "inefficient" maybe, but not bad.

Surely the polemic can continue, but it's unlikely to happen face-to-face given the ski-masks, persecutions and the military siege. In the words of Munoz-Ledo: "I don't believe that [Marcos] is someone who will remain in the political scene of the country." What, does he already have a pact with Chuayffet? A disappearance, maybe of the kind ordered by that Justice Secretary of Chiapas, that other great PRD member, Eraclio Zepeda?

Meanwhile, the powerful will continue to promise us the Apocalypse in exchange for change. It is His conclusion that it is better to avoid it and be comfortable. Others deduce, in silence that the Apocalypse is eternal and that chaos is not about to come, but is already a reality. . . .

I DON'T KNOW how to finish this so I ask Durito for help. The spectacle of his sculpture is erased by the bolts of lightning of the storm. The reluctant light makes the contrast of the shadows darker. Maybe that's why I never saw Durito come out from under the ruin, and for a moment I thought something extraordinary had happened. Durito was smoking and sitting on top of the piano.

"How did you get out from under there?"

"Simple. I was never down there. I moved to one side when the piano started tumbling. I decided instantly that no work of art deserved being on top of my body. Anyway, I am a gallant knight, and for that you need to be a soulful artist and there are few of those. Alright, what is your problem my dear Guatson?"

"I don't know how to end this letter," I say, ashamed of myself.

"That's an easy problem to resolve. Finish the way you started."

"How did I start? With a point?"

"It's elementary, my dear Guatson. It is in any book of mathematical logic."

"Mathematical logic? And what does that have to do with political morality?"

"More than you think. For example, in mathematical logic (not to be confused with algebra) the point represents a conjunction, an *and*. The point is the same as an *and*. To say A *and* B or A plus B, you write A.B. The point is not final; it is a sign of unity, of something which is added. It is defined, between one point and another, by X number of paragraphs, where X is a number which the mirror does not alter and reflects faithfully," Durito says as he arranges his papers. To the west, the sun uncovers clouds and takes over the sky.

And things being like this, this postscript comes to an end with a point which, according to Durito, does not mean the end but a continuation. Vale then: Y

P.S. So I invite you to resolve the enigma which encloses the central theme:

///

Instructions:

First. *Through the Looking Glass*, Lewis Carroll, Chapter II, "The garden of the living flowers."

Second. Each period means the end of a paragraph.

Third. Punctuation marks don't count.

Fourth. Numeric chaos in the logic of the numbers in the mirror:

1-111. 14-110. 9-109. 247-107.

11-104. 25-103. 47-97. 37-96. 3-95.

14-94. 3-89. 24-87. 22-86. 6-85.

10-84. 48-82. 21-81. 43-79. 55-78.

10-77. 49-76. 83-72. 21-71. 42-64.

6-63. 27-62. 52-61. 63-59. 13-58.

11-57. 3-56. 6-54. 101-53. 141-51.

79-50. 35-49. 32-49. 51-46. 11-45.

88-44. 12-43. 12-42. 31-41. 3-40.

24-39. 15-38. 20-37. 18-37. 17-36.

27-35. 22-33. 111-32. 7-32. 115-31.

20-31. 12-31. 5-31. 68-30. 46-30.

31-30. 12-30. 9-30. 54-29. 45-29.

12-29. 49-28. 20-28. 9-28. 40-27.

15-27. 42-22. 111-21. 91-21. 29-21.

3-21. 34-20. 6-20. 81-19. 66-19.

44-19. 36-19. 18-19. 11-19. 123-18.

90-18. 80-18. 76-18. 65-18. 43-17.

4-17. 51-15. 48-15. 28-15. 16-15.

47-14. 20-14. 8-14. 39-13. 12-13.

55-12. 54-12. 53-12. 18-11. 43-10.

25-10. 41-8. 9-6. 6-4. 1-1.

Fifth. In the mirror, chaos is a reflection of the logical order and the logical order is a reflection of chaos.

Sixth. A.A = ?

Seventh. There are seven mirrors: the first is the first. The second and third open the mystery of chaos which is ordered in the fourth. The fourth is constructed with the fifth and the sixth. The seventh is the last one.

///

Vale once again. Health, and it appears that (given trees, outlaws, and dentistry) it is not so easy to love the branch.

Subcomandante Insurgente Marcos
Zapatista Army of National Liberation
Mountains of the Mexican Southeast,
Chiapas, Mexico

THE FOURTH WORLD
WAR HAS BEGUN

SUBCOMANDANTE MARCOS

Originally appeared in *Le Monde Diplomatique*, September 1997.

Translated by Ed Emery.

THIS is Marcos's most cogent, straightforward analysis of neoliberalism, the term many use to describe the new world mercantilism, also known as globalization. It is an important description of the world after the Cold War. In Marcos's view, the US–Soviet conflict has been replaced not by a US-dominated international order, but by a chaotic scramble by global financiers and corporations to control markets. In this process, he says, nation states become mere departments of the corporate order, and politicans are reduced to "company managers." In a formulation that will surprise many, Marcos says the Zapatistas "think it is necessary to defend the nation state in the defense against globalization," and to create a "world in which there is room for many worlds."

The idea of defending the nation state against globalization positions the Left—in "advanced" as well as dependent nations—as a defender of national sovereignty against multinational corporations whose only loyalty is to the dollar sign. This is the opportunity created by the Seattle WTO protests—for disparate movements like labor, students, and environmentalists to stand for American democracy against those whose trade agreements trample the meaning of the tradition. The issue of patriotism is turned upside down politically, as great corporations are questioned over their treatment of American workers and subordination of local, state, and federal governments.

Handled properly, this is not protectionism—an attempt to protect First World wages against maquilladoras—but a defense of global democratic processes against corporate seizure and usurpation.

Marcos clearly does not believe that national democratic movements have ripened enough to assure a globalization of democracy, but that is the path he charts. For now, he writes, "pockets of resistance" are cropping up everywhere that people or ecosystems are classified as "disposable." This resistance cannot be reduced to a single class or agency of change headed by a political party, because by its very nature it represents the diversity of cultures that globalization seeks to suppress.

Here is the theoretical basis for the Zapatistas' embrace of the indigenous, the civic society, the Mexican flag, and international Zapatismo at one and the same time. The Indians are the primary, long-suffering "disposables" of neoliberalism; civil society is the web of voluntary associations made disposable by the concentration of corporate power; the national government must be rescued democratically from its fate as company management; and a globalization of resistance must be fostered against entities like the WTO and NAFTA.

Original Editor's Note: A political earthquake hit Mexico after the July 6 elections. For the first time in almost 70 years, the Institutional Revolutionary Party lost its absolute majority in the Chamber of Deputies. It also lost control of several states and of the mayorship of Mexico City. In Chiapas, the Zapatista National Liberation Army issued no directives about the elections, choosing instead to withdraw to the sheltering greenery of the Lacandón jungle. From this sanctuary the head of the ZNLA, Subcommander Marcos, sent us this original and geostrategic analysis of the new world picture.

> War is a matter of vital importance for the state; it is the province
> of life and death, the road which leads to survival or elimination.
> It is essential to study it in depth.
>
> —SUN TZU, *The Art of War*

As a world system, neoliberalism is a new war for the conquest of territory. The ending of the Third World War—meaning the Cold War—in no sense means that the world has gone beyond the bipolar and found stability under the domination of a single victor. Because, while there was certainly a defeat (of the socialist camp), it is hard to say who won. The United States? The European Union? Japan? All three?

The defeat of the "evil empire" has opened up new markets, and the struggle over them is leading to a New World War—the Fourth.

Like all major conflicts, this war is forcing national states to redefine their identity. The world order seems to have reverted to the earlier epochs of the conquests of America, Africa, and Oceania—a strange modernity, this, which progresses by going backward. The twilight years of the twentieth century bear more of a resemblance to the previous centuries of barbarism than to the rational futures described in science fiction novels.

Vast territories, wealth, and above all, a huge and available workforce lie waiting for the world's new master but, while there is only one position as master available, there are many aspiring candidates. And that explains the new war between those who see themselves as part of the "empire of good."

Unlike the Third World War, in which the conflict between capitalism and socialism took place over a variety of terrains and with varying degrees of intensity, the Fourth World War is being conducted between major financial centers in theaters of war that are global in scale and with a level of intensity that is fierce and constant.

The ineptly named Cold War actually reached very high temperatures: from underground workings of international espionage to the interstellar space of Ronald Reagan's famous "Star Wars"; from the sands of the Bay of Pigs in Cuba to the Mekong Delta in Vietnam; from the frenzy of the nuclear arms race to the vicious coups d'état in Latin America; from the menacing maneuvers of NATO armies to the machinations of the CIA agents in Bolivia, where Che Guevara was murdered. The combination of all this led to the socialist camp being undermined as a world system, and to its dissolution as a social alternative.

The Third World War showed the benefits of "total war" for its victor, which was capitalism. In the post–Cold War period we see the emergence of a new planetary scenario in which the principal conflictual elements are the growing importance of no-man's-lands (arising out of the collapse of the Eastern Bloc countries), the expansion of a number of major powers (the United States, the European Union, and Japan), a world economic crisis, and a new technical revolution based on information technology.

Thanks to computers and the technological revolution, the financial markets, operating from their offices and answerable to nobody but themselves, have been imposing their laws and worldview on the planet as a whole. Globalization is merely the totalitarian extension of the logic of the finance markets to all aspects of life. Where they were once in command of their economies, the nation states (and their governments) are now commanded—or rather telecommanded—by the same basic logic of financial power, commercial free trade. In addition, this logic has profited from a new permeability created by the development of telecommunications to appropriate all aspects of social activity. At last, a world war which is totally total!

One of its first victims has been the national market. Rather like a bullet fired inside a concrete room, the war unleashed by neoliberalism ricocheted and ended by wounding the person who fired it. One of the fundamental bases of the power of the modern capitalist state, the national market, is being wiped out by the heavy artillery of the global finance economy. The new international capitalism renders national capitalism obsolete and effectively starves nations' public powers into extinction. The blow has been so brutal that sovereign states have lost the strength to defend their citizens' interests.

The fine showcase inherited from the ending of the Cold War—the New World Order—has shattered into fragments as a result of the neoliberal explosion. It takes no more than a few minutes for companies and states to be sunk—but they are sunk not by winds of proletarian revolution, but by the violence of the hurricanes of world finance.

The son (neoliberalism) is devouring the father (national capital), and in the process, is destroying the lies of capitalist ideology: In the new world order there is neither democracy nor freedom, neither equality nor fraternity. The planetary stage is transformed into a new battlefield in which chaos reigns.

Toward the end of the cold war, capitalism created a new military horror: the neutron bomb, a weapon which destroys life while sparing buildings. But a new wonder has been discovered as the Fourth World War unfolds: the finance bomb. Unlike the bombs at Hiroshima and Nagasaki, this new bomb does not simply destroy the *polis* (in this case, the nation) and bring death, terror, and misery to those who live there; it also transforms its target into a piece in the jigsaw puzzle of the process of economic globalization. The result of the explosion is not a pile of smoking ruins or thousands of dead bodies, but a neighborhood added to one of the commercial megalopolis of the new planetary hypermarket, and a labor force which is reshaped to fit in with the new planetary job market.

The European Union is a result of this Fourth World War. In Europe globalization has succeeded in eliminating the frontiers between rival states that had been enemies for centuries, and has forced them to converge toward political union. On the way from the nation state to the European Federation the road will be paved with destruction and ruin, and one of these ruins will be that of European civilization.

Megalopolises are reproducing themselves right across the planet. Their favorite spawning ground is in the world's free trade areas. In North America, the North American Free Trade Agreement between Canada, the United States, and Mexico is a prelude to the accomplishment of an old dream of US conquest: "America for the Americans."

Are megalopolises replacing nations? No—or rather, not merely that. They are assigning them new functions, new limits, and new perspectives. Entire countries are becoming departments of the neoliberal mega-enterprise. Neoliberalism thus produces, on the one hand, destruction and depopulation, and, on the other, the reconstruction and reorganization of regions and nations.

Unlike nuclear bombs, which had a dissuasive, intimidating, and coercive character in the Third World War, the financial hyperbombs of the Fourth World War are different in nature. They serve to attack territories (national states) by the destruction of the material bases of their sovereignty and by producing a qualitative depopulation of those territories. This depopulation involves the exclusion of all persons who are of no use to the new economy (indigenous peoples, for instance). But at the same time the financial centers are working on a reconstruction of nation states and are reorganizing them within a new logic: The economic has the upper hand over the social.

The indigenous world is full of examples illustrating this strategy: Ian Chambers, director of the Central America section of the International Labor Organization, has stated that the worldwide populations of indigenous peoples (300 million people) lives in zones which house 60 percent of the planet's natural resources. It is therefore "not surprising that there are multiple conflicts over the use and future of their lands in relation to the interests of business and governments. . . . The exploitation of natural resources (oil and minerals) and tourism are the principal industries threatening indigenous territories in America."* And then come pollution, prostitution, and drugs.

*Interview with Martha García, *La Jornada*, May 28, 1997.

In this new war, politics, as the organizer of the nation state, no longer exists. Now politics serves solely in order to manage the economy, and politicians are merely company managers.

The world's new masters have no need to govern directly. National governments take on the role of running things on their behalf. This is what the new order means—unification of the world into one single market. States are simply enterprises with managers in the guise of governments, and the new regional alliances bear more of a resemblance to shopping malls than to political federations. The unification produced by neoliberalism is economic: In the giant planetary hypermarket it is only commodities that circulate freely, not people.

This economic globalization is also accompanied by a general way of thinking. The "American way of life" which followed American troops into Europe during the Second World War, then to Vietnam in the 1960s, and more recently into the Gulf War, is now extending itself to the planet as a whole, via computers. What we have here is a destruction of the material bases of nation states, but we also have a destruction of history and culture.

All the cultures which nations have forged—the noble past of the indigenous peoples of the Americas, the brilliance of European civilization, the cultured history of the Asian nations, and the ancestral wealth of Africa and Oceania—are under attack from the American way of life. Neoliberalism thus imposes the destruction of nations and of groups of nations in order to fuse them into one single model. The war which neoliberalism is conducting against humanity is thus a planetary war—the worst and most cruel ever seen.

What we have here is a puzzle. When we attempt to put its pieces together in order to arrive at an understanding of today's world, we find that a lot of the pieces are missing. Still, we can make a start with seven of them, in the hope that this conflict will not end with the destruction of humanity. Seven pieces to draw, color in, cut out, and put together with others, in order to try to solve this global puzzle.

The first of these pieces is the twofold accumulation of wealth and of poverty at the two poles of planetary society. The second is the total exploitation of the totality of the world. The third is the nightmare of that part of humanity condemned to a life of wandering. The fourth is the sickening relationship between crime and state power. The fifth is state violence. The sixth is the mystery of megapolitics. The seventh is the multiple forms of resistance which humanity is deploying against neoliberalism.

///

THE CONCENTRATION OF WEALTH AND THE DISTRIBUTION OF POVERTY

In the history of humanity, a variety of models have fought over the erection of absurdities as the distinguishing features of world order. Neoliberalism will have a place in the forefront when it comes to the prizegiving, because in its "distribution" of wealth all it achieves is a twofold absurdity of accumulation: an accumulation of wealth for the few, and an accumulation of poverty for millions of others. Injustice and inequality are the distinguishing traits of today's world. The earth has 5 billion human inhabitants: of these, only 500 million live comfortably; the remaining 4.5 billion endure lives of poverty. The rich make up for their numerical minority by their ownership of billions of dollars. The total wealth owned by the 358 richest people in the world, the dollar billionaires, is greater than the annual income of almost half the world's poorest inhabitants—about 2.6 billion people.

The progress of the major transnational companies does not necessarily involve the advance of the countries of the developed world. On the contrary, the richer these giant companies become, the more poverty there is in the so-called "wealthy" countries. The gap between rich and poor is enormous: far from decreasing, social inequalities are growing.

The dollar sign that you have drawn represents the symbol of world economic power. Now color it dollar-green. Ignore the sickening stench; this smell of dung, mire, and blood are the smells of its birthing . . .

THE GLOBALIZATION OF EXPLOITATION

One of the lies of neoliberalism is that the economic growth of companies produces employment and a better distribution of wealth. This is untrue. In the same way that the increasing power of a king does not lead to an increase in the power of his subjects (far from it), the absolutism of financial capital does not improve the distribution of wealth, and does not create jobs. In fact its structural consequences are poverty, unemployment, and precariousness.

In the 1960s and 1970s, the number of poor people in the world (defined by the World Bank as having an income of less than $1 per day) rose to some 200 million. By the start of the 1990s, their numbers stood at 2 billion.

Hence, there are increasing numbers of people who are poor or who have been made poor. Fewer and fewer people are rich or have become rich. These are the lessons of Piece 1 of our puzzle. In order to obtain this absurd result, the world capitalist system is "modernizing" the production, circulation, and consumption of commodities. The new technological revolution (information technology) and the new revolution in politics (the megalopolises emerging from the ruins of the nation state) produce a new social "revolution." This social revolution consists of a rearrangement, a reorganization of social forces and, principally, of the workforce.

The world's economically active population (EAP) went from 1.38 billion in 1960 to 2.37 billion in 1990—a large increase in the number of human beings capable of working and generating wealth. But the new world order arranges this workforce within specific geographical and productive areas, and reassigns their functions (or nonfunctions, in the case of unemployed and precarious workers) within the plan of world globalization. The world's economically active population by sector (EAPS) has undergone radical changes during the past 20 years. Agriculture and fishing fell from 22 percent in 1970 to 12 percent in 1990; manufacture from 25 percent to 22 percent; but the tertiary sector (commercial, transport, banking, and services) has risen from 42 percent to 56 percent. In developing countries, the tertiary sector has grown from 40 percent in 1970 to 57 percent in 1990, while agriculture and fishing have fallen from 30 percent to 15 percent.* This means that increasing numbers of workers are channelled into the kind of activities necessary for increasing productivity or speeding up the creation of commodities. The neoliberal system thus functions as a kind of mega-boss for whom the world market is viewed as a single, unified enterprise, to be managed by "modernizing" criteria.

But neoliberalism's "modernity" seems closer to the bestial birth of capitalism as a world system than to utopian "rationality," because this "modern" capitalist production continues to rely on child labor. Out of 1.15 billion children in the world, at least 100 million live on the streets and 200 million work—and according to forecasts this figure will rise to 400 million by the year 2000. In Asia alone, 146 million children work in manufacturing. And in the North too, hundreds of thousands of children have to work in order to supplement family incomes—or merely to survive. There are also many children employed in the "pleasure industries": According to the United Nations, every year a million children are driven into the sex trade.

The unemployment and precarious labor of millions of workers throughout the world is a reality which looks unlikely to disappear. In the countries of the Organization for Economic Cooperation and Development (OECD), unemployment went from 3.8 percent in 1966 to 6.3 percent in 1990; in

---

*Ochoa Chi and Juanita del Pilar, "Mercado mundial de fuerza de trabajo en el capitalismo contemporáneo," UNAM, Economia, Mexico City, 1997.

Europe it went from 2.2 percent to 6.4 percent. The globalized market is destroying small- and medium-sized companies. With the disappearance of local and regional markets, small and medium producers have no protection and are unable to compete with the giant transnationals. Millions of workers thus find themselves unemployed. One of the absurdities of neoliberalism is that far from creating jobs, the growth of production actually destroys them. The UN speaks of "growth without jobs."

But the nightmare does not end there. Workers are also being forced to accept precarious conditions. Less job security, longer working hours, and lower wages: These are the consequences of globalization in general and the explosion in the service sector in particular.

All this combines to create a specific surplus: an excess of human beings who are useless in terms of the new world order because they do not produce, do not consume, and do not borrow from banks. In short, human beings who are disposable. Each day the big finance centers impose their laws on countries and groups of countries all around the world. They rearrange and reorder the inhabitants of those countries. And at the end of the operation they find there is still an "excess" of people.

What you have now is a figure resembling a triangle: this depicts the pyramid of worldwide exploitation.

MIGRATION, A NIGHTMARE OF WANDERING

We have already spoken of the existence, at the end of the Third World War, of new territories waiting to be conquered (the former socialist countries) and others to be reconquered for the "New World Order." This situation involves the financial centers in a threefold strategy: There is a proliferation of "regional wars" and "internal conflicts"; capital follows paths of atypical accumulation; and large masses of workers are mobilized. The result: a huge rolling wheel of millions of migrants moving across the planet. As "foreigners" in that "world without frontiers" which had been promised by the victors of the Cold War, they are forced to endure racist persecution, precarious employment, the loss of their cultural identity, police repression, hunger, imprisonment, and murder.

The nightmare of emigration, whatever its cause, continues to grow. The number of those coming within the orbit of the United Nations High Commission for Refugees (UNHCR) has grown disproportionately from 2 million in 1975 to more than 27 million in 1995.

The objective of neoliberalism's migration policy is more to destabilize the world labor market than to put a brake on immigration. The Fourth World War—with its mechanisms of destruction/depopulation and reconstruction/reorganization—involves the displacement of millions of people. Their destiny is to wander the world, carrying the burden of their nightmare with them, so as to constitute a threat to workers who have a job, a scapegoat designed to make people forget their bosses and to provide a basis for the racism that neoliberalism provokes.

FINANCIAL GLOBALIZATION AND THE GENERALIZATION OF CRIME

If you think that the world of crime has to be shady and underhanded, you are wrong. In the period of the so-called Cold War, organized crime acquired a more respectable image. Not only did it begin to function in the same way as any other modern enterprise, but it also penetrated deeply into the political and economic systems of nation states.

With the beginning of the Fourth World War, organized crime has globalized its activities. The criminal organizations of five continents have taken on board the "spirit of world cooperation" and have joined together in order to participate in the conquest of new markets. They are investing in legal businesses, not only to launder dirty money, but also to acquire capital for illegal operations. Their preferred activities are luxury property investment, the leisure industry, the media—and banking.

Ali Baba and the Forty Bankers? Worse than that. Commercial banks are using the dirty money of organized crime for their legal activities. According to a UN report, the involvement of crime syndicates has been facilitated by the programs of structural adjustment that debtor countries have been forced to accept in order to gain access to International Monetary Fund loans.*

Organized crime also relies on the existence of tax havens: There are some 55 of these. One of them, the Cayman Islands, ranks fifth in the world as a banking center, and has more banks and registered companies than inhabitants. As well as laundering money, these tax paradises make it possible to escape taxation. They are places for contact between governments, businessmen, and Mafia bosses.

So here we have the rectangular mirror within which legality and illegality exchange reflections. On which side of the mirror is the criminal? And on which side is the person who pursues him?

---

*The Globalization of Crime, United Nations, New Yrok, 1995.

LEGITIMATE VIOLENCE OF ILLEGITIMATE POWERS

In the cabaret of globalization, the state performs a striptease, at the end of which it is left wearing the minimum necessary: its powers of repression. With its material base destroyed, its sovereignty and independence abolished, and its political class eradicated, the nation state increasingly becomes a mere security apparatus in the service of the mega-enterprises which neoliberalism is constructing. Instead of orienting public investment toward social spending, it prefers to improve the equipment which enables it to control society more effectively.

What is to be done when violence derives from the laws of the market? Where is legitimate violence then? And where is illegitimate? What monopoly of violence can the hapless nation states demand when the free interplay of supply and demand defies any such monopoly? Have we not shown, in Piece 4, that organized crime, government, and finance centers are intimately interlinked? Is it not obvious that organized crime has veritable armies on which it can count? The monopoly of violence no longer belongs to nation states: The market has put it up for auction.

However, when the monopoly of violence is contested not on the basis of the laws of the market, but in the interests of "those from below," then world power sees it as "aggression." This is one of the least studied and most condemned aspects of the challenges launched by the indigenous peoples in arms and in the rebellion of the Zapatista National Liberation Army against neoliberalism and for humanity.

The symbol of American military power is the pentagon. The new world police wants national armies and police to be simple security bodies guaranteeing order and progress within the megalopolises of neoliberalism.

MEGAPOLITICS AND ITS DWARFS

We said earlier that nation states are attacked by the finance markets and forced to dissolve themselves within megalopolises. But neoliberalism does not conduct its war solely by "unifying" nations and regions. Its strategy of destruction/depopulation and reconstruction/reorganization also produces a fracture or fractures within the nation state. This is the paradox of this Fourth World War: while ostensibly working to eliminate frontiers and "unite" nations, it actually leads to a multiplication of frontiers and the smashing apart of nations.

If anyone still doubts that globalization is a world war, let them look at the conflicts that arose out of the collapse of the USSR, of Czechoslovakia and of Yugoslavia, and the deep crises which have shattered not only the political and economic foundations of nation states, but also their social cohesion.

Both the construction of megalopolises and the fragmentation of states are founded on the destruction of the nation state. Are these two independent and parallel events? Are they symptoms of a mega-crisis about to occur? Or are they simply separate and isolated facts?

We think that they represent a contradiction inherent in the process of globalization, and one of the core realities of the neoliberal model. The elimination of trade frontiers, the explosion of telecommunications, and information superhighways, the omnipresence of financial markets, international free trade agreements—all this contributes to destroying nation states and internal markets. Paradoxically, globalization produces a fragmented world of isolated pieces, a world full of watertight compartments which may at best be linked by fragile economic gangways—a world of broken mirrors which reflect the useless world unity of the neoliberal puzzle.

But neoliberalism does not merely fragment the world which it claims to be unifying; it also produces the political and economic center which directs this war. It is urgent that we embark on a discussion of this mega-politics. Mega-politics globalizes national politics—in other words it ties them to a center which has world interests and which operates on the logic of the market. It is in the name of the market that wars, credits, buying and selling of commodities, diplomatic recognition, trade blocs, political support, laws on immigration, breakdowns of relationships between countries, and investment—in short, the survival of entire nations—is decided.

The worldwide power of the financial markets is such that they are not concerned about the political complexion of the leaders of individual countries: What counts in their eyes is a country's respect for the economic program. Financial disciplines are imposed on all alike. These masters of the world can even tolerate the existence of left-wing governments, as long as they adopt no measure likely to harm the interests of the market. However, they will never accept policies that tend to break with the dominant model.

In the eyes of mega-politics, national politics are conducted by dwarfs who are expected to comply with the dictates of the financial giant. And this is the way it will always be—until the dwarfs revolt.

Here, then, you have the figure which represents mega-politics. It is impossible to find the slightest rationality in it.

///

POCKETS OF RESISTANCE

> To begin with, I ask you not to confuse resistance with political opposition. Opposition does not oppose itself to power but to a government, and its fully formed shape is that of an opposition party; resistance, on the other hand, cannot be a party, by definition: It is not made in order to govern but . . . to resist."
>
> —TOMAS SEGOVIA, "Alegatorio"

The apparent infallibility of globalization comes up hard against the stubborn disobedience of reality. While neoliberalism is pursuing its war, groups of protesters, kernels of rebels, are forming throughout the planet. The empire of financiers with full pockets confronts the rebellion of pockets of resistance. Yes, pockets. Of all sizes, of different colors, of varying shapes. Their sole common point is a desire to resist the "New World Order" and the crime against humanity that is represented by this Fourth World War.

Neoliberalism attempts to subjugate millions of beings, and seeks to rid itself of all those who have no place in its new ordering of the world. But these "disposable" people are in revolt: women, children, old people, young people, indigenous peoples, ecological militants, homosexuals, lesbians, HIV activists, workers, and all those who upset the ordered progress of the new world system and who organize and are in struggle. Resistance is being woven by those who are excluded from "modernity."

In Mexico, for example, the so-called "Programme for Integral Development of the Tehuantepec Isthmus" is conceived as a large industrial zone. This zone would include factories, a refinery to process a third of Mexico's crude oil, and a plant to make petrochemical products. Transit routes between the two oceans would be built: roads, a canal, and a trans-isthmus railway. Two million peasants would become workers in these industrial and transportation sectors. In the same way, in the southeast of Mexico, in the Lacandón Jungle, a longterm regional development program is being set up with the object of making available to capital indigenous lands that are rich not only in dignity and history, but also in oil and uranium.

These projects would end up by fragmenting Mexico, separating the southeast from the rest of the country. They are also framed within a strategy of counterinsurgency, like a pincer movement attempting to encircle the rebellion against neoliberalism that was born in 1994. At the center are to be found the indigenous rebels of the Zapatista National Liberation Army.

While we are on the subject of rebellious indigenous peoples, a parenthesis would be in order: The Zapatistas believe that in Mexico recovery and defense of national sovereignty are part of the anti-liberal revolution. Paradoxically, the EZLN finds itself accused of attempting to fragment the Mexican nation.

The reality is that the only forces that have spoken for separatism are the businessmen of the oil-rich state of Tabasco, and the Institutional Revolutionary Party members of parliament from Chiapas. The Zapatistas, for their part, think that it is necessary to defend the nation state in the face of globalization, and that the attempts to break Mexico into fragments are being made by the government, and not by the just demands of the Indian peoples for autonomy. The EZLN and the majority of the national indigenous movement want the Indian peoples not to separate from Mexico but to be recognized as an integral part of the country, with their own rights and culture. They also aspire to a Mexico which espouses democracy, freedom and justice. Whereas the EZLN fights to defend national sovereignty, the Mexican Army functions to protect a government which has destroyed the material bases of sovereignty and which has offered the country not only to large-scale foreign capital, but also to drug traffickers.

It is not only in the mountains of southeast Mexico that neoliberalism is being resisted. In other regions of Mexico, in Latin America, in the United States and Canada, in the Europe of the Maastricht Treaty, in Africa, in Asia and in Oceania, pockets of resistance are multiplying. Each has its own history, its culture, its similarities, its demands, its struggles, and its successes. If humanity hopes to survive and to improve itself, its only hope lies in these pockets which are created by the excluded, the marginalized and those who are considered "disposable."

So what we have here is a drawing of a pocket of resistance. But don't attach too much importance to it. The possible shapes are as numerous as the forms of resistance themselves, as numerous as all the worlds existing in this world. So draw whatever shape you like. In this matter of pockets, as in that of resistance, diversity is wealth.

HAVING NOW DRAWN, colored, and cut out these seven pieces, you will notice that it is impossible to fit them together. This is the problem. Globalization has been seeking to put together pieces which don't fit. For this reason, and for others which I cannot develop in this article, it is necessary to build a new world. A world in which there is room for many worlds. A world capable of containing all the worlds.

THIS POSTSCRIPT SPEAKS of dreams couched in love. The sea rests at my side. For a long time it has shared my anxieties, my uncertainties, and many of my dreams, but now it sleeps with me in the hot night of the forest. I watch its rippling movements in its sleep and I am struck with wonder again at finding it unchanged: warm, fresh, and at my side. The stifling heat of the night draws me from my bed and guides my hand and my pen to summon up old Antonio, today, as he was many years ago. . . .

I asked old Antonio to go with me on an exploration up the river. We took only a bit of stew to eat. For hours we followed the winding riverbed, and in the end hunger and the heat began to get to us. We spent the afternoon following a herd of boars. It was almost night when we eventually caught up with them. Suddenly, a huge wild boar detached itself from the group and attacked us. Summoning up all my military know-how, I threw away my gun and climbed the nearest tree. Old Antonio was unarmed, but instead of running away he placed himself behind a thicket of canes. The giant boar ran straight at him, with its full force, and found itself caught up in the undergrowth. Before it could disentangle itself, old Antonio lifted his big old stick, and with one blow provided our evening meal.

The next morning, when I had finished cleaning my modern automatic rifle (a 5.56mm M-16 with a range of 460 meters, a telescopic sight and a drum magazine holding 90 bullets), I settled down to write my field diary. Omitting most of what had happened, I noted only: "Met wild boar. A. killed one. Height 350 meters. Did not rain."

While we were waiting for the meat to grill, I told old Antonio that my portion would serve for the festivities that were being prepared back at base. "Festivities?" he asked, poking the fire. "Yes," I said. "Whatever the month, there's always something to celebrate." And I embarked on what I thought was a brilliant dissertation on the Zapatistas' historical calendar and celebrations. Old Antonio listened to me in silence. Then, imagining that he was not finding it interesting, I settled down to sleep.

While I was still half awake, I saw old Antonio take my notebook and write something in it. The next day, after breakfast, we shared out the meat and each went our separate ways. When I reached camp, I reported back and showed the notes I had made in my notebook. "That's not your writing," someone said, pointing to the page in question. There, beneath what I had written, old Antonio had written, in large letters: "If you cannot have both reason and strength, always choose reason, and leave strength to the enemy. In many battles, it is force that makes it possible to win a victory, but the struggle as a whole can only be won by reason. The strong man will never be able to draw reason from his strength, whereas we can always draw strength from our reason."

And down below, in smaller letters, he had written "Happy Festivities!"

Obviously, I was no longer hungry and, as usual, the Zapatista festivities were indeed happy.

Subcommander Marcos.
Zapatista National Liberation Army, Chiapas, Mexico

MARCOS ON
MEMORY AND REALITY

August 1999

Translated by Irlandesa.

MARCOS begins by envisioning himself awakening to the living universe of the mountains, along with an ancient storyteller named Old Antonio, who seems both real and imaginary. He relates stories through Antonio as a link to the "first ones," then gradually applies the stories to the present situation—in this case the long students' and workers' strikes for free education at the national universities in Mexico City.

In Old Antonio's story is embedded a Zapatista understanding of war as a symbolic—or cultural—transformation. The Mexican government is attacking memory, not simply armed Zapatistas. The Zapatistas represent the oldest ancestors, those who revolted against the arrogance of Vucub-Caquix, originally the keeper of the colors, who began to believe he was the Sun and Moon himself. Two young gods, the hunters of the dawn, were sent to "hurt the mouth" of the arrogant Vucub-Caquix, followed by two old ones who used deception to pull out Vucub-Caquix's teeth and replace them with maize. They blinded him as well, and he turned into a disorderly macaw flying in the jungles of Chiapas.

The EZLN, Marcos says, is trying to wound the mouth of lies and remove its fangs, like the first ones did to the arrogant Vucub-Caquix. "They will call that struggle war, even though it is only a denunciation, an unmasking of the lie and an extinguishing of the false light that reigns there above."

There is no clearer delineation of the nature of war as seen by the EZLN. While it is a mistake to understate the importance of their armed struggle, it is more important to not overstate armed struggle as their strategy. Their weapons and alliances protect them from military annihilation so their "unmasking"—the word is deliberate—can continue to expose and resist the ethnicide confronting them. Far from seizure of the state's machinery of power, they wish to demobilize its assault on their consciousness.

Marcos describes the Zapatistas' agenda as being on behalf of "further on," an agenda which cannot be completed under the present arrangement of Mexico and the world. But how do you motivate people to fight for a future they will never see? Again, he provides a story as the motivating context, one told to him 15 years previously when the joined the EZLN. It is the story of a "crazy and foolish" old man who planted trees that grow to fruition long beyond his lifetime. The "sensible" ones—i.e. the modern pragmatists—would only do their planting for the present. Generations later, the young people discovered and came to revere a huge forest of trees, learning from the oldest living one that it had been planted by the "crazy and foolish" man. The grove is dedicated to "the first ones," those who planted for the future of the world.

With this Zapatista role of bridging to the future, bridging to other worlds, Marcos explains in graphic and humorous terms the effort to supply the striking urban students with food. Not stones, he jokes, alluding to the paranoid establishment view that the EZLN is importing weapons. Not stones, but maize. The maize that is sent will "speak the bridge that we are" instead of their having to accept tinned food.

CLOSING SPEECH AT THE NATIONAL ENCUENTRO IN DEFENSE OF THE CULTURAL HERITAGE

I scatter flowers of War, I, of the smiling face
Since I come along with war.
I am a quetzal bird and I come flying,
Through difficult passages I come along with war.
I am a beautiful blackbird with red neck,
I come flying: I come to become a flower,

I turn into a bloodstained Rabbit.
See me: I am serious now, gird your sides
I, whose eyes wink, who goes smiling.
I come from inside the flowered courtyard. See me, I am serious,
Gird your sides. I am going to become flower,
I, the bloodstained Rabbit.

—NAHUATL POETRY

Being what they were, the eves and the charged memories are
more real than the intangible present. The eve of a voyage is a
precious part of the trip.

—JORGE LUIS BORGES

August once again, and, once again, dawn. The sea is sleeping and a small trail of cloud is resting its white weariness above the mountain. Once more it begins its flight and restive flutter, but it does not reveal the stars. Up above, the great serpent is bleeding blue pearls of light. The Moon, a lady, has just finished washing her face, and she appears at the balcony, still not sure whether she is in flight or staying put. Below, next to a candle, a shadow is guarding the night and memory. Another shadow approaches him and a flame momentarily illuminates two faceless faces—a shadow of a shadow.

The cloud that was rising in flight is delayed a bit, and the light oozing from the illumined serpent stops. The midnight sun becomes a far-off torch. The moon stands still at her window, and even a falling star is stilled, neither falling nor ascending. Everything remains quiet, motionless.

Attention! Listen! Now the word reigns. . . .

OLD ANTONIO HAD just said hello with the goodbye that runs through his lungs. In spite of the cough—which I had to accompany (not just to be in solidarity, I had it as well, and although mine wasn't as deep as the Old One's, my throat and chest did indeed hurt, and they sought relief)—both of us lit up the tobacco we were carrying—the cigarette for him, the chewed-up pipe for me. Then the bridge began, which is what we call the word here. The dancing light of a candle was illuminating us, and history came from light, then from the sun, and from the morning. It is this, then.

THE HISTORY OF THE FALSE LIGHT, THE STONE, AND THE MAIZE

Long, long ago, time was still waiting for the time to make time. The greatest gods, those who gave birth to the world, went about exactly as they always went about: racing about in a rush. Because these first gods had taken much time with their dancing and singing, and they were late in making the moon and the sun, whose work was to give light and shadow to the world, which was moving very slowly. Then Vucub-Caquix, the keeper of the seven first colors, began to think that he was the sun and the moon, given that many and beautiful were the colors in which he dressed. As he flew very high, his vision could reach far, and—so it seemed to him—it could reach everything. Men and women were already moving about the land, but they had not turned out very well. The first gods had already made men and women several times and they just were not very good. It was as if the most great gods were learning, smudging the world and correcting the men and women they were creating. They lacked time, then, for the men and women of the maize to be made, the true ones.

Busy as they were, the first gods did not hear what Vucub-Caquix was saying, and that he now wanted everyone to adore him, like the luminous light. When they learned of it, the most great gods had a wonderful idea: they would call on two young gods and two old ones to put Vucub-Caquix in his place. The two boys were called Hunabku and Ixbalanque, which are the names also carried by the hunter of the dawn. The two old gods were Zaqui-Nin-Ac and Zaqui-Nima-Tziis, the creator couple. Hunabku and Ixbalanque hurt the mouth of the false sun-moon, who boasted great light, with their blowpipe. Vucub-Caquix's pain was great, but he did not fall. Then the old creators went and they offered to fix his mouth. They took out his beautiful teeth and replaced them with teeth of maize and Vucub-Caquix' face fell. They had already blinded his eyes, and he forget his lust for nobility and remained exactly as he flies these mountains now, like a macaw in disorderly flight.

And so it was; there have been, and are, those who believe themselves to be sun and moon, and they boast of great and powerful light. Such is gold, money, and political power that is raised as path and destiny. Their light blinds and transforms, makes the false appear true, and conceals the truth behind double faces. When money was made into lying gods across the land, their false priests made governments and armies so that the lie would endure. History continues to suffer and to hope that the young and the old will reach agreement in order to wound the money from the mouth of lies and to take down the bleeding fangs. With stones and maize as arms, young and old will undress the power. They will call that struggle war, even if it is only a denunciation, an unmasking of the lie, and an extinguishing of the false light that reigns, vainly.

Old Antonio remains silent and gives me his hand. Saying "I am done," he says goodbye and leaves. Old Antonio left a small stone and a solitary grain of maize in my hand.

Across the long negligee of night, thousands of lights are awaiting, waiting . . .

BLOWS THAT SEEK SILENCE

Brothers and sisters, participants in the National Encuentro in Defense of the Cultural Heritage:

We greet the ending of this first meeting in defense of memory. We know that others will follow, and that this has been just the first of many encuentros and accords that will have to be built between those of us who are resisting the buying and selling of Mexico's cultural heritage.

These have been difficult and beautiful days. The government—all of you know this now—is continuing to attack the indigenous Zapatista communities and is continuing forward with its war. By attacking us, the government knows it is attacking memory. That is the reason for its stubbornness, its cruelty, and its arrogance. What is at stake in these lands is not negligible, which you saw, throughout these days and nights, speaking, discussing, agreeing, disagreeing, singing, and dancing—which is how true encuentros are made.

It has been a great honor for us to have met you, and it has been an honor for us to see you, sharing the pain and suffering, the indignation and the rage over this new military attack against the Zapatista peoples. What the government did was to remind everyone that there is a war going on here, that there is an entire rebel people resisting, and that there is an occupation army—the federal one—seeking to guarantee the merchandise that those who are governing and ordering have already sold. The merchandise has a name: it is called national sovereignty.

It is not the first time that blows have sought to keep us silent. It is not the first time that they have failed. Now, in addition to silencing us, the blows are trying to separate us from the principal resistance movements in the country: the UNAM university students, who are defending the right to a free education and the Mexican Electricians Union, that is defending the electric industry—and yours, the communities from the National School of Anthropology and History and from the National Institute of Anthropology and History, as well as of all the persons and organizations who make up the National Front in Defense of the Cultural Heritage. All these movements and ours have something in common: the defense of history. Because of that, every attack against one of these movements is an attack against all the others.

At least, that is how we understand it. That is why we feel that the repression against the UNAM students last August 5 was also against us. That is why we have supported the mobilizations and calls by the SME. That is why we have joined with you in defense of memory and against attempts to privatize our cultural heritage.

Over the last few days, we have received some notes and letters. The compañeros have been collecting them in a little cardboard box. We read everything they had to say. That is why they say there are little talking boxes there. There are requests for interviews, for meetings, doubts, experiences, questions. The intense and difficult nature of these days has prevented us from giving to each and every one of them the response they require. We hope you will forgive us and accept our promise to respond to them as soon as possible.

Among the papers there is one that asks what the Zapatistas want; it mentions that much information has been manipulated in the media, distorting what is happening here and the path that moves and inspires us.

This is the month of August, and for us it is also the month of memory. And so I will try and respond a bit to the question: "What do the Zapatistas want?"

It is not going to be easy for them to understand us now. For some strange reason, the Zapatistas speak for a time further on. I mean that our words do not fit in the present, but rather they are made to fit into a puzzle that does not yet exist. Thus, patience is a guerrilla virtue.

Fifteen years ago I first came to these mountains. In one of the guerrilla camps, a story was told to me, at dawn—as is the law—from 15 years before. Thirty years have now gone by, in this August that is soaking us. I will tell the same story as the man who related them to me, when—between jokes about my pathetic appearance and the clown's pants I was wearing—he welcomed me to the Zapatista Army of National Liberation.

THOSE WHO CAME LATER DID UNDERSTAND

In a certain town, men and women toiled in order to survive. Every day the men and women went out to their respective jobs: the men to the fields and the bean crops; the women to the firewood and to carrying water. At times there was work that brought them together as equals. For example, men and women worked together to cut coffee when its time had come. And so it passed.

But there was a man who did not do that. He worked, but not in the fields or bean crops, nor did he go to the coffee plantations when the beans reddened among the branches. No, this man worked planting trees on the mountain. The trees this man planted did not grow rapidly; they took entire decades to grow. Other men laughed at this man and criticized him quite a bit. "Why do you work at things that you are never going to see completed? Better to work in the fields, which will give you fruit in months, and not in planting trees that will not be large until you have already died. . . . You are a fool or crazy, because you work fruitlessly."

The man defended himself and said, "Yes, it is true, I am not going to see these trees full grown, full of branches, leaves, and birds, nor will my eyes see children playing under their shade. But if all of us work just for the present and just for the following day, who will plant the trees that our descendents are going to need in order to have shelter, consolation, and joy?" No one understood him. The crazy or foolish man continued planting trees that he would not live to see grown, and sensible men and women continued planting and working for the present.

Time passed, and all of them died. Their children continued in their work, and they were followed by the children of their children. One morning, a group of boys and girls went out for a walk and found a place filled with great trees. A thousand birds lived in them and their great branches gave relief from the heat and protection from the rain. The entire mountainside was found filled with trees. The boys and girls returned to their town and spoke of this marvelous place.

The men and women gathered together and they went to the place in great surprise. "Who planted this?" they asked. No one knew. They went to speak with their elders and they did not know either. Only an old one, the oldest of the community, could tell them the story of the crazy and foolish man.

The men and women met in assembly and had a discussion. They saw and understood the man whom their ancestors had dealt with and they admired that man very much. They knew that memory can travel very far and arrive where no one can think or imagine—the men and women of that day stood in the place of the great trees.

They surrounded a tree in the center of the grove, and they made a sign out of colored letters. They had a fiesta afterward, and dawn was already approaching when the last dancers left to go to sleep. The great forest was left alone and in silence. It rained and then ceased to rain. The moon came out and the Milky Way molded its convoluted body once again. Suddenly a ray of moonlight insinuated itself among the great branches and leaves of the tree in the center. By its small light, the sign of colors that had been left there could be read:

> To the first ones:
> Those who came later did understand.
> Thanks

This story was told to me 15 years ago, and 15 years had already passed since what they told me had come to pass. Perhaps it is pointless to say it in words because we say it with acts; but yes, those who came later did understand.

And if I am telling you this, it is not just to give our regards to the first ones, nor is it just to give you a little piece of that memory that was lost and forgotten. It is to try and respond to the question of what the Zapatistas want.

We want to plant the tree of the morning. We know that, in these frenetic times of realpolitik, of fallen flags, of polls that substitute for democracy, of neoliberal criminals who call for crusades against what they are hiding and that which feeds them, of chameleonlike transformations—in these times, to say that we want to plant the tree of the morning sounds foolish and crazy, a theatrical phrase or an outdated utopia.

We know it; nonetheless, that is what we want, and that is what we are doing. How many people in the worlds that make up the world can say as we can say that they are doing what they want to do? We think there are many, that the worlds of the world are filled with crazy and foolish persons who are planting their respective trees for their respective tomorrows, and that the day will come when this mountainside of the universe that some call Planet Earth, will be filled with trees of all colors. There will be so many birds and comforts that no one will remember the first ones, because all the yesterdays that are distressing us so today will be nothing more than an old page in the old book of the old history.

In that tree of tomorrow, the other will know and respect the other others, and the false light will lose its last battle. If I were pressed to be precise, I would tell you that it is a place with democracy, liberty, and justice: That is the tree of tomorrow.

This is what the Zapatistas want. You might think that I have been vague in my response, but I have never before spoken so clearly. Times will come in which these words will fit; together, their embrace will expand and they will be heard and guarded and they will grow. That is what the words are for.

MOTION FOR POZOL!

Men and women, participants in the National Encuentro in Defense of the Cultural Heritage:

Before ending this, we want to send our greetings to, and be with, those who are far away and persecuted: the students of the National Autonomous University of Mexico.

Among the letters that spoke from the talking cardboard box, one informed us that the Independent Union of Workers of the Metropolitan Autonomous University (SITUAM) had raised 21,900 pesos as humanitarian aid for the purchase of maize for the communities in resistance. We have consulted with our chiefs from the Clandestine Revolutionary Indigenous Committee and we would like to ask the compañeros and compañeras from SITUAM to listen to the following:

It was with concern that we read in various newspaper reports that the students on strike at UNAM were eating nothing but potatoes and tinned food. This worried our compañero and compañera chiefs very much, because they are reading that the students are not eating their tortillas nor taking their pozol. "How, then, are they going to resist?" they ask me. I merely shrug my shoulders, since what I would not give for a succulent La Migaja tin of sardines. But the committees were not thinking about sardines, but about the tortillas and pozol the students would need in order to resist the bad government. After a long discussion, and not a few accounts of the advantages of pozol and tortillas, they came and told me: "The committee says to send pozol and tostadas to the students on strike."

My mouth watering, I went to the committee and asked to speak. I said that UNAM is in Mexico City and that Mexico City is very far from here. "How many checkpoints distant?" they asked me, because now the compañeros measure distances by the number of checkpoints there are between one and the other point. I told the truth, that I did not know, that there were many, but that the problem was the kilometers and the time and that the pozol would arrive sour.

"Sour!" they said and laughed, since sour pozol is a delicacy here, they say (it always gives me a bellyache). And, to the shout of "sour pozol!" ("motion for pozol!" they would say in the CGH, I believe), they took out the marimba and they made themselves a fire and heated their tostadas and then one took out his bottle of sour pozol and, yes, the party went on. I refused the pozol that they offered me, but I did have the tostadas, since I hadn't eaten. When, at last, everything returned to normal. I presented the problem again: The pozol would already be moldy when they arrived in Mexico City (yes, I was careful not to say "sour" again), ergo, it would not be a good idea to send pozol. "Very well, then," they told me. "Send them tostadas." And so I did, but then what I am about to tell you came to pass:

TOSTADAS THAT PRODUCE "BAD IDEAS"

A group of compañeros left, carrying pans of tostadas, on a mission to deliver them to the General Strike Council of UNAM and to the school assemblies, along with a message where we asked forgiveness for not having sent pozol. When crossing through the checkpoint at Guadalupe Tepeyac, a high-ranking officer stopped our compañeros and searched the cargo. He asked them who those tostadas were for, and the compas said that they were for some relatives who were studying in the city. "That's not true!" the officer responded. "It's for the strikers. Take all the tostadas away from them!" The soldiers at the checkpoint did what they were ordered. One of them took a piece of tostada and put it toward his mouth. "Don't do that, soldier!" the officer reprimanded him. "Don't you know that those are Zapatista tostadas and they produce bad ideas in those who eat them? Bury them far away from here!" And so tostadas are now prohibited by the Firearms and Explosives Law and they may not cross the checkpoints in order to go to UNAM and produce bad ideas in those who eat them. I was saddened by the failure and I so informed the committee. The committee said not to be concerned, that we would still see that the students on strike would be able to eat tostadas and take pozol in order to have the strength to resist.

THAT IS THE story. Now that we have been made aware of the support that the brothers and sisters of SITUAM have lent, the committees are asking me to ask you the following:

Take that money and carry it to Mexico City and buy maize for the CGH and for the assemblies and for the guards and for the brigades of young people who are fighting for free education. Tell them that the Zapatistas sent it so that they can eat their tostadas and pozol, if they should so desire, and not just potatoes and tinned food. Tell them that we send greetings and we hope that this maize we are sending them knows how to tell who we are, and that we are not sending them stones because they certainly have them there. We hope that they continue to be strong, that they open their hearts to all our words and that they not forget that here we care for them, admire them, and, although they are far away, we also embrace them.

This is what the Committees asked me to ask the compañeros and compañeras from SITUAM, and, as we are sure that they will say yes, let us be a bridge between two dignified movements: that of the university workers and that of the university students.

As a special service for the media present, here is a press release:

> The Independent Union of Workers of the Metropolitan Autonomous University made delivery of their aid of X tons of maize to the striking students at UNAM, through the unusual behavior of the EZLN. The Zapatistas, through the voice of their masked leader, stated that that is exactly how the Zapatistas are, unusual bridges that cross not only Mexico, they say, but all the different worlds that are in, and have been in, the world. At the end of the act, the Sup wanted to let out a belch, but a croak came out, and he opted for being the victim.

You are welcome, ladies and gentlemen of the press.

MEMORY HAS ITS OWN REALITY

Brothers and sisters:

It might appear odd that I have brought together a Nahuatl poet, Popul Vuh, and Jorge Luis Borges for this closing. Especially Borges. And, although I could say that this month is the one hundredth anniversary of his birth, that is not the reason why he is sharing space with our most ancient wise ones and storytellers. No, it so happens that a book reached my beat-up desk. The wind had played with it and it had opened it to the page entitled "August 22, 1983." I do not know if August was insinuating itself into my memory in this way, but the fact is that nature was imitating art, the words that are at the top of this writing, along with the Nahuatl, jumped out from that page. Perhaps Borges came in order to remember that cultural heritage is not just one thing and that everything has something of the universal. Or perhaps he only came to tell us, in his way, that memory has its own reality, like La Realidad that joins us together has memory. Or perhaps he only came so that he might tell us all that this is just the eve of a long voyage and that, therefore, the voyage has already begun.

In the end, we know—and it is why we are here—that the fangs of the false light will fall and, with stones and grains of maize, a tree will grow in any place in any world. Even if no one remembers, the tree will know that the first ones were necessary and they kept their word.

Meanwhile, the soil will have to continue to be prepared. We will have to be patient and despite the stupid olive green, the struggle must continue, so that the word becomes bridge and stone and maize and tree and hope of tomorrow. All of that and more is what the Zapatistas are and want.

Vale.

Salud and, although it appears that we are defending the past, in reality in La Realidad we have agreed to defend tomorrow.

Democracy!

Liberty!

Justice!

From the mountains of the Mexican southeast
By the Clandestine Revolutionary Indigenous Committee—
General Command of the Zapatista Army of National Liberation
Subcomandante Insurgente Marcos
La Realidad, Awake
Mexico, August of memory, 1999

MARCOS FROM THE UNDERGROUND
CULTURE TO THE CULTURE OF RESISTANCE

October 1999

Translated by Irlandesa.

THIS is another Marcos, jovial, relaxed, reaching out to an underground youth audience much like the Seattle protest constituency, including Rage Against the Machine, other rock groups, Herman Bellinghausen (a dedicated *La Jornada* journalist), and Javier Eliorriaga (a former Zapatista prisoner, and a national political organizer). It is the night before a projected concert, and Marcos is talking by video.

Punk or rock are clearly not his genre, nor mine. One feels he is drifting here, seeking to summarize a connection on unfamiliar ground. He could lecture them to become political, to join a liberation front, but does not. He could tap into guilt by reminding them of hunger, death, and armed struggle, but he doesn't. Disarmingly, as if he has nothing else to do, he speaks like an elder brother, or perhaps a father figure, with a spirit of perfect respect and egalitarianism. He seems to genuinely believe that, in the global underworld of opposition movements, there are no permanent hierarchies. The key is to live in opposition, and living includes laughter, dance, and music. It is a world of fantasy, inhabited by imaginary beings like Marcos' little friend Don Durito, the beetle who plans to invade Europe in a can of sardines. Many in underground movements would say that these pleasures should be deferred, but Marcos appears to welcome them.

His iconic status in the underground culture stems in part from his risking his life with a sense of humor, and his refusal to "grow up," to take "the cure" of no longer being himself. He is a living rejection of the maxim that revolutionaries become conservative through aging itself. He becomes a symbol of resistance beyond youth. He is an armed Jack Kerouac, still on the road.

///

THE SUP'S WORDS FOR THE "FROM THE UNDERGROUND CULTURE TO THE CULTURE OF RESISTANCE" ROUNDTABLE ALICIA MULTIFORUM

October 26, 1999

I would like to thank the organizers who were in charge of the Alicia Multiforum for the invitation to participate in this roundtable.

I do not have much experience in round tables. Square tables are more our specialty, as the table most certainly must be where those who are accompanying this act are seated: Zack de la Rocha, Yaotl, Hermann Bellinghausen, Nacho Pineda, a compa from the Punk Anarchy Collective, and Javier Elorriaga.

More, it is quite likely that the participants at this round table that is not round are seated on a small platform. Perhaps there is not even a table, and there are only a few chairs. Perhaps the only one who has a table is me, because they have to put the TV on something in order to show you this video.

The fact is, at this round table, those who are participating cannot see each other's faces, something that would most certainly be happening if they were at a round table that was, in fact, round. And so here we are, sitting around a round table that is not round, and facing you, which is better, because from here I'm able to see a guy whose face is the best argument for leaving the issue of round and square tables in peace, and better that I don't tell you what that look is suggesting either (*sigh*).

Where was I? Oh, yes! That here we are, facing you, at that round table that I don't know who called "From Underground Culture to the Culture of Resistance." I don't have anything against whoever called this round table that isn't round that. The problem is that word that is repeated: "*culture*." So many things fit there that, even though we are restricting them to the limits imposed by the words "underground" and "resistance," they would not do for a round table, no matter how square it might be, but rather for a great intercontinental encuentro that would last for years, without even including the time taken up in arranging the microphone, greeting the raza, or in staying asleep because someone has decided that culture can also be boring and has set about demonstrating it.

Having said that, I am not going to talk to you about underground culture, nor about the culture of resistance, nor about the bridge that most certainly joins them. In addition to leaving the issue for those who are accompanying us at that table that we are calling round even knowing that it is square, I will avoid making myself appear ridiculous and I will be able to conceal my encyclopedic ignorance on this subject. As the well-loved Don Durito of Lacandón would say, "There is no problem sufficiently great that it cannot be pondered upon." I would add to those wise words that cause the action and the commitment, "nor is there a round table that is not square."

I know that you are all anxious to know what in the hell I'm going to talk about then. More than one of you might be asking if the guitar I have by my side means that I'm going to play a song, one of those that are so honorably played in the Mexico of below, which we all are.

But no, I'm not going to play any songs. The guitar is for the surprise appearance we're going to make tomorrow, October 27, 1999, with Rage Against the Machine, Aztlán Underground, and Tijuana No at the Sports Palace. That's if they don't censor us first, or if the law doesn't show up, in which case the concert will be held in the prison closest to your hearts.

I'm going to be sincere with you, this entire initial litany has been to use up time, because the organizers made it quite clear to me that I was to speak for some 20 minutes, and I believe that 20 minutes are too long to say that I'm not going to speak to you about underground culture, nor about the culture of resistance, nor about the relationship between the one and the other.

You know? We are warriors. Some very otherly warriors, but, at the end of the day, some warriors. We warriors know a few things. We know about weapons.

So, better that I talk to you about weapons. Specifically, I'm going to talk to you about the weapon of resistance.

We, besides being warriors, are Mexican indigenous. We live in the mountains of the Mexican southeast, which is turning out to be the last corner of this country. We live like the majority of the indigenous in Mexico live—that is, very badly.

Our homes have dirt floors, our walls are of sticks or mud, and our roofs are of laminate, cardboard, or grass. One room serves for kitchen, dining room, bedroom, living room, and henhouse. Our foods are, basically, maize, beans, chili, and the vegetables that grow in the garden. For medicine we have a little popular pharmacy, poorly stocked. Doctors? In our dreams. The school, if it is not being occupied by the government's soldiers, is a hall, where up to four different groups of students coexist at the same time. The students are not very numerous, because our children start working when they're very small. Between four and five years old, the girls begin carrying wood, grinding maize, washing clothes, and taking care of their younger brothers and sisters; when they're between 10 and 12, the boys begin going to the mountain, taking care of the livestock, carrying wood, working the fields, the coffee plantations, or the pasture. Our lands are poor in two senses: they are poor because they are ours, who are poor as a matter of course. And they are poor because they yield little in the way of harvest. We have only mud and rocks; the finqueros have the good lands. The livestock and coffee that we sell to make money, we sell to the coyotes, who are a kind of intermediary, who pay us a tenth of the price of our products in the market. And so our work, in addition to being hard, is badly paid.

However, even though we live like most of the indigenous population in the country, that is, in poverty, we do not live the same as most of the indigenous population. Our poverty is the same as the poverty of the others, but it is different; it is "other" poverty. We are poor because that is what we chose. From the beginning of our uprising, they have offered us everything to get us to sell ourselves, to surrender.

If we had done so, if we had surrendered, if We had sold ourselves, we would now have good houses, good schools, hospitals, machinery for working the land, better prices for our products, good food.

But we chose not to sell ourselves. We chose not to surrender. Because it so happens that we are indigenous and we are also warriors. And warriors are warriors because they are fighting for something. We Zapatistas are fighting for good homes, good food, good health, a good price for our work, good lands, good education, respect for indigenous culture, the right to information, liberty, independence, justice, democracy, and peace. We are fighting for all of that, but for everyone, not just for ourselves. That is why we Zapatistas are warriors, because we want "For everyone, everything, nothing for ourselves."

If we had surrendered, if we had sold ourselves, we would no longer have been poor, but others would have continued to be so.

You are asking yourselves: Where is the weapon that this handsome, attractive, nice warrior was going to talk to us about? I'll tell you now.

It happened that, when they saw that we were not surrendering, that we were not selling ourselves, the government began attacking us in order to force us to surrender and to sell ourselves. They offered us many things— money, projects, aid—and if we rejected them, they became angry and they threatened us. That is how we came to understand that, by refusing to accept government aid, by resisting, we made the powerful angry. And there is nothing a Zapatista warrior likes more than making the powerful angry.

With singular joy we dedicated ourselves to resisting, to saying *no*, to transforming our poverty into a weapon of resistance.

Almost six years of war have now spoken with that weapon. With it we have resisted more than 60,000 soldiers, tanks, aircraft, helicopters, cannon, machine guns, bullets, and grenades. With it, we have resisted the lie.

If you would like me to sum it up, I would tell you that we made ourselves soldiers so that one day soldiers would no longer be necessary. We remain poor so that one day there will no longer be poverty. This is what we use the weapon of resistance for.

Obviously, it is not the only weapon we have, as is clear from the metal that clothes us. We have other arms. For example, we have the arm of the word. We also have the weapon of our culture, of our being what we are. We have the weapon of music, the weapon of dance. We have the weapon of the mountain, that old friend and compañera who fights along with us, with her roads, hiding places, and hillsides, with her trees, with her rains, with her suns, with her dawns, with her moons. . . .

We also have the weapons that we carry by nature, but it is not the time to be going around punning, much less now, when you've all become very serious. In order to chase away your seriousness, I'm going to tell you a joke—no, don't be frightened, I'm not going to tell you a joke, better that we leave that to Zedillo, who, as president, is nothing but a bad joke. No, better that I go on to the next issue that I'm going to talk to you about.

Music and Resistance. Notably rock, but not just rock. Music groups, but not just music groups. I mean, not just what we see and listen to, but also what makes our seeing and listening possible. Because the raza gets down when it listens to Rage Against the Machine, to Aztlán Underground, to Tijuana No. Or to "Durito Against the Sup" (which is a group that's going to be formed if Durito keeps on giving me whooping cough).

Where was I? Ah yes! That the raza gets down when it listens to a good music group, and then one feels ones bones and muscles being controlled by nothing other than the heart and one starts moving, shaking, jumping, a little step here and another little step there, getting together, a "prexta pa la orquestra" (I already know that everyone is thinking: son of a bitch, the Sup is talking like a pachuco from the Tin Tan or Piporro films, but, whatever, raza) well, they dance then, and they don't think about those who are making it possible for that group to be listened to, and that we have a place and a reason to dance. For example, the other day I was listening to some cuts from a group that plays heavy metal (since it so happens that I am "educating my ear," because before the war I was just into folk dances and polkas, ajua). I took a look at the liner notes to the compact disc, and I read that there are tons of people involved, in addition to those who play the music. I believe the musicians recognize the work of all these people, but those of us who are listening or dancing just don't. For example, here we are in the Alicia Multiforum and here is Zack, Yaotl, Pineda, the compa from Punk Anarchy, Elorriaga, and this video that you are being forced to watch and listen to, because what you wanted was to listen to Zack and Yaotl, and not talking exactly, but partying with a song. Good, I said here we are in this place, and whoever organized this round table that is square, whoever or whatever is responsible for the sound being heard well or badly, whoever takes care of this building, whoever keeps it going, whoever opened this space so that you and we could meet? We don't have any idea. Their place is too in the background. But, then, I'm proposing to you, for all those people who are back there, that we give them a round of applause that can be heard even in the back, and don't leave them out, because if not for them there would be neither round table, nor square, nor concert. Applaud, then.

[Applause continues]

If the applause takes a while, push "stop" on the video, because, if not, I'm going to continue and no one can fight me.

All done now? Good. The subject was, what is music and resistance. As I explained before, as far as music goes I'm just do-re-mi-fa-sol-la-ti, and I still get it wrong, but we are a bit smart about resistance. The fact is that Zapatismo and rock bring and carry something, because, if not, what are Zack and Yaotl and I doing here (because I'm also a rocker, but an old-fashioned one), sitting at a round table which, as everyone has seen, is square.

If we say that Zapatismo rebounded in rock groups and in that way produced its other and different effect, I believe we would be being unfair. We are talking about groups with a long tradition of social commitment and professional independence. What happened? Who knows. Perhaps many round tables are necessary, even though they may be square, in order to look at the issue of rock and Zapatismo.

Perhaps what happened is there was a meeting. There were words that met, but, above all, there were, and are, feelings that met. If there are songs from these groups that could easily appear to be communiqués, and if there are communiqués that could be lines to songs, it is not by virtue of who is writing them, it is because they are saying the same thing, they are reflecting the same thing, that underground "other," which, by being different, organizes itself in order to resist, in order to exist.

Because it is not just the Zapatistas who are warriors of resistance. There are many groups (and there are several gathered together here) who have also made a weapon of resistance, and they are using it. There are indigenous, there are workers, there are women, there are homosexuals, there are lesbians, there are students, there are young people. Above all there are young people, men and women, who name their own identities: punk, ska, goth, metal, trasher, rapper, hip-hopper, etcetera. If we look at what they all have in common, we will see that they have nothing in common, that they are all different. They are "others." And that is exactly what we have in common, that we are "other," and different. Not only that, we also have in common that we are fighting in order to continue being "other" and different. And we are "other" and different to the powerful; we are not like they want us to be, but rather just as we are.

And what we are—far from wanting to impose its being on the "other" or different—seeks its own space, and, at the same time, a space of meeting. The punks don't go around on a campaign demanding that all young people be punks, nor do the ska, or the goths, or the metal heads, or the trashers, or the rappers, or, certainly, the indigenous. However the Power does indeed want us to be how they want us to be, want us to dress according to the style the Power dictates, want us to talk the way he says, want us to eat what he sells, want us to consider beautiful and lovely what he considers beautiful and lovely, even wants us to love and hate the way he establishes that love and hate should be. And not just that, the Power also wants us to do all this on our knees and in silence, without going around jumping, without shouts, without indigenous uprisings, well-mannered. That is why the Power has armies and police, to force those who are "other" and different to be the same and identical.

But the "other" and different are not looking for everyone to be like they are. As if each one is saying that everyone has his own way or his own thing (I don't know how that's said now) and, in order for this to be possible, it is not enough to just be, you also must always respect the other. The "everyone doing his own thing" is both an affirmation of difference, and it is respect for the other difference. When we say we are fighting for respect for our different and "other" selves, that includes fighting for respect for those who are also "other" and different, who are not like ourselves. And it is here where this entire resistance movement—called "underground" or "subterranean," because it takes place among those of below and underneath institutional movements—meets Zapatismo.

This meeting is a meeting between warriors, among those who make resistance a weapon, and who fight with it in order to be what they are, in order to exist. When Zapatistas say "we want a world where many worlds fit," we are not discovering anything new, we are simply saying what the "other" and different who walk the worlds of below have already said.

We Zapatistas say, "I am as I am and you are as you are; we are building a world where I can be, without having to cease being me, where you can be, without having to stop being you, and where neither I nor you force another to be like me or like you." When Zapatistas say, "a world where many worlds fit," we are saying, more or less, "everyone does his own thing."

Before you start putting on airs, I'll go on to another subject on the same subject.

Because it so happens that, because we are different, we are the same. We are the same persecuted, the same despised, the same beaten, the same imprisoned, the same disappeared, the same assassinated. And it is not ours who are doing the persecuting, despising, beating, imprisoning, assassinating. It is not even the "others" from below. It is the Power and their names. Our crimes are not stealing, beating, assassinating, insulting. Nor is our crime being "other" and different. Our crime is in being so, and in being proud of being so. Our crime—which in the Power's penal code merits the death penalty—is the struggle we are making to continue being "other" and different. If we were "other" and different shamefully, in hiding, guiltily, betrayed by ourselves, trying to be—or to appear to be—what the Power wants us to be or to appear to be, then they would give us an indulgent and pitying little pat, and they would tell us that "these are things of youth, you will get over them with age." For the Power, the medicine against rebellion is time, "since it will go away with age."

What the Power is not saying is what is behind "that age" that it assumes will cure and do away with youthful rebellion: hours, months, years of blows, of insults, of jails, of deaths, of rapes, of persecutions, of neglect, a machinery working to "cure us" if we stop being what we are and if we turn ourselves into servile beings, or which will eliminate us if we insist on being what we are, without regard to calendar, birthdays, or the date on the birth certificate.

And so, then, we are all transgressors of the law. Because there is a law in this system that kills and silences those who are "other" and different. By living, by shouting, by talking—that is, by being rebels—we are transgressing that law, and we are, automatically, criminals.

Criminals that we are, we live in a rebel reality, where resistance is a bridge for us to meet, recognizing our difference and our equality. And rock is also a bridge over which those realities walk in order to meet.

In what way is rock a mirror for this very "other" and different reality? The truth is, I do not know and I do not understand. I look at and listen to groups like Rage Against the Machine and Tijuana No (to mention just those who are participating in tomorrow's concert, but knowing that there are many others, and that all of them are good — as musicians and as human beings), and I ask myself why do they do what they do, say what they say, and play what they play. I believe it would be better for them to tell us what goes on with them. Perhaps it so happens that they are also asking themselves why we Zapatistas are doing what we are doing, saying what we are saying, and playing what we are playing (although, when it comes to rock, we are fairly useless. Useless: a good name for a group or for a song. "Useless," like that, with no qualifiers, so that everyone fits, men, women, and those who are neither men nor women, but who *are*).

The reason for this video is to answer the question of why we Zapatistas are doing what we are doing, saying what we are saying, and playing what we are playing, but, since I've gone over the 20 minutes I had, it will remain open. At best, what I said earlier might help in finding the answer.

Sale, then, raza, banda, compas, chompiras, valedores, neros, gueyes, or, as that international philosopher who is now dressing as a pirate, Durito, says, "everyone doing his own thing."

Then, Elorriaga's thing shall follow, who will, in his turn, tell us whose thing is to follow, Bellinghausen's, Zack's, Yaotl's, Pineda's, the compa from Punk Anarchy's, or I don't know whose thing then, because, because they might have put me in the middle (which would be in *very* bad taste), or left me to the end, so that the raza would already be asleep and wouldn't have to hear the outrageous things I'm saying here.

Vale. Salud and (like it says on the cover of that fanzine that has the good taste to call itself Z*UPterraneo*), and with such a thing, "something doesn't smell right," which means something like "there are things and then there are things." Salud!

From the mountains of the Mexican southeast
The Sup, tuning up his guitar for the special appearance.
Mexico, "other" and different, October 1999.

TO THE RELATIVES OF THE
POLITICALLY DISAPPEARED

April 2000

ONCE again Marcos brings an original passion and lyrical style to the longstanding subject of human rights reports and speeches, the plight of relatives of "disappeared," incarcerated, tortured, and murdered political rebels. He reveals his roots in the rebellions and persecutions of the 1970s and 1980s as well. His nature imagery—oblivion is the ravine, while memory is mountain and stone, the shadowed moon a sign that something is missing—is as powerful as any environmental author. The statement that "memory is not a date that marks the beginning of an absence, but rather a tree, which planted yesterday, rises up tomorrow," exactly describes the roots of Zapatismo that cannot be severed by military force but only by public complicity in forgetting.

I dream in marble cloisters
Where, in divine silence,
The heroes stand, at rest;
At night, by the light of the soul,
I speak with them by night!
They are in line. I pass
Among the lines. I kiss
The hands of stone, the eyes
Of stone open. The beards
Of stone tremble. The stone swords
Are brandished: they weep.
The sword shudders in the sheath!
Mute, I kiss their hands.

—JOSÉ MARTÍ

///

APRIL falls with stone hand over Mexico. Sun and shadows abound during the day, and at night the moon negotiates a path mined with stars. This country now walks the path of uncertainty, that ravine, one of whose sides is threatened by oblivion and forgetting. On the other side, memory is made mountain and stone.

The dawn is plucking petals from lost lights when, in any city, in any house, in any room, in front of any typewriter, a mother (the heart of the flower of stone, hope) is writing a letter. Curious, the dawn leans over her shoulder and barely manages to steal a few lines: "and then you will imagine the sorrow that grieves me so . . . for us, the mothers, who have lived as if with a dagger plunged into our chest for so very long. . . . " The shadow brings the bowl of the pipe to the candle and lights the tobacco and the words which have already taken over the hands, which are now writing:

I did not know Jesús Piedra Ibarra, or César Germán Yanez Munoz. Not personally. From other photographs I can recognize them now in the poster in front of me, that shines a EUREKA! on the upper part. In the center, a group of men and women are carrying a large banner that reads PRESENTATION OF THE POLITICALLY DISAPPEARED, and it is filled with photographs of men and women, all young, all Mexican. Among the images, I lightly mark with a pen that of Jesús Piedra Ibarra and that of César Germán Yanez Munoz.

I examine the faces of those holding up the banner: mostly women, and it can be seen from their faces that they are forever mothers. Are? Forever? They are, and they are forever, that is for certain. The poster could be from 25 years ago, from 15, from 5 years ago, from this very day. It tells me nothing other than the firmness of those gazes, their determination, their hope.

The White Brigade, the paramilitary group with which the government conducted the dirty war against the Mexican guerrillas of the 1970s and 1980s, kidnapped Jesús Piedra Ibarra on April 18, 1975, 25 years ago. Since then, nothing has been learned of him. The Mexican Federal Army detained César Germán Yanez Munoz in 1974, 26 years ago. Since then, nothing has been learned of him. Thirty years ago, 20 years ago, 10 years ago, 5 years ago, right now in Mexico political opponents are being "disappeared."

I did not know Jesús Piedra Ibarra or César Germán Yanez Munoz, nor any of the politically disappeared men and women. Or perhaps I did know them. They had other faces and wore different bodies, but it was their same gaze. I knew them in the streets and in the mountains. I saw them raising their fists, flags, weapons. I saw them saying *no!*, shouting *no!* until they were left without voice in their throats but still in their hearts. I saw them. I knew them. Then they were confederates, compañeros, brothers, they were us. I knew them. I know them. Their feet and arms are other, but their steps are the same, their embraces are the same. I know them. I know us. Those faces are ours. Just take a black-tipped pen and paint a ski mask on the faces of those men and women.

Jesús Piedra Ibarra, César Germán Yanez Munoz. I knew their mothers. I knew Rosa, mother of César Germán, and, some time later, Rosario, mother of Jesús. I knew Rosa and Rosario, both mothers of fighters, both fighters, both seekers. Some years ago Rosa made as if she had died and went to look for César Germán under the earth. Rosario continues above, looking for Jesús. Mamas of stone, Rosa and Rosario look above and beneath the stones. They are looking for a disappeared, two, three, dozens, hundreds. . . .

Yes, there are hundreds of politically disappeared in Mexico. What were these and other men and women guilty of to deserve from their enemies, not life and liberty, but neither jail nor grave? At times a photograph is the only material thing remaining of them. But in the mothers' hands of stone, that photograph is made into a flag. And the flags are made to wave in the heavens. And the heavens are where they are raised by men and women who know that memory is not a date that marks the beginning of an absence, but rather a tree which, planted yesterday, rises up tomorrow.

Of what material can the homage be made to those anonymous heroes who have no other corner than the memory of those who share their blood and their ideals? Of stone, but not of just any stone. Perhaps of the stone of memory that their mothers were and are. Because there are mothers that are stone, stone of refuge, of strength, of home, of wall that sustains the word *justice* in their hearts.

The mothers of the disappeared are of stone. What can those ladies fear who have confronted so much, who have struggled so much? Not absence, because they have carried that for many years. Not pain, because they live with that each and every day. Not exhaustion, because they have traveled all paths time and again. No, the only thing the ladies fear is the silence with which oblivion, forgetting, and amnesia covers itself, staining history.

The ladies have no weapon against that fear other than memory. But where is memory safeguarded when a frenzied cynicism reigns in the world of politics? Where can those little pieces of history take refuge, which now appear to be only photographs, and which were once men and women with faces, names, ideals? Why does the Left of today seem to be so overwhelmed by the present and to forget its absent ones? How many of those fallen in the long night of the dirty war in Mexico are nothing other than stepping stones in the rise of the Left as alternative politics? How many of those that we are owe much to those who are not here?

Is it over? Has the nightmare that was called the White Brigade ended now? What is the government body now called that is in charge of disappearing those who are opposed to the system? Mexico: Has it done better with political disappearances since it has been "modern?" Can one speak of justice while political disappearances exist?

Those who are relatives (through blood, through ideas, through both) of the politically disappeared: Do they have company today in their anguish, in their pain, in the absences? Where are the hands and shoulders for them? Where is the ear for their rebellion? What dictionary contains their determined search that will banish forever the words "irremediable," "irretrievable," "impossible," "oblivion," "resignation," "conformity," "surrender?" The politically disappeared: Where are their executioners?

Those who disappeared them appear at the old and beleaguered house of the current politics in Mexico. They see that no one is turning around, that no eye is even turning to the forgotten chest of those who have fought so that there may no longer be a below to which one's gaze might fall. The executioners congratulate themselves then: They have been successful; they raise their cups and toast with blood the death of memory.

This country is called Mexico, and it is the year 2000. The century and millenium are ending, and the belief continues that silence makes things disappear: If we do not speak of prisoners and the politically disappeared, they will then be erased from our present and from our past.

But it is not so. With silence not only will our history vanish, but, most certainly, the nightmare will be repeated, and other mothers will be made of stone, and they will travel to all corners, above and below, saying, shouting, demanding justice.

The executioners are celebrating their impunity (and their impunity is not just that they have no punishment, it is also that the disappeared continue to be disappeared), but also the silence.

Nonetheless, not everyone forgets.

Because, further below, where the roots of the Patria take life from subterranean rivers, the defeat of the executioners is brewing.

The images that memory raises in this heart from below are of stone, and those men and women who, barely touching the strong skin of history, are rising up and speaking, have some part of stone. And there is also a bit of stone in that modest school which, in the midst of the Zapatista Realidad, where the name shines like a flag: "Jesús Piedra Ibarra School."

THE SHADOW CRUMPLES the written pages and sets fire to them with the same light with which he relights his pipe. He takes another clean page and, with concise tenderness, writes:

> April 18, 2000.
>
> Mama Stone:
> I do not know about the others, but we do not forget.
> With affection, Your Zapatista daughters and sons.
>
> PS: Best wishes to all the ladies.

Below, the dawn continues its hot embrace, while the sea arranges the breezes of her hair. Above the moon, partial, reminds us that nothing will be complete if memory is missing. And "memory" is how justice is called here.

From the mountains of the Mexican southeast.
Subcomandante Insurgente Marcos.
Mexico, April 2000

DO NOT FORGET
IDEAS ARE ALSO WEAPONS

Subcomandante Marcos

Originally appeared in *Le Monde diplomatique*, August 2000

Translated by Harry Forster.

THE purpose of this text is to fuel the debate between right and left-wing intellectuals. It does not attempt to explain relations with governments or changes in society.

PAY-PER-VIEW GLOBAL DOMINATION

The world is not square, or so we learn at school, but on the brink of the third millennium it is not round either. I do not know which geometrical figure best represents the world in its present state but, in an era of digital communication, we could see it as a gigantic screen—one of those screens you can program to display several pictures at the same time, one inside the other. In our global world the pictures come from all over the planet—but some are missing. Not because there is not enough room on the screen but because someone up there selected these pictures rather than others.

What do the pictures show? On the American continent, we see a para-military group occupying the Autonomous National University of Mexico (UNAM); but the men in gray uniforms are not there to study. Another frame shows an armored column thundering through a native community in Chiapas. Beside this, we see United States police using violence to arrest a youth in a city that could be Seattle or Washington. The pictures in Europe are just as gray.

A MEMORABLE OMISSION

Intellectuals have been part of society since the dawn of humanity. Their work is analytical and critical. They look at social facts and analyze the evidence, for and against, looking for anything ambiguous, anything that is neither one thing nor the other, revealing anything that is not obvious—sometimes even the opposite of what seems obvious.

These professional critics act as a sort of impertinent consciousness for society. They are nonconformists, disagreeing with everything—social and political forces, the state, government, media, arts, religion, and so on. Activists will just say "we've had enough," but skeptical intellectuals will cautiously murmur not enough or too much? Intellectuals criticize immobility, demand change and progress. They are, nevertheless, part of a society, which is the scene of endless confrontation and is split between those who use power to maintain the status quo and those who fight for change.

Intellectuals must choose between their function as intellectuals and the role that activists offer them. It is also here that we see the split between progressive and reactionary intellectuals. They all continue their work of critical analysis, but while the more progressive persist in criticizing immobility, permanence, hegemony and homogeneity, the reactionaries focus their attacks on change, movement, rebellion, and diversity. So in fact, reactionary intellectuals "forget" their true function and give up critical thought. Their memory shrinks, excluding past and future to focus only on the immediate and present. No further discussion is possible.

INTELLECTUAL PRAGMATISM

Many leading right-wing intellectuals start life as progressives. But they soon attract the attention of the powerful, who deploy innumerable stratagems to buy or destroy them. Progressive intellectuals are "born" in the midst of a process of seduction and persecution. Some resist; others, convinced that the global economy is inevitable, look in their box of tricks and find reasons to legitimate the existing power structure. They are awarded with a comfortable armchair, on the right hand of the prince they once denounced.

They can find any number of excuses for this supposedly inevitable outcome: It is the end of history; money is everywhere and all-powerful; the police have taken the place of politics; the present is the only possible future; there is a rational explanation for social inequality. There are even "good reasons" for the unbridled exploitation of human beings and natural resources, racism, intolerance, and war.

In an era marked by two new paradigms—communication and the market—right-wing intellectuals have realized that being "modern" means obeying one rule: "Adapt or go under." They are not required to be original, just to think like everyone else, taking their cue from international bodies like the World Bank, the International Monetary Fund, or the World Trade Organization.

Far from indulging in original, critical thought, right-wing intellectuals become remarkably pragmatic, echoing the advertising slogans that flood the world's markets. In exchange for a place in the sun and the support of certain media and governments, they cast off their critical imagination and any form of self-criticism and espouse the new, free-market creed.

BLIND SEERS

The problem is not why the global economy is inevitable, but why almost everyone agrees that it is. Just as the economy is becoming increasingly global, so is culture and information. How are we to prevent vast media and communications companies like CNN or News Corporation, Microsoft or AT&T, from spinning their worldwide web?

In today's world economy the major corporations are essentially media enterprises, holding up a huge mirror to show us what society should be, not what it is. To paraphrase Régis Debray, what is visible is real and consequently true.* That, by the way, is one of the tenets of right-wing dogma. Debray also explains that the center of gravity of news has shifted from the written word to visual effects, from recorded to live broadcasts, from signs to pictures.

To retain their legitimacy, today's right-wing intellectuals must fulfill their role in a visual era, opting for what is immediate and direct, switching from signs to images, from thought to TV commentary.

FUTURE PAST

In Mexico, left-wing intellectuals are very influential. Their crime is that they get in the way. Well, that's one of their crimes, because they also support the Zapatistas in their struggle: "The Zapatista uprising heralds the start of a new era in which native movements will emerge as players in the fight against the neoliberal global economy."† But we are neither unique nor perfect. Just look at the natives of Ecuador and Chile, and the demonstrations in Seattle, Washington, Prague—and those that will follow.

*Croire, voir, faire, Odile Jacob, Paris, 1999.
†Yvon Le Bot, "Los indígenas contra el neoliberalismo," *La Jornada*, 6 March 2000.

We are just one of the pictures that deform the giant screen of the world economy.

The prince has consequently issued orders: "Attack them! I shall supply the army and media. You come up with the ideas." So right-wing intellectuals spend their time insulting their left-wing counterparts, and because of the Zapatista movement's international impact, they are now busy rewriting our story to suit the demands of the prince.

NEOLIBERAL FASCISTS

In one of his books Umberto Eco provides some pointers as to why fascism is still latent.* He starts by warning us that fascism is a diffuse form of totalitarianism, then defines its characteristics: refusal of the advance of knowledge, disregard of rational principles, distrust of culture, fear of difference, racism, individual or social frustration, xenophobia, aristocratic elitism, machismo, individual sacrifice for the benefit of the cause, televised populism, and use of Newspeak with its limited words and rudimentary syntax.

These are the values that right-wing intellectuals defend. Take another look at the giant screen. All that gray is a response to disorder, reflected in demands for law and order from all around us. But is Europe once more the prey of fascism? We may well see skinheads, with their swastikas, on the screen, but the commentator is quick to reassure us that they are only minority groups, already under control. But it may also take other, more sinister forms.

After the fall of the Berlin wall both sides of the political spectrum in Europe rushed to occupy the center. This was all too obvious with the traditional left, but it was also the case with the far right.† It went out of its way to acquire a new image, well removed from its violent, authoritarian past, enthusiastically espousing neoliberal dogma.

SKEPTICALLY HOPEFUL

The task of progressive thinkers—to remain skeptically hopeful—is not an easy one. They have understood how things work and, noblesse oblige, they must reveal what they know, dissect it, denounce it, and pass it on to others.

---

*Umberto Eco, *Cinque scritti morali*, Bompiani, Milan, 1997.
†See Emiliano Fruta, "La nueva derecha europea," and Hernán R. Moheno, "Más allá de la vieja izquierda y la nueva derecha," in *Urbi et Orbi*, Itam, Mexico, April 2000.

But to do this, they must also confront neoliberal dogma, backed by the media, banks, major corporations, the Army, and police.

What is more, we live in a visual age—and so, to their considerable disadvantage, progressive thinkers must fight the power of the image with nothing but words. But their skepticism will get them out of that trap, and if they are equally skeptical in their critical analysis, they will be able to see through the virtual beauty to the real misery it conceals. So perhaps there is reason to hope.

There is a story that when Michelangelo sculpted his statue of David, he had to work on a secondhand piece of marble that already had holes in it. It is a mark of his talent that he was able to create a figure that took account of those limitations. The world we want to transform has already been worked on by history and is largely hollow. We must nevertheless be inventive enough to change it and build a new world.

Take care and do not forget that ideas are also weapons.

CONCLUSION

THE *purpose of these selections has been to offer and review the thinking and style of Marcos in his several moods. Other works exist that provide a fuller collection of his writings (Juana Ponce de Leon, ed.* Our Word Is Our Weapon, *Seven Stories Press, 2001, and Bardacke and Lopez, ed.* Shadows of Tender Fury, *Monthly Review, 1995).*

In conclusion, I want to suggest three powerful legacies that Marcos and the EZLN have already planted for this and future generations.

First, there is a lesson in how to live in a world with little hope and few examples. Very simply, Marcos stands for the principle that we each must know what we would risk dying for in order to know what we live for. The cynical credo of the modern world is quite the opposite, that everyone has a price. Marcos and the Zapatistas have been offered government grants and a role in the Mexican state. They have insisted on dignity and independence instead. Their armed struggle is a lesson in how to risk death on behalf of dignity, rather than of how to kill soldiers or bomb state buildings. Those who have accepted their own deaths—especially if they are gentle warriors, poets, storytellers—have a particular moral authority in a world that seems to vanquish or corrupt its heroes.

Second, his writings have energized and given direction to the worldwide opposition to corporate globalization. What seemed beyond challenge a few years ago, an ideology of modernism pretending to "the rank of a religious cult" (the term is Carlos Monsiváis's), a secular replacement for utopia and revolution, is now challenged and, in some sense, trembling in the face of an opposition by otherness that came out of nowhere. There were no well-known, established, and respectable personalities, no political parties, in the front ranks of the resistance to NAFTA and the WTO. The resistance came from the shadowy underground of the "other," from unexpected places like Las Cañadas and Seattle. Marcos and the EZLN have done more to define the global system they call "neoliberalism," and define a course of opposition, than any personality or party on the planet.

Globalization by its nature triggers a varied range of grievances depending on where its damage is done. Marcos was among the first to see, nurture, and organize the elements of globalized resistance.

Finally, Marcos and the EZLN have returned the question of the indigenous to its central place in our memory and the organization of our world. While there always has been a romantic movement concerned with indigenous culture, spirituality, and rights, the general thrust of both conservative and progressive political thought has accepted the notion of their "backwardness." The Left's tendency has been to place greater emphasis on the working class than the indigenous, viewing the latter as primitive or traditional. In *effect, the end of indigenous cultures, however tragic or brutal, was prelude to the formation of a proletariat with supposed revolutionary potential. Conservatives believed they should accelerate the process by displacing, evicting, and reorganizing the lands of the indigenous, meanwhile incorporating the survivors in various manifest destinies and civlizing missions, usually through Christian schools, name changes, and forced urbanization.*

With the emergence of liberation theology, the role of Church changed from consoling and pacifying the indigenous to organizing and defending their right to exist. The Zapatistas went further, supporting the restoration and protection of their traditional spiritual and communal practices. They did so at first of necessity, facing isolation otherwise, but then they actually seemed to assimilate into, and become able to share experiences equally with, the indigenous that they had come to lead but now were following. Marcos became a convert, and in doing so, a conduit between two spirit worlds and political realities.

The Marcos writings suggest that this is a conversion experience to which more people of the modern world should "surrender" (his word, a striking one). When the brilliant Guatemalan scholar Victor Perera chronicled the lives of the Mayans of the Lacandónes two decades ago, just as Marcos and his compañeros were establishing camps in the jungle, Perera expected to see the perishing of the Lacandónes in our lifetime. There was no alternative imaginable at the time. While expecting their demise, however, he did not share the view that they were disposable. He believed that their loss would parallel the loss of ecosystems of vital significance to the faraway modern world. He also lamented the iminent loss of the Lacandónes' cultural heritage, in which he included unique spiritual capacities. Perera speculated that with the collapse of ancient Mayan centers like Palenque and Tikal, which were designed to explore the outer cycles of the universe, the same spirit of exploration was perhaps driven inward, into "internal heavens and hells, the hidden suns and moons . . . and into the refinement of 'extrasensory' means of communication such as telepathy," for he "came to accept telepathic and even televisual communication between Lacandónes as a matter of course."*

Into this seemingly impenetrable, dying world came the six original creators of the EZLN. It is a miracle that they stayed, listened, learned the languages,

---

*Victor Perera and Robert D. Bruce, *The Last Lords of Palenque: the Lacondon Mayas of the Mexican Rainforest,* University of California Press, Berekely, 1982.

and in the end incorporated and finally externalized the feelings, thoughts, dreams, and culture of these Mayans to the wider world.

Whether this movement becomes a grand, dignified funeral procession for the doomed indigenous, a prolonged day of the dead, a spectacular shower before oblivion, or instead a reappearance of the el mundo profundo *which prevents the death sentence known as globalization, is the question this generation will address. Far from being a question of the past, what to do about the Conquest that never ended is the question of the future. The globalizers seem to think the loss of the indigenous along with their mountains, rainforests, plants, insects, and jaguars, is a necessary stage toward progress. But what if the very opposite of modern thought is the true word, that the collapse of the indigenous people and their natural world—the end of cultural diversity along with biodiversity—means the end of systems that have sustained life for thousands of years? Seen in this manner, is it not time for more of us to say* Basta *too?*

PART THREE
THE COMMENTARIES

THE LAST GLOW OF THE
MEXICAN REVOLUTION

ADOLFO GILLY

Excerpted from "Chiapas and the Rebellion of the Enchanted World" in *Rural Revolt in Mexico*, Daniel Nugent (Duke University Press, 1998).

I.

Since the time of Don Porfirio, the liberal Mexican state has claimed a pre-Hispanic Indian ancestry for itself while denying the rights common to all citizens to those Indians actually living in Mexican territory. This was in the tradition of nineteenth-century liberalism in Mexico, where since the Constitution of 1824 the Indian majority had been unevenly assimilated to the category "citizens"; only as individuals did they enjoy the supposed "legal equality" that is the recognized right of every citizen. And there they sort of remained. The law rendered them as invisible as Garabombo, Manuel Scoria's fictional Peruvian Indian.

Neither were Indians as such included in the constitutional pact of 1917. Instead they appeared in that modifying successor of liberal pedigree under the general rubric of "peasants" and "communities" with rights to land. The national project of the new Mexican state, expressed in the official ideology of *indigenismo*, involved the assimilation and absorption of the indigenous in the Mexican, and the "citizenization" of Indians through public education, state protection, and economic development.

As is well known, the province of Chiapas was left at the margin of the Mexican revolution, not even experiencing a "revolution from without," as did Yucatán. The Obregón government entered into a deal with the local landlord oligarchy, lending its political support to the maintenance of the oligarchy's domination of peasant and Indian *pueblos*. For the Chiapan oligarchy, this deal was one more step in its history of "modernization" from above without the slightest change in social relations. Railroads, highways, investment, state administration—all were laid over obscure and violent servile relations maintained by force and by ignorance about the residents of the Chiapan countryside, negated not only in their condition as Mexican citizens but even in their condition as human beings. Chiapan reality continued to be immutably faithful to what was described by Rosario Castellanos in *Ciudad Real* or in *Oficio de tinieblas*.

In a kind of suspended time, this reality reproduced colonial-period sociocultural relations of command/obedience within Chiapas even while its external appearance vis-à-vis the political system was that of the Republic. The situation of Indians during the liberal regime of Porfirio Díaz was not very different, as Eric Van Young described when referring to the doctrine of the "just war" against the Yaquis of Sonora occurring simultaneously with the installation of the monument to Cuauhtémoc on the Paseo de la Reforma:

> None of this was new, of course, but stretched far back into colonial times, offering yet another in a series of continuities in Mexican cultural history. In the colonial period, Indians for the most part were viewed by those in authority not only as children of diminished intellectual capacity but also as ignorant, lazy, drunken, vicious sodomites naturally prone to suggestion, extreme violence, and religious backsliding. Nor did this complex of attitudes toward indigenous people have much to do with Enlightenment thought, with its mania for classification, though the Enlightenment may have laid an ideological patina over the basic conceptual arsenal. It goes back much further in the history of European–native encounter, finding its roots not only in the radical otherness of American native cultures in the eyes of the Europeans but also in the daily praxis of exploitation and asymmetrical power relations. Indeed, I am tempted to remark that the expropriation seems ontologically prior to the ethnic elements.

It was against the crucial blindness of this "complex of attitudes" that the indigenous Zapatista rebellion rose up in 1994. In declarations, gestures, spatial movements, clothing, attitudes, in a vast symbolic language directed to the rest but above all to their following, they made that point; and, if it were required, the rebels would not tire of repeating it. It was summarized in one word, *dignity*.

After the revolution, exploitation and its corresponding forms of domination changed much less in Chiapas than the political and economic forms in which they were enveloped. But at least three processes occurred. First, Mexico was changing in its laws, its relations of power, and its modes of negotiating rule. Second, notwithstanding their outright rejection, Indian communities preserved their forms of internal relations—their offices, beliefs, myths, histories and, above all, their languages, their entire cultural universe—and put into place a determined constellation of forces and forms for their protected and continued use. Finally, between those two processes, a slow and unavoidable osmosis—however invisible and negated—took place, since Chiapas is in Mexico and not somewhere else.

In other words, the absence of the Mexican revolution, a "modernization" without social change, and the oft signaled "freezing" of the communities were real but not absolute. And if finally modernity burst onto the scene even more violently in the Indian rebellion of 1994, it was above all with that first demand, the strangest because the most universal and the most abstract: *dignity*.

This demand is invariably disconcerting and irritating to those who unlawfully retain power. They haven't a clue how to place it or understand it, never mind respond to it. How can one satisfy a demand if one understands neither what it is nor what the other means to say by it? Faithful to the dominant regime's system of beliefs, they essentially keep seeing Indians as they were seen in the time of Don Porfirio. Sometimes, not even people expressing solidarity with the rebels thoroughly embrace the demand of the latter, because their own experience is limited to an Enlightenment idea of the dignity of the individual (another idea not respected by the regime).

This other sense of dignity includes the dignity of the individual, but it also embraces a more ancient and more complex universe, opaque to the rational gaze of the Enlightenment but conserved alive and whole in the occult history and collective life of the communities, in their histories, myths, beliefs, and desires. It is this lived and inherited dimension, the communitarian idea of what it is to be human—which is to say, dignity as definitive of and inherent to the human condition—that nurtures the ultimate base of the moral economy of this and other rebellions of the oppressed: "perhaps an ancient fury / nameless generations / crying out for vengeance" as the song of Francesco Guccini says.

The Indian idea of community (territory, language, and history) is rooted "in the sacred order (of religious beliefs, symbols, and practices) where dominion over a locality is anchored (the political structure and history of the place) and where its time (from 'immemorial times' to the historical present) is calculated," as Van Young puts it. This order is not egalitarian but hierarchical, as are the internal relations specific to the agrarian community that guarantee its subsistence and reproduction. Respect for human beings is rooted in respect for this order, which defines the traditional norms of reciprocity, rights, and responsibilities within the community. Both the sense of dignity and those acts which negate it—humiliation, insult, affront—are lived in the same manner but have formed themselves in different worlds. It could be that the slogan of the Industrial Workers of the World at the start of the twentieth century explains this lived character better: "An injury to one is an injury to all."

It is in this feeling of injustice, of moral outrage demanding reparation from the heavens, that the roots of the rebellion of poor folk, whether urban or rural, are combined and nurtured. In moments such as these, injustice is lived as the negation of dignity (whether individual or collective), as a threat to the essence of the human condition as each community or human being conceives or imagines it. And only then does the decision to risk everything, in rebellion against a "situation that they need not, cannot, and ought not endure," as Barrington Moore puts it, ripen in the consciousness.

It is always good to recall that the slogan of Emiliano Zapata and his Liberation Army of the South was not, as many have said, "Tierra y Libertad," but rather a slogan that came out of the history of the agrarian pueblos and their relation to power: "Reforma, Libertad, Justicia y Ley." It was upon these ideas that the Zapatistas constructed their government and legislation in the pueblos of Morelos.

Justice is the word on which all the others depend. The lived context— the *material*, if you will, of insult, reparation, and reestablishment of justice—appears to escape the notice of those who want to explain the logic of rebellion above all in terms of individual interest and the commercial reasoning of the modern world. They cannot comprehend that interest and reason in a world of collective solidarities are articulated differently, nor see the community as an intelligent and thoughtful whole, a totality; even less can they see religion—that millenarian incarnation of equilibriums and reasons to be of the agrarian pueblos—as an instrument of legitimation of reason and interests. Perhaps it will be to the sacred order, an order whose ultimate essence is to be found in notions of justice and injustice, that one must go to search for the point where finally that communitarian dignity and its secular, individual, and Enlightenment version are fused: a place crisscrossed by the secret passageway of coming and going between the enchanted world and the modern word.

///

II.

Jan Rus writes that for Mayan peasants of highland Chiapas the word "revolution" is unrelated to the revolution of 1910. For them, that was little more than a civil war between two dominant factions—one local the other central—for control of the region; peasants were excluded and mistreated equally by both factions. For the Indians, the true revolution occurred during the time of President Cárdenas in the second half of the 1930s, when a partial agrarian reform, unions, and the abolition of debt peonage finally reached Chiapas.

The years between 1936 and the early 1940s are sometimes called the time of "the revolution of the Indians." This revolution was neither peaceful nor only made from above, because nothing ever changes that way. Some figures such as Erasto Urbina, a modest functionary of the cardenista government, were later local legends, leading groups of armed men who assured that a redistribution of lands and the application of legal dispositions were achieved *manu militari*. Maya Indians were finally included in the revolution: but really only as peasants and ejidatarios, less (or not at all) as Indians. The price of this limited inclusion was the subordination of the communities and settlements to the tutelage of the state, which is to say to a constitutive interchange with the Mexican state community; guardianship in exchange for protection.

The state successfully incorporated communities that had their own ancestral, corporatist traditions of social organization and politics, interlaced with community beliefs and religious offices. Out of this hybridization surged an unforeseen imbrication, different from that according to which the very same state had integrated other urban or peasant sectors. Jan Rus describes the result:

> With the passage of time, it turned out that they managed to coopt not only the native leaders who were their direct collaborators but also, ironically, the very community structures previously identified with resistance to outside intervention and exploitation: independent self-government, strictly enforced community solidarity, and religious legitimation of political power. As a result, by the mid-1950s, what anthropologists were just beginning to describe as "closed corporate communities" had in fact become "institutionalized revolutionary communities" harnessed to the state.

This incorporation, in turn, produced another result already known throughout Mexico: it converted the state into the peasants' primary interlocutor, to whom all their demands, expectations, and requests would henceforth be directed. In other words, it was no longer landlords but the state and federal governments that were left as the *true counterpart to the peasantry*. The strength of this corporatist paternalism of the state, however, which could convert the peasantry into its "favored children"—its *hijos predilectos*, to borrow a phrase from Arturo Warman—also turned out to be its weakness; for it was unable to rid itself of the stubborn and discomforting presence of the peasantry. In the years that followed, Indian communities in Chiapas, like *ejidos* and *pueblos* in other parts of Mexico, discovered not only the persons through whom to negotiate their relations with the national and local governments but, at the same time, a way in which to maintain their own customs and internal relations that would conserve roles of domination internal to the communities and at the same time be functional vis-à-vis the ruling state.

The key figure in this relationship was, of course, the local community leader, with one foot in the community and its "traditions" and the other in the PRI's system of negotiation and cooptation. His power as *principal* derived from the confidence the community conceded him as one of their own, capable of mediating with the outside world. This functionary, at the same time, accumulated income and privileges for himself and his family not always visible to the community, deriving as they did from the integrating and coopting logic of the Mexican system of domination. The more he compromised himself with the state, the more he invoked his own "Indianness" and the defense of "Indian culture."

At the nexus between the peasant community cultures and their domination by the national state there appeared, as throughout Mexico, the well-known and irreplaceable figure of the *cacique*. In the case of Chiapas, though, the system of negotiation and mediation within which the *caciques* and "power brokers" operated assumed particular characteristics. First of all, the state's domination of the Indians remained based on the isolation and enclosure of the Indian communities, set apart from the national community by language and by the racism of the Chiapan ruling oligarchy. The Mexican Constitution, which explicitly included peasants, did not cover Indians; they were excluded from the national community.

Second, the modernization of the elite and the extension of investment and capitalist relations in Chiapas during the period of economic expansion between the Second World War and the late 1960s did not modernize the exploitation of Indian communities. The appropriation of their lands and the products of their labor, feudal subjugation and servile labor

relations, and institutionalized repression remained as the methods for dealing with Indians.

Third, the specific form of the communities' subordinated absorption
into corporatist relations "froze" those communities' internal social relations, thereby preserving them little modified and in community hands.
This conservation, functional to the mode of domination and a "modernization" without social change, at the same time left the Indians in control
of the beliefs, values, and hierarchies of their own world: a world apart, subordinated to, but neither modified by nor absorbed into, the political culture of the ruling regime.

For the Chiapan elite, the apparently closed character of rural communities was an inevitable result of the "backwardness," "ignorance," and
"inferiority" of the Indians. In due time, as happened in so many other
places, this secret world, invisible to the dominators, changed from a place
of silent subordination to, first, a place of equally silent resistance and, later,
to one of secret subversion accessible only to those belonging to that world.
But, it turns out, there were tens of thousands who belonged to that world.

At the end of the 1970s, coincident in time with the national political crisis revealed in the student movement of 1968, a new period of struggle—
this time against the *caciques*—started in the Indian communities,
particularly among the Chamulas. Once again the response was repression,
the expulsion of dissidents from the communities as "enemies of tradition,"
and finally the flight of thousands of exiles to found dozens of new colonies
in San Cristóbal and in the Selva Lacandóna during the 1980s.

Also in the 1970s, a crisis was emerging within the Confederación
Nacional Campesina (CNC), the national pinnacle of mediation between
peasants and the state. Because the CNC was no longer able to fulfill its
functions—since official resources earlier destined for the peasantry were
drying up and/or being redirected toward private, commercial agriculture—
this crisis was exacerbated. In response to this process in Chiapas (and other
states), new independent organizations of *ejidatarios* and peasants formed,
launching a struggle not only for land but also for credit, access to services,
improved conditions for selling their products, etc.

The crisis of the old *caciques* and power brokers coincided with the
appearance of new local leaders, shaped by the new forms of organization
and interlocution with the state and its credit and commerce agencies (e.g.,
the Instituto Mexicano del Café, established in 1973), as well as through
the direct presence of *ejidos* and unions of *ejidos* in the market, even as
exporters of commercial crops. These leaders learned to take advantage of

differences between national and state government policies and to move effectively within the dense tangle of state plans for selective credit, which had been designed in the first place to benefit above all private producers.

The deterioration of the old corporatism and the redirection of federal agencies toward a commercial economy and away from subsidies for the cultivation of maize and coffee were dissipating the old system of state protectionism, substituting for it a more commercial relationship with federal agencies. But this purported "modernization" occurred without any substantial change in the corporatist political structures upon which were based the domination and reproduction of the national and local political regime. On the contrary, under cover of and through traditional channels of the regime, a new alliance was developing between vigorous national finance capital and the old Chiapan ruling oligarchy, the two parties linked by their investments and interests in cattle, coffee, precious hardwoods, and construction. Also during the 1970s, large oil reserves—one of the major inducements for the privatization of industry—were detected in Chiapas.

Starting with the government of Carlos Salinas de Gortari, the "modernizing" governing group sought new sustenance and support from this type of regional and international alliance, utterly distinct from the old corporatist apparatus. Privatization of public companies, foreign investment, and entering into the NAFTA would complete the consolidation of a new leading elite in Mexico. This elite nevertheless preserved the old mechanisms of corporate political control and the federal government's monopoly of power through a single party, the PRI, whose dominance had been an unwritten law since 1929. The combination of economic liberalization without political democratization would turn out to be explosive.

Meanwhile, popular movements fighting for land in Chiapas were losing any chance of success thanks to the legal consolidation of the properties of landlords, especially cattle ranchers. The government of Miguel de la Madrid (1982–88) issued 2,932 "certificados de inafectabilidad de propiedades agrícolas" (75 percent of the total number of such certificates issued since 1934) and 4,714 certificates for cattle properties (90 percent of the total for the same period). The effective conclusion of land redistribution antedated by almost a decade its legal conclusion with the reform of Article 27 of the Constitution at the end of 1991.

At the same time, the government developed policies for the cooptation of local leaders and the insertion of new experts and "influential" brokers through its credit and marketing agencies. Some of these leaders, experts, and brokers came out of old leftist organizations from the 1970s, convinced that they were actually realizing the Maoist slogan "Serve the People" in the context of the era of the market. (Some of them, along the way, "served themselves" in that ubiquitous recycling of knowledges and sources of income.) Corporatism continued to demonstrate a surprising capacity for mutation as a way of guaranteeing its reproduction in a period of change while perpetuating itself as the unsubstitutable mechanism of the political regime.

But that mechanism could not erase the parallel innovations in popular organizational forms and the presence of new and active local peasant leaders. Chiapan peasants and Indians were involved in multiple forms of mobilization: marches to cities in the state and to Mexico City, vigils in urban plazas and outside public buildings, hunger strikes, demonstrations. A new and diverse panorama was "modernizing" a social movement from below, in practice, and revitalizing its forms and autonomous decisionmaking.

The crucial point at which these movements converged and from which much of what followed took off appears to have been the First Indian Congress of Chiapas in October 1974, with representations of Tzotziles, Tzeltales, Tojolobales, and Choles. Also participating were catechists and deacons from the diocese of San Cristóbal, who brought to the Indians the influence of the church, and brought to the church the force of attraction of the demands, suffering, and exigencies of Indian religiosity. The state government initially supported the congress, but withdrew that support in the face of its radical demands and denunciations, later refusing to recognize it.

Unforeseen and unplanned by anyone, a secret plot at the margins of a worn-out corporatism was constituting itself equally in ideas and modes of belief as well as in practices such as simply being together; discussing, organizing, making decisions. This plot was opaque and resisted penetration by the regime's mechanisms of domination, even as it was in friction and permanent engagement with those mechanisms. Although the word "autonomy" was not used, an effective autonomy from the state was forming itself within that hidden world—even less perceptibly because, from without, that world had to maintain relations and exchanges with its privileged interlocutor, the power establishment.

These factors contributed to the circumstance that the state's relations with the new peasant organizations were not determined in the first place by concessions (which in any event were exhausted) but above all by repression and growing official violence to contain popular mobilizations and prevent independent organization. The repression involved direct action by state police, the federal army, and the private armies (*guardias blancas*) of the ranchers and landlords, alongside the method of encouraging rivalries over lands and boundaries within different *ejidos* and communities or exacerbating internal conflict over religious questions or prestigious offices at the heart of the communities. Thus as Antonio García de León put it: "Since 1974 Chiapas is a region aflame and dislocated, even if during twenty years this little war has been silent and silenced. . . . This cycle was initiated in March of 1974, when 40 soldiers from the 46th Battalion torched the 29 hovels in the shantytown of San Francisco in Altamirano." During the years and governments—whether federal or state—that followed, repression never let up: 120 evictions in La Frailesca in 1976 (20 people wounded, 250 jailed); rebellion in Venustiano Carranza in 1976 (2 peasants and 7 soldiers dead, many wounded, 6 women raped, 13 *comuneros* jailed); in May 1977, detentions and torture of peasants in San Quintín in the Selva Lacandóna by landowner-hired policemen, who later were ambushed and executed by the peasants; in July 1977, reprisals by the army far from San Quintín against 16 *ejidos* in Simojovel and Huitiupán, with children smothered in the attempt to escape and 2 Indian leaders thrown out of an army helicopter; in April 1978, the military eviction of Nuevo Monte Líbano, in the Selva Lacandóna (years later the source of one of the first nuclei of the EZLN), with 150 dwellings burned to the ground, 2 Tzeltales killed, and 6 tortured; in 1980, bloody evictions in Soconusco and, in May and June, peasant land invasions of 68 fincas in Sitalá, Tila, Tumbalá, Yajalón, Bachajon, and Chilón.

The military offensive peaked in July 1980. Under the command of General Absalón Castellanos, who would be governor of the state between 1982 and 1988, the army attacked the Tzeltal settlement of Wololchán, in Sibacá. Twelve Indians were killed and their bodies were burned. Wololchán disappeared, erased from the map; its residents fled to other settlements or to the forest. Antonio García de León published the following story, told by an Indian who witnessed the killing:

> And they used an apparatus unknown to me, a machine gun. A bomb goes off and explodes, and bullets are flying all over the houses. It's a terrifying thing, and that's how it went. We all said get out of here 'cos we weren't returning the fire. Some *compañeros* were left dead, a woman was left lying there. Many were wounded, even babies. Poor children and poor women: They came out of their houses like pigs, covered in mud. . . . We were treated like vile dogs, and the landlords were right there. The agreement was clear,

money gets what it needs, it was money that made the soldiers come to Wololchán.

"Money gets what it needs" says the Tzeltal, money "made the soldiers come." His reasoning is unequivocal: The law of the land is life, the law of money is death.

Between 1982 and 1987, according to Amnesty International, 814 peasants were assassinated in Mexico, most of them members of independent organizations. Seventy-five percent of those assassinations took place in states with a high Indian population—Chiapas, Oaxaca, Guerrero, Puebla, Michoacan, and Veracruz—and high levels of agrarian conflict. The bulk of these crimes figure as part of a scheme of repression in which assassination or jail is used to selectively eliminate the most outstanding leaders of those organizations. By the end of 1987, the picture in Chiapas could be summarized in five points: ranchers and landowners are better protected by the law and the government; official corporatism is in crisis; the independent opposition is growing; an Indian, not just a peasant, identity is a visible feature of that opposition; ceaseless repression is accompanied by a modernizing and paternalist language, what Thomas Benjamin has called "bloody populism."

For the majority of the one million Indians of Chiapas, the basis of their economy and their culture is access to land and the cultivation of maize and coffee. In 1990, 67 percent of the maize grown in *ejidos* and agrarian communities was destined for the market, and only 33 percent was used for subsistence. Of the 1,714 *ejidos* and agrarian communities extant in 1988, maize was the primary crop in 1,264 of them, coffee in 349. While these *ejidos* and agrarian communities comprised 41.4 percent of the workable land in Chiapas, 95.9 percent of those lands were rain-fed fields utterly lacking in capital investment and agroindustrial equipment.

The withdrawal of INMECAFE from the market in 1989, the drastic contraction of credit from the state, the increased costs of production resulting from the overvaluation of the peso, and the 50 percent collapse of coffee prices on the international market provoked a disaster for the small-scale Chiapan coffee producers. Thousands abandoned coffee cultivation between 1989 and 1993.

A similar combination presented itself to the 2.5 million maize producers in Mexico (where 80 percent of *ejidatarios* cultivate maize) and, of course, to the 74 percent of *ejidos* and agrarian communities in Chiapas where maize is the principal crop. The World Bank's demand for the elimination of price supports combined with the threat of Mexico's impending entrance into the NAFTA to create an anxious situation. As is well known, the average yield of maize in Mexico is 1.7 tons per hectare, while in the United States it is 6.9 tons. The prospect of an end to price supports and the obligation to compete on the international market was a death sentence for maize cultivators in Chiapas.

III

Two events whose importance for Chiapas was not immediately evident to many occurred in 1988 and 1989.

In 1988 an opposition candidate, Cuauhtémoc Cárdenas, the son of General Lázaro Cárdenas, won the elections for the presidency of Mexico. The perception and conviction that that was the real result were generalized from the start throughout Mexico. In an outrageous act of electoral fraud, even in the recount, Cárdenas's victory was overturned to the benefit of Carlos Salinas de Gortari. That stain of illegitimacy on Salinas's presidency would never be erased and in the end was immensely destructive. Although the rulers didn't suspect it at the time, that stain would prove to be fatal to a state community so thoroughly constituted in history as is the Mexican one. At that point, the social pact had been broken. One of the evident political manifestations of the rupture was a subsequent increase in voter abstention and a general lack of interest in elections. Those who once were hopeful had, in the next moment, given up hope.

In 1989, Patrocinio González Garrido, outstanding exemplar of one of the ancestral lineages of the "familia chiapaneca" (his father, Salomón González Blanco, had been governor 10 years earlier), was designated governor of Chiapas. Immediately he struck a deal that resulted in a fusion of the local oligarchy and the giant national financial interests that were linked to the Salinas government. The new governor continued the repressive policies of his predecessors and complemented them with the exertion of growing pressure on the diocese of San Cristóbal and its bishop Samuel Ruíz. It is well known that in private meetings Patrocinio González would boast about having at his disposal his own private FBI. If asked what that stood for, he responded: "The state police: la Fuerza Bruta Indígena."

As the neoliberal turn of the federal government was accentuated, Secretary of the Interior Fernando Gutiérrez Barrios was removed from office in January 1992. A key figure in national security affairs for 30 years, Gutiérrez apparently was opposed to the modification of Constitutional Article

130 with respect to relations between the Catholic Church and the Mexican state, and he was reluctant to go along with the wholesale abandonment of the postrevolutionary model of that state. His replacement was laden with meaning for Mexico's destiny: Gutiérrez's successor was none other than Governor Patrocinio González Garrido.

This change had at least three longterm implications, not apparent to many at the time. First, besides weakening even further the nationalist sector's links to the state apparatus, the government was left (*a*) without Gutiérrez's critical personal knowledge in matters of internal security and (*b*) without his ability and experience with respect to combining repression with negotiation. Second, it strengthened the alliance of the federal government with the Chiapan oligarchy, whose most distinguished political figure would assume the important post of secretary of the interior, responsible both for gearing up the machinery to win the presidential election of 1994 and for looking after internal affairs in Mexico during the short period leading up to the implementation of the NAFTA on January 1, 1994. Third, and possibly unappreciated by everyone except for Chiapan Indians and the movements in which they participated, Gutiérrez's replacement by González Garrido removed from Chiapas a key and well-placed figure involved in the containment, destruction, infiltration, and repression of the popular movements. Only the self-deception of supposing that their own backs were well covered could explain how the government made a move such as this.

Yet another event, though invisible to everyone except for the few participating, also occurred in 1988 and 1989. Formally established in November 1983, the Zapatista Army of National Liberation had about 100 members five years later and was totally unknown elsewhere in the country. After the electoral fraud of 1988, repeated in the 1989 state elections in Michoacán, the EZLN's membership grew over the course of the next year to some 1,300 people. In retrospect, it is difficult not to see the correlation between this unexpected expansion of EZLN ranks, the electoral fraud of 1988, the sharp expressions in the letters to Cuauhtémoc Cárdenas, and the armed seizures of town halls in Michoacán in 1989 to protest the latest fraud. They were indications of a change in the spirit and expectations of important sectors of the population.

In these circumstances an important breaking point was registered in the development of nonclandestine peasant and Indian organization in Chiapas. Toward the end of 1989 the Alianza Campesina Independiente Emiliano Zapata (ACIEZ) was formed in Altamirano, Ocosingo, San Cristóbal,

Sabanilla, and Salto de Agua. At the start of 1992 the name was changed to ANCIEZ by the addition of the word "Nacional" and the announcement of affiliates in six states of the Republic. In Chiapas it had extended its bases among the Tzotzil, Tzeltal, and Chol communities of El Bosque, Larrainzar, Chenalhó, Chanal, Huixtán, Oxchuc, Tila, and Tumbalá.

At the end of December 1991, the state police dispersed a gathering of Indians in Palenque with the usual violence — clubbings, detentions, torture. These Indians were protesting against the corruption of their municipal presidents, demanding the construction of public works and distribution of land as promised, and expressing their opposition to the reforms to Article 27 of the Constitution. The state government invoked the 1989 reform to the Chiapas Penal Code as the legal basis for the police action. Articles 129 and 135 of the new Penal Code stated that participation in unarmed collective protests constituted a threat to public order punishable by two to four years in prison.

On 7 March 1992, the Xi'Nich ("ant," in Chol) march left Palenque for Mexico City. The 400 Indian participants arrived in the capital six weeks later, after securing the support of communities in Tabasco, Veracruz, Puebla, and Mexico State along the route they traveled. The Indian question and the repression in Chiapas finally made it into the national press. The federal government promised solutions, but failed to make good on any of its promises.

On 12 October 1992, to commemorate 500 years of Indian resistance in America, thousands of Indians coming from all the towns in the surrounding region — some witnesses say as many as 10,000 — occupied the city of San Cristóbal in an orderly demonstration. The demonstrators roped the statue of the conquistador Diego de Mazariegos, founder of the Ciudad Real, and tore it down. As would later be seen in the taking of San Cristóbal on January 1, 1994, this was a kind of trial run. The thousands of Indians who later joined the ranks of the EZLN *guerrilleros* were, in large part, the very same group that had demonstrated on the quincentennial October 12. At the start of 1993, the ANCIEZ went underground.

In May 1993 there was an armed confrontation with the federal army at an EZLN training camp in the *pueblo* of Corralchén. Although the national press published the news, the government said it was unimportant and denied that there was any guerrilla activity. An image of prosperity and internal peace had to be maintained in order not to awaken worries in the United States and Canada or upset the still-awaited entrance into NAFTA on January 1, 1994. It is logical to suppose that the governments of those countries were informed of the military battle through their embassies but collaborated in maintaining silence.

The interested parties couldn't have done a better job if they had agreed in advance to guard the secret of what became the grand spectacle of the next New Year's Eve.

IV

The manner in which the indigenous communities made the decision to rebel merits its own section. Here the testimony is from Subcomandante Marcos. Between 1990 and 1992, he says, the Zapatista army "made itself bigger, made itself more Indian, and definitively contaminated itself with communitarian forms, including indigenous cultural forms. The civilian population, the civilian authorities, in this case Zapatistas, had total control of the territory. They are part of our organization, but they are civilians."

At the start of 1992 the state government's repression continued; the modification of Article 27 was a watershed for the peasants. The Zapatista civilians in the towns and villages started to let the military leaders of the EZLN know that "the people want to fight." The military leaders advised that the international situation—including in Central America—was not favorable to any attempt at revolution. To that, Marcos continues, the Zapatista civilians responded with remarks like:

"I don't know, we don't want to know what's happening in the rest of the world, we are dying and you gotta ask the people. Don't you all say that you must do what the people say?" "Well . . . yes." "Well then, let's go and ask them." And they sent me [Marcos] to ask around in the towns.

Yeah, I went to most of the *pueblos* to explain things. I told them, "Here is the situation like this: it's a situation of misery and all that; this is the national situation, and that's the international situation. Everything is lined up against us. What are we gonna do?"

They kept on discussing for days, for many days, until they took a vote and drew up the results that said: "So and so many children, so and so many men, so and so many women, so and so many say *yes* to war, and so and so many still say *no*." And the result, by several tens of thousands, was that the war would have to start, in October of 1992, with the quincentenary.

That October 12, 1992, according to Marcos, they went to the demonstration to issue "the last call for peaceful, civil struggle." After that, there were more meetings in the settlements, and in a recount done in November 1992 the decision to launch a rebellion was ratified.

In January 1993 the Clandestine Revolutionary Indigenous Committee (CCRI) was formed "to formalize the real power they had in the communities and the no less real subordination of the EZLN to the CCRI." The CCRI, whose members had the title of *comandante,* then decided "It's time" and, according to Marcos, put him in charge of military command. Preparations went on throughout 1993.

This reconstruction of the sequence of events prior to the rebellion is based above all on the version given by Subcomandante Marcos and the Zapatistas. We have to hope for or search out other sources, particularly the memories of the Indian participants, in order to corroborate it. Nevertheless the Zapatista version, in my judgment, has the ring of truth.

First of all, the sequence of the decisions has not been disputed by opposed official versions, or by any others for that matter. Second, the form of the decisionmaking process corresponds, in effect, to the modes developed in agrarian communities when facing similar circumstances, as is corroborated by history, anthropology, and the accounts and life stories of those who at one time or another have taken part in the concrete organization of rebellions by subaltern communities, especially of miners and peasants. One of the finest studies of these processes of collective reflection may be found in Leon Trotsky's history of the Russian Revolution.

Third, the declarations by Marcos made at different times, taken comparatively, permit one to deduce this probable accuracy. In his account, Marcos says (1) that the communities had been inclined toward rebellion since 1992, under pressure of their own situation and perhaps also by the long wait; and (2) that the leaders resisted rebellion, preoccupied by an international situation that they saw as unfavorable while the communities were indifferent to it. This divergence between the communities and the leaders of the EZLN could have been invented or exaggerated by Marcos in order to underscore the popular or democratic character of decision-making in a movement "from below" or in order to counterbalance official accusations that the rebellion was the simple product of outside agitators "deceiving" or "manipulating" "the masses." Nevertheless, another declaration by Marcos, in a different context, serves to confirm the difference of perception between leaders and the communities with respect to the conditions for insurrection.

In his interview with Yvon Le Bot in September 1996, Marcos says that in 1988 the leaders of the EZLN failed to evaluate "the civil insurgency of

Cardenismo" and that only many years later did they realize its magnitude and "what an impact it had had in people's consciousness." Meanwhile, between 1988 and 1989, their membership increased from fewer than 100 to 1,300. As seen earlier, this growth in the EZLN ranks at that time, along with the subsequent disenchantment with elections in the face of fraud and the repression directed against democratic movements, could be considered symptomatic of how the "impact in people's consciousness" that went unnoticed by the leadership of the EZLN translated into practice.

There existed in that moment an unexplained difference of perception between the communities and the leaders regarding the new eruption of *Cardenismo*. The communities lived and breathed *Cardenismo* and registered it as part of their experience, in their familial and social contacts, in their everyday lives, in the specific forms of their imaginary, even if they did not translate it perhaps into the words of politics. The leaders, as a natural result of the mode of thinking necessary for their own struggle, perceived *Cardenismo* as a new but predictable failure of "the electoral route," their perception being confirmed by their vocation: after electoral *Cardenismo*, insurrectional *Zapatismo* would follow. In any case, the reinforcement of EZLN ranks between 1988 and 1989 would tend to confirm that analysis.

Here two different (not necessarily contrary) ways of perceiving the crisis of the State intersect: that of the experience of the communities (and of the population in general) and that of the leaders and organizers of the revolutionary left. The communities perceive in *Cardenismo* above all else insurgency, a rupture with the regime from below; they tend not to share the electoral and institutional preoccupations of the political leaders. Those Indians were in tune with the manner and mental universe of those who wrote letters to Cárdenas threatening to take up arms in 1988 and who in effect took up arms in Michoacán one year later. The leftist leaders see above all the limits of the *Cardenista* movement: Its encompassment within a legal and electoral framework makes it difficult to fathom the depth of the fissure opened from below in the national state community as it had constituted and consolidated itself since the 1940s.

The channels through which communities, on one side, and the leadership of the EZLN (or for that matter any other left-wing organization), on the other, get their perceptions of the surrounding society are not the same; nor are the filters and the codes according to which they are interpreted. This difference, invisible to all in "normal" times when the capital decision—insurrection—is not in play, comes to light at the moment of making that decision. For that reason, while some see in the "disappearance of

the Soviet Union" a negative factor, others who are distant from that inter-
pretation of an upheaval, regarding which they are not concerned, measure by other methods—against the arc of their own lives—the maturation
of conditions for rebellion. It is here that the memory of the old-timers, as
an indivisible part of collective thought, occupies the place that, in a political framework, would be given over to doctrinal or theoretical considerations. But when all is said and done, isn't theory a generalization of
experience and, as such, of memory? And isn't an ancient memory therefore more reliable than a theory under pressure?

That having been said, it ought to be noted that, until the decision was
made to start the armed rebellion, for the EZLN leadership it was not only
logical but also, in a sense, necessary within its own legitimate categorical
universe, to maintain its particular vision of *Cardenismo* as a way to preserve
and affirm the convictions and organizing forms that would prepare the
EZLN to head the rebellion. And when that moment got closer, *la consulta*, "consulting the civilian following"—which does not exist in other
types of organizations—appears to have been the effective instrument for
correcting or equilibrating their perceptions and putting them in tune with
different visions.

A GUERRILLA WITH A DIFFERENCE

RÉGIS DEBRAY

From *New Left Review*, July/August 1996

Originally appeared in *Le Monde*,
May 1996 as "La guerilla autrement"

Translated by Elena Lledó.

AN indistinct trumpet from faraway in the middle of the night. This is how
news spread from one hamlet to another, from valley to valley, by long
sounds on the horn. Marcos and the mayor Moisés, ever cunning, sitting
under a silk-cotton tree, look at each other, inquiring. Although only a
meter away, I cannot distinguish their eyes. A second sounding. Then, the
bell of La Realidad starts to ring. It is the village-camp *tojolabal*, where we

chat nostalgically, under the huge tree. Electric lanterns light up here and there, sounds of motors, beacons to the side of the *reten*—the post of control, at the entrance to the hamlet. The Indian commander, anxious, gets up, the small escort of insurgents huddles into a semi-circle. An incursion, an unexpected attack?

Two minutes later, Moisés returns. False alarm. It was only a Red Cross jeep bringing back the corpse of a young boy, a victim of anemia. He was called Francisco, and was nine years old. Three days ago his family had taken him to the dispensary which is ten kilometers away, at the edge of the Zapatista zone. He will be buried here. Corn is increasingly scarce. Malnutrition is spreading throughout communities. A child died this morning. What does it matter since he was never really born? Among the indigenous people of Chiapas, who lack civil status, since a birth certificate is never issued, there is never a death certificate. Burials take place simply. Routinely.

Why then this sudden disturbance and this clinking of arms in the esplanades fringed by smart sheds with thatched or zinc roofs where chickens and dogs roam? In the last few weeks, the village security force has detected one or two attempts at infiltration by armed civilians. It is not now certain whether the government wants to add the martyr to the myth. It considers that to surround them and let them rot is less damaging to it than to exterminate. Still, the *guardias blancas*, the right-hand men of the big landowners, remain. One suspects that these landowners would pay dearly for Marcos's skin. Abstractly, it would in fact be the most economical solution, which would be disguised as a settling of scores between rival leaders, or as a grim story of narcos.

Of the Zapatistas' Chiapas, one thing must first be said: the guest goes there to meet the Subcommandante and surprise, he finds indigenous people. Tzotzils, Chols, Tzeltals, Tojolabals, Zoques—ancient zombies become complete citizens, with or without their faces covered with red scarves. Anonymous rebels, organized in whole communities, over an area of many tens of thousands of square kilometers, from the cold high lands of the Ocosingo, which recall the landscape of the Auvergne, to the suffocating thickness of the Lacandón jungle, which is reminiscent of the humid Amazon. A territory which is half Switzerland, half tropical. A population, with its administration, its army, its safe-conducts, its regulations. Its *municipios*, its *ejidos* (communal territories), its *milapas* (corn fields or family parcels), its wooden amphitheatres built under the open sky for large gatherings, nicknamed *Aguascalientes* (warm waters), after the revolutionary convention of 1914. Its farmyards, its horses and cows. Expecting a band of guerrillas, one runs into a community—or, in this case, a mosaic of communities.

From New York, Paris and even Mexico City, one only sees the sons of Zapata through the keyhole of the camera: a Zorro with a black balaclava helmet, a cap with three stars, a brown jersey, crossed cartridge belts, a rucksack, a Che-like pipe—why these torn boots, this badly repaired cap, I ask Marcos. "It's more *picturesque*," he answers with a wink. In such photographs, the foundation is lacking: the world of the Mayas, with its memories, its languages, its traditions, its ceremonies. With its wounds, its hunger, its new hopes. And this foundation changes everything. Marcos is the interface. The media, that necessarily personalizes issues, sees only the Occidental exterior, as the symbolic star gains in force, and certainly his style, his fables and his personalities, which issue, however, from an Oriental and hidden interior.

Guérrillero or superstar? Neither one nor the other. A creative activist. The EZLN (Zapatista Army for National Liberation) is not—anymore or yet—a guerrilla movement (despite having started as one 10 years ago after the elitist model of *foco*, the armed vanguard). It has become the organization of self-defence for some tens of thousands of excluded people—of three million inhabitants, Chiapas has a million indigenous people. And the "Sup" uses publicity, not as an aim, but a means. For him media action is Clausewitz's war applied to newspapers: the political extended by other means. He has dealt some blows to the establishment, which returns them in full measure. As is natural.

If he took printed matter as a weapon, and, at the beginning, four newspapers as interlocutors, he has also struggled with television and the mass media, ridiculing and humiliating the most powerful people, the officials, and such a bill has to be paid. When I mentioned to him that in a major evening newspaper, Chiapas is said to be the last meeting place of the international "*red jet-set*," he burst out laughing. "All's fair in love and war," he murmurs, shrugging his shoulders, "They risk turning you into an attraction. This is nothing very special, don't you think? And then, after that? Marcos will lose his image but the indigenous will gain security. That is the main point. They will have more chances to eat and fewer threats over their heads. So we say, welcome to the celebrities. We have to hold out until the rainy season. Another month and we will be saved until next year."

///

HOW CELEBRITIES ARE USEFUL

The rains start at the end of May. They turn paths to mud, making them barely passable, and obstruct the operations of the helicopter-borne commandos—the helicopter being the only serious threat, the one that the peasants have no time to warn the rebels against, as they otherwise do with the slightest movement on the ground. When a celebrity travels to La Realidad, they drag journalists with them and dissuade military expeditions. Danielle Mitterrand, while passing through Mexico, announced her arrival in the region where her foundation sent food and medicines. Marcos is delighted to meet her and thanks her. That will produce a photograph in the national press, and thus a respite, and a fissure in the media blockade.

Corn is the priority. Pursued by the army's movements, the peasants find it more and more difficult to sow and to harvest. Or to cut wood for essential heating and construction. The military, explains the Sup, tries to buy the peasants by offering them beans and milk, or flour for *tortillas*, in return for disowning the movement. The indigenous Zapatistas reject such offers. Dignity can make you hungry.

The war of images? It is more than a metaphor. Each side films the other. At 10:00 in the morning, every three days, an armored column slowly traverses La Realidad along the central dirt road. The pretext: to bring supplies to the military camp of San Quintin on the other side of the Euseba river. At the head and the tail of the convoy, a hidden soldier films with a video camera. And Zapatista sympathizers, doctors or social workers, take photographs, returning their fire. It was in this manner, it is explained, that one day an American military advisor was surprised perched on a halftrack. This lapse in etiquette before witnesses was never repeated.

The laws and constitutional guarantees—including the freedom to come and go—remain effective. A police checkpoint in Las Margaritas checks the identity of travellers, photographs them, but does not act in a particularly aggressive manner. Cars are not searched. The police drift between being brutal and good-natured. Chiapas is not a "free Republic" but a kind of state within a state, which the latter surrounds and would certainly like to suffocate, but politely, without unnecessary stridency. For the moment, this equivalent of two or three Corsicas is calm, despite acts of intimidation that here and there the soldiers permit themselves. Internecine killings occur more often in neighboring states, in Guerrero and Oaxaca, than in this zone of virtual combat. The balance of power defines the situation.

Since 1988, throughout Mexico, the deaths of 421 left-wing militants have been recorded. A low-intensity civil state, Mexico is no longer a dictatorship, without being a democracy. Chiapas is neither at war nor at peace. The rebels form neither a clandestine band nor a registered political party. Arms are there to ease negotiation, having first made it possible. Today the authorities talk with outlaws who otherwise they would hunt down. A liaison agent between the interior minister and the rebels, Javier Elorriaga, arrested at the start of the offensive of February 1995, is today sentenced to 14 years in prison. The indigenous people, often illiterate, have as representatives and guests at the negotiating table the cream of the academic intelligentsia—anthropologists, historians, and lawyers. Guerrillas who make the effort not to shoot; an army that occupies but avoids confrontation. Victory goes to whoever, in this standoff, does not break the truce. Whoever fires first will have lost, since the battle is more psychological than military.

For a revolutionary, the middle ground is not a comfortable place to be. It traps Marcos in the unpleasant dilemma of either being criminalized if he renews combat—which erupted only once, on January 1, 1994 (the day when the free-trade treaty with Mexico's northern neighbor took effect), when he occupied the big cities of the state, and there were 50 deaths—or of being relegated to folklore if he remains with his arms at his feet. Turned into the diabolical figure of a murderer if he responds to military pressure closing in; ridiculed as a bluffer if he reacts by withdrawing. How can one escape from the trap? By emerging from the perimeter, by increasingly nationalizing the stakes. The second round of the negotiations no longer concentrate on the indigenous question but on the very structure of the regime. An explosive program—for which the Zapatistas will have served as detonators.

"Chiapas," says Manuel Camacho, the ex-minister of foreign affairs appointed by then-president Salinas to restore peace after the insurrection of January 1994, "is the laboratory for the democratization of the country." Supported by public opinion, Camacho was able to avoid the worst. The hard-liners of the PRI, the state party, wanted war without rhetoric. Ten years earlier, the young Camacho, then a senior civil servant, had prepared a project of agrarian reform for Chiapas. Under the pressure of the *caciques, el señor Presidente* discreetly buried the planned reforms. Result: the explosion.

PURITANISM IN THE REVOLUTION

Marcos has the history of Mexico running through his veins. A strange libertarian who thinks in patriotic terms, he commands a hierarchical army and reacts in communitarian, not individualist terms. For the new Zapatism, going by the rustic nature of the leader at least, is based on the same equation as the old one: the Gospel plus the poncho, the missionaries' biblical tradition plus the agrarian tradition of the uprooted Indians, everything at the service of a religion of the motherland. As in 1910, the restitution of land and the expulsion of the merchants from the temple are the major aims of the uprising.

The religious imprint is evident, up to the puritan and disciplined execution of order in the plantations, islands of order with something, at least in La Realidad, of the Jesuits' "reductions" of Paraguay. Even small presents to individuals are prohibited; only the community gives and receives. This is how corruption can be prevented. One recognizes a Zapatista village especially by the fact that in the streets no child stretches out their hand, whereas in Chamula, which is still under the control of traditional *caciques*, the visitor is harassed by flocks of little barefoot beggars in rags. Alcohol is banned. Drugs are also out, that goes without saying. Nudity is prohibited. There are separate approaches to the river for men and women, where one bathes in the evening beside the horses. Everybody has to wash himself, some in underpants, some in shirt and bra. Everything is spelled out with signposts and placards. There is a little church for communion on Sundays. A dispensary, a school. Dormitories with hammocks. Small altars where the Virgin of Guadalupe faces a lithograph of Zapata hung on shanty walls. Frugal nutrition: black beans and tortillas. No electricity. In the evening, one can hear communal singing under the trees, preceding the sleep of the just. Ecologists and the pure of heart will find themselves at home on the edge of the Lacandón jungle. An ideal holiday camp—at least as long as the army keeps its distance, since each new garrison brings the impurities that the evangelism of the rebels, hardly warlike, has tried to exclude: marijuana, tequila, and prostitution.

On the façade of the church of the diocese of San Cristóbal, which was once the see of Bartolomé de las Casas, the Indians' defender in the sixteenth century, one can still distinguish the stains of rotten eggs and fruit furiously thrown by the *coletos*, the hardcore anti-Zapatistas. Don Samuel Ruíz, the bishop, has bodyguards. This "red" bishop, disapproved of by the Vatican, has been in office for 36 years. The government had asked Rome to recall him even before the village was taken over by the Zapatistas, until they realized that because of his prestige among indigenous people, he was best placed to act as an intermediary between the state and the rebels.

Today he is attending an episcopal council. It is his Dominican deputy, Gonzalo Ituarte, who receives me. He has spent 12 years in the midst of the *comunidades*. In the vestry-offices one can see the portraits of previous popes, one of John XXIII, though not of John Paul II—surely due to lack of space. We touch on the cold civil war, the local oligarchy's accusations against the church, and the first incidents of the revolt at the time of the celebration of the five-hundredth anniversary of the discovery of America when the statue of a conquistador in the village square was toppled by the Indians.

"I disagree with armed struggle," he says to me, "but I understand the causes. The Zapatistas fight for the same thing that we do. If I would reason as a theologian, I would talk of a 'just war.' The social situation was unbearable. But what is a just insurrection if everybody is exterminated? Look at Guatemala, for instance. One hundred and fifty thousand deaths in twenty years. And fifty thousand refugees among us." For the rest, there is no trace of discouragement in this small, jovial and lively man who holds communion with martyrs and saints, and who thinks that "life, like the Spirit, always triumphs in the end."

The next morning, a warm and spectacular welcome at La Realidad, the regular meeting point for visitors, when Marcos and his people come to drag me from a refreshing rest in a hammock, and we depart on horseback in the direction of the forest. A brief hour of trotting through half-bare hills. Then we arrive at a camp in a glade, neat and camouflaged, which reminds me of that in Nancahuazu 30 years ago. The deafening chirring of crickets and insects. Sentinels all around. Tacho, a member of the clandestine Indian revolutionary committee, joins us. We start talking about the *humano* and the *divino*, as it is said in Spanish, of human and religious relationships within communities.

Tacho is Catholic but that is not important here. A secular outlook is necessary to avoid confrontation between ethnic groups and to maintain unity. People explain how the army attempts to divide in order to rule, by opposing one sector or faith against the others. Marcos, who has a quick and calm way of speaking, without lyricism, listens to my objections while smoking his pipe with a meditative expression. He explains how much the extent of international solidarity has surprised him and how much also he has been surprised by the attacks from old revolutionaries of Central America, with the exception of the Guatemalans. How difficult it is to want to belong to everybody and to nobody in the game of mutual exclusions among the international Left, and how much the Indian cause needs oxygen from outside to steer clear of any fundamentalist or racial turn.

I ask Marcos if the Internet can give technological wings to the internationalism of yesteryear? "To the sympathizers, yes, but I myself can not use it. With satellite tracking I would have a bomb on my head in eight minutes." The Chechen leader Dudayev did not take such precautions. "At the beginning," he continues, "we thought we would not have to be around for too long; then we discovered we were only a symptom, a fragment of a protest movement much larger than us, which stretched overseas." Some months earlier, despite the news blockade, a million and a half Mexicans responded in the villages to a referendum about what should be conceded to the rebellion.

What will be necessary to make him lay down arms and take off the balaclava? When will he consider the aim of the war attained? "The day," he answers, "when an Indian will enjoy the same rights as a white in every corner of the republic; the day when the party-state system is finished and when *election* will no longer be a synonym for *fraud*. Today, an opponent is either killed or bought off: That is what has to change." "Don't hold your breath," I remark.

In the meantime, will they be able to hold out? "In the worst case, we will return to the forest. We have already resisted for ten years. We can plunge once more into the catacombs for another ten years or more. The regime underestimates us militarily. All the better for us. It is true, we are wearing ourselves out. But the others are worn out faster than us. Everybody here is vulnerable but we are a bit less so than the government, this one or any other. Time is on our side. The economic situation is not about to change. Without any doubt we will finish by succeeding. The only problem is," he adds laughing, "that we do not know what we will do afterwards."

WRITING TO ROBIN HOOD

Strange mixture of self-confidence and programmatic modesty, Marcos, who never misses an occasion for ridicule, does not give the impression of being full of himself. This is certainly a virtue when one, while still alive, has acquired a little of the kind of legend that posthumously hung around Che. From all directions, this fugitive receives the mail of a president to which he can obviously not reply, and which, moreover, has to be burned in the most dangerous moments. There are all kinds of things. Letters of detained people from all corners of the world asking him to come and liberate them—he opened the prisons in Chiapas during the first days of the insurrection. Letters from authors of plays which are never performed, of apprentice novelists in search of publishers, of social reformers who in their paranoia seek a brother. But also, and more seriously, from widows and orphans. The role of Robin Hood has its inconveniences, especially in the absence of secretaries. Belonging to that odious species of temperate sleepers who can be content with four hours a night, Marcos, with the assistance of an electric lantern, conscientiously devours books and other printed matter, as in the good old days. There are delays that become advances. A bookseller in San Cristóbal de las Casas, whispered to me on our way back: "Since the Zapatistas, people here watch less television. They come to buy books. My business is doing better."

To arrive at the capital is like jumping from the Orinoco to La Defense. Chiapas belongs to North American Mexico like Guyana belongs to the French Republic: the same flag, another planet. Questions rain down on the newcomer. About strategy, style, the color of his eyes, alliances, the danger the movement represents. . . . Nobody here, friend or enemy, doubts that the movement has the art of never being where it is expected. To surprise, to destabilize, is perhaps not enough for a political strategy, but it is sufficient in the sense that no politics can afford to ignore it.

Is this the old dogmatic Left reemerging unscathed from the ruins? The dormant seed of Fidel concealing a sectarian authoritarianism? An astute manipulation of regimented Indian masses? A master of the society of the spectacle? A classic *caudillo* refreshed by postmodern humor and the reading of Cortazar, or the first representative of an eventual post-caudillism? All this is open to controversy.

"He amazes me for the worst and for the best," Octavio Paz confides, yet without tenderness for revolutionary Caesars and resistant to Left naiveté. "The spectacular side annoys me a little, but his capacity to establish quite profound links with the Indian groups is admirable. What I would like, is that he would enter political life and that he would help in the democratic transition." I leave the welcoming library of the great poet and historian for a dinner with friends. There, Carlos Fuentes does not beat about the bush: "He is a fine man, full stop. He has changed the history of this country. I appreciate him, I admire him, and I say it openly."

Dismissing his beheaded Colombia, where not only terrorists imagine him as the last recourse and the president-in-waiting, García Márquez states—"No question about it, if I put myself forward, they could elect me and that would be a real catastrophe." He nods assent, smiling: Marcos is a comrade of the Left but a Colombian cannot mix himself up in the internal affairs of Mexico. "Surely the most interesting personality of this country"—which counts for a lot, I say to myself—adds Julio Scherer, the doyen of Mexican journalists. "He was also, for a moment, the most important but the aura has dwindled away. History can change horses. Things move fast."

"He has let his moment pass, it's a pity," agrees Jorge Castañeda, the respected analyst and politician of the center Left. "He does not like me, and yet I like him a lot," Porfirio Munoz Ledo flings the words out. He presides over the left party of the legal opposition, the PRD: "If he lets himself become cut off from the real country by the small radical left group that has become his court circle, this will be a great loss for Mexico." Other fellow guests join in, and then we're off for the rest of the night. This intense town is not made for those who go to bed early

Mexico 1996. End of the reign, end of the regime, end of an epoch. The oldest party state in the world, founded in 1929, hesitates to turn the page. The United States restlessly observes its southern border where millions of *braceros* made hungry by the crisis push behind the barbed wire. Of these two countries, which will conquer the other? Which culture will sweep away its competitor? Nothing is definitively decided. For the moment the cul-de-sac is evident: a government that does not govern anything, or almost nothing; small villages that fall into dissidence; agitated streets, demanding a settling of accounts; technocrats educated in Yale or MIT lining up numbers on paper and on Sirius. A new social pact is pursued on all sides. Some predict a storm, others a slow deterioration.

"Welcome to hell": so the Sup greeted the new president after his election. When he received me amidst the Zapatista *comandancia*, on a horse, with that sense of brilliance that characterizes him, the film-loving prophet took me by the arm and took me to see, at the other side of a ravine, a square of forest in flames: The Tojolabal peasants clear forest by burning. "Life is cruel, don't you think? Fire must pass over the land for the grain to grow. You cannot construct if you do not first destroy." It crosses my mind that cultivation by fire exhausts the land and devastates the best forests but, after all, it is he who knows the territory. I say nothing and in the night I watch the burning, this metaphor of the apocalypse.

POWER FROM BELOW

"We do not want a revolution imposed from the top: It always turns against itself. We are not a vanguard. We are not here to close things down but to start renew our efforts," he repeated to me in the camp. "Our aim: to give voice to civil society, everywhere, under all its forms, in all its fronts. We are neither the only ones nor the best ones. We do not have the truth or the answer to

everything. Provided we raise good questions, that is enough for us. . . ."
This statement, "and now it is your turn to play" ends 50 years of the self-
proclaimed vanguard. Take to arms but prefer stimulation to confrontation:
This is the first originality. To pose as a national force without aiming for
state power, without appetite for the role of deputy, governor or president:
the second paradox. "Politics with a difference": It is disconcerting, provoking, problematic. But naturally of concern to all those, beyond Mexican
borders, who risk the bitter struggle of the exercise of power and of a will
to justice.

It is in the nature of Indian communities—of Asiatic character—that
power rises from below. This cult of consensus, this "all together or nothing" attitude has made its mark on the small band of hierarchical and self-
confident Guevara supporters who, in the old manner, plunged into the
unknown in 1984. These whites came to convert the Indians to the revolution, as their ancestors did in the old days, to the Gospel; and, voila, it is
the Indians who have converted them to another conception of the world,
horizontal and modest. Those who came from the city brought with them
a sense of the individual, of the nation, and beyond, of the wider world; the
natives a sense of harmony, of permanent referendum, of listening.

Each element deconstructs and reconstructs itself in contact with the
other. This cross-breeding of two microcosms has meant progress for both.
Zapatism is the exact opposite of, and surely the antidote to, the Sendero
Luminoso in Peru. "If we finish by disappearing," Marcos insists, "then, yes,
it would be brutal and without hope. It would be Yugoslavia in the Mexican South. The Federal State would no longer have anyone to talk to but
enemies." This suspicious dissidence probably plays a unifying and constructive role. It unites in the nation forces which otherwise would risk separation, make it explode.

A rebel of limits, one sends him on his way always with his fire-break of
a nickname: the romantic. The man with the balaclava reassures one with
his down-to-earth side, a sense for practical detail moderating the indispensable megalomania—necessary, I imagine, to endure "the long voyage
from suffering to hope," of 11 years of mosquitoes, black beans and clandestine work, of a decade with damp feet, without chocolates or press conferences. And now, the order of the day? "To win," he answers, "And to find
corn." No rhetoric in this poet, he speaks willingly about death, though he
does not seem to have any predilection for suicide. One foot in the camp
of the longterm Indian struggle, the other in that of the hurrying people of
the metropolis.

It is difficult, this large space between distant memory and urgent issues. Which will dominate the other, the long timespan of the Mayas or the short-term concerns of the yuppies? Hamlet, *that is the question.* Oral cultures have a slow rhythm; one deliberates, taking one's time, step by step. In Zapatista territory, away from the disorder of premature cities, it is always necessary to wait, under rain or sun; the indigenous people consult and let the hours pass with a smiling indifference.

To refuse the sights and the delights of power, in imitation of a demonstrative Left, protesting and moralizing, while simultaneously adopting the methods of force, in imitation of a voluntarist Left without illusions, that combination is an unusual challenge. For the management of dissidence and the assimilation of opponents, the Mexican system is the best in the world—if the Soviet Communist Party had sent an information-gathering mission to the PRI, the Soviet Union would certainly still be standing. No steel plate does not dissolve in this stomach. The rebels know it. The Zapatistas—neither guerrillas nor political party—one could see in this a way of fleeing the test of reality and responsibility.

Let us rather ask us if these Mexicans are not in the process of inventing a new realism. A rather good way of not extinguishing the rebellion's fire under the ashes of the state. To assume to the end the role of the defender of the oppressed, but by threatening to make a nuisance of themselves, and by publicizing a certain preparedness to rise to extremes, and not only by marches in the streets. It is the equivalent of the weak dissuading the strong. Could it be a third line between radical, verbal incantation and democratic-realist resignation? Locally this works. Without promising the Earth, the Zapatistas mobilize. They have transformed hundreds of thousands of people-objects into the subjects of history.

That, at least, is what I said to myself, near to Oventic in the Altos, while watching the pride with which a small, 16-year-old militiaman was looking at us, lost in the haze, with hood and khaki uniform. He was stoically posting guard with his comrades in front of *Aguascalientes III*, one of the places set up by the indigenous inhabitants to receive the thousands of foreigners expected this year for the meeting of "galaxies against neoliberalism." After having made us wait for an hour behind barbed wire, which was the time needed to go to consult the superior ranks by radio—to verify that there was a general agreement that we could cross the sacred fence—he took us on a tour of the result of several months work by bare hands: kitchens, canteens, dormitories, everything in wood palisades cut on the spot, and placed against the hill, an amphitheater of board benches around a vast open space of clay—the equivalent to *Aguascalientes I,* destroyed by the army in Guadalupe Tepeyac. "For a week, the soldiers search for confrontation with our forces. But we have given our word that we will respect the cease-fire," he looks us straight in the eye. *"Nuestras fuerzas, nuestra palabra"* [Our strength is our word]. The adolescent's eyes shone with pride.

Mexico has 100 million inhabitants, and only 15 million indigenous people. The rebels, if they are not to rot where they stand, will have to multiply the bridges between the marginal and the majorities, clandestine operators and legalists. A simple "Wretched of the Earth, unite" attitude will not overturn neoliberalism today; the Zapatistas do not claim to have discovered the key to the dilemma, they do not have a doctrine. But in San Cristóbal, in the Indian market, a *corrido* announces at the top of his voice on a radio-cassette: "Marcos is everybody, Marcos is a comrade." "The end of utopias," this then was not a surrender, but a return to the essential: resistance.

NORTHERN INTELLECTUALS
AND THE EZLN

DANIEL NUGENT

Originally appeared in *Monthly Review*, July 1995.

IN recent decades, important trends in social and cultural analysis have been qualified with the prefix "post." Today social scientists, for instance, are expected to know something about poststructuralism, postmodernism, post-Fordism, and even something called post-Marxism. A situation once identified as "colonial" is said by some to have been supplanted by another, called "postcolonial." Whatever the virtues of these perspectives—for the challenges they present to conventional understandings, for generating new forms of critique—they are of little value for understanding contemporary historical developments; worse, they have introduced a vocabulary and form of presentation that obscure considerably more than they reveal.

Other essays outline the main characteristics of postmodernist "discourse." For present purposes, it will be enough to cite a particularly compelling example to illustrate how this discourse is now being applied to what used to be called the "Third World." That example is found in the work of Gayatri Spivak, who once remarked that "Class is the purest form of signifier," implying that class is a "pure" linguistic symbol in the sense that it has no concrete referent in the material world.* From the vantage point of the sort of linguistic theory on which so many postmodernist discourse analysts draw, the quality of the referent is less important than the location of concepts like class in relation to other "signifiers." So Spivak is able to say, for instance, that "socialism" has "no historically adequate referent" in India, by which she means that Indian socialism did not originate in a truly indigenous tradition of socialist discourse. Aijaz Ahmad has recently commented on this observation in a way that nicely captures the postmodernist notion of "history." To be told that socialism has no "historically adequate referent" in India, he remarks, would come as a big surprise to all those millions of Indians who, for reasons having to do with their own experience of their own domestic capitalism and their own situation in its class divisions, regularly vote Communist. The "historical referent" for Indian socialism, in other words, is not some disembodied imperial "discourse" but Indian capitalism and a political practice "undertaken within India by Indian political subjects."

That is one way of summing up the difference between postmodernism and Marxism. It isn't that Marxism is uninterested in language, discourse, or meaning, and the best historical-materialist work deals precisely with the many different concrete referents that words like "class" or "work" can have in specific historical conditions. But here I simply want to underline that Marxism can understand the practices through which meanings are produced in relation to the actions of people on and in the world and not just in relation to other meanings. Practices are undertaken in particular places at particular times by particular subjects in particular conditions, and these have to be studied historically.

REVOLUTION ON THE INTERNET

Say, for instance, we want to analyze Mexican society, whether viewed through the prism of the Mexican revolution of 1910, or the neo-Zapatista

*Versions of this paper were presented as talks in New Haven; Zamora, Michoacan; and Chicago in the autumn of 1994, and in Austin, Texas in March, 1995. Thanks to Gil Joseph, Eduardo Zarate, José Lameiras, Alexandra Stern, Bryan Roberts, and Guillermo de la Pena for those invitations. For the rest I have relied on the support, insight, and criticism of my collaborators in Tucson, Arizona, Raquel Rubio Goldsmith and Eva Zorilla Tessler.

revolution in Chiapas starting on January 1, 1994, or the crisis of the state and the ruling party in recent months. A starting point would be to recognize that Mexico has long been a "postcolonial society." Mexico has moved along temporally—if not developmentally—from an earlier colonial condition for almost two centuries. Yet one of the most striking features of the ways in which political power is organized socially and experienced subjectively throughout Mexico—whether in the "advanced" northern state of Chihuahua or the "backward" southeastern state of Chiapas—is that it is and remains a profoundly colonial or, in a pinch, neocolonial rather than unequivocally postcolonial form of power. Neither the Wars of Independence and the Wars of the Reform during the nineteenth century, nor the revolution of 1910 and the "reforms" of Salinastroika in the period 1988–1994 during the twentieth century, signaled irreversible, radical breaks with the past. Rather, they are moments in a sustained process of transformation. That series of political transformations was associated with a series of economic transformations that established the specific form of Mexican capitalism. The language of "pre" and "post," which pretends to be about historical change, actually disguises these processes of transformation by carving up history into discontinuous and disconnected units.

Nevertheless, the lure of intellectual fashion is so great that scholars who two decades ago worked with peasants in Mexico and wrote about social movements, rural class formation, and the permanent character of the primitive accumulation of capital in dependent, peripheral states now author postmodernist essays and books with titles (e.g., *Hybrid Cultures*) and themes (the metaphor of a salamander to organize reflections on Mexican history) that have more in common with magical realist literature than with historical materialist analysis. This is not to suggest that magical realism—say, the novels of Gabriel García Márquez or Isabel Allende—has nothing to tell us, and that only historical materialism can reveal the Truth. It is only to underline the radical differences between literary and historical ways of relating to social reality.

Perhaps it should come as little surprise that some postmodern/postcolonial critics seem, or pretend, not to know that the arenas of discourse in which their work circulates are at several removes from the social reality they purport to represent. The privileges now enjoyed by intellectuals in the North have been so reduced that many seem to be compensating by providing to themselves an inflated sense of their own importance and the significance of purely intellectual or "discursive" practices. Nonetheless, the distinction between what is being talked about and how it is being talked about remains important. As Gabriel García Márquez is reported to have said to Carlos Fuentes while discussing the turn taken by internecine struggles within the ruling party in Mexico in the early months of 1995, "We are going to have to throw our books into the sea. We've been totally defeated by reality." If a litterateur can get the point, why can't a literary theorist?

Yet postmodern concepts and assumptions, even casual turns of phrase, have a real seductive power over many intellectuals; and the freewheeling adoption of a postmodern vocabulary is having especially insidious effects on the study of current historical developments. This is particularly evident in the boatloads of material published about the EZLN uprising in Chiapas, the rebellion of the damned in the South that woke up the world on the morning of January 1, 1994. In the rush to issue accounts of this seemingly unprecedented and original popular uprising, the expression "postmodern" fell quite easily from the pens and mouths of many commentators. More than a year after the EZLN challenged the power of the Mexican state, meanwhile, we read on *The New York Times* Op-Ed page that "the Mexican Meltdown of 1995 is the first postmodern economic crisis."

Beside an unending stream of English-language publications providing profiles of the EZLN or its spokesperson Subcomandante Marcos, several computer networks devoted solely to distributing information about the EZLN have appeared as well. It's as though the circulation of information, the communication and production of commentaries in the English-language book and electronic media, is mirroring the production by impoverished Chiapan peasants-become-artisans of "Marcos" and "Ramona" dolls, the small wooden figures clothed not in traditional Mayan garb but in the outfits of the EZLN, complete with miniature ski masks and wooden rifles.

It is perfectly in keeping with the postmodernist worldview that a major theme in accounts of the Chiapan rebels has to do with the media of communication through which "we" in the North learn about, and relate to, the EZLN. "In Marcos's prose," writes specialist Deedee Halleck, "one senses an expertise and familiarity with computer-based text, if not directly with e-mail." Putting things this way (which assumes that guerrillas are freely able to tap into electric power lines in a state in which, though it generates half the hydroelectric power in all of Mexico, most towns are not wired for electricity) diverts attention and analysis from an explicit consideration of the actual goals and accomplishments of the neo-Zapatistas and their connection to other currents within Mexican, Latin American, and North American society. It shifts attention instead toward the postmodern world of digital simultaneity. In being asked to assess "what effect the e-mail activity [has] had on actual events," we are presented with the image of "new icons of romantic rebellion" "bursting through . . . TV screens" and the powerful effect of "the Zapatista presence on the Internet."

Asserting that the multiple messages resonating "within the nocturnal hacker community" have a palpable historical effect fits perfectly the notion that neo-Zapatismo is indeed a "postmodern political movement." Focusing on, even celebrating, the EZLN's use of modems, fax machines, and e-mail suggests that their most distinctive feature as a political movement is to have shifted the object of struggle from control of the means of production to control of the means of communication; revolutionary ideals are to be advanced by the free exchange of rebel-friendly software and communications packages. But this way of thinking about the rebellion tends to block out the years of organizing that preceded January 1, 1994. To assert the fundamental "postmodernity" of the EZLN is not really to analyze "actual events" in Chiapas. It is more a way of allowing some intellectuals to appropriate these events, to situate these complex historical developments on their own (intellectual) terrain, to assimilate them to a discourse that permits computer-literate academics to feel good about themselves.

A POSTMODERN POLITICAL MOVEMENT?

Particularly disconcerting is the manner in which claims regarding the postmodernity of the EZLN are repeated by people on the left. An example that springs to mind is Roger Burbach's essay on the "Roots of the Postmodern Rebellion in Chiapas" published in the *New Left Review* last summer, where the EZLN is described as "a postmodern political movement" that attempts "to move beyond the politics of modernity."

Once past these introductory remarks, Burbach presents a compelling, competent, and concise description of the neocolonial background to the 1994 uprising. Drawing on recent research by anthropologists, sociologists, and political scientists familiar with the region, Burbach presents an analysis that is not particularly "postmodern" in either form or structure. He demonstrates that the rebellion occurred in Chiapas when it did because a particular form of capitalism has been adopted in this region of the world. Outlining the ways labor migration is related to the alienation of the peasantry from the land, how commercial agriculture, especially of coffee production, is buffetted by fluctuations in international commodity prices, and how strategic relocations of squatters are engineered by the Mexican state while large landowners and ranchers continue to rely on hired gun thugs (the guardias blancas), Burbach gives some substantive content to the notion of "combined and uneven development."

Nevertheless, in its opening and closing paragraphs, where the assertion of the fundamental "postmodernity" of the EZLN is repeated time and again, the essay is symptomatic of what can happen when northern intellectuals, even those on the Left, become enchanted by a sort of postmodernist identity politics. This adoption of postmodern vocabulary and categories of analysis winds up revealing more about academic politics in the North than it does about the situations these analyses are meant to explain. I think it is worth closely examining some of these passages in Burbach's article in order to appreciate fully the absurdities to which such analyses can lead.

The opening paragraph begins thus:

> The Indian uprising in Chiapas that burst upon the world scene in January is a postmodern political movement. The rebellion is an attempt to move beyond the politics of modernity. . . .

It is difficult to see how a rebel army of peasants, aware of itself as the product of 500 years of struggle, that quotes from the Mexican Constitution to legitimate its demand that the president of Mexico immediately leave office, that additionally demands work, land, housing, food, health, education, independence, liberty, democracy, justice, and peace for the people of Mexico, can be called a "postmodern political movement." How can the EZLN move beyond the politics of modernity when their vocabulary is so patently modernist and their practical organization so emphatically premodern? Their democratic command structure is a slow-moving form of organization—requiring as it does direct consultation and discussion with the base communities in five or six different languages—which is difficult to reconcile with postmodernist digital simultaneity. Do their demands include a modem and VCR in every jacale or adobe hut in Mexico? No. Is their chosen name "The Postmodern Army of Multinational Emancipation" or "Cyberwarriors of the South"? No. They are the Zapatista Army of National Liberation. Emiliano Zapata (not a "free-floating signifier" but a specific historical subject), who led the peasants of Morelos from 1911 until his assassination in 1919 in recovering control of the land and driving out the caciques/foreign political bosses, is a very unlikely postmodern hero.

Here is the conclusion of the opening paragraph: "Even more fundamentally, [the rebellion] seeks to end the victimization of Indians by centuries
of western modernization." Again, there is little particularly "postmodern"
about struggling to that end (quite apart from the fact that premodern forms
of exploitation are alive and well and continue to be major targets of struggle). Here it becomes increasingly difficult to get a grip on what is supposed
to be postmodern. What is the "modernization" which the neo-Zapatistas are
resisting! Does it have something to do with capitalism? Would any anticap-
italist struggle be postmodern? For that matter, since one of the major con-
ceits of postmodern discourse is that capitalism doesn't exist, at least as a
systematic totality, it hardly makes sense to talk about a postmodern anti-
capitalism. And since it is unclear what historical conditions are being
opposed by a postmodern politics, we are left with the impression that the
neo-Zapatista program is a kind of historical utopianism, a pipe-dream of virtual reality, rather than a pragmatic response to real historical conditions.

Nor is our understanding of postmodernity or of the EZLN much advanced
by the following: "The uprising led by the EZLN . . . comes in the wake of the
collapse of the 'modern' bipolar world of the post Second World War era and
the ideological exhaustion of most national liberation movements. . . ."

Burbach here appears to be assuming that the collapse of the "Communist world" signaled the end of modernism. But it is not at all clear what
is supposed to be postmodern about that extremely tentative great leap forward of neoliberal ideology, the market, and policies oriented toward capitalist economic restructuration; in some important respects it may
represent a triumph of "modernism." And from an altogether different point
of view, it is possible to view the triumph of modernism in an optimistic
light. As Marshall Berman has written:

> 1989 was not only a great year, but a great modernist year. First, because
> millions of people learned that history was not over, that they had the capac-
> ity to make their own history—though not, alas, in circumstances chosen by
> themselves. Second, because in the midst of their motions, those men and
> women identified with each other: even in different languages and idioms,
> even thousands of miles apart, they saw how their stories were one story, how
> they were all trying to make the modern world their own. I fear that vision
> has faded from our public life.

One thing demonstrated by Chiapas 1994 is that the vision to which
Berman refers, almost nostalgically, has once again been drawn into focus

by the appearance of neo-Zapatismo, the forthright clarity of the communiqués from the CCRI-CG (Clandestine Revolutionary Indigenous Committee—General Command), and the writings of Subcomandante Marcos. At the same time, and particularly in Chiapas, there still remain bipolar axes of difference—women and men, capital and labor, North and South, Indian and white—through which people's lives are organized, and disorganized, and made miserable. In a sense, then, the " 'modern' bipolar world of the post–Second World War era" is stronger—and more vicious, more destructive, more retrenched—than ever. The most serious problem facing "most national liberation movements"—including the EZLN—may not be ideological exhaustion but rather the threat of physical extermination.

In any case, it is difficult to determine the ideological resources available to participants in such movements when their own voices are muted and their own practices are obscured by the superimposed discourses of northern academics. If such movements derive their meaning only from the terms of academic discourses, how different is the conservative claim that the EZLN is led by "outside agitators" from the supposedly radical claim that the EZLN is a "postmodern political movement?"

THE EZLN AND THE STATE

Maybe what really identifies the EZLN as a postmodern movement for Burbach is this: "What distinguishes the EZLN from its predecessors is that it is not bent on taking power in Mexico City, nor is it calling for state socialism."

But in addition to being a curious reason for regarding the movement as postmodern, this is straightforwardly and simply wrong—wrong about the EZLN, and wrong about its predecessors. First, in their declaration of war in late 1993, the first order from the General Command of the EZLN to its military forces was to "Advance to the capital of the country, defeat the Mexican Federal Army . . . and permit the liberated peoples to elect, freely and democratically, their own administrative authorities." Second, from the time of the conquest and even before, Mexican history has been wracked by large-scale popular uprisings and rebellions by peasants and Indians. A key feature of these mobilizations is that most were, precisely, not "bent on taking power in Mexico City." Perhaps that's why the peasants and Indians invariably lost, why each rural revolt has ended with the victory of the dominant class.

Whatever the extent of violence exercised during earlier popular uprisings, there has often been a strong antimilitaristic streak running through them, and an even stronger repudiation of the power of the state, whether colonial or neocolonial, patrimonial or capitalist. Two obvious examples that spring to mind are the popular armies led by Emiliano Zapata and Francisco Villa between 1911 and 1920. But neither Villismo and Zapatismo [Mark I] were "bent on taking power in Mexico City"; nor were either of them calling for "state socialism." To try to forge a new basis for social life in a way that is grounded in the experience and responds to the demands—or the requirements for living—of los de abajo, of the misnamed *marginados* (who are in fact not the least bit "marginal" to the continuing reproduction of specific forms of exploitation) is hardly to call for state socialism. In any event, "state monopoly capitalism" is a more accurate term for the sort of social system Burbach correctly insists the neo-Zapatistas are repudiating.

At any rate, throughout the world peasant movements have tended to regard the state as alien and distant, and typically their revolts have been directed not at the seizure of state power but at the replacement of an alien form of rule by a different social order. Hence it could be argued that the failure to aim for state power is rather more pre- than postmodern. If Burbach is right about the neo-Zapatistas' relation to the state, then the EZLN is typically premodern; but if he is wrong, than it is more modern than "postmodern."

The other side of this coin is Burbach's claim that the EZLN's objective "is to spark a broad-based movement of civil society in Chiapas and the rest of Mexico that will transform the country from the bottom up."

It is undeniable that the EZLN is distinguishable from other popular social movements in Mexico in the last 60 years in its success at not only precipitating "a broad-based political and ideological dialogue" but also in actively mobilizing large groups of people. It is no less certain that the current effort is not without precedents outside the conventional circuits of power that flow to and from the state and the ruling party. Many Mexican activists and popular organizations—some more visible and predictable than others—share the objective of generating a broad-based movement to transform society from the bottom up. Alongside human rights organizations, peasant coordinadoras, and the popular organizations that sprang out of the rubble of the earthquakes in Mexico City in 1985, are the unofficial and independent trade unions, the millions of people who voted for Cuauhtémoc Cárdenas in 1988, and movements such as the peasant mobilizations in the northern state of Chihuahua in the 1980s that linked up with peasant mobilizations in Chiapas, just as others had a century earlier.

What distinguishes the EZLN, then, is not its objective, but the genuinely unprecedented success with which its initiative has been embraced and taken seriously by many currents in Mexican society.

Yet however unprecedented the EZLN's apparent success up to now (in April 1995), it is still hard to see what this has to do with its postmodernity. Broad-based movements in Mexican society have both "modern" and "premodern" antecedents, and organization in "civil society" has long been a staple of popular mobilizations. When in his concluding section Burbach again insists that the EZLN's "postmodernist perspective" is demonstrated by "the demand for authentic democracy, and transforming society from the bottom up," one can't help wondering why good old Marxist socialism, with its commitment to securing human emancipation and a thorough democratization of society beginning with "freely associated direct producers" would not be the epitome of postmodernity.

The attempt to pin the postmodern label on the EZLN is shot through with contradictions, which are nicely summed up in the following observation:

> Another central factor facilitating this revolt's postmodernity is that it is not a rebellion against a typical autocrat or dictator like Batista or Somoza, but a movement that traces its lineage back to the early twentieth-century Mexican revolution.

To begin with, it is unclear exactly what Batista or Somoza are supposed to typify. But the main thing is that the rebels—communicating in languages understood only by themselves and a handful of anthropologists, linguists, missionaries, and former Maoists—yet again appear pretty premodern and the enemy they have identified manifestly modern. What distinguishes the EZLN, even by this account, is not their postmodern redefinition of temporality, space, and experience itself, but, on the contrary, their sense of palpable connection with a tradition. Burbach's observation that "The struggle of the EZLN . . . [is] over how to mobilize the population to recapture the county's revolutionary ideals" certainly captures something important about what the neo-Zapatistas are trying to accomplish and how they are self-consciously building upon past struggles of historical peasantries in Mexico. But that observation neatly and decisively subverts his claims for the EZLN as a "postmodern political movement."

So where does this leave us? The language of postmodernity has added nothing to our understanding of Chiapas. If anything, it has obscured and detracted from what is valuable in Burbach's account. It is especially depressing to observe this effect in an otherwise illuminating and politically sympathetic study, and it is a measure of the price we have to pay for this surrender to fashion. Instead of bringing us closer to an understanding of a complex social movement, it simply serves to underline the profound distance between postmodern intellectuals and the activists or supporters of the EZLN.

Why not interject some remarks of a Chihuahuan peasant, asked whether people in northern Mexico, followers of Francisco Villa, had joined the revolution in 1910 to recover control of their land? "Put it that we now have land," replied Cruz Chavez in 1986, "but that was a fight. And justice? And freedom? When will we get that? Can you tell me? Look, we're gonna die of old age without seeing them, because the more time that passes, justice and freedom only get worse in our country."*

Now I can imagine at least two different ways of connecting these remarks to what is happening in Chiapas today. We could simply take Cruz Chavez's words with those of Subcomandante Marcos and measure them both against some abstract repertoire of signifiers to find out, for example, whether they are pre- or postmodern discourses. Alternatively, we could consider these discourses historically, comparing the ways in which words like "freedom" and "justice" figure in their respective vocabularies, and how they relate to their concrete and changing historical referents, their material and social conditions, their political practices and struggles. We could consider as well how the labor process in Mexican agriculture has or has not changed since 1910, how political democracy has or has not advanced. And we could explore the ways in which the EZLN is trying in practice to answer the questions posed by Cruz Chavez in a different region of Mexico, under different historical conditions, and building differently on a long history—including the 1910 revolution—of political struggle.

In the first case, it is hard to see how our objective as intellectuals could be anything else than to appropriate those discourses, to claim them as our own. In the second, we would simply be trying to understand and explain. The latter objective is in some ways more modest. At least it is less likely to exaggerate the power of intellectuals, because it acknowledges that we are

---

*Interview with Cruz Chavez Gutierrez in El Tascate, Namiquipa, Chihuahua, July 1986. This man was the grandson of an earlier Cruz Chavez, who led the town of Tomochic, Chihuahua, in a briefly successful and still influential armed uprising against the Mexican state in the early 1890s.

talking about social and political practices undertaken by specific people other than ourselves, instead of claiming that our own discourse is the only real practice, our academic discourse the only real politics.

Derek Sayer has suggested that "we might want to consider the possibility that the status of 'organic intellectual' of anything other than a ruling class might just be a contradiction in terms." However difficult it may be to accept, this suggestion does have the virtue of acknowledging both the limits and the grounding of intellectual activity. Something approximating, however remotely, the determinative power that postmodernist intellectuals claim for their own discursive practices—the power to create reality itself—is, in the real world, possible only for servants of a ruling class, with the power of the state underwriting their discourses. The rest of us should be content to see our intellectual activity function as a critical instrument, as a challenge to ruling ideologies, maybe as a guide to political action when possible, but above all as a way of enhancing or broadcasting, but not replacing, the voices of those who oppose oppression.

AS TIME GOES BY
"Marcos," or The Mask is the Message

JOSÉ DE LA COLINA

Originally appeared in *Letras Libras*,
February 1999.

Translated by Shayna Cohen.

IN the first days of January 1994, between the two celestial myths of Santa Claus and the Three Wise Men, television cameras brought before our eyes the immediate, earthly myth of a just leader, streamlined against a landscape of rustic peasants, misery, rebellion, and immobilized rage. It was an invasion of painful and ominous images. Beside the protagonist—or around him but in a second plane or an adjoining plane—clustered a frieze of undifferentiated secondary actors, the justifiers and the defenders, doubtless the descendants of underdevelopment and misery, those who are traditionally made to pay for the broken dishes, the sacrificables to a Revolution longed for as the raison d'être of history, already distorted into (capital) True Men by a propaganda as skillful as it is Manichean (employing as its method, though sublimating it, an ethnic appeal from indigenous Chiapans). Some of these true men, the constituents of the Zapatista Army of National Liberation, also came masked, and even if that was not necessary, they were certainly (and would continue to be) predestined to a chronic anonymity: The majority of the time, the hero, the super-subcomandante, went to speak and have pictures taken on behalf of them, more than as one of them. It was a troop whose soldiers had clearly been taught guerrilla methods, given arms — or wooden facsimiles of guns, because the important thing was that the effect be spectacular — and at the risk of their lives, they showed the world a scenario that had, until then, only been shared among the everyday local color: underdevelopment, hunger and violence.

The protagonist had come forth from the jungle as if from a grand historical obscurity, as if from a revolt founded on insult, propelled by a thirst and hunger for justice that really exist in Chiapas. And, as a sudden myth, which he himself constructed and offered up ("I am a myth of genius" he would say a little later, with the auto-irony that is his trademark), he invaded television screens, the front pages of the papers, the Internet, the national political scene, and the world's attention — particularly that of Europe, which from the easy chair of a blasé life was unexpectedly entertained by folklore in arms: an adventurer, virile, sweet, Third World-esque and with an old-but-new look. His emergence introduced the first — and maybe the only — Latin American (or maybe even international) chiefs or rebel leaders or historic champions, who in addition to digging (as many have done) into the flashiness of a pseudonym or a nom de guerre, used the romantic prestige and the melodrama of a mask or a veil (a ski mask) as a pledge to the obscurity more characteristic of the heroes in movies or comic strips (Zorro, Fantomas, Cruz Diablo, Batman, El Santo, El Mil Mascaras) than of verifiable, real world terrorists (to the degree that the news really certifies them as such), such as fundamentalists in the Middle East or the heads of ETA.

In reality, the mystery surrounding the name and face has disappeared. The ski mask served not to negate Marcos's identity but to highlight the photographability of his eyes, framing them as a little window, granting them the privilege of a perpetual close-up, accentuating his presence with a touch of mystery. The mask also allowed the nullification of Rafael Sebastián Guillén and the creation of another man, "Marcos," and another face, represented exclusively by a mystical, masked gaze: mythic, photogenic. In a single look, the face synthesized a hero who, from our first perception, seemed to have sprung from nothing into an immediate semi-god or a flash of lightning without end. Aside from the mask, this lofty leader's corporeal decoration is a constellation of symbolic objects: the cartridge belts worn in an X "like that of Emiliano Zapata," the lit pipe as a distinctive amulet of an intellectual, a handkerchief tied about his neck perhaps in coquettish remembrance of Pol Pot, the barrel of a shotgun at his shoulder, indicating that this thing is seriously happening, and some auxiliary new age technology attached to his belt, signaling that this is an era of an intercommunicated planet, and in his carriage, this pacifist discourse, a warlike curriculum in which the media will be the battlefield.

Since his entrance (almost an apparition, an epiphany) "Marcos" has presented himself with a quality of visual fetishism, selling himself as an icon destined to nourish the new revolutionary imagination in all its novelty and velocity. He risks entering into a museum of modern kitsch as a pastiche of Che Guevara (who also ended up being kitsch). But, for the time being, he has triumphed in an illusory, captivating act. The image was the message, the spirit became material in the figure, the personality was the mask. And didn't Monsiváis say, "Marcos without the ski mask is not admissible, is not photographable, is not a living legend?" Moreover the mask has generated a fascinating dialectic between Outside and Inside. From the outside Marcos offers himself up as a mere man on a warpath—no one and everyone (all of the wronged Chiapan Indians, for example); from the inside, in the end, as Elena Poniatowska said, he is "this man who has a god inside him, and he is called Marcos."

So the mask—the object that transformed the until-now-obscure Rafael Sebastián Guillén into the radiant, errant knight "Marcos," the proof of the possibility of mobilizing revelation to revolution, and at the same time a receptacle of divine manifestation, of a redeeming discourse—is in fact the message: "All can be Marcos," says the ski mask, the nom de guerre. "And you will be like gods," whispers that nice little beetle Durito, Marcos's primary interlocutor until recently.

And so, already, there we have it: mask = message. And message = spectacle.

Anticipating the unblushing ecstasy of Madame Danielle Mitterand (who would have ordered the hero to return to the jungle mounted on his horse, just as he came, so she could contemplate the flavor of it in all its plastic grandeur) and preceding the sense of show-business that movie director Oliver Stone (who arrived in Chiapas intent on Hollywoodizing the champion), a tourist, thanking (for the unexpected enrichment of his tour) an event as Latin, as picturesque, as romantic as Marcos's first apparition, he breathed forth (into cameras and microphones) a phrase as foolish immediately as it was lucid in the long run. The exclamation didn't eulogize or vituperate but simply defined the specter: "What a showman!" This showmanship, capable of commanding a grand opera in a full jungle (thus the showboat of the Intergalactic Encounter or the "National Democratic Convention of Aguascalientes," with a public of falsified fans, compromised artists and intellectuals and journalists), amounted to extended explosions of torrential prose, prophetic, playful, mournful, accusatory, political, lyrical and at times vulgar: a soliloquy, from colloquial rhetoric or poetry of Chiapan Indians to the grandest, lyrical tirades of brilliant poets or the narrative abilities of "magical realism," passing through a Marxism jumbled with subliminal citations from Foucault, Althuser, and right up to Derrida, through the Third World's resuscitated ideology, modernist indigenism and the recurring call to a semi-Gramscian civil society which consists of no-one-knows-what but is useful for what it is. (The distrustful witness suspects that "Marcos" means by "civil society" the allied bureaucrats that the communists call fellow travelers or necessary fools and that vernacular Mexican language calls *paleros*.)

"Marcos" is the sudden, red blaze in the firebreak of the "end of history" and the beginning of globalization. It is alleged that post-history has left, to the detail of a pinpoint, the common people with a new, brilliant guide, a variant on the head of state, this time in a local, national, international, and Internetic format. The masked protagonist's talent for using the media, for reproducing and propagating the recourse of his discourse, and even the double discourse (demanding peace, having declared war), has merit in that it made evident the fundamental power of the word. Collegiate, knowledgeable, and a debater of neopositivism, already the chief has said (as recorded by an old fellow student) that "the things that exist, in the meantime, are named." His movement, framed by the Zapatista Army of National Liberation, apart from one or two acts of real war and apart from the coercion and exaction that guerillas exercised upon unconvinced indigenous people (those for whom it suffices to *not* be EZLN-istas, to transform them, whether they want it or not, into deplorable PRI-istas who must be punished for this supposed wicked affiliation), exists above all because of a declaration of war and an avalanche of manifestos and proclamations "from the Lacandón jungle." For the most part, it was born verbally. It came into existence by means of the word, but principally by means of the word of Marcos, the mouthpiece who, in the name of all, erected himself as protagonism's involuntary martyr, all the time occupying the microphone—and sadly he feels obligated to steal the show.

The voice is not everything. In writing the word is elevated to the nth power, and Marcos has written profusely. (The caricaturist Magu, reproaching him for a period of inaction, went so far as to ask him if the uprising had only been armed so that *La Jornada* would publish his lengthy speeches, live from the jungle).

The guerilla insurrection is essentially a perpetual manifesto and an infinite series of pamphlets written by Marcos (on paper or on Internet screens) and put on stage, in people of flesh and bone, within the miserable and magnificent Chiapan scenery and under the eyes of the world. It is the power of the word and of fiction, even if the cost in real blood—as often the blood of the True Men as that of commonplace indigenous people (who are also true ones but without capitals)—is so high and lamentable.

ONCE AGAIN,
THE NOBLE SAVAGE

JEAN MEYER

Originally appeared in *Letras Libras*, March 1999.

Translated by Jay Miskowiec.

NOBODY likes to admit the end of their noble dream, whether it's called the "City of the Sun," the "City of God," the "New Jerusalem," or the "Kingdom of Liberty." The difficulty of accepting the harsh reality that this world under the moon is not, nor can it be, the Garden of Eden explains the prodigious echo awakened by the cyberguerrilla Marcos and the EZLN [the Zapatista Army of National Liberation]. Out of nowhere they resuscitated the apparently forgotten messages of Robin Hood and Heraclio Bernal, of Bartolomé de las Casas and Emiliano Zapata, of Cuauhtémoc and Che Guevara, of Cochise, Geronimo, and Fidel Castro. In both Mexico and Europe awoke the millenarian hope of the "end of history, " a hope that didn't signify so much the triumph of "neoliberalism" and "globalization" as the advent of the Reign. Which reign? That of liberty, equality, and fraternity. One needn't be more precise: each person is free to dream his or her own utopia. Christian or communist, anarchist or authoritarian, horizontal or vertical, it really doesn't matter. The indigenous or Indian dimension, absent from the EZLN's initial agenda, surfaced as soon as Marcos measured its importance against the hope rediscovered in Mexico and even more so in Europe, especially Catholic, Latin Europe — France, Italy, Spain. For many people, the young and not so young, through the Mexicans of Chiapas the Americas returned to being the New World and Marcos became Sir Hope. Thus we have had two characters, two phantoms, running through Europe: the Indian and Revolution.

Leszek Kolakowski taught me that Marx was an Old Testament prophet and a German philosopher whose (utopian) "fantasy" of the emancipation of all humanity through class struggle, which, in Lenin's case, was followed to the letter, didn't lead to liberation but to absolute social subjugation. Before Marx, the French Revolution, at least in its Jacobean or ultra-Jacobean thrust (that of Gracchus Baboeuf, known as Graco: an absolutely ancient 2,000-year-old revolutionary agenda!) had demonstrated how the path of the generous, liberating utopia led toward the Reign of Terror. It took me a few years to learn the lesson.

For that reason the neo-Zapatista message doesn't resonate within me: I have learned something from history and the frequent return of certain good men, and I'm not 16 or 20, ages which magnify revolutionary stirrings. Still, Alain Touraine is older than I am and what's happening in Chiapas has rejuvenated him extraordinarily. In 1992 he didn't hesitate to proclaim that "the epoch of revolutions has ended, economic rationality is the sign of contemporary modernity. . . . As a result of the failure of totalitarian regimes, our view has changed radically. After having thought that revolution was the best path to create modernity, 30 or 50 years later we reached the historical — not theoretical — conclusion that this politicization of the economy, this mixing together of everything, was leading to ruin."

Touraine is among the famous who went to "revolutionary" Chiapas, who participated in the International Encounter for Humanity and Against Neoliberalism. He showed his enthusiasm for the "armed democrat" Marcos: "History will recall the physical, political, and intellectual courage of Subcomandante Marcos, a sociologist on horseback, a mixed-blood among Indians, a Mexican patriot and a militant global revolutionary, who risks his life in order to once again unite, in Latin America and elsewhere, revolutionary struggle and political liberty."

On various occasions Régis Debray has been critical about his revolutionary past and his apology for the armed path of revolution after revolution. He distanced himself from the Cuban and other revolutions, even from the once tutelary figures of Fidel and Che, but the heat from Marcos's torch reignited him.

Long sensitive to the "media of fascination," Debray possibly admired Marcos more for his communication genius than as a guerrilla. He also recognized, no doubt, the university colleague who is an Internet expert, who in a few days of shooting obtained more worldwide news coverage than Guatemalan or Colombian guerillas have in 30 years.

But let's leave aside Régis Debray, who didn't take long to return to his permanent skepticism. There are thousands of young and not so young people who form the international network of *Ya Basta!* with all its Catholic, Protestant, socialist, and communist aid committees: in two words, Christians and leftists. They are telling us that revolutionary, millenarian, religious (Christian or non-Christian) hope hasn't died. This hope moves a great number of the NGOs and churches that continue to wait for God to judge history in the form of revolution, purifying fire, the sword of the archangel Michael. The five-sided star—that of the Bolsheviks and Mao— is present, along with the cross and the Virgin of Guadalupe: Marxist revolution and Christian revolution.

And thus in pilgrimage come nuns, mother superiors, priests, and ministers, as well as leaders of the Italian Communist Party and the wife of a French president, not to mention so many young people attracted by the personality of Marcos and his allusions that are as much sexual as theoretical. To speak of this new altar to the personality of a masked man (the nonexistent knight) would lead us too far off track, but it can't be separated from the revolutionary idea. I say "idea," but that's not the right word; better "idea-passion." The most powerful idea-passion of the twentieth century, made even stronger because it redoubled the bet apparently lost in the nineteenth century, is undoubtedly revolution, whether red, brown, or black. The fall of the Berlin Wall and the USSR, that period from 1989–91, was for many something like the death of the gods in a time of polytheism, or the death of God in a Nietzschean time that is our own as well. It left those believers orphaned, at least until 1994 when Marcos returned to preach the good news, with something that sounded at bottom like the Shining Path, a reference not lost on everyone.

The sermon's echo is understood in Mexico: The Left had lost all hope in face of the accumulated successes of the young Carlos Salinas de

Gortari, who seemed invincible; the PRI would retain power until 2012 or 2108, said the least pessimistic. As Bertrand de Grange and Maite Rico wrote: "Marcos, like the little boy in the story, dared point out that the emperor really had no clothes." And a regime like the Mexican, which since 1914 had based its legitimacy on the Revolution, which had made Emiliano Zapata into a revolutionary idol, had to be very sensitive to the sermon. President Salinas himself, sincerely enamored with the figure of Zapata, was rudely shaken.

If the word "revolution" belongs to Mexican nationalism and civicism, the Cuban Revolution was and continues to be for the most recent generations the October Revolution of Latin America. If Europe still stirs thinking of its October, how much more do Mexico and Latin America thinking of La Moncada, Fidel, Che . . . and Marcos, the latter's most recent reincarnation. Cuba was for a European generation "the Cuban fiesta," for a Latin American generation "the first free territory of the Americas." And so, up until today, Fidel continues to be practically untouchable for a certain sector of the Left, that which could never renounce the socialist fatherland and revolutionary violence. If a few "leftist intellectuals" have changed their position after the events of 1989–91, few have publicly recognized their error. Many remained silent, stupefied, consternated, until January of 1994 when Marcos brought them a fantastic gift: Utopia had not died; a new free land existed in America, in Mexico, in Chiapas.

Pablo Gonzalez Casanova hadn't lost faith. In 1992 he wrote, "Perhaps not since Montesquieu has one conceived of a popular and democratic balance of powers, sovereignties and autonomies as efficient and feasible as the Cuban." He was one of the first to celebrate the good news proclaimed by Marcos: Once again collective redemption was possible through the defeat of liberalism, in a felicitous alloy of Marxism, Christianity, and aboriginalism. Hadn't the same author written, "If the ruling classes make religion into the opiate of the masses, revolutions reclaim its liberating character. They experience faith and the struggle for liberation as one sole commitment . . . the Eucharist is linked to the liberating and pastoral experience lived in the flesh itself. Political analysis is elaborated before and after mass. The atrium is also the agora."

Revolution as a millenarian utopia and liberation theology, which is no less utopian, no less millenarian, encountered each other in Chiapas in order to create, once again, the "new world," the Americas. Once again at least for the Catholics, because for revolutionaries this is something new, the "Indian" recuperating his quality of the "noble savage," free of all the sins of the individualist, bourgeois, liberal world. Moreover the noble savage, the ancient *gens angelicum* (the society, the people, the celestial, angelical nation) of the seventeenth century Franciscans had been transformed into the "good revolutionary." By starting to fight, the Indian, Subcomandante Marcos, and Bishop Samuel Ruíz took up again, perhaps without realizing it, an old dispute of New Spain between Creoles, ranch owners, miners; captains on one side, ecclesiastics on the other.

This new episode would have greatly interested Carlos Rangel because it confirmed his thesis concerning the intersection of the errors of Latin Americans about themselves and the errors of Europeans about Latin America. The persistence of both equivocations explains the audience for Marcos. The narcissistic perspectives of Europeans have always inflated Latin America's aberrations and illusions. This is obvious when it's a matter of European enthusiasm for a certain Latin American novel or painting, but the same thing occurs with regard to the social sciences or politics.

Jean Francois Revel, who was quite hard on Mexico (and rightly so) in 1952, quite severe about the totalitarian temptation (and rightly so) in 1975, said that ideology is the twin sister of pathology. He said as well, that for Europeans, "America is like a mirror of their own obsessions, the repulsive in the case of North America, the oniric in the case of South America. Thus shortly after the ruin of the imaginary 'revolution' of 1968, Europeans looked for the realization of their dreams in guerrilla movements: Tupamaros, Montoneros, Guevaristas, and later the Shining Path or the Sandinista totalitarianism inspired and sustained by Castro. . . . The European left awaited from Latin America, and the Third World in general, the revolution which it had been denied. . . . In 1994 it found new support for its insurgent dreams in Mexico, in the EZLN of Subcomandante Marcos."

How many European youths who on January 1, 1994, knew nothing at all about Mexico, much less the name Chiapas, immediately got drunk on the new literary genre created by Marcos? With enthusiasm and generosity they picked up the cry, "Ya basta!" (Enough is enough!). And their Mexican brothers, too, those the same age as well as the veterans of the previous leftist generations, and at one time the vast majority of Mexican society, or at least the urban society of the megalopolis: It's certain there exists in the middle class a (latent) bad conscience in face of the poor. Suddenly there appeared the distant image of the poor *par excellence*, the poor dressed in all their virtues, a potentially messianic poor—the Indian, the root of our nationality, the Indian as the quasi-Christ, presented to the world by a

Robin Hood and a Bartolomé de las Casas no less media-savvy than his rival and alter-ego of the mask and pipe.

Mexico, France, Italy, and Spain are Catholic countries that have been able to find in the revolutionary spirit the same passion that stirred Marx and Engels, and centuries earlier Joaquin de Fiore: the old Christian apocalyptic millenarianism. This ancient utopian impulse, periodically rejuvenated in the Americas, "the continent of revolutions," and in Mexico, "the land of volcanoes," has again been shared by Christians and non-Christians, the young and the not so young, all impatient to put an end to the reign of evil. They share the belief that the present world is bad and that its salvation will be absolute or it won't be at all. The old world can't adjust, and has to be finished off in order to reach the new world. Who, if not the original inhabitants, those who have their roots in the Americas ("the new world"), is called to redeem humanity?

Suddenly the "Indian" finds himself promoted to the dignity of being the revolutionary agent and the new "proletariat." The Catholic Church from both Mexico and abroad starts again down a path it took centuries ago, and the leftist messianics follow on this route that is new to them. As much a certain Mexican nationalism as a certain European internationalism fulfills the sacrament of this new but quite ancient undertaking of, once again, "redeeming the Indians."

An old European dream, one that never had anything to do with American reality, has been reactivated in Chiapas by a bishop who, in principle, never dreamed of revolution but of barring the way to Protestants, and by a guerrilla who, in principle, never promoted any kind of Indianism, but rather sought out "the weakest weak." Liberation theology made the bishop approach the guerrilla and the indigenous catechists made the guerrilla approach the bishop. The two were incompatible rivals, but the enthusiasm of their European and Mexican partisans prohibited any apparent rupture. Such partisans find in Marcos and Don Samuel a historic mythology in action; with them are revived those from the sixteenth century whom Alfonso Reyes called "the leftist fathers of the Americas," men like More, Campanella, Erasmus, Vives, and Valdés. The words of Vasco de Quiroga resound once again:

"For not in vain, but with great cause and reason, is it called here the New World, and it is the New World: not because it has been newly found, but because in its people and almost everything it resembles the first age, the golden age . . . the first age, the golden age, has become, through our malice and the great greed of our nation, worse than the iron age."

VOICES FROM THE JUNGLE
Subcomandante Marcos and Culture

ELENA PONIATOWSKA

Originally appeared in *Distant Relations*. Trisha Ziff (Ed.)
(Smart Art Press, 1995)

Translated by Ellen Calmus.

IT is reasonable, just, and necessary in Latin America that suddenly in the hills, among the oaks of the forest, on the mountain, desperate men and women from the deepest reaches of the jungle, from the deepest reaches of abandonment, rifles held high, cry out that Indians and peasants also have the right to live. Latin America is at war, a war of the poor against the rich. It is a muffled, latent, dark, primitive war—the continuing awful struggle of those who have been forgotten, a war interspersed with long years of truce. The poor have a limitless endurance; they helplessly observe the way they are pushed aside, until one day one of them or someone on their side stands up and says, "enough, no more, better to die." It is only when this mass becomes dangerous that its existence is recognized.

In Mexico the past is not past; the past never dies. Every day we experience the Conquest in the flesh. Five hundred years have not elapsed since the arrival of the Conquistadors. In 1995, Indigenous Latin Americans are treated just as they were in 1519; they share the same exact living conditions. Our country is racist, sexist, classist. In *Resistencia y Utopia: 1528–1940* (*Resistance and Utopia*), Antonio García de León, a historian of Chiapas, writes the same story that was written by the first bishop of Chiapas, Fray Bartolomé de las Casas, in his *Breve Crónica de la Destrucción de las Indias Occidentales* (*A Brief Chronicle of the Destruction of the West Indies*). Don Samuel Ruíz, the current bishop and worthy successor of Fray Bartolomé, is mocked in Mexico as well as in the Vatican for his defense of the Indians. On the streets of Mexico City and in the larger cities of Chiapas, they put up posters with his photo: DANGEROUS CRIMINAL and WANTED FOR BETRAYING HIS COUNTRY. There have never been such campaigns of harassment against anyone else in the country. He is hated by the rich Chiapanecans, who say that he is the comandante of the Zapatista forces, and that Marcos is his subcommander. Since 1960, when he was assigned the diocese of San Cristóbal by Pope John XXII, Samuel Ruíz has chosen to work on behalf of the poor—and in Latin America to choose to work with the poor is a crime; liberation theology has been demonized. In 1993 Samuel Ruíz was investigated by the Vatican on the initiative of Bishop Bernard Gantin, a black African from Zaire (of all people), head of Latin American Affairs in the Vatican, but it wasn't until 1995 that *L'Osservatore Romano* admitted that all Bishop Ruíz had done was to concern himself with "the fair demands of the poor exploited masses of his diocese."

Time has not passed in Chiapas. B. Traven, the German writer who lived in Mexico for many years until his death in 1969, could write the same novels today that he wrote in the 1930s, not to mention his *Estudio Antropológico de Chiapas* (*An Anthropological Study of Chiapas*). His books about the jungle, *Gobierno* (*Government*), *La carreta* (*The Cart*), *Marcha a la montería* (*The March to the Hunt*), *Trozas* (*The Logs*), *La rebelión de los colgados* (*The Rebellion of the Hanged*), *El General* (*The General*), and *Puente en la selva* (*A Bridge in the Jungle*) are terrifyingly current. Nothing has changed—nothing. Well, something has happened: The rain forests have been nearly annihilated by fortune hunters, timber dealers, cattle ranchers looking for pasture, coffee growers, and landowners, who, unlike the Indians, have no close relationship with nature—they use heavy machinery, they don't know how to grow cacao in the shade of larger trees, they don't know how to live in the jungle without destroying it, they don't take care of the jungle flora and fauna.

Since 1519 Mexico has gone through a long process, a confrontation between two equally great cultures. Yet, one of these cultures did everything in its power to annihilate the other, tear it out by its roots, destroy its temples, break its back. Since then Mexico has not ceased to be a colonized country. The Church of Nuestra Señora de los Remedios, one of the largest churches in the state of Puebla, was constructed on top of a pyramid larger than that of Kofú in Egypt. It measured 488 meters wide by 62 meters tall; its splendor covered an area of 17 hectares. The Spanish church mounted the Aztec temple as Cortez mounted Malinché, but Nature was wise enough to preserve underground the vestiges of our splendid past. The gods still throb under Mexican soil, and Coatlicue and Huitzilopochtli compete with the other saints; when we want rain we all pray to Tlaloc. The Zócalo, with its National Palace and Cathedral, was built in the sixteenth century on top of the Templo Mayor, and the latest excavations further confirm (as if further confirmation were possible) the legitimacy and validity of pre-Columbian Mexican society.

Colonization is perhaps the worst thing that can happen to a people, though it is now said that we Mexicans use this as an excuse for not succeeding, for acting like underage children, for lying, cheating, and not being able to solve a single one of our problems. Our huge country, instead of becoming greater, has lost territory. We sold Texas and California to the United States and nothing happened, nobody rose up in arms (in spite of the fact that we lost our best and most fertile land). After 200 years of independence, we are inferior to our past—not because we lost the land, but due to a condition we share with the rest of Latin America: We are in debt. There is violence behind each Latin American state, ancestral violence and economic violence. We are living on borrowed money, and this gives our life a sense not shared by other lives, the sense of punishment. Our metaphysical insecurity dates from the Conquest and today is transformed into our condition as debtors, as men and women who walk in chains.

For the past 65 years, we Mexicans have been guided by our Holy Revolution, our Blessed Revolution, our Enlightened Revolution. Revolutionary rhetoric has permeated not only the predictable, cardboard speeches of the ruling party, it has permeated our entire lives. In our newspapers the term "Mexican Revolution" appears as often as the word "Mexico." We can't say "Mexico" without saying "Revolution." Nevertheless, the minute there is a revolutionary uprising, official condemnation is unanimous; the Zapatistas turn out to be the cause of all our evils. Among other evils is our punishment by "big money": Mexico began its last presidential administration with two billionaires, but it ended up with 14. The country of revolution is the land of the big fortunes. The fortunes of Brazil and other Latin American countries pale next to the large Mexican fortunes. Only the Arab oil fortunes are greater.

In response to official history, there were grassroots uprisings (the student movement of 1968 had a profound influence on the political life of Mexico, giving rise to a number of grassroots movements), and popular heroes emerged. First it was Zapata, with his cry of "Land and Liberty" in the revolution of 1910. Emiliano Zapata distributed the land of Morelos in 1910 after building an army out of a bunch of peasants. "The land belongs to the farmer," he said to all the poor and to the hacienda owners. Hated by the rich, venerated by the poor, Zapata died without knowing that he had begun one of the most far-reaching movements in Mexico—Zapatismo—or that 85 years later, in Chiapas, a group made up almost entirely of Indians would show that Zapatismo is still alive.

On January 1, 1994, a leader emerged who combined the roots and characteristics of previous leaders—Emiliano Zapata, Rubén Jaramillo, Lucio Cabañas, Genaro Vásquez Rojas—but who took on areas the others never mastered. First, he had a whole series of modern resources the others never dreamed of, such as modern information technology. Insurgent Subcomandante Marcos, he calls himself. The figure of Che Guevara fertilized the field, and a new caudillo has arrived, not mounted on horseback but borne on a great flood of romanticism. The name "Marcos," they say, is made up of the initials of the towns in Chiapas that the Zapatistas took on January 1: Margaritas, Altamirano, La Realidad, Chanal, Ocosingo, and San Cristóbal. One hundred combatants of the Zapatista army stationed themselves in the Plaza de las Armas. They took the National Palace, destroyed its files of land ownership, and finished off its bureaucracy. Unlike Zapata, Marcos has his own news agency. There in the deepest Lacandón jungle or somewhere in the mountains of the southeast, as he himself describes his location, he knows everything, he reads everything, from T. John Perse to Shakespeare, whose sonnets he quotes in the original English. He has found a way to not only be better informed than his predecessors, but even better informed than city dwellers, and he sends his communiqués by modem to selected newspapers. A ski mask is an essential part of his charisma. It serves less to conceal his face than to reveal his character. His critics say that Che Guevara always showed his face, but the subcomandante shows his face through his letters, his famous communiqués, which reveal much more than if we were able to see his nose, which we know is large, his beard, which we know is thick, his eyes, whose loving expression we have all seen, his pipe, and his very recognizable voice. In Mexico the police know everything, and what they don't know they ask the FBI or the CIA, who usually know ahead of time what will happen in our country. After January 1 Marcos became the most charismatic man in Mexico: nobody can match his ability to convoke an audience for an event. On his own, with his one-man news agency, he uses instruments of communication and persuasion, which in his hands acquire an aspect of the "ideal," becoming instruments at the service of a cause—not because they are owned by Marcos but because they put cybernetics at the service of those who have never had anything, who have never seen a computer in their lives. Computers, thanks to the "Sub," as they call him, turn out to be a democratizing factor. It seems to me that putting modern technology within reach of the poorest people is, in a way, an advancement of the cultural process; with Marcos, the much-bandied-about "modernity" sought by Mexico through NAFTA [the North American Free Trade Agreement] first began to penetrate the Mexican jungle.

What is Marcos's language? Accused of being sentimental, kitsch, simplistic, a pamphleteer, of writing soap operas, Marcos tells stories in a language everybody can understand. Sometimes he reminds us of Saint-Exupéry. He talks to those around him—the children, old Antonio, the peasants, the men and women who followed him to the mountains to become Zapatistas—and his writing reflects their thoughts. His stories are stories of the soil. Helping the poorest and most downtrodden to be heard is an act of culture, and that is what revolution is about these days. There is an essential book about Chiapas, *Juan Pérez Jolote* by the anthropologist Ricardo Pozas, but we have learned almost nothing since that book—not withstanding Rosario Castellanos's *Balún Canán, Oficio de Tinieblas* (*Mass for the Dying*) and *Ciudad Real* (*Royal City*). For the world to suddenly flood into such a state as abandoned as Chiapas is a cultural revolution.

The Zapatistas are also echoed in the media, mainly in the Mexican newspaper *La Jornada*. Marcos, allowing himself the luxury of censorship (and to the applause of many), has refused access to the most powerful television monopoly of the country: Televisa. It would seem that, thanks to Subcomandante Marcos, a cleansing of Mexico's often corrupt communications media is taking place, and Mexican journalists, inspired by the process, are trying to redeem their media. For a few months romanticism ranged the copy desks of a number of Mexican newspapers, and many reporters returned from Chiapas to Mexico City in an exalted state, saying their visions of the world and of themselves had been turned upside down.

Marcos's language is the language of a man who has survived the jungle and knows it well, a man who has eaten snakes when he could get them, a mestizo who gets sick to his stomach and has had an enormously difficult time getting used to the tropics. His language is new in Mexican politics; it is the beginning of a new way of doing politics—which is certainly a cultural phenomenon. Far from resorting to the usual calumnious political rhetoric, nothing in Marcos's speech reminds us of the speech of senators and congressmen. The language of Marcos, a mestizo, can clearly be understood by everyone; he shares the language of the men, women, and children of Chiapas. Marcos is familiar with the bites of the Chechem fly, or "evil woman," which causes delirium in its feverish victims; he knows about the dangerous Bac Ne snake, or "four noses." He knows how to find a path through the jungle in the rain where the branches of the trees form an immense green umbrella; he knows about walking for hours at a stretch carrying a 40-kilo backpack on his shoulder; he knows how to pitch a tent and tighten his belt for days; he knows how to live with other people; and he especially knows how to think. His language is the language of hard daily life, life connected to the soil: the language of survival. The language of politicians, from local representatives to the president of the republic, is the language of bureaucracy. Marcos writes from the soil and constantly speaks of his relationship with the trees, with the sunset, with the cold early morning hours, with the *zacate estrella* (star grass), with old Antonio, with Moi, Tacho, Monarca, Durito, with the inhabitants of Chiapas. He talks to the mountains and the tall trees, to crickets and beetles, and that is why we feel his words resonate inside us and we hear them to be true.

The Zapatista demands as expressed in their Lacandón Jungle Declaration were cultural: work, land, housing, food, health, education, independence, freedom, democracy, and peace. They asked that all indigenous languages be declared official Mexican languages, and that the teaching of these be required in primary, secondary, and high schools as well as in the universities; they also asked that their rights and dignity as indigenous peoples be respected, and that their cultures and traditions be taken into consideration. They want the discrimination and contempt they have suffered for centuries to stop. They demand the right to organize and govern themselves autonomously, because they do not want to be subject to the will of powerful Mexicans and foreigners. They want their justice to be administrated by the indigenous people themselves, according to their customs and traditions, without intervention from illegitimate, corrupt governments.

Can a handful of poorly armed men and women (2,300 Zapatistas) change the cultural system of a country, educate that country, and make it grow? In a country hungry for figures worthy of looking up to, the element of ethics in Marcos's identity is definitive. He has not only taken power, he has made our young people grow up, he has raised our society's consciousness, he has made that society participatory. Thanks to him—and I don't blush to say it—I think we are better people. At least Marcos hasn't lied to us, he has not betrayed anybody, and he has lived according to his ideas, which seems to be a lot to ask in our country. He stayed in the jungle for 11 years, he has shared and continues to share the Indians' living conditions, he means what he says, and he keeps his word. His war is *sui generis*, as he said himself on March 6 in a letter addressed to Miguel Vásquez, a boy from La Paz, Baja California:

/// III

One fine day we decided to become soldiers so that some day soldiers would not be necessary. That is, we chose a profession which is suicidal, since its objective is to disappear: soldiers who are soldiers so that one day nobody would have to be a soldier. Obvious, no?

The Zapatistas chose to start their war on January 1, 1994, the day the North American Free Trade Agreement took effect. They took over the Plaza de Armas in San Cristóbal de las Casas without frightening the tourists on their Christmas holidays—this was so much the case that Marcos told some tourists who were going to the beach at Cancún that he hoped they would have a good time, and he told some others who planned to go to the archeological site at Palenque that the road was closed and, not without humor, added: "Excuse the inconvenience, but this is a revolution."

The fact that the tourists had not noticed means that the tranquility of San Cristóbal was not disturbed to an alarming degree by armed men in ski masks, wearing crossed bandoliers, and even carrying submachine guns. From the first moment, Subcomandante Marcos's style was not to kill whoever stood in his way. His guerrilla warfare was distinguished by being more political than military.

The government responded to the Zapatista offensive with violence. The war lasted 12 days, the army going so far as to drop bombs; afterward, they razed the land to get rid of any supplies with which civilians might support the Zapatistas. The international press discovered that Mexico was not a First World country but still remained in the Third World. The truth of the Zapatistas penetrated deeply into public opinion. Demonstrations by students, professors, housewives, and poor people were what stopped the army's genocidal attacks against the Zapatista Indians. Responding to public pressure, President Salinas said he would pardon the rebels. Subcomandante Marcos replied with one of the most impressive of his communiqués (which have crossed oceans and received answers from Germany, the United States, Canada, Spain, Italy, France, England, El Salvador, Switzerland, Brazil, Holland, Chile, Norway, Japan, Puerto Rico, Panama, South Africa, and Ireland):

Why should we ask for pardon? What are they to pardon us for? For not dying of hunger? For not being quiet about our misery? For not humbly accepting the gigantic historic burden of contempt and abandonment? For having taken up arms when all other ways were closed to us?

For ignoring the Penal Code of Chiapas, the most absurd and repressive penal code in living memory? For having demonstrated to the rest of the country and to the whole world that human dignity is alive and can be found in its poorest inhabitants? For having prepared ourselves well and conscientiously before we began? For carrying guns into battle instead of bows and arrows? For having previously learned how to fight? For all of us being Mexicans? For most of us being Indians? For calling on Mexicans to fight in every way possible to defend what is theirs? For fighting for freedom, democracy, and justice? For not following the patterns of previous guerrilla groups? For not giving up? For not selling out? For not betraying each other?

Who should ask for pardon, and who is to grant it?. . . . Those who filled their pockets and their souls with declarations and promises? The dead, our dead, so mortally dead of a "natural" death—that is, of measles, whooping cough, dengue, cholera, typhoid, mononucleosis, tetanus, pneumonia, malaria, and other gastrointestinal and pulmonary delights? . . . Those who treat us like foreigners in our own land and ask us for our papers and our obedience to a law of whose existence and justice we know nothing? Those who tortured us, put us in jail, murdered us, or made us disappear for the serious "infraction" of wanting a piece of land, not a big one, just a piece of land on which we could produce something to fill our stomachs?

Who should ask pardon, and who is to grant it?

One of Subcomandante Marcos's proposals to Mexican citizens was the creation of a cultural space: a library in the jungle. Marcos and his Zapatistas provided the labor and the raw material, the citizenry supplied the maintenance and continuity. Through collection drives, young people contributed several thousand books, and a number of university students traveled in caravans to the Lacandón jungle to work as librarians. Now the library has ceased to exist; it was burned by the Mexican army. What harm was there in a library? Why not leave it for the people of Guadalupe Tepeyac, to whom it belonged? Were they trying to erase a symbol, the symbol of the Zapatistas?

Those who join the Zapatista National Liberation Army have to have finished elementary school. Zapatistas know how to read and write. If they read slowly in public, or if they stumble over certain words when giving a speech or reading a statement to the press, this is due to the fact that their first language is Tzeltal or Tzotzil. Education is a required topic of discussion for them, since one of their main proposals is to achieve literacy among the population—but they want to be the ones who teach the population to read and write. Our book-learned education is characterized by its removal from reality. For example, Mexican children are currently taught that every child should sleep in a room with the window open. Knowing as we do that 40 million Mexicans live (with their families) in two-room dwellings, whose only opening is a door onto the street—who are the children targeted by the official textbook? The last thing to be taught in rural schools is "know-how," and many children drop out of school by the third grade precisely because their schools have no relationship with their reality.

The most important cultural phenomenon brought about by the Zapatistas is their new attitude toward Indian women. For both young Indigenous women and those over 35 years old (because at 35 they are already old), to become a Zapatista is their best life option. Among the Zapatistas they feel respected. They used to work as maids, weavers, or embroiderers, and they were not paid half what their work was worth. Subcomandante Marcos has said:

> We take good care of our women because, since they are malnourished, we don't want them to lose too much blood when they have their periods. Here in the Zapatista Army, the penalty for rape is death. A man who rapes a woman is sentenced to death by firing squad. Fortunately, we have not yet had to send anyone to be shot. Zapatista women can choose the man they want to marry. Before, they were the ones chosen. They have the right to control their own bodies, and use a variety of methods of contraception, since they can't have children in the jungle. They can now look their husbands in the eye; they have become true partners.

Rosario Castellanos once told how on one of her journeys to Chiapas she met an Indian returning from the forest with his bundle of firewood, riding on a burro. Behind him, also with her bundle of firewood, his wife followed on foot. Rosario asked him, "Why do you travel comfortably seated, while your wife follows behind you, on foot?"

Unperturbed, the Chiapanecan answered, "Ah, that's because she doesn't have a burro!"

We could say now that, thanks to the Zapatistas, the Indian women of Chiapas finally have a burro.

CHIAPAS,
LAND OF HOPE AND SORROW

José Saramago

Originally appeared in *Le Monde Diplomatique*,
March 1999.

Translated by Barbara Wilson.

A few weeks before he was awarded the 1998 Nobel Prize for Literature, Portuguese writer José Saramago went to Chiapas with Brazilian photographer Sebastião Salgado, to meet Subcomandante Marcos and report to the world on the sufferings of the Indians of southern Mexico. He met a proud people who have refused to give up hope. The Zapatistas with their National Liberation are insisting on autonomy—but not secession or separatism. Notwithstanding, the 1996 San Andrés accords failed to materialize into the hoped-for law to amend the constitution. Two years ago negotiations were broken off and since then the government has tried to bring the Zapatista forces to their knees with a combination of aid programs and counterinsurgency measures using armed civilian groups. In the violence that has followed over 100 have died.

IN 1721 Charles-Louis de Secondat, Baron de Montesquieu, asked with an assumed simplicity that in no way masked a bitter sarcasm: "Persians? How on earth can anybody be Persian?" It is nearly 300 years since he wrote his celebrated Persian Letters and we still have not managed to find an intelligent answer to this most fundamental question in the long history of human relations. We fail to understand how anybody could have been "Persian" then, and, as if that were not absurd enough, could still obstinately persist in being "Persian" now, when the whole world is conspiring to persuade us that the only truly desirable thing in life is to be what we like to call "Western"—a general and deceptively handy term (Western values, fashions, tastes, habits, interests, enthusiasms, ideas). The alternative, if worse comes to the worst and one cannot rise to those sublime heights, is to become some kind of "Westernized" hybrid by dint of persuasion or, failing all else, force.

To be "Persian" is to be foreign, different—in short, not like us. The mere existence of "Persians" has been enough to upset, confuse, disorganize and generally throw a spanner in the works of our institutions. "Persians" may even go to the intolerable lengths of disturbing the very thing all governments hold most dear—their sovereign right to rule in peace. The Indians in Brazil (where being landless is another way of being "Persian") were and still are Persians; the Indians in the United States were but have now almost ceased to be Persians; the Incas, Mayas, and Aztecs were Persians in their day and so are their descendants, wherever they may be. There are Persians in Guatemala, Bolivia, Colombia, Peru, and the unhappy land of Mexico.

There, the relentlessly questing lens of Sebastião Salgado sought out and recorded these moving and arresting images that speak to us so directly. How is it, they ask, that you "Western" and "Westernized" people of North and South, East and West—you who are so cultivated, so civilized, so perfect—still lack the intelligence and sensibility to understand us, the Persians of Chiapas?

For it is, in the end, a question of understanding. Understanding the speaking look in the eyes, the grave expression on the faces, the simple way of being together, feeling and thinking alike, weeping the same tears, smiling the same smile. Understanding the way the sole survivor of a massacre places her hands like protecting wings on the heads of her daughters, understanding this unending river of the living and the dead, the spilling of blood, the rebirth of hope, the fitting silence of people who have been waiting hundreds of years for respect and justice, the contained anger of people whose patience has finally run out.

Six years ago, in obedience to the dictates of the neoliberal "economic revolution" masterminded from outside and ruthlessly enforced by the government, amendments to the Mexican constitution put an end to the distribution of land, and to any hope the landless peasants may have cherished of having their own patch of ground. The native peoples believed they could defend their historic rights (or customary rights, if you think Indian communities have no place in Mexican history) by banding together to form civil societies—societies, strange as it may seem, still marked by a refusal to countenance any form of violence, even such violence as would be perfectly appropriate to their situation.

These societies have always had the support of the Catholic Church, though to little avail. Their leaders and representatives have all been thrown into prison. There has been an increase in systematic, implacable, and brutal persecution by the state and the great landowners—united in the defense of their interests and privileges—and the Indians have continued to be forcibly expelled from their ancestral lands. As a last resort they often had to flee to the mountains or take refuge in the jungle and it was there, in the deep mists of the hills and valleys, that the rebellion was to take root.

The Indians of Chiapas are not the only people in the world to be humiliated or oppressed. In every age and every place, regardless of race, color, custom, culture, or religious belief, humankind has always been ready to humiliate and oppress people it still, by a sad irony, persists in calling its fellow men and women.

We have invented things not found in nature: cruelty, torture, contempt. In an abuse of reason, we have divided humanity into irreconcilable categories: rich and poor, masters and slaves, strong and weak, learned and ignorant. And, within each of these divisions, we have created subdivisions, so that the pretexts for despising, humiliating, and oppressing are endlessly varied and perpetuated.

In recent years, Chiapas has become a place where the most despised, humiliated, and oppressed people in Mexico have been able to regain that dignity and honor they had never entirely lost. It is a place where the heavy rock of age-old oppression has shattered, making way for an endless funeral cortege of the dead led by a procession of the living—new and different people, today's men, women and children asking only that their rights be respected—their rights not just as members of the human race but as Indians now and in the future.

They rebelled and took up arms, but their chief weapon was the moral force that only honor and dignity can maintain in the mind when the body is prey to the hunger and poverty it has always known.

Beyond the uplands of Chiapas, there is not just the Mexican government, there is the whole world. Every attempt has been made to persuade us that this is just a little local trouble that can be brought under control by a strict application of national laws—laws which, as we have seen once again, are deceptively malleable and can be adapted to suit the strategy and tactics of the economic powers and the political powers that serve them. But the issue that is being fought out in the mountains of Chiapas and the Lacandón jungle extends beyond the frontiers of Mexico. It touches the hearts of all those who have not abandoned, who never will abandon their hopes and dreams and their simple demand for equal justice for all.

As that remarkable man who goes by the name of Subcomandante Marcos once wrote, the rebel demands "a world that will contain countless worlds, a world both unified and diverse." Dare I add, a world that will uphold the inalienable right of everyone to be "Persian" for as long as they like and be beholden to no one.

The mountain ranges of Chiapas are certainly among the most spectacular landscapes I have ever had the privilege of seeing. But they are also a hotbed of violence and crime. Thousands of natives, driven from their homes and lands for the unpardonable crime of showing silent or open support for the Zapatista National Liberation Front (EZLN) are crowded into makeshift camps. There is little or no food, the small amount of water that is available for the refugees is almost always polluted, and adults and children alike are ravaged by diseases such as tuberculosis, cholera, measles, tetanus, pneumonia, typhus, and malaria. Meanwhile, the public authorities and medical services turn a blind eye. A military force of almost 60,000 men—a third of the Mexican Army—is currently occupying the state of Chiapas on the pretext of maintaining public order. This explanation is belied by the facts. If the Mexican army is protecting a section of the native population and even giving them training, weapons, and ammunition, it is generally because they are members of the Institutional Revolutionary Party (PRI) which has held sway for 70 years almost without a break. It is no coincidence that these paramilitary groups are formed for the sole purpose of doing the dirtiest work of all—attacking, raping, and murdering their own people.

Acteal* was yet another episode in the terrible tragedy that began in 1492 with the arrival of the conquistadors. For 500 years in Iberian America the native peoples have been passed from pillar to post—from the soldiers who killed them to the masters who exploited them and the everpresent Catholic church which took away their gods but could not crush their spirit. I use the term "Iberian" advisedly, not to exonerate the Portuguese and Brazilians, who took over the genocidal operation that reduced the three or four million Indians living in Brazil in the Age of Discovery to barely 200,000 in 1980.

After the Acteal massacre, the simple words "We are winning" began to be heard on the radio. Anyone who was unaware of what was going on might have thought this was an insolent and provocative piece of propaganda put out by the murderers. But no, it was a message of encouragement, a call to take heart, going out on the air and uniting the native communities as if in an embrace. While they mourned their dead, 45 more

---

*A massacre in Chiapas on 22 December 1997, in which 45 alleged Zapatistas, mainly women and children, were killed.

to add to five centuries of slaughter, those communities stoically raised their heads and told each other, "We are winning." For to survive humiliation and oppression, contempt, cruelty and torture cannot but be a victory—a great victory, the greatest of all, being as it is a victory of the spirit.

Eduardo Galeano, the distinguished Uruguayan writer, tells how Rafael Guillén,* before he became Subcomandante Marcos, went to Chiapas and spoke to the Indians but they did not understand him: "Then he went into the mist, he learned to listen and so to speak." The mist that stops us seeing is also the way to the world of those who are not like us, the world of Indians and Persians. We must stop talking, we must look and listen, and then perhaps we will be able to understand.

---

*According to a statement issued by the Mexican ministry of the interior on February 9, 1995, the real name of "Subcomandante Marcos" was Rafael Guillén, born in Tampico in 1957.

UNMASKING**MARCOS**

ILAN STAVANS

Originally appeared in *Transition*,
Spring 1996.

Tout révolutionnaire finit en oppresseur ou en hérétique.

—ALBERT CAMUS

THE Subcomandante Insurgente Marcos, or *El Sup*, as he is known in Mexico. His skin is bleached, whiter than that of his compañeros. He speaks with palpable erudition. The sword *and* the pen: He is a rebel, yes, but also an intellectual, a mind perpetually alert. And like some ranting dissenter, he is always prepared to say No: No to five centuries of abuse of the indigenous people of Chiapas and the nearby Quintana Roo in the Yucatán Peninsula. No to the sclerotic one-party state that has mortgaged Mexico and her people for generations, and for generations to come.

No, No, and No.

El Sup is also like Sisyphus, or possibly like Jesus Christ: He bears on his shoulders an impossible burden, the aspirations and demands of an embattled people. He must know, in his heart, that the rock is too heavy, the hill too steep; his efforts will change very little in the way people go about their lives south of the Tortilla Curtain. His real task, the best he can do, is to call attention to the misery of miserable men and women.

He isn't a terrorist but a freedom fighter, and a peaceable one at that. He took up arms because debate is unfruitful in his milieu. He is a *guerrillero* for the 1990s who understands, better than most people, the power of word and image. He uses allegories and anecdotes, old saws and folk tales, to convey his message. Not a politician but a storyteller—an icon knowledgeable in iconography, the new art of war, a pupil of Marshall McLuhan. As he himself once wrote, "My job is to make wars by writing letters."

El Sup is a tragic hero, a Moses without a Promised Land. He stands in a long line of Latin American guerrilla heroes, at once real and mythical, an insurrectionary tradition stretching back nearly half a millennium. Figures like the legendary Enriquillo, who orchestrated an uprising among aborigines in La Española around 1518, about whom Fray Bartolomé de las Casas writes eloquently in his *Historia de las Indias*. And Enriquillo's children: Emiliano Zapata; Augusto César Sandino, the inspiration for Daniel Ortega and the Sandinistas; Simón Bolívar, the revolutionary strategist who liberated much of South America from Spanish rule and who dreamed in the 1820s of La Gran Colombia, a republic of republics that would serve as a Hispanic mirror to the United States of America; Tupac Amaru, the Peruvian Indian leader of an unsuccessful revolt against the Iberians in 1780, whose example still inspires the Maoists in Peru; Edén Pastora, *Comandante Cero*, an early Sandinista guerrillero turned dissenter; and, of course, Fidel Castro and Ernesto "Che" Guevara. A robust tradition of revolutionaries, overpopulated by runaway slaves, *indios*, *subversivos*, muralists, and disenfranchised middle-class intellectuals.

El Sup: newspaper columnists and union organizers credit him for the wakeup call that changed Mexico forever. He had gone to Chiapas in 1983 to politicize people. "We started talking to the communities, who taught us a very important lesson," he told an interviewer. "The democratic organization or social structure of the indigenous communities is very honest, very clear." He fought hard to be accepted, and he was, although his pale skin marked him as an outsider. ("Though the preeminent spokesman of the Zapatista movement, he could never aspire to a position greater than subcomandante, as the highest leadership positions are customarily reserved for Indians.) The next 10 years were spent mobilizing peasants, reeducating them and being reeducated in turn. The rest, as they say, is history.

And rightly so: after all, on the night of January 1, 1994, just as the so-called North American Free Trade Agreement, NAFTA, among Canada, the United States, and Mexico, was about to go into effect, he stormed onto the stage.

Lightning and thunder followed.

It was a night to remember. As José Juárez, a Chiapas local, described it, "It was on New Year's Eve when President Carlos Salinas de Gortari retired to his chambers thinking he would wake up a North American. Instead he woke up a Guatemalan."

No, said the Subcomandante. Mexico isn't ready for the First World. Not yet.

Everywhere people rejoiced. ¡*Un milagro!* A miracle! A wonder of wonders! So spoke Bishop Samuel Ruíz García, the bishop of San Cristóbal, whose role in the Zapatista revolution angered conservatives, but who was endorsed by millions worldwide, turning him into a favorite for the Nobel Peace Prize.

With his trademark black skintight mask, El Sup was constantly on television. *Un enmascarado:* Mexicans turned him into a god. Since pre-Columbian times Mexico has been enamored of the mask. A wall between the self and the universe, it serves as a shield and a hiding place. The mask is omnipresent in Mexico: in theaters, on the Day of the Dead, in *lucha libre*, the popular Latin American equivalent of wrestling. And among pop heroes like El Zorro, El Santo the wrestler, and Super Barrio, all defenders of *los miserables*, masked champions whose silent faces embody the faces of millions.

Suddenly, the guerrilla was back in fashion. The "news" that the Hispanic world had entered a new era of democratic transition had been proven wrong. Once again weapons, not ballots, were the order of the day. Within the year, the lost "motorcycle diary" of Che Guevara was published in Europe and the United States—a record of a 24-year-old Che's travels on a Norton 500 from Argentina to Chile, Peru, Colombia, and Venezuela. A free-spirited, first-person account unlike any of his "mature" works, it recalled Sal Paradise's hitchhiking in Jack Kerouac's *On the Road.* El Sup had discovered new territory: the revolutionary as easy rider.

El Sup had a rifle, yes, but he hardly used it. His bullets took the form of faxes and e-mails, cluster bombs in the shape of communiqués, and nonstop e-mail midrashim through the Internet. He wrote in a torrent, producing hundreds of texts, quickly disproving Hannah Arendt's claim that "under conditions of tyranny it is far easier to act than to think." In less than twelve months, during sleepless sessions on the word processor in the midst of fighting a war, El Sup generated enough text for a 300-page volume. And he sent it out without concern for copyright. His goal was to subvert our conception of intellectual ownership, to make the private public and vice versa.

He was a master at marketing. By presenting himself as a down-to-earth dissenter, a nonconformist, a hipster dressed up as soldier, he made it easy to feel close to him. To fall in love with him, even. In one communiqué, for instance, he addresses the Mexican people:

> Brothers and sisters, we are the product of 500 years of struggle: first against slavery; then in the insurgent-led war of Independence against Spain; later in the fight to avoid being absorbed by North American expansion; next to proclaim our Constitution and expel the French from our soil; and finally, after the dictatorship of Porfirio Díaz refused to fairly apply the reform laws, in the rebellion where the people created their own leaders. In that rebellion Villa and Zapata emerged—poor men, like us.

In another, he writes to his fellow Zapatistas:

> Our struggle is righteous and true; it is not a response to personal interests, but to the will for freedom of all the Mexican people and the indigenous people in particular. We want justice and we will carry on because hope also lives in our hearts.

And in a letter to President Clinton, El Sup ponders:

> We wonder if the United States Congress and the people of the United States of North America approved this military and economic aid to fight the drug traffic or to murder indigenous people in the Mexican Southeast. Troops, planes, helicopters, radar, communications technology, weapons, and military supplies are currently being used not to pursue drug traffickers and the big kingpins of the drug Mafia, but rather to repress the righteous struggle of the people of Mexico and of the indigenous people of Chiapas in the southeast of our country, and to murder innocent men, women, and children.
>
> We don't receive any aid from foreign governments, people, or organizations. We have nothing to do with national or international drug trafficking or terrorism. We organized ourselves of our own volition, because of our

enormous needs and problems. We are tired of so many years of deception and death. It is our right to fight for a dignified life. At all times we have abided by the international laws of war and respected the civil population.

Since all the other compañeros of the Zapatista National Liberation Army were more modest, El Sup stole the spotlight. He was unquestionably *la estrella*. And his enigmatic identity began to obsess people. His education, some said, is obviously extensive. He must be a product of the *Distrito Federal*, the Mexico City of the early 1980s.

Was he overwhelmed by the outpouring of public affection? "I won't put much stock in it," he told one interviewer.

> I don't gain anything from it and we're not sure the organizations will, either. I guess I just don't know. About what's going on. I only get an inkling of what's going on when a journalist gets angry because I don't give him an interview. I say, "Since when am I so famous that they give me a hard time about being selective, and the lights, and I don't know what all." That is pure ideology, as they say up there, no? We don't have power struggles or ego problems of any kind.

Being selective: *el discriminador*. But his ego, no doubt, is monumental. He courted attention relentlessly. By 1995, stories circulated that internal struggles within the Zapatistas were growing, fought over El Sup's stardom.

Meanwhile, unmasking El Sup became a sport. Who is he? Where did he come from? I, for one, thought I knew, though not through any feat of journalistic prowess. I haven't been to the Chiapas jungle since the Zapatistas launched their rebellion. And if he is who I think he is, I haven't spoken to him since long before his communiqués began streaming from the Lacandón rain forest.

The clue to his identity came in early 1995, after Salinas had ceded power to his successor, Ernesto Zedillo Ponce de León, in the aftermath of a series of political assassinations that had rocked the PRI, the governing party. The enemy grew restless. El Sup had become too dangerous. And too popular! He was better known than any politician. He commanded more attention than any of the soap operas on Mexican TV, the opiate of the Mexican masses. Enough was enough. It was time for him to go.

Desenmascarar. What the Mexican government performed was an ancient ritual at the heart of the nation's soul: the unmasking. Quetzalcoatl was unmasked by the Spaniards, Sor Juana by the Church, and Pancho

Villa by a spy. To unmask can mean to undo, or to destroy, but it can also mean to elevate to a higher status: Every six years, as the country prepares to receive its new president, the head of the PRI literally unveils his successor before everyone's eyes.

In the public eye—El Sup's own terrain—Mexican government revealed his true self: Rafael Sebastián Guillén Vicente, a 37-year-old former college professor. A revelation, indeed, which El Sup immediately disputed . . . before vanishing into the night. Just like that, he disappeared. Off the TV screens. Out of the spotlight. He became a nonentity: *un espíriru.* Other Zapatistas replaced him in the high command of the Zapatista army.

In Mexico, of course, the government is always wrong; that is, since it promotes itself as the sole owner of the Truth, nobody believes it. And yet, El Sup might well be Guillén. I personally have no trouble equating the two. They sounded the same, right down to their rhetoric—a language I learned at the Xochimilco campus of Mexico City's Universidad Autónoma Metropolitans (UAM), the decidedly radical school where Guillén taught. In discussing his communiqués with several old college friends, we were struck by the similarities between his postmodern tongue and the often hallucinatory verbiage at Xochimilco, full of postscripts and qualifications and references to high and low, from modernist literature and academic Marxism to pop culture. El Sup said his idols were the nationally known "new journalists" Carlos Monsiváis and Elena Poniatowska, whom my whole intellectual generation deeply admired and whose own works trespass intellectual boundaries with glee. When asked to describe the books that influenced him, he would cite the 1970s writing of Octavio Paz, Julio Cortázar, Mario Vargas Llosa, and Gabriel García Márquez, although he would be careful to distance himself from the right-wing politics of Paz and Vargas Llosa.

El Sup mooned journalists with his writings. His speeches, like the authors we studied at UAM, seamlessly mix fiction with reality, becoming masterful self-parodies, texts about texts about texts. In a reply to a letter from the University Student Council of the University National Autónoma de Mexico (UNAM), he writes that with great pleasure the Zapatistas have received the students' support. He asks them to get organized following the pattern of the Zapististas, and concludes—

> If you accept this invitation, we need you to send some delegates so that, through an intermediary, we can arrange the details. We must organize everything well so that spies from the government don't slip through. And if you

make it down, don't worry about it. But keep up the fight over where you are, so that there can be justice for all Mexican people.

That's all, men and women, students of Mexico. We will be expecting a written response from you.

Respectfully,

From the mountains of the Mexican Southeast.

P.S.: El Sup's section: "The repeating post-script."

Another postscript follows, and then more and more.

P.P.S.: As long as we're in the PS.'s, which of all the "University Student Councils" wrote to us? Because back when I was a stylish young man of 25 . . . there were at least three of them. Did they merge?

P.S. to the P.S. to the P.S.: In the event that you do (whew!) take the Zócalo, don't be selfish . . . . Save me some space where I can at least sell arts and crafts. I may have to choose between being an unemployed "violence professional" and an underemployed one, with underemployment wages (much more marketable that way, under NAFTA, you know).

P.S. to the nth power: These postscripts are really a letter disguised as a postscript (to hide it from the Attorney General's Office and all the rest of the strongmen in dark glasses), but of course, it requires neither an answer, nor a sender, nor an addressee (an undeniable advantage of a letter disguised as a postscript).

Nostalgic P.S.: When I was young (Hello, Attorney General's Office. Here comes more data), there used to be a lightly wooded place between the main library, the Facultad de Filosofa y Letras, the Torre de Humanidades, Insurgentes Avenue, and the interior circuit of Ciudad Universitaria. We used to call that space, for reasons obvious to the initiates, the "Valley of Passions," and it was visited assiduously by diverse elements of the fauna who populated at 7 P.M. (an hour when those of good conscience drink hot chocolate and the bad ones make themselves hot enough to melt); they came from the humanities, sciences, and other areas (are there others?). At that time, a Cuban (Are you ready, Ambassador Jones? Make a note: more proof of pro-Castro tendencies) who used to give lectures seated in front of piano keys the color of his skin . . . and who called himself Snowball, would repeat over and over, "You can't have a good conscience and a heart. . . . "

Final fortissimo P.S.: Have you noticed how exquisitely cultured and refined these postscripts are? Are they not worthy of the First World? Don't they call attention to the fact that we "transgressors," thanks to NAFTA are striving to be competitive?

"Happy Ending" P.S.: Okay, okay, I'm going. This trip is coming to an end, and the guard, as usual, is still asleep and some one is tired of repeating "is anybody out there?" and tell myself, "Our country . . . and what is your answer?"

EL SUP'S UNCONVENTIONAL style was a commonplace at UAM in the early 1980. I was a student there at the time, the same time that Guillén, about five years my elder, was teaching. Some of my friends took classes with him, remarking on his sharp intellect and infectious verbosity. Crossing paths with him in hallways and cafeterias, I remember him as bright and articulate.

Well-known as an incubator for Marxist, pro-Cuba, pro-Sandanista activity, UAM's Xochimilco campus had been built by the government in the early 1970s. It included two other campuses in far-flung corners of the city. It was built in an attempt to dilute the massive student population at UNAM, the oldest institution of higher learning in the country.

In her book, *La noche de Tlatelolco*, Poniatowska chronicled the protests of 1968. It was UNAM's student body, some 30,000 strong, who led the protests, which were brutally crushed in the massacre at Tlatelolco Square. El Sup, although not Guillén, was born during that massacre—a ritual birth, an origin in which his whole militant odyssey was prefigured. If the revolution couldn't be won in the nation's capital, he would join the unhappy peasants in Chiapas and Yucatán—he would become an urban exile.

When Xochimilco opened, it immediately superseded UNAM in antigovernment militancy. It became a magnet for subversive artists, would-be guerrilla fighters, and sharp-tongued political thinkers. The place was known for its unorthodox educational methods, and fields of study often lost their boundaries. Professors not only sensitized us to the nation's poverty and injustice, they encouraged us to take action. Friends would take time off to travel to distant rural regions and live with the indigenous people.

Most eventually returned, but many didn't—they simply vanished, adopting new identities and new lives.

Injustice, inequality, freedom of speech—we wanted changes. "Down with the one-party system!" We would take advantage of cheap fares and travel to Havana, to become eyewitnesses to the profound transformation that had taken place in a corner of the Hispanic world. The Sandinistas in Nicaragua captured our attention and love. We admired their courage and identified with intellectuals like Julio Cortázar, Ernesto Cardenal, and Sergio Ramirez, who had put their literary careers on hold to work for the Nicaraguan government, or who had orchestrated international campaigns to support the Sandinista fight. We were excited—and we were blind. Our personal libraries were packed full with Marxist literature. Our writers were busy fashioning a style in which art and politics were inseparable. We disregarded any argument that tried to diminish our utopian expectations.

Indeed, finding bridges between political theory and activism became a sport. Those of us who studied psychology embraced the antipsychiatry movement and were expelled from asylums for allowing patients to go free. I, for one, worked with a metropolitan priest, Padre Chinchachoma, who devoted his ministry to homeless children. He believed that to help the children he needed to live among them, in Mexico City's garbage dumps—foraging with them for food, making and selling drugs for money, and occasionally engaging in acts of vandalism. I read Padre Chinchachoma's books with great admiration. He was my messiah, my Sup before El Sup.

Xochimilco—exciting, contradictory. Our teachers were dissatisfied middle-class Mexican leftists, exiled Argentinean intellectuals, and other Latin American émigrés. Our idols were Che Guevara, Felix Guattari, Antonio Gramsci, and Herbert Marcuse. Wealthy professors urged us to agitate among peasants in the countryside. And, what's more, we were aware that the government perceived our radicalism, our animosity, as productive.

In fact, it wanted our hatred. Its rationale was clear: If adolescents in the Third World are always full of antigovernment feeling, they should be provided with a secluded space to vent their rage. They'll scream, they'll organize, but as long as they're kept in isolation, nothing will come of it. And so we did, investing our time and energy in countless hopeless insurrectionary projects. But it wasn't a waste of energy. Something great did come out of it: El Sup.

I left Mexico in 1985, but I often look back at my years at UAM as a turning point. Between the pen and the sword, I thought I was wise for choosing the pen. But El Sup was even wiser: He chose both.

My politics and artistic views have changed somewhat. I have become a critic and scholar and have adopted a new language. In the process, I acquired a new mask of my own: I became part Mexican and part North American—at once both and neither.

Evidently, El Sup is also an academic, although a less reticent one. I was the coward, the egotist. He was the hero. We are both bridges—across cultures, across social classes. I chose the library as my habitat, while he made Mexico itself his personal creation.

So what if he is Guillén, and vice versa? Simply that his unmasking has served its purpose: El Sup has faded away from public attention. His once-omnipresent visage now appears infrequently, if at all, a haggard reminder of the still miserable conditions in the South.

Now there's talk of him, El Sup, becoming a leftist candidate in national politics. But history has little room for heroes shifting gears, and even less for legends who undress themselves. Besides, no career is more discredited in Mexico than that of a politician. Better to vanish: Only then will his trademark become truly indelible. Or better still: to become a novelist. After all, Latin America is depressing in its politics, but vivid in its imaginings. Viva El Sup, the intangible—a giant of the imagination.

CHIAPAS: THE INDIANS' PROPHET

ENRIQUE KRAUZE

Originally appeared in *Letras Libres.*
Reprinted in *The New York Review of Books,*
December 16, 1999.

Translated by Hank Heifetz.

Rebellion in Chiapas: An Historical Reader
by John Womack, Jr.
372 pages, $17.95 (paperback)
published by New Press

Marcos: La genial impostura
by Bertrand De la Grange and Maité Rico
472 pages, 104 pesos (hardcover)
published by Mexico City: Editorial Aguilar

*Religión, política y guerrilla en Las Cañadas de la Selva
Lacandóna*
by Maria del Carmen Legorreta Díaz
333 pages, 91 pesos (hardcover)
published by Mexico City: Editorial Cal y arena

1.

Four days after the Zapatista uprising on New Year's Day 1994 in the impoverished state of Chiapas, a reporter interviewed one of its peasant soldiers, a prisoner of the Mexican Army, and asked why he was fighting. "I want there to be democracy, no more inequality," he said. "I am looking for a life worth living, liberation, just like God says." John Womack Jr. uses these words as the epigraph to his book *Rebellion in Chiapas: An Historical Reader.*

The speaker was José Pérez Méndez, a Mayan peasant like all the common soldiers of the Zapatista Army of National Liberation (the EZLN), and his statement conveys much of the impetus of the rebellion, whose leaders were not Mayan chiapanecos but urban university graduates, like Subcomandante Marcos himself. They had been planning the uprising for 10 years, with the original intention of establishing a guerrilla foco (center) in Chiapas, in territory under their control, from which they hoped a revolution could spread. But the rebellion became something quite different: an event and a movement that could go nowhere militarily but has received extraordinary national and international attention. Now, more than five years later, the eventual fate of Zapatismo is still uncertain, and Mexico will enter the year 2000 with the as yet unresolved problem of, in the words of the Mexican intellectual Gabriel Zaid, "the first postmodern guerrilla war."

THE ZAPATISTA SOLDIER José Pérez Méndez had good reason to want democracy. For the Partido Revolucionario Institucional (PRI), which has governed Mexico uninterruptedly for 70 years, the "backward" state of Chiapas was a secure reserve of votes in national elections, giving the PRI, on average, 97 percent of the ballots. The "electoral victory" was engineered through efficient methods of fraud: vote buying, false ballots substituted for the real thing in areas where the government party felt threatened, and strong pressure from powerful local interests to "vote the right way." The machinery of the corporate state had links with all levels of power in Chiapas, from the Indian caciques, or political bosses, of small villages and communities all the way up to the dominant class—the owners of the coffee plantations and the cattle ranches, the lumber barons operating in the tropical forests, and other financial interests.

Pérez Méndez was one of many thousands protesting against the extreme social inequality in Chiapas. The state has immense natural resources. As of 1994 it was the primary producer of coffee, cattle, and cacao in Mexico, third in hydroelectric power, fourth in natural gas resources. And yet of its population of 3.7 million as of 1994 (of which 27 percent are Indian, divided among four major groups of ethnic Mayans), 50 percent were undernourished, 75 percent earned less than the Mexican minimum wage (then defined as $1,500 per year), and 56 percent were illiterate. In Los Altos ("The Heights") and the Lacandón jungle—centers of Zapatismo—the conditions were even worse, intensified by a population density of 76 inhabitants per square kilometer, almost double that of the rest of the state. And in these regions, close to 80 percent of the population is Indian.

Perhaps the greatest justification for Pérez Méndez's militancy lies in the daily affront to his dignity. (Womack's "a life worth living" is a translation of *una vida digna*, which can also be rendered as "a life with dignity.") Mexico is a country which for four centuries has undergone the most successful process of ethnic and cultural mixing in the Americas, but the ancient region of the Mayan civilization in Mexico, comprising primarily Chiapas and Yucatan, has been an exception from the very beginning. Racial discrimination, exploitation, and servitude have flourished through the centuries in its haciendas and cities. And they have bred ferocious ethnic wars.

THE CONTINUED PRESENCE of the Zapatista movement may not have lessened the economic inequalities of Chiapas (recent studies are not available), but there is no doubt that it has given the image of Indians (about 10 percent of the total population of Mexico) greater dignity, and brought their problems to the center of national attention. The shock of the Zapatista uprising of 1994 surely helped to intensify the demand for democratic change in the country. Faced with the threat that Mexicans might again be drawn to revolutionary action as they have been in the past, the people who hold power in Mexico, particularly the PRI, for the very first time opened up a real possibility of democratic electoral competition. At the same time, the political left, represented by the Partido de la Revolución Democrática (PRD)—a coalition of various forces including socialists, former Communists, and dissident defectors from the PRI—could cleanly distance itself from the idea of armed revolution (strongly favored by some sectors of the left since the late 1960s) and take clearer form as a social-democratic party contending politically for power.

The Zapatistas themselves, however, have shown an ambivalent, sometimes hostile, attitude toward electoral democracy, and this has had disastrous results. In the municipal elections of 1995, for instance, they instructed their followers not to take part in the voting, which both proved damaging to the PRD, the party that had shown the most respect for them, and also helped the PRI win elections they might otherwise have lost. In that same year, the Zapatistas chose not to respect the outcome of a citizens' referendum conducted nationwide by sympathetic groups in which 1.5 million voters asked them to disarm and join the political process. Again, in 1997, they discouraged their followers from voting in the midterm elections, once more delivering many municipalities to the PRI. On the other hand, the Zapatistas have actively promoted the spontaneous establishment of "independent municipalities," taking over villages controlled by the PRI. This has led to violence on both sides.

IN HIS INTRODUCTION to *Rebellion in Chiapas*, a collection of 32 documents ranging from colonial arguments and pronouncements dating from the sixteenth century to the latest EZLN communiqués from the jungle, John Womack Jr. explores the complicated, and sometimes paradoxical, unfolding of the Zapatista movement. He credits the government of President Carlos Salinas for its considerable investment in Chiapas before the rebellion, and for having rapidly decreed a cease-fire after the initial outbreak, instead of moving on to crush the movement, an option strongly favored by some of his advisers. Womack shows less sympathy for the policies of the present government of Ernesto Zedillo, whom he blames for delaying, and ultimately blocking, a solution to the conflict, even though both parties signed the agreement of San Andrés in 1996, which called for the withdrawal of most of the Mexican army stationed in Chiapas and the disarming of the Zapatistas.

Womack says (and he is partly right) that Zedillo did not carry out the accords because he felt that a continuing military presence and the mere passage of time would erode the will and the prestige of the Zapatistas. It is also true, and not discussed by Womack, that the provision advocating autonomy for Indian ethnic communities and their "uses and customs" ran into widespread opposition within the government, which feared that if power within the communities were to fall completely into the hands of local Indian leaders and come to serve the prejudices of majorities unused to tolerating dissident opinions, local autonomy would not only "subvert the political order" but also cause real harm to individual rights.

With 40,000 government troops still deployed in the regions involved in the Zapatista uprising, Chiapas is today engaged in a frozen war. But another, more sporadic, civil war continues, on a smaller scale, a war within the Indian population itself, between the Zapatistas' supporters and their opponents. Some of their opponents are paramilitary groups linked directly to the PRI or to powerful local bosses. But others have political disagreements with the Zapatistas or reflect old resentments or newly inflamed family land disputes.

On December 22, 1997, in the tiny settlement of Acteal, one of these villages divided between factions, an appalling massacre took place. Forty-five defenseless people (21 women, 15 children, and 9 men) were murdered. The dead were all members of Las Abejas, "The Bees," a citizens' organization sponsored by the diocese of San Cristóbal and sympathetic to the Zapatistas. The victims were praying at a local shrine when the killers launched their attacks. Two explanations for the slaughter have been offered. According to a communiqué issued by Subcomandante Marcos and the Zapatista army, it was a clear case of "ethnocide," of "a state-sponsored crime . . . approved by the federal and local governments," as part of the ongoing "low intensity war" against the Indians of Chiapas. The assassins were described as "paramilitary" groups directly armed by the state.

The official government report admits a "limited complicity" of "local police forces" but claims that the crime was committed by other Indians, supporters of the PRI who were bitterly opposed to the local pro-Zapatistas because they had created an "autonomous municipality" in the zone and had taken over its major resource, a bank of sand and gravel used as filler for road construction. The government report describes a civil war, a wave of looting and robberies, violent assaults, killings, and acts of revenge committed by both sides. It sketches a fierce conflict not so different from a number of ancient feuds among the Indians, where the communal system of values can show its negative side in the rejection of dissent, leading frequently to expulsions or even attempts to exterminate the dissenters.

Both versions convey much of the truth. Local government officials, not only the local police, shared far more responsibility for the crime than they admitted. The killers were allowed to organize and arm themselves despite warnings about what they might do. They were paramilitaries, but not federally sponsored gunmen. Like their victims, they were local Indians, working for a political boss connected to the PRI who was seeking revenge for the death of one of his sons in a recent encounter. On December 14, the boss, Jacinto Arias Cruz, former PRI mayor of the town of Chenalhó, was sentenced to 35 years in prison for organizing the massacre. Twenty-three of the killers were convicted with him. In the polarized situation of present-day Chiapas, the possibility of similar massacres continues to be very real.

WOMACK'S COLLECTION OFFERS English-speaking readers the opportunity to demystify the conflict by introducing a broad historical perspective. And it corrects an overemphasis on the charismatic Subcomandante Marcos by also concentrating on a person whose work in Chiapas preceded Marcos by 25 years, Bishop Samuel Ruíz of San Cristóbal de las Casas.

Without an understanding of Samuel Ruíz's long years of evangelical labor, the Zapatista rebellion cannot be adequately comprehended or evaluated. Using sources in the original Spanish, including some of the documents that Womack translates as well as other books and articles and a number of interviews I conducted in Chiapas, I have come to a somewhat different view of Ruíz's work, though Womack and I agree on the vital importance of the religious factor to what has happened, and is happening, in Chiapas.

Bishop Samuel Ruíz, who has recently retired at the age of 75 after almost 40 years as bishop, has carried through the most successful practical application in all of Latin America of the liberation theology that developed out of Vatican Council II convened by Pope John XXIII in 1962. Because of him, hundreds of thousands of Indians in the state of Chiapas have "become conscious" of the conditions of oppression under which they live. This is obviously a great good, but the impressive pastoral work of Samuel Ruíz has had other results as well, some more controversial.

2.

Hanging on a wall of Bishop Samuel Ruíz's office in the episcopal building in the highland city of San Cristóbal de las Casas is a folk-style painting that depicts an imaginary encounter between Samuel Ruíz and his remote precursor: Fray Bartolomé de las Casas, the great apostle to the Indians of the sixteenth century. The artist has presented the pair almost as twins, except for the eyeglasses Samuel Ruíz is wearing.

Bartolomé de las Casas, the "protector of the Indians," was the first priest ordained in the New World and the third bishop of San Cristóbal. The painting not only brings together the two men but recalls, as well, the traditional filial relationship in Mexico between priests and Indians, which began in 1524 when Hernán Cortés summoned the Franciscan missionaries to Mexico. Hidalgo and Morelos, the nineteenth-century leaders of the War of Independence against Spain, were both priests; and their armies, at least in the first stage of the rebellion, were largely Indian. Chiapas, which is a living museum of Mexican history, seems the perfect place for the resurgence of a very Mexican figure, the rebel priest who may invoke the neo-Thomist doctrine of the "Just War," as a last resort of the oppressed against their oppressors.

ACCORDING TO DON Samuel, the grim reality that he encountered when he arrived in Chiapas in 1960 was not "generically distinct" from what had profoundly shaken the soul of his great predecessor more than four centuries before. In one community he was informed that all the children had died almost overnight as the result of an epidemic wrongly diagnosed by the official health services. In some haciendas, owners whipped their resident peons; in San Cristóbal de las Casas, bastion of the coletos (a term used for the white upper class, especially within this city), Indians would still step off the sidewalks to let whites pass and could still hear themselves addressed with the same words of racial contempt that had assaulted the ears of Fray Bartolomé four centuries ago: "Indian dogs!"

To put an end to what Las Casas called the "unlawful treatment of the Indians," both bishops took energetic action. They brought to the diocese priests who shared their concern. Both called on members of the Dominican order, which, like the Franciscans, had come to the New World as a preaching order actively seeking converts. From the first, certain Dominicans showed a greater critical awareness of the injustice and cruelties inflicted upon the Indians, and they were the first to voice doubts about the moral legitimacy of the Conquest.

Both bishops also had to deal with significant resistance from local ecclesiastics: Fray Bartolomé from members of other preaching orders, Samuel Ruíz from the old monsignors and other conservative priests who were shocked when he would refuse to sleep in the "big house" of a hacienda and would choose instead to spend the night in the modest home of a peon. Both would come to praise, and idealize, the values and customs of the Indians, arguing that they had lived in a better society whose harmony had been subverted by the Conquistadores and, more recently, by exploiters and power brokers from outside the Indian communities.

"He is a prophet who creates prophets," says Miguel Concha, director of the order of the Dominicans in Mexico, about Bishop Ruíz. And Don Samuel has produced many prophets in his diocese: thousands of lay teachers of doctrine, called "catechists," the great majority of them Indians, who for three decades have been sowing (they would also say receiving) the "Word of God" in their small communities. The new "catechist" movement in Chiapas, Ruíz's creation, can be seen as a variation on traditional conversion: the propagation of doctrine by personal teaching in an effort to make the Indians conscious of their oppression.

This evangelical effort has been at the heart of the political changes that have shaken Chiapas before and since 1994. Fray Toribio de Benavente (known as Motolinía), a famous Franciscan opponent of Bartolomé de las Casas, expressed his fear that Las Casas's ideas would someday be "read by the Indians." This is precisely what Samuel Ruíz and his catechists have succeeded in doing.

3.

Don Samuel Ruíz was the first-born son of poor parents. His mother and father met as braceros, migrant grape-pickers in California. His mother was there illegally, as a "wetback." They married and returned to Mexico, where their son Samuel was born in 1924, in Irapuato, within the highland basin of the bajío to the north of Mexico City. This zone (along with Jalisco to the west) forms the very heart of Catholic Mexico. During the late 1920s (the era of the uprising of Catholic peasants called Cristeros against the anticlerical government of President Plutarco Elias Calles) and the 1930s, his father, now a small grocer, was not only pro-Cristero but also a Sinarquista, a member of a home-grown Mexican movement that was deeply Catholic but can also legitimately be described, in its racism and exclusivism, as fascist.

The movement was strong in León, where Samuel Ruíz entered a seminary in 1937, at the age of 13. The young Samuel Ruíz saw Sinarquismo as "a movement that shook things up, a necessary step in the civic and political education of society." He is very far from that position now. The direct ideological descendants of Sinarquismo—the dangerous and profoundly antidemocratic movements of the Catholic far right—are fiercely opposed to social Catholicism, to Samuel Ruíz and the theology of liberation. But coming from a Sinarquista family, he had an early acquaintance with an ideology that rejected the secular state in favor of a religious community.

In 1947, after studying at the Seminary of León, Samuel Ruíz entered the Colegio Pio Latinoamericano in Rome, a key center for the training of Latin-American priests. He seemed well on his way to a relatively cloistered career as a church theologian when, at the Biblical Institute of Rome, he studied biblical exegesis and began, as he would later say, "to half understand that the Bible is the only book written for a poor people in search of the promised land."

He returned to Mexico in 1952, and in 1954 he became rector of the Seminary of León. Five years later, he was appointed bishop of Chiapas — the poorest, most socially backward state in the Mexican republic. He would become one of the 2,692 bishops to attend the historic conclave that changed much of the direction of the Catholic Church, the Second Vatican Council.

Shortly before the Council began, he had his first transforming "revelation," his emotional response to one of the major themes Pope John presented as a preamble to the conference: the declaration that it was to be in the developing countries, in the "Third World," that the Church would discover what it really was and what it really had to do. For the bishop of Chiapas, this exhortation implied a mandate: "It clarified and determined the essential mission of the Church: if it does not maintain an adequate relationship with the structural world of poverty, it is no longer the Church of Jesus Christ."

IN 1964, RUÍZ decided that his diocese was much too large for him to deal effectively with social problems. So he cut it in two: the dioceses of Tuxtla and, what would become his own, of San Cristóbal de las Casas, 48 percent of the state, including by far the majority of its Indian population. Then, three years later, Samuel Ruíz divided his diocese into six administrative zones, based in part on ethnic differences.

In 1962 Ruíz invited groups of Dominicans into Chiapas, most of them dedicated to the new directions within the Church. By 1966, these "apostles" had established the Mission to the Chamulas, which would undertake, along with their normal priestly duties, the construction of a health center and workshops for arts and crafts, a night school for teaching women about health care and other domestic skills, and a communal farm. But it was the opening of schools for training and organizing Indians as "catechists" that was the decisive step in implementing the new evangelism. Ruíz celebrated

Mass at one or another of these schools every Sunday. By the 1970s, more than 700 catechists had been trained, and there would be many more in the years to come.

Liberation theology for Latin America—the "Preferential Option in Favor of the Poor"—received its classic articulation at the Second Conference of Latin American Bishops held in Medellín, Colombia, which Ruíz attended in the critical year of 1968. The new theology incorporated some aspects of Marxist analysis: the class struggle as an objective fact, capital as the product of alienated labor, and especially the explanation of the underdevelopment of the so-called Third World as a direct product of the development of the so-called First World. In addition, the liberation theologists would try to discover "the Plan of God" in the Bible, and attempt to "activate the transforming energy" of biblical texts. The new theology called for peaceful struggle to resolve the problems of the poor and the oppressed but—in line with the neo-Thomist definition of "a just war, to avenge a wrong so serious that it is impossible to heal it in any other way"[*]—did not exclude the use of violence as a last resort.

4.

The communities of Las Cañadas—a region laced with deep ravines within the Lacandón Jungle, which was to become a center of the Zapatista movement—were established by immigrants from elsewhere in Chiapas beginning in the Fifties. Most of these immigrants had been peons on estates bordering on the jungle who were forced out when the government began encouraging the spread of cattle ranches by giving the landowners financial incentives to switch from farming. The local oligarchy, the landowners and the politicians of the PRI, who were deeply imbued with a master–servant notion of the economy and a racist view of society, lobbied locally and nationally against government land-distribution efforts, and they hired gunmen to prevent the peons from settling on unused lands within their estates. Other immigrants were workers who had lost their places on the coffee

---

[*]See Norberto Bobbio, Nicola Matteucci, and Gianfranco Pasquino, *Diccionario de Política*, in two volumes (Mexico City: Siglo XXI, 1991), Book Two, pp. 1557–1563. The classic formulation of the sixteenth-century theologian Francisco de Vitoria, invoked by both left- and right-wing Catholic militants during this century, is quoted here, including the following passage:

> In no way could the world remain in a fortunate state, and what is more, we would arrive at the worst state of things, if tyrants . . . could inflict injuries and oppress the good and the innocent and if it were not permissible for the latter to repel their aggressions and give them a good lesson.

plantations in the south of the state, as the growers began to hire cheaper Guatemalan labor. For many Indians, emigration to the jungle seemed their only hope. Between 1950 and 1980, the population of the Lacandón jungle nearly tripled, from fewer than 80,000 souls to about 225,000.

The catechists also moved into Las Cañadas, where they began to apply a new method for "sowing" questions and "harvesting" responses that was partly inspired by the ideas of the Jesuit-trained Brazilian educational reformer Paulo Freire—especially in his key work *Pedagogy of the Oppressed* (1970). Freire called for the encouragement of independent (and potentially transformative) thinking and expression from illiterate peoples; he wanted them to be taught to read and to be self-sufficient in their judgment. In the words of Fray Gonzalo Ituarte, who was then vicar of the diocese, a truly liberating education should center on "the appropriation of the Word. . . . The Word of God summons me to recreate the world not for the domination of my brothers but for their liberation." Put into practice in Chiapas, the process came to be called "The Word of God" and the catechizer would be given the name *tijuanej*, which in the Tzeltal Maya language means "the animator, the provoker, the stimulator."

Javier Vargas, a member of the Marist order and a leading teacher and director of the catechists, was on one of his frequent inspection tours through the Ocosingo region near the Lacandón jungle when it occurred to him that the experience shared by the jungle's new inhabitants, including the catechists, was that of a new Exodus: the departure from the estates, the long and dangerous period of wandering through the jungle, and the eventual building of new villages. Inspired by the parallel, which brought the biblical world ever closer, Don Samuel and Vargas, along with other workers of the diocese, decided to replace the traditional Catholic catechism of fixed doctrinal questions and answers with a new catechism, more in accord with Vatican II, which would express "all the sources of the Word of God, the Bible, and tradition," but also "the history of the Indians as they record it, their traditions, their culture, wherein is the seed of 'the Word of God.' "

The result was a document fundamental to the conversion of the Indians to an indigenous form of the theology of liberation: *We Are Seeking Freedom: The Tzeltales of the Jungle Proclaim the Good News*. The text (a translation of which is included in Womack's book) is based on collective conversations between catechists and Indians, originally held in Tzeltal Mayan and later translated into Spanish and issued in 1971 by the diocese as a modest book of a little more than 100 pages. It contains prayers, songs, and readings of various kinds organized around the theme of oppression.

Four types of oppression are described: economic, political, cultural, and religious. The book uses many citations from the New Testament and the prophetic books of the Old Testament to support specific arguments. For example, economic oppression, which the emigrants to the Lacandón jungle had experienced on the haciendas, is compared to Pharaoh's Egypt within the context of an appeal to God:

> You said to the ancient Israelites when they were living as slaves: "I have seen the sufferings of my people. I have heard them weep and ask me for aid. I come to liberate them from their oppressors and carry them to a fine and spacious land that offers many fine fruits." (Ex., 3:7–8). Because of this we have come together to ask you, O Lord, to help us as well, to be of aid to us!

The oppression is also political because the laws favor the rich; it is cultural because the caxlanes (non-Indians) despise the languages and cultures of the Indians, who as a consequence fall into the error of despising themselves. And it is religious because conventional religious practice concentrates far too much on external acts of worship, and this undermines the strength of men and does no real honor to God.

To offset these the community must be strengthened: "We live in community, we have a culture, we are worth a great deal. . . . The community is life, it carries me to freedom. . . . The good Christian is he who makes the world grow for the good of his brothers. . . . " And more. God Himself is present in the community. He speaks through those who speak and, in a sense, He is the community. The catechism of the Exodus concludes with a question: "What are we to do?"

IN 1974, IN honoring the five-hundredth anniversary of the birth of Bartolomé de las Casas, the state government of Chiapas inadvertently set the stage for a further step toward action. It convoked a National Indian Conference (Congreso Nacional Indígena), which was undoubtedly meant to be one of the feel-good cultural events that are a common feature of Mexican official calendars. The state authorities asked the diocese for help in organizing the conference, which Samuel Ruíz provided. The results were unexpected.

Months before the conference, six representatives of the diocese visited numerous Indian villages and settlements, encouraging them to take part. Fourteen hundred delegates attended, representing more than 500 communities, most of them in Chiapas. The sessions dealt with specifically

Indian problems and were conducted in Chiapas's four major Indian languages. For many Indians, it was their first experience outside their closed worlds. It was also the first major public conference in Chiapas at which the Indians themselves discussed their problems without the restrictive presence and interference of the government. During one session, an old man wept, because "no one had ever asked him anything in his whole life."

The delegates agreed on the need for major improvement on four issues: the protection of Indian land rights, programs for health and for education, and greater protection of the Indian communities from exploitation. A speaker linked the conference to the work of the catechists and dubbed this assembly "the son of the Word of God." It was followed by meetings throughout the country and even trips by a delegation of Indians and activists to the US and Canada. A newspaper was started and a hymn was composed with versions in all four languages: "We advance as a single heart,/As a single heart we are building our liberation."

A few political organizers attended the conference, men of the Left, some of them radicalized by the "Olympic massacre" of students at the Plaza of Tlatelolco in Mexico City in 1968. They had been in Chiapas, says Javier Vargas, "more invisible than visible . . . not that they were living there clandestinely—it was that they smelled, they felt, the social force of the Chiapas Indians." They were in a sense the older brothers of men like Subcomandante Marcos, who was 11 years old in 1968. It was they who were mostly responsible for the Marxist phrases and ideas in some of the documents produced by the conference (excerpted by Womack), but they were by no means its leaders. The overwhelming force of language, argument, and moral will clearly came from the Church. And in view of the history of Chiapas's abandonment, and the resultant weakness of its political institutions, it was natural enough that the leadership be taken by an archaic institution and by a bishop who was a "convert" and on a mission to protect the Indians.*

INSPIRED PRIMARILY BY the catechist movement and by a new social consciousness charged with the certitudes of religion, many of the Indians of Chiapas, especially in the Lacandón jungle, began to make demands on what they perceived as a hostile government. Faced with the growing wave of requests for the partition of lands or for formal acknowledgment of small

---

*For a more extended description of the conference, see Jesús Morales Bermúdez, *Memoria del Congreso Nacional Indígena*, Anuario del Instituto Chiapaneco de Historia, Mexico City, 1991.

land tenancies, the local authorities responded with threats, often carried out, of expulsion and violence. They did not understand that a new kind of community was forming in the jungle—more austere, more united, and much more combative.

An absurd decree issued in 1972 by the national government of President Luis Echeverría contributed even more to the community's cohesion. The decree was presented as an act of "historical restitution" to the "last survivors" of the Maya culture: the Lacandón tribesmen who had been living for many years as hunters and gatherers in the jungle. While an area of 614,321 hectares (about 1.5 million acres) was given to the Lacandóns, a total of 66 families, the decree was, in part, a smokescreen for the government's gift of exclusive lumbering rights to big Mexican companies. The welfare and lives of the almost 4,000 Indian families now settled in the region were threatened by this decree, and they began the hard struggle against it.

Toward the end of the 1970s, the diocese made another important move, creating a new category of church workers among the Indians, with new theological and political responsibilities. These were the deacons, known as tuhuneles, or "servants," who, while laymen like the catechists, could offer the sacraments of baptism, extreme unction, and the Eucharist, and could also serve as marriage witnesses in the name of the Church. This new office, which could be filled for life and was open to married men, was received by the Indians with great enthusiasm. It responded to a centuries-old aspiration in the region—the desire, in the words of one tuhunel, "to have our own leaders, our own priests, our own religion."

For Samuel Ruíz and his diocese, the tuhuneles were conceived largely as a step toward a return to primitive Christianity. "Without vainglory," Don Samuel said to me in a recent interview, "I can affirm that if an anthropologist were to visit these communities, he would see that the figures of the catechist and the tuhunel almost stem from the tradition and form part of [the Indian communities'] own culture."

IN PRACTICE, THE goals of Samuel Ruíz reflect both his longing for the communitarian "primitive Church" and his commitment to the Church as it later developed. By the 1970s, the bishop was fully exercising the three implicit aspects of his office: prophet, priest, and king. As a prophet, he lashed out at injustice in his preaching and announced the hope of liberation. As a priest, he cared for his flock, offering them consolation and guiding them toward an awareness of the holy. As king, he allowed himself to be treated as a sovereign to whom his people rendered homage. He had become known to his people—and addressed in person and writing—as Tatic, the Tzeltal Mayan affectionate form for "father." Villages would prepare a month in advance for his visits. The women sewed special dresses for the occasion, while the men worked to prepare a proper house for Tatic's stay. On the day of his arrival, a line of men and a line of women formed to kiss his ring. They slaughtered cattle for a large meal in honor of Tatic, and when he celebrated Mass they sang praises for the prospect of liberation through God and the Gospels.

In 1974, when Ruíz turned 50, he published a short book of impressive erudition, *The Biblical Theology of Revelation*, in which he described the Indians of Chiapas as the collective body of Christ, devoted to saving society and themselves. In it he envisioned reality (or at least the reality of Chiapas and the Third World, the heart of his theology of liberation) as involving, on the one hand, oppression and oppressors and, on the other, a poor, oppressed people and a God who deals with injustice and offers them a way to oppose it.

But the teaching of the Word of God may exclude those who disagree. In some of the annual reports submitted by the catechists of the Tzeltal area to Bishop Ruíz and now stored in the diocesan archives, there are references to those groups who cannot easily form part of the growing community, and who must be "changed" in order to be included. There are, for instance, those who resist the new teaching methods, those who are described as having "ideological differences," those who are influenced by Protestant sects, those who disagree politically, those who do not speak their minds in discussions. These comments foreshadow much of the present situation in Chiapas.

5.

The success of the catechists, and later of the deacons, in dealing not only with sacred matters but with the harsh daily problems of the poor, suggested to Ruíz the need for a more explicitly political organization that could make use of the critical energy growing in the Indian communities. Early in 1976, during a visit to Torreón in the border state of Chihuahua in the north, Ruíz met a group of young militants who called themselves "Maoists," having been influenced by Chinese Marxist belief in the importance of organizing the peasantry, although not by the Maoist commitment to armed revolution. Their leader was Adolfo Orive, a left-wing economist who had spent time in China. His organization, Línea Proletaria, advocated the transformation of social relations, not military struggle. Its young activists were university graduates who had worked as organizers among poor squatters living in Central Mexico, in Torreón, Durango, and Monterrey. They worked mostly on practical matters, such as trying to improve squatters' housing, increase their water supply, and bring them electricity. "It seemed to me that [Orive] possessed clarity of thought," Ruíz remembers. He was impressed.

He invited the group, some 30 young activists, to Chiapas, and they began working in the villages alongside representatives of the diocese. They began various modest projects, such as helping the peasants to produce honey which they could sell, and negotiating with the federal government to enable the Indians to sell coffee directly without the participation of rapacious "coyotes" (middlemen).

In the campaign for the peasants' liberation, another small group, the CIOAC (Central Independiente de Obreros Agrícolas y Campesinos), some of whose members had joined the Communist Party, succeeded in organizing hundreds of peasants on its own. In contrast to "the struggle step by step" (lucha paso a paso) of Adolfo Orive's brigadistas, however, they favored and carried out a "struggle by forceful action" (lucha al golpe), occupying land that belonged to the haciendas, and resisting attempts to dislodge them.

By 1978, Orive's brigadistas, the "northerners," succeeded in winning the support of a few thousand catechists, who felt that these organizers could make tangible social improvements. But problems arose between the brigadistas and the diocese. The "northerners" at first had relied on the diocese—its organizations, its priests, nuns, and catechists—to gain the confidence of the local population. But then, to the bishop's dismay, they began to bypass the Church and moved independently into the communities. Moreover, Ruíz and the leaders of his catequistas saw the commercial contacts they had established with the federal government as "compromising." They accused the brigadistas of being reformistas and compared their projects to the "Golden Calf" of Exodus, a "deception" that would only delay the struggle of the communities to liberate themselves from oppression.

Despite the diocese's distrust, the brigadistas continued their activity into the early 1980s. They founded an organization called the Unión de Uniones, which was able to conclude agreements with the government for a credit union to help finance grassroots projects for the production and sale of coffee. Thousands of Indian peasants became small stockholders in this

bank. When the economic crisis of 1982 bankrupted the Mexican government following a collapse in the oil boom and caused the price of Chiapas
coffee to plummet, the brigadistas lost much of their popular support, and
Orive and some of his comrades went back north. Behind them they left in
place the Unión, a functioning organization that would soon prosper again
with aid from the central government, especially after 1988.

Meanwhile the diocese intensified its own political activities. Events in
Central America during the late 1970s and 1980s seemed to strengthen the
argument for the lucha al golpe: the increase in military terror in
Guatemala, the guerrilla action in El Salvador, the victory of the Sandin-
istas in Nicaragua, and the assassination in Chiapas of Samuel Ruíz's
friend, Bishop Oscar Arnulfo Romero, while celebrating Mass. In 1980,
Ruíz created a more radical organization, known as SLOP (*root* in Tzeltal
Mayan), drawn from among the catechists closest to him.

SLOP was a clandestine group, and many of the details of its members'
activities are still not known. It was clearly meant to be a core group to prepare for a possible armed rebellion, in line with the revolutionary aspirations
that were spreading through South and Central America in the 1970s and
1980s. SLOP had the major assignment of creating armed "self-defense"
units for the Indian villages (the word *autodefensa* in Spanish is a general
term for the initial stages of nongovernmental armed organization). Lacking expertise in the use of weapons, they would eventually turn to another
group of outsiders who had moved into the Lacandón jungle in 1983.

These outsiders were the remnants of a guerrilla movement, the
National Liberation Front, which had been founded in 1969 in the northern city of Monterrey. Their leaders were university graduates, Marxist revolutionaries who, in the early 1970s, had tried to create a guerrilla foco
within the Lacandón jungle. In 1974, however, the Mexican Army had
attacked and almost completely destroyed their force. Among the few
survivors who left Chiapas were Fernando Yañez, the brother of the movement's founder. He would return 10 years later to reestablish a guerrilla
movement, accompanied by younger militants, including a student of philosophy born in Tampico, probably in 1957. This was Rafael Sebastián
Guillén Vicente, who had written his university thesis on Althusser and
would later become famous under the pseudonym of Subcomandante Marcos. Now, in the early 1980s, the group revived their organization and
began recruiting local Indians. They became known as the EZLN, the Zapatista Army of National Liberation.

Bishop Ruíz was well aware of the nature and history of this movement before he made the decision to work with them toward the goal of social revolution. In Chiapas during this period, knowledgeable observers spoke of the "four roads" to social progress: the "Word of God" (that is the diocese itself and its organization); the moderate and reformist Unión de Uniones (later to become ARIC, the Asociación Rural de Interés Colectivo); the EZLN, and SLOP. For Bishop Ruíz, all "four roads" were valid routes to the goal, but the diocese itself was to remain paramount. For six years (1983–89) the four groups worked together, SLOP and the Zapatistas organizing in the villages and the Union de Uniones/ARIC providing much of the money, diverted from government funds.

The interplay among these organizations and the various options they represented—all of them considered valid at the time, including armed revolt—is epitomized in the person of Lázaro Hernández. He was the "deacon of deacons," the most important Indian leader of the diocese, and he joined the EZLN in 1984, under the pseudonym of Jesús, while remaining a leader of SLOP. He received clandestine military training at EZLN camps elsewhere in Mexico and, at the same time, became secretary-general of the moderate ARIC. (Opposed to the tactic of immediate military action, he left the Zapatistas in 1993, and has now become a political boss linked to the PRI.)

In this setting and in the radical atmosphere produced by guerrilla warfare in Central America, many catechists and deacons began to believe in the prospect of an armed uprising, in the idea that "the Word of God" and the need to change society were leading to a religious imperative to "take up arms," an option in the Catholic tradition of the "just war"—as it is in many religions, from some Protestant sects to Hinduism. In her book *Religión, política y guerrilla en Las Cañadas de la Selva Lacandóna*, Maria del Carmen Legorreta, an adviser for many years to the Unión de Uniones, has collected statements by former partisans of Zapatismo that trace how the catechists' preaching was slowly sliding toward the acceptance of armed rebellion. In the words of one of these ex-Zapatistas:

> You would come to the conclusion [from what the catechists said] that the people of God fought with weapons, not because it said so in the Bible but because that's the direction they developed out of the questions, about arms, about all the old prophets, how they too struggled in Egypt, they rescued the native peoples who were suffering in their work like servants, like slaves; so what could they do to liberate themselves? Why were they able to free

themselves? Because they believed in God, they believed in the armed struggle. . . . Everything the priests told you was believed, because people trusted the Bishop.

Toward the end of the 1980s, however, the diocese and the secular radical movement of the EZLN came into conflict. By 1988, Subcomandante Marcos was the second-in-command within the clandestine Zapatista hierarchy, becoming number one six years later. Aside from the obvious question of the power of the different groups (a similar question but a much more serious one than the problem a decade earlier with the brigadistas), the confrontation had much to do with the "unmasking" of Subcomandante Marcos's hostility to religion. Marcos was known to have officiated at "revolutionary marriages" and to have commented frequently that "God and his Word are worth zilch" (*valen madres*). According to Legorreta, Bishop Ruíz, faced with the growing influence of Zapatismo, decided to use SLOP to offset that influence. According to Bertrand De la Grange and Maité Rico, in their *Marcos: La genial impostura*, a book highly critical of Zapatismo, the SLOP leaders began to intensify their criticism of the Zapatistas, saying that "Marcos is a mestizo, he's not poor, and why should we let him give us orders?"

SLOP also tried to buy more arms on the Mexican black market to strengthen its position and to prevent the "armed option" (the *lucha al golpe*) from being left solely in the hands of the Zapatistas. Marcos began to act against Zapatismo's opponents. Whole families were expelled from their villages or shunned by their neighbors, and there is evidence that pro-Zapatista deacons refused the sacraments to Indians who would not join or support the EZLN. It was the beginning of the split between Zapatistas and non-Zapatistas that is the source of the endemic civil war within Chiapas.

The Zapatistas were shaken by the collapse of the Berlin Wall, which undermined popular faith in their traditionally Marxist ideology (though they would soon adopt an "indigenist" line, concentrating on the unity of all the Indians of Mexico rather than on world revolution). But even after the fall of East European communism, the EZLN was able to retain its strength among the sons of those who had made the exodus to the jungle. These young men dreamed of a transformation in their lives: "After the war, it is we who will give the orders," one of them said. As for Samuel Ruíz, Marcos is said to have called him a modista—a word that can mean "seamstress" or "fashion designer"—because the bishop followed the "fashions"—*modas*—of the moment, meaning that Ruíz in the 1980s had seen armed struggle as a possible alternative, a "just war" that would help to move his flock to the Promised Land, but with the fall of communism he changed his mind.

Ruíz was reacting to the new geopolitical reality of Central America, where prospects were visibly growing weaker for a successful lucha al golpe. He broke with the Zapatistas at this time (and only for a time) around the issue of the armed revolt as a tool, but not as a possibility to be totally dismissed. The Zapatistas were moving toward a tactical decision with which he did not agree and they were moving toward it independently, expanding their power partly at the expense of the diocese.

Events were steadily advancing toward the Zapatista uprising of January 1, 1994. Marcos made his now famous statement, "Here there will be no Word of God, here there will be no government of the Republic, here there is going to be the Zapatista Army of National Liberation." Samuel Ruíz made a telling comment, "These people have arrived to mount a saddled horse," the horse of social revolution that he himself had saddled.

SOME OF THE actions of the Salinas government gave the Zapatistas more verbal ammunition. They argued that NAFTA threatened to flood Mexico with cheap farm products from the north, cutting the income of Mexican peasants. The changes in Article 27 of the Constitution, permitting members of the ejidos—common lands protected from sales—to sell their land to private owners, seemed to be even more threatening, a betrayal of agrarian reform, the "supreme achievement" of the Mexican Revolution. The Zapatistas spread the word that the government's action would cause further impoverishment and the devastation of the peasants and Indians of Mexico.

On August 6, 1993, 5,000 Zapatistas staged battle maneuvers in the jungle, even while Don Samuel was preaching against the EZLN as "that cursed organization which advocates war and death" and urging his catechists and deacons to teach that "the armed project is a project of death, contrary to God, who chooses a road of life." Yet much of the sophisticated diocesan radio network remained available to the Zapatistas before, during, and after the rebellion. And that same year, when a military detachment came upon a Zapatista encampment in the jungle and exchanged fire, killing several Zapatistas and taking many of them prisoner, it was Don Samuel who intervened to secure their freedom.

The Salinas government began to accelerate the flow of money into Chiapas. The former Unión de Uniones, now ARIC, tried with some success to revive the reformist goals of the brigadistas 10 years later: they built a number of primary schools, introduced new coffee-growing projects, and partly reversed the legislation assigning exclusive privileges to the Lacandón tribesmen in the jungle.

But while many Indians continued to believe in the lucha paso a paso, others sold their cattle to buy arms. The Zapatistas were able to retain 40 percent of their followers, despite the infusions of government money and despite Ruíz's now open opposition.

6.

In some of their sermons before the rebellion, Don Samuel and his vicar, Gonzalo Ituarte, used drawings of trees to illustrate world and national politics. One drawing shows, from the roots up, the elements of "the capitalist government which controls," beginning with landowners, bankers, businessmen, etc., passing through the trunk of political parties and institutions and rising to the top where the various media—as the instruments of ideology—are represented. The second is a compact history of the relationship between the Indians (*pobre*, "the poor man") and the diocese (Sk'op, or God). Another tree is much simpler. The diocese organization SLOP forms the roots, the peasants are the trunk, and the summit of the tree is plagued by a *majanté*, a "parasite" marked "Z" for Zapatismo, which threatens to consume both trunk and roots.

The Church's visual and verbal admonitions proved fruitless. When the majanté began their rebellion in January 1994, they gained considerable national and international sympathy. In his first public statement after the uprising, Samuel Ruíz gave a measure of legitimacy to the movement, his words fully in line with his commitment to the supreme value of social equality: "The truth is that for the Indians, tired of the promises made by government, there was no other way out but that of the gun. They were driven beyond what they could stand, though we do think that there are alternatives." What did he mean by alternatives? In part perhaps further organization, different sorts of pressure. More important, however, the term is deliberately vague, as Ruíz's rhetoric often has been (which is true as well of the Church in general and of all Mexican rhetoric, even when something very real is screened behind the elegant words).

It is nevertheless clear that the bishop's attitude toward government has not changed since the rebellion. When I first met him, in 1994, he commented on the impending national and local elections: the National Action

Party (PAN) was a party that represented the interests of the upper and middle classes, he said. The Democratic Revolutionary Party (PRD) claimed to speak for working people, but the experience of England showed that workers were fully capable of voting for conservatives. As for the governing party, the PRI, it wasn't even worth discussion. "There are no acceptable schemes," he said quietly. "We have to search for national articulation beyond the political parties. What is most important is that 'civil society' manifest and express itself. I am hopeful that a miracle will happen. If not, there will be an inmolación" (the Spanish word suggesting not only revolution but martyrdom). He maintained that position when I last saw him, a year ago: The electoral process in Mexico offered no reasonable way to reform the country.

Yet in January 1994, when President Salinas unexpectedly declared a cease-fire after almost two weeks of fighting, both the government and the Zapatistas requested Ruíz's mediation in the peace talks. The Zapatistas still respected him, while the government recognized him as a useful intermediary. In 1994, Mikhail Gorbachev recommended the bishop for the Nobel Peace Prize, which he might have won if peace had really come to Chiapas. But now, almost six years later, the Mexican army remains in place, while Zapatistas and non-Zapatistas continue to confront each other uneasily and sometimes violently in many villages.

7.

I ended my last interview with Don Samuel a year ago feeling that I had met a true incarnation of Isaiah or Amos, the righteous prophet of God. Yet I also felt that he lives in a different world from mine. While his struggle for social justice over so many years has been impressive and moving, his attitude toward compromise and toward violence remains ambiguous.

To me the danger in Ruíz's view of the world is not only that it leaves little room for dissent. By helping to polarize a community, it can lead to potentially explosive situations, as happened in the massacre at Acteal. It can also serve to intensify the exclusiveness of traditionalist communities like those of the Chiapas Indians. And it can feed the temptation (a constant danger in Mexican history) toward martyrdom as a means of triumph over defeat.

One of Samuel Ruíz's most loyal converts, Father Raúl Vera, is scheduled to replace him, although there is speculation that the Vatican will appoint a more conservative bishop, as it did some years ago in Chihuahua and Cuernavaca. In either event, Ruíz's successor will greatly influence the future of Chiapas, and the impact of the Chiapas problem in Mexico. It may be that the EZLN leaders are waiting until the year 2000, hoping for the election of a center-left government with whom they might more easily deal. At the present moment, this does not seem likely. It will be essential for the next government—whether PRI, PAN, or PRD—to conclude a final settlement in Chiapas. The best option for the Church in Chiapas and for Zapatismo itself would be to recognize the growing enthusiasm for electoral democracy, to participate in the elections of the year 2000, and to struggle, electorally and democratically, for legislation that could help the many poor of Mexico, and particularly the Indians, who are often the poorest among them.

If Zapatismo remains a guerrilla movement in a state of passive waiting, it will continue to lose force and sooner or later have to come to a negotiated agreement like those that ended the guerrilla wars in Central America. And, on the side of the Church, the new bishop of San Cristóbal de las Casas—whoever he may be—will have the responsibility of determining the direction of the Chiapas Church. The odds are still good that the elections of 2000 will be the most democratic in the modern history of the country. In that event all the elements of Mexican society, including the Zapatistas and the Church in Chiapas, will have to adjust to this new reality, which—if the election goes reasonably well—could create a national government (and a precedent) with the controls and accountability that are necessary for democracy to develop and maintain itself in Mexico.

"SEEDS OF THE WORD" IN CHIAPAS
An Interview with Bishop Samuel Ruíz García

GARY MacEOIN

Originally appeared in *National Catholic Reporter*,
February 18, 2000.

Bartolomé de las Casas was named first bishop of what is now San Cristóbal de las Casas, Chiapas, Mexico, in 1543. The diocese then embraced most of the heartland of the Mayan civilization with its pyramids, its sophisticated astronomical and mathematical discoveries, its domestication of corn (maize). Within four years he had been forced into exile by the Spanish settlers because of his defense of the indigenous inhabitants.

The 33 bishops who followed Las Casas did little to change matters. They baptized, taught a few simple prayers in Latin, and promised eternal happiness as reward for a life of misery.

Bishop Samuel Ruíz García came to Chiapas in 1960 with the same mentality. Ruíz recalls, "I traveled through villages where bosses were scourging debt-slaves who did not want to work more than eight hours a day, and all I saw were old churches and old women praying. 'Such good people,' I said to myself, not noticing that these good people were victims of cruel oppression."

Ruíz was fortunate. The Second Vatican Council (1962–65) and the Medellín Conference of Latin American bishops (1968) opened new horizons. Just as the second half of the twentieth century saw the end of the colonial era, he began to envision the end of ecclesiastical imperialism in Latin America, Africa, and Asia.

Ruíz learned the languages. He spun off more than half the state into two new dioceses, keeping for himself the most deprived area with 1.5 million inhabitants, most of them indigenous people who speak several Mayan languages. These people, hitherto despised, responded enthusiastically to his invitation to tell him what they expected of the church.

A thousand communities representing 400,000 people prepared the agenda for a Congress of the Indigenous held in 1974. The objective, as defined by Ruíz, was to let the people speak. In three days of discussion in four Mayan languages, with simultaneous translation organized by themselves, 1,250 delegates told the church what they expected from it: a catechesis that would encourage the recovery of and respect for the people's historical memory, its ministries, symbols, and values, and specifically the development of an indigenous clergy.

The Congress proclaimed the right of the indigenous to land, education, and health, the right to organize their own cooperatives, to secure adequate transport from farm to market and to process and commercialize their products. They were the same demands the Zapatista rebels would formulate 20 years later.

Ruíz's liberation theology and preferential option for the poor were shaking the foundations of an unjust society and a colonial church. The power brokers of Chiapas, who saw the church as protector of their privileged status, were outraged. It was not long until a papal nuncio, Bishop Girolamo Prigione, teamed up with government officials to get rid of Ruíz. The Zapatista rebellion in 1994 saved Ruíz when he became the only person the Zapatistas would accept as negotiator. Eventually, Ruíz was given a coadjutor with right of succession, Bishop Raúl Vera López. Far from curbing Ruíz, however, Vera López within a year had become a solid supporter of Ruíz's views. So Vera López apparently had to be sacrificed. He was removed from Chiapas to a diocese to the north.

Few in Mexico accept the official Vatican explanation that Vera López was removed "for purely ecclesiastical reasons." Carlos Fazio, author of a biography of Ruíz, wrote in the Mexico City daily *La Jornada* that the motives were "political and ideological," an authoritarian decision of Vatican Secretary of State Cardinal Angelo Sodano who rejected the judgment of Papal Nuncio Justo Mullor.

Whoever takes over as bishop will inherit a diocese where the people have a special awareness of their place in the broader church because of Ruíz. How he has implemented his discovery that the "seeds of the word" were already present in the mountains of the Mayan people before the Europeans arrived is the subject of the following interview given to Gary MacEoin, Ruíz biographer and Latin America expert, in November 1999. The interview was minimally edited for space considerations.

MacEoin: The center of gravity of the church has moved from the so-called Western World (European civilization) to the so-called Third World, the world of poverty, in which European dress appears alien, even hostile in the light of historical experience. In this context I'd like to ask three questions. To what extent have you been able to inculturate the church in the Mayan culture? How much further do you think it is possible to go within our present canonical structures? How much further do you think it is desirable to go, assuming the appropriate canonical changes?

Ruíz: Let me start with a very general reflection. The church has an official position on this issue, so that we don't have to seek justifications or undertake investigations to find the answer. The gospel must be incarnated in every culture. The African bishops—and also the Canadian bishops—raised this issue at the Second Vatican Council. The Latin American bishops touched on it at Medellín, [Colombia, 1968], went deeper into it at Puebla [Mexico, 1979], and still deeper at Santo Domingo [Dominican Republic, 1992], where there is an official mention. The bishops of Africa, Asia, Canada, and the United States have also raised it on various occasions. Pope John Paul has also referred to it more than once—at Oaxaca [Mexico], Yucatán, and Mexico City—as something already in progress. The Department of Missions of CELAM [the Federation of Latin American Bishops' Conferences] has held reunions, as have other church entities, seeking to determine specific approaches. In this way, reflection and practice are coming closer together. We must conclude, accordingly, that an evangelical content exists that is not identified with any given culture. The gospel was not born in the West. It was born in the East, and with a specific dress.

For the primitive church the challenge of evangelization was to decide whether Romans or pagans who became Christians had to undergo the circumcision mandated by Mosaic Law. Peter and Paul were agreed that, since Mosaic Law had ended, this was not necessary. Peter, however, out of deference for converts from Judaism, did not eat pork, washed his hands, and observed all the other ceremonies laid down by Mosaic Law when he ate with [Jews]. But when he ate with pagans from the Roman Empire who had become Christians, he ignored the prescriptions of Mosaic Law. So Paul told him that this inconsistent conduct could easily give scandal and needed to be clarified.

Before long the conflicting practices created pressures that required the first ecumenical council, the Council of Jerusalem, to provide a solution. The problem we are now dealing with is accordingly not a new one but rather an old problem that recurs. What happened then was that the Christianity that started in the East passed to the West and became incarnated in Western culture.

Because of the form it assumed during a long period of insertion, incubation, and presentation in the Roman Empire, it ended up by producing what was called the Western Christian culture.

When Christianity later sent missionaries to China or other parts of the world, they brought with them not only the gospel but the Western way of life. They offered the "Christian culture" as the only dress in which Christianity could be clothed.

MacEoin: Even church architecture.

Ruíz: Of course. It was natural. When missionaries came to this continent, they took it for granted that they had to present Christianity through the forms of Western culture. This meant that no opportunity for interreligious dialogue arose 500 years ago. Christianity did not dialogue with the pre-Colombian religions. Its theology rejected the possibility that there was anything good in them.

MacEoin: All the works of the devil.

Ruíz: Exactly. Shadows of error and darkness of death was how the missionaries described them, using the words of a psalm. Now, however, with the Vatican Council we have a new situation and are questioning the attitudes of the past. Both here and on other continents there is the same concern to distinguish the gospel from its cultural dress. Of course, the cultural dress is not irrelevant for the individual, because we all seek and express our personality through our culture. But because cultures are different in different parts of the world, the gospel message must be incarnated in each.

However—and this is the third point as regards your first question—we have to recognize with the council that there is not a presence of Jesus Christ until an evangelization occurs. What all world cultures have is a revealing presence of God, what the Greek and Latin Fathers called the seeds of the word—*semina verbi*—hidden in those cultures. In consequence, evangelization (and inculturation) is not—forgive the expression—an attempt to determine how many goals from your culture you can score in the indigenous culture, how much of Western culture the indigenous culture can tolerate. The objective is rather to recognize the presence of a salvific process, an Old Testament like that of the Jewish people, an Old Testament of this cultural group, through which God has revealed himself. Recognition of this presence of God means that this is a salvific process that continues forward to the explicit encounter with Jesus Christ announced and testified to by the church.

A cardinal prefect of the Congregation of the Evangelization of Peoples put it this way: "The theological reflection, the thinking of the people of a given culture, is not simply a trampoline on which Christianity can bounce. It is part of the content of the gospel mission." In other words, we must start from the position that a salvific line of progression—*una trayectoria salvifica*—exists. As Paul says in the Acts of the Apostles, God has allowed himself to be revealed salvifically to the different peoples until the time comes when all these peoples are called to form a people of peoples, which is the new people of God.

The theory is accordingly clear. Practice depends on a variety of circumstances, not just on the disciplinary aspect. To take the case of the Mayan people of Chiapas, this is a people that continue to exist as such but has lost many elements pertinent to its self-identification. So we are now engaged in a process that may appear regressive, namely, a search for the foundations of its identity, because when a people is conquered, it loses its own history and is left with only that of its conqueror. This historic situation has also caused it to lose many characteristic notes of its culture. I recall a recent tragic experience. Some friends were talking to an indigenous young woman about Jesus Christ. "I don't want to hear another word about Jesus Christ," she screamed, pressing her hands hard against her ears. "What I want is to be allowed to find out who I am." So that she could then determine for herself her path to the future.

What this means is that the indigenous peoples did not have time to engage from within their cultural identity in a dialogue with a religion from outside. They lost not only their identity, but the right to have an identity. They had to accommodate. In order to be Christians they had to live schizophrenically, with a deeply hidden ethnic identification while identifying in public with a Western culture. That moment of schizophrenia is disappearing on the continent. The indigenous peoples are emerging with an awareness of their identity.

What is going to happen now . . . is that if the Christian churches or Christianity do not quickly recognize this process of revelation in the cultures and present a Christ in whom the seeds of the word become explicit, the indigenous are not going to find an identity in Christianity but will instead seek their identity in pre-Colombian religions. And their unity will not flow from their Christian identity but from a cultural identity, even if understood very differently. And this is what is uniting the indigenous peoples.

I think that this kind of evolution is occurring throughout the continent. People are identifying themselves as indigenous, not as Christians or non-Christians. It follows that if Christianity succeeds in taking this step of recognition of the salvific process and honors the encounter with an announcement of a Christ already present in some way in every culture, then we will have taken a step forward in what we hope for the continent. The church will have been enriched by the cultural experience of all these peoples. Having recognized the presence of God in these cultures, it will begin to make this presence of God a critical element of its own culture and move forward toward the elimination of present anti-values so that it can live more fully its own cultural identity.

We are still dealing with a preliminary aspect of your first question. Let us move on to the final part, which asks, How far has this intra-ecclesial process already gone? I think it is advancing in fundamental ways. First of all, the indigenous peoples understand that they have to recover their cultural identity, or to live it if they have already recovered it. They also understand that this is not a favor or a concession, but simply their natural right to be recognized as belonging to a culture that is distinct from the Western culture, a culture in which they have to live their own faith.

Many different groups are working in this direction. Some are Christians evangelized a long time ago who have forgotten the forms in which they expressed their beliefs. They are trying to recover their identity by means of their ways of thinking and the language they still retain, to see how they can live their Christian values with the elements of their culture that they still retain. They are changing rapidly as they recover their religious books, etc. There is here the risk of taking a step backward. The majority, however, understand that they have to look at their past and their identity, but as now read from their new historic situation. That is to say, from Christianity, so that they do not seek an identity that remains a hostage of the past without recognizing the present in which they are living.

There are other religious groups that have not fully advanced to Christianity, surviving as hidden individuals who continued to live their pre-Colombian religious beliefs. These are on the path of the so-called Indian theology, which reflects not Christian theology but that of their own religion. They are preparing for the interreligious dialogue that did not take place 500 years ago.

MacEoin: Expressed in Christian concepts?

Ruíz: That depends. Some were never evangelized, never had contact with the settlements, for example, in the forests or in the Andes. Others were in contact with the settlements and for long periods were unable to profess their faith openly. They found ways to use Christian symbols. They are now reformulating their pre-Colombian faith to enable themselves to engage in dialogue with Christianity.

MacEoin: As is happening in Brazil, for example.

Ruíz: Yes, and in other places. We are making progress. I think we are making serious progress. . . . In Chiapas, we have some 8,000 catechists, most of whom are conscious of this situation. They are engaged in specific studies to determine how the values of their culture can be expressed in Christian faith, how they can live this faith. For example, the value of marriage, what are the cultural attitudes to marriage, in order to find out how best to express the values of the sacrament through their own cultural signs. That's moving ahead.

Other issues arise. Something that didn't happen before, something that is a result of the presence of the gospel, is the movement of indigenous women. This has resulted from serious reflection, not a rejection—as in some feminist movements—of the opposite sex, a reflection on how the female sex was rejected. So now the woman is saying: "This is my territory. Don't invade it." In the San Cristóbal diocese at least we have a movement that includes men. To enable the women to come together for discussions and reflections, the men have to stay home and take care of the children. This means that husband and wife go forward together on this road. Here we have a new fruit of an evangelizing program.

We also have 311 indigenous catechists who have been ordained deacons. But the road to the priesthood remains a problem. What we have come to understand is that in all indigenous communities in the continent, from Alaska to Patagonia, human maturity is measured not by years but by the experience the person has in the smallest social structure, the family. They ask, "How can an individual who does not have the experience of managing a family and living in a family have the qualities needed to speak to an entire community?"

I think of a young man, a catechist, 28 or 29 years old. We were at a meeting of catechists, some of them older people. They were discussing an image. Should they take it to San Cristóbal to be painted or should they bring the artist to the community to have the work done here? This young catechist began to sum up the various viewpoints as if about to make his contribution. An older man sat looking at him intently, then interrupted him: "You child, how dare you open your mouth?" He was devastated. He never opened his mouth for the rest of the meeting. He was a talented young man, the head catechist in the community. But he was not married.

MacEoin: So what do they really think about the priests?

Ruíz: There is a Western priesthood and a Western Christianity that they continue to accept. They accept it the way it came and they similarly accept the priest. That's where we are. I have the crucial experience of two indigenous seminarians. Conscious as I was of this situation, I said to them: "You have to work your way here locked into two cultures, and I'd like to help you to take that step." They understood what I was saying. One of them, who had a good grasp of theology, said, "Excuse me, my bishop, but I can't continue here. I want to be a priest, but not a priest from the outside. I have come to understand my culture. Before I did not understand it. Now I feel and am an indigenous person. And I feel that I will be accepted by my indigenous brothers and sisters—but tolerated rather than accepted. They will accept me because I come from the Western culture as a mestizo priest. But that's not what I want. I want to be a priest of my culture, of my own culture." And so he left. He is working now as a member of our team.

MacEoin: And the other seminarian?

Ruíz: He left, too. One of them is now involved in social work, and the other works for the diocese. There are other situations where they swallow their pride and go on to ordination. But the pull of their culture is strong. I remember the trauma of one. "I came to the seminary," he told me. "In a matter of three or four days, the rector asked me: 'Do you have a spade somewhere 'round here?' Then he took a spade and began to dig as if about to plant a tree. I took the spade, and with my soutane hitched up to my belt, I asked if I should continue to dig. 'That's enough,' he said. 'We're not going to plant a tree. Just toss your Indian complexes into that hole, cover them up, and be the same as the rest of us.'

"I felt like a fish that had to live out of the water. And I learned to live out of the water. But after I was ordained, my bishop sent me to my place of origin. My parents were still there, and I had forgotten the language they spoke. And the people rejected me because I was a traitor to the community. I had abandoned my culture for a different one. Then I forced myself to relearn the language and made every effort to assimilate the culture again. So one day they said to me: 'Father, we can now see that this brother really wants to be with us.' Then, about a week later, I hear the music of the community band coming toward the parish house. That's strange, I say to myself. There is no saint's day, no festival. What's up? It's not my saint's day. Where are they off to? Next I see the community president approaching, followed by the band and the entire community.

"They stop at the door. 'Brothers,' I ask, 'what's the celebration?'

" 'Nothing special, padrecito. We just want to tell you how happy we are because you are now indeed an Indian, and you are telling us and we understand that you want to live with us.'

"Then the municipal president steps forward. 'As a recognition of this fact,' he said, 'here is my daughter for you to marry.'

"I thought the house was shaking. It was like an earthquake." Then he laughed: "And, you know, she wasn't too ugly. So I said to them: 'Let me see what the bishop says.' The bishop didn't help me much. 'Look,' he said, 'do you want me to change the whole law of the church just for your case?' "

You can see that this priest had come to understand the psychological *corrida* [journey] of his people, and the level of confidence they had reached. And that is the tremendous problem we have in this continent. We can continue to have Indians who are ordained priests after having passed through a mechanism of transculturation that we call seminaries. We already have these kinds of priests, mestizo priests of indigenous origin, but they are not indigenous priests. For that they would have to undergo a formation within their own cultural situation. There is some progress in this direction, but high-up people are afraid. We need theological reflection and a strong and serious anthropological revolution before this step can be taken.

There is still, however, an even more interesting issue here than any of these, an issue not yet considered. Some points have been touched on, but we have ahead of us here a bigger earthquake. Jesus Christ was not a priest according to the Law of Moses. He was a layperson. He did not belong to the tribe of Levi. Instead, he was a priest according to the order of Melchizedek. This was a pagan priesthood, not a Jewish one, and it may have anteceded the Jewish priesthood, because the Jewish people did not exist until after their liberation from Egypt. In its beginnings the Christian church operated with a certain level of autonomy, because Jesus ordained his disciples after the supper. At the Last Supper—it is noted that it was after the supper, that is to say, after the Jewish supper was ended—he instituted the sacrament of the Eucharist and also established those who were to continue this celebration. For some time they continued on the margins of Judaism. They went to the Temple to pray while celebrating the Eucharist in people's homes. As Christianity gradually grew, it moved to differentiate itself from the Jewish priesthood. Later on, however, the Catholic church returned to the model of the Jewish people. My bishop's miter comes from that old priesthood.

The expectation now is that—if we are talking about the incarnation of the church in the cultures—when the indigenous peoples of this continent enter as autochthonous [indigenous] churches, their priesthood will be able to merge with the priesthood of Christ according to the order of Melchizedek, and not according to the Jewish priesthood. This calls for a profound study, but from the viewpoint of theology it is an extremely rich situation. I do not mean that the Jewish priesthood has not served up till now, but it is not the cultural model. It is not according to the order of Melchizedek. . . . In the priesthood according to the indigenous cultures, it is clear that we are not engaged in just a cultural discussion, but also in a transcendental and novel theological one. That means that it is not in the same line as the discussions in Europe and elsewhere on whether or not priests can be married, as they are in the Eastern Catholic churches. It is not a discussion of theological schools, but of the concrete application of what the council said. That means that it is not simply an abstract theological discussion but a call to apply what the council said. It is true that the road may be hard, but the theory is clear. We have no problem about justifying our position. What we have to do is to promote a practice that is already fully justified by pastoral theological positions.

MacEoin: We are simply talking of applications?
Ruíz: Correct, absolutely correct.

MacEoin: In Chiapas, what about the sacrament of matrimony. Are people looking for cultural forms?
Ruíz: What happened, when we began to talk about incarnating the church in the cultures and to explain what this meant to the people, almost immediately all the sacraments began to acquire a community dimension that they previously lacked. Previously, people said: "I want to arrange first Communion for my child," [and] "I want to have my child baptized on such a day." All that stopped. Baptisms are arranged by the community. And, as the communities are small, everyone is involved in the preparation and celebration. They look into the practices of the parents and godparents to ensure that they are living a Christian life. The entire community witnesses the ceremony and testifies that this child should be baptized because the parents and godparents understand what baptism means.

MacEoin: How long does all this take?
Ruíz: It varies. Three months in some places, up to a year in others. They all know each other. When there are families that have not been practicing the faith regularly, they take more time to ensure that they understand clearly the commitment they are making.

The same happens with marriages. When the individual approach ended, interesting things happened. I remember a women's meeting I attended. One of the women was saying: "In the past my mother and father would sell me. They waited until they had a certain quantity of wood or beef or whatever, so that they could offer my hand to the family that asked for me. And it never occurred to them to ask me whether I liked the boy or not." I was watching a process of liberation in a very concrete context. And they are looking for external signs. They have not yet found them, because their culture was crushed so totally. Marriage in their tradition was destroyed.

Although so many customs were lost, some are being recovered in one way or another. For example, we are trying to reach the point—I think we are almost there—of not distinguishing between a customary marriage and a Church marriage so that they would no longer be separate events, and also that the marriage would be recognized civilly without any additional ceremony. This is a process that is moving forward gradually in the whole continent. And already they have regained a community aspect. I have a concrete instance. A Marist brother who left his congregation but continued to work in the diocese decided to marry.

MacEoin: His name?

Ruíz: Vargas, Javier Vargas. He tells the community in which he is living. "Brothers, I am about to marry, but I want to tell you that I want to continue to accompany you. Tell me, what do you think?"

They say: "Well, we have to see what is the woman like and to find out if she also wants to stay here." When she came, they asked: "Sister, are you ready to serve wherever needed?" She agreed to undertake the normal preparation. It lasted three months, with the indigenous who had themselves been instructed by Javier conducting her instruction. They married and they continued to work in that community for several years, fully accepted by the community, until they had to leave for the education of their children.

MacEoin: As regards the Eucharist?

Ruíz: Without the Eucharist, without a priesthood that gives them the Eucharist, there will be an imported priesthood. A distribution of the Eucharist by deacons has strengthened the power of the community greatly. But for this it is still necessary to have a eucharistic celebration. That is what it means to be autochthonous. The council says that to be autochthonous is to be able to reflect the faith in all your cultural forms, to express it with your own values and also to have your own ministers within your own culture. It speaks even of autochthonous bishops, autochthonous priests and bishops. In this way a church comes into being with its own means. The word autochthonous does not mean autonomous and it does not mean independent. What it means is to be able to express your own culture, which has suffered down the centuries. I think that in this way I have answered your other questions.

MacEoin: Have you reached this point or are you in a process that can move a distance farther but has a final goal that it is not possible to reach?

Ruíz: We cannot get to that point at the present time, but we are moving. . . .

MacEoin: Is a situation possible in which the married couple would be the priest?

Ruíz: That's what we are talking about. That is what is on the table. A priesthood according to the culture. It would still be within the church, because in the church we have married priests. It is accordingly something that is indisputable.

MacEoin: For us it's a rather novel concept.

Ruíz: In the Western church. But not in the Catholic church. It's normal in the Eastern church. That's the way it is in the Eastern church.

THE ZAPATISTAS:

The Challenges of Revolution in a New Millennium

MIKE GONZALEZ

Originally appeared in *International Socialism*,
December 2000

REACHING A CROSSROADS

There were those who argued that the fall of the Berlin Wall would mark the beginning of a new era when a full blown capitalism, allowed to roam freely across the face of the globe, would finally be allowed to bring prosperity to every corner of the earth. The myth fell to pieces on the Basra Road, where the evidence of the methods of capitalism's expansion was exposed to a watching world audience by CNN. In the period that followed the abandonment of Africa, the brutal imposition of neoliberal economic strategies, and the disintegration of Russia ushered in a period of aggression that continued through the Balkans and beyond.

What was unclear in those early years of the 1990s was where and in what form resistance would express itself. In reality, of course, the struggle against the depredations of capitalism had not relented for a moment—the Palestinian Intifada continued unabated through the so called "end of history," the landless and homeless of Brazil began their occupation of empty spaces throughout that vast country, and South Africa celebrated the overthrow of apartheid.

And yet many on the left seemed transfixed by the idea that revolution was no longer possible—as if the possibility of the mass overthrow of capitalism was inextricably linked to those brutal bureaucracies of Eastern Europe which claimed the legacy of workers' revolution while savagely repressing any attempt by their own workers to organize in defense of their own class. The struggles against capitalism continued unabated, but they were now described as "new social movements," a designation which seemed to distance them from any class content and from any general understanding—those much-derided "grand narratives" that sought out the laws of motion that linked and connected apparently disparate phenomena. And it was true that on the surface many of these forms of organization appeared to arise out of local issues or to make a virtue of the fact that they had no program for a general social transformation. They were environmentalist or ethnic or rights movements with no prescription for the reorganization of society as a whole.

NEW YEAR'S DAY 1994

Then on January 1, 1994, just after midnight, the local and the global coincided in a way whose enormous symbolic power was impossible to ignore. While the presidents of Mexico and the US and the prime minister of Canada prepared to launch the North American Free Trade Agreement (NAFTA), a rising of indigenous communities in a remote part of southern Mexico—the state of Chiapas—seized the headlines. The EZLN—the Zapatista Army of National Liberation—issued its first communiqué.

The celebration was almost immediate. John Berger and Roger Burbach were among those who proclaimed this "the first postmodern revolution." What was it that so attracted the disappointed sections of the old Left to the Zapatistas? And why did an insurgent Chiapas later become such a central feature of the emerging new movement grouped around the condemnation of global capital and its destructive incursions into every corner of the world?

At one level, the particular history of Chiapas illustrated how remorseless and pervasive was the process of globalization; on another, that same history exposed in the harshest light the actual consequences of those global program of economic integration and "rationalization" masked by anodyne terms like "structural adjustment." Duncan Green quotes *The Economist*, a journal that can usually be relied on to tell the truth to its own supporters among the ruling class: "Stabilization and structural adjustment have brought magnificent returns to the rich." Those returns, of course, represented a redistribution of wealth across the world. In the specific case of Latin America, for example, "60 million new names were added to the roll call of those living in poverty in Latin America," according to statistics provided by the Economic Commission for Latin America (CEPAL) between 1990 and 1993. By 1997 that figure had increased to the point where 36 percent of all households lived below the poverty levels defined by UNESCO.

In broad brush strokes these inelastic statistics translated into an increasingly repeated general picture. Multinational corporations encroached further and further into lands previously given to subsistence agriculture or food production, using them for the cultivation of export crops with advanced technologies. At the same time the much cheaper food imports from the United States—maize in particular—undermined that area of agriculture too. A particularly poignant example was the shift of the Salvadorean economy towards flower production at the expense of food growing lands. The little land given to food production was increasingly polluted by the highly toxic fertilizers employed to accelerate the growth of the flowers. The same process was repeated on a much larger scale throughout the continent.

Those agricultural workers or peasant farmers expelled from the land drifted toward the expanding city slums in search of casual work which, as often as not, meant joining the ghostly armies of *ambulantes*—street sellers selling contraband goods or chewing gum or consumer durables, or fire-eating and tumbling in front of snarling rows of cars at traffic lights. Or they joined the roaming gangs of young muggers or drug dealers who ranged the streets of almost every Central American town after 1990. In the countryside unemployment grew even more rapidly than in the cities, and extreme poverty made its reappearance there. A resurgent tourism brought a new market for sun and sand and the multiple aspects of "service" which involved Latin Americans in selling one or several of their physical attributes in exchange for the indispensable dollar—indispensable because the other aspect of structural adjustment was the systematic dismantling of public services, health, and education. As each of these became privatized, they also became available to a limited dollar-earning clientele. No one escaped—not even Cuba, despite its many claims to have escaped the remorseless laws of survival in the global market.

The North American Free Trade Agreement represented in some ways a second stage in that process of integration and adjustment. It was "the first ever regional trade agreement between a First and a Third World economy"—even though Mexico was one of the largest of the nonmetropolitan economies—"a crucible in which advanced technology, subsistence farming, global finance capital, massive underemployment, and contrasting legal and political systems are mixed for the first time." What NAFTA guaranteed was the removal of all tariff barriers and restrictions on foreign investment, even for state procurement. In agriculture all tariffs would be fully removed within 15 years, spelling the effective disappearance of all but the most large-scale sugar, maize, and vegetable growing enterprises. Even Mexico's most symbolically sacred area—oil production—was partially opened,* and the financial industry had already opened significant areas to foreign involvement—insurance and the stock market, for example—before eliminating all and any financial barriers by 2007.

Then-president Carlos Salinas de Gortari was a late but enthusiastic convert to NAFTA. The enormous personal fortune he accrued and his ubiquitous involvement in all manner of dirty tricks, including the elimination of his competitors and political opponents, may explain his conversion. Furthermore he was the president of the PRI, the Institutional Revolutionary Party which had governed Mexico in one form or another since the 1920s and which constituted effectively the political machinery of the state.

---

*Oil production had been entirely controlled by foreign companies before the Mexican Revolution of 1910, and was only nationalized in 1938 by the populist President Cárdenas, despite the fact that the post-revolutionary constitution of 1917 made the subsoil an inalienable national resource. In theory that remains at least partly in force as the national oil corporation PEMEX still monitors exploration—but all secondary production, including refining, is open to private (including foreign) investment.

It was in every sense a bureaucratic dictatorship whose six-yearly election of a new president indicated only a transfer of power between components of the governing elite. So when Salinas announced that "what was most satisfying at the end of the day is that we achieved a balance that is good for all three countries," he had every reason to assume that with this degree of political and economic control the victims of the new agreement would not interfere with NAFTA's much-vaunted official launch.

He was quite extraordinarily wrong.

THE RISING OF THE RED BANDANNAS

The armed movement that took the town of San Cristóbal de las Casas, capital of the southern Mexican state of Chiapas, could not have been more of a contrast to the snappily suited bevy of international businessmen and politicians (Clinton and Salinas among them) who had gathered to sign the NAFTA documents. These were indigenous people, members of the 21 or so ethnic groups who occupied the areas in and around the Lacandón forest near the border with Guatemala. They spoke a number of languages. Their weapons were limited to rifles—and some of the insurrectionaries carried only wooden facsimiles. Their dress was often handmade—blankets made locally, rough sandals, woollen balaclavas to hide their faces. What could be more remote from the world of consumer goods and multinational capital flows that concerned the NAFTA signatories—especially since they spoke Tojolobal and Tzotzil and K'iche rather than the English of the global market? Yet in their apparently remote region the talks conducted in comfortable air-conditioned offices shaped and impacted directly on their everyday lives. The distance was only apparent. The global market's steel grip held their lives in thrall too.

The ethnicities to which they belonged constituted some of the 10 million or so indigenous people of Mexico—people whose conditions of life and standards of living were among the very lowest on the continent. Of the 3 million or so residents of Chiapas at that time, one third were illiterate—overwhelmingly indigenous people. Half the population lived in homes without running water, again most of them members of ethnic minorities. Disease was rampant, life expectancy lower than any other section of Mexico's 90 million population, and 39 percent of the population of the state earned less than the minimum wage, with infant mortality—at nearly 55 per 1,000—among the highest in the country, if not in the region. As the First Declaration of the Lacandón Forest put it:

///

We have been denied the most elemental instruction, in order thus to use us as cannon fodder and loot the wealth of our country without any care for the fact that we are dying of hunger and curable diseases; without any care for the fact that we have nothing, absolutely nothing; no roof worthy of the name, nor land nor work, nor health, nor food, nor education; without the right to elect our authories freely and democratically; without independence from foreigners, without peace or justice for ourselves or for our children.

Today we say *Basta! Enough!*

Yet Chiapas produced half of Mexico's hydroelectricity, was the largest coffee exporting state, and produced the second highest quantities of oil after Veracruz. It was also increasingly important as a cattle producer. The contrast speaks for itself.

The data, however, conceal a specific historical experience which lies at the roots of the Zapatista movement and to some degree explains its characteristic forms of organization and its symbolic language.

In the mid-1930s, under the populist presidency of Lázaro Cárdenas, one of the key demands of the peasant revolutionaries led by Zapata finally began to be fulfilled—the expropriation of agricultural land and its redistribution in the form of communal holdings called *ejidos*. Through the 1940s the redistribution continued, though the land given over to ejidos in Chiapas tended to be marginal land, distant from roads and infrastructural services and often previously uncultivated, in the Lacandón forest and the river basins. The recipients were largely indigenous communities. As Chiapas's agricultural economy grew through the 1960s and 1970s, cattle raising became the most important area of activity—and while the ejidos did raise some cattle they were mainly sold as calves to the big cattle-raising estates producing for the national and international market. Indeed ejido land was itself increasingly sublet to larger individual farmers or to the big estates—even though that was specifically forbidden by the originating legislation. By the 1970s many ejido members found themselves working as wage laborers on land of which they were the nominal collective owners. In the same decade cattle production doubled (from 2 million to nearly 4 million head), occupying more and more land, and an oil boom drew growing numbers from the land to the boomtowns of northeastern Chiapas. At the same time growing demand for electricity from an expanding urban economy in a period of boom led directly to the flooding of 100,000 hectares (a quarter of a million acres) of fine farmland.

There was resistance, of course. Bishop Samuel Ruíz, nominated to his post despite the vehement objections of the conservative church, had already organized a peasant conference in October 1974 at which 527 delegates represented 327 indigenous communities. The main issues the congress addressed concerned the aggressive encroachment of the big cattle estates onto communal land, the corruption of government officials and their involvement with the big landowners, and the absence of labor rights for plantation workers. The Indian communities and farmers described how local officials controlled access to markets on the one hand and credit on the other, an exploitation reinforced by an absence of cultural rights (fundamentally the right to use their own language) and an astonishing lack of even the most basic health facilities. The response of the government to the congress in practice was given with the murder by the Army of six peasants shortly afterward.

Tensions were exacerbated by the crisis of the early 1980s which began with the devaluation of 1982. The government of de la Madrid (1982–1988) marked the first steps in the move toward the full-blown policies of structural adjustment introduced by the Salinas regime. So the rescue of the Mexican economy organized by the international financial institutions and private US capital not only involved incurring a massive debt, but also carried with it conditions and strings which de la Madrid enthusiastically applied. The result was a collapse in the value of wages of close to 40 percent, cuts in social spending of over 40 percent, a rise in unemployment of 15 percent (from 9 percent to 24 percent of the economically active population) and a rampant program of privatization. The overall outcome was a dramatic redistribution of wealth toward the rich—with labor's share of GDP falling from 41 percent to 29 percent.

In Chiapas itself the general picture applied in extreme forms: 400 percent more cattle were exported between 1982 and 1987, yet the number of herds fell significantly—the industry was becoming concentrated in fewer and fewer hands. The abolition of the state INMECAFE agency put small coffee growers at the mercy of the intermediaries acting on behalf of the international market—the result would be the virtual collapse of small coffee production. Throughout this period the communities resisted, organized, and fought back. The government, for its part, introduced occasional reforms and redistributions of land. But in no case were these intended to fundamentally alter the patterns of land ownership or income distribution. In its usual way, the state and the PRI, its political expression, used grants of land to ejidos and the provision of subsidies as instruments of patronage and methods of political control—a local client leadership was established for whom subsidies and land titles were rewards for their allegiance to the PRI. Although this often succeeded in confusing and dividing the burgeoning grassroots resistance, it could not stop the growth of independent organizations like the Zapatistas. In 1989–1990 the PRI governor of Chiapas, Patrocinio González Garrido, himself a wealthy cattle baron, embarked on a repressive campaign against the organizations of indigenous resistance while simultaneously appropriating communal lands and small farms for absorption into the big agricultural estates. Peasant protests were broken up by armed gangs, communal rights ignored, the movement's leaders snatched and imprisoned. In 1991 a group of women from Ecatepec staged a protest sit-in in central Mexico City, and the following year the violent repression of a meeting of indigenous organizations provoked a six-week march by 400 people from Palenque to Mexico City which finally broke the conspiracy of silence.

THE RISE AND RISE OF ZAPATISMO

Those who saw the Zapatista movement as a virtually spontaneous outburst against neoliberalism and its strategies were quite simply wrong. The EZLN was a movement about whose actual founding date there still seems to be some disagreement, but which had been established at the very least five years before the rising of 1994. More importantly it drew on 20 years of virtually continuous and determined struggle on the part of a range of communities and organizations against the depredations visited upon them not so much by a particular tactical decision as by the development of Mexican capitalism itself. The fact that most of those involved in the resistance held to indigenous cultural traditions and spoke Spanish imperfectly did not absolve them from the processes of accumulation agreed and organized in profoundly different circumstances by people who had nothing in common with them. Nor did the often low level of technology they employed in a usually labor-intensive system of production, or the absence of even the most elementary social provisions signify that they stood outside the circles of reproduction of an international capitalist system. But it did serve to indicate how very remote they were from any system of representation—a political voice, of which their multiple and little-understood ethnic languages came to symbolize their lack.

Yet 1992–1994 did mark a qualitative change in the character of peasant organization and struggle in Chiapas. It is worth repeating that, while it may fit with a largely Western mythology about how the oppressed begin to resist, it is simply not true that the transformation of indigenous struggle in the region was spontaneous or instinctive. It does not fit with a model of the rising of the innocents, a last-ditch defence of ancient and enduring forms of life. This was a population who had struggled to function within a modern economy, and in the face of the relentless assaults of the representatives of an aggressive global capitalism which had long since penetrated even into the remotest corners of the Chiapas region.

What 1992 did mark, however, was an important change in the forms of struggle and in the ideology of peasant insurrection. A key element was the decision by Salinas to revoke Article 27 of the Mexican Constitution; it was a decision of deep resonance and far-reaching significance. Article 27 referred to the promise of agrarian reform and the right of communal ownership—under the reformed article land could be bought and sold and the state's commitment to land reform was officially ended. True, Article 27 had more often been observed in the breach—but it nevertheless had remained as a defining expression of the ideal nature of the state. It was the banner of the radical wing of the Mexican Revolution of 1910–1917 whose slogan—*Tierra y Libertad* (Land and Liberty)—was personified by the leader of the peasant insurrectionaries, Emiliano Zapata.*

The subsequent survival of the postrevolutionary Mexican state, a political compromise between the new political class born of the period of military struggle and parts of the old landed oligarchy, depended in large part on its ability to maintain ideological hegemony and political control over the agricultural workers and the peasantry on the one hand, and the burgeoning working class on the other. The prelude to the forging of the new state was the murder of Zapata himself, in 1919, for he would not tolerate the consensus that might draw him into a new ruling elite but would abandon forever the commitment to the socialization of land. It has been argued that Zapata was a peasant revolutionary, whose concerns were limited to a radical agrarian reform and who was unable to break out of that limited

---

*Frank McLynn's recent account of that movement, *Villa and Zapata: A Biography of the Mexican Revolution* (London, 2000), is a perceptive and extremely readable and refreshingly non-academic account of the role of the peasant armies in the events of 1910-1917. Useful general histories of the movement are Adolfo Gilly's *La Revolución Interrumpida* (Mexico City, 1971) the title means "The Interrupted Revolution," but the English translation, published by Verso, is simply called *The Mexican Revolution*. Beyond that there is a huge bibliography on the Mexican Revolution, comprehensively reviewed in the bibliographical essay at the end of McLynn's book.

frame of reference to address the connections between the separate areas of class struggle—and that consequently his movement was little more than a jacquerie, a peasant rising. Adolfo Gilly among others provides the evidence that in the course of the armed struggle Zapata's vision evolved, developed, and was deeply transformed. But the circumstances and pace of that change, and the asymmetries between political developments elsewhere and within Zapata's own movement, both provide the narrative structure of the history of that "unfinished revolution" and suggest parallels between the experience of Zapata himself and the movement that took his name some 80 years later.

Zapata's base was in the state of Morelos, south of Mexico City, and the neighboring province of Puebla. Morelos was a center of the expanding sugar industry of early twentieth century Mexico; the growth of the plantations occurred at the expense of the rural communities who owned and worked the land, often communally, to produce largely food crops. As the plantations expanded their land was invaded and stolen with the active support of the notorious *guardia rural*, the armed rural guards commanded and controlled by Mexico's dictator of 30 years, Porfirio Díaz. The revolutionary manifesto which Zapata produced in Februrary 1911, the *Plan de Ayala*, expressed the demands of his class of small farmers and their communities for communal land rights and political freedom. In forging an alliance with sections of the old landowning class, the rulers of the new Mexican state turned against the rural movement.

In late November 1914 Zapata and Villa entered Mexico City and ended the attempt by Victoriano Huerta to restore the old regime. For a month or two they effectively held control of the government. But neither had envisaged the conquest of state power, and they withdrew to their regional strongholds. But there was no doubt that their presence in the capital had frightened the new bourgeoisie—they had expelled the counter-revolutionary threat of Huerta, but having done so they themselves now became the obstacle to the forging of a new national state. Within a month Carranza, a wealthy landowner and a state governor under the Díaz dictatorship, became the leader of the new Mexico. His national project was well defined in an early decree recognizing the right to private ownership of the land. It was consistent, therefore, that he should see it as his first task to mobilize forces against Zapata and Villa, including the infamous Red Batallions of workers mobilized against Zapata. As the military assault on Zapata progressed he was driven further and further into his Morelos redoubt and to a large extent besieged there.

At the same time, however, Zapata and his advisers were enacting a series of decrees and creating a range of organizations within the besieged province which suggested that Zapata was moving rapidly in an increasingly radical direction in his social and political thinking. Under siege from a national army, Zapata began to recognize the necessity of an alliance between peasants and workers, for the socialization of land and property, and for radical democratic forms. He was no unlettered peasant in any case—he had been aware of and in contact with anarchist ideas from an early age. Their distrust of the bourgeoisie and emphasis on mass action clearly convinced him, but their refusal to address issues of political power and the control of the state go far to explain Zapata's decision to withdraw from Mexico City (and from the battle for the conquest of power) early in 1915. His critical reappraisal of that experience was now (tragically) taking place under siege conditions and with few possibilities of making contact with the urban working class movement.

That experience, that history, has an unmistakable resonance for the end-of-century inheritors of Zapata's mantle.

A ROAD LESS TRAVELED

The armed action on that January day in San Cristóbal was limited and quite rapidly contained—though there were other simultaneous actions against local police stations and barracks elsewhere in the region known as Las Cañadas, roughly the Lacandón forest. In fact it was not the EZLN's first armed action. The decision to move to armed struggle had been taken at a meeting of indigenous community leaders in 1992. The timing of that agreement responded to the decisive abandonment of Article 27 of the Constitution; the state could no longer be seen as a potential defender of indigenous land rights; nor, as the experience of the previous four years of González Garrido's governorship had shown in particular, could any of its representatives be relied on to defend the rights or representations enshrined elsewhere in the constitution.

Yet it had remained an almost wholly secret war until January 1, 1994—despite the impact of the protest march of 1992 which for the first time brought the rural struggle to the heart of the capital. Then the limited armed actions provoked an extraordinary and rapid response outside Chiapas, which almost certainly restrained Salinas from the repressive military response he and previous presidents had employed as their prime instrument for addressing the problems of the people of Chiapas. This time he announced on January 12, 1994 a unilateral cease fire by the government. Within six weeks, on February 20, peace talks began in San Cristóbal under the auspices of Bishop Samuel Ruíz. It was then that the negotiating committee of ski-masked Zapatistas, wearing indigenous dress, became an internationally recognized phenomenon. Chief among them was their central spokesperson, the Spanish-speaking Subcomandante Marcos. Though he appeared to be the leader of the movement, he insisted that he was speaking on behalf of a Clandestine Revolutionary Committee whose elected membership reflected the spectrum of communities and ethnicities that made up the Zapatista National Liberation Army.

Alma Guillermoprieto ascribes the reluctance of the Mexican government to move against the Zapatistas entirely to the impact of Marcos:

> The huge, and lifesaving outpourings of support in favor of a group that was essentially unheard-of less than two weeks earlier, and that espoused the violent overthrow of the state, was almost as astonishing as the rebellion itself. It would have been inconceivable without the communiqués and declarations of the man who at the time professed to be merely the "spokesperson" of the insurrection, Subcomandante Marcos.

The role of Marcos is undoubtedly central, though the debate about his politics and his significance in the struggle has generated rather more heat than light. But Guillermoprieto herself makes the kind of assertions that would be repeated in the months after the insurrection across the world. That the movement was "unheard-of." By that she means that it was not known outside Chiapas—and the temptation is therefore to assume that it had not existed at all before a variety of external enthusiasts seized hold of the Zapatista cause. As I tried to show earlier, both Zapatismo and its component communities in struggle had quite a long history. Secondly she asserts that the EZLN "advocated the violent overthrow of society"; yet other enthusiastic supporters proclaim that "unlike almost all previous revolutions, the Zapatista revolution does not aim to take power."* The contradiction is fundamental.

---

*From J. Holloway and E. Peláez's Introduction to their edited volume, *Zapatistas* (London, 1998). This truly terrible collection is illustrative, in a wholly negative way, of some of the confusions that Zapatismo generates. Let me make it clear that I don't make this judgment because I disagree with its political viewpoint, but because it has no viewpoint at all. It is an attempt to imitate the idiosyncratic eclectic style of Marcos himself—which I suspect is inimitable—and to make a virtue of imprecision, moralistic rhetoric, and political ambivalence. And on the way it does Zapatismo itself a disservice even in its own terms.

Marcos learned his politics during the Mexican student movement of 1968, which ended in savage repression on the eve of the Olympic Games of that year—when 500 or more students were gunned down in cold blood during a public meeting at Three Cultures Square, Taletelolco, in Mexico City on October 2. Those leaders of the movement who were not killed or imprisoned and tortured often went into hiding to escape their government persecutors. The 1968 student movement was beset by political argument. The new generation of student leaders, clearly influenced by some of the anti-Stalinist notions filtering through from Europe and in particular from the US, were clearly deeply suspicious of the corrupt authoritarian regimes personified by Mexico's current president, Díaz Ordaz. The Communist Party, for its part, had long been compromised for its complicity with elements of the ruling group and its collusion with the extraordinarily corrupt Mexican trade union leadership. The revolutionary socialist tradition, for its part, had few advocates in Mexico. If there was a beacon of revolutionary hope it was Cuba, nourished by a Mexican national revolutionary mythology enshrined above all in Zapata—the symbol of an uncorrupted revolutionary ideal.

It was logical, therefore, that Maoism should take root among the generation of student revolutionaries seeking an international ideology embedded in a nationalist tradition and adapted to the withdrawal into the countryside that followed the repression of 1968. A document produced in mid-1968 in the course of the student movement in the capital presaged that future direction. It was called "Hacia una Política Popular" ("Toward a Popular Politics"), written by Adolfo Orive, a university lecturer at Mexico City's UNAM and the group's acknowledged leader. The "people" to which it referred reflected a politics of alliances based on a bloc of several classes defined by their common exclusion from the state.

The organization's "mass line" was bitterly critical of the existing organizations of the Left, which it saw as having only tenuous roots in the mass movement and of being locked into an antagonistic but permanent relationship with the PRI.

After the crushing of the student movement some student activists attempted—unsuccessfully—to create guerrilla groups in Chihuahua in the north and Guerrero (where there already existed an armed local resistance movement led by Genaro Vázquez) in the south. Those influenced by PP (Política Popular), however, moved into other areas, to work particularly with peasant groups, squatters, and student groups. Their general political strategy—the "mass line" mentioned earlier—was critical of armed struggle and profoundly skeptical of the Leninist conception of the party. Their *política de dos caras* (politics on two fronts) was directed at a kind of political organization on the margins, away from the threat of state repression and immersed within the mass movements. The method of organization—deriving in part from the experience of 1968–was what was called *una política asambleísta'*—direct democracy through mass meetings. René Gómez and Marta Orantes, for example, were two young Maoist agronomists who went to Chiapas around 1974 to help to prepare the Indigenous Congress organized by Bishop Ruíz. Some eight years later another activist from the same political tradition would arrive in the area and begin the construction of the EZLN—Marcos.

The alliance between Maoist activists and representatives of liberation theology like Samuel Ruíz may at first glance seem a curious one. But it is certainly my view that these two disparate political currents shaped the political rhetoric which would later become such an object of fascination for the supporters of the Zapatistas around the world. What the two perspectives shared was an insistence on direct democracy and self activity, and a clear reaction against the Stalinist variants of Communism whose sorry history of compromise with dictatorships and state bureaucracy was particularly striking in Mexico, though it was a phenomenon repeated throughout the continent. That anti-Stalinism expressed itself as a deep hostility to the concept of the revolutionary party, or the caricatures of a Leninist model which had proliferated in Latin America's more recent history. For the Maoist currents, too, Cuba's absorption into the Soviet bloc ensured that neither Cuba itself, nor the kind of guerrilla politics which it had espoused up to 1968, could offer an alternative. That suspicion of authoritarianism and emphasis on self activity, together with a strong sense of moral purpose, also characterized the ideas of "liberation theology"—a current of thought that emerged out of a savage critique of the role of the Catholic Church in defending dictatorship and legitimating oppression. Expressed at two Bishops' Conferences at Medellin, Colombia (1967), and Puebla, Mexico (1969), the new theology was perhaps personified by Camilo Torres, the young Colombian priest who "opted to struggle with the poor," joined the guerrillas, and was killed in 1965. Priests now emerged in the leadership of mass organizations of struggle throughout Latin America—and defended their use of arms where the repression was most bitter, as in Guatemala, El Salvador, and Colombia.

In fact, the struggles of the 1980s produced a series of internal conflicts between organizations and their leaders. Separate Maoist factions within

Chiapas each accused the other of factionalism and authoritarianism. Marcos and the EZLN had begun military training for "self defence," of which many sectors of the church were deeply suspicious. On the other hand, and paradoxically, it was the liberation priests who were most suspicious of the contact with official agencies (for credit, land negotiations, services, etc.) which many of the Maoist cadres advocated as part of their "politics on two fronts" strategy. As the strains and tensions developed through the 1980s, a new factor entered the equation. An aggressive Protestant evangelism was particularly active in Guatemala, where military ruler Rios Montt was a born-again Christian, and in Nicaragua, where over 100 sects organized opposition to the Sandinistas. They began to organize in Chiapas in the same period, exploiting suspicions of a radical Church among some of the better off peasants, raising issues of gender discrimination and particularly of contraception among women who had become increasingly self-confident precisely because of their role in the struggles of those years.

And yet, despite the spreading influence of Protestant fundamentalism and liberation theology's profound suspicion of the Mexican state on the one hand, and resistance to armed struggle on the other, by 1993 the majority of Chiapas's indigenous population were ready for war—and the EZLN would lead it, as the manifestation of the democratic determination of the communities themselves.

But what kind of war?

What began as a violent insurgency in an isolated region mutated into a nonviolent though no less disruptive "social netwar" that engaged the attention of activists from far and wide and had nationwide and foreign repercussions for Mexico.

The term "social netwar" is certainly not one with which I was familiar. But it points to that element of Zapatismo that has so fascinated those beyond Mexico. While wearing Indian dress and presenting themselves to the world through the multiple languages of indigenous Mexico, the Zapatistas—and Marcos in particular—have used the Internet as a free communications highway. The paradox is moving and in some curious way quite beautiful. The US military who generated this many-branched information superhighway to facilitate internal communication can hardly have intended it to be used to generate solidarity for an armed struggle in an isolated redoubt in southern Mexico. There was also something about the nature of the messages that Marcos sent that caught the imagination. The language of Zapatismo was a curious mixture of registers; it was clearly familiar with the categories of political debate and modern economics, yet the communiqués were also full of a visionary language more usually associated with religious rhetoric as well as myths and parables which clearly originated in the oral cultures of the region.

Above all it had a powerful moral charge. Here were the very poorest addressing the wealthiest and most powerful directly. The messages from Marcos were able to leap the encircling troops (some 12,000 of them) that Salinas immediately sent to Chiapas. If Salinas agreed to a ceasefire just 12 days after the rising, we can assume that he did so believing that the Zapatistas, who had by now returned to their communities, could be besieged, strangled, and eventually overrun. The fact that they were not undoubtedly has to do with their ability to speak to a listening world, and to the almost instantaneous movement of solidarity and support that they generated, particularly among students and workers in Mexico City.

For Salinas, moving into an election year and with the eyes of the world focused on Mexico, Chiapas was a problem. His chosen candidate, Colosio, was murdered in March for reasons still unknown. The head of the PRI, Ruíz Massieu, was murdered three months later. In Chiapas the negotiations in San Cristóbal beginning on 21 February attracted massive media attention and a growing stream of tourists curious to see these "rebels down from the hills." The industry in Marcos dolls and memorabilia began very quickly.

The armed confrontation between the Zapatistas and the Mexican state had already ceased. In the nearly seven years since the rising the number of Mexican armed personnel in the area has quadrupled, the encirclement of the Zapatistas is now almost complete, their area of control has been reduced and continual inroads into their communities have left many dead and those left alive deprived of water, electricity, and physical access to the outside world. Yet there has been no resumption of war (other than the "netwar").

When Marcos and the negotiators returned to the communities with a peace agreement at the end of March 1994, the supporters of the EZLN rejected the agreements. The timing was highly significant, coming as it did some three months before voting began for the national presidential elections. Ernesto Zedillo, Salinas's nominee to replace the murdered Colosio, was the PRI's candidate—a virtual guarantee, at least up till then, of an overwhelming victory. The other candidates were Vicente Fox, a right-wing businessman and candidate of the Catholic party, PAN; and Cuauhtémoc Cárdenas, son of the president who had distributed land for the first time, and candidate for the PRD (Revolutionary Democratic Party), a coalition organization embracing social democrats, some Left nationalists, and a number of ex-members of the PRI who had followed Cárdenas out in 1987. In the 1988 election Cárdenas was seen as the great hope of the left—a champion of reform, democratisation and change. Although the candidate was anything but inspiring in his public appearances, he did manage to gather the support of wide sections of Mexican society seeking change; had the vote-counting computer system not inexplicably crashed just as the final votes were in, he would almost certainly have won.

In the intervening six years he had lost much of his symbolic significance. He was a reformer, perhaps, but within the system rather than outside it. Time and again the PRD had negotiated with Salinas rather than opposed him, and the wide range of struggles against Salinas's economic policy had not always been able to count on his support. For Cárdenas, the Zapatistas presented him with a golden opportunity to reestablish his oppositional credentials. As the elections approached, the PRD opportunistically identified with the widespread popular support for the Zapatistas throughout the country. From the point of view of a besieged Zapatista enclave in Chiapas, speaking across the airwaves to a massive audience but unconnected in any organizational way to them, the PRD was offering a network of contacts beyond Chiapas. At the same time, Marcos was not blind to the fact that the PRD was using the movement for electoral purposes, and he tried to elicit undertakings from Cárdenas that he would carry through the 32 original demands that the EZLN had placed before government negotiators in February. In the event, Cárdenas lost the election again and then turned his attention to the powerful post of mayor of Mexico City, which he did win three years later. By the year 2000 his support had declined and Fox, candidate of the PAN, won a largely democratic election.

Much has been written about the frequently paradoxical nature of Marcos's lengthy bulletins to the world. Often poetic, personal, analytical, and mythic at the same time, their curious and lyrical language has often been celebrated as a new political language for a postmodern revolution. The origins of the movement marry a sense of the economic and political realities of globalization with a visionary quality of high moral content that echoes with the metaphors of religious language. Marcos's occasional excursions into fable or children's stories are charming and often powerful in their simplicity. But the paradoxes and internal contradictions also suggest a pluralistic vision, a notion of a political and imaginative space in which different views, visions, and strategies for change can coexist without resolution. Aesthetically, it is pleasing and complex. Politically, it is paralyzing.

The concepts derived from the struggles of previous decades persist here — centrally in the evasion of the question of power. It is a curious quality in a revolutionary organization that it does not seek power. What then is the nature of the revolution they advocate? At one level, the demands are absolutely clear and correspond to the needs and interests of many of the individuals and communities of the region — particularly as far as land on the one hand, and the recognition of indigenous political and cultural rights on the other are concerned. At the same time, the experience of recent times has led them to a profound distrust of the intentions and integrity of the Mexican state — an extremely well founded suspicion. That would explain the rejection of the March 1994 agreements and subsequent accords.

But if one thing has become incontestably clear as a result, in part, of the Zapatista rising itself, it is that there is no space outside the system — globalization does not tolerate free territories.* Like every major struggle, the origins of Zapatismo lie in specific local conditions, but the movement's claim is that it is part of a global process and a global resistance. If at first, and in the hope that Cárdenas might occupy the presidential palace in Mexico City, the EZLN placed its demands upon the Mexican state, there could be little hope that a Zedillo presidency would not pursue objectives in any way different from those of his predecessor.

It was presumably with that in mind that the Zapatistas convoked the Convention of August 1994 in the Lacandón forest. The meeting attracted many supporters to the specially built grass amphitheater deep in Zapatista territory. For many of them the long walk through the jungle carrying their own plate, fork, and spoon will certainly have been a novel experience. Equally it raised the national profile of the Zapatistas. But the movement was already at an impasse in many ways. The PRD was demonstrably an electoral organization whose sole concern was winning elections. Their commitment to Zapatismo was not a principled one. Equally, it was clear that the confrontation between the Zapatistas and the Mexican state had already reached a stalemate. The level of popular support and sympathy the EZLN enjoyed could hardly be higher, yet it was physically trapped inside Chiapas. More importantly it was ideologically enclosed too. Its local roots

---

*Two examples to reinforce the point. For nearly 10 years the resistance of El Salvador fought a heroic struggle against massive US-provided military material, creating free territories in various places, particularly Morazán, in the process. Since the peace accords of 1990 there are no more free territories and El Salvador is fully integrated into the global economy. In Colombia, where such territories do exist under FARC and ELN control, they are the object of a rising military siege abetted and funded by the US.

were firm, its representativity unquestioned, and its claim for rights just by any standards. Morally, it dominated the high ground—especially in contrast to a government, now run by Zedillo, which was as corrupt as its predecessors and as committed to a full neoliberal agenda of rising unemployment, falling living standards, full and rapid privatization, cuts in public spending, and a free market in all commodities—including land.

There is little doubt that the balance of political elements within the Zapatista message began to change by late 1994—the emphasis on the issue of indigenous rights was combined with the increasingly central demand for autonomy. As George Collier put it, the Zapatistas were beginning to negotiate with the government as a parallel national movement.

In some sense, as the encirclement tightened around Chiapas, the Zapatistas were moving toward the opposite conclusion from the one that Zapata himself had begun to reach during the siege of Morelos. Any encounter between the Mexican state, nearly 50,000 of whose troops are currently in Chiapas, and the Zapatista enclave would be an absurdly unequal one. The state's concern was not necessarily with the Zapatistas themselves, but rather with the resonance they might have beyond the state of Chiapas. As Zedillo's economic policies began to bite, there was growing discontent and pockets of fierce resistance began to emerge. Yet there was also a collapse in levels of union membership—a result of a long history of manipulation of trade unions by the PRI and the presidency. The regular *Consultas*— popular plebiscites—organized by the supporters of the Zapatistas confirmed again and again the enormous level of support for Chiapas. But if, as John Ross suggests, the Zapatistas's original appeal to the PRD had been intended to address the mass of its working class supporters directly, that had manifestly failed to develop into any form of national organization.

Defined as a class movement, the Zapatistas could develop joint actions of class defense and coordinated struggles. Defined as a national movement, in however direct a way, the Zapatistas were constrained to calling for support for their actions at the very time when a vicious official siege was making it virtually impossible for them to move at all. And massacres like Acteal, where 45 people were murdered by the army and/or pro-government peasant activists, were signals that the army could encroach whenever it wished—although it was clear that the government favoured a slow but silent campaign of attrition, cutting off or polluting water supplies, making movement through or into the Zapatista areas virtually impossible, cutting electricity, denying medical services, and so on. The symbolic power of the Zapatistas was unabated, their actual ability to act increasingly contained.

In the rest of the country structural adjustment and NAFTA are producing exactly the results its instigators anticipated. As the Mexican economy grows and plays host to foreign investors in growing numbers, 50 percent of the population live in poverty and 15 percent beneath the extreme poverty line. Forty million Mexicans are undernourished—10 million have no access to health care whatsoever.

This points up the central dilemma in the Zapatista experience. If the early alliance with the PRD suggested a hope of a reform of the state, then that hope now lies in ruins. As the rest of Latin America has discovered, social democrats or nationalist revolutionaries who find themselves administering programs of austerity and structural adjustment become neoliberals with unnerving speed. Zedillo, of course, had no such credentials—but Cárdenas presented his candidacy for the 2000 elections on the basis of his ability to carry through exactly such programs—hence his early willingness to present a joint platform with the candidate of the PAN, Vicente Fox, an erstwhile Coca Cola executive and the candidate of the industrial and manufacturing business sector. In the event, Fox won the election and Cárdenas remains as leader of a loyal opposition—still proposing occasional joint projects.

The language of rights, which has increasingly dominated Zapatista rhetoric, also presumes an intermediary state, or the existence of neutral agencies. The role has been filled at the level of political debate by NGOs, which have also attempted to plug some of the holes left by the abandonment of public services by the new alliance of state and private capital. But they are by definition unable to propose an alternative project for the state. Thus all the lobbying in the end comes down to whether those who walk hand in glove with global capital are willing from time to time to offer a crumb or two of justice. But it is a contradiction in terms to expect redistributionist policies or social justice from governments whose very survival depends on administering programs designed to accumulate an increasing proportion of wealth in the hands of powerful international economic actors.

WISHING AND HOPING

The Zapatista movement has generated movements of solidarity across the world. At one level it has coalesced around a defense of the oppressed—the exemplary victims of neoliberalism and corporate greed. That is their symbolic power. An anarchist friend of mine suggested to me after Seattle that "this was all because of the Zapatistas." Did he mean their example? In part that is what he meant—but beyond that he saw them as representatives of a new politics. Zapatismo does not seek power, only justice; Zapatismo does not acknowledge leaders, but it is democratic in the extreme; Zapatismo is not a party, but a living and changing movement; Zapatismo has used the Internet to create an international connection between all those who reject a capitalism red in tooth and claw.

The moral authority of Marcos is, of course, enormous. But it also has political implications. Where does solidarity with Zapatismo lead its supporters politically? In Mexico itself there are some 29 sites of armed struggle now, with the state of Guerrero—as poor and brutalized as its southern neighbor—chief among them. The magnificent student strike at UNAM in Mexico City (1999–2000) lasted for nearly a year in its struggle against the destruction of free education. It raised Zapatista slogans in its frequent assemblies. Yet throughout that year there was no suggestion of coordinated action. Solidarity—sympathy—replaced organization.

"New social movements" have been defined as "popular movements" which see the people as the central actors and have "institutional demands" which they address to the existing power. This may well characterise Zapatismo, but it is also clear that their demands have been ignored. As Vicente Fox prepares to take power as the first non-PRI president in 60 years, it is absolutely clear that he will not in any sense change the political arrangements in Mexico—or listen to Chiapas.

For the EZLN and its supporters, December will be a crunch moment. It is then that Vicente Fox will take power, and then that his evasive response to questions about his intentions in Chiapas will no longer work. At one point he said that he would "resolve the Chiapas question in 15 minutes" but it remains to be seen what kind of solution he had in mind. Nevertheless, it would be a reasonably secure guess that his agenda will not include agrarian reform, a redistribution of wealth to the poorest, increased public spending, a solution to the problems of Mexico's poor, full employment, or a state of rights.

It is inconceivable that the communities of Chiapas should be asked to continue to resist the silent war of attrition to which they have been subject for years. They remain an example of heroic resistance to oppression which has quite rightly inspired all those who are united against global capitalism. What has to be acknowledged, however, is that they are not in a position to provide political leadership for the movement that has celebrated their example.

Zapatismo has raised important questions that must concern the Left. The issue of authentic democracy and the accountability of leaders to those on whose behalf they speak is a principle that has been at the heart of the socialist movement since the Paris Commune and the organization of the Soviets in 1917. That proletarian democracy was proclaimed by regimes which created grotesque caricatures of it is a historical distortion we have to deal with and acknowledge, patiently explaining why authoritarian bureaucratic rule was the absolute contrary of all that revolutionary socialists stand for. Suspicion of party organization derives from the same source—yet without coordinated and disciplined organization to match the self-awareness of a capitalist class fighting for its interests on every front simultaneously, the producers cannot use the enormous power they have as a collective. For in the end, the issue is power—the control of society by the producers. The renunciation before the fact of any claim to lead society in new and different directions is an entirely moral (if not moralistic) posture, and one that will under no circumstances draw a similar response from the ruling classes across the world. There is not a choice between power or its absence. The only choice available is on the question of which class holds power.

The decade that produced the Zapatistas unmasked the real workings of the capitalist system; it exposed the limits of nationalism where capitalism is resolved to act globally, and it made manifest that capitalism by its nature is driven solely by the impulse to accumulate. Underpinning much of the Zapatistas' political language is a rhetoric of rights, but that is posited on the assumption that a capitalist state is governed by principles and laws rather than class interests. Since 1990 Latin America has seen regime after regime come to power, led by ex-revolutionaries or social democrats, and bearing aloft a banner promising democratization, social justice, and truth. The decade ends with those slogans still unfulfilled and the democrats who replaced the military regimes hopelessly compromised with the imperatives of capitalism. It is time to revisit the theory of permanent revolution, which acknowledged the international character of class struggle while recognizing that it would erupt in every case in local or national contexts, and confronted the fact that only a revolutionary proletariat can fulfill the democratic tasks and create the egalitarian future that Marcos describes so movingly in his speeches and stories.

OF LOVE, MARRIAGE, CHILDREN, AND WAR

GUIOMAR ROVIRA

Originally appeared in Women of Maize: Indigenous Women and the Zapatista Rebellion.

EZLN women have challenged indigenous tradition deeply on gender issues. They can decide not to take a husband, and as soldiers they must avoid getting pregnant, although they do not renounce sexual activity. It is a million miles from village life, where a girl is expected to get married and have children. Major Ana Maria is very familiar with this reality:

> They get married very young, at 13 or 14, often against their will. That's why the EZLN Revolutionary law on Women includes the right to choose a partner without obligation. This law was proposed by the women from the villages and we all supported it. In some places, if a young man likes a young girl he doesn't go and ask her if she likes him, but goes straight to her father and asks to have her. He brings along a liter of rum and says, "I want your daughter." By the time the girl realizes, she's already been sold off. The women are forced violently. Many women cry their way to the groom's house or to the altar, you know, because they don't want to, they don't agree. You can't just have a boyfriend or date like in the city; tradition makes that a sin.

The wedding tradition of the Tzotziles in Los Altos de Chiapas is a lengthy procedure. In the testimonial book *A Wedding in Zinacantan*, by Juan de la Torre López, Anselmo Pérez explains:

> Many years ago, when a young boy reached engagement age, first he offered his respects to his father and mother, presenting them with a bottle of rum, and requesting they ask for the hand of the girl on his behalf.

If they agree to do so, the boys parents gather six or seven *Jak'oletik* or "askers" and their wives, plus an old lady to take charge of delivering the presents to the bride's father, another lady to take charge of the drinks and three more men to pour the rum. The ritual of visiting the girl's home takes a long time while her father is treated with food, fruits, favours and most of all, rum. The only one who doesn't appear at all in the traditional wedding is the bride, who is totally overlooked. Says Anselmo Pérez, "They don't ask their daughter whether she wants to marry or not: the father and mother decide."

A positive answer leads to courtship. However, the bride doesn't get close to the groom at any time; they don't even exchange a word. It's her father who the groom has to please, to whom he gives presents, whom he chats with, in whose company he drinks a lot of rum and for whom he will labor for several months. This was the old traditional way. In some ways it did provide some knowledge of the man to whom the daughter was to be given and she at least got used to seeing him during "courtship."

But the passing of time, and poverty, allowed only the worst of the old traditions to persist. The father considers himself the lord and master of his daughters and selling them at any point is socially acceptable, as can be seen in Hacia el Ahlan K'inal. Dominga, from Huixtán, didn't want to go with her parents to settle the forest. Her mother says:

> My husband got pissed off because Dominga didn't obey. So he talked to a man who was asking to marry her. If she doesn't come along I'm going to sell her to that man, he thought. Dominga didn't want to get married, but since my husband had the money already she went away in tears with her new husband.

After the uprising, assemblies were held to discuss women's rights. They complained of their parents' harshness in arranging their daughters' marriage:

> Sometimes girls are asked for when they are still very young, and the parents don't think clearly, they sell the daughter for money, or give her away to a man when she is just eleven or twelve years old. A girl that age can't cope with the duty of looking after a husband and she goes back home. Parents who understand this wouldn't marry us off before we are grown-ups because it is very difficult to look after a husband and children when we are poor.

But what chance of avoiding her destiny does a girl have when she's already been sold by her father to a man she doesn't like? With the rigid social rules of the indigenous communities, none. Where to run to? How to face the terror of a first night with a man she does not know or love?

Captain Irma found a way of dealing with the impasse. She ran off along with her brother and joined the ranks of the EZLN. There, some years later, she fell in love with and married a rebel.

In May 1994 indigenous women gathered together in San Cristóbal and pronounced themselves in agreement with the Zapatista law that says they can't be forced to marry. "Before, women were exchanged for a cow. But marriage has to be the woman's free choice."

Some concluded, "When we don't want to marry, it is better to discuss it with our parents and the man and not be forced, because that ruins a girl's life, especially when children come later on."

The picture is not always so bleak. Juana Hernandez, from San Juan Chamula municipality, recounts how lucky she was: "I married of my own free will; my mother didn't force me. Our custom is just to live together, no church or registry office."

A 17-year-old Tzotzil boy, Pedro, who works as a gardener, asked me one morning for some money. He needed 50 pesos to buy all the things his father-in-law requested in exchange for his daughter: four cases of soft drinks, eight kilos of meat, five kilos of sugar, ten liters of rum, three bags of coffee. She is also 17 and according to Pedro, in order to get her to marry him he abducted her: "I took her out of her house, just like that," but he points out it was with her agreement.

> The thing is, I don't have a father. My father drank a lot of rum and he died. I started working when I was just eight, that's how I learned to work. My mother and my brothers and I all became Protestants.

Now Pedro has to pay the dowry to his partner's father and that will formalize the marriage; they won't go to a church or a registry office. At the beginning the father-in-law was requesting money, but with the help of Maria Auxiliadora, a Protestant pastor in the neighborhood of San Cristóbal, he was convinced to follow custom and take goods instead. Pedro says that if he has a daughter he will do the same and demand a dowry.

The anthropologist Andris Medina discusses the common practice of abduction (which is also rape in many cases) as a way of getting married, in *Tentjapa: Family and Traditions of a Tzeltal Town*.

> Abduction is another way of reducing the burden of the dowry. It usually takes place at village parties. The prospective boyfriend keeps an eye on the girl he likes and goes to wait for her on her way back home and at the right

moment he grabs her and takes her off into a field, where they will spend the night. This happens after the girl has accepted the male's courtship. The day after the abduction, the boyfriend will go to her house to talk to her relatives, bringing several liters of rum and hoping for a positive reception, because her relatives can take revenge and beat him up. Some *ladinos* from the town say that years ago abduction of women was more frequent and spectacular, the women being grabbed in the market and dragged off to the man's house.

HELL AT THE IN-LAWS

When an indigenous woman gets married she has no preparation for sex, because reproductive issues and anything erotic are taboo. They face this experience alone, when they are still little more than children.

Furthermore, men have been educated in such a way that they would never feel required to show any special care or give any kind of explanation to their wives. They simply "use them" as one often hears it said. One night, hardly containing her laughter, Azucena asked us, men and women alike: "What about you, have you been used?" Although as a Zapatista she lives another way of life and while she was directing her question to a male photographer, the expression is indicative in that it usually refers to women.

Sexual pleasure is unknown to them. "That is not done, it's not traditional," asserted Sebastiana fiercely during the late 1995 government negotiations. To make matters worse for the newlywed, tradition dictates that she live with her in-laws. Overnight the young girls become the focus of the suspicion of an alien household and are often exploited too. Far from their mothers and relatives, they enter a universe in which they are strangers. Often, however hard they try, they will be treated with contempt. Women say that it is common for the in-laws to encourage the husband to beat his wife. In most cases, they agree, "my husband's family and my husband take me for a servant."

Women are brought up to put up with everything uncomplainingly. The speech of the bride's parents in the Tzeltal town Oxchuc, on the eve of her departure, goes like this, according to Martin Gómez Ramirez in *Ofrenda a los ancestros en Oxchuc*:

Now the birthplace will be left forever, for she is leaving for another home, to another house, in other lands, in other places; because her parents so desired, they have allowed it to be so, now her husband's parents will become hers. Now listen, my girl, to what I'm about to tell you, hear what my lips say, what my heart commands: "So, my daughter, be good, put your best foot forward, don't gossip, don't lie, don't criticize your father-in-law, don't reproach your mother-in-law either or slander your fellows, or gossip as you go about your business, or swear. Now that you're getting married, obey the commands of your father-in-law, your mother-in-law, your husband, don't ever be arrogant. Listen first to what you are told, so that you can comply correctly. Only in that way will they be content, only if you obey with your hands and feet, but if you slander or defame your father-in-law, judge your mother in-law, reproach your fellows, judge your brother-inlaw's wife, disrespect your husband, then illness will come, evil will come to your family. Don't call the Devil upon you, don't attract the Devil, please, my daughter. If you have listened to what we've told you I shall be contented, I'll be satisfied because then there won't be gossip nor will you bring shame on our family."

Sometimes, however, the woman can't bear the situation or is childless. Anthropologist Andrés Medina looks at the causes of separation between Tzeltals, including sterility and the in-laws. In the former case the woman has lost her worth, so she can be returned like defective goods:

> The dissolution of the domestic group by the separation of the couple is a relatively frequent phenomenon in family life. The most critical moment is that between the wedding and the birth of the first child. . . . The absence of children leads to separation, and sterility, in most cases, is blamed on the woman. Separation between a husband and wife with no descendants means that her relatives have to give back all the wedding presents. If there are children, the woman goes back to her parents' home bringing the youngest baby, who needs the mother's milk. If there are older ones, they stay with their father and his family. There are basically two reasons for separation when there are children: failure of either spouse to fulfill familial responsibilities, or conflict between the wife and the husband's relatives, which ends with the woman returning to the parental home.

Deep in the Lacandón forest, in the Tojolabal community of La Realidad, eighteen-year-old Berta has had to go back to her mother's house. While she breast-feeds her daughter and serves beans to her three-year-old son, she wipes away her tears and tells how she ran away from home because she could no longer stand being ill-treated by her in-laws, who were given to shouting, constant scolding, malicious gossip, and even beating. For young, efficient, intelligent Berta, accustomed to hard work, life became a nightmare. She cried every day, and however hard she tried she couldn't stop her in-laws' criticism. Sometimes Ruth, her mother, came along with her to the maize field. Her beautiful daughter's tears and the purple rings around her eyes made her sad, but she couldn't do anything; that is the custom. One night, Berta decided to go to her mother's with her two children. Her mother, aunt, and grandmother live together, three single women who understood the young girl's desperation.

Ruth, Felisa, Teresa, and Berta depend upon Ruth's eldest son, who lives with them, plus his wife and a little boy. They carry firewood, help to harvest other people's maize for a small portion of it, load it on their shoulders, look for firewood, sow, plow the land, find a way to get some beans and feed the four small children and a fifth on the way.

Berta was terrified, thinking her husband might come to take away her children. Tradition dictates that the man takes the females and the woman the males, but the girl-baby is still breast-feeding and Berta wanted to keep both of them. It appears that these women from La Realidad have had poor luck in finding a partner. Ruth tells us that her husband was a murderer, a madman who would kill anyone because according to him, a sorcerer had put the evil eye on him. "They adored Satan because they had no God." Besides, Ruth wasn't his first wife—he had another wife and he had killed his father-in-law. His violent behavior is described by Ruth: "He threatened to kill me too." The murderer was shot dead. It happened in a community right next to La Realidad, called Guadalupe Los Altos. He was going to finish off a young lad who he decided was bringing misfortune. The lad climbed up a tree to try to escape. His wife was nearby and saw him being shot at and thought he was dead. She ran to tell her family and a group of men went to lay an ambush for Ruth's husband—"He was hunted like a deer on the road," says Ruth—and his days were over.

Ruth was able to breathe freely from then on. "He had killed five or six times and drank a lot," she recalls. She didn't think of getting married again, she was better off alone and of course, had peace of mind, "and we'll always have a little pozol if nothing else," she told herself. "There were other men who were interested but not enough, because of my family and my children."

Felisa, Ruth's sister, has a three-year-old boy. Her son's father left her for another woman and went to live in Las Margaritas. He's never given her any money to help her support the child. There seems to be little chance of beautiful, 30-year-old Felisa marrying again. The strict social code of a small village refuses an "abandoned" woman the chance of beginning again. Felisa has thought of looking for a job as a maid in the city, but Teresa, her wise old mother, appeals to her common sense. What will she and her little boy find? Exploitation, pain, hard work, abandonment, and only distance from everything they have here, community, family, nature. At least they have pozol. . . . Where in Tuxtla are they going to find pozol like they make in La Realidad? And Maseca brand tortillas? No way.

LOVE IN THE EZLN

It is May 1994. Rigoberta and Captain Cristóbal are together now, assigned to the same unit. Rigoberta is very young—she might be 17, Cristóbal, 26. They cuddle and caress furtively from dusk until dawn. Other times, she sits on his lap, her arms around his neck. They ask us reporters to take a picture of them before we leave their camp for the city. They want to have a picture of themselves together. They put on their balaclavas, step away from each other and say "Ready." It seems they want to be separate but together in the same picture. "Move closer!" we shout; and shyly one of them puts the arm around the other's shoulder. It doesn't matter. A picture of them rolling around together in a corner of the camp would have been better. Nevermind, in the picture their eyes, the only exposed bit of their faces, are shining with all the love, happiness, and hope in the world.

Quick-witted, wisecracking Captain Maribel explains how lovers get engaged in the Zapatista army:

> When a *compañero* loves a *compañera*, the first thing he has to do is ask the commanding officer for permission. "Well, I like that *compañera*, I love her." Then when he goes to talk to her, she already knows he has permission. Why ask the commanding officer? Well because that way they find out if another *compañero* is already involved.

Maribel has been a rebel for nine years. There are more ways, she explains:

> There are two ways here in the EZLN: One is that the couple gets together and that's it, we have a party and celebrate, we already know they are married and therefore the couple has to be respected. The other way is that they sign an agreement saying they're getting married of their own free will, that nobody forced them to and that the most important thing in their relationship will be their work and not their partner. We women in the EZLN know that our work is what has to be done well, because we won't be

here forever together. Sometimes the *compañero* has to go to work in one place and the *compañera* in another. Or it can happen that the *compañero* is a captain and so is the *compañera* and they have to stick to their units. Then they just meet when there's a chance to be together. That also causes trouble, because sometimes the man gets uptight imagining what his *compañera* might be doing . . . They imagine all sorts of things. But we correct mistakes collectively, so that problems can be dealt with out in the open.

Maribel tells of the significance of collective participation in the ritual:

When the *compañeros* sign the agreement, the commanding officers present stand to attention with those of us at the celebration, we cross our rifles and they walk underneath. This also means that we defend their marriage and we are happy fighting along with them and we have a party and— bingo!—they are married.

The rebel troops in Los Altos have the same practice. The commanding officer of the area narrates:

If someone wants to get married, if a woman likes a *compañero*, she goes and asks permission of the commanding officer to see if she can get him to go out with her and if a man likes a *compañera* he asks permission and the officer says yes or no, and first they have to check if the *compañera* or the *compañero* is already taken.

Traditional indigenous communities are shocked at the ease with which people get together in the EZLN. Explains Ana Maria:

In the EZ, if we are attracted to a *compañero*, we are given permission to get to know each other for a while, to go out together and then perhaps decide to get married.

Permission may be given for a couple to be married in a religious ceremony, with their family present, but it depends on the particular circumstances. Divorce is not penalized; the couple just split up and communicate the fact to their superior officer. Also, if a woman says "I do not want to be with so-and-so anymore" and he goes on harassing her, the officer will separate them in order to avoid trouble.

Mixed marriages between rebels and civilians are also occurring. In January 1995, a year after the uprising and a month before the February military raid, Captain Maribel said:

> Not long ago a *compañero* got married, here in town. First of all we had to ask for the parents' permission. Then the guy and the girl started dating and we began to prepare a party with the whole community and then they got married. However, the *compañera* has to join the rebel ranks. In this case, she had already thought of becoming a member of the EZLN so it wasn't a problem. She was ready to do that, she was part of the militia.

During the 13 months when the EZLN "liberated" a large part of the forest, the rebels coexisted with the villagers. According to Maribel, who is head of the youth group in charge of cultural activities, dances, theater, and Zapatista songs, the young girls from various communities joined the militia.

> All the young girls came into the militia. Of course there were chose who don't want to and don't, it all depends on the person. They said: "I'm going to participate here, and go step by step," that's how the *compañeras* participate. So we start to see coexistence between rebels and civilians. It's a good thing, because the community itself understands and supports it.

Have you married? Captain Maribel answers:

> Yes. I decided to have a relationship with a *compañero*, I got married; with permission and in front of all the *compañeros*. However, there are always difficulties, we had problems, wanted to get divorced and we did, no problem.

That is as much as she wishes to say about her personal life. In another forest ravine, in 1994, Lieutenant Azucena says:

> I got married three years ago, on May thirteenth. The *compañeros* lined up, crossed their rifles, and Captain Martin and I walked underneath. We signed an agreement and they threw a party with food. But even if you get married it isn't like in the villages—we are soldiers, and you know sometimes we'll get together but each one has his job and it mustn't matter if your husband goes away.

///

MATERNITY, CONTRACEPTION, AND ABORTION

In Chiapas maternity is seen as a woman's primary mission. When a young woman gets married she knows she has to "give children." If for any physical reason she is incapable of having children, she becomes a frustrated woman and is viewed as such by all. Marriage, often loveless, is in reality a socioeconomic contract based upon procreation. It is believed that fertility is a divine blessing, granted by that ultimate female deity, the moon. Women who can't have children are punished by the gods, they are excluded and are frequently the object of contempt.

One of the characters in *Oficio de tinieblas*, by Rosario Castellanos, tackles the social issue of infertile women:

> Catalina Díaz Puiljá, at 20 years already withered and aged, had been gifted to Pedro by her parents from childhood. At first there was happiness. Being without a child was seen as natural. However, later, when the girls she spun with, carried water and firewood with, started walking with heavier tread (carrying their own weight and that of the one inside them), when their eyes softened and their bellies swelled up like balloons, then Catalina touched her empty hips, hated her light step and looking quickly behind her saw that she had left no footprint. She became distressed, thinking that she would be remembered thus by the village. From then onward she could not find rest. . . . And the moon didn't turn white, as for the women who conceive, but was tinted red like the moon of the spinsters and widows and the women of pleasure.

The Mayans say that women's fertility depends on the moon. Its cycles presage the human and agricultural reproductive cycle. The moon is the holy mother—*ch'ul metik* in Tzotzil—the mother of the sun. A full moon is considered the best moment for conception and therefore for sexual relations. "Some indigenous people believe most women menstruate during the new moon and are more fertile at full moon," explains William Holland in *Mayan Medicine in Los Altos de Chiapas*.

Sex for procreation within marriage is what is considered normal. Everything else is considered a sin by most people.

Lawyer Marta Figueroa stresses the importance of reproduction:

If you sterilize indigenous women you take away the only value they have in the eyes of the community, therefore they can no longer be part of the community.

The Zapatistas, however, came to shake up the old order of things. The rebels are girls of reproductive age who renounce this stage of womanhood to devote themselves to the struggle, without renouncing sex. An abyss separates them from the parochial mindset of their mothers. "We can't have children in the Zapatista Army. We use condoms," says 20-year-old Azucena, amused.

Captain Maribel adds:

> We can't have children here because conditions do not permit it. We can't look after them. However, some compañeras have got pregnant. They go back to their communities to have the child, then they decide whether they want to come back.

She stresses that the girls choose their contraceptive method.

> The pill or injections, whichever she wants. At the beginning we had trouble getting them, but recently—January 1995—some compañeras have given us some more.

The pill can have side effects. Many of the women are rounded, maybe because in the EZLN they have regular daily food, which they didn't have in their villages or maybe it is due to the monotonous diet. Maribel agrees: "Yes, it is hard with the pill, because at the beginning we all get headaches, but after a while the compañeras get used to them."

Major Ana Maria explains that the army women are an exception:

> In the rebel army we can't have children because we are constantly on duty, moving from one place to another and because our job is to fight for the people. It would be very difficult to bring up a baby in the mountains. Therefore, we have family planning. However, if a compañera wants to have a baby, she goes to live with her family and has it. If she wants to come back afterward she leaves her mother or her mother-in-law to look after the baby. There have been many cases in which compañeras have got pregnant by

accident, they've had the baby and left it with their family because they want to continue in the struggle.

Contraceptives are available in the EZLN, but according to Ana Maria, in the indigenous communities, "They don't exist, they are unknown." On the issue of abortion she adds:

> Parents are careful that their daughters do not get pregnant. Young girls are so afraid of their parents that they don't even talk to boys. Nevertheless, many girls do get pregnant and they have the baby, but it isn't easy to get an abortion and if someone does have one she doesn't tell. . . . Abortion is an issue we don't discuss or mention at all. There is a belief that abortion is wrong. It would be like perverting tradition.

A reporter from *La Jornada* asked Ana Maria, in the cathedral in San Cristóbal, what happens if they have the possibility to abort, as one out of five women of fertile age in rural Mexico has had an abortion. She answered:

> The fact that a tradition or a belief exists doesn't mean it can't change. For now it is not allowed in the communities, it's punished, women who abort are punished. What happens often is that the girl goes to a midwife or a natural healer and asks to have an abortion for fear of her family and of being beaten. In the communities that I know of, the people doing it are fined or they catch the man who got her pregnant and lock him up for a few days and then fine him or make him pay for the girl's medical care.

TRADITIONAL MEDICINE

In Los Altos de Chiapas, in contrast to elsewhere in Mexico, female mortality is higher than male mortality. Many die in childbirth. There are no reliable statistics, however, because many indigenous women do not have a birth certificate. And in such cases, no one bothers to register the death, because "they didn't exist." In her *Indigenous Medical Practice*, Graciela Freyermuth writes that in Chamula death during pregnancy is covered up and other causes given officially. It is also a curious fact that women never tell their husbands about pregnancy because they consider it shameful.

The indigenous concept of health embraces more than the physical condition, including relations with one's neighbors, religious responsibilities, and upholding tradition.

If you steal or kill then you have sexual dreams. If you speak badly of someone or neglect your duties or argue with your neighbors then illness follows.

In Los Altos people also think that you can catch a disease on the road because of jealousy, you can fall down and "lose your spirit into the earth," because of dreams or witchcraft. The power of physical and spiritual healing is attributed to the *ilol*, an experienced natural healer. Knowledge is usually passed from one generation to the next. As Freyermuth writes, an ilol "knows which [diseases] have been caused by the wind, the thunder, the devil or water or through dreams, envy, food or unacceptable social behavior. Through the pulse he can feel a blood current going to the heart and mind." The ilols claim they can find out everything related to the patient, from the illness itself to the social rule transgressed. They use magic, herbs, fortunetelling, laying-on of hands, and some allopathic medicines.

The ilol uses a wide range of treatments. There are rites such as calling the lost soul, passing the handle of the corngrinding stone over the pregnant woman's body during prolonged labor, or sacrificing hens; prayers in caves, at church, at home, or where the disease was caught; or else candles, rum, "blowing," physical manipulation, animals, stones, and most of all plants can be used. The latter can be either drunk as tea, or eaten raw, ground with water or made into a paste, used in baths, suppositories, powders, or heated on the corral.

THE HEALER ALSO decides in which direction the altar has to be set so that the prayer will bring about the cure, what color and size the candles should be, and the right time of day.

When a midwife is also an ilol and a herbalist, she is as qualified as you can be in Tzotzil medicine. Her services will be frequently requested and many sick people will call at her house to be treated. She charges very little. Working as an ilol allows a woman to expand her knowledge and the areas she can work in.

A very important element of the indigenous cosmology is the belief in a lower world, a hell, and a series of threatening forces which loom over the lives of men and women. There is a sense of fatality that at the same time acts as an iron form of social control. Any infraction of community rules will be punished by supernatural forces. Researcher Vrilliam Holland R. points out in his book *La medicina maya en los altos de Chiapas* that "someone who cuts himself, falls over, fights a friend, strikes his wife, breaks a bone, loses or forgets something" is considered a victim of the gods of death.

Mayans believe that when a person is born an animal is also born, which will become his *nagual* or partner throughout his life until death, when they both die. Their destinies are inseparable. The animal and the human share the same spirit if not the same flesh. Whatever happens to one will happen to the other: power, illness, pain, or death. The Tzotziles believe that these animals live in sacred mountains, separated into families. When a woman marries a man, her nagual leaves its parents' sacred mountain and goes to live at the husband's. If an indigenous man or woman goes to live far away, in the city, and becomes half ladino, rejecting indigenous traditions, then their animal partner goes to one of the faraway unknown mountains of the white people. This person will no longer be acknowledged by the Indians as their nagual lives elsewhere.

THE ROLE OF THE INDIGENOUS MIDWIFE

In Chiapas 70 percent of pregnant women in the urban areas go to a midwife, whereas in the countryside the midwife takes care of practically every birth. A. Medina tells,

> It is believed that the moon decides when the children will be born, so when there's a new moon people say "the moon has gone to bring more children to the mothers' wombs." The protection of the moon is requested and is used to determine gestation dates. When a woman feels she is pregnant she looks at the size of the moon, and then calculates nine months. During that time pregnant women pray to the moon for a healthy birth. Prayers are intensified if labor is late.

The Tzotzil have guarded their traditions more zealously than any other group. Childbirth is pretty much forbidden territory for ladinos or outsiders. Birth is a ritual ceremony, always accompanied by *posh*—homemade rum—colored candles, incense, and smoke. Women give birth at home, fully clothed. The newborn emerges from between the folds of the *nagua*, the woolen skirt. Tzotzil women rarely give birth laying down. Usually they stand or squat, hanging onto their husband's neck—that is his contribution to the labor. Sometimes the father and other relatives take shifts in providing the strenuous support required. The whole family, their guests and the midwife celebrate the birth with prayers, chanting, and huge quantities of posh. In the Tzeltal town Tenejapa, Medina writes that, "birth is a personal occasion witnessed only by the midwife and the husband and sometimes also his mother. The husband supports the woman from behind so she can give birth squatting."

Indigenous birth rites vary slightly. In Tenejapa:

> The natural healer cuts the umbilical cord off the baby and hangs it from a nearby tree and the placenta is placed on the household fire. The baby is bathed in warm water and the father chews a little chili, putting a bit of it on the baby's lips to prevent them staying black. For the first three days after the birth the mother rests and the relatives keep company outside, around a makeshift fire. They say this is to prevent the child from "diseases," because this is when s/he is most exposed. . . . For 20 days the woman drinks warm water and is considered weak.

In the Lacandón forest, traditions are more diluted. In the course of settlement many ancient indigenous traditions were abandoned. Women were forced to face a hostile world, far from any facilities, in an unknown habitat and climate. The first arrivals had to give birth without their mothers, in extreme conditions, in an unfamiliar world.

TERESA, TOJOLABAL MIDWIFE

Teresa arrived with the first settler families. After climbing hills, crossing fields, and clearing their path through the undergrowth with machetes, they happened upon the valley they would call La Realidad. It was covered in thick vegetation, huge trees and thick shrubs and there was water. The Tojolabal people had walked for days, carrying their few belongings on their backs: a machete, a blanket, some tortillas, and the hope of land. They built La Realidad with their own hands, by the sweat of their brow. Step by step, in that inhospitable valley inhabited by pumas and malaria-carrying insects, humble straw and timber houses were built. With much effort they managed to channel the river that now winds through the village bringing water close to the dwellings. They had created a clearing for settlement.

As time went by Teresa became a grandmother and the town's midwife. "Nobody taught me. It was something I wanted and was able to do but I only discovered this when I was about thirty years old."

One of this Tojolabal woman's gifts, which the doctors who have met her have been unable to explain, is that she can manipulate babies from breech position in their mother's belly. She has never had to do a caesarean. In addition, Teresa states she has never lost a single child during labor. Who taught her? How did she learn? Teresa dreamed she was making clay pots, she says they were very pretty pots, and she was modeling them with her hands. Later, when she touched the pregnant woman's belly she let herself be led by those dreams and modeled again. Gesturing with her gentle but worn hands she explains:

> Let's say this banana is the baby and it is in breech position—this is the head and this is the bottom. If he is like this inside the mother, you take a little ointment and turn the baby like this to move him down. Then you have to search for the head and turn it round and then lift the bottom into the right position, bottom up and the head in the vagina.

This grey-haired old lady discovered her gift through dreams:

> I don't know what happened, I just dreamed a lot, I dreamed of very pretty little pots, I see them shining and inside them there are like a lot of little ribbons and beads of different colors. It seems it is my fate to become a midwife. Those are my dreams. I believe God gave me a task, a job to do. But I've stopped dreaming since I've become a midwife.

A long history of poverty, isolation, and complete absence of medical care led her to discover her ability. Near La Realidad, at Guadalupe Los Altos, where she went often with a niece who was pregnant and who the midwives wanted to have an abortion.

> They have a midwife there, but I don't think she knew what to do. My niece was about four months pregnant. She'd already bought the remedy, a bottle of wine, I don't know what kind, and they were going to give it to her to make her abort.

///

It was superstition that led her to want to get rid of her child: "Her midwife said the child was an animal, that it wouldn't be human, but a frog or a pig, that was what the people taking care of her said."

So the frightened girl went to see a natural healer and she told her sister-in-law that she would go and get the remedy. "All right, but be careful," answered the latter. It happened that Teresa had arrived in town that day.

The girl's sister-in-law asked her, "Your aunt arrived yesterday, didn't she? Why don't you talk to her?"

"Oh, because I don't know if she knows what to do."

"She does, she took care of me, my baby was in breech position and she turned him around."

Then the girl, whose name is Margarita, went to ask permission from her father-in-law, "My aunt Teresa arrived yesterday and she knows how to help. Why don't we ask for her help?"

"Well, dear," said her father-in-law "if you want to ask for her help I'll do it tomorrow."

Teresa continues the story: The old man didn't delay, he came the next day. At that time my husband didn't know I was delivering babies. As I came back from gathering maize, the old man arrived.

"Where is my little brother?"

"You sit down, he'll be right back."

"Well, we'll talk when he comes."

He sat down there with his bag. I wondered: "why does he want to see my husband?" When my husband arrived with his horse (he had been to get maize), they unloaded and sat down to rest. He took out a big bottle of rum and a glass.

"So, my brother, I come on behalf of your niece, for she says Teresa here knows how to help those who are . . . pregnant."

"I know nothing of that."

My husband turned around and asked me: "Is it true you know about pregnancy?"

"I don't really know, but I'm learning."

"If you know how to do it, then help my niece too."

On the next day I went there. First they gave me coffee. Then I went to see Margarita.

"How are you?"

"I'm pregnant but people say it's not going to be human."

"How come it won't be human? Isn't the father human then?"

"Yes, but I've been told that maybe it's going to be some sort of frog or a pig."

"But how can you believe them?"

"Yes, but who knows?"

"Let's see what we can do for you."

She went to her bed and I looked at her. I told her, "Don't be afraid, you're all right, you're pregnant, you're all right."

"Then if I'm all right, I don't have to have an abortion?"

"No, you don't, you're all right and I'm going to help you."

So I kept visiting her. When she was due I wasn't there, there was another midwife there, a man, and he attended her and she had a healthy baby girl.

Many years have passed since then. Now, says Teresa, "I'm granny to all the children, I have about two hundred grandchildren!"

After that incident her services began to be requested:

> That's how people in my town knew I was a midwife, after the people already knew here. Then they came to ask me for help and to look after their women. . . . I thought to myself: "how am I going to manage to help the women? And how do I hold the baby?" But then I thought, "well, I've already been through that, I myself have children, I know my body and other women's bodies are no different."

She recalls her own childbirths:

> I'm pregnant, I go to get my maize, carry firewood and then I'm in bed, my baby boy or girl is already there with me. When my family notices I've had my baby with me for two days already. It's easy, yes, it is easy to have children. The hard thing is to lose them. I have seven children, but not all of them survived. Four died; only three girls survived.

Although Teresa insists she is a midwife by vocation, there is a family tradition, which is often the way. "My mother and father were midwives and they were good at it as I am now: There are three of us now, my brother and also my sister who is here in Santa Rita now."

A doctor visiting La Realidad was so amazed by her work that he decided to learn from her. He told her: "Doña Teresa, you know your people's ways which is something that no medical course teaches us. You are self-taught but it is also your destiny. You work with me and I'll help you as much as

I can." Theresa says, "So I worked with him. He gave me all my equipment, but when he went and other doctors came, I didn't want to continue with them. They weren't good with patients."

Teresa continued to receive pupils; doctors who had graduated from the best Mexican universities. She taught them to deliver babies. "They came here often, asking for support, and saw how I manipulate babies in breech position and then started to do it too."

In these places, childbirth always takes place at home, in bed, without undressing. Felisa, Teresa's daughter, was horrified that when she was in the hospital she saw women about to give birth wearing just a white gown, open at the back. For an indigenous woman to be undressed by someone else is one of the worst things that can happen to her. Felisa explains:

> We don't take off our clothes here. We give birth the way we are, with clothes on and then you get changed afterward. The next day they come to bathe us with warm water, at home. In the hospital it's awful.

Teresa carries out a ritual, less complicated than the Tzotzil one:

> When the baby is born a little "promise" is lighted, a little candle for good health. I bathe him with good soap and warm water and clean him up neatly. I cut the umbilical cord with a razor blade. I dab on surgical spirit, press the cord, and tie it up again. The piece attached to the baby has to be tight so it won't bleed. I cut it in the middle, then I cauterize it with a candle so it won't bleed. You wash him well, clean him with a cloth, put the nappy on, the baby vest, shawl, everything. You give him to his mother, who is there lying down. Then he is passed on to the father, the grandfather, each of them give him a kiss and after that, depending on the time, you tell him good morning or good afternoon.

The husband is inside, and witnesses the birth. "He helps the mother," says Teresa. The floor of the forest huts are made of earth. The placenta will stay there:

> When the baby is ready, we make a hole in the earth and bury the placenta, so it stays inside the house.
>
> If the baby is born with the umbilical cord tied around his neck, it is because the mother forgot to untie the leather headband she uses when hauling firewood. That's why a pregnant woman has to be mindful of many details.

Teresa knows how to use herbs. "There aren't any contraceptive herbs, it's against nature. Rather, the herbs are used for the opposite, to beget children, which is the greatest gift."

Teresa doesn't have a set fee for deliveries. "I'm happy because people see that I do my job because I want to. So if they want to they give me ten or five thousand (old) pesos." Other midwives, men (because there are a few) or women, have set fees. Teresa says that there are people who charge 100 new pesos for a boy's birth. (One new peso is worth 1,000 old pesos). If it happens to be a girl, the price is half, 50 new pesos. The campesinos always prefer to have a boy than a girl.

The names for the newborns are chosen by the family; their favorite names or something with an international flavor. Thus, in La Realidad we found a Clinton and Floriberta and even Donaldo. Outside the forest, in the cold lands, the Tzeltal people from Oxchuc have two surnames from birth. The formal (Spanish) one, usually Morales, Santiz, Gómez, Méndez, López, or Encino, and then the indigenous one, which varies but is related to the moment of birth or the pregnancy. For example, the position of the stars can determine the newborn's name. If the birth occurs in bright sunshine the child will be called *K'aal*, writes Martin Gómez Ramirez in *Offering to the Ancestors in Oxchuc*. Or if the mother dreams of an animal, plant, or object during the pregnancy, this will be the paternal surname for the first born and those that follow. Gómez Ramirez points out: "It is also said that right after the birth the parents examine the placenta carefully and patiently to see the shape and color in the middle."

There is a story of a man given the surname K'ulub, meaning locust, because when he was born the placenta was bright green. Gómez Ramirez also relates that:

> If a man or a woman dreams of any part of the human body, let's say *chinbak*, which means knee, then that was the surname given to the newborn. However the Gómez of Oxchuc not only have k'ulub, but a relationship with plants, animals, and other objects because they dreamed of them or imagined them.

MARCOS:
MESTIZO CULTURE ON THE MOVE

MANUEL VÁZQUEZ MONTALBÁN

Originally appeared in *El Pais*,
February 22, 1999.

Translated by Ed Emery.

TWO years ago Subcomandante Marcos announced to Spain's TV cameras, in the presence of Georgina Cisquella and Pere Joan, that he was giving up reading my Carvalho novels, because when he was deep in the forest the recipes that my hero cooked just made him hungry. I made a promise to the subcomandante that I would include pre-Columbian recipes in my novels, and they would be eaten deep in the Lacandón forest.

One day someone handed me a couple of letters. One was addressed to me and the other to Carvalho: "To: Manuel Vázquez Montalbán and/or Pepe Carvalho, La Rambla, Barcelona Catalunya, Spain. From: Insurgent Subcomandante Marcos, Chiapas, Mexico." The first was headed by a quotation from *Don Quixote* and continued in the characteristically striking style of the subcomandante, who has been marked out by various of Mexico's literati as a great writer in the making. He said that he had read some of my books, including *Murder on the Central Committee* and *The Prize*. The second letter announced a series of forthcoming *encuentros*, and jokingly inquired if I might be able to bring down a few sausages. I wrote back to say that I would travel across to Chiapas from Cuba while I was working on my book *Y Dios entró en La Habana*.

Shortly afterward came the slaughter of the Zapatista indigenous community in Acteal, killed by paramilitaries acting on the orders of local PRI bosses. It wasn't even known if Marcos was still alive. Then all of a sudden up he popped again with his July Declaration. In a powerful letter he condemned the hypocrisy of the Mexican government and the present world order. He quoted Antonio Machado, or rather his creation Juan de Mairena, the greatest liberal thinker of all the liberal thinkers that ever were: "We should expect a man who is a public figure to be true to his mask, but sooner or later he has to show his face."

Marcos spoke mockingly of the "mask" of the sovereignty of the Mexican state—a state that has sold thousands of nationalized companies in order to meet the bill of modernity—and the sham of democracy in a country that is full of disappeared people and paramilitary gangs run by local politicians.

The subcomandante quotes Shakespeare, Carlos Fuentes, Galeano, and Miguel Scorza. He acknowledges his debt to my "Pamphlet from the Planet of the Apes" when he quotes: "The operation of discrediting critical reason was carried out by a group of intellectual 'beautiful people,' composed mainly of onetime young philosophers, one-time young sociologists and onetime young leaders of public opinion who have learnt the way to the master's dining table and have learned the lessons of the paid hack."

These gentlemen create the climate for repression, and the PRI and its thugs provide the guns. At the same time campaigns have been launched to discredit Bishop Samuel Ruíz (described as being a fundamentalist), Marcos himself (accused of being an imposter), and even Rigoberta Menchú, once hailed as a hero by Salinas de Gortari. There has also been a campaign in defense of national sovereignty, apparently leveled against the volunteers who have been traveling to Mexico to end the scandal of the *desaparacidos* (disappeared people) in Mexico, whereby that country has become what Amnesty International describes as a "black hole in the protection of human rights."

In its 1997 report Amnesty offers a revealing geography of the violation of human rights worldwide. It is clear that the worst offenders are countries that are in the throes of neoliberal modernization. The Zapatista guerrillas appear to be under siege in their forest, but in fact it is they who have laid siege to the PRI government and the decaying ghost of the PRI party-state. This explains why in early 1999, for instance, a journal such as *Letras Libres*, following the spirit of Octavio Paz in *Vuelta*, devoted its first two editions to the government's campaign against Zapatismo. Similarly *Proceso* published a special edition to highlight the way in which Zapatismo has contributed to breaking the trick mirror of Mexican reality. Not to mention the interview which Juan Gelman did with Marcos, a real two-sided lesson in literary theory.

I've read enough of this subcomandante to know that he's not inclined to conventional Marxist-Leninist rhetoric. It is as if he has turned his back on that "acoustic continuity" which Sloterdijk discusses in *Im Selben Boot*

("In the Same Boat")—an acoustic continuity which is an end in itself, which will die with the tribe that endorses it, and which destroys nothing, especially when it speaks the language of destruction. Marcos has found a way of imbuing demands with a new poetry, because he takes as his starting point the real historical subject of social change: the person who has been globalized, standing up against the globalizers.

That explains why I'm here, in a hut in La Realidad, an indigenous community in which Indians live together with a group of foreign observers. These are young men and women—today Catalans and Italians—who have paid their own fares to get here, who eat the same humble food as their hosts, in the same sunlight and by the same candlelight when it gets dark. They work with them every morning, going out onto the road to record the threatening passage of military convoys. They photograph them. They ask them not to enter La Realidad itself in order not to create bad feeling among the Indians. Or they may work doing woodwork or helping to build a turbine. They share the everyday lives of these people.

The PRI mass media accuse them of fomenting revolt, or burning the forest, or even of taking away Mexican soil in their rucksacks. Such was the hostility generated by the arrival of the international observers in March 1998 that many of the volunteers feared action by the paramilitaries, and traveled on foot through the Lacandón forest to the Guatemalan border.

I've come here because I was drawn by the possibility of meeting Marcos. That has meant running the gauntlet of military checkpoints. Are you a writer? Are you intending to write about Chiapas? I bring the *subcomandante* four kilos of Guijuelo sausage, some nougat, a copy of *Y Dios entró en La Habana* and I await the signal that will come from the forest once night falls. A Zapatista captain arrives. He wears the Zapatistas' trademark balaclava and leads two horses. One is for Guimar Rovira, a journalist who is Catalan by birth and Mexican by family connections, and who is traveling with me as photographer. The other is for me, who has never ridden a horse in his life. The captain notices this fact—but more importantly so does the horse. It eyes me first with disdain, and then with anxiety. Then it casts me in the role of a latter-day Indiana Jones and takes me up hill and down dale, across a little river and followed for part of the journey by a dog that had caught a whiff of the sausages.

Suddenly we arrive at a clearing in the forest. Marcos appears, together with his compañera Mariana. They both wear balaclavas. He asks us not to describe Mariana or photograph her. As I hand over the sausages and the book she watches with the same air of amusement with which Marcos lets it be known that he is not Dr. Livingstone and I am not Stanley. Further-more, he lets it be known, he is not the Tarzan of the Lacandón Forest and Mariana is not his Jane.

On a table made of small branches, built specially for the occasion, we set out the basis for two or three interviews, while Guiomar films and takes photos. Marcos produces an emergency tape recorder in case mine breaks down. He watches me and corrects my clumsy efforts with the tape recorder with the careful attentiveness of an expert in film and recording. His hands are broad and the palms are roughened by the 13 years that he has spent in the forest. But he has the fingers of a professor of philosophy. I explain that at this point I shall only be writing a short article, but that later I intend to expand that into a major article, a book or a pamphlet. He is much taken with the word "pamphlet"—*panfleto*.

"Maybe it'll turn out like your *Panfleto desde el planeta de los simios* . . ."

Q. "I have studied the five declarations that you have issued, and what surprises me is the notably vanguardist character of your revolution. Monsiváis says that rather than a vanguard you represent a meaningful minority. You don't operate in the vanguardist manner of a minority that sees itself as possessing some total truth. Partly from a learning process that has involved contact with the indigenous peoples and partly from your desire to make a revolution for them, you have taken on board the people's language and their energy for change."

A. "We see ourselves as a group that posed a series of demands and was lucky because those demands happened to coincide with and mirror demands arising elsewhere in the country and in other parts of the world. The merit of the EZLN (Zapatista National Liberation Army) is that it has succeeded in finding the wavelength to produce this set of reverberations—first in urban Mexico and among the peasants of Mexico's countryside. But also in other countries, in the excluded minorities of other countries. The slogan "¡Ya basta!" found a sympathetic echo in other places. We were lucky that we were able to tune in and communicate with those groups, and also because those groups felt themselves involved in and strengthened by what we were saying."

Q. "In part the worldwide crisis of the Left stems from a confusion over who is now the historical subject of change, since the industrial proletariat has been broken apart and deconstructed as a historical subject. In your case, ethnicity—the indigenous peoples, the two-time losers—becomes the historical subject. You denounce the world's wrongs on the basis of what is immediate and obvious, and not by doing what the traditional revolutionary Left would have done, superimposing a schema of national or international class struggle."

A. "We came to the forest like a classic revolutionary elite in search of that subject—the proletariat in the classic Marxist-Leninist sense. But that initial approach was not adequate to deal with the reality of the indigenous communities. They have a different substratum, a complex prehistory of uprisings and resistances. So we modified our approach interactively. There is a 'before' and 'after' of the Zapatista movement in relation to 1994.

"The EZLN was not born from approaches that arrived from the city. But neither was it an approach deriving exclusively from the indigenous communities. It was created out of a mixture, a (Molotov) cocktail, out of a culture shock which then went on to produce a new discourse, a mestizo movement that is critical and emancipatory. What we are arguing is that historical change cannot be allowed to proceed at the expense of the exclusion of a given sector of society.

"That necessarily implies political, social and economic costs for a country, and also for the whole world. The world is never going to be a homogeneous place. We have to respect the right to difference. And this is what the excluded are saying: 'Either you take account of us and our rights, or you'll be stuck with us as a noise in the apparent harmony of the new international order.' "

Q. The emergence of the Zapatista movement coincides with the proclamation of Mexico's arrival onto the international scene with the signing of the North American Free Trade Agreement (NAFTA). That was the point when the Zapatista movement erupted, giving the lie to this happy modernizing scenario. Was that intentional?

A. "It was the historical process itself which paved the way. Neoliberalism and globalization in Mexico are based on a lie: We can join the First World as long as we don't include all sectors of society, as long as we eliminate those who don't fit with the neoliberal standards of the marketplace. At the moment when we were making our entry into the First World, tens of millions of indigenous peoples were being left out of the account, plus several million poor people. It was as if they were not actually Mexicans, because they had certainly been treated as such.

"It was neoliberalism that provoked the indigenous people into revolt, given the brutality with which it began to implant itself in 1982, putting an end to the pseudo-revolutionary ambiguity of the PRI. It was neoliberalism not Zapatismo that posed the choice between disappearance and death or struggle and survival. That was what led to the First Declaration from the Lacandón forest, and the Zapatista uprising.

"Obviously there has been a process of organization, because as you know a guerrilla movement doesn't become successful simply by big words but by its ability to generate support and fight back. It has to find the right conditions to set down roots among the population. Indigenous people are very much opposed to this society of waste and dissimulation which has been created through the plunder of natural resources and the sale of the country's economic apparatus to the multinationals."

Q. "The indigenous rebellion is simultaneously a set of demands and a metaphor. Its demand is to be given a place among the majority. At the same time it is a metaphor for the social losers of globalization who are demanding a new set of rules for the game."
A. "The Zapatista indigenous movement is a symbol of resistance to being sacrificed in a world that is becoming standardized. In this world other differences are taken on board and so cease to be differences, or they are eliminated. That's why the indigenous movement has won the sympathy of sectors that are seemingly very different, such as young people, anarchists, immigrants, the reorganized Left, the displaced people of our world, in Europe, in the United States, and in Mexico. That's why these volunteers come here. And even though they're foreigners they have a tremendous understanding with the indigenous peoples, despite the fact of not speaking their dialect, and the fact that they don't have their culture, or even their stature—physically, I mean.

"We were very lucky. The way that money was working at the world level was seen as a fraud, and this created a lot of resentment.

But we wanted to go further and organize a politics which went beyond rancor. We go a lot deeper than fundamentalist movements, even though that's what some Mexican intellectuals accuse us of being.

"We're not looking for any kind of revenge. We're fighting for a society in which there will be a place for us, but that doesn't mean that we are trying to make everyone the same as us. We're not saying that everybody has to be indigenous, and that everything that isn't indigenous has to disappear. Imagine the contempt of this system—they couldn't even be bothered trying to to con the Indians. Why not? Because the Indians were supposed to disappear. With other productive sectors—the middle classes, the students, the intellectuals—they tried to pull the wool over their eyes. With the Indians they didn't even bother. But now they've changed their minds. Now suddenly they're talking about 'bringing them on board.'"

Q. "A Guatemalan writer told me that until the age of 50 he didn't even notice that indigenous peoples existed—and that was in a country where they're 50 percent of the population: 'I didn't recognize them as people. Ever since I was a kid, I'd seen them in my house, as servants, and I'd seen them in the streets, but I'd never seen them as people like the rest of us.'"

A. "Here the idea was that the Indians would simply disappear—or maybe some of them would be preserved as a tourist attraction. That's why the Lacandón forest is what it is, a kind of breathing-space in a far corner of the country."

Q. "Zapatismo offered a new mirror so that Mexico no longer had to see itself in the distorting mirror of a modernity based on a lie. To an extent it also represented the real face of the world—the real face of the disaster of neoliberalism."

A. "That was something that we only understood afterward. What we wanted to show was that Mexico's entry into the First World was built on a lie. Not only a lie for the Indians—as was shown by the economic, political, and ethical crisis of 1994–95—but also a lie for the middle classes and the working classes, as we used to say. And also a lie for a significant sector of the business community.

"We were lucky. When we drew up our platform it happened to coincide with the shattering of that lie. And at the same time these lies are also being rejected — or beginning to be rejected — in other countries which are dumping a large part of their history and their marginalized populations: for instance the Southern and Eastern immigrants who are waiting at the doors of Europe, the Latino migrants into the United States, the young and unemployed all over the world, and the cultural problems of a Europe that finds itself under attack from the cultural project of the Anglo-Saxons.

Q. "You're offering a non-falsifying mirror not only for Mexico but also for the rest of the world. The delightful character that you've created, the the philosopher-beetle Durito, has suggested that you invade Europe aboard a sardine can."

A. "I said no, because I would have had ended up doing the rowing. . . ."

Q. "When people used to ask Sciascia why he always wrote about Sicily he would reply 'Because Sicily is the world.' Mexico too is the world, and the Indian represents the figure of the two-time loser under globalization."

A. "A lot of people made fun of the First Declaration of the Lacandón Jungle when we said that we intended to march on Mexico City. Our arguments were heard in every town and city in Mexico, and they mobilized civil society, that section of society which ought to be the historic subject of change. What we didn't achieve by our arguments was achieved by the breakdown of the political system. The PRI started fighting among themselves, and at that point we discovered the massive corruption of Salinas de Gortari, the prophet of the First World.

"We are now mobilizing 5,000 Zapatistas thoughout Mexico to build toward our big consultation in March, to reaffirm the demands of the indigenous peoples. Our arguments have reached out to people all over the world. They have helped people to understand and denounce the trick mirror that offers us history with a happy ending and a globalization that is made to suit the globalizers. 'Here we are, and here we stay!' And now we're getting this prism effect, a multi-mirror effect on all sides. It wasn't made by us — the seeds of this situation were already there in the memory of the indigenous peoples and their oppression."

III

Q. "The cultural offensive conducted by neoliberalism during the past 15 years has been an offensive against historical memory and against utopia. For neoliberalism the elimination of memory means that history no longer has causes, no longer has guilty parties. And eliminating utopia means that the present and the predetermined become the only choices open to us. You are asking for a fairly modest utopia—that the Constitution and democracy should be inclusive of everyone. But surely, to make constitutions all-inclusive is a subversive act which oligarchies and the established order could not survive."

A. "We are not putting forward any particular economic model. Let's say that the Zapatista project is more about an ethical sense of politics rather than a program for government, which is what a political party would present. Zapatismo is different from traditional revolutionary movements. We don't want power. We want equality and difference to be taken seriously. When we talk about the restoration of memory, it is part of our fight against the one-dimensional nature of the present, which only serves the interests of the upper classes: They want us to forget that they are the same thieves and crooks as yesterday, forget that today they're making you the same promises that they made yesterday and then never fulfilled. As for utopia, what social change in the history of the world was not brought into being by utopianism? None."

Q. "Neoliberalism is also a utopia, but nobody has ever seen the worldwide happiness that it's supposed to bring. . . . "

A. "But to bring about the world order that they're planning they will have to eliminate or exclude a large part of humanity. They'll have to abolish their history, and also abolish nation-states, so that they don't resist the economists' plans. Like the utopia in *Blade Runner*—instead of a world we'll have one big business, with layer after layer of managers, right down to the level of workers and consumers. But there is resistance, and it's coming from the excluded sectors. In one place it's indigenous peoples, in another migrants, homosexuals, lesbians, women, young people, the unemployed. . . . All these sectors are being forced to define themselves as buyers or sellers. It's the only choice that's offered them: 'If you don't buy or sell, then for us you don't exist.' "

///

Mariana's voice interrupts to tell us that the airplane is coming. And there it is, the military aircraft that arrives every afternoon. Flying over the forest, as does the military helicopter that appears every morning. We postpone the rest of our conversation for 24 hours. Next time, comandante Tacho and major Moisés will also be present. As we travel back through the deepest darkness of night I recall some paragraphs from the letter that I wrote to Marcos at the end of 1998:

I regret the hungers, real or imagined, which Carvalho caused you, and I think we'll have a problem overcoming the obstacles that separate us by means of sausages. Maybe people and words can get through, but I'm not sure about the sausages—these days customs officers seem more worried about pig diseases and cholesterol than about theories or ideologies. But none of us can close our eyes to the seriousness of your circumstances because the evidence of its dramatic nature is in the news every day. My project is to reflect those circumstances out to the world and show how they represent a real choice: either solidarity or barbarism. You have constructed an unimpeachable ethical reference point and that is what makes you dangerous, in a cultural and political marketplace that has become so ethically devalued. It also represents something new after the unhappy and inevitable demise of the dialectic of political blocs which ended up creating a globalization of double standards of truth and morality, double-talk, and double accounting. The liberatory project has to be related back to the concrete situations which make it such a necessity, the real collective necessities brought about by inequality and injustice. The strength of the Zapatistas is that your thinking is not based on the false truth of an ideological leftover that was defeated in the Third World War, but on the blatant fact of the disorder which capitalism creates in its present phase, when it no longer has a watchdog to keep it in line. That explains the irritation that your way of proceeding provokes among the messianic caste of intellectuals, whether it's intellectuals from the old days of Marxism-Leninism or from the new days of neoliberalism based on genetic engineering. You people are a noise on the wavelength of *pensée unique*. Long live noise!

The *subcomandante* is forced to be rather theatrical by the nature of his surroundings, and also as a response to the false choice between a modernization which seeks to impose uniformity and the leftovers of the semantic shipwreck of Marxism-Leninism. He is the enlightened mouth-piece—very enlightened—of a set of very basic insurgencies: the Indian as both reality and metaphor of the globalized person; and *mestizaje* as something desirable rather than simply unavoidable.

FROM MARCOS TO DON VÁZQUEZ MONTALBÁN

An extract from the letter sent by *subcomandante* Marcos to Vázquez Montalbán in December 1997:

> Some weeks ago I read your article in the Mexican paper *La Jornada* (on the "nation state," or rather on its definition), and I have taken out my type-writer in order to write you a few thoughts that your writing stirred in me—but most of all to say hello.
>
> So here I am, writing to ask you to do me a couple of favours (in addition to actually reading this letter, of course).
>
> For example I wanted to ask you to greet Pepe Carvalho on my behalf. Tell him that I bear him no ill feeling for the torment that I experienced during those first years in the mountains (1984–90), when I read his gastro-nomic, amatory, and detective adventures. To such an extent do I bear no grudge that I am preparing a long piece which I am sure will be a delight to children and grownups alike when they see Pepe Carvalho and the Super-intendent cooperating in a globalized correspondence in order to solve a highly complicated criminal case. . . .
>
> Following different paths you and I both find ourselves dealing with the themes that you raise in your articles: globalization, the death throes of the nation state, the social development of Europe, the Europe of the financiers, the nature of the Left in this period, etc. This nightmare (which they're try-ing to sell us as the best of all possible worlds, and which is both the same and different whether it's in America or Europe) threatens us with the most terrible of destruction: the destruction of historical memory.
>
> And perhaps that's the reason why, here, Power is trying to destroy those peoples who have historical memory as their guide and banner: the Zapatista indigenous movement. In the town of Chanalhó, in Chiapas, paramilitary gangs (trained, paid for, and directed by the Mexican government and by the decomposing corpse of the PRI) have set about hunting down rebel Indians like in the times of the Conquista. Their desire for peace and a powerful determination to survive has led to our comrades fleeing to the mountains. While you read these lines more than 4,000 refugees, living and dying under

the open skies far from their homes, are the proof that the peace rhetoric of this government is simply a clumsy mask to hide a war against history. . . .

There must be another way. We are fighting in order to find it, and we are sure that you are doing the same. For that reason I would like to ask you to join us in moving ahead on two fronts: what we can do to solve the puzzle of the seventh mirror*– and what we can build through a shared analysis of globalization and its consequences.

*See page 250.

AGAINST THE GREAT DEFEAT
OF THE WORLD

JOHN BERGER

Originally appeared in *Race and Class*,
October 1998–March 1999.

IN the history of painting one can sometimes find strange prophecies— prophecies that were not intended as such by the painter. It is almost as if the visible by itself can have its own nightmares. For example, in Breughel's *Triumph of Death*, painted in the 1560s and now in the Prado museum, there is already a terrible prophecy of the Nazi extermination camps.

Most prophecies, when specific, are bound to be bad, for, throughout history, there are always new terrors. Even if a few disappear, yet there are no new happinesses—happiness is always the old one. It is the modes of struggle for this happiness which change.

Half a century before Breughel, Hieronymus Bosch painted his *Millennium Triptych*. The left hand panel shows Adam and Eve in Paradise, the large central panel describes the Garden of Earthly Delights, and the right hand panel depicts hell. And this hell has become a strange prophecy of the mental climate imposed on the world, at the end of our century, by globalization and the new economic order.

Let me try to explain how. It has little to do with the symbolism employed in the painting. Bosch's symbols probably came from the secret, proverbial, heretical language of certain fifteenth-century millennial sects, who believed that, if evil could be overcome, it was possible to build heaven on earth! Many essays have been written about the allegories to be found in his work. Yet if Bosch's vision of hell is prophetic, the prophecy is not so much in the details—haunting and grotesque as they are—as in the whole. Or, to put it another way, in what constitutes the space of hell.

There is no horizon there. There is no continuity between actions; there are no pauses, no paths, no pattern, no past, and no future. There is only the clamor of the disparate, fragmentary present. Everywhere there are surprises and sensations, yet nowhere is there any outcome. Nothing flows through: Everything interrupts. There is a kind of spatial delirium.

Compare this space to what one sees in the average publicity slot, or in a typical CNN news bulletin, or in any mass media commentary. There is a comparable incoherence, a comparable wilderness of separate excitements, a similar frenzy.

Bosch's prophecy was of the world-picture that is communicated to us today by the media under the impact of globalization, with its delinquent need to sell incessantly. Both are like a puzzle whose wretched pieces do not fit together.

And this was precisely the phrase which Subcomandante Marcos used in an open letter about the New World Order last year.* He was writing from the Chiapas, southeast Mexico. I cannot do justice in a few lines to his full analysis. He sees the planet today as the battlefield of a Fourth World War. (The Third was the so-called Cold War.) The aim of the belligerents is the conquest of the entire world through the market. The arsenals are financial; there are nevertheless millions of people being maimed or killed every moment.

The aim of those waging the war is to rule the world from new, abstract power centers—megapoles of the market, which will be subject to no control except that of the logic of investment. "Thanks to computers and the technological revolution," he writes, "the financial markets, operating from their offices and answerable to nobody but themselves, have been imposing their laws and worldview on the planet as whole. Globalization is merely the totalitarian extension of the logic of the financial markets to all aspects of life." Meanwhile, nine-tenths of the women and men on the planet live with the jagged pieces which do not fit.

---

*See page 270.

"What we have here is a puzzle," writes Marcos. "When we attempt to put its pieces together in order to arrive at an understanding of today's world, we find that a lot of the pieces are missing. Still, we can make a start with seven of them, in the hope that this conflict will not end with the destruction of humanity. Seven pieces to draw, color in, cut out, and put together with others, in order to try to solve this global puzzle." So vividly does this recall the jaggedness in Bosch's panel that I half expect to find there these seven pieces.

The first piece Marcos names has the shape of a dollar sign and is green. The piece consists of the new concentration of global wealth in fewer and fewer hands and the unprecedented extension of hopeless poverties.

The second piece is triangular and consists of a lie. The new order claims to rationalize and modernize production and human endeavor. In reality, it is a return to the barbarism of the beginnings of the industrial revolution, with the important difference that the barbarism is unchecked by any opposing ethical consideration or principle. The new order is fanatical and totalitarian. (Within its own system there are no appeals. Its totalitarianism does not concern politics which, by its reckoning, have been superseded but global monetary control.) Consider the children. One hundred million in the world live in the street; 200 million are engaged in the global labor force.

The third piece is round like a vicious circle. It consists of enforced emigration. The more enterprising of those who have nothing try to emigrate to survive. Yet the new order works night and day according to the principle that anybody who does not produce, who does not consume, and who has no money to put into a bank is redundant. So the emigrants, the landless, the homeless are treated as the waste matter of the system—to be eliminated.

The fourth piece is rectangular like a mirror. It consists of an ongoing exchange between the commercial banks and the world racketeers, for crime, too, has been globalized.

The fifth piece is more or less a pentagon. It consists of physical repression. The nation-states under the new order have lost their economic independence, their political initiative, and their sovereignty (the new rhetoric of most politicians is an attempt to disguise their political, as distinct from civic or repressive, powerlessness). The new task of the nation-states is to manage what is allotted to them, to protect the interests of the market's mega- enterprises and, above all, to control and police the redundant.

The sixth piece is in the shape of a scribble and consists of breakages. On the one hand, the new order does away with frontiers and distances by the instantaneous telecommunication of exchanges and deals, by obligatory free-trade zones (such as the North American Free Trade Association), and by the imposition everywhere of the single unquestionable law of the market; and, on the other hand, it provokes fragmentation and the proliferation of frontiers by its undermining of the nation-state—for example, the former Soviet Union, Yugoslavia, etc. "A world of broken mirrors," writes Marcos, "reflecting the useless unity of the neoliberal puzzle."

The seventh piece of the puzzle has the shape of a pocket, and consists of all the various pockets of resistance against the new order that are developing across the globe. The Zapatistas in southeast Mexico are one such pocket. Others, in different circumstances, have not necessarily chosen armed resistance. The many pockets do not have a common political program as such. How could they, existing as they do in the broken puzzle? Yet their heterogeneity may be a promise. What they have in common is their defense of the redundant, the next-to-be-eliminated, and their belief that the Fourth World War is a crime against humanity.

The seven pieces will never fit together to make any sense. This lack of sense, this absurdity, is endemic to the new order. As Bosch foresaw in his vision of hell, there is no horizon. The world is burning. Every figure is trying to survive by concentrating on his own immediate need and survival. Claustrophobia, at its most extreme, is not caused by overcrowding, but by the lack of any continuity existing between one action and the next which is close enough to be touching it. It is this which is hell. The culture in which we live is perhaps the most claustrophobic that has ever existed; in the culture of globalization, as in Bosch's hell, there is no glimpse of an elsewhere or an otherwise. The given is a prison. And faced with such reductionism, human intelligence is reduced to greed.

Marcos ended his letter by saying, "It is necessary to build a new world, a world capable of containing many worlds, capable of containing all worlds."

What the painting by Bosch does is remind us—if prophecies can be called reminders—that the first step toward building an alternative world has to be a refusal of the world-picture implanted in our minds and all the false promises used everywhere to justify and idealize the delinquent and insatiable need to sell. Another space is vitally necessary.

First, a horizon has to be discovered. And for this we have to refind hope against all the odds of what the new order pretends and perpetrates.

Hope, however, is an act of faith and has to be sustained by other concrete actions. For example, the action of *approach*, of measuring distances and *walking toward*. This will lead to collaborations that deny discontinuity. The act of resistance means not only refusing to accept the absurdity of the world-picture offered us, but denouncing it. And when hell is denounced from within, it ceases to be hell.

In pockets of resistance as they exist today, the other two panels of Bosch's triptych, showing Adam and Eve and the Garden of Earthly Delights, can be studied by torchlight in the dark. . . . we need them.

I would like to end by quoting the Argentinian poet, Juan Gelman:

Death itself has come with its documentation
We're going to take up again
The struggle
Again we're going to begin
Again we're going to begin all of us
Against the great defeat of the world
Little *compañeros* who never end
Or who burn like fire in the memory
Again and again and again.

RESOURCES

THE following publications were the source of many of the pieces published in *The Zapatista Reader*. Readers are encouraged to visit these websites where subscription details and sample articles can be found:

The Nation Magazine (www.thenation.com) America's leading journal of radical and dissenting opinion, which includes Alexander Cockburn, William Greider, Christopher Hitchens, and Katha Pollitt among its regular writers.

In These Times (www.inthesetimes.com) Lively, Chicago-based radical biweekly.

La Jornada (www.jornada.unam.mx/) Mexican daily newspaper with absolutely indispensable coverage of Chiapas; a pole of attraction for many of Mexico's leading leftist intellectuals (Spanish language).

Proceso (www.proceso.com.mx/) Leading Mexican weekly magazine.

The New Republic (www.tnr.com) Leading center-right weekly magazine.

The Irish Times (www.ireland.com) Leading Irish daily newspaper.

NACLA (www.nacla.org) The North American Congress on Latin America is an invaluable resource that provides in-depth coverage of Latin American affairs that goes beyond the coverage one associates with the mainstream media; muckracking, insightful, and challenging.

Brecha (www.brecha.com.uy/) Radical Uruquayan weekly.

Letras Libras (www.letraslibres.com) This elegant, liberal monthly — "against the authoritarianism of the right and left" — is a successor to Octavio Paz's *Vuelta* magazine. Edited by Enrique Krauze, it is Paz-ian in tone and is an intellectual embarrassment of riches, containing work from some of the world's leading writers and thinkers.

El Financiero International (www.elfinanciero.com.mx/) Mexican Financial daily newspaper (Spanish language).

Le Monde Diplomatique (www.en.monde-diplomatique.fr/) The world's leading socialist monthly newspaper, published from France with many foreign language editions, including an excellent English edition edited by Wendy Christianssen.

New Left Review (www.newleftreview.org) Leading Leftist theoretical journal edited by Perry Anderson.

Red Pepper (www.redpepper.org.uk/) British left-wing monthly.

National Catholic Reporter (www.natcath.com/) Lively and continually surprising weekly newspaper devoted to national and international affairs from an independent, broadly Catholic angle.

El Pais (www.elpais.es/) Distinguished Spanish daily newspaper (Spanish language).

International Socialism (www.istendency.org/isj.html) Revolutionary Socialist quarterly, published by the British Socialist Workers Party.

Race and Class (www.homebeats.co.uk) Monthly journal published by the Institute for Race Relations in London.

The Guardian (www.guardian.co.uk) The UK's leading liberal daily newspaper with an excellent team of radical columnists including Paul Foot, George Monbiot, Naomi Klein, Francis Wheen, Gary Younge, and Charlotte Raven.

Monthly Review (www.monthlyreview.org) Marxist monthly journal, respected for its coverage of political economy and international affairs.

The New York Review of Books (www.nybooks.com/nyrev/) Premiere US journal of letters, published 20 times a year.

Cambio (www.cambio.com.co) Colombian news weekly, owned by Gabriel García Márquez (Spanish language).

The following list of resources is admittedly incomplete and partial but the joy of visiting these sites are the incredible range of links they include.

ZAPATISTA WEBSITES

EZLN (www.ezlnaldf.org/index.php) The official EZLN website (Spanish language).

¡Ya Basta! (www.ezln.org/acerca.en.html) A private, nonprofit site devoted to the EZLN.

Struggle Site (flag.blackened.net/revolt/mexico/ezlnco.html) Contains EZLN communiqués in English.

SOLIDARITY/POLITICAL/NGO GROUPS

Mexico Solidarity Network (www.mexicosolidarity.org/)
Accion Zapata (www.utexas.edu/students/nave/)
Global Exchange (www.globalexchange.org/)
School of Americas Watch (www.soaw.org)
Fray Bartolomé Human Rights Center (www.laneta.apc.org/cdhbcasas/)
La Lutta (www.lalutta.org)

MEDIA/INFORMATION

La Crisis (www.la-crisis.com) Spanish language.
Latin American Alliance (www.latinsynergy.org/latininfo.htm)
New Internationalist (www.oneworld.org/ni/) Alternative press online.
Latin American Network Information Center (www.lanic.utexas.edu) Latin
    American information, esp. politics, media, and culture
Clarin (www.clarin.com) Argentenian daily (Spanish language).
CounterPunch (www.counterpunch.org)
NarcoNews (www.narconews.com) Excellent, muckraking website on war
    on drugs edited by Al Giordano

WRITERS

Manuel Vázquez Montalbán (vespito.net/mvm/indesp.html) Spanish lan-
    guage.
Paco Taibo II (vespito.net/taibo/) Spanish language.

ACKNOWLEDGMENTS

Tom Hayden: I wish to thank Carl Bromley of Nation Books for his extraordinary grasp of both the substance of this book and the countless tasks necessary to bring it to fruition. He was truly a co-editor. I also wish to thank Katrina vanden Heuvel, editor of *The Nation*, for her commitment from the very beginning. Thanks also to Guillermo Mayer, my former legislative deputy in Sacramento. Mexican-born, he guided me through an eyewitness experience in Chiapas and was instrumental in the process of choosing and translating many of the essays included here.

Carl Bromley: Thanks to my compañeros Justin Vogt, Shayna Cohen, and Russell Cobb for their extraordinary assistance and expertise in helping to shape this book: from research, translations, advice, and making international phone calls for me, they were indispensable; Antonino D'Ambrosio and the LaLutta.Org crowd for technical assistance; Art Winslow for his intuition; Roane Carey, Bruce Shapiro, Marc Cooper, Alejandro Munoz, Scott Sherman, Ilan Stavans, Jorge Mancillas, and David Brooks and Tania Molina from *La Jornada* for advice and expertise; Jay Miskowiec from Aliform Publishing in Minneapolis; Tom Hansen from the Mexico Solidarity Network; Irlandesa; Monique Lemaitre; Pascal Beltran Del Rio at *Proceso*; Dan Weaver at Nation Books; Sarah Chamberlain, Ham Fish and Taya Grobow at The Nation Institute; Claude Misukiewicz at *Monthly Review*; Ghadah Alrawi, Dan O'Connor, and Neil Ortenberg at Thunder's Mouth Press; Victor Navasky, Betsy Reed, Sandy McCroskey, Peggy Suttle, Mary Taylor Schilling, Danielle Veith, and Hillary Frey at *The Nation*; Daniel Singer and Jeanne Singer; Roger and Anita Bromley; Stephen Hyde; and Stefanie Ameres.

PERMISSIONS

WE gratefully acknowledge all those who gave permission for written material to appear in this book. We have made every effort to trace and contact copyright holders. If an error or omission is brought to our notice we will be pleased to remedy the situation in future editions of this book. For further information, please contact the publisher.

ABOUT THE CONTRIBUTORS

Homero Aridjis is one of Mexico's leading poets and novelists. He was born in Contepec, Michocan, Mexico, in 1940 to a Greek father and Mexican mother. Two collections of his poetry have appeared in English, *Blue Spaces* and *Exaltation of Light*, and three novels: *Persephone, 1492: The Life and Times of Juan Cabezón of Castile* (for which he was awarded the Grinzane Cavour Prize), and *The Lord of the Last Days: Visions of the Year 1000*. His work has been translated into 10 languages. Twice the recipient of a Guggenheim Fellowship, he has taught at Columbia University, New York University, and Indiana University. He has been Mexican ambassador to the Netherlands and Switzerland, and he is the founder and president of the Group of 100, an international environmental organization of writers, artists, and scientists. He is the president of PEN International and lives in Mexico City.

John Berger is an art critic and Booker Prize–winning novelist. He is the author of *Ways of Seeing*, which was based on the celebrated and enormously popular BBC TV series. Berger was born in North London but has lived in France for more than 40 years where he has worked on a diverse range of projects. He studied art at the Central Art School and later in Chelsea. In the early 1950s he began to write weekly art criticism for the *New Statesman* and *Tribune*. He has published a number of novels, the first of which, *A Painter of Our Time*, was published in 1958. He won the Booker prize in 1972 for G which tells the story of a person traveling round Europe in the years before the first world war. Along with his fictional work and art criticism he has written and appeared in films; collaborated on theater projects; and written political and cultural essays, medical philosophy, poetry, and studies of photography.

Pascal Beltran Del Rio is the Managing Editor of *Proceso*. He was the Washington correspondent from 1994 to 1999. He has a degree in journalism from the National University of Mexico and is the author of *Michoacán: Ni un paso atrás. La política como intransigencia*, about elections in the state of Michoacán (1993). He teaches journalism at the Universidad Iberoamericana in Mexico City and is a commentator for radio and TV news in Mexico.

Salvador Carrasco was born and raised in Mexico City. After studying at the National Autonomous University of Mexico's Center for Film Studies, Carrasco attended New York University's Tisch School of the Arts, from which he graduated in 1991, receiving the distinguished Founders Day Honors Award. After graduating from NYU, he embarked on his first feature film, *The Other Conquest* (*La Otra Conquista*), an epic drama about the Spanish Conquest of Mexico as perceived by an Aztec Indian. It would take Carrasco and his producing partner, Alvaro Domingo, many years and unbelievable hardship to complete this independent film, which many critics have hailed as a masterpiece. He was also the editor of the Spanish-language cultural magazine, *Litoral*, which published a wide range of international writers and visual artists. Carrasco's essays and poems in both Spanish and English have been published in books, newspapers and magazines.

José de la Colina was born in Spain and became a Mexican citizen in 1941. Octavio Paz called him a "unique writer" whose prose is among "the best in Mexico". He has published several volumes of stories, essays, criticism, and film history, among them *Ven caballo gris*, *La lucha con la pantera*, *La tumba india*, *Viajes narrados*, and *Miradas al cine*. He is a member of the editorial board of *Vuelta* and director of the Semanario Cultural of the newspaper *Novedades*. The book *Objects of Desire* gathers interviews of Luis Buñuel conducted by De la Colina.

Régis Debray traveled to Cuba, taught philosophy at the University of Havana, and, after lengthy conversations with Fidel Castro, wrote *Revolution in the Revolution?* (1967), a primer and intellectual treatise on guerrilla warfare which was an international bestseller. In April 1967, Debray was captured in Bolivia while accompanying a guerrilla force under Ernesto "Che" Guevara's command and was sentenced to 30 years in prison but he was pardoned in 1970 after an international campaign. He sought refuge in Chile, where he wrote *The Chilean Revolution* (1972) after interviews with Salvador Allende. Later he became an adviser on foreign affairs to French President François Mitterrand and from the mid-1980s to the mid-1990s held a number of official posts in the French president's office. He is the author of a short biography, *Charles De Gaulle: Futurist of the Nation* and *Media Manifestos: On the Technological Transmission of Cultural Forms*.

Eduardo Galeano is a Uruguayan writer, reporter, and novelist whose works include the trilogy *Memory of Fire*, *Open Veins of Latin America*, *Days and Nights of Love and War*, *We Say No: Chronicles 1963–1991*, and his essay/memoir about soccer, *Soccer in Sun and Shadow*.

Gabriel García Márquez won the Nobel Prize for literature in 1982. He is the publisher of *Cambio* magazine, a Colombian weekly news magazine. His books include *One Hundred Years of Solitude*, *Autumn of the Patriarch*, *Love in the Time of Cholera*, and the recent, nonfiction *News of a Kidnapping*.

Adolfo Gilly is a renowned scholar of Mexican politics. His recent publications include *Chiapas: La Razón Ardiente, Ensayo sobre la Rebelión del Mundo Encantado* (1997) and *México, el Poder, el Dinero, y la Sangre* (1996). From 1997 to 1999 he served as adviser to Mexico City Mayor Cuauhtémoc Cárdenas.

Mike Gonzalez is a Senior Lecturer in Hispanic Studies at Glasgow University, Scotland, who specializes in Spanish-American culture, literature and history, film and music. His interests include the Mexican novel and modern poetry, as well as the role of music in Latin American culture. He is the editor of the *Collins Concise Spanish Dictionary* and the author (with David Treece) of *The Gathering of Voices: The Twentieth Century Poetry of Latin America*. He has helped produce courses for the BBC, especially *Sueños* and he recently edited the Routledge Encyclopedia of Latin American Culture (edited with Dan Balderston and Ana M. Lopez). He is an active member of the Scottish Socialist Party.

Alma Guillermoprieto is the author of *The Heart that Bleeds* and *Samba*. She writes about Latin America for various publication in the United States and England, and is a regular contributor to *The New Yorker*.

Tom Hansen is the National Coordinator of the Mexico Solidarity Network, a coalition of eighty-eight organizations supporting struggles for justice, dignity, democracy and human rights in Mexico and the US. He also serves as co-Director of the Chiapas Media Project, a bi-national partnership that develops alternative media capacities with indigenous communities in Chiapas, Mexico.

Luis Hernandez Navarro is the editor of the Op-ed page and columnist at the Mexico City daily paper, *La Jornada*

Naomi Klein is an award-winning journalist, based in Toronto. Her articles have appeared in the *New York Times*, the *Village Voice*, *The Nation*, the *New Statesman*, *Newsweek* and *The Baffler*. Her book *No Logo: Taking Aim at the Brand Bullies* was an international bestseller. She is a columnist for the *Toronto Globe and Mail* and *The Guardian* (London).

Andrew Kopkind joined *The Nation* in 1982 where he was an associate editor and senior political writer until his death in 1994. As a reporter for the *New Republic* in the 1960s he introduced SNCC and SDS to a national audience, as well as covering the emerging Black power movement, the counterculture and the anti-Vietnam protests. He was also the *New Statesman's* US correspondent during this period. His essays are collected in *The Thirty Years' War: Dispatches and Diversions of a Radical Journalist 1965-1994*.

Enrique Krauze is a famous Mexican writer whose short biographies of Mexican leaders have sold over a million copies. He has served as co-editor of the intellectual journal, *Vuelta*, and has also written for the *New York Times*, *Time*, the *Wall Street Journal*, *New Republic* and other publications. He is a leading advocate of democratic reform in Mexico and is the author of *Mexico: Biography of Power—A History of Modern Mexico 1810–1996*.

Saul Landau, scholar, author, commentator, and filmmaker, is the first recipient of the Hugh O. La Bounty Chair for Interdisciplinary & Applied Knowledge at California State Polytechnic University, Pomona. He is known for his work on foreign and domestic policy issues, Native American and South American cultures, and science and technology. He has produced 40 films on social, political and historical issues, and worldwide human rights, for which he won the Letelier-Moffitt Human Rights Award, the George Polk Award for Investigative Reporting, and the First Amendment Award, as well as an Emmy for "Paul Jacobs and the Nuclear Gang." Saul Landau has written over ten books, short stories, and poems and is currently working on a detective novel. He received an Edgar Allen Poe Award for "Assassination on Embassy Row," a report on the murder of Orlando Letelier.

Jorge Mancillas, a writer and activist based in Los Angeles, is a Regional Service Coordinator for the California Faculty Association and a columnist for the Mexican weekly *La Crisis*. He was previously the Southern California Political Director for the Service Employees International Union, and a legislative aide to Senator Tom Hayden. He was a neurobiologist and professor with the UCLA School of Medicine, Department of Anatomy and Cell Biology and Director of a laboratory at UCLA's Brain Research Institute. Prior to that, he was a staff scientist at the Salk Institute in La Jolla and at the MRC's Laboratory of Molecular Biology in Cambridge, England. He was born and raised in Ensenada, Baja California, Mexico. He is currently writing *Rebels, Angels, and Assassins: The Struggle for Power in Mexico*.

Michael McCaughan is the Mexico Correspondent of the *Irish Times* and has written for *The Guardian*.

Gary McEoin is a writer who specializes in Latin American and the Catholic Church. He is the author of *The People's Church: Bishop Samuel Ruíz of Mexico and Why He Matters* and editor of *The Papacy and the People of God*.

Jean Meyer is a historian and researcher at the Centro de Investigación y Docencia Económica (Center of Economic Research and Teaching), a specialist on religious and peasant movements and on Eastern Europe, and the author of *La Cristiada*.

Carlos Monsiváis is one of Mexico's most celebrated journalists and social commentators. He is the author of *Amor Perdido* [Lost Love], *Escenas de Pudor y Liviandad* [Scenes of Frivolity and Shame], *Entrada Libre* [Free Entry], and *Rituales del Caos* [The Rituals of Chaos]. *Mexican Postcards*, an English-language collection of his essays edited by John Kraniaukas, was published by Verso in 1997.

Andres Oppenheimer is a foreign correspondent and a member of the *Miami Herald* team that won the 1987 Pulitzer Prize. He is the author of *Castro's Final Hour, Bordering on Chaos*, on Mexico's crisis, *Crónicas de héroes y bandidos*, and *Ojos Vendados*.

Octavio Paz, the poet and essayist, was born in 1914 in Mexico City. Paz began to write at an early age, and in 1937, he traveled to Valencia, Spain, to participate in the Second International Congress of Anti-Fascist Writers. Upon his return to Mexico in 1938, he became one of the founders of the journal *Taller* (Workshop), a magazine which signaled the emergence of a new generation of writers in Mexico as well as a new literary sensibility. In 1943, he traveled to the USA on a Guggenheim Fellowship where he became immersed in Anglo-American Modernist poetry; two years later, he entered the Mexican diplomatic service and was sent to France, where he wrote his fundamental study of Mexican identity, *The Labyrinth of Solitude*, and actively participated (together with Andre Breton and Benjamin Peret) in various activities and publications organized by the surrealists. In 1962, Paz was appointed Mexican ambassador to India: an important moment in both the poet's life and work, as witnessed in various books written during his stay there, especially, *The Grammarian Monkey* and *East Slope*. In 1968, however, he resigned from the diplomatic service in protest against the government's bloodstained supression of the student demonstrations in Tlatelolco during the Olympic Games in Mexico. After that Paz continued his work as an editor and publisher, founding two important magazines dedicated to the arts and politics: *Plural* (1971–1976) and *Vuelta*, which has been publishing since 1976. He won the Nobel prize in 1991.

Elena Poniatowska, the essayist, journalist, and novelist, is of Polish and Mexican descent and was born in Paris, France in 1932. She has been living in Mexico since 1942 and became a citizen in 1969. After being schooled both in Mexico and the United States, she began her literary career as a journalist with the daily *Excelsior* in 1953, and has since been contributing articles, essays, and chronicles to other major newspapers such as *Novedades*, *La Jornada*, *El Financiero*, *El Dia*, *El Nacional*, and *The News*, as well as for magazines the likes of *Siempre*, *Revista Mexicana de Literatura*, *Punto*, *Proceso*, *Nexos*, *Vueita*, *Fem*, and *Revista de la Universidad*. In Mexico, she has been recognized with the Javier Villaumutia award, a distinction she declined, and was twice honored with the Mazatlan Award for Literature (1972 and 1992). She is the first woman to have received the national award for journalism (1979) and holds additional distinctions in this field such as: the El Porvenir (1986), the Manuel Buendia (1987), and the national Juchiman awards. Her work was recongnized in Colombia with the Premio Internacional Proartes in 1997 and, in Chile that same year, with the Gavriela Mistral award.

Ignacio Ramonet is the Director of *Le Monde Diplomatique* and a Professor at the University of Paris-VII.

John Ross won the 1995 American Book Award for his *Rebellion from the Roots*, the first volume in English to look at the roots of the Zapatista rebellion. His latest book is *The War Against Oblivion: Zapatista Chronicles 1994-2000.* Other Mexico books include *The Annexation Of Mexico—From the Aztecs to the IMF, In Focus Mexico,* a political guidebook, and *Tonatiuh's People,* a novel of the Mexican cataclysm. Ross also pens a weekly on-line newsletter "Mexico Barbaro," a grassroots report from the Mexican underbelly. He continues to function as Mexico correspondent for the *LA Weekly,* the *SF Bay Guardian,* the *Texas Observer, Noticias Aliadas* (Lima), *Gemini News Service* in London, and *Sierra Magazine.* Considered a younger Beat poet in the late 1950s, Ross has eight chapbooks of poetry in and out of print, including "Whose Bones," "Jazzmexico," and the brand-new "Against Amnesia."

Guiomar Rovira is a journalist writing for, among others, the Spanish newspaper *El Mundo.* She was in San Cristóbal de las Casas on new Year's Day 1994 and witnessed the Zapatista Rebellion. She has also published *Zapata Lives.*

José Saramago was born in Portugal on November 18, 1922 and published his first novel, on the poor peasants of his native province Alentejo, in 1947. An unquiet spirit, a militant communist in search of the truth, he took an active part in the revolutionary movement that followed the overthrow of the Salazar regime in April 1974. He was awarded the Nobel prize for literature on October 8, 1998, in recognition of his lifelong concern with social justice. The following titles are available in English: *Baltasar and Blimunda, Year of the Death of Ricardo Reis, Stone Raft, Manual of Painting and Calligraphy, The Gospel According to Jesus Christ, A History of the Siege of Lisbon,* and *On Blindness.*

Joel Simon worked as correspondent in Mexico until 1997. He is the author of *Endangered Mexico: An Environment on the Edge* (Sierra Club Books, 1997). He is currently the deputy director at the Committee to Protect Journalists in New York.

Ilan Stavans teaches at Amherst College and is an editor of the literary journal *Hopscotch*. His books include *The Hispanic Condition*, *Tropical Synagogues*, *The Oxford Book of Latin American Essays*, *The One-Handed Pianist*, *The Oxford Book of Jewish Stories*, *The Inveterate Dreamer: Essays and Conversations on Jewish Culture*, and *The Essential Ilan Stavans*.

Paco Taibo II is a prodigious novelist, essayist and biographer. His enormously popular detective novels featuring Hector Belascoaran Shayne, a grumpy, one-eyed private eye, have been described by Scott Sherman in *Boston Review* as "subtle meditations on Mexico's history and culture, x-rays revealing the inner workings of the country's political system." He is also the author of a recent biography *Guevara Also Known as Che*. In his novel *Same Clouds* Taibo makes an appearance and tells Belascoran: "I've spent the last thirteen years fighting the system. I was in the student movement in '68, I was active for a while in leftist politics, I worked with the unions, with factory workers, organizing, putting out magazines, pamphlets. . . . I've never been interested in just making myself a bunch of money. I never worked for the PRI. . . . when I fucked up I never got anyone killed, and if I fucked somebody over it was out of ineptitude and stupidity and not because I'd sold out or was an asshole. No one ever paid me not to do what I believed in."

Manuel Vázquez Montalbán is Spain's most popular writer. He is a novelist, poet, essayist, and cookbook writer. His most famous character, the Barcelona detective Pepe Carvalho, first appeared on the crime literature scene in 1970. In 1981 he won the French Grand Prix for Detective Fiction. His novels *include Murder in the Central Committee, Southern Seas, Off Side, An Olympic Death*, and *The Angst-Ridden Executive*. He is also the author of *Marcos: El senor de los espejos*.

Bill Weinberg is the author of *Homage to Chiapas: The New Indigenous Struggles in Mexico* and the editor of World War 3 Report (www.ww3report. com).

JoAnn Wypijewski, a former senior editor of *The Nation*, is a writer based in New York City. Her work has appeared in *The Nation, Harper's, Il Manifesto, Ms.*, and *The Progressive*. She is the editor of *Painting by Numbers Komar and Melamid's Scientific Guide to Art; The Thirty Years' War: Dispatches and Diversions of a Radical Journalist 1965-1994* by Andrew Kopkind; and the author of a forthcoming book on the new Star Wars military program, to be published by Verso.